Thematic Catalogues in Music

The first printed thematic catalogue.
William Barton's *Book of Psalms in Metre* (London: G.M., 1645)

Thematic Catalogues
in Music

An Annotated Bibliography

*including printed, manuscript, and in-preparation
catalogues; related literature and reviews; an essay
on the definitions, history, functions, historiography,
and future of the thematic catalogue*

by BARRY S. BROOK

CITY UNIVERSITY OF NEW YORK

Published under the sponsorship of the *Music Library Association*
and *RILM Abstracts of Music Literature.*

PENDRAGON PRESS

HILLSDALE, NEW YORK

By the Same Author

La Symphonie française dans la seconde moitié du XVIIIe siècle.

The Breitkopf Thematic Catalogue, 1762-1787.

Musicology and the Computer; Musicology 1960-2000: a practical program.

Perspectives in Musicology (with Edward O. D. Downes and Sherman Van Solkema).

RILM retrospectives

A series of annotated bibliographies sponsored by RILM (International Repertory of Music Literature)

No. 1   Thematic catalogues in music.

No. 2   French dissertations in music, by Jean Gribenski et al. (in preparation)

No. 3   The iconography of music, by Frederick Crane (in preparation)

No. 4   International congress reports in music (in preparation)

Library of Congress Cataloging in Publication Data

Brook, Barry S
  Thematic catalogues in music, an annotated bibliography.

  (RILM retrospectives, no. 1)
  "Published under the sponsorship of the Music Library
Association and RILM abstracts of music literature."
  1. Music--Thematic catalogs--Bibliography. I. Title.
II. Series: International Repertory of Music Literature
(Organization) RILM retrospectives, no. 1.
ML113.B86   016.78   72-7517

Contents

Reproductions

On the definitions, history, functions, historiography, and future of the thematic catalogue

The thematic catalogue is a powerful research and bibliographic tool. It arranges a body of music in a systematic order and provides positive identification in a minimum of space and symbols. It derives its power from the use of 'incipits,' or musical citations of the opening notes. For most music, an incipit of no more than a dozen *pitches* is required. When *rhythmic values* accompany the pitches, the incipit's 'uniqueness quotient' is astonishingly high. (It would not be surprising if the figure were close to 98 or 99 percent, except for folk music, where a tune may have many variants.)

A musical work, printed or manuscript, may be identified by composer, its title, opus number, key, instrumentation, movement headings, first line of text, date, publisher, dedicatee, plate number, etc. No one of these, indeed no combination of these, can provide as certain an identification as an incipit. Here are some illustrations of why this is so: two different composers' names may appear on three sets of manuscript parts of the same concerto grosso. An anonymous 15th-century three-voice motet with Latin text may also appear as a French chanson entitled *L'amant douloureux*. A composer may write a dozen trio sonatas in D major, three of them with the movement sequence, allegro-andante-presto. A concert aria found in a library in Vienna, in the key of F, may turn up in Prague in the key of G, and with added horn parts. Two printings of a set of quartets may be given different plate numbers by the same publisher. Two publications of the same opera, in different cities, may bear different titles, and dedications to different patrons.

Finally, a set of six symphonies may be published in Amsterdam with one opus number, in Offenbach with another, and in London without any at all within a series of periodical overtures.

By contrast, the incipit rarely leads one astray. Even transposed works can be readily identified in properly organized incipit files. In dealing with anonymi and with works of disputed authorship, the incipit becomes indispensable - as a catalogue without them will readily demonstrate. In short, the collection, classification, transposition, and lexicographical ordering of the incipits into thematic catalogues have enabled scholars to solve a myriad of otherwise insoluble problems, and have provided musicians, librarians, students, biographers, and program annotators with an invaluable reference tool.

A word is in order about the term, *thematic catalogue*, which has been in semantic difficulties for two centuries. Webster defines its etymological sire, *theme*, as a 'central idea', a 'subject or topic of discourse', etc. Similarly, in music a theme is usually defined as 'a principal melodic feature in a composition'. However, when the word *theme* is used in its adjectival form as part of the term *thematic catalogue* or *thematic index*, it virtually always means 'beginning' or 'incipit'.1

In the late eighteenth century the French title 'Catalogue thématique', meaning 'incipit index', appeared in print all over Europe. It was first used by Hummel in 1768, and then by Pleyel in 1789, by Imbault in 1792, and by Artaria in 1798. (Both Hummel and Pleyel cautiously added the words 'ou commencement'.) Christian Ulrich Ringmacher employed the term for the first time in German, in the prefatory note to his *Catalogo* in 1773; "Mit vielem Vergnügen gebe ich hiermit denen Musikliebhabern gegenwärtigen gedruckten thematischen *Catalogum* [his emphasis] meiner Musikalien heraus,..."2 Bland, in 1792 and 1800, was the first to use the English titles 'thematic catalogue' and 'thematic index'. In all of these instances what were catalogued were incipits, not *true* themes. This has remained the case until today. Indeed, in the relatively few instances when true themes or motives rather than incipits are catalogued, the adjective, 'thematic', is usually avoided in the title, e.g.: *Symphonic Themes* by Burrows and Redmond (New York,

---

1. This metamorphosis has not occurred in other fields; a 'thematic index' to a book in history or medicine provides a guide to the principal ideas or topics that appear throughout the volume.

2. See no. 1065 for a description of this catalogue; on questions of primacy, cf. Otto Erich Deutsch, "Thematische Kataloge", *Fontes Artis Musicae* V/2 (1958) 75.

1942), *Dictionary of Musical Themes* by Barlow and Morgensten (New York, 1949), and *Themensammlung musikalischer Meister-werke* by Schiegl and Schwarzmaier (Frankfurt am Main, 1967).

The semantic confusion probably arose because in the later 18th century when the terms 'theme' and 'thematic catalogue' were first regularly used, compositions almost **always** *began* with their main theme. The 18th century words 'theme' and 'themata' were thus synonymous with what has (only in recent decades) come to be called 'incipit'; they were used interchangeably with 'initia', 'beginnings', 'commencements', 'anfänge', and 'subjects or first few bars'. (It can even be argued, not altogether illogically, that in music it was the word 'theme' rather than the term 'thematic catalogue' that took on a new meaning.) Breitkopf may **well** have been the first to use the word theme or 'themata' in this sense. In 1762, in the *Nacherinnerung* of the Parte Ima of his *Catalogo delle Sinfonie* (p. 29) he writes, "I have tried to make them [the works catalogued] recognizable by their *themes* [*themata*, his emphasis]... to differentiate one from another as one differentiates books by their titles". Mozart used the same word in a letter to his sister dated 19 December, 1787, "...will you please note down **the theme**s [themata] of the pieces I have sent you from Vienna and send them to me so that I may not send you anything twice over?" (transl., Emils Anderson).

Undeniably, it would have made for greater lexicographical tidyness if the hundreds of catalogues in this volume that bear the title 'thematic' had instead, and from the beginning, been named 'incipit index'. There have been a handful of thematic catalogue compilers who have resisted the word 'thematic' in favor of such more etymologically defensible titles as *Beginnings* (Barton, no. 73), *Initia* (Kerll, no. 655, Thannabauer, no. 1302), *Subjects* (Bland, no. 123), *Anfangs-Verzeichnis* (Ludwig/Gennrich, no. 764), *Aavangsmaten* (Duquesnoy, no. 326), and *Incipitkatalog* (Hell, no. 579). As Alphons Ott put it, none of these terms has succeeded in dethroning 'thematic catalogue'[3]

In preparing this volume, the title, *Incipit catalogues and indexes*, was considered. Because this might compound the confusion, and would seem to exclude catalogues of true themes, it was decided to let *Thematic Catalogues in Music* stand. Two centuries of usage, sufficient for the most scrupulous of lexicographers, has validated the commonly accepted meaning of the term. Furthermore, this name, retaining some of its ambiguity to the end, allows for the in-

3. "Thematische Verzeichnisse" *Die Musik in Geschichte und Gegenwart*, XIII cols. 311-21 (see no. 934).

clusion of catalogues of true themes, literature about cataloguing, etc.

We have defined 'thematic catalogue' in the broadest of terms as a grouping of incipits, themes, or melodic formulas presented in any type of notation (syllables, neumes, tablatures, etc.) or code or computer input language (graphic, numeric, *Plaine and Easie,* etc.). Included in this volume, therefore, are listings for all manner of printed and manuscript thematic indexes, dictionaries, compilations, and tables of contents, as well as for collections of true themes and motives--in brief, for any 'catalogue' that may be of documentary significance. A 'theme' is defined as a principal melodic idea of a composition, longer than a figure or a motive, and to some extent complete in itself. An 'incipit' (musical) is defined as the opening notes of a piece, usually only those of the principal melodic voice; when the bass line or other voices are also given, these are referred to as a double or multi-stave incipit. A 'text incipit' is of course the opening words of a vocal work and we have used 'texted incipit' to mean a musical incipit with text underlay.

Early history and function

The early history of the thematic catalogue may best be outlined in terms of its functions, of which it is possible to discern at least nine.[4]

MNEMONIC AID. This type of thematic index helps the performer recall the beginnings of a well-known body of tunes or melodic formulas. The tonaries of the 9th to 11th centuries (see no. 1310) belong in this category. These treatises--French medievalist, Michel Huglo, has inventoried 400 of them--often contain musical incipits to guide the reader in choosing the proper tone or formula to connect the end of the psalm verse with the antiphon. These must be considered the earliest examples of thematic catalogues.

Curiously, the first *printed* thematic catalogue had a similar function. In 1645, William Barton published *The Book of Psalms in Metre... all following the common tunes at this day used in, and about London...* (no. 73), a 304-page collection of Psalm texts; on a single page contains "The

---

4. For an historical perspective on the early history of the thematic catalogue, the reader may wish to consult the chronological tables of *Manuscript thematic catalogues before 1830* and *Printed thematic catalogues before 1830* that appear as appendices to this essay.

beginnings of [22] G[eneral] and P[articular] tunes now used in London" (see reproduction in the frontispiece of this volume). Most of the psalm texts have one, two, three asterisks and can be sung to one or another of the similar- ly-marked popularly-sung melodies. This type of thematic index survives in our day in handwritten incipit lists used on occasion by song leaders and café pianists.

TABLE OF CONTENTS. This is an incipit index appearing together with a printed or manuscript volume of musical pieces as a guide to its use. The first-known index of this type was prepared by Hendrich Lübeck in 1598 as part of a 115-leaf manuscript volume containing 202 trumpet sonatas and fanfares (see no. 763 and accompanying reproduction). Thematic tables of contents have become commonplace in nine- teenth and twentieth-century editions of the works of major composers, e.g. Beethoven sonatas, Chopin mazurkas. Such indexes have been omitted in this Bibliography unless they are of special historic interest or include incipits not covered more fully elsewhere; in the case of some minor com- posers, the only thematic catalogues available for them are of this type.

GUIDE TO A COMPOSER'S OWN OUTPUT. This type of cata- logue serves not only to put order into a composer's works, but as a hallmark of his authorship, and even as a procla- mation against counterfeiters. The latter was the object- ive of what is probably the first catalogue of an indi- vidual composer's works. In 1686, Johann Kaspar Kerll pub- lished a set of Magnificat versets for organ, *Modulatio organica* (see nos. 655,193), to which he attached a ten-page thematic catalogue entitled, *Subnecto initia aliarum Compos- itionum...*[5] It contained 32 incipits for 22 of his other keyboard works (i.e. not works from the *Modulatio*) which, he said, he had seen "in more than one place..., ascribed to someone else". With this catalogue Kerll was thus asserting his authorship and publicizing his wares at the same time.[6] It was not until almost a century later that other composers began to follow suit, e.g. Johann Georg Schürer (1765, see

---

5. Kerll's thematic catalogue *preceded* what may be the first printed non- thematic catalogue of a single composer's works, Johann Theile's *Opus musicalis compositionis* (Merseburg: Gottscheck, 1708). It lists some 44 Masses, Magnifi- cats, and Psalms, with brief descriptive comments, e.g., *Stylum modernum elabo- rate,...Stylo antiquo Ecclesiastico*. See Johann Mattheson, *Critica Musica*, II, 58-59; and E.J. Mackey, *The sacred music of Johann Theile*. (Ph.D. diss: Univ. of Michigan, 1968) 59-60, 319ff.

6. See Kerll's preface, *Ad lectorum* (no. 655), translated in no. 193, B. Brook, "The earliest printed thematic catalogues", *Larsen Festschrift* (Copen- hagen, 1972) p. 110.

nos. 1185-96); Haydn (1765-1805, no. 510, the *Entwurf Katalog*); and Mozart (1784-1791, no. 856, *Verzeichnüss aller meinen Werke vom Monath Febraio 1784 bis Monath...1..*[15 November, 1791], which has been printed and reproduced in facsimile no fewer than ten times.) Early nineteenth century examples of composers' own catalogues include those of Johann Joseph Roesler (before 1813, no. 1093) and George Gerson (1823, no. 446). In the 19th century, the cult of individuality furthered the use of chronologically ordered opus numbers. Beethoven was the first great composer to do so systematically.[7] This tendency reduced the need for composers to prepare their own thematic catalogues.

INVENTORY OF LIBRARY HOLDINGS. In the eighteenth century, the contents of many large church, court, and private music collections were catalogued thematically for obvious practical reasons. Such catalogues could be arranged by date of acquisition, by composer's name, or by storage shelf. The earliest known example of a thematic library catalogue was begun in 1720, for the Prussian general Friedrich Otto von Wittenhorst-Sonsfeld (today both catalogue and collection are located in the Herdringen Castle, see no. 581). Other examples include catalogues of the library at Rheda, 1750 (no. 1046); the Gimo collection in Uppsala, 1750 (no. 1325); Maria Anna of Bavaria, 1750 (no. 884); **Herzogenburg,** 1751 (no. 582); Brtnice [Pirnitz], ca.1752 (no. 1940); **Osek,** 1754 (no. 933); Filipo Ruge, Italian flutist in Paris, ca. 1757 (no. 1121); Kromeriz, 1759 (no. 699); Olomouc, 1759 (no. 926); etc. Even when such catalogues list works or entire collections that have been lost, as they often do, they may assist in the identification of anonymi and in the tracing of patterns of music dissemination.

Among the earliest examples of *published* thematic library catalogues are those by Coussemaker of the anonymous Masses in Cambrai, 1843 (no. 216); by Haberl of sacred works of the Capella Sixtina in the Biblioteca Apostolica Vaticana 1888, (no. 1096); and by Kade of the great collections in Schwerin, 1893 (no. 1192). In recent years, the considerable growth in thematic library cataloguing, including that for RISM, represents a major advance for research (see index under *thematic catalogues of collections* and *thematic catalogues of library holdings*). Much remains to be done however in the field as we shall point out below.

COPYING FIRM ADVERTISEMENT. These display incipits of works on hand on the premises of the establishment, works

7. See Lenore Coral (no. 257) p. 9.

that are available to be copied at so much per page. Three such catalogues are known: the Breitkopf *Catalogo* (Leipzig, 1762-87) with over 888 pages and 14,000 incipits in six parts and 16 supplements (no. 167); the Ringmacher catalogue (Berlin, 1773) with 628 incipits (no. 1065); and the lost Christian Gottfried Thomas *Catalogus,* which was issued in manuscript copies from 1778 onward (no. 1304).

The significance of such catalogues is in inverse ratio to their numbers. Catalogues of published works are inventories of prints that once existed in multiple copies; in the majority of instances at least one of these copies can be located. Catalogues of manuscripts often deal with unica or 'near unica'; when these are lost the catalogue's incipits may be the only evidence of a composition's existence or the only method, as with some library catalogues, of identifying anonymous and doubtful works.

The Breitkopf Catalogue, about which I have written elsewhere (Introduction to the Dover reprint edition number 167c), is possibly the most important single bibliographic aid to 18th-century research by its size, breadth of coverage, and sociological import. Despite its inaccuracies, it remains indispensible for dating and attribution.

This bibliography shows that it can no longer be called the "first printed thematic catalogue",--as it has from Burney to Deutsch--but the "lustre and significance" of Breitkopf's great accomplishment is not diminished one whit by this loss of primacy (see no. 193; the earlier catalogues are Barton's and Kerll's).

PUBLISHING FIRM ADVERTISEMENT. These catalogues present incipits of the firm's own printed or engraved works. One composer or a whole roster may be represented; and on a single leaf or in a large volume. The earliest example of such a catalogue appears to be that of J.J. and B. Hummel, published in Amsterdam in 1768-74 (see no. 608). Its title is informative: *Catalogue thématique ou commencement de touttes les oeuvres de musique qui sont du propre fond de J.J. & B. Hummel, publié à la commodité des amateurs, par où ils pourront voir, si les pièces qu'on leur présente pour original, n'ont pas déjà été imprimées.* Others were published by Corri in Edinburgh in 1779, ...*songs*...*from operas* (no. 262), Bland in London, 1790-93 (no. 123), Bossler in Speyer, 1790-94 (no. 152.1), Imbault in Paris, ca. 1792 (no. 615), Artaria in Vienna, 1798 (no. 30). The earliest publishers' catalogues of the works of individual composers include Forster's *Catalogue of the works of Giuseppe Haydn,* London, 1786? (no. 511); Artaria's *Catalogue thématique* of Pleyel's chamber works [Wien, 1789] (no. 975); and Hoffmeister's listing of his own flute compositions, Wien, 1800 (no. 594).

The early nineteenth century saw the great flowering of this type of catalogue. E.g., those of Mozart (London: Monzani, 1805, no. 861); Mauro Giuliani (Steiner, 1815, no. 452), Beethoven (Hoffmeister, 1819, no. 83), Moscheles (Probst, 1825, no. 850), Czerny (Diabelli, 1827, no. 274), Gelinek (André, 1820?, no. 441), Mendelssohn (Breitkopf & Härtel, 1843, no. 813), Schubert (Diabelli, 1852, no. 1178), Schumann (Schuberth, 185-, no. 1184), Chopin (Breitkopf & Härtel, 1855, no. 741). In some instances the catalogues were prepared or corrected by the composers themselves (e.g. Moscheles and Liszt). Similar publishers' catalogues continue to be produced in our time. In mid-19th-century the high season of publishers' sales catalogues was reached. The next step is in the direction of the scholarly catalogue which we will come to as the ninth and final function below.

LEGAL DOCUMENTS. Contracts, bills of sale, *inventaires après decès*, etc., have made use of incipits for positive identification. Two such documents by Haydn are known, one with 20 incipits, "I acknowledge to have received seventy pounds [from William Forster, London publisher] for 20 symphonies, sonatas...composed by me...", 1786 (no. 512, see also no. 514). There are five by Boccherini, including his *Catalogo delle opere da me... cedute in tutta Proprieta al Sigr Ignazio Pleyel,* 1796 (no. 132, see also 130-31,133-34). Similar documents exist concerning Michael Haydn (no. 561f), Mayseder (no. 798), and Moscheles (no. 851). A famous example of an estate inventory is that for C. P. E. Bach, *Verzeichniss des musikalischen Nachlasses...,* 1790 (no. 38).

COMPILATION OF TRUE THEMES. Such catalogues often contain extended quotations and may serve for analysis (e.g., of Sibelius' music, nos. 1215-16); as a 'guide' for the music lover (e.g., to concerto themes, no. 208, or to symphonies, no. 207); or as a pedagogical tool (e.g., solo trumpet passages "grouped into various levels of...rhythmic, ornamental...problems...", no. 383).

MUSICOLOGICAL DOCUMENTATION. Thematic catalogues prepared with scholarly thoroughness and accuracy represent a new direction in cataloguing that began about 1850. Such catalogues may be related in function to some of those previously mentioned, but primarily they serve as the essential, initial step in the solution of historical, analytical, and musico-sociological problems. They may be based on a genre, a form, a period, a country, a region, a publishing house, a library, an individual composer, a group of composers, or a specific monumental or complete works edition. They may be buried in the supplement to an unpublished dissertation or represent the efforts of many scholars working collectively on a major union-cataloguing project. As a type they are the most important and most numerous thematic catalogues of our time. Today the most frequent piece of advice given graduate students embarking on the preparation of many types of theses and dissertations is: "The first thing to do is to compile a thematic catalogue".

Recent history

The model for the new scientific approach was Ludwig Ritter von Köchel's *Chronologisch-thematisches Verzeichniss* of Mozart's works. He began his research on his great catalogue in the early 1850's and published it with Breitkopf & Härtel in 1862. Köchel went far beyond the mere listing of a work's title, date, instrumentation and opening bars. He provided such additional information as location of autographs, listings of early editions, references to literature about the work, and multiple-stave incipits for all movements. Köchel was able to profit from the work of that prodigous collector and music bibliographer, Aloys Fuchs, who made his own extensive thematic index of Mozart's output available to him. Fuchs, who was also the compiler of over 20 other incipit indexes,[8] began his cataloguing efforts around 1830 and continued until shortly before his death in 1853. He may well be considered the father of our documentary approach to thematic cataloguing despite the fact that virtually none of his catalogues were published in his lifetime. Today they survive in manuscript in the Deutsche Staatsbibliothek in Berlin; several of them have never been superceded.

The new direction in cataloguing dramatized by Köchel coincided with the 19th century expansion in the discipline of musicology and the publication of the great complete works editions especially in Germany. The stream of catalogues that appeared during the next half century thereafter, often prepared in conjunction with complete works editions; they included indexes for Beethoven, Spohr, von Weber, Schubert, Schumann, Mendelssohn, Bach, Glinka, Saint-Saens,

8. Pages from three of them have been reproduced as illustrations in this book, e.g. Corelli (no. 408), Marcello (no. 782), and Spohr (no. 1229). For a discussion of Fuch's life, library, and cataloguing work, see articles by Friedrich Wilhelm Riedel (no. 1153-54) and Richard Schaal (no. 1159).

Čajkovskij, Brahms, Gluck, C. P. E. Bach and finally Dvorak (which was published in 1917). Rarely however did any of these approach the Köchel catalogue in scholarship. Most remained closer in purpose and coverage to publishers' sales catalogues. (F.W. Jähn's detailed work on Weber is a notable exception that, as Alexander Hyatt King points out, "has remained unapproached as a source book".[9]

During the recovery period after the First World War, few catalogues appeared. In the thirties and forties the tempo increased somewhat with catalogues for Reger, Kreisler, Volkmann, and Domenico Scarlatti, as well as a number of facsimiles of 18th century manuscript catalogues, especially Jens Peter Larsen's invaluable *Drei Haydn Kataloge in Faksimile*, which came out in 1941. It was not until the 1950's and the post-war resurgence of musicological activity that the full impact of Köchel's innovations began to be felt. At last there appeared definitive scholatly thematic catalogues of the works of Bach (Schmieder), Beethoven (Kinsky), Schubert (Deutsch), Couperin (Cauchie), Haydn (Hoboken), Boccherini (Gérard). Many others are currently in the making as may be seen (marked by asterisks) in the pages of this book.

Historiography

If we may seem to have entered upon the thematic catalogue's golden age, we are doing so with a minimum of historiographical support. Too few studies have been made of the history and problems of thematic cataloguing; and there has been only limited debate on the merits of different methods of catalogue presentation and incipit classification, on questions of inclusion and exclusion of information, on the use of non-conventional, machine-readable notational codes.

Among the few classic articles contributing to an understanding of the history and function of the thematic index are those by Wilhelm Altmann, Otto Erich Deutsch, Wolfgang Schmieder, A. Hyatt King, and Nanie Bridgman; more recent contributions, some with useful discussions of computer applications, have been written by Friedrich Wilhelm Riedel, Jiří Fukač, Lenore Coral (her master's essay), Jan La Rue, Mary Rasmussen, Murray Gould, Harry Lincoln, Lawrence Berstein and Franklin P. Zimmerman. A fine lexicographical

---

9. See "The past, present, and future of the thematic catalogue", *Monthly Musical Record* LXXXIV (1954) p. 40. Mr. King's admirable essay has been a source of inspiration to my own, both in content and title; it includes a more detailed survey of 19th and early 20th century developments than is to be found here.

offering is **Alfons** Ott's "Thematische Verzeichnisse" in *Die Musik in Geschichte* und *Gegenwart*.[10]

The question **of what** to include and exclude in a definitive thematic catalogue of a composer's works has been aired by Alexander Hyatt King in his previously-mentioned article (footnote 9). His hopes for a thoroughgoing discussion of his scheme, between compilers and users, has unfortunately not been realized. There is no more effective way to re-open the question than to restate his outline, with Mr. King's kind indulgence, in its entirety. "Any plan", he writes, "...must be flexible, in order to suit the needs of widely differing composers in different epochs. A scheme for all the necessary sections of a catalogue might be based on the following principles:

> (a) [*Title, author, date*]
>   1. Conventional title, with opus or identification number.
>   2. Reference to standard or complete edition.
>   3. Author of words, or other source of text for vocal works.
>   4. Date and place of composition.
> (b) [*Incipits*]
>   1. Incipits of each movement, with number of bars in each.
>   2. Note on difference, if any, between autograph or primary MS. source and standard printed editions.
> (c) *Autographs*
>   1. Location, including correct shelf or class mark if it is in a public, permanent collection.
>   2. Number and measurement of folios with, in the case of fragments, the number of bars on each leaf.
>   3. Transmission; owners and dates; successive prices, if known.
> (d) *Copies*
>   1. Those contemporary, or nearly so, with the autograph, if containing variants or composer's own markings.
>   2. Later ones, according to importance, especially if autograph is lost.
> (e) *Editions*
>   1. The first edition, with conventional title, wording of title-page number, date if any, imprint and price.
>   2. Later editions, only if published in the composer's lifetime, and containing changes made by him.
>   3. Arrangements made by the composer, or others in his lifetime, if containing changes sanctioned by him.
>   4. Posthumous editions, only if containing changes sanctioned by the composer.
> (f) *Notes*. Confined to bibliographical matters, affecting the interaction of any or all of (b) - (e).
> (g) *References*
>   1. Confined to important passages in the standard biography, in all editions and translations.
>   2. Books and articles in all languages, confined to those of real merit and originality.[11]

---

10. All of these contributions appear in the Bibliography under the authors' names and are marked with the following symbol: □

11. *Op. Cit.,* pp. 45-46.

One addition, an important one to my mind, should be made to Mr. King's outline. In section *(g) References* (or perhaps in section (b) as number 3) I suggest the inclusion of: References to contemporary catalogues, both thematic and non-thematic. Similar outlines should be drawn for library, regional, genre, publisher's and union catalogues.

In folk music classification and indexing Scheurleer's famous *Preisfrage*[12] of 1899, "Welche ist die beste Methode, um Volks- und volkmässige Lieder nach ihrer melodischen (nicht textlichen) Beschaffenheit lexikalisch zu ordnen?" (no. 1162) launched an important and as yet unresolved discussion (see Koller, no. 676; Krohn, no. 698; Heinitz, no. 570; Elscheck and Stockmann, no. 354).

In the area of non-conventional, typewriter, and machine-readable notation, there has been considerable activity. The present author's efforts to demonstrate the usefulness of the *Plaine and Easie* code have engendered a variety of helpful responses and counter-proposals. The ideal requirements for such a code were originally (1963-64) set down as follows:

(1) It must be speedy, simple, absolutely accurate as to pitch and rhythm. It should be as closely related mnemonically to musical notation as possible, so that it appears natural and right, avoiding arbitrary symbols. It should require only a single line of typewriter characters without the need for back-spacing or for a second pass over the line. It should be usable by non-musicians with only a few minutes of instruction. It must be easily recognizable as music from the symbols alone and immediately retranslatable, without loss, into conventional notation.

(2) It must be applicable to all western music from Gregorian chant to serial music.

(3) It must be internationally understandable and universally acceptable.

(4) It must be so devised as to be readily transferable to electronic data-processing equipment for key transportation, fact-finding, tabulating and other research purposes.[13]

A number of effective codes have been developed in recent years. Among those in extensive use today, in addition to *Plaine and Easie*, are Madame Bridgman's system, Ingmar Bengston's *Numericode*, Stephan Bauer-Mengelberg's *Ford-Columbia language*, and the code used by Franklin P. Zimmerman.

12. The prize was a complete set of the works of Sweelinck.
13. B. Brook and M. Gould, "Notating music with ordinary typewriter characters (A Plaine and Easie Code System for Musicke)" (no. 187); see also B. Brook, "The simplified *Plaine and Easie* code system for notating music; a proposal for international adoption" (no. 188, with reproduction of summary version).

Outlook

Of the requirements listed above, the one that has not been fulfilled thus far -- and may not ever be -- is that of universal acceptance. Although this would have simplified the exchange of data and the merging of data-banks by computer, the lack is not too great. Not only does each system have practical advantages of its own, but machine-readable coding in one language may, if required, by translated into another for merging, sorting, and rearranging. Clearly, the potential of data processing for thematic catalogues is enormous. Unfortunately, the realization of that potential has been disappointing. It has been about ten years since wide interest in machine processing of musical data first developed. It may take still another decade or more before the miracles that then seemed 'around the corner' will have come to pass. I am not speaking of promising, or even completely successful 'pilot projects'--we have had enough of those--but rather of full-fledged, dependable operations capable of handling vast quantities of musical data, and with all programming and data-storage difficulties a thing of the past. Such operations must be accompanied by an ability to transform coded musical notation into elegant and inexpensive photo-composed pages, and to transpose and extract parts automatically.

Computerized data-processing is obviously ideally suited to the manipulating, sorting, and classifying of the large quantities of data being collected by the current union cataloguing projects reported in these pages. These include folk music archives with as many as 35,000 incipits (nos. 298, 711, 653.1, 436); card indexes of Renaissance polyphony (nos. 173, 733-34, 1334); of 18th century symphonies (nos. 282, 712); of 55 archives in Bohemia and Moravia totalling over 160,000 incipits (no. 1003) etc. The directors of several of these projects have made extensive use of data-processing and others are planning to do so.

As automation techniques develop further and are put into practice on a large scale, we may anticipate increased assistance in the solution of many of the problems associated with thematic cataloguing, e.g. identification, construction of concordances, arrangement into various systematic orderings, etc. It is regrettable that the International Repertory of Musical Sources, the most ambitious musical cataloguing project of our time, was not able, for reasons of time, personnel, and publication cost, to include incipits in its Series A/I (Single printed works before 1800) now in the process of publication. (My preference would have been strongly in favor of the inclusion of incipits in an inexpensive coded form, no matter what the difficulty, at least for the works not otherwise identifiable in standard thematic catalogues. Cataloguing of such works without their incipits is, in my view, incomplete and must eventually be redone.)

Fortunately, it has been decided to attempt to include incipits in the RISM cataloguing now under way for Series A/II (Pre-1800 manuscripts). To do otherwise would have been disastrous. Printed works may be identified and dated by various means, e.g. opus number, publisher's name and address, plate number, newspaper advertisements, etc.); manuscripts have relatively few such controls and therefore *require* incipits. In the pages of this book, under numbers 1068 to 1089, the reader will find descriptions of the progress of RISM A/II cataloguing in twenty countries. Since the decision to include incipits was made only recently and since before that decision came, several important countries had already completed their work, there are major national gaps in coverage. It will require much time and extensive funding to bring this potentially invaluable bibliographic tool into being. Meanwhile for specific questions relating to pre-1800 manuscripts, it is often possible to consult a country's national files in person or by letter (addresses are included in the entries under RISM).

Source research is a relatively finite field. It is not outside the realm of hope and possibility that by the end of this century, music historians and bibliographers will have caught up with their literary and art-historical brethren in the control of (at least) their early sources. In achieving this end, the 'complete' thematic catalogue will, with computer assistance, play a central and indispensable role. It can do so by providing, in a given field, a complete and accurate distillation of all available musical, analytical, literary, contextual, and chronological information.

Appendix A

Manuscript Thematic Catalogues before 1830

[Key: **Composer**, COMPILER, Library (country), *Title*]

Date		No.
ca. 900-1100	*Tonaria* by REGINO of Prüm, ODO of Clugny, GUIDO d'Arezzo, etc.	1310
1598	LÜBECK, Hendrich. [*202 trumpet 'sonatas' and fanfares for Christian König zu Dänemark*]	763
ca. 1728-1760	Herdringen (D). *Des Herren General Major Frey Herrn von Sonsfeldt Musicalisches Cathallogium*	581
1750	Rheda (D). *Catalogi musici...Waldhorn...Violin...Flaut... Hautbois...Clavecin...Violoncelle...*	1046
1750	Rheda (D). *Catalogi musici...Deutsche Cantates und Arien... Italiänische und Frantzsische Cantates*	1046a
ca. 1750	Uppsala, Gimo Collections (S). *Catalego di Musica Mandata à Casa*	1323
ca. 1750-1765	Karlsruhe (D). [*Catalogues A-C and E*]	641-44
ca. 1750-1790	München (D). *Catalogo De Libri di Musica Di S.A.S.E. Maria Anna, Elettrice de Bavaria...Arie, Oratori, Serenata...*	884
1751-17?	Herzogenburg **(A)**. *Catalogus Selectorium Musicalium chori Ducumburgensis...*	582
ca. 1752	Brtnice [Pirnitz] (CS). *Inventario per la Musica*	194
1753	HUND, Joannes. *Catallogus Symphoniarum et triosonantium*	612
1754	Osek (CS). *Syllabus seu Catalogus perutilis...*	933
ca. 1757	Ruge, Filippo. *Catalogue de la Collection symphonique...*	1121
1759	Kroměříz (CS). [*Thematic catalogue*], (cf. Olomouc)	699
1759	Olomouc (CS). *Cathallogus über die Hochfürstlichen Musicalia und Instrumenten*	926
1759	SHARP, William, James, and Granville. *Sharp Catalogue*	1212
1761	**Tartini, Giuseppe** (ALMERI), *Tutti motivi de concerti...*	1278

1784-   Haydn, Michael. (Strnischtie), *Themata Michael Haydn'scher*   566
  1855   *Messen...*

ca. 1785? Viotti, Giovanni Battista. *Concerti Viotti, Concerti*   1341
           Giernovigh

1786   Haydn, Joseph. [*Contract with William Forster, publisher*]   512

1787   Melk (A) (HELM). *Catalog delle Sinfonie, Concerti, Quintetti,* 808
           Quartetti, Trio, ed. Soli

1790   Bach, Carl Philipp Emanuel. *Verzeichniss des musikalischen*   38
           Nachlasses des Verstorbenen Capellmeisters C. P. E. Bach

1790   Klosterneuburg (A). (SCHMIDT). *Catalogus...*   668

ca. 1790? Klosterneuburg (A). *Musicalien Verzeichniss*   667

ca. 1790? Praha, Krakovský z Kolovrat (CS). *Verzeichniss Aller*   994
           Musicalien...

ca. 1790? Haydn, Joseph. *Indice tematico Delle Sinfonia a grande*   509
           orchestra...

1790-92   Haydn, Joseph (KEES). *Catalogo Del Sinfonien...*   513

1790-92   Melk (A). (HELM). *Catalogo delle Sinfonie, Concerti,*   809
           Quintetti, Quartetti, Trio ed Soli

1791   Salzburg (A). *Catalogus Musicalis in Ecclesia Metropolitana:* 1130
           Archivium

1792   Praha, Zatec (CS). *Catalogues Musicaliorum Chori e Ecclesia...*999

after   London (GB). BURNEY, Charles, *Index in notation to the 6*   757
  1794   *vols. of Dr. Tudway's MS collection of English Church*
           Music (1715-20) in the British Museum

1794-   Ljubljana (YU). *Musicalien-Catalog der Philharmonischen*   745
  1804   *Gesellschaft in Laibach...*

1795   Haydn, Joseph. [*Agreement with Johann Peter Salomon, London*   514
           Impressario...]

1796   Freising (D). *Themata...Kirchen und Kammer Musicalien...;* 399,400
           Supplement: Themata von jenen Musicalien...

1796   Boccherini, Luigi. *Nota delle opere non date ancora a*   131
           nessuro [contract with Pleyel]

1796   Boccherini, Luigi. *Catalogo delle opere da me Luigi*   132
           Boccherini cedute in tutta Proprieta al Sigr. Ignazio Pleyel

1797   Boccherini, Luigi. *Nota della Musica Mandata a Parigi l'anno*   130
           1790 o 1791

1797   Boccherini, Luigi. [*Act of Sale of op. 40-43*]   133

1799   Boccherini, Luigi. [*The Act of Sale of the Six Piano*   134
           Quintets, Op. 56]

ca. 1800   Wein (A). Freudenthal. *Catalogue Des Diverses Musiques*   1405

ca. 1800   **Hasse, Johann Adolf.** *Catalogo della Musica di Chiesa*   500

ca. 1800   Berlin, Deutsche Staatsbibliothek. [*Thematischer Catalog der* 111
            Voss-Buchsen]. Handschriften

ca. 1800   Basel (CH). Universtätsbibliothek, *Sarasin Collection*   76

ca. 1800?   **Seidelmann, Franz.** *Thematischer Catalogus derer Kirchen*   1198-99
            Musicalien...; Catalogus...

ca. 1800?   Berlin, Deutsche Staatsbibliothek (D). [*Vocal works, 18th C.*] 110

ca. 1801   **Naumann, Johann Gottlieb.** *Verzeichniss der Kirchen*   898
            Musicalien...

ca. 1802?   **Sperger, Johann Matthias.** *Tema von Contrabass Concerte,*   1226
            1225; Catalog über verschückte Musicalien

1804   Donaueschingen (D), Fürstlich Fürstenbergische Hofbibliothek. 309
            Copia Verzeichniss Nr. 12

1804   SEITZ, Alpius. *Liederbüchlein...*   1204

1805   **Haydn, Joseph;** ELSSLER, Johann. *Verzeichniss aller derjenigen* 516
            Compositionen...

after 1806 **Haydn, Michael.** *Catalogus omnium operum ecclesiasticor...*   562.1

1807   Seitenstetten (A). *Index Missarium...*   1203

ca. 1809   Praha. Kačina (Kuttenberg) (CS). *Catalogo; Catalog der*   990-93
            Kirchen Musicalien; Catalog der Opern Oratorien und
            Einzelnen Singstücken; Catalog der Harmonie Stücke und
            Türkische Musik

ca. 1810   Praha...Clam é Gallas. *I Catalogo Delle Carte di*   987-88
            Musica...; II Catalogo

ca. 1810-   München...*Königliche Hofcapelle. Catalog über Saemtliche*   885
1850   *Kirchenmusik...*

1811   Eisenstadt (A). (PRINSTER). *Catalogue...Vespers,...Litanies,..*350
            Te Deum,...Hymnes des Miserere,...

ca. 1812   **Schuster, Joseph.** *Catalogus deren Kirchen Musicalien...*   1188

ca. 1813   **Roesler, Johann Joseph.** [*Autograph thematic catalogue of*   1093
            his works]

1814   **Haydn, Michael.** (RETTENSTEINER). *Catalog über die Bekannten* 568
            Compositionen des Herrn Michael Haydn...

1820   **Haydn, Joseph.** *Verzeichniss der Symphonien...welche bei*   520
            Carl Zulehner...

1820   **Hummel, Johann Nepomuk.** *Werke von...Hummel Welche Artaria*   610

1820-25   Melk (A). (HELM?). *Catalogo delle Sinfonie, Concerti,*   810
            Quintetti, Quartetti, Trio ed Soli

Appendix B

Printed Thematic Catalogues before 1830

1800   Hoffmeister, Franz Anton. *Catalogue thématique de touts les*   594
          Oevres pour la Flute traversiere...(Wien: chez l'auteur)

1802   Haydn, Joseph. *Collection...des quatuors...*(Paris: Pleyel)   515

ca. 1805 Mozart, W.A. *Catalogue thématique...* (London: Monzani)   861

ca. 1806 Haydn, Joseph. *Quatuors pour deux violons, alto et basse,*   517
          mis en collection; Table thématique (Paris: Sieber)

181-   Fesca, Friedrich Ernst. *Thematisches Verzeichniss der compo-*   374
          sitionen von Friedrich Fesca... (Leipzig: Peters)

18-?   Fesca, Friedrich Ernst. *Catalogue thématique des...quintetti*   375a
          et quatuors (Paris: Richault)

ca. 1810 Haydn, Joseph. *Collection complette des quatuors; catalogue*   518
          thématique... (Vienna: Artaria)

1815   Giuliani, Mauro. *Thematisches Verzeichniss der sämtlichen*   452
          Original - Werke... (Wien: Steiner)

1815?   Haydn, Joseph. *Catalogue thématique de tous les quatuors*   519
          (Paris: Janet et Cotelle)

1818-22   Boccherini, Luigi. *Table thématique...des quintetti...*   135
          (Paris: Janet et Cotelle)

1819   Beethoven, Ludwig van. (Hofmeister) *Thematisches Verzeichnis...* 83
          Instrumentalmusik... (Leipzig: Hofmeister)

1819   Giuliani, Mauro. *Catalogue thématique des oevres* [sic]   453
          (Wien: Artaria)

182-?   Bergiguer, Benoit Tranquille. *Catalogue thématique...*   103
          (London: Monzani & Hill)

ca. 1820- Beethoven, Ludwig van. *Catalogue thématique...works for the*   84
   1825   *Pianoforte* (London: Monzani & Hill)

ca. 1823 Beethoven, Ludwig van. *Catalogue thématique...*(London: Preston) 85

ca. 1824 HODSOLL, William (publisher). *Catalogue thematique...sympho-*   589
          nies and overtures by Mozart, Haydn, Rossini, Pleyel, etc.

1824   London, Philharmonic Society. (CALKIN). *Catalogue of the lib-*   758
          rary belonging to the Philharmonic Society (London: Maund)

ca. 1825 Fesca, Friedrich Ernst. *Themes de tous les quatuors et quint-*   375
          teti (Paris: Henry)

1827?   Czerny, Carl. *Verzeichniss (thematisches) der Werke...* (Wien: 274
          Diabelli)

ca. 1827 HODSOLL, William (publisher). *Catalogue thematique of sympho-*   590
          nies and overtures by Mozart, Haydn, Beethoven, Himmel,
          Weber, Mehul;...by A. Romberg, Pleyel, Winter, Rossini,   591
          Kreutzer, Handel, Paer and Mozart (London)

1829   Boccherini, Luigi. *Table thématique des quintetti* (Paris: 136
          Janet et Cotelle)

1830?   Onslow, George. *Catalogue thématique des quatuors et quin-*   927
          tetti (Paris: Pleyel)

Acknowledgments

This book is dedicated to my graduate students, past, present, and future.

Without their assistance, and that of scores of friends and colleagues, this volume would have had to appear under someone else's name. It was conceived in the 1963-64 *Bibliography and Research Techniques* seminar at Queens College of the City University of New York. Compilation was begun at that time as a methodological exercise. (The nine year gestation period is entirely my responsibility, as are all remaining errors and omissions, which I had naively hoped to eliminate 'almost completely', but which continued to present themselves in droves until the hour read 11:59, and beyond.

The *Queens College Supplement to the Music Library Associations's Check List of Thematic Catalogues (1954)* appeared in 1966. Its 45 pages added 230 entries to the 362 in the *Check List*. I quote from its introduction: "The original...*Check List*...was a model of scholarly precision and of the kind of cooperative effort that alone can make such a venture possible...The need for updating the out-of-print 1954 *Check List*... has long been manifest...The Supplement is designed to help prepare for the eventual publication of a new, up-to-date annotated bibliography of and on thematic catalogues. The Supplement is no finished product: it presents only a portrait of work-in-progress and a plea for additions and corrections." Similar pleas were published in a dozen journals and dispatched in a thousand letters.

The answers, from librarians about manuscript catalogues, from music department heads regarding unpublished dissertations, and from individuals preparing new indexes were invaluable. My heartfelt thanks are hereby extended to all who so kindly responded. Special thanks are most gratefully tendered:

To my [then] students who, following the publication of the *Queens College Supplement*, helped immeasurably in the checking, rechecking and annotating of entries, in particular, Madeleine Hogan, Nancy Herman, Dorothy Austin, and Drora Pershing Maynard.

To the students from the City University Graduate School who more recently assisted in various ways in the seemingly unending process of beating the manuscript 'into final shape', Vered Cohen, John Backo, Lois Gertzman, Murray Citron, and Carl Moskovic; to Margaret Grupp, Associate Editor of *RILM Abstracts* and doctoral candidate at New York University, whose ability to decipher German script from (often poorly-exposed) microfilm copies of 18th century catalogues is little short of uncanny;

and most particularly to Richard Viano, who 'keyboarded' the entire manuscript, did a splendid job of researching, and wrote a number of the entries himself.

To those American colleagues who generously shared their expertise and their files, in particular Jan LaRue whose great work with thematic catalogues--18th century and union--is reflected in many entries; Ruth Watanabe, chairwoman of the MLA committee on thematic indexes (successor to Helen Joy Sleeper's earlier committee); and Cecil Adkins, compiler of *Doctoral Dissertations in Musicology*. To Walter Gerboth and James Pruett, former and present chairmen of the MLA publications committee, for whose many tips and slips I am most grateful; Carol Bradley, whose excellent formatting suggestions improved the shape of the entries; Robert N. Freeman, who helped with Melk; Owen Jander who did likewise with WECIS; as did Bathia Churgin with some rare catalogues from Karls-ruhe; and to Ruth Hilton, whose bibliographic skill solved many problems.

To European colleagues whose specialized knowledge and unfailing cooperation helped unravel a myriad of mysteries; to Alfons Ott, who made available the new information he had gathered since the publication of his MGG article on thematic indexes; Karl-Heinz Köhler who piloted me through the Aloys Fuchs' materials in the Berlin Staatsbibliothek and provided essential microfilm; to Kornel Michałowski, Teresa Chylińska, and Maria Prokopowic who helped with Polish catalogues; to Cari Johans-son, Åke Davidsson, and Anders Lönn, who did the same for those of Swe-den; to Nanna Schiødt, Torben Schousboe, and Dan Fog of Denmark; Alexan-der Hyatt King and Robert Dearling of Great Britain; István Kecskeméti and Iván Pethes of Hungary; Milena Galuškova, Theodora Strakova, Emil Hradecky, Milan Poštolka, Oldřich Pulkert, of Czechoslovakia, and most particularly, to Jiří Fukač who kindly sent me detailed descriptions of many 18th-century Czech thematic inventories.

To Robert Münster in Munich, Erich Thurmann of Münster, and Alexan-der Weinmann of Vienna, whose intimate knowledge of their countries' musical sources was always at my disposal; to Gertraut Haberkamp who contributed information about a hundred obscure catalogues and corrected errors in a hundred others. To Georg Feder and Horst Walther, who sent in important additions to the entries on Joseph Haydn; to Jens Peter Larsen who carefully checked the entire Haydn section, twice. To Charles Sherman who is responsible for many Michael Haydn entries. To Donald McCorkle who unscrambled the Brahms catalogue tangle; and to Pierluigi Petrobelli who did the same for Tartini. To C., F. and S. of Pendragon Press, and to Lisa and Jim who pitched in.

In closing, may I reiterate my plea for suggestions, corrections and additions. Newly published catalogues should of course be reported to *RILM abstracts*, co-sponsor, with the Music Library Association, of this volume. Such abstracts together with all other information will be incorporated in a future edition, which I can only hope will bear another editor's name.

Barry S. Brook

New York, 1972

Using the Bibliography

MAIN HEADINGS

All items in this Bibliography are entered under name of a composer, library, publisher, compiler, or author, as main headings.

INDIVIDUAL COMPOSER'S CATALOGUES appear under the composer's name (in bold face capital letters, dates added).

BACH, JOHANN SEBASTIAN, 1675-1750

COLLECTIVE CATALOGUES of works by more than one composer appear under:
    a) *Library*, when its holding, in whole or part, is being indexed (In bold face, city's name in capitals, MS call number added if applicable.)

FIRENZE, Biblioteca Riccardiana: Ms. 2794

    b) *Publisher*, when his output is inventoried. (In bold face, last name in capitals, the word *publisher* added.)

BLAND, John (publisher)

    c) *Compiler*, when more than one library or one publisher is involved. (In bold face with last name in capitals, the word *compiler* added.)

HATTING, Carsten E. (compiler)

LITERATURE ABOUT THEMATIC CATALOGUES appears under the author's name. When related to a specific catalogue, the item is entered immediately following the catalogue it describes. When the item discusses cataloguing in general, it is entered under the author's name as a main heading. (In medium roman type, last name in capitals.)

KING, A. Hyatt

N.B. Where two or more catalogues (or articles) share the same main heading, they bear different numbers and are placed in chronological order. However, entries for a catalogue's subsequent editions, supplements, and related literature, are grouped together with the parent catalogue and share its number but with a letter added.

INDENTED SUB-HEADINGS

Composer, library, or **publisher** as main heading:

a)   COMPILER, **title,** bibliographical citation of source.
b)   **Title** of thematic-catalogue-portion of item (omitted if this is
             a self-contained catalogue, hence identical to a.)
c)   Annotation, reviews, references.

Compiler as main heading:

a)   **Title,** bibliographical citation of source.
b)   **Title** of thematic-catalogue-portion of item.
c)   Annotation, reviews, references.

AUTHOR as main heading:

a)   **Title,** bibliographical citation of source.
c)   Annotation.

> N.B. In an annotation, it is assumed, unless otherwise stated, that
> all incipits are single staff, and are given only for the opening
> movement. A number in parentheses following a composer's name indi-
> cates the number of incipits for that composer contained in the cata-
> logue. An annotation in quotation marks is by the compiler of the
> catalogue annotated, usually from correspondence he or she has sent
> in.

NUMBERING

Items that have decimals added to their number are *separate* entries
(added after initial numbering was made).

Items that have letters added to the number are *related* entries (e.g.
second edition, supplement, descriptive literature).

SYMBOLS

manuscript or *typescript* (symbol omitted when dissertation is available for sale in microfilm or xerox)

in preperation (location or affiliation of compiler added when available)

literature (about thematic catalogues or cataloguing)

Library of Congress (catalogues used in uniform titles on the catalogue cards of the Library of Congress)

Abbreviations

A	Austria	Jahr/Jg.	Jahrgand
Apr	April	Jb.	Jahrbuch
Aug	August	*l*	leaves
B	Belgium	L.A.	Los Angeles
b.	born	MA	Master of Arts
bap.	baptised	Mar	March
Bd.	Band, Bande	Mass.	Massachusetts
Bibl.	biblioteca, Bibliothek, bibliothèque, etc.	Md.	Maryland
		MGG	Die Musik in Geschichte und Gegenwart
c.	century (siècle, Jahrhundert)	MM	Master of Music
ca.	circa	MS,MSS	manuscript, manuscripts
Calif.	California	N	Norway
CH	Confédération Helvétique (Switzerland)	N.C.	North Carolina
		n.d.	no date (sans date, ohne Jahr)
Co.	Company	N.J.	New Jersey
Col.	column	NL	Netherlands
Cs	Czech	no.	number
CS	Czechoslovakia	Nov	November
C.U.N.Y.	City University of New York	n.p.	no place (sans lieu, ohne Ort)
d.	died	N.Y.	New York
DA	Dissertation Abstracts	Oct	October
DDT	Denkmäler deutscher Tonkunst	op.	opus
		p.	page, pages (seite, seiten)
De	German		
Dec	December	P.	Press
DMA	Doctor of Musical Arts	Penn.	Pennsylvania
diss.	dissertation	PL	Poland
DTB	Denkmäler der Tonkunst in Bayern	Pt	Portugese
		rev.	revised
DTÖ	Denkmäler der Tonkunst in Oesterreich	RISM	(see RILM)
		S	Sweden
ed.	editor, edition, edited (Herausgeber, Ausgabe, redacteur, etc.)	Sept	September
		sér.	series
		Soc.	Society
En	English	Sv	Swedish
enl.	enlarged	t.	tome
f.	following (page)	trans.	translate, any form
f	folio	U.	University
F	France	U. Micro	University Microfilms, Ann Arbor, Michigan
fasc.	fascicle		
facsim.	facsimile	US	United States of America
Feb	February	v.	volume, volumes (Band, Bände)
fl.	florished		
Fla.	Florida	Va.	Virginia
H	Hungary	vln.	violin
I	Italy	WECIS	Wellesley Edition Cantata Index Series
Inc.	Incorporated		
Jan	January	YU	Yugoslavia

PERIODICAL ABBREVIATIONS

ActaMusicol	Acta musicologica Int	PIMG	Publikationen der internationalen Musikgesellschaft
AfMW	Archiv fur Musik- wissenschaft BRD		
AMZ	Allgemeine musika- lische Zeitung	RassegnaMCurci	Rassegna musicale Curci I
Analecta- Musicol	Analecta musico- logica Int	RBelgeMusicol	Revue belge de musi- cologie B
BJ	Bach-Jahrbuch DDR	RItalMusicol	Rivista italiana di musicologia I
Börsenbl	Börsenbl. fur den Deutschen Buch- handel	RILM	Répertoire Interna- tional de Littéra- ture Musicale
Brio	Brio GB	RMI	Rivista musicale italiana I
Consort	The consort GB		
CurrentMusicol	Current musicology USA	RMusicol	Revue de musicologie F
FontesArtisM	Fontes artis musicae Int	SchJMW	Schweizerisches Jahr- buch für Musik- wissenschaft
GalpinSocJ	Galpin Society journal GB		
HaydnStud	Haydn Studien BRD	SIMG	Sammelbände der internationalen Musikgesellschaft
HudR	Hudební rozhledy CS		
HudVeda	Hudební věda CS		
IM	Istituzione e Monu- menti dell' Arte Musicale Italiana	StudMusicol	Studia musicologia H
		SvenskTMf	Svensk tidskrift för musikforskning S
JAmerMusicol- Soc	Journal of the Ameri- can Musicological Society USA	TVerNederMg	Tijdschrift van de Vereniging voor Nederlandse Musiek- geschiedenis NL
JResearchMEd	Journal of research in music education USA	VfMW	Vierteljahrsschrift für Musikwissen- schaft
KmJB	Kirchenmusikalisches Jahrbuch BRD	ZfMW	Zeitschrift für Musikwissenschaft
MCourier	Musical Courier		
MDisciplina	Musica disciplina INT	MOpinion	Musical opinion GB
MEducatorsJ	Music educators journal USA	MQ	Musical Quarterly USA
		MR	Music review GB
MensMelodie	Mens en melodie NL	MTimes	Musical times GB
Mf	Die Musikforschung BRD	NeueZM	Neue Zeitschrift für Musik BRD
MfMG	Monatshefte für Musikgeschichte	Notes	Notes, Music Library Association, USA
MGes	Musik und Gesell- schaft DDR	Organo	L'organo I
		ÖsterreichMz	Österreichische Musikzeitschrift A
MLetters	Music and letters GB		

LIBRARY ABBREVIATIONS

A - ÖSTERREICH

Ee	Eisenstadt, Esterházy-Ar- chiv
H	Herzogenburg, Chorherren- stift Herzogenburg, Bibliothek und Musik-

	archiv
HE	Heiligenkreuz, Zisterzien- serstift
KN	Klosterneuburg, Augustiner- Chorherrenstift
LA	Lambach, Benediktiner- Stift Lambach

M	Melk an der Donau, Benediktiner-Stift Melk
R	Rein, Zisterzienserstift, Bibliothek
SCH	Schlägl, Prämonstratenser-Stift, Schlägl
SEI	Seitenstetten, Stift
SF	St. Florian, Augustiner-Chorherrenstift
Wdo	Wien, Zentralarchiv des Deutschen Ordens
Wgm	--Gesellschaft der Musikfreunde in Wien
Wh	--Pfarrarchiv Hernals
Wkann	--Sammlung Prof. Hans Kann
Wkh	--Kirche am Hof
Wn	--Österreichische Nationalbibliothek (ehem. K.K. Hofbibliothek) Musiksammlung
Wp	--Musikarchiv, Piaristenkirche Maria Treu
Wst	--Stadtbibliothek, Musiksammlung
Ww	--Pfarrarchiv Währing
Wweinmann	--Privatbibliothek Dr. Alexander Weinmann

B - BELGIQUE/BELGIE

A	Antwerpen (Anvers)
Ba	Bruxelles (Brussel) Archives de la Ville
Bc	--Conservatoire Royal de Musique, Bibliothèque
Br	--Bibliothèque Royal Albert 1er
BRc	Brugge (Bruges) Stedelijk Muziekconservatorium, Bibliotheek
Gc	--Koninklijk Muziekconservatorium, Bibliotheek
K	Kortrÿk, St. Martinskerk
Lc	Liège (Luik), Conservatoire Royal de Musique, Bibliothèque
Lu	--Université de Liège, Bibliothèque
M	Mons (Bergen), Conservatoire Royal de Musique, Bibliothèque
MEa	Mechelen (Malines), Archief en Stadsbibliotheek
MEs	--Stedelijke Openbare Bibliotheek
Tc	Tournai (Doornik), Chapitre de la Cathédrale, Archives

CH - SCHWEIZ (CONFÉDÉRATION HELVÉTIQUE/SUISSE)

Bu	Basel, Öffentliche Bibliothek der Universität Basel, Musiksammlung
E	Einsiedeln, Kloster Einsiedeln, Musikbibliothek
SGs	St. Gallen, Stiftsbibliothek
SGv	--Stadtbibliothek (Vadiana)
Zz	Zürich, Zentralbibliothek, Kantons-, Stadt-, und Universitätsbibliothek

CS - ČSSR (CZECHOSLOVAKIA)

Bm	Brno, Moravské múzeum-hud. hist. oddeleni
BRe	Bratislava, Evanjelícka a.v. cirkevná knižnica
BRhs	--Knižnica hudobného seminára Filozofickej fakulty univerzity Komenského
BRnm	--Slovenské národné múzeum, hudobné oddelenie (mit den Beständen aus Kežmarok und Svedlár)
BRu	--Universitní knihovna
J	Jur pri Bratislava, Okresný archív, Bratislava-vidiek
KO	Košice, Městský archív
KRa	Kroměříž, Zámecký hudební archív
KRE	Kremnica, Městský archív
L	Levoča, Rímsko-katolícky farský kostol
Mms	Martin, Matica slovenská, Literárny archív
Mnm	--Slovenské národné múzeum, archív
N	Nítra, Štátní archív
NM	Nové Mesto nad Váhom, Rimsko-katolícky farský kostol
Pnm	Praha, Národní múzeum -hud. oddeleni
Pr	--Československý rozhlas - hudebni archív Ruzná provenience
Sk	Spišská Kapitula, Katedrálny rímsko-katolícky kostol-Knižnica Spišskej Kapituly
TR	Trnava, Dóm sv. Mikuláša

D - DEUTSCHLAND

AB	Amorbach, Fürstlich Leiningische Bibliothek
B	Berlin, Staatsbibliothek (Stiftung Preussischer Kulturbesitz)
BAR	Bartenstein, Fürst zu Hohenlohe-Bartensteinsches Archiv
Bds	Berlin, Deutsche Staatsbibliothek (ehem. Kgl. Bibliothek; Preussische Staatsbibliothek; Öffentliche Wissenschaftliche Bibliothek)
DL	Delitzsch (Sachsen-Anhalt), Museum, Bibliothek (Schloss)(ehem. Heimatmuseum)
DO	Donaueschingen, Fürstlich Fürstenbergische Hofbibliothek
DS	Darmstadt, Hessische Landes- und Hochschulbibliothek (ehem. Grossherzoglich Hessische Hofmusik-Bibliothek, Grossherzoglich Hessische Hof- und Landesbibliothek, Musikabteilung)
HL	Haltenbergstetten, Schloss uber Niederstetten (Baden-Württemberg), Fürst zu Hohenlohe-Jagstberg'sche Bibliothek
HR	Harburg über Donauwörth, Fürstlich Öttingen-Wallerstein'sche Bibliothek, Schloss Harburg
KA	Karlsruhe, Badische Landesbibliothek, Musikabteilung
KNhi	Koln, Joseph Haydn-Institut
LB	Langenburg (Württemberg), Fürstlich Hohenlohe-Langenburg'sche Schlossbibliothek
LEu	Leipzig (Sachsen), Universitätsbibliothek der Karl-Marx-Universität, Fachreferat Musik
Mbs	München, Bayerische Staatsbibliothek (ehemals Königliche Hof- und Staats-bibliothek), Musiksammlung
MÜs	Münster (Westfalen), Santini-Bibliothek (übernommen in die Bibliothek des Bischöflichen Priesterseminars)
MÜu	--Universitätsbibliothek
OB	Ottobeuren (Allgäu), Bibliothek der Benediktiner-Abtei
Rtt	Regensburg (Bayern), Fürstlich Thurn und Taxissche Hofbibliothek
RAd	Ratzeburg (Schleswig-Holstein), Domarchiv
RH	Rheda (Nordrhein-Westfalen), Fürst zu Bentheim-Tecklenburgische Bibliothek (übernommen nach Universitätsbibliothek Münster)
S	Stuttgart, Württembergische Landesbibliothek (ehemals Königliche Hofbibliothek)
SI	Sigmaringen, Fürstliche Hohenzollernsche Hofbibliothek
SWl	Schwerin (Mecklenburg), Mecklenburgische Landesbibliothek (ehem. Mecklenburgische Regierungsbibliothek), Musikabteilung
ZL	Zeil (Bayern), Fürstliche Waldburg-Zeil'sches Archiv

DK - DANMARK

Dsch	Dragor, Privatbibliothek Dr. Camilio Schoenbaum
Kc	København, Carl Claudius' Musikhistoriske Samling
Kk	--Det kongelige Bibliotek
Kmk	--Det kongelige danske Musikkonservatorium
Kt	--Teaterhistorisk Museum
Ku	--Universitetsbiblioteket 1. afdeling
Kv	--Københavns Universitets Musikvidenskabelige Institut
Ou	Odense, Odense Universitetsbibliotek
Sa	Sorø, Sorø Akademis Bibliotek

F - FRANCE

Pc	Paris, Bibliothèque du Conservertoire national de musique (now in Pn)
Pn	--Bibliothèque nationale

GB - GREAT BRITAIN

Cu	Cambridge, University Library
Lbm	London, British Museum
Ob	Oxford, Bodleian Library
Och	--Christ Church Library

H - MAGYARORSZÁG

Bb	Budapest, Bartók Béla Zeneművészeti Szakközepiskola Könyvtára
Bl	--Liszt Ferenc Zeneművészeti Föiskola Könyvtára
Bn	--Országos Széchényi Könyvtár
KE	Keszthely, Országos Széchényi Könyvtár, "Helikon"-Könyvtára
PH	Pannonhalma, Musicotheca Jesuitica

I - ITALIA

AN	Ancona, Biblioteca comunale "Benincasa"
MO1	Modena, Liceo Musicale O. Vecchi

NL - NEDERLAND

At	Amsterdam, Toonkunst-Bibliotheek
AN	Amerongen, Archief van het Kasteel der Graven Bentinck
DHgm	Den Haag, Gemeente Museum
DHk	--Koninklijke Bibliotheek
'sH	'S Hertogenbosch, Archief van de Illustre Lieve Vrouwe Broederschap
Uim	Utrecht, Instituut voor Muziekwetenschap der Rijksuniversiteit
Usg	--St. Gregorius Vereniging, Bibliotheek

S - SVERIGE

K	Kalmar, Gymnasie- och Stiftsbiblioteket
L	Lund, Universitetsbiblioteket
M	Malmö, Stadsbiblioteket
N	Norrköping, Stadsbiblioteket
ÖS	Östersund, Jämtlands Läns Biblioteket
Skma	Stockholm, Kungliga Musikaliska Akademiens Bibliotek
Sma	--Svenskt musikhistoriskt arkiv
Ssr	--Sveriges Radio, Musikbiblioteket
St	--Kungliga Teaterns Biblioteket
STr	Strängnäs, Roggebiblioteket
Uu	Uppsala, Universitetsbiblioteket
V	Västerås, Stifts-och Landsbiblioteket
VI1	Visby (Gotland), Landsarkivet
VX	Växjö, Stifts-och Landsbiblioteket (ehem. Stifts-och Gymnasiebiblioteket)

US - UNITED STATES OF AMERICA

BE	Berkeley (Cal.),University of California, Music Library
CIhc	Cincinnati (Ohio), Hebrew Union College Library
LC	Washington, (D.C.), Library of Congress, Music Division
NYcg	New York (N.Y.), Graduate Center, City University of New York
NYpl	--New York Public Library at Lincoln Center
NYpm	--Pierpont Morgan Library
NYqc	--Queens College of the City University, Paul Klapper Library, Music Library

ABEL, CARL FRIEDRICH, 1723-1787

1   HELM, Sanford M. Carl Friedrich Abel, symphonist; a biographical,
    stylistic, and bibliographical study (PhD diss.: U. of Michigan,
    1953) 378p. Univ. Micro. no. 5677. (typescript)
        Thematic index of Abel's instrumental music, 328-64.
            Arranged by key with incipits of all movements.

2   BEECHEY, Gwilym. Carl Friedrich Abel's six symphonies, Op. I4,
    MLetters 51/3 (Jul 1970) 279-85.
            Incipits for all movements of the Op. 14 symphonies.

3   KNAPE, Walter. Bibliographisch-thematisches Verzeichnis der Kompo-
    sitionen von Karl Friedrich Abel (1723-1787), Verlag des Herausgebers
    W. Knape, Cuxhaven 1 (1971) x, 299p.
            Double staff incipits for all movements of 46 symphonies,
            15 concertos, 18 string quartets, 37 string trios, 32 sona-
            tas, etc. Works arranged by genre.

4   DEARLING, Robert (Dunstable, Bedfordshire). [Thematic catalogue]
▽   Index cards. Compiled 1971 (manuscript).
            Incipits for 46 symphonies and 18 quartets.

ADAMS, Robert Lee (compiler)

5   The development of a keyboard idiom in England during the English
    Renaissance (PhD diss.: Washington U., St. Louis, 1960) 3v., Univ.
    Micro. 60-4680. (typescript)
        Thematic index of English virginal music, v. III, 1-337.
            Index assembled from contemporary manuscript collections such
            as Parthenia, Fitzwilliam, etc. Themes are entered alphabe-
            tically by composer. Contains a manuscript index (p. 338-94)
            listing the contents of the sources used. Pages 395-406 con-
            tain a title index.

Key: ✷ in preparation; ▽ manuscript; □ literature; ✷ Library of Congress

ADLGASSER, ANTON CAJETAN, 1729-1777

6   RAINER, Werner. **Das Instrumentalwerk A.C. Adlgassers nebst Biographie**
▽   **und Werkverzeichnis** (PhD diss.: Innsbruck, 1964) 200*l*. (typescript)
          Thematisches Verzeichnis, 95*l*.
                Over 100 incipits of 8 Masses, 2 Requiems, Offertories, Ves-
                pers, hymns, etc., 22 oratorios, 11 sinfonias, concertos and
                chamber music.

6a   --- **Anton Cajetan Adlgasser.** Ein biographischer Beitrag zur Musik-
☐   geschichte Salzburgs um die Mitte des 18. Jahrhunderts, *Mitteilun-*
          gen der Gesellschaft für Salzburger Landeskunde CV (1965) 205-37.
                First (non-thematic) portion of the dissertation.

6b   --- *Mozart-Jahrbuch* XXXX (1962/63) 280-91.
☐   Index of the works, but without incipits.

AGOSTINI, PIER SIMONE, ca. 1650-?

7   JANDER, Owen (Wellesley, Mass.). **Thematic catalogue,** to be published
✱   in the *Wellesley Edition Cantata Index Series*. (see no. 1400).

ALBÉNIZ, ISAAC, 1860-1909

8   BARULICH, Frances (New York U.) **The piano music of Isaac Albéniz**
✱   **(1860-1909)**
          Thematic index, Appendix.
                Multiple staff incipits for all movements, études, individual
                dances etc. for each work within a suite or collection. There
                will be approximately 200 works covered (each piece within a
                suite or collection being counted as one work). The entries
                will be arranged in chronological order.

ALBERO, SEBASTIAN, fl. 1750

9   SHEVELOFF, Joel Leonard. **The keyboard music of Domenico Scarlatti:**
          A re-evaluation of the present state of knowledge in the light of
          the sources (PhD diss., Music: Brandeis U., 1970) 3v.: xiv, 688p.
          Univ. Micro. no. 70-24,658. (typescript) (see no. 1158).
          Thematic index to the thirty sonatas of Sebastian Albero, v. 3,
          Appendix D, 546-51.
                Two staff incipits of the thirty single movements for key-
                board as found in the MS source Venezia, Biblioteca Marciana,
                9768. "All we know about Albero is that he was a court organ-
                ist in Madrid in 1747 and again in 1751 (from pay receipts),
                that British Museum Additional 31553 containing 44 sonatas
                purportedly by Domenico Scarlatti was copied out for Albero
                in the late 1740's, and that the manuscript volume of his
                thirty keyboard sonatas was executed by the same hand that
                copied out the great Venezia and Parma sets of MSS of Scar-
                latti's sonatas."

ALBERTI, DOMENICO, ca. 1710-1740

10   EITNER, Robert. **Domenico Alberti,** *Quellen-Lexicon* I (Leipzig:
      Breitkopf & Härtel, [1898])
          Thematisches Verzeichnis der 8 Sonaten, 84.
              Incipits for 8 sonatas originally published as Alberti's
              8 sonate per cembalo, Op. 1 (London: Walsh, 17--). Giuseppe
              Jozzi published a second edition, as his own compositions,
              in Amsterdam (1761). *8 sonate pour clavecin* (see no. 636.1)

10a   --- 2. verbesserte Auflage (Graz:Akademische Druck u. Verlagsanstalt
      1959).

11   WÖRMANN, Wilhelm. **Die Klaviersonate Domenico Albertis,** *ActaMusicol*
      XXVII (1955) 84-112.
          Thematisches Verzeichnis, 97-98.
              Incipits for all movements of 24 one-and two-movement works.

ALBINONI, TOMASO, 1671-1750

12   GIAZOTTO, Remo. **Tomaso Albinoni. Musico di violino dilettante**
✧   **veneto** (Milan: Bocca, 1945) 351p.
          Indice tematico, 323-51.
              Incipits for each movement of his sonatas, concertos, sin-
              fonias, and suites.

13   TALBOT, Michael. **The instrumental music of Tomaso Albinoni (167I-**
▽   **174I)** (PhD diss.: Cambridge U., 1968) 3v.(typescript)
          Thematic catalogue, v. II, 1-99.
              Approximately 550 incipits for all movements, including
              sections in contrasted tempi within a movement. "A source
              list mostly on even-numbered pages alternates with a cata-
              logue proper on odd-numbered pages."

14   DEARLING, Robert (Dunstable, Bedfordshire). **[Thematic catalogue]**
▽   Index cards (manuscript).
              Supplements Giazotto's catalogue by 30 works.
              Reported in 1971.

ALBRECHT, Constantin (compiler)

15   **Thematisches Verzeichnis der Streich- und Clavier-Trios, Quartette**
      und Quintette von Haydn, Mozart, Beethoven, Schubert, Mendelssohn-
      Bartholdy, und Schumann, chronologisch geordnet und metronomisirt von
      [C.A.] (Leipzig: Forberg; Moskau: Jurgenson, 1890) xx, 66p.

ALBRECHTSBERGER, JOHANN GEORG, 1736-1809

16   FUCHS, Aloys. **Thematisches Verzeichnis sämtlicher Compositionen**
▽   (D Bds: MS no. 18). (manuscript)
              One of many manuscript catalogues prepared by Fuchs. (see no.
              1159)

17   FUCHS, Aloys. **Thematisches Verzeichnis von J.G. Albrechtsbergers**
▽   **sämtlichen Compositionen** (D Bds: HB VII Mus. ms. theor. K. 405)[44p.]

Double and single staff incipits for 206 instrumental works
and sacred vocal compositions: sonatas, quartets, trios, preludes, Masses, Graduals, Offertories, etc., organized roughly
according to genre.

18   FUCHS, Aloys. Themat. Verz. der Kompositionen von G. Albrechtsber-
▽   ger von A. Fuchs 1838 (D Berlin: Ms. 4° 97)(manuscript)

    Reference: Robert EITNER, Quellenlexicon 1, 96.

19   WEISSENBAECK, Andreas. Thematisches Verzeichnis der Kirchenkompositionen von Johann Georg Albrechtsberger, *Jahrbuch des
Stiftes Klosterneuburg*, VI   (Wien and Leipzig: W. Braumuller,
1914) 1-160.
    Part I (dated works in chronological order) gives vocal
incipits for all voices with Latin text and instrumentation.
Part II (undated works) gives incipits of all sections of
masses, offices, and liturgic hymns. 279 compositions
indexed by title and by Esterhazy and Klosterneuburg
holdings.

20   SCHRAMEK-KIRCHNER, Alexander Matthias. Johann Georg Albrechtsbergers
▽   Fugenkompositionen in seinen Werken für Tasteninstrumente (PhD diss.:
Wien, 1954) 3v., 251l.; l. 253-501; 26p., 4l., 133l., 82l. (typescript)
    Thematisches Verzeichnis J.G. Albrechtsbergers Kompositionen für
Tasteninstrumente, v. 3, 82l.
    Single and double staff incipits of preludes, fugues, ver-
sets, etc. arranged by opus number (1-30), then followed by
works without opus number.

21   SOMFAI, László. Albrechtsberger-Eigenschriften in der Nationalbibliothek Szechenyi, Budapest, *Studia Musicologica*, I/1-2 (1961)
175-202; IV/1-2 (1963) 179-190; IX/1-2 (1967) 191-220.
    [Thematic catalogue of the instrumental works]
    Part I: Symphonies, concertos, and chamber music for 4 and
5 instruments; Part II: Chamber music for 3 instruments;
Part III: Chamber "sonatas" that consist of prelude and
fugue movements. Arrangement is chronological within genres.
Incipits of each movement, instrumentation.

d'ALESSANDRO, RAFFAELE, 1911-1959

21.1 MARETTA, Luise (Bern). [The life and work of Raffaele d'Alessandro
*   (1911-1959)]
    [Thematic catalogue].

ALFVÉN, HUGO, 1872-1960

22   RUDÉN, Jan Olof. Hugo Alfvén: Käll-och verkförteckning [Hugo
*   Alfvén: list of sources and works]. To be published in 1972 or
1973.
    Contains a chronological list of works, with incipits
given for each movement. Includes folk music noted
down by Alfvén.

ALTMANN, Wilhelm (compiler)

23   Orchester-Literatur-Katalog; Verzeichnis von seit 1850 erschienenen
      Orchester-Werken. 2. vermehrte Auflage (Leipzig: Leuckart, 1926)
              Contains the following thematic indexes: Händel: Concerti
              Grossi, p.19-20; 158-9; Haydn: Symphonien, 21-30; Mozart:
              Symphonien, 46-51, Klavier-Konzerte, 215-18.

ALTMANN, Wilhelm

24   Über thematische Kataloge. *Bericht über den Internationalen Musik-*
□   *wissenschaftlichen Kongress der Beethoven-Zentenarfeier* (Wien: Univer-
      sal Edition, 1927) 283-89.

d'ANGLEBERT, JEAN HENRY, 1628-1691

25   Pièces de clavecin, *Publications de la Société Française de Musico-*
      logie, 1. sér. VIII (1934) 161p.
              Table [of contents], 155-61.
                    151 incipits of keyboard chaconnes and overtures, as well as
                    d'Anglebert's transcriptions of "other airs" by Lully.

ANGLÈS, Higini (compiler)

26   La Música de las cantigas de Santa María del Rey Alfonso el Sabio;
      facsímil, transcripción y estudio critico (Barcelona: Biblioteca
      Central, 1943) 2v.
              Capitulo VII: Indice Temático de las Melodías, v. II, 115-26.
                    Thematic index of the melodies, all anonymous. Modern clefs,
                    non-mensural transcription for the 402 cantigas and 22 extra
                    incipits from the appendices.

AOSTA, Italy. Biblioteca del seminario

26.1   VAN, Guillaume de. A recently discovered source of early fifteenth
      century polyphonic music, *MDisciplina* II (1948) 5-74.
                    Contains a thematic catalogue of the 70 *unica* in the Aosta
                    Codex, including works by Berken, Binchois, Bloym, Brabant,
                    Brassart, Dunstable, Grossin, G. Le Grant, J. Le Grant, Loque-
                    ville, Nelbeland, Power, Sarto, Sovesby, and Zacharias.

ARCADE, EUGÉNE, 1867-?

27   DÉDÉ, fils. Eugéne Arcade, Chef d'orchestre au Concert-Parisien,
      compositeur né à Bordeaux le 12 Janvier 1867 (New York: Victor
      Genez) folio, n.p. (US LC: ML 134/.D30 A2)
              [Thematic catalogue].

ARLT, Gustave O.

28   Lexicographical indexing of folk melodies, *Modern Philology* XXVII/2
□   (1929) 147-54.

ARNOLD, SAMUEL, 1740-1802

29   DEARLING, Robert (Dunstable, Bedfordshire). [Thematic catalogue]
▽   Index cards (manuscript).

"Incipits for 34 operatic overtures (from early editions in the
British Museum), supplementing Cudworth by 31 works." (see no.
273)

ARTARIA (publisher)

30   Catalogue thématique de Haydn, Mozart, Clementi et Pleyel (Wien:
Artaria, 1798).

ASPELMAYER, FRANZ, 1728-1786

31   RIESSBERGER, Helmut. **Franz Aspelmayer (I728-I786)** (PhD diss.: Inns-
▽   bruck, 1954) 184, xliii*l*. (typescript)
Thematischer Katalog der Instrumentalwerke Aspelmayers, [147]-
184.
> Over 150 incipits for all movements of 4 symphonies, 13
> string quartets, 19 trios and divertimenti for 2 violins
> and bass, concertos, etc. Works arranged by genre.

AUGSBURG, Bibliothek der Fuggerschen Domänenkanzlei

32   KROYER, Theodor. **[Thematic catalogue]**   (On loan by the *DTB* to D
▽   Mbs) 234*l*. Compiled 1918-1919. (manuscript)
> One of the many inventories prepared by the compiler under
> Adolf Sandberger's direction for the *Denkmäler der Tonkunst
> in Bayern*. This is an important catalogue of 900 works,
> mostly MSS. Includes listings for many unknown composers
> and numerous little-known or lost works. Composers: Moli-
> tor, Brandl, Michel, Georg Lang, Banhard, Bachschmidt, Franc.
> Ign. Kaa, Jaumann, Zach, Weinrauch, Righini, Brixi, Anfossi,
> Meinr. Spiess, Schlecht, Dischner, Mozart, Neubauer, C.H.
> Graun, Giov. God. Seifert, P.Sixt. Bachmann, Fischer, M.
> Haydn, J. Haydn, J. Demharter, Frigl, Xav. Heel, Beecke,
> Martin, Giov. Hayde, Salieri, Holzmann, L.B. Witzka, Jos.
> Schnabel, Gerard Martin, Sales, Sacchini, Dirmayr, Matth.
> Fischer, Fürst Anselm Victor Fugger, Drexel, Gretry, Gluck,
> C.L. Röllig, Triklir, Hofmeister, Reichardt, B. Schermer,
> Matthias Pauser,Schlicht, Wenceslav Ranque, Wolfg. Schaller,
> Freden, Vogler, Violand, Schwindl, Rosetti, Gyrowetz, Mez-
> ger, Gius. Martin, Krommer, Kospoth, Loeffler, Paul Struck,
> Paul Wranitzky, J. Amon, M. Clementi, Canabich, Dittersdorf,
> P. Theodorus, Händel, Vanhal, Pleyel, Mislivecek, Bach, Giu-
> seppe Bieling, N.Piccini, Schmidt, Sophi, La Motte, Holzbauer,
> Joh. Nep. Hummel, Georg Anton Dosch, J.M. Malzat,Isf. Kettner,
> Lechner, Jommelli, Angeber, Cherubini, Plac. Braun, Fortuna-
> to Cavallo, Giulini, Ant. Hammer, Zöschinger, Bororolli,
> Pausch, Laube, Madlseder, Mango, Winter, Starck, Traetta, Ul-
> linger, Sardini, Bill, Palestrina, Preindl, Eybler, Bonav.
> Witzka, Sandl, L. Schneider, Adlgasser, Toeschi, Witt, Giov.
> Plac. Rutini, Schroeter, C.H.Rink, Knecht, A. Müller, Rei-
> cha, Schmittbaur, Ph. Eder, Jos. Thoma, Sterk__, Frederic,
> Ferd. Ries, Kaesermann, Beethoven, G. Hemmerlein, J.F.G.
> Beckmann, Gius. Sardi, Kneferle, Boccorini, Joh. André, Him-
> mel, Tartini, Viotti, Leop. Kozeluch, Fesca, Cimarosa, Hiller,
> Giov. Batt. Borghi, Mich. Demler, Guglielmi, Hasse, C.M. We-
> ber, Benda, Andreozzi, Lampugnani, Majo, Schubart, Nicolai,

Bucher, J.S. Mayr, Harder, Dürniz, F.J. Miller, Schuster,
Paisiello, Rust, Paer, Giac. Tritto, Tozzi, Naumann, Carlo
Monza, Mortarelli, Joh. Nic. Tischer, Kirmayr, C.F.Beck.

Reference: Robert MÜNSTER, Die Musik im Augustinerchorherrenstift Beuerberg von 1768 bis 1803 und der thematische Katalog
des Chorherrn Alipius Seitz, 55. (see no.1205).

AUMANN, FRANZ JOSEPH, 1795-?

33   DORMANN, Peter (Mainz). Thematischer Katalog
*

AVISON, CHARLES, 1709-1770

34   STEPHENS, Norris L. Charles Avison, an eighteenth-century English
composer, musician and writer (PhD diss.: U. of Pittsburgh, 1968)
x, 349, 11p. Univ. Micro. no. 69-4106.(typescript)
    Thematic catalogue, 11p.
      Incipits for all movements of all known works with and with-
out opus numbers. Supplement for doubtful works. Entries
give information on MSS and published editions.

BACCAY, Dalmidio Alberto (compiler)

35   Musica regional y metodo [Regional music and its formulas] (Buenos
Aires: Luis Lasserre, 1967) 98p. (*RILM* 67/2180^{dm})
    [Thematic catalogue].

BACH [unidentified as to first name]

36   KAST, Paul. Die Bach-Handschriften der Berliner Staatsbibliothek,
Tübinger Bach-Studien II-III (1958) 161-64. (see nos. 40b & 64b)
    Incipits of 45 instrumental works by unidentified Bachs.

BACH family

37   SCHNEIDER, Max. Thematisches Verzeichnis der musikalischen Werke
der Familie Bach, *BJ* IV hrsg. von Arnold SCHERING (Leipzig et al:
Breitkopf & Härtel, 1907) 103-77.
    This first installment of the catalogue indexes works by
Heinrich (p. 105-09), Johann Michael (p. 109-32), and Johann
Christoph Bach (p. 132-77). Two-stave incipits for all movements of vocal and instrumental works. Lost works included,
sources given.

37a   --- Reprint (New York: Johnson Reprint, 1967)

Key: * in preparation; ▽ manuscript; □ literature; ☆ Library of Congress

BACH, CARL PHILIPP EMANUEL, 1714-1788

38   Verzeichniss des musikalischen Nachlasses des verstorbenen
Capellmeisters C.P.E. Bach...(Hamburg: G.F. Schniebes, 1790) 1-52.

38a   --- Reprinted by Heinrich MIESNER, *Bach Jahrbuch* XXXV (1938)
         103-36; XXXVI (1939) 81-112; XXXVII (1940-1948) 159-81.
            The thematic index of keyboard and instrumental works is
            contained in part I of the *Bach Jahrbuch* reprint, XXXV
            (1938) 107-36. Works arranged by genre.

39   WESTPHAL, Kurt. **Catalogue thématique des Oeuvres de Carl Philipp**
▽   **Emanuel Bach** (D Bds) 105p. (manuscript)
            Incipits arranged by genre for solo and ensemble, keyboard,
            and vocal works (partially thematic). Provides dates.

40   WOTQUENNE, Alfred. **Thematisches Verzeichnis der Werke von C.P.E.**
☆   **Bach** (Leipzig: Breitkopf & Härtel, 1905) 109p.
            Internationally accepted standard catalogue. Incipits of
            instrumental music arranged chronologically within genre
            with instrumentation provided. Melodic incipits of vocal
            music with text underlay.

40a   --- Reprint (Wiesbaden: Breitkopf & Härtel, 1964).

         Reviews: OeMZ XXIV (Feb 1969) 110.

40b   --- Supplement in Paul KAST, **Die Bach-Handschriften der Berliner**
Staatsbibliothek, *Tübinger Bach-Studien* II-III (1958) 153-56.
         48 incipits of vocal and instrumental works.

41   MIESNER, Heinrich. **Philipp Emanuel Bach in Hamburg; Beiträge zu**
seiner Biographie und zur Musikgeschichte seiner Zeit (Heide, 1929)
136, [14]p.
       Themenverzeichnis, Notenanhang, [14]p.
            Includes comparisons of themes of C.P.E. Bach with those of
            J.S. Bach, W.A. Mozart, and others, with excerpts from auto-
            graph MSS.

42   JACOBS, Richard Morris. **The chamber ensembles of C.P.E. Bach**
using two or more wind instruments (PhD diss.: U. of Iowa, 1963)
xvii, 293p. Univ. Micro. 63-7926 (typescript)
            Includes corrections and addenda to the standard thematic
            catalogues, and relevant errors and omissions in Wotquenne
            thematic list of works of C.P.E. Bach.

43   SUCHALLA, Ernst. **Die Orchestersinfonien Carl Philipp Emanuel Bachs**
nebst einem Thematischen Verzeichnis seiner Orchesterwerke (PhD
diss.: Mainz, 1968) (Dissertationsdruck: Augsburg, 1968) 295p.
       Thematisches Verzeichnis aller Orchesterwerke C.P.E. Bachs,
       163-286.
            Incipits organized by Wotquenne numbers. Contains a con-
            cordance table for comparison with the original "Nachlass"
            catalogue, and with the catalogues of Wotquenne, Westphal,
            and Bitter. Over 300 double staff incipits for all movements
            of 52 clavier concertos, 2 oboe concertos, 4 flute concertos,
            3 cello concertos, 19 sinfonias, 15 sonatas, etc.

44   HELM, Eugene (U. of Maryland). A new thematic catalogue of the
*   works of C.P.E. Bach.
            "Incipits for the complete works as gathered in 15 countries
            and nearly 200 libraries with descriptions of manuscript
            and printed sources. About 2500 incipits, of all movements,
            each on a single staff. Arranged by medium of performance.
            With selective lists of modern editions. Completion expected
            in 1972."

BACH, JOHANN BERNHARD, 1676-1749

45   ARNESON, Arne Jon. The orchestral ouvertures of Johann Bernhard
▽   Bach (1676-1749) (MA diss.: U. of Wisconsin, 1969) 2v. (typescript)
            Thematic index of his orchestral overtures in D, G, e and g,
            76-79.
                "The work consists of discussion, analysis and scholarly
                editions of the overtures."   Contains 41 incipits.

BACH, JOHANN CHRISTIAN, 1735-1782

46   SCHÖKEL, Heinrich P. J.C. Bach und die Instrumentalmusik seiner
      Zeit (PhD diss.: Ludwig-Maximilians Universität, München, 1922)
      (Wolfenbüttel: Kallmeyer, 1926) 203p.
            Thematischer Katalog der Instrumentalwerke J.C. Bachs, 177-203.
                Incipits arranged by genre and then by opus number. Loca-
                tion of MS is given when known.

47   TUTENBERG, Fritz. Die Sinfonik J.C. Bachs (Wolfenbüttel-Berlin:
      Kallmeyer, 1928) 387p.
            Thematischer Katalog der Bachschen Sinfonien, 369-87.
                65 incipits of opera overtures, other overtures, symphonies,
                and sinfonies concertantes, with bibliographical information.

48   TERRY, Charles Sanford. John Christian Bach (London: Oxford U.
      Press, 1929) xvi, 373p.
            John Christian Bach's works, vocal and instrumental: thematic
            catalogue, [193]-361.
                Gives incipits according to genre of the sacred and secular
                vocal, orchestral, chamber, violin, piano, and military
                music. Dates of composition, publishers, occasions of
                performance, and sources are included.

48a   --- 2nd ed., with a forword by H.C. Robbins LANDON (London, New
      York: Oxford U. Press, 1967) 1v, 373p.
                Contains important corrections to the thematic catalogue
                in the first edition. (see also no. 51)

49   WHITE, Joseph A. The concerted symphonies of John Christian Bach
      (PhD diss.: U. of Michigan, 1953) 2v. Univ. Micro. 58-3750 (typescr)
            Thematic index of symphonies, v.I, part 3, 313-19.
                Incipits of each movement for 15 concerted symphonies.
                Library locations of MSS given.

50   DOWNES, Edward O.D. The operas of Johann Christian Bach as a re-
▽   flection of the dominant trends in opera seria 1750-1780 (PhD diss.:
      Harvard U., 1958) 3v.(typescript)
            Thematic index [of the operas], v. 3, Appendix A, 2-74.

Detailed thematic index to the individual numbers in all
Bach's operas, plus a few arias and overtures he is known
to have written for insertion into opere serie by other
composers. Organized alphabetically by opera. Gives melodic
incipits of highest voice for vocal numbers with text underlay, and incipits of first violin or highest wind for all
movements of instrumental numbers.

50a   --- Revision projected by Downes for publication by Harvard U. Press.

51   KRABBE, Niels. **The symphonies of John Christian Bach.** A biblio-
▽   graphical survey, with a discussion of the problems of authenticity
       and chronology (PhD diss.: U. of Copenhagen, 1967) 227p. (typescript)
           Thematic-bibliographic catalogue of John Christian Bach's symphonies,
           25-163.
               Incipits for all movements of 51 genuine symphonies and 20
               spurious or doubtful symphonies followed by comments on, and
               corrections or additions to, Terry's catalogue. (see also no.
               48a)

51.1   --- **J.C. Bach's symphonies and the Breitkopf Thematic Catalogue,**
       Festskrift Jens Peter Larsen 1902 ⅛ 1972. Studier udgivet af Musik-
       videnskabeligt Institut ved Københavns Universitet (København: Wil-
       helm Hansen Musik-Forlag, 1972) 233-54.
               Investigates the authenticity of the works attributed to J.C.
               Bach in the Breitkopf catalogue, as well as works by him but
               attributed to other composers. Contains numerous incipits.

52   VOS, Marie Ann. **The liturgical choral works of Johann Christian
       Bach** (PhD diss.: Washington U., 1969) 2v., Univ. Micro. 69-
       22565. (typescript)
           Thematic index, v.2, 1-67.
               26 works are inventoried with instrumental and vocal
               incipits for all movements.

53   DEARLING, Robert J. (Dunstable, Bedfordshire). **Thematic catalogue
▽   of J.C. Bach's symphonies, overtures, and sinfonie concertanti**
       Compiled 1972. (manuscript)
               Divided into three sections: I.) "79 works listed in key or-
               der (C,D,E flat, E, etc.) in single-stave incipits for first
               movements only, showing title, scoring, editions (cross-in-
               dexed to Section 2), tempo indications of all movements, cata-
               logue references (Terry, Tutenburg, Schökel), and where re-
               quired, notes concerning authenticity, etc. Section 2: Edi-
               tions of Symphonies and Overtures, enumerating the contents
               of early editions and cross-referencing works which appeared
               in more than one edition. Section 3: Outlines of the con-
               tents of Terry, Tutenburg, and Schökel by reference to the
               numbers in Section 1."

53.1   STARAL-BAIERLE, Ilse Susanne. **Die Klavierwerke von Johann Christian
▽   Bach** (PhD diss.: Graz, 1971) (typescript)
           Thematischer Katalog der Klavierwerke Bachs, 223-303.

BACH, JOHANN CHRISTOPH FRIEDRICH, 1732-1795

54   SCHÜNEMANN, Georg, ed.   **J.C.F. Bach. Die Kindheit Jesu (I773);
       Die Auferweckung Lazarus (I773),** *DDT* 56/1 (Leipzig: Breitkopf & Här-
       tel, 1917) xxxiii, 110p.

54   Thematisches Verzeichnis der Werke von J.C.F Bach, ix-xvii.
      96 incipits arranged by genre; dramatic works (1), sacred
      (14), secular vocal (23), keyboard (30), chamber music (14),
      symphonies (14). Detailed bibliographic information and
      location of autographs included.

--- New edition edited and revised by Hans Joachim MOSER (Wiesbaden:
Breitkopf & Härtel, 1959) xxxvii, 110p.

BACH, JOHANN SEBASTIAN, 1685-1750

55   Thematisches Verzeichniss/ über,/ sämtliche Compositionen von/ Johann
▽   Sebastian Bach/ Cantor in Leipzig/ Geb. 21. März 1685 + 28. Juli
      1750/zusamengestellt/ von/ Aloys Fuchs in Wien/ 1839./ 156p. (some
      blank) (manuscript)
            Double staff incipits for all the works of Bach, arranged by
            genre. Compositions for clavier and organ, instrumental mu-
            sic, and vocal music.

56   Johann Sebastian Bach's Werke, hrsg. von der Bach-Gesellschaft (Leip-
      zig: Breitkopf & Härtel, 1851-1926) Jg. 27/2; Jg. 46.
      Die Gesangeswerke Bach's...Die Instrumentalwerke Bach's. Thema-
      tisches Verzeichniss.
            The second half of Jg. 27 is a complete thematic index of
            church cantatas no. 1-120 in numerical order, with two staff
            incipits of all sections of each work. Jg. 46 is a thematic
            index of cantatas 121-191, and all of Bach's other vocal and
            instrumental works by genre. An alphabetical index and in-
            dex of first lines is included.

56 a --- Reprint (Ann Arbor: J.W. Edwards, 1947).

56 b --- Reprint in progress (Gregg Press).

56 c --- Reprint in microfiche (University Music Editions).

56 d --- Reprint in miniature score form (Kalmus).

57   Thematisches Verzeichniss der Instrumentalwerke von Joh. Seb. Bach.
      Auf Grund der Gesammtausgabe von C.F. Peters (Leipzig: Peters,
      [1867]) Anhang I, 89p.
            Pages 5-88b contain a thematic index of Bach's instrumental
            works, divided into categories by medium.

57a   --- 2nd edition edited by Alfred DÖRFFEL [1882] iv, 92p.

58   TAMME, Carl. Thematisches Verzeichniss der Vocalwerke von Joh. Seb.
      Bach. Auf Grund der Gesammtausgaben von C.F. Peters und der Bach-
      Gesellschaft (Leipzig: Peters, 1890) xvi, 156p.
            Thematic index to Bach's vocal music in 13 sections according
            to genre.

58a   --- Reprint [193-]

58b   --- Reprint (New York: Franklin, ca. 1972).

59   HOCHSTETTER, Armin. Die Symmetrie im Aufbau der Orgelpräludien von
▽   Joh. Seb. Bach. Ein Beitrag zur Entwicklungsgeschichte der Orgel-
      musik. (PhD diss.: Wien, 1928) viii, 210l. (typescript)
      Verzeichnis der Werke in Anfängen, 60-69.
            44 single and double staff incipits of preludes, fugues,
            fantasias, toccatas, etc.

60 [McALL] May deForest Payne. **Melodic index to the works of J.S. Bach**
(New York: G. Schirmer, 1938)
> An index of 3636 themes given in Bach's actual tonalities,
> plus finding charts based on the design formed by the first
> four notes of different pitch in each theme. Concordance
> of numbers used by Peters and Bach-Gesellschaft editions.

60a Revised and enlarged edition by May deForest McALL (New York: Peters,
1962) 138p.
> *Reviews: National Association of Teachers of Singing Bulletin*
> XX/1 (1963) 38; *Organ Institute Quarterly* XI/2 (1965) 23;
> Elizabeth TRUSTAM, *Brio* II/1 (1965) 22-23.

61 DRINKER, Henry S. **The Bach chorale texts in English translation**
(New York: Association of American Colleges, 1941) xii, 105p.
  Melodic index to the 389 chorales, 83-105.
> Incipits indexed in a system based on mode, first and re-
> peated notes, direction of progression, and time signature.
> Chorales are numbered according to Bernhard Friedrich Rich-
> ter's edition of the *389 chorales of J.S. Bach for mixed
> chorus* (Breitkopf & Härtel, 1898)

62 SCHMIEDER, Wolfgang. **Thematisch-systematisches Verzeichnis der**
✡ **Musikalischen Werke von Johann Sebastian Bach,** *Bach-Werke-Verzeichnis*
(BWV) (Leipzig: Breitkopf & Härtel, 1950) xxii, 747p.
> "A complete thematic index of all the known works of Bach,
> organized by genre and by instrumentation, giving for each
> work the author of the text, if any, instrumentation, puta-
> tive date of composition, a brief description,...the nature
> and last known (1945) whereabouts of the sources, any other
> Bach works with which it shares material or works of other
> composers upon which it is based, the principal editions,
> and a list of the references to the work in literature."
> *Notes* VIII/1 (Dec. 1950) 156-59.
> *Reviews: Monthly Musical Record* LXXX (Oct 1950) 198-200;
> *MTimes* XCI (Oct 1950) 394-95; Alfred DÜRR, *Musica* IV (Dec
> 1950) 484-88; Friedrich BLUME, *Mf* IV/2-3 (1951) 220-23;
> W.C. de JONG, *MensMelodie* VI (Nov 1951) 350.

62a --- 2. Unchanged re-editions (1958, 1961).

62b --- 3. Designated as the 3rd edition (Wiesbaden: Breitkopf & Härtel,
1966).

62c --- 4. Auflage. 2 volumes considerably enlarged and corrected.
*

BACH, WILHELM FRIEDEMANN, 1710-1784

63 **Wilhelm Friedemann Bach [Thematic catalogue]** (D Bds: HB VII, Mus.
▽ ms theor. K. 497) [5p.](manuscript)
> Incipits for a small selection of miscellaneous works.

64 FALCK, Martin. **Wilhelm Friedemann Bach.** Sein Leben und seine Werke
✡ mit thematischem Verzeichnis seiner Kompositionen (Leipzig: Kahnt
Nachf., 1913) iv, 170, 31p.
  **Thematisches Verzeichnis der Kompositionen von Wilhelm Friedemann
Bach,** part IV, 31p.
> Incipits for all movements of 106 vocal and instrumental
> works, organized according to genre and key, with spurious
> works added at the end of each group.

64 a   --- New edition by Wilibald GURLITT (Lindau: Kahnt, 1956) 170, 31p.

64 b   --- Supplement in Paul KAST, **Die Bach-Handschriften der Berliner Staatsbibliothek,** *Tübinger Bach-Studien* II/3 (1958)
      Bei Falck nicht verzeichnete Werke, 157-60.
        Contains an Incipit Verzeichnis of Bach family MSS.

BACHMANN, Alberto (compiler)

65   **Les grands violinistes du passé** (Paris: Fischbacher, 1913) 468p.
        Contains thematic lists of works by the following composers:
        Baillot, Bériot, Corelli, Ernst, Geminaini, Joachim, Kreutzer,
        Laub, Leclair, Lipinsky, Locatelli, Nardini, Paganini, Rode,
        Sarasate, Spohr, Tartini, Vieuxtemps, Viotti, Vivaldi, and
        Wieniawski. Listings are incomplete. See under individual
        composers for details.

BAILLOT DE SALES, PIERRE-MARIE-FRANÇOISE, 1771-1842

66   BACHMANN, Alberto. **Les grands violinistes du passé** (Paris: Fisch-
      bacher, 1913) 468p. (see no. 65)
        48 incipits from his "Méthode" for violin, p. 7-13.

BARBIREAU, JACQUES, ca.1470?-1491

67   SAAR, Johannes du. **Het Leven en de Composities van J. Barbireau**
    [The life and works of J. Barbireau] (Utrecht: W. de Haan, 1946)
    210p.
      De Composities van Barbireau, 29-31.
        Incipits of each voice in Masses, chansons, and a motet,
        with bibliographic information giving location of MSS in
        libraries.

BARLOW, Harold; MORGENSTERN, Sam (compilers)

68   **A dictionary of musical themes** (New York: Crown, 1948) 642p.
        Lists 10,000 themes, by composer and genre. Works are
        selected chiefly from instrumental music available on
        records up to time of publication. Alphabetical finding
        index with themes transposed to C major or C minor is in
        letter notation. Not concerned with incipits as such,
        but with all the important themes of works listed.

        Reviews: Notes V (1948) 375-76; W. McNAUGHT, *MTimes* (1949)185.

68 a   --- Reprint (London: Williams & Norgate, 1949) 656p.

68 b   --- Reprints (1957, 1966).

68 c   --- **Dizionario dei temi musicali,** ed. by H. Dahnk. (Milano: Sormani,
    1955)
        Reviews: Rassegna Musicale XXVII (Mar 1957) 82-83.

69   **A dictionary of vocal themes** (New York: Crown, 1950) vi, 547p.
        Indexes 8,000 themes, and also contains a melodic index
        in letter notation, with themes transposed to C major or
        C minor.
        Reviews: Thomas FAULKNER, *Étude* LXIX (Apr 1951) 7-8;
        C.S., *MAmerica* LXXI (July 1951) 33; H.H., *MOpinion* LXXIX

(June 1956) 539; Eric BLOM, *MLetters* ,XXXVII (July 1956)
291-94; John WARRACK, *MTimes* XCVII (July 1956) 359.

69a --- Reprint (London: E. Benn, 1956).

69b --- Reprint. A dictionary of opera and song themes, including
cantatas, oratorios, lieder, and art songs (New York: Crown, 1966).

BARTENSTEIN, Schloss Bartenstein. Fürst zu Hohenlohe-Bartensteinsches
Archiv, *see* HALTENBERGSTETTEN no. 483

BÁRTFA, Hungary (currently Bardejov, Czechoslovakia): Bártfa Collection

70 MURÁNYI, Róbert Árpád (Budapest). [Thematic catalogue]
*   Thematic catalogue of the collection now deposited in the
National Library (Országos Széchényi Könyvtár) in Budapest.

BARTLETT, Loren Wayne (compiler)

71 A study and checklist of representative eighteenth century concertos
and sonatas for bassoon (PhD diss.: State U. of Iowa, 1961) 274p.
U. Micro. 61-5544. (typescript)
Thematic index, Appendix, part II.
Lists opening themes of all concerto and sonata movements
in 120 manuscripts and printed works covered by the study.

BARTÓK, BÉLA, 1881-1945

72 SUCHOFF, Benjamin. Computer applications to Bartók's Serbo-Croatian
□   material, *Tempo* LXXX (Spring 1967) 15-19.
A lexicographical index (prepared with a computer) of the 75
melodies contained in Béla Bartók's *Serbo-Croatian Folksongs*
and the analysis of the derived data for variant relation-
ships, classification procedures, and aspects of folk style.

BARTON, William (compiler)

73 The book of psalms in metre (London: G.M., 1645) 304p. [see reproductions of title page on p. 15, of catalogue page on frontispice]
The beginnings of G[eneral] and P[articular] Tunes now used in
London, *f* [A6] *verso*.
This appears to be the first printed thematic catalogue. It
is found on a single page (see frontispice of this bibliography) of a 304-page volume, 5 3/4 by 3 1/4" in size. [Edi-
tions of the book vary; an earlier edition (possibly the
first), printed in 1644 (copy in New York Public Library),
does not contain the thematic catalogue page.] It contains
no fewer than twenty-two tightly-spaced incipits, all eight
diamond-shaped notes in length, except for two which have
only six notes. There are fifteen "general tunes" most of
them with one, two, or three asterisks, and seven "particular
tunes" that have first-line titles only. The psalm texts are
similarly labelled thus indicating the tune to which they may
be sung.

Reference: E. BACKUS Catalogue of music in the Huntington Library (San Marino, Calif., 1949) item 1889.

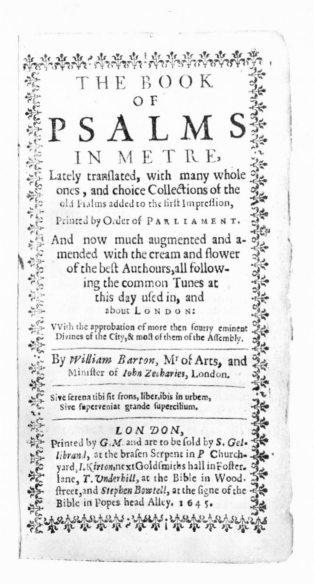

II. Barton, *Book of Psalms...*, 1645, title page, no. 73

73a   --- BROOK, Barry S. The earliest printed thematic catalogues,
☐   *Festskrift Jens Peter Larsen 1902 14/VI 1972.* Studier udgivet af
Musikvidenskabeligt Institut ved Københavns Universitet (København:
Wilhelm Hansen Musik-Forlag, 1972) 103-12.

BASEL, Universitätsbibliothek

74   RICHTER, Julius. **Katalog der Musik-Sammlung auf der Universitäts-Bibliothek in Basel (Schweiz).** Verzeichnet und beschrieben im Jahre 1888. (Leipzig: Breitkopf & Härtel, 1892) 104p.
        Musik-Handschriften, 25-82.
            Incipits are given only for works not otherwise easily
            identifiable (in 1888). Includes over 200 incipits, using
            original clefs and notation, of works by Senfl, Isaac,
            Willaert, etc..

75   REFARDT, Edgar. **Thematischer Katalog der Instrumentalmusik des I8. Jahrhunderts in den Handschriften der Universitätsbibliothek Basel**
        Publikationen der Schweizerischen Musikforschenden Gesellschaft, Ser.
        II, v. 6. (Bern: Paul Haupt, 1957) 59p.
            Alphabetical list, by composer, of manuscripts in Basel Uni-
            versity Library; gives publishers, dates, instrumentation,
            and incipits of works not thematically catalogued elsewhere
            in published literature (e.g. *DTÖ*). Includes surviving
            materials from the Sarasin collection (see no. 76) Com-
            posers: Abel, Barbella, Barriere, Bauer, Beck, Behm, Ber-
            nasconi, Borghi, Bühl [Pichl], Cambini, Campioni, Cannabich,
            Carcani, Champein, Chartrain, Chiesa, Conti, Danzi, Davaux,
            Davesnes, Eisenmann, Ferrandini, Gallimberto, Gassmann, Gos-
            sec, Gretry, Haydn, Hemberger, Hoffmeister, Jommelli, Lam-
            pugnani, Leduc, Lucchini, Martini, Michl, Monsigny, Monza,
            Nardini, Pelissier, Piazza, Piccini, Pleyel, Polaci, Puglia-
            ni, Questorino, Ragazzi, Ricci, Rinaldo da Capua, Riso,
            Roeser, Rugge, Saint-Georges, Sala, Sammartini, Schmitt,
            Schmittbauer, Schwindl, Solnitz, Sozzi, Sperger, Spourni,
            Karl Stamitz, Sterkel, Tartini, Torti, Valle, Wagenseil,
            Wanhall.
        Reviews: Hans Heinrich EGGEBRECHT, *Musica* XII (May 1958)
        310-11; Hellmut FEDERHOFER, *Mf* XI/2 (1958) 244-45.

76   **Katalog d. Luk. Sarasin Mus. Slg.** (CH Bu: Handbibl. Kunst. d 119)
▽   432 numbered pages of which ca. 340 are blank. Compiled ca. 1800
      (manuscript) Microfilm copy in US NYcg.
            This collection, originally belonging to a late 18th cen-
            tury patron of music, is now in the Basel Universitäts-
            bibliothek (see REFARDT above for a description of the
            catalogue and the incipits of the extant works). The origi-
            nal Sarasin MS catalogue contains incipits for a number of
            lost works not in Refardt. Genres include: overtures (p. 1-
            56), quartets (88-89), trios (138-40), solo works (194-95),
            quartets (207-08), arias (347). A list of composers with
            cross-references to the catalogue appears on pages 377-432.
            Composers inventoried are: Alday l'aine 6, Aresne 1, Aubert
            4, Bach 12, Emanuele Barbella 1, Francesco Beck 28, Berna-
            sconi 1, Ferdinando Bertoni 1, Bianchi 1, Cannabich 2,
            Chiesa 3, Gio. Pietro Crispi 9, Alessandro Danesi 2, Daube 1,
            Davaux 6, Fiamenghino 1, Fils 14, Fr. Fiorillo 3, Galimber-
            ti 2, Galuppi 1, F.L. Gassmann 18, Gentura 1, Gio. Batta
            Gerrascio 1, Giulino 2, Gluck 1, Fr. Gius. Gossec 10,
            Grau 1, Guglielmi 4, Hemberger 3, Gius. Heyden 14, Hey-
            mann 1, Holzbauer 10, Jarnowick 1, Jomelli (Jomella) 1,
            Giacomo Cristoforo Kachell 3, Luckese 1, Bartolomeo Lus-
            trini 1, Girolamo Mango 1, Martino 2, Giuseppe Michel 6,

Miroglio il Giovane Oppera 6, Giacomo Insanguine delle
Monopoli 2, Carlo Monza 2, W.A. Mozart 1, Pietro Nardini
Napoletano 3, Ottani 1, Gaetano Piazza 1, Piccini 7,
Ignace Pleyel 40, Polaci 2, Tomaso Prota 2, Pugliani 1,
Pugnani 5, Questorino 1, Franc. Saverio Richter 3, Abaté
Rici 2 Rinaldo da Capua 1, Paolo Riso 4, Ant. Sacchini 1,
Sala 1, St. George 2, Fr. Schlecht 2, Schmidt in Roma 3,
Federico Schwindel 2, Fred^{co} Schwindlin 1, Gio. Batta
Scolari 1, Stadler 1, Stamitz (Carlo Stametz) 18, Gius.
Toeschi (Toueschi) 14, Romaso Traetta 1, Pietro Valle 1,
Federico Vanhall 1, Giorgio Vogl 1, Wagenseil 5.

BAUER-MENGELBERG, Stefan

77 **The Ford-Columbia input language,** *Musicology and the computer,* Barry
☐ S. BROOK, ed. (New York: City University of New York Press, 1970) 48-
52.
> A summary of an input language designed to be used for photo-
> composed printing of music, and being presently employed in
> several thematic cataloguing projects. (see nos. 733 & 734)

BAYARD, S.P.

78 **A miscellany of tune notes,** *Mélanges--studies in folklore,* S. THOMP-
☐ SON (1957) 151-76.

BECQUART, Paul (compiler)

79 **Musiciens néerlandais à la cour de Madrid. Philippe Rogier et son
école (1560-1647).** *Mémoires de l'Académie Royale de Belgique* XIII/4
Classe des Beaux-Arts (Bruxelles: Palais des Académies, 1967) 368p.
  Incipit Musicaux, 299-336.
> Cites 100 musical incipits (from 66 archival documents), in
> old notation, all parts, of Flemish composers at the Spanish
> royal music chapel in Madrid under Philip II. Works inven-
> toried as follows: Ph. Rogier motets (nos. 1-22), chansons
> (23-26), masses (27-35), motets (36-48), leçons (49-53);
> Étienne Bernard chansons (54-55); Englebert Turlur motets
> (56-58); Géry de Ghersem motet (59); Nicolas Dupont "répons"
> (60); M. Romero (61-65), psaumes(66-70), motets (71-72),
> other works (73-95, 96-98),villancicos (99-100).

BEECKE, IGNAZ NOTKER von, 1733-1803

80 MUNTER, Friedrich. **Ignaz von Beecke und seine Instrumentalkom-
▽ positionen** (PhD diss.: München, 1921) 85*l*., p. 85-91, *l*. 92-96.
(typescript)
  **Thematisches Verzeichnis der Instrumentalkompositionen von
  Beecke,** 85-91.
> Incipits for 21 symphonies, 8 concertant sinfonies, serenades
> and partitas, 17 string quartets, 6 clavier concertos, 26
> clavier sonatas, 8 violin sonatas, 6 trios, etc.

81 SCHECK, Helmut. **Die Vokalkompositionen von Ignaz von Beecké**
▽ (Zulassungsarbeit für die künstlerische Prüfung für das Lehramt
an Höheren Schulen) (München, 1961) 84*l*., 9*l*. Notenanhang (typescript)

Thematisches Verzeichnis der Vokalkompositionen von I. von
Beecké, 9*l.*
> 99 incipits for 20 music dramas, 9 church compositions, 22
> cantatas, 44 Lieder and songs.

BEETHOVEN, LUDWIG VAN, 1770-1827

82
▽
Oeuvres de Beethoven./ Catalogue thématique. (A Wst) 103p. (manuscript). Microfilm copy in US NYcg.
> Incipits (single, double, or multiple staff) for works ar-
> ranged first by opus number, then works without opus number.

83
HOFMEISTER, Friedrich. Thematisches Verzeichniss der Compositionen
für Instrumentalmusik welche von den berühmtesten Tonsetzern unseres
Zeitalters erschienen sind. Heft I: Louis van Beethoven, mit dessen
eigenen Tempo-bezeichnungen nach Mälzl's Metronome. (Leipzig, 1819)
25p.
> Early thematic index of Beethoven's instrumental music
> through Op. 102. Items arranged by genre according to
> ensemble. Includes an index of arrangements.

83 a
--- "Durchschossenes Exemplar mit zahlreichen Ergänzungen von Aloys
Fuchs" cited on p. 214 of Friedrich Wilhelm RIEDEL, Die Bibliothek
des Aloys Fuchs. In: Hans Albrecht in memoriam, Wilfried BRENNECKE;
Hans HASSE , eds. (Kassel: Bärenreiter, 1962) 207-24.

84
Catalogue thématique of L.V. Beethoven's works. For the pianoforte
(London: Monzani and Hill, ca. 1820-25) 2p. (GB Lbm: Hirsch IV.
1112. (5.))
> *Reference:* HUMPHRIES, Charles; SMITH, William C. Music pub-
> lishing in the British Isles (Oxford: Blackwell, 1970)237.

85
Catalogue thématique of Beethoven's works (London: Preston, 1823
or later) 1p. (GB Lbm: Hirsch IV 1112 (8)).
> *Reference:* HUMPHRIES, Charles; SMITH, William C. Music pub-
> lishing in the British Isles (Oxford: Blackwell, 1970) 264.

85.1
▽
FUCHS, Aloys. Nachweisung über einige Autographe (D Bds: Kat. ms.
510) 13*l*. (manuscript).

> *Reference:* SCHAAL, Richard. Quellen zur Musiksammlung Aloys
> Fuchs, *Mf* XVI (1963) 71. (see no. 1159)

86
Thematisches Verzeichniss der im Druck erschienenen Werke von Ludwig
van Beethoven (Leipzig: Breitkopf & Härtel, 1851) 167p.
> Gives incipits in piano reduction of each movement of pub-
> lished works. Organized in order of opus numbers, followed
> by works without opus numbers arranged by genre. Contains
> extensive bibliographic information, plus a supplement of
> spurious works. Excluded are out-of-print works and compos-
> itions which appeared as supplements in periodicals and
> books. Published anonymously, this edition was probably
> compiled by C. Geissler.

86 a
--- 2. verm. Aufl. Zusammengestellt und mit chronologisch-biblio-
graphischen Anmerkungen versehen von G. NOTTEBOHM (1868) iv,
220p.

86b   --- Anastatischer Druck der 2. Aufl. Nebst Bibliographie von Emerich
          KASTNER (1912).

86c   --- Ergänzt von Theodor FRIMMEL (1925).

86d   --- Reprint of 86c. (Walluf bei Wiesbaden: Sändig, 1972)

87   **Catalogue des oeuvres** (Thematic catalogue advertised in a catalogue
      by Artaria, 11/29/1856).
                    Reference: Alexander WEINMANN, **Vollständiges Verlagsverzeich-
              nis Artaria & Comp.** (Wien: L. Krenn, 1952) 154.

88   THAYER, Alexander W. **Chronologisches Verzeichnis der Werke Ludwig
      van Beethoven's** .(Berlin: F. Schneider, 1865) viii, 208p.
              Incipits for works not included in the 1851 Verzeichnis, and
              for canons, fugues, Scotch, Welsh, and Irish melodies, march-
              es, dances, etc. (see no. 86)

89   PROD'HOMME, Jacques Gabriel. **La jeunesse de Beethoven (I770-I800)**
      (Paris: Payot, 1921) 371p
          **Catalogue thématique [des oeuvres composées à Bonn et à Vienne
          de I782 à I800]**, 323-71.
              Themes or incipits of each movement of 125 early works, in
              piano reduction and with instrumental indication. Includes
              keyboard, vocal, and instrumental works in approximate
              chronological order, preceded by a chronological catalogue
              and a concordance with the Thayer and Nottebohm catalogues.

      --- Reprint (Paris: Librairie Delagrave, 1927).

90   HAAS, Wilhelm. **Systematische Ordnung Beethovenscher Melodien,**
      Veröffentlichungen des Beethovenhauses in Bonn VII and VIII
      (Bonn: Beethovenhaus; Leipzig: Quelle & Meyer, 1932) 16p., 618
      col., 28p.
              Catalogue of ca. 5700 melodies including incipits of move-
              ments, themes, and internal passages, transposed to C major
              or A minor. A code gives original key, tempo, instrumenta-
              tion or vocal identification, and page reference to the
              Gesamtausgabe.   Organized by rhythm (part I) and by melodic
              pattern (part II).

91   BIAMONTI, Giovanni. **Catalogo cronologico di tutte le musiche de
      Beethoven** (Roma: Mezzetti, 1951) v. I, 1781-1800, 585p.
              Chronological list of incipits and musical examples from
              works of the years indicated, with a non-alphabetical index.

91a   --- **Schema di un Catalogo generale cronologico delle Musiche di
      Beethoven, I78I-I827** (Roma: Mezzetti, 1954) 186p.
              Contains only a handful of incipits.

91b   --- **Catalogo cronologico e tematico delle Opere di Beethoven comprese
      quelle inedite e gli abbozzi non utilizzati** (Torino: Ilte, 1968)
      xxx, 1201p.
              Incipits on several staves.
                    Reviews: Jack WESTRUP, *MLetters* LI/2 (Apr 1970) 195-98.

92   BRUERS, Antonio. **Beethoven; catalogo storico-critico di tutte le
      opere** 4th enlarged edition (Roma: G. Bardi, 1951) 679p.
          Indice tematico, 581-643.
              Incipits arranged by opus number. Concordance to the num-
              bering of Beethoven's works by different scholars, 645-58.

93 KINSKY, Georg; HALM, Hans. **Das Werk Beethovens. Thematisch-biblio-**
☆   **graphisches Verzeichnis seiner sämtlichen vollendeten Kompositionen**
(München-Duisburg: G.Henle, 1955) xxii, 808p.

> Divided into two parts: works with and works without opus
> numbers. In the latter part, the first initial of each of
> the words in the German title, Werke ohne Opuszahl, is used
> as a prefix to the cardinal number (i.e. WoO 4). Supplement
> includes doubtful and falsely attributed works. Entries
> give information on MSS and published editions.
>
> *Reviews:* Otto ALBRECHT, *Étude* LXXIV (Dec 1956) 8-9; Willy
> HESS, *Musica* XL (Mar 1956) 235-36; Willi KAHL, *Mf* CXVII (Oct
> 1956) 486-89; Donald W. MacARDLE, *Notes* XIII (Mar 1956) 280-
> 82; Robert SABIN, *MAmerica* LXXVI (July 1956) 28; Max UNGER,
> *NeueZM* CXVII (Oct 1956) 577-78; Otto KINKELDEY, *JAmerMusicol-
> Soc* X (Summer 1957) 119-24.

BELLA, JÁN LEVOSLAV, 1843-1936

94 ZÁVARSKÝ, Ernest. **Ján Levoslav Bella, život a dielo** (Bratislava:
Vydavatelstvo Slovenskej akadémie vied, 1955) 497p.
**Tematický soznam skladieb J.L. Bellu [Thematic catalogue of
works]**, 363-464.

> Works include opera, cantatas, orchestral works, solo and
> chamber music, songs, choral music, sacred vocal music
> (Catholic and Protestant), and unfinished or lost works.

BENDA family

95 LORENZ, Franz (Berlin). **Die Musikerfamilie Benda,** v. 1 (Berlin:
*   Verlag de Gruyter, 1967) Volumes II and III to be published.
[Thematic catalogue], v. III, ca. 600p.

> Incipits for the complete works of Franz (1709-1786),
> Johann Georg (1713-1786), Joseph (1724-1804), Georg (1722-
> 1795), Friedrich Wilhelm Heinrich (1724-1814), Friedrich
> Ludwig (1746-1792), Karl Hermann Heinrich (1748-1836)
> Benda. Also includes Maria Carolina Wolf, born a Benda,
> and Juliane Reichardt (1752-1783), also born a Benda,
> and her daughter Louise Reichardt (1779-1826). Provides
> full bibliographical apparatus.

BENDA, FRANZ, 1709-1786

96 LASERSTEIN, Alfred. **Franz Benda, sein Leben und seine Werke** mit
▽   thematischem Verzeichnis seiner Kompositionen, photographischen
Beilagen und zahlreichen Kopien. Ein Beitrag zur Geschichte der
Instrumentalmusik im 18. Jahrhundert (PhD diss.: Breslau, 1924)
v, 200p. (typescript)
Thematischer Katalog sämtlicher Werke, 94-141.

> Incipits for all movements of 109 violin sonatas with
> accompaniment, 10 concertos, 11 symphonies, and collected
> études and capriccios.

97 MURPHY, S.N.J.M.,Sister Therese Cecile. **The violin concertos of**
▽   **Franz Benda and their use in violin pedagogy,** parts I & II (PhD
diss.: U. of Southern California, 1968) vii, 379, 152p. (typescript)
Appendix A. Thematic catalogue, 362-376.

> Incipits for all movements of 28 concertos.

BENDA, GEORG, 1722-1795

98   LÖBNER, Karl-Heinz. Georg Benda (1722-1795); sein Leben und sein
▽   Werk mit besonderer Berücksichtigung der Sinfonien und Cembalo-
     konzerte (PhD diss., Musicology: Martin Luther U., Halle-Wittenberg,
     1967) (typescript).
          Thematic catalogue of symphonies and concertos.

BENGTSSON, Ingmar

99   Numericode: a code system for thematic incipits, *SvenskTMf* XLIX (1967)
☐   5-40.
          After a special heading indicating key or mode, metre, and
          first melody tone with absolute octave mark, pitch and dura-
          tion are indicated in two separate lines. Pitch is coded by
          the numerals 1-7 (tonic is always 1). Sharps and flats are
          indicated by "+" and "-" following the pitch numeral. Tied
          notes are indicated by an equals sign, bar lines by a slash,
          and rests by an "o". Duration is represented by the same
          numerals used in the *Plaine and Easie Code* (see no. 188, and
          illustration on p. 43). Triplets, duplets, etc., are coded
          with the time value in parentheses.

100 Incipitkatalogisering- några meddelanden [Incipit cataloguing; a
☐   report], *Svenskt musikhistoriskt arkiv* Bulletin. Vol. 5, p. 20.
          Summary notices of incipit cataloguing in progress at the
          Library of the Royal Swedish Academy of Music, the Swedish
          Music History Archive and the Swedish Center for Folksong
          and Folk Music Research. [Kungl. Musikaliska akademiens
          bibliotek, Svenskt musikhistoriskt arkiv, Svenskt visarkiv].

BENNET, Lawrence (New York U.)

101 Italian cantata composers employed by the Habsburgs, c. I690-c.I740
*   Thematic catalogs of Italian cantatas.
          The catalogue is divided into two sections: 1.) Bononcini
          (Giovanni Maria and his two sons Giovanni and Antonio Maria)
          and 2.) other cantata composers employed by the Habsburgs at
          the turn of the 18th century. Part one will contain incipits
          for 24 cantatas by Giovanni Maria Bononcini, 375 cantatas by
          Giovanni Bononcini, and approx. 31 cantatas by Antonio Maria
          Bononcini (to be published in *WECIS*, 1974). Part two will
          contain incipits for the cantatas of Caldara, Badia, Conti,
          Porsice, and Ziani, and will probably be published by *WECIS*
          c. 1975.   (see no. 1400)

BENVENUTI, Giacomo (compiler)

102 Andrea e Giovanni Gabrieli e la musica strumentale in San Marco, *IM*
     I-II (Milano: Ricordi, 1931-2) 2v.
        [Thematic index]
              V. I (8p. inserted between p. cxlvii and p. 1) contains mul-
              tiple staff incipits for all sections of works by A. Gabrieli
              G. Gabrieli, and Annibale Padovano. Genres included are arias,
              battaglie, ricercare, madrigals, motets, and psalms. V. II
              (p. iii-viii) contains multiple staff incipits for all sec-

tions of the 14 canzonas and two sonatas in G. Gabrieli's
Sacrae Symphoniae of 1597.

BERBIGUIER, BENOÎT TRANQUILLE, 1782-1838

103   Catalogue thématique of T. Berbiguier's works (London: Monzani &
       Hill, [182-?])
              One side of one folio leaf.

BERG, ALBAN, 1885-1935

104   PERLE, George. Representation and symbol in the music of Wozzeck,
       _MR_ XXXII/4 (Nov 1971) 281-308.
              20 Leitmotives with assigned titles, generally on a single
              staff. "We will classify as a _Leitmotiv_ any characteristic
              musical idea that occurs in more than one scene and that
              acquires an explicit referential function in the drama
              through its consistent association with an extra-musical
              element...the list is not in any sense a definitive one."

105   PAZ, Silvia (Queens College of the C.U.N.Y.) Thematic catalogue
 *   of the works of Alban Berg
              Multiple staff themes for all sections of works, published
              and unpublished. Will include annotated bibliography and
              discography. Ca. 150p.

BERGGREEN, Andreas Peter (compiler)

106   Folksange og-melodier nedskrevet på 56 små kort [Folksongs and folk
 ▽   melodies written on 56 small cards] (DK Kk: mu 7004. 1376) (manu-
       script)
              Single and double staff incipits for folksongs and melodies
              from 17th-19th centuries. Compiled late in the 19th century.

BÉRIOT, CHARLES de, 1802-1870

106.1 BACHMANN, Alberto. Les grands violinistes du passé (Paris: Fisch-
       bacher, 1913) 468p.
              [Table thématique], 15-16.
              List of works includes incipits for nine violin concertos.

BERKELEY, California. University of California at Berkeley

107   DUCKLES, Vincent; ELMER, Minnie; PETROBELLI, Pierluigi. Thematic
       catalogue of a manuscript collection of eighteenth-century Italian
       instrumental music in the University of California, Berkeley Music
       Library (Berkeley: University of California Press, 1963) 403p.
              Contains themes from some 990 manuscripts of 1062 instrumental
              works by 82 eighteenth-century composers, plus 75 anonymous
              compositions. In addition, three separate thematic catalogues
              accompanying the manuscript collection are cited (p. 384-85)
              which cover 292 works by Tartini; 42 by Straticò; 4 by Viotti
              and 5 by Giernovigh (see nos. 450,1263-64, 1280-81, 1341)

Reviews: Arthur HUTCHINGS, *MLetters* XL/3 (1963) 261-63; Ake
DAVIDSSON, *RMusicol* L/129 (1964) 246-47; Mariangela DONÀ,
Musica d'Oggi VII/2 (1964) 64; Richard D.C. NOBLE, *Consort*
-/21 (1964) 325-26; B. R. *MOpinion* LXXXVII (Feb·1964) 283;
Denis STEVENS, *MTimes* CV/- (Jul·1964) 513-14; Charles CUD-
WORTH, *GalpinSocJ* -/18 (1965) 140-41; Donald W. KRUMMEL,
Notes XXII/3 (1966) 1025-26.

BERLIN, Deutsche Staatsbibliothek : **Ms. K. 546 (catalogue)**

107.1 [Thematic catalogue]   (D Bds: Mus. ms. theor. K 546) 41p. (manu-
▽   script). Without date or title page. Microfilm copy in US NYcg.
           This manuscript is probably of Salzburg origin. Two-thirds
           of the catalogue are incipits for the church music of Eber-
           lin; the remaining third contains incipits for sacred works
           by Michael Haydn. (Masses, Graduals, Offertories, Vespers,
           Litanies, etc.). In between the two, there appears an in-
           sert entitled "In der Domkirche zu Salzburg befinden sich
           folgende Werke", with incipits for works by Adlgasser (17),
           and Fischietti (4), and a numerical summary without incipits
           for Eberlin.

BERLIN, Deutsche Staatsbibliothek: **Ms. K. 584 (catalogue)**

108   [Symphonies, 18th c.]   (D Bds: HB VII, Mus. ms. theor. K. 584) [9p.]
▽   Microfilm copy in US NYcg. (manuscript)
           Incipits for "Sinfonies" by Graun (45), Bach (7), Benda (4),
           Kohne (2), Boetticher (1), Schultz (1), and Ledzig (1).

BERLIN, Deutsche Staatsbibliothek: **Ms. K. 728 (catalogue)**

109   [Instrumental works, 18th-19th c.]   (D Bds: HB VII, Mus. ms. theor.
▽   Kat. 728) [7p.] Microfilm copy in US NYcg. (manuscript)
           Incipits for miscellaneous works by Mozart (10), Beethoven
           (10), Onslow (31), and Mendelssohn (13).

BERLIN, Deutsche Staatsbibliothek: **Ms. K. 860 (catalogue)**

110   [Vocal works, 18th c.] (D Bds: HB VII, Mus. ms. theor. Kat. 860)
▽   [32p.] Microfilm copy in US NYcg. (manuscript)
           20 large-scale works, mainly operas, by Holzbauer (4),
           Trajetta (3), Jomelli (2), Salieri (2), Demajo (1),
           Gasmann (1), Piccini (2), and Gluck (5). Incipits are
           provided for all sections of each work.

BERLIN, Deutsche Staatsbibliothek: **Voss-Buch**

111   [Thematischer Catalog der Voss-Buchschen Handschriften (Partituren)]
▽   Musik-Catalog. Enthaelt: Die Thema's der Partituren zur Vocal=auch
      Vocal mit Instrumentalmusik. (D Bds: HB VII, Mus. ms. theor. Kat.
      26) [207p.] Compiled ca. 1800. Microfilm copy in US NYcg. (manu-
      script)
           Double staff incipits for vocal works, mainly sacred, by a
           a wide variety of composers ranging from the Renaissance to
           the Classical period (Palestrina, Agricola, J.S. Bach, Tele-

mann, Clementi, Mozart, and many others). Arranged alphabetically by composer. Incipits for a group of anonymous
works are appended.

BERLIN, Deutsche Staatsbibliothek: Codex Mus. Ms. Z. 21

111.1 EITNER, Robert. Codex Mus. Ms. Z. 21 der Königlichen Bibliothek zu
Berlin, *MfMG* XXI (1889) [93]-102.

> Lists the contents with incipits given in an alphabetic no-
> tation, including, among anonymous works, themes by Adam von
> Fulda, Agricola, Aulen, Beham, Busnois, Des Prez, Finck, Flor,
> Gerstenhaus, Hofhaimer, Isaac, Jacobit, Resinarius, and Volck-
> mar.

BERLIN, Deutsche Staatsbibliothek: Mus. ms. 40024

111.2 PÄTZIG, Gerhard. Das Chorbuch Mus. ms. 40024 der Deutschen Staatsbibliothek Berlin. Eine wichtige Quelle zum Schaffen Isaacs aus der
Hand Leonhard Pämingers. *Festschrift Walter Gerstenberg zum 60. Geburtstag* (Wolfenbüttel & Zürich, Möseler Verlag, 1967) 122-42.

> Partially thematic. The compiler suggests that, contrary
> to Eitner, all the works in this MS are by Isaac except
> for one by Senfl. Those in the hand of Päminger are copies
> of works by Isaac.

BERLIN, Joachimstalsches Gymnasium

112   EITNER, R.; JACOBS, R. Thematischer Katalog der von Thulemeier'schen
Musikalien-Sammlung in der Bibliothek des Joachimsthal'schen Gymna-
siums zu Berlin (Leipzig: Breitkopf & Härtel, 1899) (Beilage zu den
MfMG, 30-31, 1898-99) 110p.

> Incipits of works by: K.F. Abel, G.M. Alberti, J.S. Bach, K.
> P.E. Bach, J.C. Bach, F. Benda, C.S. Binder, L. Boccherini,
> A. Bon, J. Boutmy, C.A. Campion, A. Corelli, G. Coretto, E.
> Eichner, J.F. Fasch, I. Fiorillo, P. Fischer, Forster, E.Fox,
> B. Galuppi, F. Gasparini, F. Geminiani, C.E. Graf, J.G. Graun,
> K.H. Graun, Guilain, G.F. Händel, J.H. Hasse, J. Haydn, Hein-
> rich, Heinrici, J.W. Hertel, K. Hockh, B. Hupfeld, J.G. Ja-
> nitsch, H.P. Johnson, K. Kerle, J.P. Kirnberger, Kirwitz,
> Krause, Kuhn (H.L.?), J.F. Lampe, A. Lotti, J.B. Lutter, Mar-
> tinetti, Martino, J. von Mattheson, W.A. Mozart, C. Nichel-
> man, G. Paesiello, B. Pasquini, J.C. Pepusch, Pfeiffer, N.
> Piccini, A. Pogllietti, J.J. Quantz, A. Razazzi, P. Ricci,
> G.F. Richter, K. Rodenwald, J.H. Rolle, G. le Roux, C.F.
> Ruppe, G. Rush, A.M. Scaccia, C. Schaffrath, C.F. Schale, J.
> A. Scheiber, Scherer, F. Schwindl, G.A. Sorge, Stamitz, Ste-
> phens, G. Tartini, G.P Telemann, A. Vivaldi, J.K. Vogler, G.
> J. von Vogler, G.J. Wagenseil, J.B. Wendling, F. Zappe, G.B.
> Zingoni, and works by anonymous composers.

BERLIN, Staatsbibliothek-Stiftung Preussischer Kulturbesitz: Bokemeyer

113   KÜMMERLING, Harald. Katalog der Sammlung Bokemeyer, *Kieler Schriften
zur Musikwissenschaft* XVIII (Kassel: Bärenreiter, 1970) 423p.
Katalog der Musikaliensammlung von Heinrich Bokemeyer (1679-

I75I), die sich heute in Berlin, Staatsbibliothek Stiftung
Preussischer Kulturbesitz, befindet.
  1839 incipits of sacred and secular works of the 16th-18th
  centuries (cf. *MGG* II, col. 80)
  Reviews: Richard H. HUNTER, *Notes* XXVIII (1971).

BERLIN, Staatsbibliothek—Stiftung Preussischer Kulturbesitz: Pretlack

114   JAENECKE, Joachim (Frankfurt/M.). **Repertoire-Untersuchungen der**
*   **Musiksammlung Pretlack, Stiftung Preussischer Kulturbesitz** (PhD
      diss. in progress).
        Will include a thematic catalogue of the Pretlack Collection
        given recently to the Stiftung Preussischer Kulturbesitz.
        The collection contains manuscripts of the period ca. 1740-
        1770, mostly instrumental music (symphonies), and also some
        arias, etc.

BERLIND, Gary; LOGEMANN, George W.

115   **An algorithm for musical transposition** (New York: New York U. Insti-
□ ▽   tute for Computer Research in the Humanities, 1967) (typescript)
        Useful in the transposition of incipits to C major or C mi-
        nor, e.g. with the *Simplified Plaine and Easie Code*. (see
        no. 188)

BERNABEI, ERCOLE, ca.1620 (to 1622)-1687

116   KATZBICHLER, Emil. **Über das Leben und die weltlichen Vokalwerke**
      des Ercole Bernabei I622-I687, Hofkapellmeister in München von I674-
      I687 (PhD diss.: München;   München: Musikverlag Emil Katzbichler,
      1963) 127p.
        Thematisches Verzeichnis der Werke Ercole Bernabei's, 117-25.
          Incipits of all secular and sacred vocal works arranged al-
          phabetically **according to** text incipit.

BERNSTEIN, Lawrence F.

117   **Data processing and the thematic index,** *FontisArtisM* XI/3 (1964) 159-
□   65.
        An historical survey of thematic indexing, its problems and
        itemized possibilities of their solution by the use of
        modern electronic equipment.

BERNSTEIN, Lawrence; OLIVE, Joseph P.

118   **Computers and the 16th-century chanson; a pilot project at the Uni-**
□   **versity of Chicago,** *Computers and the Humanities* III/3 (Jan 1969)
      153-61.

BEROUN, Czechoslovakia. Okresný archív

118.1 HOLEČEK, Jaroslav. **Hudební sbírky děkana J.A. Seydla a Tekly Pod-**
*   **leské-Batkové. Okresní Archív Beroun** [Musical collection from the
       estate of Dean J.A. Seydl and of singer Tekla Posleská Batková.

State archive in Beroun]. To be published in the *Artis Musicae An-
tiquioris Catalogorum Series,* 1973-74.

BERTONI, FERDINANDO, 1725-1813

119   HAAS, Ingrid. **Ferdinando Bertoni. Leben und Instrumentalwerk** (PhD
▽   diss.: Wien, 1958) 2v., 89*l*.; *l*.90-271. (typescript)
         Das Instrumentalschaffen, 2 fold-out leaves.
              17 incipits for 3 symphonies, 6 string quartets, 6 sonatas
              for clavier and violin, 1 duet for 2 flutes, 1 cembalo sonata.

BERWALD, FRANZ, 1796-1868

120   CASTEGREN, Nils (Lidingö, Sweden) **A thematic catalogue of Franz**
*   **Berwald's works**
              Thus far, Berwald's dramatic music and some of his orchestral
              works have been covered.

BESOZZI, CARLO, 1738-1791

121   NIMETZ, Daniel. **The wind music of Carlo Besozzi** (PhD diss., Musi-
▽   cology: U. of Rochester, 1967) 2v. (typescript)
         Thematic catalogue, v. II, ii-iii.
              Incipits for 24 sonatas with tempo indications.

BEUERBERG, *see* SEITZ, nos. 1204-1205

BINDER, CHRISTLIEB SIEGMUND, 1723-1789

122   FLEISCHER, Heinrich. **Christlieb Siegmund Binder** (Regensburg: G.
✡   Bosse, [1941]) 173p.
         **Thematisches Verzeichnis der Werke von Christlieb Siegmund
         Binder,** 131-60.
              The appendix is an incipit catalogue of all movements of
              the complete works arranged by genre, and within genre by
              date, with names of dedicatees. Included are: solo key-
              board works (35), chamber works (20), concertos for key-
              board and orchestra (37), and orchestral works (3).

BLAND, John (publisher)

[John Bland's publishing house (1776-1795) with about 12,000 engraved
plates, changed hands to Lewis, Houston and Hyde (1795-1797); Frances Linley (1797-1798); and Robert Birchall (1798-1819). Together,
they published an interesting series of thematic catalogues, preceded
in England only by those of John Corri.]

123 **Catalogues of subjects or beginnings of the several works, for the
    harpsichord, piano forte, & organ, which are printed and sold by J.
    Bland** (London: [1790-1793?]).
              Appears with different headings. For example, the last issue
              of 1790 bears the title "Index to 48 Nos of Bland's harpsi-
              chord collection without Accmpts." (actually contains inci-
              pits for only 47 periodical issues).

124   Thematic catalogue of French songs (London: ca. 1792) 1p. (GB Lbm:
       B.M.H. 1601. c (11.))

         Reference: HUMPHRIES, Charles; SMITH, William C. **Music pub-**
         lishing in the British Isles (Oxford: Blackwell, 1970) 76.

125   Catalogue of subjects or beginnings of Bland's colln. Divine Music
       (London: Ca. 1793) 3p. (GB Lbm: B.M.H. 117)
                 Incipits of sacred vocal music with text underlay (psalms,
                 hymns, etc.).

         Reference: HUMPHRIES, Charles; SMITH, William C. **Music pub-**
         lishing in the British Isles (Oxford: Blackwell, 1970) 77.
         Includes facsimile of page 1.

126   Catalogue of subjects of beginnings of Italian songs, etc. (London:
       Lewis, Houston, Hyde, ca. 1796) 1p. (GB Lbm: B.M.G. 811. (3.))

         Reference: HUMPHRIES, Charles; SMITH, William C. **Music pub-**
         lishing in the British Isles (Oxford: Blackwell, 1970) 212.

127   Bland's collection (continued by F. Linley) of sonatas, lessons,
       overtures, capricios, divertimentos & c. for the harpsichord or pi-
       ano forte, without accompts. by the most esteemed composers, No. 36
       (London: F. Linley, [1796?])
                 On the back page of each piece in this "periodical" of works,
                 published monthly, there appears a thematic catalogue of a-
                 vailable pieces in the collection. Linley reprinted earlier
                 numbers from the original plates, but used the current, most
                 complete, thematic catalogue plate for the last page. On the
                 back of "No. 36 to be continued Monthly, and contain 10 pa-
                 ges, Price 1^S/6^d" there are listed 48 works by Pleyel, Lin-
                 ley, Clementi, and Nicolai.

128   Thematic index to Bland's (continued by Birchall) harpsichord col-
       lection (London: Birchall, ca. 1800) 1p. (GB Lbm: B.M.g. 443.r.
       (1.))

         Reference: HUMPHRIES, Charles; SMITH, William C. **Music pub-**
         lishing in the British Isles (Oxford: Blackwell, 1970) 74.

BLOW, JOHN, 1649-1708

129   CLARKE, Henry Leland. **John Blow (1649-1708) last composer of an**
▽   **era** (PhD diss.: Harvard U., 1947) 4v.   (typescript)
           Thematic index, v.3, 798-818.
                 Keyboard and concerted works arranged by key. Includes
                 doubtful and spurious works.

BOCCHERINI, LUIGI, 1743-1805

130   Nota della musica mandata a Parigi l'anno 1790 o 1791 (F Pc: MS. 1612)
▽   (manuscript)
                 "This catalogue lists the 110 works bought by Pleyel in 1797
                 after laborious negotiation. They had previously been ceded
                 to a certain M. Boulogne, who was believed to have perished
                 during the course of the French Revolution."
         Reference: Yves GÉRARD, **Catalogue of the works of Luigi**
         Boccherini, p. 684 (see no. 140)

131 Nota delle opere non date ancora a nessuno (Roma: Paola Ojetti
▽   Collection) Compiled 1796. (manuscript)
        "This document served as the basis for the first negotiation
        to be concluded between Boccherini and Pleyel. It contains
        56 works, classified by year, without opus numbers. A
        note at the end of this catalogue indicates that two works
        will be completed at the end of the year (1796) which will
        bring the number of works for sale to 58." Reproduced in
        Bollettino Bibliografico Musicale (June 1930) and in Arnaldo
        Bonaventura, *Luigi Boccherini* (Milano-Roma, 1931).

        Reference: Yves GÉRARD, Catalogue of the works of Luigi
        Boccherini, 683-84 (see no. 140)

132 Catalogo delle opere da me Luigi Boccherini cedute in tutta Pro-
▽   prieta al Sig^r Ignazio Pleyel (London: collection of the heirs
    of Stefan Zweig) Compiled 1796. (manuscript)
        The above 58 works are catalogued by opus number without
        any indication of the year.

        Reference: Yves GÉRARD, Catalogue of the works of Luigi
        Boccherini, p. 684 (see no. 140)

133 [The act of sale of op. 40-43] (US NYpm) Dated 21 Feb 1797. Copy
▽   in US NYcg. (manuscript) [reproduction of op.42 on opposite page]
        A contract for his works sold to Pleyel. Incipits with
        tempo markings for the 26 compositions.

134 [The act of sale of the six piano quintets op. 56] (Paris: Germaine
▽   de Rothschild Collection) (manuscript)
        Sale was arranged through the French embassy in Madrid.
        23 June 1799. Reproduced in Gérard plate 5.

        Reference: Yves GÉRARD, Catalogue of the works of Luigi
        Boccherini, p. 684 (see no. 140)

135 Table thématique de la collection des quintetti de Boccherini
    (Paris: Janet et Cotelle, [1818-1822]) 2*l.*
        93 incipits of quintets ordered by their appearance as
        published by Janet et Cotelle.

136 Collection des quintetti de Boccherini (Paris: Janet et Cotelle,
    1829)
        Table thématique des quintetti, 2p., 1st vln part.
            96 incipits with concordance of opus and collection numbers
            and information as to original key, tempo, dynamics, and
            instrument if other than 1st violin.

137 PICQUOT, Louis. Notice sur la vie et les ouvrages de Luigi
    Boccherini (Paris: Philipp, 1851) iii, 135p.
        Liste thématique de tous les ouvrages de Boccherini, restés
        inédits, classés chronologiquement dans leur ordre de com-
        position, 105-32.

137a --- New edition. Louis PICQUOT, Boccherini. Notes et documents
    nouveaux par Georges de SAINT-FOIX (Paris: Legouix, 1930) 203p.
        [Thematic catalogue], 151-81.
            A chronologically arranged thematic catalogue of 366
            diverse instrumental compositions, of which 74 are un-
            published. Resumé of catalogue, p. 183-85. Includes
            list of available editions.

Opera 42.   Tre Quintetti. = grandi

1º. All.º Moderato.

2º. And.º Con moto.

3º. All.º Moderato.

= Due Quartettini. =

1º. All.tto Moderato.

2º. Andante.

Sinfonia Grande.

Corni.

Ottetto Notturno. Lento.

Un Quintettino. And.º Lento.

Fine.

In tutto 26. Pezze, che unite alle 84. dell'altro

Catalogo formano pezze = 110. =

Luigi Boccherini.

Mano propria.

Nous Emmanuel Louis Joseph Dhermand

III. Boccherini, [Act of sale] Opera 42, 1797. no. 133

138   AMSTERDAM, Ellen I. **The string quintets of Luigi Boccherini**
        (PhD diss.: U. of Calif., Berkeley, 1968) 183p. U. Micro. 69-14, 833.
           Thematic catalogue, 141-77.
               125 incipits for the string quintets.

139   GÉRARD, Yves. **Catalogue of the works of Luigi Boccherini,** under the
☆   auspices of Germaine De Rothschild (London: Oxford U. Press, 1969)
        716p.
              Over 1,400 incipits for all movements of the complete works,
              including spurious and doubtful works. Arranged by genre
              with full bibliographical apparatus including autographs,
              MS copies, library locations, etc.

              Reviews: Charles CUDWORTH, *MLetters* LI/3 (July 1970) 302-
              04; *MTimes* CXI (Mar 1970) 279-81; *RItalianaMusicol* IV (Mar-
              Apr 1970) 353-55; *RMusicol* LVI (1970) 96-97.

140   ALMEIDA, Antonio de (Paris). **[Thematic catalogue of symphonies]**
▽   (manuscript) Xerox copy in US NYcg.
              Incipits for 30 symphonies, arranged by opus number.
              Provides instrumentation, tempo indications for all
              movements, date of composition. Includes two doubtful
              compositions. This catalogue is to be published with
              editions of Boccherini symphonies by Doblinger as edited
              by the compiler.

BOLOGNA, Archivio di S. Petronio

141   PAGANELLI, Sergio. **[Thematic catalogue]** (manuscript) File cards.
▽   Incipits for manuscripts located in this archive. Genres
              inventoried are: polyphonic music (16th-17th c.); concerted
              music (voice and instruments), sacred (Masses, Psalms, etc.
              with incipits for every section) from 17th-18th c.; all arias,
              duets, trios, choruses from motets, cantatas, oratorios, and
              serenatas from 17th-18th c.; all movements of 17th-18th c.
              instrumental music.

BOLOGNA, Biblioteca Universitaria: MS 2216

142   WOLF, Johannes. **Geschichte der Mensural Notation von 1250-1460**
        (Leipzig: Breitkopf & Härtel, 1904) 3v.
           [Thematic index], v. 1, 199-208.
              Index of Bologna MS Bibl. Universitaria 2216, including works
              by Antonius de Civitate, Arnaldus, Binchois, Ciconia, Dufay,
              Dunstable, Feragut, Grossin, A. de Lantins, H. de Lantins,
              Nicolaus de Capua, Power, Prepositi, Brixiensis, and Rezon.

BOLOGNA, Civico Museo Bibliografico-Musicale [formerly Liceo Musicale G.B. Martini]

143   GASPARI, Gaetano. **Catalogo della Biblioteca del Liceo Musicale di**
        Bologna (Bologna: Romagnole dall' Acqua, 1890-1945) 5v.
          [Thematic catalogue], v. 4 (1905), 147.
              Contains a few themes, including those for eight sonatas for
              violin and basso by Lorenzo (?) Somis.

143a   --- Reprint.

144   GALLICO, Claudio. **Un canzoniere musicale italiano del cinquecento**
       (Firenze: Olschki, 1961) 213p.
              Complete thematic catalogue of the manuscript in Bologna,
              Conservatorio di Musica G.B. Martini, with musical and text
              incipits and significant bibliographical references. Indices
              of names and composers, and tables of the manuscripts.

              Reviews: H. Wiley HITCHCOCK, *Notes* XVIII/4 (1961) 578.; (a.
              bon.), *RassegnaMCurci* XXXI/2 (1961) 143-44; Cecil ISAAC,
              MQ XLVIII/4 (1962) 534-37; Nanie BRIDGMAN, *RMusicol* XLIX/126
              (1963) 120-21; Walther DÜRR, *Mf* XVII/2 (1964) 191-93.

145   PEASE, Edward. **A report on codex Q16 of the Civico Museo Biblio-**
       grafico Musicale (formerly of the Conservatorio Statale de Musica
       "G.B. Martini"), Bologna, *MDisciplina* XX (1966) 57-94.
              Thematic index, 64-90.
              131 multiple staff incipits of French and Italian chansons,
              motets, one mass, caccie, and 2 Latin treatises, in original
              notation. Alphabetical index of textual incipits and table
              coordinating original, later, and editorial pagination pre-
              cedes the thematic index.

BONNO, GIUSEPPE, 1710-1788

146   SCHIENERL, Alfred. **Die kirchlichen Kompositionen des Giuseppe Bonno**
▽   (PhD diss.: Wien, 1925) 2v.: 118, 59*l*., 2 fasc. (typescript)
              Thematisches Verzeichnis zu den kirchlichen Kompositionen des
              Giuseppe Bonno (1710-1788), 59*l*.
                     Approximately 350 double staff incipits for all movements of
                     30 Masses, 2 Requiems, Offertories, Responsories, etc.

146a   --- **Giuseppe Bonnos Kirchenkompositionen,** *Studien zur Musikwissenschaft.*
☐   Beihefte der *DTÖ* 15 (1928) 62-85.
              Without incipits.

147   BREITNER, Karin. **Giuseppe Bonno und sein Oratorienwerk** (PhD diss.:
▽   Wien, 1961) 174*l*. (typescript)
              Thematischer Katalog und Verzeichnis der weltlichen Vokalwerke,
              110-49.
                     Multiple staff incipits for all numbers (arias, duets, reci-
                     tatives, etc.) of 4 Azione sacre (*Eleazaro; San Paolo in Atene;*
                     Isacco, Figura del Redentore; Giuseppe Riconosciuto). All
                     other works are listed without incipits.

BONONCINI, GIOVANNI BATTISTA, 1670-1747

148   HUEBER, Kurt. **Die Wiener Opern Bononcinis von I697 - I7IO** (PhD diss.:
▽   Wien, 1955) 3v., 130*l*.; *l*. 131-264; 84p. (typescript)
              Thematischer Katalog der Wiener Opern von Giovanni Bononcini, v.3.
                     Incipits for all numbers (overtures, arias, duets, etc.) of
                     17 operas. Arranged chronologically.

149   LINDGREN, Lowell (Harvard U.). **Giovanni Bononcini** (PhD diss. in prep)
*   Comprehensive catalogue for the operas.

150   --- **Giovanni Bononcini [Thematic catalogue]**
*   An elaborate thematic catalogue of the arias.

BOSSE, Detlev (compiler)

151   Untersuchung einstimmiger mittelalterlicher Melodien zum "Gloria in
      excelsis Deo", *Forschungsbeiträge zur Musikwissenschaft* 2 (Regens-
      burg: Gustav Bosse, 1968) 102p.   (*RILM* 69/481[bm])
              Part 2 is a catalogue of incipits and sources of 56 mono-
              phonic Gloria melodies from the 10th-18th c. (non-mensural).

BOSSI, CESARE, last quarter of the 18th c.

152   DEARLING, Robert J. (Dunstable, Bedfordshire). [Thematic catalogue]
▽   Index cards (manuscript)   (see no. 282)
              Incipits for 16 overtures to Ballets in GB Lbm editions.

BOSSLER, Heinrich Philipp (publisher)

152.1 [Thematic publisher's catalogues] (Speyer: Bossler, 1790-1794).
              Reference: O.E. DEUTSCH, Thematische Kataloge, (see no. 297).

BOYCE, WILLIAM, 1710-1779

153   Cathedral music; being a collection in score of the most valuable
      and useful compositions for that service, by the several English
      masters of the last 200 years (London: Novello, c. 1849) 4v.
          Thematic catalogue of Dr. Boyce's services, anthems, etc., v. 1,
          viii.
              Incipits of the 61 anthems listed in the work.

153a --- 2nd ed. Vincent NOVELLO, Boyce's services and anthems (London:
      Novello, 1858) v. IV, verso of p. vii of the preface.

154   STEVENS, Denis. [Thematic catalogue] (GB Ob: Ms Mus. Sch. D 230a/b)
▽   (manuscript)
              Incipits for works by Boyce in the Bodleian Library, Oxford.

155   BRUCE, Robert J. (Bodleian Library, Oxford)   A thematic catalogue
*   of the music of William Boyce I7II-I779
              Single and multiple staff incipits for all movements and
              sections of approximately 1,600 instrumental and vocal
              works. All extant music, both printed editions and music
              in manuscript, arranged by the following genres: (1) Sacred
              vocal music: hymns, services, anthems, Saul and Jonathan,
              Solomon; (II) Odes (43 court odes and other odes); (III)
              Music for the theatre; (IV) Songs; (V) Glees, rounds, and
              canons; (VI) Instrumental music.

BRAHMS, JOHANNES, 1833-1897

              [Until recently, the standard thematic catalogue of Brahms'
              works was that first published by Simrock in 1887, and there-
              after in at least five editions. Donald M. McCorkle, who is
              making a long-range study of Brahms' music, has kindly pro-
              vided annotations for the Simrock entries. See below for the
              latest Brahms cataloguing efforts.]

156   [Thematic catalogue] (D Bds: HB VII, Kat._ms. 521) [196p.] n.d.
▽   An incomplete catalogue. Double and multiple staff incipits

for only those opus number through op. 76, and for a small
group of works without opus numbers appended to the main
part of the catalogue.

157   [Simrock Brahms Verzeichniss I] **Thematisches Verzeichniss der bisher
im Druck erschienenen Werke von Johannes Brahms.** Nebst Systematischem
Verzeichniss und Registern (Berlin: N. Simrock, 1887) 134p.
>   This edition contains *Werke mit Opuszahl* through Op. 101 and
>   eight *Werke ohne Opuszahl (Mondnacht, Deutsche Volkslieder*
>   Heft I-II, *Volkskinderlieder, Choralvorspiel und Fuge, Fuge
>   in As moll, Studien für das Pianoforte, Gavotte von C.W. Gluck,
>   Ungarische Tänze).*

157a [SBV II] **Thematisches Verzeichniss sämmtlicher im Druck erschienenen
Werke von Johannes Brahms.** Nebst Systematischem Verzeichniss und
Registern (Berlin: N. Simrock, 1897) 175p.
>   This second issue is an enlargement of the original edition
>   to include the additional works composed and published through
>   1897. The title page was altered, and some important changes
>   and additions incorporated within the original page-plates.
>   Forty-one new plates were engraved to accomodate the extra
>   compositions and expanded catalogues and indexes. New pages
>   105-40 were inserted between original pages 104-05; pagination
>   of original pages 105-34 changed to 141-75.

157b [SBV III] --- Neue Ausgabe (Berlin: N. Simrock, 1902).
>   This extremely rare "new issue" is a reprint of the 1897 issue
>   with altered title page and numerous additions of arrangements
>   made by other musicians incorporated within the entries by
>   added lines of type. Alterations in the page-plates were
>   made to change Breitkopf imprints in favor of Simrock, to
>   substitute some later editions for originals, and to add some
>   transposed editions for high and low voices. The prices
>   quoted here are the same as in SBV II. Otherwise, it is
>   almost as accurate as SBV II, but very misleading to the
>   uninformed user.

157c [SBV IV] ---Neue Ausgabe (Berlin: N. Simrock, G.M.B.H., 1903)
>   The first issue of the reorganized Simrock firm (*Gesellschaft
>   mit Beschränkter Haftung*). Here further alterations have
>   been made without any notice, although the arrangements and
>   editions which differ from those in SBV II are apparently
>   the same as those listed in 1902, but with altered prices.
>   The most significant alteration is the addition of Op. 122,
>   which was added as p. 127. To justify the pagination, p. 127-
>   151 were renumbered as p. 128-52 by using one former blank
>   leaf (counted as p. 152). More misleading than SBV III.

157d [SBV V] --- Neue vermehrte Ausgabe, (Berlin: N. Simrock, G.M.B.H.,
1904)
>   An altered reprint of SBV IV, with the same types of alter-
>   ations as before. Incorporated are newer arrangements by
>   other musicians for harmonium, harp, etc., as well as minia-
>   ture score editions (for the first time); some more original
>   editions have been deleted. French texts appear for some
>   vocal works. Some price changes appear without notice. A
>   particularly misleading and unreliable catalogue.

157e [SBV VI] ---Neue vermehrte Ausgabe (Berlin: N. Simrock, G.M.B.H., 1910)
Final issue, a varied reprint of the previous issue, not otherwise a "new enlarged issue", but still further removed from
the authority of Brahms. Numerous new arrangers and transcri-
bers appear with added editions of adaptations.

158 EHRMANN, Alfred von. **Johannes Brahms: Weg, Werk und Welt** (Leipzig:
Breitkopf & Härtel, 1933) xii, 534p. Supplement, vi, 180p.
Thematisches Verzeichnis seiner Werke, Supplement, 1-164.
Incipits arranged by opus number, works without opus number,
and posthumously discovered and doubtful works. Indexed categorically and alphabetically. Annotated incipits in score
or piano reduction with instrument indication for all movements. Both orchestra and solo entrance incipits given in
concertos. Includes all bibliographic information.

159 Solo songs of Johannes Brahms.....English texts by H.S. Drinker
(New York: Association of American Choruses, 1946) 3v.
Melodic index to the Brahms solo songs, v. 3, Appendix, 44p.
Incipits are transposed to C major or A minor, and classi-
fied according to rhythmic and melodic shape.

160 BRAUNSTEIN, Joseph. **Thematic catalogue of the collected works of
Brahms** (New York: Ars Musica Press, 1956) 187p.
The catalogue includes all of Brahms' original works plus
his own arrangements, with and without opus numbers. Publication dates given; titles and text incipits indexed. The
editor's statement that it was "a revision and enlargement
of the fourth edition of 1907" is open to question. There
was no fourth edition (*Auflage) per se* of SBV, though there
was an undesignated fourth issue *(Ausgabe)* in 1903. No other
reference to a 1907 issue has been found. The revision in-
volved " was mainly a process of eliminating material, by
which the collation data for the original editions and the
statement of supplementary specifications, materials, and
arrangements, other than Brahms' own, were eradicated before
reprinting the catalogue; the enlargement consists entirely
of titles and incipits, with a slight bit of chronological
data, for posthumous editions. All of this was photograph-
ically borrowed without acknowledgment mostly from Ehrmann's
Thematisches Verzeichnis. For the imprints of original editions in the identification headings, the too-often incorrect
information printed in the issues of SBV following 1902 is
retained without comment." (McCorkle)
Reviews: MEducatorsJ XLIII (1957) 77; Robert SABIN, *MAmerica*
CXXVI (Dec 1956) 34; Helen Joy SLEEPER, *Notes* XV (Dec 1957)
106-07.

161 FELLINGER, Imogen (Köln).   [Thematisches Verzeichnis]
*

162 KROSS, Siegfried. **Thematisch-bibliographisches Verzeichnis sämtlicher
* Werke von Johannes Brahms** (To be published, Tutzing: Schneider)

163 McCORKLE, Donald M.   [Thematic catalogue]
*   Part of a larger study of manuscript sources.

BRANT, PER, 1714-1767

164   BENGTSSON, Ingmar. Anteckninger om Per Brant. III. War Brant ton-
       sättare? [Notes on Per Brant. III. Was Brant a composer?], *SvenskTMf*
       XLVII (1966) 5-61.
           [Thematic catalogue]
                   Incipits of 19 compositions, many of which are dubious,
                   grouped according to their probable degree of authenticity.
                   Two attributed to Brant are also traced to A. Brioschi and
                   H. Roman.

BRATISLAVA, Slovenské národné múzeum v Bratislave

165   [Central catalogue of Slovakian musical-historical sources]
  ▽   A thematic cataloguing project, begun in 1966, that includes
               sources up to 1918 that originated in the ČSR and are pre-
               served in Slovakia. Will also include foreign sources in
               Slovakia that relate to Slovakian music history. Omits
               chant literature and monumental collections using archaic
               forms of notation. Most inventoried sources derive from
               music collections of the 18th and early 19th centuries
               (primarily sacred vocal and instrumental music and secular
               instrumental works). To date, 12 such collections have
               been examined. An incipit catalogue is essential for Slo-
               vakian sources since many of the compositions are anonymous.
               Goals of the cataloguing project also include providing
               data for *RISM* and building up a microfilm archive of the
               catalogued sources. (see no. 1073)

BRAV, Ludwig (compiler)

166   Thematischer Führer durch klassische und moderne Orchestermusik zum
       besonderen Gebrauch für die musikalische Film-Illustration, mit einer
       Abhandlung: die Praxis der Bearbeitung und Besetzung für kleines
       Orchester (Berlin: Ed. Bote & G. Bock, 1928) 130p. Title as given
       on paper cover; title on page 1 is as follows: "Thematischer Führer
       durch die Orchestermusik des Verlages Ed. Bote und G. Bock. Zum
       besonderen Gebrauch für Film, Bühne, Konzert."
           Thematic index, 1-93.
                   Incipits of each section or movement of 276 works written
                   for stage and film by the following composers: Albert, Arbos,
                   Auber, Audran, J.S. Bach, Bauer, Baussnern, Becce, Beethoven,
                   Benedict, Berger, Berlioz, Bial, Blech, Brüll, Dawes, Deppe,
                   Dvorak, Ego, Elukhen, Erdmann, Ertel, Eulenberg, Fischel,
                   Flotow, E. Franck, Geisler, U. Giordano, Godard, Gounod,
                   Graener, Grünfeld, Händel, Hofmann, Hösslin, Humperdinck,
                   S. Jones, Kahn, Kienzl, Klughardt, F. Koch, Labinsky, Lalo,
                   Langert, Lecocq, Leoncavallo, Lewandowski, Liapounow, Liszt,
                   Lortzing, Maillart, Mahler, Mascagni, Mattausch, Mendelssohn,
                   Meyerbeer, Mlynarski, Moszkowski, Nicolai, Norem, Offenbach,
                   Paderewski, Paepke, Pirani, Radeche, Raff, Rameau, Redern,
                   Reger, Respighi, Reznicek, Rossini, Rothstein, Rubenstein,
                   Rudorff, Schillings, Schjelderup, Schmalstich, Schubert,
                   Schumann, Smetana, Spialek, Spinelli, J. Strauss, R. Strauss,
                   Suppé, Taubert, A. Thomas, Trapp, Tschaikowsky, Urban, Vieux-
                   temps, Watermann, Weiner, Witteborn, Weis, Wendland, Wolf,
                   Zamecnik.

IV. Breitkopf, *Catalogo delle sinfonie...* (Leipzig, 1762),
title page and page 22, no. 167

BREITKOPF, Johann Gottlob Immanuel, 1719-1794 (compiler)

167   Catalogo delle sinfonie, partite, overture, soli, duetti, trii, quattri e concerti per il violino, flauto traverso, cembalo ed altri stromenti, che si trovano in manuscritto nella Officina musica di Giovanni Gottlob Breitkopf in Lipsia (Leipzig, 1762-1765) 6 parts: 32, 48, 34, 24, 24, 38p.

167a --- Supplemento I-XVI (1766-1787) 56, 44, 36, 32 & 8, 32, 32, 40, 40, 40, 28, 36, 44, 32, 58, 82, 46p.

> Together, the six parts and 16 supplements comprise one of the largest and most important printed thematic catalogues of music. Its total of 888 pages contain approximately 14,000 incipits by over 1000 composers. Indicates composer, title and instrumentation, plus text underlay for some 1200 vocal works. Because this large compilation appeared over a 25 year period, it has proved invaluable for dating, as well as identification of anonymi, etc.

167b --- MEYER, Kathi. Early Breitkopf & Härtel thematic catalogues of
☐   manuscript music, *MQ* XXX (Apr 1944) 163-73.

> Discusses 25 thematic and non-thematic catalogues published 1760-1787 by J.G.I. Breitkopf [without Härtel].

167c --- BROOK, Barry S. ed. The Breitkopf thematic catalogue; the six parts and sixteen supplements 1762-1787, with introduction and indexes (New York: Dover, 1966) xxvii, 888, xxix-lxxxi.

> This one volume reprint edition provides supplementary over-all pagination which facilitates use of specially prepared indices. The introduction discusses the background of the catalogue and its compiler, and evaluates its accuracy of dating and attribution.
>
> *Reviews:* Owen ANDERSON *Music Journal* XXV/- (Nov. 1967) 52; Gugliemo BARBLAN *RItalianaMusicol* II/2 (1967) 402; Richard D.C. NOBLE *Consort* -/24 (1967) 332; Marc PINCHERLE *RMusicol* LIII/2 (1967) 190-91; Alexander WEINMANN *ÖsterreichischeMZ* XXII (Nov. 1967) 676; Quaintance EATON *Music Clubs* XLVII/3 (1968) 47-8; Donald W. KRUMMEL *Notes* XXIV/4 (1968) 697-700; Edward OLLESON *MLetters* XLIX (July 1968) 253-4; Stanley SADIE *MTimes* CIX (Dec 1968) 1121; Bernard E. WILSON *JAMS* XXI/3 (1968) 400-04; Tomislav VOLEK *HudVěda* 2 (1969) 212-14; Klaus HORTSCHANSKY *Mf* XXIJI/3 (1970) 363.

167d --- BROOK, Barry S., ed. The Breitkopf Thematic Catalogue: corri-
*   genda supplement

> This publication will list the corrections, clarifications, identifications of anonymi, double parentage conflicts, etc. that have been found by, or sent in to, the editor of the reprint edition (see p. xv of the introduction to that edition, no. 167c). The editor will welcome corrigenda of all sorts.

167e --- DEARLING, Robert J. [Cross-reference to the Breitkopf Catalogue]
☐   *Haydn Yearbook,* in press.

> Annotated list covers all Haydn's works in the Breitkopf Catalogue, plus information surrounding other composer's symphonies, quartets, and allied works.

BREITKOPF & HÄRTEL (publishers)

168   **Catalogue of works for orchestra** (Leipzig, London, New York, 1903)
          Thematic catalogue of Haydn and Mozart symphonies published
          by Breitkopf & Härtel, p. 28-36.

168a --- London, 1912.
          Contains the following thematic catalogues: Symphonies of
          Beethoven, Haydn, Mendelssohn, Mozart, Schubert, Schumann,
          Sibelius and Weingartner published by Breitkopf & Härtel,
          p. 49-61; Piano concertos by Beethoven, Hafden Cleve, Mozart,
          p. 16-17; Violin compositions by Mozart, p. 19; Violoncello
          concertos by Julius Klengel, p. 20; Orchestral works by J.S.
          Bach and Händel, p. 35-38.

169   **Catalogue of chamber music** (Leipzig, London, New York, [1906])
          Thematic lists for the following: String quartets of Haydn,
          Beethoven, Mozart, Mendelssohn, Schubert, and Schumann, p. 49-
          53; Pianoforte trios of Haydn, Beethoven, Mozart, Mendelssohn,
          Schubert, and Schumann, p. 54-56.

170   **Führer durch die Volksausgabe Breitkopf & Härtel** (Leipzig, [1910?])
      296p.
          Contains a thematic list in the appendix, p. 281-96.

171   **Guide through the Breitkopf edition** (New York, [1911?]) 182p.
          The appendix contains thematic lists, p. 143-82 of Mozart
          and Haydn sonatas for piano, piano solo or duet reductions
          of the symphonies, sonatas for violin and piano, and the
          string quartets of each composer which were published by
          this firm. Also a thematic list of the Breitkopf "Conserva-
          toire Collection" edited by Henry GERMER with works by:
          Beliczay, Blumner, Bock, Brüll, Damm, Duvernoy, Fielitz,
          Förster, Gauby, Götze, Gulli, Hornemann, Huber, Jadassohn,
          transcriptions of Wagner by Liszt, works by Liszt, Mächtig,
          Merkel, Messer, Nürnberg, Sitt, Bruch, Heller, Röntgen,
          Stihll, Vogel, Junkelmann. Arranged by collection number.

172   **Orchestermusik** (Leipzig, [1931]).
          Supplement contains a thematic catalogue of works by Atter-
          berg, J.S. Bach, Beethoven, Bruch, Cleve, Friedrich der
          Grosse, Händel, Haydn, Hubay, Klengel, Mendelssohn, Mozart,
          Rosetti, Schubert, Schumann, Sibelius, Spohr, Weingartner,
          and Zilcher.

BRESLAU, *see* WROCŁAW

BRIDGMAN, Nanie (compiler)

173   **[Catalogue thématique de la musique vocale polyphonique des XVe et**
▽   **XVIe s.]**
          A MS card catalogue maintained and continuously updated in
          the Départment de la Musique of the Bibliothèque Nationale
          in Paris. (Instrumental music is not included.) The cata-
          logue was begun in 1949, and follows the principles of clas-
          sification and codification as described the compiler in a
          series of articles (see nos. 174-77)

The catalogue thus far contains over 12,000 cards, which
will be the basis for a volume of *RISM* now in preparation.
Included are: 1) all of the "fonds ancien" (prints and MSS)
of the Département de la musique of the Bibliothèque
nationale, including also the "fonds du Conservatoire";
2) MSS of the Département des manuscrits de la Bibliothèque
nationale; 3) MSS of the period covered from other French
and foreign libraries.

BRIDGMAN, Nanie

174   L'Établissement d'un catalogue par incipit musicaux, *MDisoplina*
☐   IV/1 (1950) 65-68.
> Laments the lack of interest in compiling thematic cata-
> logues of all periods and offers a system of notating in-
> cipits.

175   À propos d'un catalogue central d'incipits musicaux, *FontesArtisM*
☐   I (1954) 22-23.
> A brief statement in favor of a centrally located thematic
> catalogue for libraries.

176   Le classement par incipit musicaux, histoire d'un catalogue, *Bulletin*
☐   *des Bibliothèques de France* IV/6 (1959) 303-08.

177   Nouvelle visite aux incipit musicaux, *ActaMusicol* XXXIII/2-4 (1961)
☐   193-96.

BRIOSCHI, ANTONIO, active ca. 1770

178   DEARLING, Robert (Dunstable, Bedfordshire). [Thematic catalogue]
▽   Index cards (manuscript). (see no. 282)
> Incipits for 53 symphonies, concertini, overtures, and
> sonatas for strings à 3 or à 4.

BRIXI family

179   NOVÁK, Vladimir. Zur Katalogisierung von Werken der Familie Brixi
> [Remarks on the cataloguing of the works of the Brixi family], *Mf*
> XXII/3 (July-Sept 1969) 335-37. (*RILM* 69/ 122ᵃp)
>> A thematic catalogue of the works of the Brixi family has
>> been compiled with the aid of a computer. Composers include:
>> František Xaver Brixi, Šimon Brixi, Victorin Brixi, Jeronym
>> Brixi, and Jan Josef Brixi.

BRNO, Hudební odděleni Zemského Musea: Catalogue-Valtice (Feldsberg)

180   [Thematic catalogue] (CS B) 50p. Compiled 1770-1790. (manuscript)
▽   Microfilm copy in D K jhi.
> Bass incipits for Masses, Litanies, Offertories, Vespers,
> Salve Regina, Ave Regina, Regina Coeli, Te Deum, Requiems,
> Stabat Mater and symphonies.

BRNO, Hudební odděleni Zemského Musea: Catalogue-Prag 1829

181   Inventarium der Instrumenten und Musicalien des Kirchenmusicchores
▽   der barmherzigen Brüder zu den heiligen Aposteln Simonem et Judam
in Prag aπ: 1829 (CS B) 36p. (manuscript). Microfilm copy in D K
jhi.

Incipits for Masses, Offertories, motets, Requiem, Regina
Coeli, and Salve Regina.

BRNO, Moravské Múzeum, *see* RAJHRAD

BRNO, Sv. Jakub

183   [Thematic catalogue] (CS; City Archives of Brno: 16/5) 134 fol.
▽   untitled (manuscript).
            Inventory of music in the church of St. Jacob, Brno. Begun
            in 1763, with entries apparently until 1782. Contains 933
            consecutively numbered items, 738 of them original entries,
            195 added later, with composer's name, data on instrumenta-
            tion and voice parts, incipits for the thorough-bass. Or-
            ganized into 28 groups according to liturgical function and
            number of voices: Missae, Veni Sancte Spiritus, Stabat Mater,
            Lytaniae, Requiem, Vesperae, Completoria, psalms, hymns,
            Offertories, Salve Regina, and Te Deum Laudamus. Consists
            of 360 anonymous works and 573 attributed works. The follow-
            ing composers are represented: Adlgasser 1, Albrectsberger
            (Albrechtberger) 2, Aufschneiter 1, Auman 1, Baradies 1,
            Bassany 1, Beyer 6, Boocus (Booccus) 3, Boog 1, Borpora 1,
            Brixi 3, Brixides 1, Bruneder 5, Caldara 75, Rinaldo di
            Capua 1, Carl 11, P. Carolo è Scholis 1, Conti 7, Cordella
            (Cordela) 2, Domberger (Domberg, Domborg, Donberger) 19,
            Ehrenhardt (Ehrnhardt, Ernhardt, Ehrenhart, Ehrnhart) 5,
            Erath 1, Eysenbach 1, Fux 32, Galuppi 1, Gottwald (Gottwaldt)
            2, Graff 3, Grasel 1, Graun 2, Peregrino Gravani 33, Tobia
            Gsur 4, Guretzky 2, Habegger (Habbegger) 7, Haberhauer
            (Habrhauer) 4, Hasse 3, Heyden (Heydn) 16, Hoffmann (Hoff-
            man) 5, Holtzbauer 3, Guntheri Jacobi 1, Leopoldo Jepser
            dilletante Vienensi 2, P.Josepho à Scta Clara Wiennensi 3,
            P. Josepho a S. Elisabetha 1, Patre Josepho Augustino 4,
            P. Justo Joseph 1, Klyma (Klima) 2, Kohaut 2, Cajetano
            Kolberer 1, Köller 1, Krottendorffer 1, Laube 7, Lohelio 3,
            Lotti 1, Ruperti Mayer 2, Miller 2, Mona 1, Navratil 3,
            Neymann 1, Novotni 2, Orber 1, Orbesser 1, Ötel (Öetel,
            Öettl, Öttel) 6, Pach 1, Pergolesi 1, Joannis Pez 1,
            Pfeiffer 1, Pichler 5, Pruneder 1, Reinhardt (Reinhard) 26,
            Reütter (Reutter) 46, Ruziczka 1, Saigl 1, Salieri 1, Saari
            1, Seeman (Semann) 2, Seuche 2, Scheibl (Scheibel, Sheibl)
            19, Schenk (Schenck) 4, Schmidt (Schmid, Schmit) 25, Rdo
            Patre Simon 2, Sonnleitner (Sonnlaitner) 4, Strasser 1,
            Sylvano 1, Tuma (Tumma, Thuma) 8, Friderico Treytler 3,
            Umstadt (Umstatt) 8, Wachter 4, Francesco Widerhoffer 1,
            Widman 2, P. Flor: Wrastil 6, Zacher 2, Zechner (Zecher)
            69, Ziannj 7, Zigler 1.

BRODY, Charles G.; RIEDEL, Johannes   (U. of Minnesota)

184   A computer aided study of Ecuadorean urban music (1970)(typescript)
□▽   "Discussion and application of computer to three matters:
            1) To use the computer to catalog the compositions by title,
            composer, author, and melodic incipit; 2) To use the com-
            puter as a tool to abstract information from the pieces for
            evidence of subtypes within the repertoire; 3) To develop

computer programs which could by useful in retrieving information from similar repertoires of other Latin American
nations."

BROOK, Barry S. (compiler)

185   La symphonie française dans la seconde moitié du XVIIIe siècle
(Paris: Publications de l'Institut de Musicologie de l'Université
de Paris, 1962) 3v.
     Index thématique arrangé par tonalités et temps, v. I, 511-73.
     Index alphabétique des incipits transposés en do majeur ou do
     mineur et indiqués par lettres, v. I, 574-84. Catalogue théma-
     tique et bibliographique, v. II, 1-726.
          Volume I includes a compact *Index thématique* with incipits,
          arranged by key and meter, for approximately 1200 symphonies
          by 156 French composers from 1740-1830. These incipits are
          transposed into C major or C minor and indicated by letters
          and alphabetically arranged. This volume also contains chap-
          ters on the thematic catalogues of M. le Comte D'Ogny and
          Ruge-Seignelai (see nos. 921 and 1121   ). Volume II is
          a complete bibliographical and thematic listing of the same
          materials, this time by composer with biographical informa-
          tion, catalogue references, location of sources, etc.
          Composers: Alday l'aîné, Alday le jeune, Alexandre, d'Ambre-
          ville, Aubert, Azais, Bailleux, Baillot, Bambini, Barrière,
          Barthélémon, Baudron, Beck, Bédard, Berbiguer, Bernardy de
          Valernes, Bernasconi, Bertheaume, Bertin, Berton, Bideau,
          Blainville, Blasius, Blois, Bonnet, Bordet, Bréval, Bullant,
          Burckhoffer, Cambini, Canavas, P.J. Candeille, Emilie Can-
          deille, Caraffe, Carassié, J.G. Cardon, J.B. Cardon, Cardonne,
          Catel, Chambray, Chardiny, Chartrain, Chrétien, Corrette,
          Croix, Cupis, Dalvimare, Dauvergne, Davaux, Davesne, Désau-
          giers, Désormeaux, Devienne, Domnich, Ducreux, Dupont, Du-
          vernoy, le Comte de F***, Fakaerti, Fortia de Piles, Frédéric,
          Garnier, Gaviniès, Glachant, Godecharle, Gossec, Grénon,
          Grétry, Guénin, Guignon, Guillemain, Guillemant, Guillon,
          Herbain, Herold, J.B. Jadin, L.E. Jadin, Janson, Jumentier,
          Jupin, Kreutzer, L'Abbé le fils, Lacépède, La Croix, Lalloyau,
          Lamoninary, Laurent, Le Brun, Le Duc, Leemans, J.X. Lefèvre,
          Théodore Lefèvre, Lejeune, Jemaire, Le Roy, Lochon, Lottin,
          Magnien, Mahaut, Mangean, Martin, Massoneau, Mathurin, Mé-
          hul, Meunier, Milandre, Miroglio, Mondonville, Monroy, Mon-
          signy, Montillot, J.B. Moulinghen, L.C. Moulinghen, G. Navoi-
          gille, J. Navoigille, Ozi, Papavoine, F. Parisot, A. Parisot,
          Pélissier, Philidor, Pierlot, Pinaire, Plessis, Pleyel,
          Procksch, Prot, Quentin, Ragué, neveu Rameau, Rebel, Rendeux,
          H.J. Rigel, Rigel (fils), Rigel (frère), Roeser, Rose,
          Rousseau, Roy, Roz, Ruge, Ruge (fils), Saint-Georges, le
          Baron de Sanes, Schencker, Schobert, Simon, Sohier, Solère,
          Spourny, Talon, Tapray, Tarade, Thomelin, Touchemoulin, Tra-
          venol, de Tremais, Tulou, Vachon, Vandenbroeck, Vibert, Wider-
          kehr.

          Reviews: Jan LaRUE, *MQ* XLIX/3 (1963) 384-88; Marc PINCHERLE,
          RMusicol XLIX/126 (1963) 131-33; Frederick STERNFIELD, *MLet-
          ters* XLIV/4 (1963) 388-90; Robert STEVENSON, *Notes* XX/3 (1963)
          466-69; Ingmar BENGTSSON, *SvenskTMf* XLVI/- (1964) 157-61;
          Bathia CHURGIN, *JAMS* XVII/2 (1964) 224-27; H.C. Robbins LAN-
          DON, *Mf* XVII/4 (1964) 435-39.

186   Thematic catalogue of the symphonie concertante (multiple concerto),
 *   I730-I830 . Index cards

BROOK, Barry S.; GOULD, Murray

187   Notating music with ordinary typewriter characters (a plaine and
 ☐   easie code system for musicke)(Flushing, N.Y.: Queens College, 1964)

187a --- Reprinted in *FontesArtisM* XI/3 (1964) 142-55.
              With added commentaries by Jan LaRue, Ingmar Bengtsson,
              Nanie Bridgman, Rita Benton and Paule Chaillon-Guiomar,
              p. 155-59, discussing the merits of the notation. This
              code has been superceded by *The simplified plaine and
              easie code system* (see next entry).

BROOK, Barry S.

188   The simplified plaine and easie code system for notating music, a
 ☐   proposal for international adoption, *FontesArtisM* XII/2-3 (May-Sept
       1965) 156-60. [for summary of the code see reproduction opposite]
              The *Plaine and Easie* code, usable with and without a com-
              puter, is now being employed in a number of thematic cata-
              loguing projects. (see nos. 817, 965, 1000, & 1122)

188a The plaine and easie code, *Musicology and the computer*, Barry S.
 ☐   BROOK, ed. (New York: City University of New York Press, 1970) 53-56.
       A summary, with slight emendations of no. 188.

188b The plaine and easie code: summary. (New York: City University of
 ☐   New York, 1967, 1970) 1p. (mimeographed) [reproduction opposite]
              A one-page condensation of no. 188.

189   Utilization of data processing techniques in musical documentation,
 ☐   *FontesArtisM* XII/2-3 (May-Sept 1965) 112-22.

190   Some new paths for music bibliography, *Computers in humanistic
 ☐   research: readings and perspectives*, Edmund A. BOWLES, ed. (Engle-
       wood, N.J.: Prentice-Hall, 1967) 204-11.

191   Music bibliography and the computer, *Computer Applications in Music*,
 ☐   Gerald LEFKOFF, ed. (Morgantown, W. Va.: West Virginia University
       Library, 1967) *RILM* 67 1282.

192   Music documentation of the future, *Musicology and the computer*,
 ☐   Barry S. BROOK, ed. (New York: City University of New York Press,
       1970) 28-36.

193   The first printed thematic catalogues, *Festskrift Jens Peter Larsen
       1902 14/VI 1972*. Studier udgivet af Musikvidenskabeligt Institut ved
       København's Universitet (København: Wilhelm Hansen Musik-Forlag,
       1972) 103-12.
              Discussion of the 18th century meaning of the terms "theme"
              and "thematic catalogue"; description of the first two,
              thus-far-known, thematic catalogues, one by William Barton
              published in 1645 in his *Book of Psalms* (see no. 73) and
              the other by Johann Kaspar Kerll published in 1686 as a
              supplement to his *Modulatio Organica* (see no. 655).

The PLAINE and EASIE Code

[Summary]

EXAMPLE: Beethoven, 5th Symphony, 3rd movement, cello.

,,4G / ,C E G /'2C 4E / 2D ,4#F/ 2.G _/ G /

(Allegro, bBEAminor, 3/4)

Duration: Given in numbers, 1 2 3 4 5 6 7 8 9 0, for both notes and rests. The numbers precede pitch letters and *remain in effect* crossing bar lines, *until a different duration number appears* .

1	whole note or rest	8	eighth	5	64th
2	half note or rest	6	16th	7	128th
4	quarter, ditto	3	32nd	9	Breve
				0	Longa

Dotted notes indicated by period: 2. C dotted half note C

Rests indicated by a hyphen: 4C-2- = ♩ 𝄽 ━

Ties by underline or plus sign : 2C_4C [or 2C+4C] = ♪♩

Triplets and other unusual rhythmic groupings are enclosed in parentheses preceded by total duration number: 4(8 CDE)

Fermata indicated by parentheses around a single pitch or rest: (C)

Pitch: Given in letters: A B C D E F G.

Accidentals immediately precede pitch letters as in conventional notation: Sharp ♯ [or X] . Flat b [or Y] . Natural n [or N] . Double sharp x [or XX] . Double flat bb [or YY] .[5]

Register (Octave Placement) indicated by commas or apostrophes placed in front of duration and pitch symbols and *remaining in effect until a different register sign appears.*

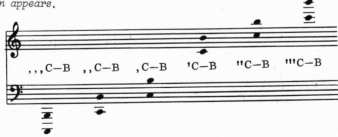

,,,C—B ,,C—B ,C—B 'C—B "C—B '''C—B

Additional Symbols:

/ Bar line	// Double bar line	t [T] Trill
g [Q] Grace note; cue notes	/-/ Full measure rest	/-3/ Three measure rest
/:/ [/R/] Repeat preceding measure	/:2/ [/R2/] Repeat 2 measures preceding	

8.68 ABC DEF GAB Repeat rhythmic pattern
(i. e. , 2 or more successive duration numbers)
for each succeeding group of pitches: etc.

[N. B. :Alternate keypunch symbols in brackets]

BROOK (Nov. ,1970)

BRTNICE [Pirnitz] castle

194   Inventario/ per/ la musica   (CS Bm: sign. G 84) 95ℓ.   Compiled ca.
▽   1752. (manuscript)
        A damaged and incomplete copy of musical sources in castle
        Brtnice (Pirnitz) in Moravia. Description: composer's name,
        number, title, instrumentation, musical incipit, text inci-
        pit. Contains the following genres: concertos, cassations,
        divertimenti, symphonies, solos, Masses, Litanies, and Offer-
        tories. 1061 incipits arranged in alphabetical order by
        composer: Anonymous 9, Abbas 1, Adolfati 1, Agrell 1, Mauro
        Alai 3, Arbesser 4, Auman 2, Barba 2, Beer 7, Bencini 4,
        Beretz 2, Bernasconi 1, Bioni 4, Bononcini 2, Boog 1, Briuio
        1, Brixi 6, Bruscha 1, Caldara 22, Carlo 5, Clyma 4, Contini
        1, Cziardini 1, Czernohorski 1, Erber 3, Faitelli 1, Ferrari
        2, Fiamenghino 2, Fillnbaum 3, Fistr 6, Gasmann 8, Gebel 1,
        Giulini 1, Gluck 1, Gottvalt 1, Grauser 3, Gron 1, Gsur 3,
        Gvicardelli 1, Hager 1, Hass 2, Hasse 24, Haydn 9, Hellman
        2, Hendl 1, Herger 1, Hoffman 2, Holtzbauer 23, Jacobi 3,
        Jomeli 2, Jacomelli (Iacomeli) 2, Janoussek 1, Kayser 9,
        Klausek 1, Knechtl 2, Kohaut 10, Kreider (Kreüder) 2, Küffner
        6, Lampugnani 2, Lasnel 2, Laube 33, Leclair 1, Leo 4, Loca-
        telli 5, Lohelio 10, Van Maldere 4, Malvasi 2, Martini 9,
        Mikuletzki 13, Miller 5, Mitcha 4, Monn 6, Müller 15, Neruda
        1, Novak 24, Ordonez 3, Orsler 75, Pajer 2, Pasteris 2,
        Pergolesi 3, Pichler 1, Pirk 1, Porpora 3, Porsile 2, Porta
        1, Predieri 15, Prustman 3, Ragazzi 8, Rauscher 1, Reinhardt
        5, Reitter 30, Richter 6, Ripl 1, Rüdl 1, Ruziczka 2, Sari 1,
        Sciasi 1, Scotur 1, Sedlaczek 15, Scheibl 1, Schenk 3, Schle-
        ger 6, Schmidt (Schmid) 27, Schramek 86, Schreger 1, Sonnleit-
        ner 5, Stamitz 19, Stietina 1, Suchanek 3, Tallman 1, Tardini
        5, Terradellas 1, Tessarini 13, Timer 1, Tuma 36, Ucielini 4,
        Umstat 5, Vachter 1, Vagenseil 34, Valpert 4, Vanhal 16, Vin-
        ci 5, Vivaldi 16, Waigerth 2, Weichenmahr 2, Weltz (Veltz)
        117, Werner 4, Zani 55, Zechner 33, Zucari 5.

194a   --- STRAKOVÁ, Theodora. Hudba u brtnických Collaltů v.17. a 18.
□ ▽   století [Music in Pirnitz, the residence of the Collalto family,
        in the 17th and 18th centuries]   (PhD diss.: U.J.E.P., Brno, 1967)
        2v: 196; 51p. (typescript)
        An analysis of the Brtnice catalogue includes a comparison
        with other important inventories of Moravian and Austrian
        provenance.

BRUCKNER, ANTON 1824-1896

195   AUER, Max. Anton Bruckner; sein Leben und Werk (Zürich: Amalthea-
        Verlag, 1947) 86p.
        Notenbeispiele, unindexed supplement.
        Incipits and musical examples for 32 works discussed in bio-
        graphy. Text underlaid in vocal examples.

196   WALKER, Arthur D. (Manchester, England). Thematic catalogue of the
*   works of Anton Bruckner
        Incipits to the complete works will include passages which the
        composer revised.

BRUNETTI, GAETANO, ca.1740-ca.1808

197 Catalogue thématique des oeuvres inédites, la plupart autographes,
▽   de Gaëtano Brunetti, Ier violon du roi d'Espagne Charles IV.
     Xerox copies in US NYcg and US NYqc. (manuscript)
                    Incipits of 39 sonatas, 7 duos, 3 theme-and-variations, 23
                    divertissements, 50 quartets, 43 quintets, 34 symphonies, 4
                    symphonies concertantes, 1 scena, and 1 variation for wood-
                    winds. Tempi, many dates, and some dedications given. MS
                    in the library of Aristide Wirsta, Bourg-la-Reine, Seine,
                    France.

198 BELGRAY, Alice B. Gaetano Brunetti: An exploratory bio-bibliograph-
▽   ical study (PhD diss., Musicology: U. of Michigan, 1970) 264p.(typescript)
        Thematic catalogue of the violin sonatas of Gaetano Brunetti,
        Part II, 125-206.
                    Incipits for all movements of 59 sonatas (bass line given
                    when necessary), and 3 Adagios Glosados (alternate second
                    movements). Information is provided for 9 missing sonatas.

BRUNI, ANTONIO BARTOLOMEO 1751?-1821

199 CESARI, Gaetano et al.   Antonio Bartolomeo Bruni, musicista
     cuneese (Turin: S. Lattes, 1931) 221p.
        Indice tematico, 69-78, 210-15.
                    Incipits for 1st violin parts of string trios and for all
                    movements of the violin sonatas.

BRUXELLES, Bibliothèque Royale: Ms. 5557

200 STEVENS, Denis. [Thematic catalogue] (B Br: Ms. 5557) (manuscript)
▽   Incipits of late 15th century liturgical music.

BRUXELLES, Bibliothèque Royale: MSS 288 and 11239

201 PICKER, Martin. The chanson albums of Marguerite of Austria, MSS
     228 and 11239 of the Bibliothèque Royale de Belgique, *Annales Musi-
     cologiques* VI (1958-1963) 145-285.
        [Thematic catalogue], 196-259.
                    A collection of song manuscripts of La Rue, Josquin, Agrico-
                    la, de Orto, Weerbecke, and anonymous associates of Marguerite
                    of Austria, with index and incipits.

201a --- Full transcriptions of the chansons appear in a volume bearing
     the same title as the above article (Berkeley: U. of California Press,
     1965) 505p.

BRYDEN, John R. (compiler)

202 Incipit title, thematic, and selected melodic pattern index of the
▽   chant in contemporary liturgical books of the Roman Catholic Church
     (Wayne State U., 1962) 249p. (manuscript) (see no. 604)
                An alphabetical notation is employed.

45

BUCAREŞTI, Ciprian Porumbescu Conservatory

203   COSMA, Viorel. **Manuscrise muzicale româneşu în Biblioteca Conserva-
       torului "Ciprian Porumbescu" din Bucureşti** [Rumanian musical manu-
       scripts in the Library of the Ciprian Porumbescu Conservatory of
       Bucharest], *Études de musicol* V (1969) 269-309. (*RILM* 69/116ap)
              Description of the collection, followed by a thematic cata-
              logue.

BUDAPEST, Országos Széchényi Könyvtár

204   LaRUE, Jan. **[Symphonies and concertos, 18th c.]** [4p.] (manuscript)
▿   Incipits for over 100 18th-century works (most of them MS,
              several prints) housed in the Széchényi Library. Indicates
              call number and instrumentation, as well as conflicting
              attributions where appropriate. The following composers
              are inventoried: C.P.E. Bach, Giov. Bach, Cannabich, Domenico
              Cimarosa, Dittersdorf, Giovanni Dressler, Cornelius Heinrich
              Dretzel, George Druschezky, Eybler, Fils, Jean Fuchs, Florian
              (F.L.) Gassmann, Gayer, Giarnovik, Georg Glantz, F.J. Gossec,
              Antoine Heberle, L. Hoffman, Hoffmeister, Holtzbauer, F. Aman-
              do Ivanschitz, Ferd. Kauer, Körtzl, Krommer, Franc. Kurzweil,
              Malter [v. Maldere], Paul Maschek, Nicoletto Mestrino, Gio-
              vani Nisle, Ordenitz, F. Paer, Pichl (Pichel), Pleyel, Ricci
              de Festone, P. Rode, G. Sarti, Carlo Schiringer, Schragner,
              Schroetter, Schuster, Giov. Sperger, Stainmez (Steinmetz),
              Süssmayr, Vanhal (Vanhall, Wanhall, Wanhal), Viotti, Wagenseil
              (Wagenseill), Wendt, Winkler, Winter, Wranitzky, Gius. Ziegler,
              Zimmermann. Also several anonymous works.

BURGSTEINFURT, Fürstlich Bentheimsche Bibliothek

205   THURMANN, Erich. **[Thematic catalogue of manuscripts in the Fürst zu
▿   Bentheimschen Musikaliensammlung Burgsteinfurt]** (Entire collection
       on loan to D MÜu since 1966) Index cards. Compiled 1970. (manu-
       script)
              Incipits, arranged alphabetically by composer, for 734 MSS.
              Composers include: Agrell, L. Alessandri, Andreozzi, Anfossi,
              Asioli, C.P.E. Bach, J.C. Bach, F. Bianchi, F. Blangini,
              Boieldieu, C.P. Bonasegla, C.A. Cartellieri, L. Caruso, Cheru-
              bini, Cimarosa, F. Devienne, Dittersdorf, K.K. Eder, G. Fari-
              nelli, J.A.L. Fatken, V. Federici, V. Fioravanti, A. Galletti,
              F.J. Garnier, P. Gaveaux, N. Gellert, Gluck, J. Goettling, F.H.
              Graf, C.H. Graun, J.F. Grenser, Grétry, F. Grünbein, P. Gug-
              lielmi, J. Haydn, F.A. Hoffmeister, A. Janitsch, G. Jarnovick,
              N. Isouard, W. Justuz, J.F. Klöffler, F. Krommer, Laue, L.A.
              Lebrun, F. Lucas, Lully, F.C. Magnus, D. Mancinelli, P.H.Masch,
              J.S. Mayr, Méhul, Metzger, W.A. Mozart, A.E. Müller, Mussini,
              Myslivecek, S. Nasolini, J.G. Naumann, J. Otto, F. Paer, G.
              Paisiello, S. Palma, S. Pavesi, W. Pichl, J. Pleyel, V. Pucitta,
              J.F. Reichardt, A. Retzel, V. Righini, A. Romberg, F.A. Rosetti,
              P.P. Roslaub, G. Rossini, A. Sacchini, J.F. de Salin, G. Sarti,
              Schröder, J. Schuster, J.G. Schwanenberger, A. Stamitz, C. Sta-
              mitz, F.v. Stengel, C.G. Toeschi, J.B. Vanhal, J.C. Vogel, J.
              Weigl, J.B. Wendling, C.W. Westerhoff, P. Winter, P. Wranitzki,
              N. Zingarelli.

205 a --- KRUTTGE, Eigel. Geschichte der Burgsteinfurter Hofkapelle I756-
□ ▽   I8I7 (PhD diss.: Bonn, 1924) (typescript).

BURHARDT, Stefan (compiler)

206   **Polonez. Katalog tematyczny** [Polonaise. Thematic catalogue], Maria
 *   PROKOPOWICZ and Andrzej SPÓZ, editors, (Kraków: Polish Music Publi-
       cations, v. 2, ca. 1972)
              Contains all known polonaises written within 1792-1830.
              Arranged in alphabetical order giving ca. 800 fully
              harmonized incipits, date of composition, autograph,
              editions, transcriptions, and literature. Includes ca.
              1500 composers.

BURROWS, Raymond; **REDMOND**, Bessie C. (compilers)

207 **Symphony themes** (New York: Simon and Schuster, [1942].295p.
              Indexes the themes of 100 symphonies from the works of Bax,
              Beethoven, R.R. Bennett, Berlioz, Bloch, Borodin, Brahms,
              Bruckner, Chaikovskii, Chausson, Copland, Dvorak, Elgar,
              Franck, Glazunov, Goldmark, Hadley, Hanson, Harris, Haydn,
              E.B. Hill, Honegger, d'Indy, Mahler, D.G. Mason, Mendelssohn,
              Mozart, Prokofiev, Rachmaninov, Saint-Saëns, Schubert, Schu-
              mann, Shostakovich, Sibelius, Sowerby, Strauss, Stringham,
              Vaughan Williams. Works listed are those frequently performed
              or readily available on records; data on scores, recordings,
              related articles and program notes is given p. 56-261.

              Reviews: W. McN. *MTimes* XCII/- (Sept 1951) 466-67.

208 **Concerto themes** (New York: Simon and Schuster, 1951) 296p.
              Principal themes of all movements listed. Indexed accord-
              ing to concerto titles, keys, and solo instruments. 144
              concertos by: Addinsell, J.C. Bach, J.S. Bach, Bartok,
              Beethoven, Berg, Berlioz, Bliss, Block, Boccherini, Brahms,
              Bruch, Chausson, Chopin, Corelli, Debussy, Delius, Dohnanyi,
              Dvorak, Elgar, Falla, Franck, Gershwin, Glazunov, Goldmark,
              Grieg, Hadley, Handel, Haydn, Hindemith, Ireland, Khatcha-
              turian, Lalo, Liszt, Macdowell, Mendelssohn, Milhaud, Mozart,
              Paderewski, Paganini, Prokofiev, Rachmaninoff, Ravel, Rubin-
              stein, St. Saens, Schumann, Shostakovich, Sibelius, Spohr,
              Stravinsky, Tschaikowsky,Vaughan Williams, Vivaldi, Walton,
              Weber, and Wieniawski.

              Reviews: International Musician L/- (Nov.1951) 31; *Musical
              Courier* CXLIV/- (Oct 1951) 28; *MTimes* XCII/- (Sept 1951) 406-
              07; *Violins and Violinists* XII/- (Aug 1951) 225; *Musical
              America* LXXII/- (Feb 1952) 278; *Music Teacher and Piano
              Student* XXXI/- (Mar 1952) 161.

BUSONI, FERRUCCIO, 1866-1924

209 KINDERMANN, Jürgen. **Thematisch-chronologisches Verzeichnis der
     musikalischen Werke von Ferruccio Busoni** (Regensburg: Bosse, 1971)
     ca. 500p.

BUTTSTETT, FRANZ VOLLRATH, 1735-1814

210   KERN, Hans. Franz Vollrath Buttstett (I735-I8I4). Eine Studie zur
      Musik des Spätbarock (Würzburg: Triltsch, 1939) xii, 97p.
          Thematisches Verzeichnis der erhaltenen Werke Franz Vollrath
          Buttstetts, [69]-93.
              Vocal and instrumental incipits of all movements for church
              cantatas, piano pieces, and songs.

BUUS, JACOB, d. 1565

211   BREITNER, Walter. Jacob Buus als Motettenkomponist (PhD diss.: Wien,
▽   1960) 183*l.* (typescript)
          [Thematic catalogue], 161-69.
              39 double staff incipits for both sections of each motet of the
              Primo Libro de Motetti 1549, and 2 motets in collections.

BYRD, WILLIAM, 1542/1543- 1623

211.1 ZIMMERMAN, Franklin B. Thematic and first-line indexes to the complete
*   works of William Byrd. Computer produced.

ČAJKOVSKIJ, PETR IL'IČ, 1840-1893

212   JURGENSON, Boris, ed. Catalogue thématique des oeuvres de Peter
      Tschaikowsky (Moscow: Jurgenson, [1897])168p.
              Works arranged in order of opus numbers, followed by those
              without opus numbers, theater and posthumous works. Includes
              indexes in French by medium, and alphabetical indexes in
              French and Russian of vocal works. Piano reduction incipits
              plus texted voice parts (Russian and German) of all movements,
              acts and scenes, with instrumentation, tempi, dynamics, dates,
              publishers, and dedications. Reprints: N.Y.,194-;London,1965

CALDARA, ANTONIO, 1670-1736

213   FUCHS, Aloys. Materiale zur zusammenstellung eines thematischen
▽   Catalogs über sämtliche Werke des Antonio Caldara...(D Bds: HB VII,
      Kat. ms. 526; microfilm copy in US NYcg) Compiled 1830-1852. In 2
      parts: 15, 10p. (manuscript)
              Draft for a catalogue of Caldara's works. Incipits for vo-
              cal works organized by genre. Incipits omitted for most of
              the second part, from which the above title is derived.

214   GREENWOOD, Barrie; PRITCHARD, Brian W. (Christchurch, New Zealand).
*   Checklist and thematic catalogue of the works of Antonio Caldara
              Incipits for over 1,200 works have so far been catalogued.
              The catalogue will be divided into sacred and secular works,

Key: * in preparation; ▽ manuscript; ☐ literature; ✪ Library of Congress

and further subdivided by genre. Will provide title and
catalogue number, scoring (vocal and instrumental), location
of autograph, location of other MSS copies, details of all
printed editions and location of 18th century editions.

CAMBINI, GIOVANNI GIUSEPPI, 1746-1825

215   TRIMPERT, Lutz. **Die konzertanten Quartette von Giuseppe Cambini.**
✡   *Mainzer Studien zur Musikgeschichte,* Bd. I (Tutzing: Hans Schneider,
     1967) 328p.
          Verzeichnis der Quartette G. Cambinis, Anhang, 243-323.
               Chronological thematic catalogue of first movements of 174
               quartets with tempo indications of other movements. In ad-
               dition, there are 39 incipits from "Quatuors d'Airs...", i.e.
               quartet arrangements of popular tunes. The appendix also
               includes a non-thematic index of his other compositions,
               vocal and instrumental.

               Reviews: Musikhandel XIX/2 (Mar 1968) 86; Howard BROFSKY,
               Notes XXVI (Sept 1969) 31-33.

CAMBRAI, Bibliothèque municipale

216   COUSSEMAKER, Edmond de. **Notice sur les collections musicales de la
     Bibliothèque de Cambrai** (Paris: Techener, 1843) 40p.
          [Thematic list], Appendix, 33-40.
               Incipits of 50 anonymous Masses with titles.

CAMBRAI, Bibliothèque municipale: MS 125-128 (olim 124)

217   DIEHL, George K. (La Salle College, Phila., Pa.). **Cambrai MS 125-**
*   **128 (olim 124)** In progress dissertation, 2v.
          Thematic catalogue, v. II.
               Incipits of all voices (in original notation) of the 229
               compositions in the MS with the standard bibliographical
               apparatus.

CAMBRIDGE University, Fitzwilliam Museum

218   FULLER-MAITLAND, J.A.; MANN, A.H. **Catalogue of the music in the
     Fitzwilliam Museum, Cambridge** (London: Clay, 1893) 257p.
               36 vocal and instrumental MS themes, 13 multiple staff in-
               cipits of keyboard MS themes. Works by: C.P.E. Bach, Bevin?
               Blow?, des Buissons, Corelli, C. Gibbons?, Handel, Palestrina,
               D. Scarlatti, Tartini, and Vittoria. Date, size of page,
               and folio number are given.

CAMERLOHER, PLACIDUS von, 1718-1782

219   ZIEGLER, Benno. **Placidus von Camerloher** (Freising: F.P. Datterer,
     1919) 140p.
          Thematischer Katalog der Instrumentalkompositionen, 135-40.
               Incipits (handwritten form) for all movements of 65 works,
               grouped according to genre (flute sonatas, trio sonatas, and

sinfonias). Works in genre groups arranged by ascending
fourths. Designation and location of MS given. Supplemented
by MAYER (see below).

219a --- Supplement in Matthias MAYER, **Placidus von Camerlohers Kirchen-**
musik und Bühnenwerke, *Jahrbuch 1964 für Altbayerische Kirchen-*
geschichte. Deutingers Beiträge Band 23/3 (München: F.X. Seitz,
1964) 119-62.
Thematisches Verzeichnis der kirchenmusikalischen Werke Camer-
lohers und Thematisches Verzeichnis jener Triosonaten und Sym-
phonien Camerlohers, die bei Z[iegler] nicht aufgeführt sind,
145-62.
81 incipits for 28 Masses, 15 offertories, 10 motets, 8 antiphons. 100 incipits for all movements of 30 symphonies and
3 trio sonatas.

220 DEARLING, Robert J. (Dunstable, Bedfordshire). [Thematic catalogue]
▽   Index cards (manuscript) (see no. 282)
Incipits for 98 symphonies, string sonatas, concertini, etc.,
supplementing Ziegler's list by some 30 works.

CAMPIONI, CARLO ANTONIO, 1720-1793

221 FLOROS, Constantin. **Carlo Antonio Campioni als Instrumentalkomponist**
▽   (PhD diss.: Wien, 1955) 2v., 124, 11*l.* (typescript)
Thematischer Katalog der Instrumentalwerke, v. 2.
165 incipits for all movements of opus 1-8, all on 11 large
leaves.

CANNABICH, CHRISTIAN, 1731-1798

222 WOLF, Jean K. (New York U.) **The symphonies and orchestral trios**
*   **of Christian Cannabich**
Thematic index
Incipits of authentic and spurious works, with numbering
based of the probably original and chronological order of
numbers appearing on the parts at the Bayerische Staatsbibliothek, München.

CANNICIARI, (DON) POMPEO, 1670-1744

223 FEININGER, Father Lawrence. **Catalogus thematicus et bibliographicus**
Pompei Canniciari operum sacrarum omnium, *Repertorium liturgiae*
polychoralis II (Tridenti: Societas Universalis Sanctae Ceciliae,
1964) viii, 207p.
Incipits of all voices, organ (figured bass), and any instrumental parts of all of Canniciari's sacred works. Arranged
by genre, with title index.

Reviews: Edwin HANLEY, *MQ* LIII/2 (1967) 270-76; Wendelin
MULLER-BLATTAU, *Mf* XXI/1 (1968) 140-41.

CAPROLI [CAPRIOLI], CARLO, ca. 1615-1673

224 CALUORI, Eleanor (Manhattan School of Music, N.Y.). [Thematic
*   catalogue] To be published in the *Wellesley Edition Cantata Index*
Series.

CARISSIMI, GIACOMO, 1605-1674

225 ROSE, Gloria. **The cantatas of Carissimi** (PhD diss.: Yale U., 1960)
▽   241p.(typescript)
        Thematic index

225a Giacomo Carissimi [Thematic catalogue of cantatas] *The Wellesley*
     Edition Cantata Index Series, fasc. 5 (Wellesley: Wellesley College,
     1966)
                Divided into 2 parts: 5a-cantatas by Carissimi, 5b-cantatas
                attributed to Carissimi. Texted incipits arranged alphabet-
                ically by text. Each entry gives sources, concordances,
                modern editions, probable dates of composition, authors of
                texts where known, and a brief description of form.
                Reviews: Claudio SARTORI, *Notes* XXIII/4 (1967) 734-37.

CASALE MONFERRATO, Archivio Capitolare

226 CRAWFORD, David E. (U. of Michigan). **Sixteenth century repertory of**
▽   **eight manuscripts of sacred polyphony in the Archivio Capitolare at**
     Casale Monferrato. Index cards (manuscript)
                Multiple staff incipits, all sections, for about 260 works
                by : Archadelt, Barra, Berchem, Bruhier, le Brun, Cellavenia,
                Compère, Danglon, la Fage, Festa, Fevin, Gascogne, Genet
                (Carpentras), Giaches de Wert, Duke Guglielmo, Gonzaga,
                L'Heritier, Jachet of Mantua, Jannequin, Madis, Maffoni,
                Maistre Jhan, Mimot le Petit, Misonne, Morales, Moulu, Mouton,
                Penet, des Prez, Prioris, Richafort, la Rue, de Sermisy, de
                Silva, Victoria, and Willaert. "The call numbers for the
                eight manuscripts at Casale Monferrato are inadequately in-
                dicated in the archives....my designations are as follows:
                C̲, D̲(F̲) [also known as D], D̲(M̲) [also known as M], G̲, L̲,
                N̲, P̲(E̲) [also known as P], and s̲.s̲. [senza segnatura]."

CAVALLI, PIER FRANCESCO, 1602-1676

227 CLINKSCALE, Martha Novak. **Pier Francesco Cavalli's Xerse** (PhD diss.:
▽   U. of Minnesota, 1970) 2v. in 3: 893p. (typescript)
                "Appendices describe the Italian and French MSS of *Xerse.*
                and present an index of all thematic material in the con-
                certed pieces."

CAZEAUX, Isabelle

228 **Classification and cataloguing,** *ALA, Manual of Music Librarianship*
☐   (1966) 30-57.
                Discusses (p. 43) inclusion of thematic incipits (in alpha-
                betical, numerical or conventional music notation) on cata-
                logue cards.

CESTI, ANTONIO, 1623-1669

229 BURROWS, David Lamont. **The cantatas of Antonio Cesti** (PhD diss.:
     Brandeis U., 1961) 254p. U. Micro. 62-1214.(typescript)

[Thematic index of the cantatas], Appendix II.
> Includes a thematic index of Cesti's cantatas and miscella-
> neous sacred compositions including those of doubtful attri-
> bution.

229a --- Antonio Cesti. Thematic catalogue of fifty-five cantatas, *The
Wellesley Edition Cantata Index Series,* fasc. 1 (Wellesley: Wellesley
College, 1964)
> Includes doubtful attributions as well as cantatas. Textual
> and vocal incipits given. Some analytical diagrams of com-
> positions.
> *Reviews:* Claudio SARTORI, *Notes* XXIII (1967) 734-37.

CHAIKOWSKY, *see* ČAJKOVSKIJ

CHAILLEY, Jacques

230 Un procédé de codification alphabétique des timbres de chansons,
☐ *Fontes ArtesM* XI/3 (1964) 166-67.
> Alphabetical codification of melodies, employing the German
> notation letters A-H. Transposed to C major or A minor. Use
> of capital and lower-case letters to differentiate the octaves.
> A slash through the letter indicates a flat (except for B
> flat), underlining a letter indicates a sharp. Grouping of
> letters and spaces between groups indicates rhythm. Melodies
> are codified by first phrase only, and are arranged in alpha-
> betical order.

CHAILLEY, Jacques; ADLER, I.; FEDOROFF, Y.; WALLON, S.

231 Le catalogage des documents ethnomusicologiques sonores (disques et
☐ bandes) de l'Institut de Musicologie de Paris, *FontesArtisM* IX/2
(1962) 76-78.
> A system for classifying ethnomusicological stylistic data,
> with particular regard for records and tapes.

CHALLIER, Ernst (compiler)

232 Sonaten-Tabelle. Eine nach Tonarten alphabetisch geordnete Aufstellung sämmtlicher Clavier Sonaten von Clementi, Haydn, Mozart
(Berlin: Ernst Challier's Selbstverlag, 1882) 13p.
> Double staff incipits for all movements of the clavier sonatas
> of Clementi, Haydn, and Mozart.

232a --- 2nd edition (Berlin: Ernst Challier's Selbstverlag, 1884)
232b --- 3rd edition (Berlin, I887)
232c --- 4th edition (Geiben, I907)

CHARENTON, EDMOND, 1827-1901

232.1 DÉDÉ, père. Edmond Charenton, compositeur né à la Nouvelle Orléans
(E.V.) le 20 Nov. 1827 mort à Paris le 4 Janvier 1901 (New York:Vic-
tor Genez) folio, n.p. (US LC: ML 134/.D29/A2)
> [Thematic catalogue].

CHARPENTIER, MARC ANTOINE, 1634-1704

233   ÉCORCHEVILLE, Jules. Catalogue du fonds de musique ancienne de la
☆   Bibliothèque nationale, v. 4 (Paris: Terquem, 1912)
          [Thematic catalogue], v. 4, 2-74.
              Ca. 420 multiple staff incipits.

234   HITCHCOCK, H. Wiley (Brooklyn College of C.U.N.Y.) Catalogue raisonné
*   of the works of Marc-Antoine Charpentier
              Incipits of the more than 500 works, with descriptions of
              lengths, performance-resources required, major divisions of
              large works. Organized by genre, and by approximate chronol-
              ogy within each genre. Data on variant copies, editions,
              phonorecordings, etc.

CHERUBINI, LUIGI, 1760-1842

235   FUCHS, Aloys. In Göttweig Benedictine Monastery (Austria), there
▽   is a copy of Auguste BOTTÉE DE TOULMON'S Notices des manuscrits
      autographes de Luigi Cherubini (Paris, 1845) with Fuchs' MS addi-
      tions of incipits ("Durchschossenes Exemplar mit thematischen In-
      cipits von Aloys Fuchs").(manuscript)

      Reference: Friedrich Wilhelm RIEDEL, Die Bibliothek des Aloys Fuchs
      in Wilfried BRENNECKE and Hans HASSE, eds., Hans Albrecht in memori-
      am (Kassel: Bärenreiter, 1962) 207-224, see p. 212.

236   WHITE, Maurice Lynn. The motets of Luigi Cherubini (PhD diss.:
      U. of Michigan, 1968) 188p. Univ. Micro. 69-2406.(typescript)
          [Thematic index], Appendix I.
              "Collated according to the limitations of the term motet"
              defined as "settings of texts employed in the Roman Church,
              independently presented from the liturgy although often
              drawn from it." (*DA* XXIX/8 [Feb 1969] 2746-47A)

236.1 PARKER, C. Gerald (Kent State U., Ohio). A thematic catalogue of
*   the instrumental music of Luigi Cherubini

CHESTER, J. & W., Ltd. (publisher)

237   WOOD, Henry J., ed. Reference book of miniature scores with thematic
      list of the symphonies and chamber music works of the great masters
      (London: Chester, [1924])
              A thematic list of symphonies and chamber music, p. [37]-[66],
              of the following composers: J.S. Bach, Beethoven, Brahms,
              Dvořák, Händel, Haydn, Liszt, Mendelssohn, Mozart, Schubert,
              Schumann, and Tschaikowsky. These catalogues are virtually
              the same as the Eulenberg catalogue (see no. 362)

237a --- 2nd ed. (?).
237b --- 3rd ed. (1930).
237c --- 4th ed. (1933).
237d --- 5th ed. (1936).

CHOPIN, FRYDERYK FRANCISZEK, 1810-1849

238 Thematisches Verzeichniss der im Druck erschienenen Compositionen
von Friedrich Chopin (Leipzig: Breitkopf & Härtel, 1852) iv, 44p.
> Multiple staff incipits arranged by opus number (1-65),
> followed by 7 works without opus numbers and those with
> posthumous opus numbers (66-74). Includes names of pub-
> lishers and dedicatees, plus an index by title and number.

238a --- Neue umgearb. und vervollständigte Ausgabe 1879.
238b --- Unverändert 1888.

239 FRITSCH, E. W. Thematisches Verzeichniss der in Deutschland im
Druck erschienenen Instrumental-Compositionen von F. Chopin, mit
Beifügung der Textanfänge seiner Lieder. In alphabetischer Ordnung
und mit Angabe der Arrangements, Preise und Verlagsfirmen. (Leipzig:
E.W. Fritsch; Breitkopf & Härtel,[1870]) xvip. Also published in *Mus.
Wochenbl., Organ für Tonkünstler und Musikfreunde* I (1870) xvip.
> Double staff incipits, all movements; arr. by genre and title.

240 GANCHE, Edouard. The Oxford original edition of Frédéric Chopin
(London: Oxford U. Press, [1932]) 3v.
Thematic index written by Frédéric Chopin and Franchomme for
the complete works collected by Jane Stirling and corrected by
Chopin, v. I, 4p. facsimile before p. 1.
> Two staff incipits of all piano works arranged by opus
> (including opus posthumous) numbers. The three volume
> edition also contains printed plates of incipits preceding
> each section (préludes, études, etc.).

241 BROWN, Maurice J.E. Chopin, an index of his works in chronological
order (New York: St. Martin's Press; London: Macmillan Ltd., 1960)
xiii, 199p.
> Double staff incipits in chronological order. Appendices
> give data on publishers, first and subsequent editions, dedi-
> cations, poets of Chopin's songs, autographs, and bibliography.
> Systematic and general index.
>
> *Reviews:* MLetters XLII/1 (1961) 72; MEducatorsJ XCVII/5
> (1961); Igor KIPNIS, *American Record Guide* XXVIII (Jun 1962)
> 816-17; Hans F. REDLICH, MR XXIII/1 (1962) 67-68;Willi KAHL,
> Mf XVI/3 (1963) 299-300; MTimes LVI (Jan 1965) 28-30.

242 BATES, August. Chopinowskie hobby angielskiego kucharza [Chopin-
hobby of an English cook], *Ruch Muzyczny* III/4 (1962)
> Thematic catalogue of Chopin's works prepared in the form of
> graphic shapes by August Bates.

243 KOBYLAŃSKA, Krystyna. Thematisches Werkverzeichnis (Duisburg-München
* Henle).

244 Katalog tematyczny dzieł F. Chopina [F. Chopin, thematic catalogue
* of works], ed. by the *Chopin Society,* Josef M. Chominski, ed. (Kraków: Polish Music Publication, ca. 1972)

CICONIA, JOHANNES, ca. 1335-ca. 1411

245   WOLF, Johannes.   Thematisches Verzeichnis der Werke des Johannes
      Ciconia aus Lüttich, *Tijdschrift der Vereeniging voor Noord-Neder-*
      lands Muziekgeschiedenis VII/2 (Amsterdam: Muller, 1904) 8p. fol-
      lowing p. 307.
              Incipits, old notation and original clefs, for all voices
              of 32 vocal works. Includes text incipits and library
              sources.

246   CLERCX, Suzanne.   Johannes Ciconia, un musicien liégeois et son
      temps (vers. I335-I4II), *Académie Royale de Belgique. Classe des*
      Beaux-Arts. Mémoires, sér. 2, t. 10, fasc. 1a-1b (Bruxelles: Palais
      des Académies, 1960) xxiii,144p.; 198p.
              Inventaire, 51-63.
              Makes corrections and additions to Wolf (see no. 245).
              Incipits, in old notation, for the 42 works of Ciconia
              arranged by genre: madrigals 4, ballades italiennes 11,
              chansons françaises 2, canons 2, parties de messe 10,
              motets 13. Provides text incipit, number of voices,
              MS sources, annotation, and modern editions.

CINCINNATI, Hebrew Union College: Birnbaum Collection

247   BIRNBAUM, Edward. [Thematic catalogue] (US CIhc)(catalogue cards)
▽   Birnbaum's unfinished attempt at cataloguing European
             Synagogue music (1700-1910) deposited in the Hebrew Union
             College Library. Approximately 7,000 file cards with musical
             incipits arranged by first words of Hebrew text. Provides
             bibliographical references.

247a WERNER, Eric. The Birnbaum Collection of Jewish Music, *Hebrew Union*
□   *College Annual* 18 (1944) 420-24.

CLARKE, JEREMIAH, ca.1673-1707

248   TAYLOR, Thomas F. (U. of Michigan). Thematic catalogue of the works
*   of Jeremiah Clarke
              Ca. 250 incipits of all movements in works which are clearly
              subdivided. Will include indices of manuscript and printed
              sources. Approximate length— 70 typewritten pages.

CLEMENS NON PAPA, JACOB, ca.1500-ca.1556

249   SCHMIDT, Joseph. Die Messen des Clemens non Papa, *ZfMW* IX (Dec 1926)
      129-58.
             [Thematic catalogue]
             Transcribed incipits or themes of sections of masses with
             original text underlay, lists of masses printed and in MSS
             in European libraries, and information on motet or chanson
             phrases on which they were based.

CLEMENTI, MUZIO, 1752-1832

250   Clementi Werke (A Wst: MH 9176/c) [17p.] (manuscript). Microfilm
▽   copy in US NYcg.

Double staff incipits for 89 works, mainly sonatas, for piano or chamber ensemble with piano.

251   ALLORTO, Riccardo. Le sonate per pianoforte di Muzio Clementi;
       studio critico e catalogo tematico. Historiae Musicae Cultores.
       Biblioteca XII   (Firenze: Olschki, 1959) 147p.
          Catalogo tematico, 60-138.
                  Two staff incipits of first movements only, with tempi and
                  time signatures given for other movements, arranged by opus
                  number. Data on autographs, editions, dates, publishers,
                  dedications, and selected discography.

                  Reviews: Kathleen DALE *MLetters* XLI/1 (1960) 58-61; Jan
                  LaRUE *Notes* XVII/4 (1960) 572-73.

252   TIGHE, Sister Alice Eugene. Muzio Clementi and his sonatas surviving
       as solo piano works (PhD diss.: U. of Michigan, 1964) 260p. U. Micro
       64-12, 693. (typescript)
          [Thematic index]
                  "The final part of the dissertation presents a brief descrip-
                  tion of 14 significant sonatas and a thematic index of each
                  movement of these 14 works"

253   TYSON, Alan. Thematic catalogue of the works of Muzio Clementi
       (Tutzing: Hans Schneider, 1967) 136p.
                  "The aim... is to provide a brief guide to the identification
                  and numbering of Muzio Clementi's compositions, and to add
                  only the essential information about textually significant
                  editions of his published works." (From the preface.) Incipits
                  are arranged in order of the composer's opus numbers, with
                  notes on location of autograph sources.

                  Reviews: *Musikhandel* XIX/3 (Apr 1968) 142; Kathleen DALE,
                  MLetters XLIX/3 (July 1968) 231-33; Stanley SADIE, *MTimes*
                  CIX (July 1968) 634-35; Franz GRASBERGER, *ÖsterreichischeMz*
                  (Feb 1969) 110; François LESURE, *RMusicol* LIV/1 (1968) 121;
                  Leon B. PLANTINGA, *MQ* LIV/2 (1968) 257-63; Donald W. KRUMMEL,
                  Notes XXV/4 (1969) 725-26; H.C. Robbins LANDON, *Mf* XXII/3
                  (1969) 390.

COLEMAN, CHARLES, d. 1664

254   MEYER, Ernst Hermann. Die mehrstimmige Spielmusik des I7. Jahr-
 ☆   hunderts in Nord- und Mitteleuropa.   (Kassel: Bärenreiter, 1934)
       258p. (see no. 821)
          [Thematic catalogue of fantasias by Coleman], 149.
                  Incipits for 1 fantasia à 5 and 5 fantasias à 6.

COLLINS, Walter S.

255   A new tool for musicology, *MLetters* XLVI (1965) 122-25.
 ☐   Describes a beginning by the author of the use of a computer
                  in correlating thematic data for the music of Thomas WEELKES
                  (1575-1623).

COPERARIO, JOHN, ca. 1575-1626

256   MEYER, Ernst Hermann. Die mehrstimmige Spielmusik des I7. Jahr-
 ☆   hunderts in Nord- und Mitteleuropa. (Kassel: Bärenreiter, 1934)

258p. (see no. 821   )
[Thematic catalogue of fantasias by Coperario], 149-52.
> Incipits for 10 fantasias à 3, 9 fantasias à 4, 57 fanta-
> sias à 5, 5 fantasias à 6.

CORAL, Lenore

257 An historical survey of thematic catalogues with special reference
□▽ to the instrumental works of Antonio Vivaldi (MA thesis: U. of
Chicago Graduate Library School, 1965).(typescript)
> The first two chapters (27p.) discuss the history, function,
> and current developments in thematic cataloguing. Chapter 3,
> on Vivaldi was later expanded and published, see no. 1357.

CORELLI, ARCANGELO, 1653-1713

258 BACHMANN, Alberto. **Les grands violinistes du passé** (Paris: Fischbacher, 1913) 468p.(see no. 65)
> **Table thématique d'oeuvres de Corelli**, 20-77.
>> Incipits for all movements of 60 sonatas, 12 concertos, and
>> the Folies D'Espagne Variations; arranged by opus number.

259 PINCHERLE, Marc. **Corelli** (Paris: Alcan, 1933) 242p.
> **Oeuvres manuscrites ou gravées attribuées à Corelli**, 233-38.
>> Incipits of eight sonatas and one concerto grosso, with
>> descriptive text.

260 RINALDI, Mario. **Arcangelo Corelli** (Milano: Curci, 1953) 523p.
> **Indice tematico**, 473-501.
>> Incipits for each movement of concerti for string orchestra,
>> arranged by opus number. Tempi and scoring given. Second
>> index of works attributed to Corelli, with locations of
>> autographs, primary references, and dates.

261 MARX, Hans Joachim (Musikwissenschaftliches Seminar der Rhei-
*   nischen Friedrich-Wilhelms-Universität, Bonn) **Thematisch-bibliographisches Werkverzeichnis Arcangelo Corellis.**
> To include in addition to the known works a number of
> newly discovered compositions plus doubtful ones critical-
> ly evaluated. This thematic index will be published as
> a supplement to the Gesamt-Ausgabe after 1972. (Köln:
> Arno Volk Verlag).

CORRI, John (publisher)

262 **A select collection of the most admired songs, duetts, etc. from
operas of the highest esteem, etc.** (Edinburgh: Corri, ca. 1779)
> One of the earliest examples of thematic lists in Great
> Britain. John Corri's father, Domenico, was the actual
> publisher.

> *Reference:* HUMPHRIES, Charles; SMITH, William C. **Music pub-
> lishing in the British Isles** (Oxford: Blackwell, 1970) 32.

CORTONA, Biblioteca Comunale: Chansonnier

262.1 NETTLES, W.Earle. **The Cortona Chansonnier** (MM Thesis, Indiana U.,
1966) 183p.
> **Thematic catalogue**

COUPERIN, FRANÇOIS, 1668-1733

263 CAUCHIE, Maurice. **Thematic index of the works of François Couperin**
(Monaco: Lyrebird Press, Louise B.M. Dyer, [1949]) 133p.
> Published editions are arranged chronologically. Two staff
> incipits are given for all movements with text underlays
> for vocal compositions, dates of composition, complete
> scoring, full titles and dates of original editions, and
> information on modern editions and recordings. Posthumous
> works separately listed in approximate order of composition.
>
> *Reviews:* Robert DONINGTON, *MLetters* XXXII/- (Apr 1951) 157-58.

264 HOFMAN, Shlomo. **L'Oeuvre de clavecin de François Couperin le grand,
étude stylistique** (Paris: A.& J. Picard, 1961) 231p.
> Catalogue thématique des pièces de clavecin de François Couperin
> le grand, 209-29.
> Multiple staff incipits for all movements of 27 keyboard
> suites.

CRAMER, JOHANN BAPTIST, 1771-1858

265 **Oeuvres/ de J.B. Cramer** (A Wst: MH 9175/c) [17p.] (manuscript).
▽ Microfilm copy in US NYcg.
> Double staff incipits for 71 works, mainly sonatas, either
> for solo piano or for chamber ensemble with piano.

266 GRAUE, Jerald C. (Eastman School of Music, Rochester, N.Y.). **Thema-**
＊ **tic catalogue**
> Incipits for ca. 500 works.

266.1 TYSON, Alan (London). **The works of John Baptist Cramer**
＊   **Thematic catalogue**
> Index card file for study purposes. No plans for publi-
> cation at present.

CROES, HENRI-JACQUES de, 1705-1786

267 CLERCX, Susanne. **Henri-Jacques de Croes, compositeur et maitre de musîque
du prince Charles de Lorraine,** *Académie Royale de Belgique.* *Classe des
Beaux-Arts.* *Mémoires,* 2. ser., t. 7, fasc. 3 A-B (Bruxelles: Palais des
Académies, [1940]) 2v.
> **Catalogue thématique,** v. 2, xxv-xlviii.
> Incipits for: A.) all movements of published instrumental
> works with opus numbers, **and** B.) MS instrumental and vocal
> works plus a list of lost works with incipits for 58 Mass
> movements, the first 38 of which are taken from a thematic
> catalogue found in the Chapelle Royale.

CROFT, WILLIAM, bap. 1678-1727

268 FERGUSON, Howard; HOGWOOD, Christopher. **Thematic index of the**
▽ **keyboard works** (manuscript)
> "Prepared in connection with their forthcoming edition.
> It is not proposed to publish the index, but MS copies
> are in the possession of Dr. Ferguson and Mr. Hogwood."

CSEBFALVY, K.

269   Systematization of tunes by computers, *StudMusicol* VII (1965) 253-57.
☐

CUCUËL, Georges, (compiler)

271   Études sur un orchestre au XVIIIme siècle   (Paris: Fischbacher, 1913)
      62, 54p.
              Contains the following thematic indexes: Gossec, Symphonies,
              [39]- 49; Proksch, Symphonies, [59]-60; Schenker, Symphonies,
              [53].

272   La Pouplinière et la musique de chambre au XVIIIe siècle (Paris:
      Fischbacher, 1913) 456p.
              Contains thematic lists of works by Alberti (p. 369),
              Gossec (p. 362-64), and Schenker (p. 364-65).

CUDWORTH, Charles L. (compiler)

273   English eighteenth-century symphonies, paper and thematic index
      (London: RMA, 1953) 31-51, ix, XXXVp. The original paper "The
      English symphonists of the Eighteenth century" was published in
      the *Proceedings of the Royal Musical Association* LXXVIII (1952)
      31-51. The "Thematic Index...", an appendix to v. LXXVIII of the
      Proceedings, appeared as a separate pamphlet published with the re-
      printed original article, under the overall title above.
          Thematic index of English eighteenth-century overtures and sym-
          phonies, X, XXXV.
                  List A, "Finding list of source material", includes descrip-
                  tions of MS and printed sources, and a list of works arranged
                  by composer giving classification and library locations.
                  List B, "Thematic index", XI-XXXV, provides 158 incipits of
                  symphonies and overtures arranged alphabetically by composer.
                  Composers include: Arne, Michael; Arne, Thomas Augustine;
                  Arnold, Samuel: Bates, William; Boyce, William; Clarke,
                  Richard; Collett, John: Crotch, William; Dibdin, Charles;
                  Fisher, John Abraham; Greene, Maurice; Haigh, Thomas; Hook,
                  James; Howard, Samuel; Jackson, William; Kelly, Thomas A.
                  Erskine, 6th Earl of; Linley, Thomas, the younger; Marsh,
                  John; Mazzinghi, Joseph; Moze, Henry; Norris, Thomas; Reeve,
                  William; Rush, George; Shaw, Thomas; Shield, William; Sme-
                  thergell, William; Wesley, Samuel; Valentine, John; Yates,
                  William.

CZERNY, CARL, 1791-1857

274   Verzeichniss (thematisches) der Werke von C. Czerny (Wien: Diabelli
      et C. [1827?]).

DAÇA, ESTEBAN [DAZA, ESTEBAN], 16th c.

275 PURCELL, Ronald C. (San Fernando Valley State College). Esteban
*   Daça, 'El Parnasso": analysis, transcriptions and commentary
     (MA diss.: in progress)
             Will include a thematic index to the fantasías.

DALAYRAC, NICHOLAS, 1753-1809

276 DEARLING, Robert J.(Dunstable, Bedfordshire). [Thematic catalogue]
▽   Index cards (manuscript) (see no. 282)
             Incipits for 24 operatic overtures (from early editions in
             the British Museum).

DAMILANO, Don Piero (compiler)

277 Fonti musicali della lauda polifonica intorno alla metà del Sec. XV
▽   Collectanea Historiae Musicae III (Firenze: L. Olschki, 1963) 59-
     90.
             Incipits for all voices, in old notation, of 92 works.
             Composers include Busnois and Dufay.

DANKOWSKI, WOJCIECH, b. ca. 1760-1765-d. 18..?

278 IDASZAK, Danuta. Źródła rękopismienne do mszy żałobnych Wojciecha
     Dankowskiego [Manuscript sources of the funeral masses of Wojciech
     Dankowski], Muzyka II/4 (1967) 16-28.
         [Thematic index], 20-28.
             Multiple staff incipits for all sections of three Requiem
             Masses.

DARMSTADT, Hessische Landes- und Hochschulbibliothek

279 [Thematic catalogue of a part of the extant 18th century Manuscripts]
▽   (D DS) ca. 300 cards (manuscript).
             Incipits for concertos, cantatas, symphonies, etc. Com-
             posers represented are as follows: Abel, Agrell, Aleotti,
             Alessandri, Allegri, Anfossi, Angiolini, Apell, Ariosti,
             J. Chr. Bach, J.S. Bach, C.Ph.E. Bach, Backofen, F. Benda,
             G. Benda, Benoit, Beringer, Bertali, Bieler, Bodinus, Boller,
             Borrosini, Brioschi, A. Caldara, Cammerloher, Cannabich,
             Chiesa, Conti, Dalai, W.G. Enderle, J.S. Endler, Friedrich
             C. Erbach, Ernst Ludwig Landgraf von Hessen, Fasch. Ferran-
             dini, Friedrich II, J. Fuss, Fux, Giraneck, J.G. Graun, C.H.
             Graun, Chr. Graupner, Händel, Hasse, Heinichen, Holzbauer,

---

Janitsch, Jomelli, Kammel, Kobrich, Koelbel, Lebrun, Ludwig
VIII, B. Marcello, Marchi, Mehrscheidt, Pachelbel, Petri,
Pfeiffer, Piccinni, Polazzi, Porsile, F.X. Richter, Sartorius,
Schetky, Seckendorff, Sollnitz, Stamitz, Süssmayr, Telemann,
Vogler, Winter.

DART, Thurston (compiler)

280   The cibell. *RBelgeMusicol* VI/1 (Jan-Mar 1952) 24-30.
        21 incipits of cibells (English dance form, 1690-1710) for
        various instruments and from various sources.

DASER, LUDWIG, 1525-1589

281   KELLOGG, King. **Die Messen von Ludwig Daser** (PhD diss.: Ludwig-
        Maximilians-Universität, 1935; München, 1938) 67p.
        Verzeichnis der Messen von Ludwig Daser, 3-13.
          Cantus firmus incipits of 22 Masses, with library location
          of MSS and information on cantus firmus origins.

DEARLING, Robert J. (Dunstable, Bedfordshire)

282   [Thematic catalogue of 18th century symphonies] Index cards (manu-
▽   script)
          The index contains over 15,000 cards taken from the standard
          thematic catalogues of single composers, library collections,
          and from 18th century editions of symphonies and overtures in
          the British Museum. The index will be expanded to include
          modern editions (since 1800) and the British Museum's MS col-
          lection. Incipits are in "thematic alphabetical order to
          throw up cross-attributions." Includes incipits for over
          1,000 composers.

DEBUSSY, CLAUDE-ACHILLE, 1862-1918

283   VALLAS, Léon. **Claude Debussy et son temps** (Paris: Alcan, 1932)
        394p.
          Liste des oeuvres de Claude Debussy, lxxxiiip. inserted between
        380-81.
            Multiple staff incipits arranged in generic groups of pub-
            lished and posthumous works. Complete bibliographical
            apparatus given.

283a ––– **Claude Debussy: his life and works,** trans. by Marie and Grace
        O'BRIEN (London: Oxford U. Press, 1933).

284   JAROCIŃSKI, Stefan; LESURE, François. **Catalogue thématique des**
*   **oeuvres et bibliographie** (Kraków: Polish Music Publications, ca.
        1974)
          Contains all his musical and literary works in chronological
          order giving fully harmonized incipits. Bibliography lists
          the works printed in France and abroad between 1883-1970.

DECOURCELLE, Paul (compiler)

285   Catalogue thématique extrait du répertoire des concerts de Monte-Carlo
      (Nice, 1900) 131, ivp.
              Contains the first page (in reduced size) of ca. 125 salon
              pieces in piano or piano-and-violin score, with index by
              title.

DEERING, RICHARD, ca. 1580-1630

288   MEYER, Ernst Hermann. Die mehrstimmige Spielmusik des I7. Jahr-
✠   hunderts in Nord- und Mitteleuropa   (Kassel: Bärenreiter, 1934)
      258p. (see no. 821)
              [Thematic catalogue], 152.
                  Incipits for 8 fantasias à 5, and 3 fantasias à 6.

DELALANDE, MICHEL-RICHARD, 1657-1726

289   DUFOURCQ, Norbert, ed. Notes et références pour servir à une his-
      toire de Michel-Richard Delalande, surintendant, maître et composi-
      teur de la musique de la chambre du roi, sous-maître et compositeur
      de la chapelle royale (1657-1726). Établies d'après les papiers
      d'André Tessier, précédées de documents inédits, et suivies du
      catalogue thématique de l'oeuvre. Published by the students of the
      Séminaire d'Histoire du Conservatoire National de Musique de Paris
      (Paris: A. & J. Picard, 1957) 356p.
              [Thematic catalogue], 28I-356.
                  Incipits arranged by "Musique Réligieuse" and "Musique Pro-
                  fane", in addition to important themes throughout a composi-
                  tion. Full bibliographical apparatus is provided.

DELDEVEZ, Edouard M. E. (compiler)

290   Curiosités musicales (Paris: Didot, 1873) 272p.
              Thematic indexes of the symphonies of Beethoven (p. 174-
              77), Haydn (p. 29-53), and Mozart (p. 73-81).

DEN KERCKHOVEN, ABRAHAM VAN, 1627-1702

291   LYNCH, William D. A stylistic study of organ works attributed to
▽   Abraham van den Kerckhoven (D.M.A., Performance: U. of Rochester,
      1969) 2v. (typescript)
              Thematic catalogue,
                  364 double staff incipits for all movements of organ works
                  in the manuscript 3326 II, Brussels Royal Library. This
                  MS is the only secondary source for the music of Abraham van
                  den Kerckhoven, along with music of many of his contemporaries.
                  Provides full bibliographical apparatus.

DENSS, ADRIAN, 16th-17th c.

292   LOBAUGH, H. Bruce. Three German lute books (PhD diss., Musicology:
      U. of Rochester, 1968) 2v. U. Micro. 68-13,806 [see also no. 746]
              Florilegium (Cologne, 1594), v. II, Appendix, 1-31.

A thematic index or transcription in full of the fantasias
and dance pieces only (i.e. Nos. 86-148). A total of 65
pieces appear, either in full (16) or in the thematic index
(49). Incipits for "interior movements" are included in the
thematic index (a total of 64 incipits, including 4 vocal).
Works include 8 fantasias, 7 galliards, 6 passamezzo suites,
18 allemandes, etc..

DESSAUER, JOSEPH, 1798-1876

293   SERTL, Otto. **Joseph Dessauer (1798-1876) ein Liedmeister des Wiener**
▽   **Biedermayer** (PhD diss.: Innsbruck, 1951) iv, 174, 130l. (typescript)
     Thematisches Verzeichnis der Werke des Komponisten Joseph Des-
     sauer (1798-1876), 130l.
          Incipits for operas, choruses, lieder, instrumental works,
          and pianoforte works 2 and 4 hands. Information is given
          for sources, periodical and book literature, and total num-
          ber of measures in each movement. Multiple staff incipits
          for all movements arranged by genre.

DEUTSCH, Otto Erich

294   **Music bibliography and catalogues,** *The Library* XXIII/4 (Mar 1943)
□   151-70.
          Describes the state of music bibliography and cataloguing
          techniques.

295   Preface to **Schubert, Thematic catalogue of all his works in chrono-**
□   **logical order** (London: Dent; New York: Norton, 1951) ix-xx. (see no.
     1181).
          Includes a brief history of some thematic catalogues and an
          examination of earlier Schubert thematic catalogues.

296   **Theme and variations, with bibliographical notes on Pleyel's Haydn**
□   **Editions,** *MR* XII/1 (Feb 1951) 68-71.
          Discussed the issue of "theme" vs. "incipit." Briefly traces
          the history of thematic catalogues to Pleyel's Haydn catalogue
          (1802).

297   **Thematische Kataloge,** *FontesArtisM* V/2 (1958) 73-79.
□   Discussion of the word "theme"; survey, analysis and criticism
          of the modern thematic catalogues; bibliography of 5 items.

DEUTSCH, Walter

298   **Erfahrungen bei der Anlage eines Melodien-Registers,** *Jb. des Österr.*
□   *Volksliedwerkes* VII (1958) 52f.; X (1961) 55f.

298.1 **Das Melodien-Register der Österreichischen Volksliedarchive,** *Öster-*
□   *reichischeMz* XVIII (Feb 1963) 89-94.
          Ten examples in explanation of the procedure used in the
          classification, formulation and organization of the incipits
          of the material in the Österreichischen Volksliederarchiven.

DIABELLI, ANTONIO, 1781-1858

299   KANTNER, Leopold. **Leben und Kirchenkompositionen von Antón Diabelli,**
▽   mit thematischem Katalog seiner Werke (PhD diss.: Wien, 1957) v,

270, 55*l.* (typescript)
Thematischer Katalog seiner Werke, Part II, 11-55.
Themes for each separate movement of Masses, Graduals, and
Offertories, with information pertaining to chronology,
sources of MSS, and printed editions.

DIBDIN, CHARLES, 1745-1814

300   DEARLING, Robert J. (Dunstable, Bedfordshire).   [Thematic catalogue]
▽   Index cards (manuscript). (see no. 282)
Incipits for 24 operatic overtures (from early editions in
the British Museum), supplementing Cudworth by 21 works.
(see no. 273).

DICKSON, Casper Gregory (compiler)

301   A melodic index to hymn tunes based on the simple sol-fa music
▽   notation (US Wc: ML 128/.H8D5). Approximately 8225 cards, 12½ x 7½
cm. in 8 boxes, author's MS cards. Boxes I-IV, titles; V-VI, composers; VII-VIII, melodies.(manuscript)
Melodies, Boxes VII-VIII.
The first index card in Box VII provides the following
description of cataloguing method:" Dickson simple sol-fa
music notation. Main octave (plain) drmfslt, lower octave
(caps) DRMFSLT, upper octave (dieresis) drmfslt, TIME 1 beat.
(period) ½ beat, (comma) ¼ beat (semicolon) after note or
under rest mark. Accidentals= sharp (#), flat(*b*)."
Slight changes in the system are found on the catalogue cards
themselves.

DIEHL, Katherine S. (compiler)

302   Hymns and tunes; an index (New York: Scarecrow Press, 1966) 1,185p.
Index V, melodies, a systematic index
Catalogues 78 hymnals. Cross indexed by first lines, authors,
composers, tune names and variants.
Reviews: Armin HAEUSSLER, *The Hymn* XVIII/1 (1967) 27-28;
R. M. LONGYEAR, *JResearchMEducation* XV/3 (1967) 240.

DIJON, Bibliothèque municipale: MS 295

303   MORELOT, Louis Stéphen. De la musique au XVe siècle.   Notice sur
un manuscrit de la Bibliothèque de Dijon (Paris: Didron, 1856)
lxiv, 338p.
Table thématique des pieces contenues dans le manuscrit 295 de
la Bibliothèque de Dijon, xv-xxiv.
Incipits, mainly of chansons, of Dijon MS 295 [517], including
works by Barbireau, Busnois, Caron, Compère, Dunstable,
Ghizeghem, Morton, Okeghem, and Tinctoris.

DITTERS VON DITTERSDORF, CARL, 1739-1799

304   KREBS, Carl. Dittersdorfiana (Berlin: Paetel, 1900) 182p.
✡   Verzeichniss der Werke Ditters v Dittersdorfs, [55]-144.
Incipits for most of the 234 instrumental works, and some

of the keyboard and sacred vocal works. Extensive information on compositions and contemporary evaluations.

305 GRUPP, Margaret (New York U.). **Dittersdorf's first movement form**
*   **as a measure of his symphonic development** (PhD diss. in progress).
      Includes a thematic catalogue of authentic as well as
      doubtful and spurious symphonies, organized according to
      key and to interval relationships of the first-movement
      incipits. Provides incipits for all movements of each
      work and cites relevant bibliographical information (e.g.
      18th c. MS and print sources, 18th c. catalogue references,
      dates, instrumentation, modern editions).

306 PULKERT, Oldřich (Praha). **[Thematic catalogue]** (manuscript)
▽   Incipits for all sections of 550 compositions found under
      the name of Dittersdorf. Genres include: operas, oratorios,
      operettas, Singspiel (35), symphonies (205), instrumental
      concertos (47), wind partitas and chamber works (96),
      sacred arias and sacred vocal works (130), Masses and Re-
      quiems 21, Litanies (6), smaller works (8). Uses Hoboken
      catalogue as a model. (see no. 555)

DÖBBELIN, Rosmarie (Basel)

306.1 [Thematic catalog of South German, essentially secular, manuscripts
*   of the early 16th century (particularly of the Codex Pernner= Regens-
       burg, Proske-Bibl., C 120)]

DOLES, JOHANN FRIEDRICH, sen, 1715-1797

307 BANNING, Helmut. **Johann Friedrich Doles; Leben und Werke.** *Schriften-
      reihe des Staatlichen Instituts für Deutsche Musikforschung* V (Leip-
      zig: Kistner & Siegel, 1939) 267p.
         Thematischer Katalog der Werke von J. F. Doles sen, Appendix A,
      183-265.
            300 texted incipits for all voices, arranged alphabetically
            within the following genre: solo songs and hymns; motets and
            choral works; chorales, psalms, and cantatas with instrumental
          · accompaniment or figured bass; passions and oratorios; Masses;
            keyboard and organ works. Instrumentation, and location of
            parts and autographs given.

DOLES, JOHANN FRIEDRICH, jun, 1746-1796

308 BANNING, Helmut. **Johann Friedrich Doles; Leben und Werke.** *Schriften-
      reihe des Staatlichen Instituts für Deutsche Musikforschung* V
      (Leipzig: Kistner & Siegel, 1939) 267p.
         Thematischer Katalog der Werke von J. F. Doles jun, Appendix B,
      266-67.
            Incipits for a song, choral air, mass, and six sonatas for
            clavicembalo, with location of parts and autographs.

DONAUESCHINGEN, Fürstlich Fürstenbergische Hofbibliothek

309 Copia Verzeichniss Nr. 12 der fürstlichen Musikalien, Pulte Instru-

▽   mente etc. im Monat Junij 1804, with added entries until 1816 (D DO)
     12p. (manuscript). Microfilm copy in D KNhi.
          Incipits for works by the following composers: Brandl, Canna-
          bich, Clementi, Cibulka, Cartellieri, Cherubini, Dittersdorf,
          Fiala, Foyler, Gyrowetz, Guenin, Gossec, Graff, Gluck, Gros-
          heim, Joseph Hadyn, Hoffmeister, Hennet, Hoffstetter, Krommer,
          Kozeluch, Kospoth, Loeffler, Mozart, Maschek, Neubaur, Pleyel,
          Pichl, Rosetti, Sterkel, Scheider, Vanhall, Vogel, Wranitzky,
          Winter, Fränzle, Zimmermann. Addenda: Beethoven, Cherubini,
          Mehul, Fischer, Gryowetz, Mozart, Müller, Beer, Marcello,
          Winter, Pleyel.

310   SCHOENBAUM, Camillo (Denmark).   Bohemica in der Fürstlich
▽   Fürstenbergschen Hofbibliothek in Donaueschingen. Thematischer
      Katalog. 14p. (manuscript) Compiled 1959. Copy in US NYcg.
          Incipits for works, mostly instrumental, by the following
          composers: Francèsco Alessio 9, Fr. X. Brixi 2, Gius.
          Fiala 32, A. Filtz 6, Adalbert Gyrowetz 22, Leopold
          Kozeluch 6, F. Krommer 20, Vinz. Maschek 1, Mitscha 1,
          Franz Neubauer 12, Wenzel Pichl 16, Pokorni 1, J.W. Raf-
          fael 1, Ant. Rosetti 29, Joh. Stamitz 2, J.B. Vanhal 14,
          Paul Wranitzky 9. Proyides call numbers and instrumenta-
          tion. Added is a list of prints without incipits.

DOUGLASS, Robert S. (compiler)

311   The keyboard ricercare in the baroque era (PhD diss.: North Texas
      State U., 1963) 2v. U. Micro. 64-3800. *DA* 24 (1964) #10, p. 4222.
          Thematic index, v. 2.
          Incipits for all keyboard compositions discussed in v. 1
          utilizing imitative counterpoint, including: ricercare,
          canzona, cappricio, fantasia, fugue, tiento, and choral
          fugue.

DRAGONETTI, DOMENICO, 1763-1846

312   SLATFORD, Rodney (London) Thematic catalogue of works
*   Over 600 incipits catalogued as of 1970.

DRESDEN, Sächsiche Landesbibliothek

313   Catalogo della Musica di Chiesa composta da diversi Autori seconde
▽   l'Alfabetto. Armaro III^{za}. Principiando della Littera S fine al Z
      con l'aggiunta degl'Autori senza nome (D Dl) 91l. Compiled 18th c.
      Copy in US NYcg. (manuscript)
          The MS was compiled in the 18th century and revised in 1812
          by Franz Schubert of the Dresden Schuberts. Pages 15-65 in-
          clude incipits for the sacred music of Johann Zelencka, and
          pages 66-89 contain incipits of about 100 unidentified works.
          Other composers represented are: Schwanenberg, Tarantino,
          Tassis, Turini, Agostion Uhlick, P. Urio, Pietro Valle,
          Vignati, Villicus, Vitalli, Vogler, Zabradeczkij, and P.
          Zieler.

DRESDEN; Sächsische Landesbibliothek: MS HB III 787a [catalogue]

313.1 [Operas, 18th c.] (D Dl: Bibl. Arch. HB III 787a) [v], 188p. (manu-
▽   script). Microfilm copy in US NYcg.
          Music and text incipits for the various numbers of each
          opera. Composers: Piccini (18), Boroni (5), Galuppi (6),
          Zametti (1), Radicchi (1), Allessandra (1), Monti (1), As-
          taritta (1), Fischietti (2), Scolari (2), Guglielmi (Giugli-
          elmi) (8), Anfossi (8), Schuster (5), Felicini (1), Armen-
          dola (1), Valentini (1), Rutini (1), Sacchini (3), Gassmann
          (Gasmann) (2), Naumann (5), Salieri (5), Gazzaniga (4),
          Borghi (1), Crisspi (1), Scarlatti (1), Ottani (3), Traetta
          (Trajetta) (2), Marcello (2), Sarti (2), Paisiello (6), Seÿ-
          delmann (3), Cimarosa (4).

VI. Dresden, [*Operas, 18th c.*], no. 313.2

DRESDEN, Sächsische Landesbibliothek: MS HB III 787b [catalogue]

313.2 [Operas, 18th c.] (D Dl: Bibl. Arch. III HB 787b)[xvi], 654p. (manu-
▽   script). Microfilm copy in US NYcg.[reproduction,preceding page]
        Music and text incipits for the various numbers of each opera.
        Includes the following composers: Fioravanti (2), Gnecco (1),
        Nicolini (2), Spontini (2), Federici (1), Pavesi (2), Generali
        (1), Morlacchi (3), Zametti (2), Astarita (1), Conti (1),
        Chinas.(1), Fabrizi (2), Storace (2), Martin (2), Mozart (3),
        Haydn (11), Tritta (1), Portogallo (4), Weigl (6), Süssmayr
        (Siessmayr) (1), Winter (4), Paer (18), Mayr (8), Anfossi (8),
        Schuster (11), Felici (2), Naumann (7), Radicchi (1), Mar-
        cello (1), Borghi (1), Crispini (1), Cimarosa (20), Amendola
        (1), di Capua (1), Valentini (1), d'Astratto (1), Pitticchio
        (1), Bianchi (1), Piccini (18), Boroni (5), Galuppi (6), Fis-
        chietti (2), Scolari (2), Guglielmi (Giuglielmi) (14), Rutini
        (1), Sacchini (3), Gassmann (Gasmann) (2), Scarlatti (1), Ot-
        tani (3), Traetta (Trajetta) (2), Sarti (5), Paisiello (13),
        Seÿdelmann (6), Salieri (13), Gazzaniga (5), Gert (?) (1),
        Maroti (1), d'O...(1), plus several illegible names.

DRESDEN, Sächsische Landesbibliothek: MS HB III 787e [catalogue]

313.3 Catalogo/ De libri Numerato Musicali/ D.S.A.R. M.A. D. de B./(D Dl:
▽   Bibl. Arch. HB III 787e) viii, 99p. Compiled 18th c. (manuscript)
     Microfilm copy in US NYcg.
        Incipits for arias, opera numbers, etc., by the following
        composers: Jommelli (43), Manna (21), Hasse (238), Terra-
        dellas (12), Cocchi (12), Capua (9), Lampugnani (8), Gluck
        (2), Giaÿ (2), Battoni (14), Bernasconi (7), Wagenseil (2),
        Micheli (1), Pescetti (12), Graun (6), Vicentino (1), Car-
        cani (2), Perez (5), Chiarino (1), Maggiore (4), Bertoni (4),
        Abbos (9), Albertis (2), Galuppi (6), Pergolesi (1), Bulli
        (7), Santarelli (1), Porta (1), Porpora (1), Leo (1), Razzoni
        (1), Pescetti (2), Verracini (12), Scolari (2), Conti (2),
        Anonymous (23). Also includes listings, without incipits,
        for Ferrandini, Vinci, Abaco, and Hasse.

VII. **Dresden**, *Catalogo de libri numerato*, 18-?, no. 313.3

314   Kirchen Musikalien des Herrn Kapell Meister Marlachi [sic] et Rastrelli
▽   [und] Mozart (D D1) 19p. Compiled after 1827. Copy in US NYcg
      (manuscript)
              Pages 2-13 contain incipits of sacred works by F.G.B. Mor-
              lacchi (1784-1841). In the middle of p. 13 is the note
              "Ritter Joseph Rastrellis junior [sic] sämtlicher Kirchen-
              compositionen segue." Across the top of pages 18-19 are in-
              cipits for all movements of a Mass in C by Mozart.

315   Ubersicht sämtlicher Herren Compositeur und deren Werke (D D1) 58p.
▽   Compiled c. 1855. Copy in US NYcg (manuscript)
              Incipits for sacred works primarily by K.G. Reissiger (1798-
              1859). Includes at least one work for each of the following
              composers: Barbieri, Antonio Benelli, Dotzauer, Joseph Eybler,
              Händel (acquired 1820), Hauptmann, J. Haydn, Hummel, Krebs,
              Joseph Michl, Miltitz, Julius Otto, Rothe, J.P. Schmidt, Fried-
              rich Schneider, K.M.v. Weber, Zingarelli.

DRESSLER, GALLUS, b. ca. 1530

316   LUTHER, Wilhelm Martin. Gallus Dressler. Ein Beitrag zur Geschichte
      des Protestantischen Schulkantorats im 16. Jahrhundert, *Göttinger
      Musikwissenschaftliche Arbeiten* 1 (Kassel: Bärenreiter, 1941) 165p.
      Thematisches Verzeichnis, 154-65.
              Incipits use simple letter code. C^1 for the first octave
              above middle C, C^2 for the second octave, etc.

DRUSCHETZKY, GEORG, 1745-1819

317   WEINMANN, Alexander (Wien). Georg Druschetzky
*   Catalogue of collected works (mostly thematic).

DUFAY, GUILLAUME, ca. 1400-1474.

319   HABERL, Franz X. Wilhelm du Fay *VfMW* I (1885) 475-483.
      [Thematic catalogue of works in the] Bibliothek des Liceo musi-
      cale und der Universität in Bologna
              Incipits in letter notation, arranged by title, of 87 of
              Dufay's works in MSS in the two libraries. Gives number of
              the voices employed.

319 a --- Also issued separately as v. I of HABERL's Bausteine zur Musik-
      geschichte (Leipzig: Breitkopf & Härtel, 1885)

DUFF and HODGESON, (publishers)

320   Musical index of favorite songs (London: 1849) 1p. (GB Lbm: B.M.
      H. 377. (12.))

321   Musical index of Samuel Lover's popular songs (London: 1849)1p.
      (GB Lbm: B.M.H. 377. (11.))

              Reference: HUMPHRIES, Charles; SMITH, William C. Music pub-
              lishing in the British Isles (Oxford: Blackwell, 1970) 364.

DUNNING, Albert (Syracuse U.)

322 Thematic catalogue of I8th century canons
*   Only for research use. No publication intentions.

DUNSTABLE, JOHN, c.1370-1453

323 STAINER, Cecie. Dunstable and the various settings of "O Rosa
     Bella", *SIMG* II (1900-1901) 8-15.
         Thematic list of Dunstable's compositions.
             Incipits in original notation of each vocal part of 46
             compositions, with library location.

324 BUKOFZER, Manfred. Über Leben und Werke von Dunstable, *ActaMusicol*
     VIII (1936) 111-19.
         Ergänzungen zu Dunstables Werkverzeichnis.
             Supplement to Stainer's catalogue identifies and locates 54
             compositions, giving incipits of some in original notation.

DUNWALT, Gottfried (compiler?)

325 Catalogo Musicalium Godefridi Dunwalt 1770 (GB Lbm: Hirsch. IV.1081)
▽   [iii;137p.] (manuscript)
             Incipits (mostly single staff, a few double staff),for 558
             instrumental works (symphonies, concertos, quartets, etc.)
             arranged by genre for each of the following composers: Abel,
             Bach, Boccherini, Bode, Bohme, Campioni, Cannabich, Davaux,
             Ditters, Eichner, Filtz, Frentzel, Galliotti, Giardini, Gos-
             seck, Heyden [Haydn], Hoffman, Holtzbaur, Kammel, Kennis,
             Kreutzer, Lolli, Nicolai, Pesch, Pfeiffer, Pugnani, Reinartz,
             Ricci, Richter, Riegel, Schiatti, Schmitt, Schwindel, Stametz,
             Toesqui [Toeschi], Vanhal, Vanmalder [van Maldere], Wreda,
             and Zach. Compiled in Köln 1770; formerly in the possession
             of Gottfried Dunwalt.

DUQUESNOY, CHARLES-FRANÇOIS-HONORÉ-LANCTIN, 1759-1822

326 CORBET, August. Onbekende Werken van Charles Duquesnoy, *RBelgeMusi-*
     col II/2 (1948) 44-51.
         Aavangsmaten van de te Antwerpen weergevonden Werken [Opening
         measures of works found in Antwerp].
             Incipits, 5 to 8 measures long, of 23 compositions in
             chronological order in so far as they can be dated.

DÜRRENMATT, Hans-Rudolf; GOULD, Murray; LaRUE, Jan

327 Die Notierung thematischer Incipits auf "Mark-Sense-cards", *Fontes-*
☐   *ArtisM* XVII/1-2 (Jan-Aug 1970) 15-23.
             Discusses the notation of thematic incipits on mark-sense-
             cards.

DUŠEK, FRANTIŠEK XAVER, 1731-1799

328 SÝKORA, Václav Jan. František Xaver Dušek. Život a dílo. (Praha:
     Státní nakladatelsk krásné literatury, hudby a umění,1958) 290p.

Uplný tematický soupis skladeb F.X. Duška, 195-283.
    Incipits for all movements of sacred and secular works,
    arranged by genre with text underlay for vocal works.
    Full bibliographical apparatus given.

DUŠEK, JAN LADISLAV [DUSSEK, JOHANN LADISLAUS], 1760-1812

329   Oeuvres de J.L. Dussek (A Wst: MH 9174) 87p. (manuscript). Micro-
▽   film in US NYcg.
            Staves and titles, along with publisher and price, were set
            down, but only 3 incipits were entered.

330   CRAW, Howard Allen. A biography and thematic catalog of the works
       of Jan Ladislav Dussek (PhD diss., Musicology: U. of Southern Calif.,
       1964) 498p. U. Micro. 64-9611.(typescript)
          Thematic catalogue, 204-394.
            Incipits of works listed in chronological order by opus num-
            ber. Includes information on dates of composition or publi-
            cation, scoring, v. no. in Breitkopf & Härtel collected works
            edition, MS locations, editions, first performances, and pub-
            lished reviews.

DVOŘÁK, ANTONÍN, 1841-1904

331   ŠOUREK, Otakar. Dvořák's Werke, Skladby Dvořákovny; ein vollständiges
       Verzeichnis in chronologischer, thematischer und systematischer Anord-
       nung (Berlin: Simrock, [1917]) Pt. II, 104p., In De and Cs.
            Multiple staff incipits for all movements or acts of over
            100 works, arranged by opus number, followed by those without
            opus numbers and unpublished works. Includes dates of com-
            position, publisher, instrumentation, piano editions, and
            adaptations.

331a   --- (Kassel: Alpor-Edition, 1960).

332   BURGHAUSER, Jarmil. Antonín Dvořák, thematický katalog, biblio-
*   grafie, přehled života a díla [Thematic catalogue, bibliography,
       survey of life and work] (Prague: Státní nakladatelství krásné
       literatury, hudby a umění, 1960; Kassel: Alpor Edition, 1960) 735p.
       In Cs, De, and En.
            Complete and exhaustive catalogue, chronologically arrnaged,
            with separate catalogues of compositional studies, unfinished
            works and sketches, catalogue of parts written in Dvorak's
            own hand. Included also are lists of works according to opus
            number, Dovorak's own list of works, location of manuscripts
            and a separate index. There is also a discography.

            Reviews: E. M. von ASOW, *NeueZM* CXXII/-(Jul-Aug 1961), *Ös-
            terreichischeMZ* XVI/- (Mar 1961) 131-32; John CLAPHAM, *MLet-
            ters* XLIII/4 (1962) 352-55; Andrew PORTER, *MTimes* CIII (Dec
            1962) 848; *HudR* XVI/18 (1963) 760-61.

DVOŘÁK, Vladimír (compiler)

333   Hudobná pozostalost' Miloša Ruppeldta v Univerzitnej knižnici v
       Bratislave [Miloš Ruppeldt's bequest to the University Library
       in Bratislava] (Bratislava: U. Library, 1967) 191p. (*RILM* 67502)
            Incipits and descriptions of 198 autographs, with all cur-
            rent bibliographical information.

EBERL, ANTON, 1765-1807

334 EWENS, Franz Josef. **Anton Eberls Leben und Werke.** Ein Beitrag zur Musikgeschichte in Wien um 1800 (Dresden: Limpert, 1927) 124p.
    Thematisches Verzeichnis der Werke Eberls, 113-22.
        59 incipits of complete works: sonatas, concertos and symphonies.

335 WHITE, A. Duane. **The piano works of Anton Eberl** (1765-1807)
▽ (PhD diss.: U. of Wisconsin, 1970) (typescript)
    Thematic catalogue of Eberl's works, Appendix I, 115p.
        "This catalogue provides for almost every work incipits for each movement, information given by previous scholars, all that is known about autographs, manuscript copies and printed editions, and the names of libraries where these are preserved." In addition to the piano works, incipits are given for 4 piano concertos, 5 symphonies, 23 chamber works, 12 Lieder, 5 larger vocal works, and 8 stage works.

EBERLIN, JOHANN ERNST, 1702-1762

336 HERBORT, Heinz Josef. **Die Messen des Johann Ernst Eberlin** (PhD diss.:
▽ Münster; Münster: Kramer, 1961) 275p., 3ℓ.(typescript)
    Der Thematische Katalog und der Quellenbericht, 25-157.
        Double staff incipits for all movements of 58 Masses.

EBRACH, Germany. Katholisches Pfarramt: Zisterzienserkloster Collection

336.1 LAUGG, Rudolf. **Studien zur Instrumentalmusik im Zisterzienserkloster**
▽ **Ebrach in der 2. Hälfte des 18. Jahrhunderts** (PhD diss.: Erlangen, 1953) 169ℓ. (typescript)
    Themen- und Stimmblätter-Verzeichnis der in Ebrach vorhandenen Instrumental-Werke, 141-58.
        119 incipits for all movements of symphonies, concertos, and chamber works in print and manuscript, formerly in the Zisterzienserkloster, now deposited in Katholisches Pfarramt Ebrach. Composers: G. Agrell, L. Boccherini, Pl.v.Camerloher, J.M. Dreyer, W.G. Enderle, A. Filtz, E.A. Forstmeyer, I. Pleyel, W. Schaller, Schmitt, F. Schwindl, K. Stamitz, F.X. Sterkel, J.J. Umstatt, J.B. Wanhall, and anonymous works.

ECCARD, JOHANN, 1553-1611

337 PRAETORIUS, Ernst. **Ein unbekanntes Erstlingswerk Johann Eccard's,**

SIMG VII (1905-1906) 114-18.
   Überschriften und Anfänge, 116-18.
      Tenor voice incipits in white mensural notation from a part-
      book of Eccard's *Zwentzig newe Christliche Gesänge*, printed
      in 1574.

ECHELARD, Donald Joseph, (compiler)

338   A thematic dictionary and planning guide of selected solo literature
▽   for trumpet (PhD diss.: U. of Montana, 1969) ii, 377p. (typescript)
      Incipits for all movements of 702 "available original trumpet
      solos, arrangements of original solos and arrangements of
      trumpet solo sections taken from larger orchestral composi-
      tions...With each set of thematic excerpts the composer,
      arranger or editor, title, accompanying medium, publisher,
      range, meter signatures employed, scale patterns employed,
      rhythmic problems, length in measures, number of measures
      rest given the soloist, ornamental problems, and miscellaneous
      problems are listed. The planning guide is a series of indices
      wherein the solos are grouped, by number, into various levels
      of metric, rhythmic, ornamental, and miscellaneous problems..."

EDELMANN, JOHANN FRIEDRICH, 1749-1794

339   BENTON, Rita. The instrumental music of Jean-Frédéric Edelmann,
    FontesArtisM XI/2 (1964) 79-88.
      Thematic catalogue.
      Incipits from 15 collections of chamber music in which the
      keyboard plays the dominant role. Provides list of early
      editions, and primary and secondary sources.

340   KIDD, Ronald R. The sonata for keyboard with violin accompaniment
▽   in England (1750-1790) (PhD diss.: Yale U., 1967) (typescript)
     Works of J.F. Edelmann, 94-100.
      Incipits for instrumental works which complement those
      found in *DTB* XVI done by Riemann. "I have attempted to
      collate Riemann's material with that included in Reeser's
      MGG article, plus further additions of my own. I include
      incipits only for those not included by Riemann. Also,
      this includes only published material and does not include
      any thematic material for the dramatic work of 1781 (Op.11)"

EDINBURGH, Advocates Library : Scone Antiphonary

341   STEVENS, Denis. [Thematic catalogue]   (GB, Edinburgh Advocates
▽   Library: MS. 5/1/15) (manuscript)

EDSON, Jean Slater (compiler)

342   Organ preludes: an index to compositions on hymn tunes, chorales,
    plainsong melodies, Gregorian tunes and carols (Metuchen, N. J.:
    Scarecrow Press, 1970) 2v.
       Incipits for 3000 "master" tunes, covering 50,000 composi-
       tions. "Section I lists the composers (alphabetically),

their nationalities and dates, titles and publishers of the
compositions, and the tunes on which the compositions are
based. Section 2 lists the Tunes (alphabetically), gives
a source of the tune, an incipit, Zahn number where available, variant names for the tunes, and then lists the composers (alphabetically) under the tune name or variant on
which they wrote a composition."

EGENOLFF, Christian, 1502-1555

343   BRIDGMAN, Nanie. **Christian Egenolff, imprimeur de musique,** *Annales
      Musicologiques* III (1955) 77-177.
        In this monograph of the German printer there is an inventory
        in facsimile p. 100-177 of incipits of chansons in the Réserve
        Vm^7 504 collection of the Bibliothèque Nationale, Paris, with
        concordances and observations.

EGGERT, JOACHIM NIKOLAS, 1779-1813

344   TYBONI, Börje. **Något om J. H. Eggerts kammarmusik [On J. H. Eggert's**
▽   **chamber music]** (MA diss.: Uppsala U., 1951) 58p. (typescript)
        Includes a thematic catalogue of the chamber works.

EHRESHOVEN, Schloss

345   **[Musiksammlung der ehem. Bibliothek des oberbergischen Schlosses**
▽   **Ehreshoven]**   Compiled ca. 1790?. (In possession of Paul Mies, Köln)
      34p. (manuscript). Microfilm copy in US NYcg.
        A fragmentary catalogue with no title page and two different
        paginations. Incipits for: numbers 17-50 of Gluck's *Alceste*
        all the numbers of J.C. Bach's *Temistocle*, Schweizer's *Al-
        ceste*, Fischietti's *Il Dottore*; two cantatas by Graun
        and Jomelli; 70 incipits for arias by Jomelli arranged by
        key; arias by Anfossi, Bach, Bertolda, Brusa,Bertoni,Galuppi,
        Gluck, Giardini, Guglielmi, Hasse, Holzbauer, Lattilla,
        Maésivo, and Manzuoli; incipits of 10 sacred pieces by Jo-
        melli; arias by deMajo, Piccini, Paesiello, Pergolesi, Pam-
        pani, Porpora, Sacchini, Traetta, Valentini,Vansuiten, Cas-
        tel, Mancolini, Cte di Sickingen, Borghi, Salieri, and Ron-
        caglia; incipits for 34 sinfonias "à 2 orchestre" by Bach,
        Cannabich, Di Sicking[sic], Holzbauer, Majo, Mislévecek,
        Paesiello, Piccini, and Traetta; incipits for chamber works
        by Cannabich, Holzbauer, Hayden, Hubert, Mislivveck, and
        Rigel; quintets by Cannabich (2) and Holzbauer (2); sextets
        by Holzbauer (2); incipits for 24 balletti by Aspelmeyer,
        Cannabich, Sickingen, Deller, Holtzbaur, Jomelli, Rodolfo,
        Rigel, and Toeschi.

EICHNER, ERNST, 1740-1777

346   REISSINGER, Marianne. **Die Sinfonien Ernst Eichners (I740-I777),**
      Neue Musikgeschichtliche Forschungen v. 3 (Wiesbaden: Breitkopf &
      Härtel, 1970) 268p.
        Thematisches Verzeichnis der Sinfonien Ernst Eichners, 232-50.

Incipits of all movements for 31 symphonies arranged in chronological order with number of measures for each movement.

EICHNER, ERNST, 1740-1777

347 KAISER, Fritz (Mainz). **Thematischer Katalog der Werke von Ernst**
*   **Eichner.**
            Almost finished, but no arrangements for publication as yet.

EICHSTÄTT, Germany. Benediktinerinnenabtei St. Walburg

348 WALLNER, Bertha Antonia. **[Catalogue]** (On loan by the *DTB* to D Mbs)
∇   Compiled ca. 1910-1930. (manuscript)
            One of many partially thematic inventories prepared by the
            compiler under Adolf Sandberger's direction for the *Denk-*
            mäler der Tonkunst in Bayern.

EICHSTÄTT, Germany. Bibliothek Schlecht

349 WALLNER, Bertha Antonia. **[Catalogue]**   (On loan by the *DTB* to D
∇   Mbs) Compiled ca. 1910-1930. (manuscript)
            One of many partially thematic inventories prepared by the
            compiler under the direction of Adolf Sandberger for the
            Denkmäler der Tonkunst in Bayern.

EISENSTADT, Esterházy-Schlossarchiv

350 PRINSTER, Anton. **CATALOGUE/ raisonné des/ Vespers, des Litanies, des**
∇   **Te Deum des/ Hymnes des Miserere/ qui se trouvent/ dans les archives**
     des musique[s] d'église/ de son...LE PRINCE REGNANT/ NIKOLAS ESTER-
     HAZY (A E: 406) 110*l*. Compiled 1811. (manuscript)
            Served as the working catalogue of the reigning prince. Com-
            piled and written by Prinster (1777-1862), horn player in Es-
            terházy. Incipits for works by the following composers: Gäns-
            bacher, J.N. Fuchs, Vogler, Tuma, Werner, Albrechtsberger,
            Reutter, Naumann, Boog, Freytag, Seuche, M. Haydn, J. Haydn,
            Spangler, Friebert, Zimmermann, Graun, Cimarosa, Paumann,
            Jaumann, Reinhardt, Schacht, List, Novotni, Preindl, Pichl,
            Hasse, Heidenreich, Henneberg, Hummel, Hoffmann, Habegger,
            Hendl, Gyrowetz, Benno, Csaky, Graf, Wanhal, Polzelli, Cheru-
            bini, Strasser, Saller, Schuster, Suderell, Sonnleitner, Dre-
            xel,Ziani, Schmidt, Gassmann, Aumann, Reinhardt, Rieder,
            Paunzan, Krottendorfer, Keinz, Liberati, Pater Joseph, Gsur,
            Fischer, Grasel, Czech, Arbesser, Donberger, Ziegler, Wast-
            riel, Richter, Oecl, Carl.

EITNER, Robert; ERK, Ludwig; KADE, Otto (compilers)

351 Einleitung, Biographien, Melodien und Gedichte zu Johann Ott's
     Liedersammlung von I544, Eitner*PGfM* IV (Berlin: Liepmannssohn,
     1876) [89]-238.
            Contains the melodies, arranged alphabetically by text,

of works by Arnold, von Bruck, Breitengraser, Dietrich, Eckel, Hellinck, Isaac, Mahu, Müller, Paminger, Reyter, Senfl, Stoltzer, Wannemacher.

ELIAS, JOSEPH DE, 1680-1750?

352   LEVASSEUR de REBOLLO, Yvonne (U. of Pittsburgh).   The keyboard works
*   of Joseph De Elias (PhD diss. in progress)
        [Thematic catalogue]
        A preliminary listing of the works being catalogued can be
        found in the author's MS monograph *A study of some organ
        works of Sr. Don Joseph Elias* (U. of Pittsburgh, 1966: M.
        812).

ELLINWOOD, Leonard

353   Tune indexing, *The Hymn* I/4 (1950) 13-18.
☐   Discusses hymn-tune indexing and proposes method for future
        indexing. New edition proposed along the lines of McALL's
        Melodic index to the works of J.S. Bach. Mentions some in-
        dices of hymn-tunes published 1902-1966. (See also SANDERS
        no. 1138).

ELSCHEK, Oskár; STOCKMANN, Doris (editors)

354   Methoden der Klassifikation von Volksliedweisen. Symposia II (Bratis-
☐   lava:Slovenska Akademia vied, 1969) 155p. (*RILM* 69/3353^{bs})
        Papers read at the 1st session of the Study Group for Folk
        Music Systematization at the congress of the International Folk
        Music Council (Bratislava, 1965). The authors are as follows:
        Jaroslav MARKL, Zu einigen Fragen des folkloristischen Musik-
        Katalogs; Wolfgang SUPPAN, Das Deutsche Volksliedarchiv und
        die Katalogisierung von Volksweisen; Walter WIORA, Zur Methode
        der vergleichenden Melodienforschung; BIELAWSKI, Ludwig and
        STESZEWSKI, Jan, Zur Klassifikation der polnischen Volkslie-
        der; Ladislav GALKO and František POLOCZEK, Systematik der
        formbildenden Elements der slowakischen Volkslieder; HOŠOV-
        SKIJ, Volodymyr,Die Aufbauprinzipien des Elementarkatalogs
        der rhythmischen Versstrukturen; VETTERL, Karel and GELNAR,
        Jaromir, Die Melodienordnung auf der Basis der metrorhythmi-
        schen Formgestaltung; ELSCHEKOVÁ, Alica, Technologie der
        Datenverarbeitung bei der Klassifizierung von Volksliedern;
        JÁRDÁNYI, Pál, Die neue Ordnung der ungarischen Volkslieder;
        DEUTSCH, Walter, Die Gesetze der Tonalität und das Melodien-
        Register; KVĚTOVÁ, Radana, Die neue Ordnung der tschechi-
        schen Volkslieder vom Standpunkt der Melodie-Inzipiten; RA-
        JECZKY, Benjamin, Die Melodieordnung der "Monumenta monodica
        Medii Aevi I. "

ELSCHEKOVÁ, Alica (compiler)

355   General considerations on the classification of folk tunes, *StudMusi-
☐   col* VII (1965) 259-62.

356   Methods of classification of folk tunes, *Journal of the Internation-
☐   al Folk Music Council* XVIII (1966) 56-76.

ENCINA, JUAN DEL, 1468-1529

357 ZIMMERMAN, Franklin B. (U. of Pennsylvania) Thematic and first-
line indexes of the complete works of Juan del Encina (1970)
Incipits for each main section of a work. The first-line
index is a complete literary concordance, containing quite
a number of Encina lines which appear in various "ensaladas"
of later time. Prepared in form of computer print-out

ERDMANN, Hans; BECCE, G.; BRAV, L. (compilers)

358 Allgemeines Handbuch der Film-Musik (Berlin-Lichterfelde: Schlesinger,
1927) 2v.
Thematisches Skalenregister, v. 2, ii, 226p.
Indexes 3050 themes according to type of expression. Various
sources and composers.

ERKEL, FERENC, 1810-1893

359 MAJOR, Ervin. Ferenc Erkel műveinek jegyzéke. Bibliográfiai
kisérlet [A list of Ferenc Erkel's musical works. Bibliography
experiment] (Budapest: Légrady ny., 1947) 19p.

ERLEBACH, PHILLIP HEINRICH, 1657-1714

360 LEHN, Edgar vom. The sacred cantatas of Phillip Heinrich Erlebach
(PhD diss.: U. of North Carolina, 1958) 211p. LC No.: Mic 58-5973.
Thematic index, Appendix, 117-211.
Incipits for all sections and movements of MS sources of
Erlebach's 23 extant sacred cantatas.

ERNST, HENRI-GUILLAUME, 1814-1865

361 BACHMANN, Alberto. Les grands violinistes du passé (Paris: Fisch-
bacher, 1913) 468p. (see no. 65)
[Table thématique], 83-84.
List of works includes 3 incipits.

EULENBURG, Ernst (publisher)

362 Eulenburg's kleine Partitur-Ausgabe. Thematisches Verzeichnis
(Leipzig & Wien: Eulenburg, [1901?]) 48p.
Incipits for works in the following sections: I. Chorwerke,
II. Orchester, III. Konzerte, IV. Kammermusik, V. Klavier-
werke. Virtually the same as Chester (no.237)

362 a --- 2. Ausgabe,[192-?].

362 b --- 3. Ausgabe,(ca. 1936) 54p.

362 c --- 4. Ausgabe, Payne's kleine Partitur-Ausgabe No. 999. Thematisches Verzeichnis (Leipzig: Eulenburg, n.d.) 54p.
This edition omits section V.

d'EVE, ALPHONSE, 1666-1727

363   SCHROEDER, A. E. **Mededeling over Alphonse d'Eve** [Information on
       Alphonse d'Eve], *RBM* I (1946-1947) 127-32.
            Thematische Catalogus.
                 Incipits (instrumental except for 3 vocal) of d'Eve's masses,
                 motets, and other sacred compositions. Eight are from MSS
                 in the Royal Music Conservatory in Brussels and the Flemish
                 Royal Music Conservatory in Antwerp, and 17 are from printed
                 works in the Royal College of Music in London.

EXPERT, Henry (compiler)

364   **Les Maîtres musiciens de la renaissance française** [Section 2]
       (Paris: Leduc, 1900)
            Bibliographie thématique, [v.] 3, 8.
                 Indexes the two Attaingnant collections of 1529 (*Trente
                 et une chansons musicales*) and 1528-1530? (*Trente et
                 sept chansons musicales*), including themes by Consilium,
                 Courtois, Deslouges, Dulot, Gascongne, Godebrye, Hesdin,
                 Janequin, Lombart, Sermisy, Sohier, and Vermont.

EYBLER, JOSEPH, 1765-1846

365   OELSINGER, Franz. **Die Kirchenmusikwerke Joseph Eybler's** (PhD diss.:
▽   Wien, 1932) 111*l*. (typescript)
            Thematischer Katalog, 18-40a.
                 115 double staff incipits for 31 Masses, 1 Requiem, 32 Gradu-
                 als, 23 Offertories, 7 Te Deums, hymns, Antiphons, etc.

FALCK, Marguerite (Paris)

366   **Catalogue thématique de la musique du Théâtre de la Foire**
✱

FAMOUS MUSIC CORPORATION (publisher)

367   **Famous favorites: a select song list** (New York: Famous Music Corp.,
       1967) 40p.
                 240 incipits of songs from the Paramount film music cata-
                 logues.

FASCH, JOHANN FRIEDRICH, 1688-1758

368   ENGELKE, Bernhard. **Johann Friedrich Fasch: sein Leben und seine**

Key: ✱ in preparation; ▽ manuscript; ☐ literature; ✵ Library of Congress

Tätigkeit als Vokalkomponist (Halle: Kaemmerer, 1908) 88, 12p.
   Thematischer Katalog der erhaltenen Vokalwerke, 12p.
      The 12-page supplement gives incipits of 85 items.

369   SCHNEIDER, Clemens August. Johann Friedrich Fasch als Sonatenkompo-
      nist. Ein Beitrag zur Geschichte der Sonatenform (PhD diss.: Münster,
      1936; Cologne: Elsner, 1936) 73, 28p. Notenteil.
         Thematischer Katalog der Instrumental-Sonaten von J.F. Fasch,
         28p. in pocket.
            Incipits of each instrumental part and continuo for each
            movement of the sonatas. Locations of autographs and
            sources of publication given.

370   KÜNTZEL, Gottfried. Die Instrumentalkonzerte von Johann Friedrich
▽   Fasch (PhD diss: Frankfurt am Main; Tutzing: Schneider, 1965)
      261p.
         Thematisches Verzeichnis der Konzerte von Johann Friedrich
         Fasch, 200-09.
            67 double staff incipits for all movements of concertos
            for one or more instruments with orchestral accompaniment.

FEDERHOFER, Hellmut

371   Alte Musikalien-Inventare der Klöster St. Paul (Kärnten) und Göss
☐   (Steiermark),*Kirchenmusikalisches Jahrbuch* XXXV (1951) 97-112.

FELLNER, Rudolph (compiler)

372   Opera themes and plots (New York: Simon & Schuster, 1958) 354p.
         "The complete stories together with over 1,000 musical
         motives and themes from arias, duets, etc., of 32 of the
         world's greatest operas."

FERRABOSCO, ALFONSO, ca. 1575-1628

373   MEYER, Ernst Hermann. Die mehrstimmige Spielmusik des I7. Jahr-
✠   hunderts in Nord- und Mitteleuropa. (Kassel: Bärenreiter, 1934)
      258p. (see no. 821)
         [Thematic catalogue], 152-53.
            Incipits for 25 fantasias à 5, 10 fantasias à 6, 3 In-
            nomines à 5, 2 Innomines à 6.

FESCA, FRIEDRICH ERNST, 1789-1826

374   Deuxième sinfonie, oeuvre IO (Leipzig: Peters, [181-])
         Thematisches Verzeichnis der Compositionen von Friedrich Fes-
         ca, mit Tempobezeichnung nach Mälzl's Metronome, separate leaf.

375   Collection des quatuors et quintetti pour le violon (Paris: Chez
      Henry, [ca. 1825]) 301p. (vln 1 part)
         Thèmes de tous les quatuors et quintetti, vln 1 part, p. [1].
            1st violin incipits of 19 quartets (including 3 for flute &
            violin) and 5 quintets.

375a Collection de quintetti et quatuors (Paris: S. Richault, [18-?])

&atalogue thématique des ouvrages contenus dans la Collection de quintetti et quatuors, 1st vln part, p. 1.
> Incipits for quintets, op. 8, 9, 15, 20, 22, and quartets, op. 1-4, 7, 12, 14, 36-38.

375 b --- [Complete list of the works of F.E.Fesca](Leipzig:Hofmeister,184-)

FESCH, WILLEM DE, 1687-1757?

376   BREMT, Fr. van den. **Willem de Fesch (1687-1757?) Nederlands Componist en Virtuoos; Leven en Werk.** Université Catholique, Louvain. *Recueil de Travaux d'Histoire et de Philologie* sér. 3, fasc. 35 (Louvain: Bibliothèque de l'Université, 1949) v, 348p.
> **Thematische Catalogus,** [189]-222.
>> Handwritten incipits of songs with Italian text, songs with English text (both introductory and vocal incipits), all movements of instrumental works (in order of opus nos.), a Mass, and a cantata.

376a   --- *Académie Royale de Belgique. Classe des Beaux-Arts. Mémoires,* t. 5, fasc. 4 (Louvain: Bibliothèque de l'Université, 1949) 348p.

FICKERT, Emil (compiler)

377   **Thematisch-analytische Bibliographie der praktischen und theoreti-**
▽   **schen Kammermusik-Werke 1750-190., Trio bis Dezett** (A Wn) (manuscript)
> *Reference:* A. Weinmann, **Die Wiener Verlagswerke von Franz Anton Hoffmeister,** *Beiträge zur Geschichte des Alt-Wiener Musikverlages* Reihe 2, Folge 8 (Wien, 1964) 15.

FIELD, Christopher D.S. (compiler)

378   **The English consort suite of the seventeenth century** (PhD diss.:
▽   U. of Oxford, 1970) 3v. (typescript)
> **Thematic catalogue, v. II, 1-33.**
>> "It covers the fantazia-suites and related works of composers working in England during the 17th century, arranged in alphabetical order by composers. (Full details of the sources of these suites and their groupings are given in volume I). Incipits are to all movements, and total 762. Named composers are: John Birchensha (12), John Coprario (73), Christopher Gibbons (34), John Hingeston (160), John Jenkins (184), William Lawes (48), Matthew Locke (209), and Christopher Simpson (12)."

FIELD, JOHN, 1782-1837

379   HOPKINSON, Cecil. **A bibliographical thematic catalogue of the works of John Field, 1782-1837** (London: the author, printed in Bath by Harding Curtis, 1961) xxiii, 175p.
> Incipits (p. 3-147) of 67 works arranged chronologically. Publication information included with bibliographical notes.
> *Reviews:* Oliver NEIGHBOUR, *MLetters* XLIII/2 (1962) 139-41; Nicholas TEMPERLEY, *MTimes* CIII/- (1962) 239; Willi KAHL, *Mf* XVI/3 (1963) 300-01; Donald KRUMMEL, *Notes* XX/2 (1963) 221-22.

FILTZ, ANTON, 1730-1760

380   ZEHELEIN, Klaus (Frankfurt). Thematischer Katalog der Kammer-
*   musik

FINAZZI, FILIPPO, 1710?-1776

381   MÜLLER [von Asow], Erich H. Angelo und Pietro Mingotti; ein Beitrag
zur Geschichte der Oper im XVIII. Jahrhundert (Dresden: Bertling,
1917) xvii, 141, cccxp.
     Thematisches Verzeichnis der Werke von Filippo Finazzi, Anhang V,
part 2, ccvii-ccxvii.
       52 incipits, one or more staves, for all movements of cantatas,
odes, arias, symphonies, and one sonata.

FINCK, HEINRICH, 1445-1527

382   EITNER, Robert, ed. Heinrich Finck (I5. Jahrhundert). Eine Sammlung
ausgewählter Kompositionen zu vier und fünf Stimmen, bestehend in
deutschen geistlichen und weltlichen Liedern, Hymnen, und Motetten.
Nebst sechs Tonsätzen von seinem Grossneffen Hermann Finck (1527 bis
1558), *Publikation älterer praktischer und theoretischer Musikwerke*
VIII (Berlin: Trautwein, 1879) 110p.
     Thematisches Verzeichniss der in vorliegender Sammlung nicht
aufgenommenen Kompositionen Heinrich Finck's, 107-10.
       35 incipits of hymns, motets, sacred and secular songs. Num-
ber of voices and MS sources are provided.

382a --- Reprint (New York: Broude Bros., 1966).

FINK, Heinrich (Duisburg)

383   Musik für das Bassetthorn. Thematischer Katalog.
*

FIOCCO family

384   STELLFELD, Christine. Les Fiocco, une famille musiciens belges aux
XVIIe siècles (Bruxelles: Palais des Académies, 1941) *Académie
Royale de Belgique. Classe des Beaux-Arts. Mémoires*, 2. sér., t.7,
fasc. 4. 172p.
     Catalogue thématique, 145-60.
       One and two staff incipits arranged first by genre then by
source for the following: Pierre-Antoine Fiocco (p. 147-52)
33 motets, 4 masses, 3 airs italiens, 3 chamber; Jean-Joseph
Fiocco (p. 153-56) 16 motets, 1 mass; Joseph-Hector Fiocco
(p. 157-60) 22 motets, 3 masses, and 3 lamentations.

FIRENZE, Biblioteca Nazionale Centrale: Magl. XIX, 176

385   Becherini, Bianca. Autori minori nel codice fiorentino Magl. XIX,
176, *RBelgeMusicol* IV (1950) 19-31.
     [Thematic index], 27-29.
       Incipits in syllable notation of the contents of the MS in
the Magliabechiano Collection. Composers include: Ćaron,

Dufay, P. de Domarto, Xaulin [Raulin], Morton, Busnois,
Mueron [G. Mureau], Bellingan [Bedingham], Lepitet basque,
Fede, Okeghem, Tinctoris, Arnolfo, Arnolfo Schard, Michelin
[Michelet], and Simonet.

FIRENZE, Biblioteca Nazionale Centrale: Magl.XIX, 107 bis

386 Florence Biblioteca Nazionale Centrale MSS (Magl XIX, 107 bis). An
▽   inventory and thematic catalogue (Harvard U., Cambridge, Mass.: Advanced Seminar in Musicology, under the direction of Gustave Reese,
1967) 78*l*. (typescript)
> Texted incipits of the 51 surviving chansons in this early
> 16th century chansonnier, with concordances in 79 contempor-
> ary MSS and incunabulae, and an extensive bibliography of
> secondary sources and modern editions. Included are transcrip-
> tions of 3 chansons with critical commentary. Composers re-
> presented in the inventory are: Brumel, Busnois, Cardinal de
> Medici, Compère, Dufay, Escobar, Encina, Hayne van Ghizeghem,
> Isaac, Japart, Josquin, Ninot le Petit, Obrecht, Vaqueras,
> Wrede.

FIRENZE, Biblioteca Riccardiana: Codex 2356

387 PLAMENAC, Dragan. The "second" chansonnier of the Biblioteca Riccardiana (Codex 2356), *Annales Musicologiques* II (1954) 105-87.
   Table of incipits-concordances-remarks, 128-71.
> Music and text incipits for 72 chansons in original notation.
> Composers represented include: Caron, Dufay, Hayne, Morton,
> Ockeghem. Single and multiple staff incipits.

FIRENZE, Biblioteca Riccardiana : Ms. 2794

387.1 [Thematic catalogue of Ms. 2794, Florence, Biblioteca Riccardiana]
▽   (New York: C.U.N.Y. Graduate School, 1972; prepared by students under the direction of Prof. Edward R. LERNER).(manuscript)
> Incipits and concordances of this 15th century parchment
> manuscript containing 73 secular and sacred compositions
> for 3 and 4 voices with French and Latin texts. Composers
> include: Dufay, Ockeghem, Fresneau, Hayne, Agricola, Com-
> père, Josquin and Pietrequin, with additional compositions
> that can be attributed to Busnois and Jannes Japart.

FISCHIETTI, DOMENICO, 1729-ca. 1810

388 Thematisches Verzeichnis der Werke von Fischietti (D Berlin: MS. fol.
▽   69) (manuscript)
> This catalogue was not located in the Berlin Staatsbibliothek,
> and its whereabouts is unknown. Eitner states: "Thematisches
> Verzeichnis der Werke von Fischietti in Berlin (Sign.: Ms.
> fol. 69)".

Reference: EITNER, Robert, Quellenlexikon III, 471.

ENGLÄNDER, Richard. Domenico Fischietti als Buffokomponist in
Dresden, *ZfMW* II (1920) 321-34.
389   [Thematisches Verzeichnis der] komischen Opern,
> Themes dispersed through article for sinfonie or overtures
> to four comic operas.

FISCHOF, JOSEF, 1804-1857

390 KLEINLERCHER, Herbert. **Josef Fischof. Leben und Werk** (PhD diss.:
▽   Wien, 1948) 2v., 167*l*.; *l*. 168-206 (typescript)
     Werkverzeichnis und thematischer Katalog, v.2, 189-204.
> 21 multiple staff incipits of available Lieder, waltzes for
> clavier.

FÖRSTER, EMANUEL ALOIS, 1748-1823

391 LUDWIG, Franz. **Förster: Thematisches Verzeichnis hergestellt von**
▽   **Franz Ludwig** (D Bds: Mus. ms. theor. Kat. 554) [134p] Microfilm
     copy in US NYcg. (manuscript)
> Catalogue of works mainly in the possession of Countess
> Contin de Castel-Seprio (née Eleonore Förster): music for
> keyboard, instrumental ensemble, and voice. Incipits for
> all movements in score, often with annotation.

392 WEIGL, Karl. **Zwei Quartette, drei Quintette,** *DTÖ* Jg 35/1 Bd. 67
     (Wien: Artaria, 1928) 99p.
     Thematisches Verzeichnis der Kammermusikwerke, 3p. following
     p. vi.
> Incipits arranged in chronological order by genre, with
> references to sources and location of original MSS.

392a --- Reprint (Graz: Akademische Druck- und Verlagsanstalt, 1960)

FORSTER, JOSEF, 1833-1907

393 NEMETH, Carl. **Josef Forster. Leben und Werk** (PhD diss.: Wien, 1949)
▽   257, Anhang 99*l*. (typescript)
     Thematischer Katalog, Anhang, 71-83.
> 23 multiple staff incipits of 2 Masses, 1 Offertory, opera
> fragments, Lieder, etc.

FRANCISCI, MILOSLAV, 1854-1926

394 MUNTÁG, Emanuel. **Miloslav Francisci. Hudobná pozostalost'** [Miloslav
     Francisci. Musical bequest] (Matica slovenská v Martine, 1965) 11p.
> Incipits in full score for the beginnings of 4 operas.

FRANCK, CÉSAR, 1822-1890

395 MOHR, Wilhelm. **Caesar Franck,** 2. ergänzte Auflage (Tutzing: Schneider,
     1969) 345p.
     Werkverzeichnis, [203]-345.
> Over 100 multiple staff incipits for all movements of works
> arranged by genre (chamber music, clavier music, opera, ora-
> torios, etc.).

FRANKFURT am Main, Staats- und Universitätsbibliothek

396 SCHMIEDER, Wolfgang. **[Thematic catalogue]**
*   Incipits, on index cards, of the library's holdings.

FRÄNZL, IGNAZ, 1736-1811

397   WÜRTZ, Roland. Ignaz Fränzl. Ein Beitrag zur Musikgeschichte der
       Stadt Mannheim, *Beiträge zur Mittelrheinischen Musikgeschichte*, 12
       (Mainz: Schott's Söhne, 1970) 114p.
          Thematisches Verzeichnis der Werke Ignaz Fränzls, 72-104.
             55 incipits, mostly double staff with some single staff entries,
             of the complete works (5 symphonies, 7 violin concertos,
             4 flute quartets, 6 trios and 1 mass.).

FRAUENWÖRTH auf FRAUENCHIEMSEE (Germany), Kloster

398   [Thematic catalogue]
*   Incipit catalogue in preparation under the auspices of the
          Deutschen Forschungsgemeinschaft (DFG), under the general
          direction of Robert MÜNSTER.

FREIBURG im BREISGAU: Deutsche Volksliedarchiv, Inzipit-Katalog, *see no.*711.

FREISING (Germany), Dom [Catalogue I]

399   Themata/ Von allen vorhandenen Kirchen und Kammer/ Musicalien welche
▽   in der den I. Setpber [September] 1796 neu/ verfassten Designation
       enthalten sind (D Kreisarchiv München: Handschriftensammlung HL III
       F. 41 nr. 1) [39p.] (manuscript)
             Manuscript catalogue of musical sources at the court of the
             Prince-Bishop of Freising. Incipits for 472 sacred and se-
             cular 18th century works comprising the collections as of
             1796. The catalogue is all the more important now since
             the collection it inventories was scattered when seculari-
             zation occurred. Composers include the following: Adolfati,
             Anfossi, Aspelmäyr, Bach, Bachschmid, Bayer, [Peyer], Beke,
             Bergolesi [Pergolesi], Binder, Boccherini, Brixi, Bugnani
             [Pugnani], Cambini, Camerlocher, Canabich, Cavi, Cimarosa,
             Cirri, Compagnoli, Corri, Dallenthl, Demler, Dischner, Dit-
             ters (Dittersdorf), Dobrüs, Drexel, Eder, Eichner, Fiala,
             Fichtl, Fontenet, Ivanschiz, Freger, Galuppi, Giordani,
             Giulini, Gossec (Gossek), Graun, Greis, Gretrÿ (Greatrÿ),
             Grua, Guglielmi, Guillon, Hafeneder, Haltenberger, Hasse,
             Haÿdn, Hochmaÿr, Hoffmann, Hoffmeister, Holzbauer, Hueber,
             Jomelli, Kerpen, Kneferle, Kozeluch, Kunzman, Lang, Laucher,
             Lederer, Leichman, Lechner, Lockelÿ, Luca, Luz, Majo, Mal-
             zat, Martini, Martino, Masi, Mensi, Michl, Mislivecek, Mon-
             tano, Montenelli, Mozart, Neubauer, Nauman, Neuser, Nico-
             lini, Nitschar, Paisello (Paieselo, Pajeselo, Pajesello),
             Perger, Pergolesi (Pergolese, Bergolesi), Pertoni [Bertoni],
             Peÿer (Beÿer), Piccini, Pichel, Pleÿel, Porta, Prixi [Brixi],
             Rebeuch, Reindl, Reutter, Righini, Rosetti (Rossetti), Ros-
             poth, Sacchini, Sales, Salieri, Sarti, Sartini, Schlecht,
             Schmid, Schmidbauer, Schretter, Schuster, Sopis, Stainmez,
             Stauber, Sterkl, Sternkopf, Stökl, Taÿber, Toeskÿ, Trajetta,
             Ullinger, Vanhal, Vogl (Vogel), Vogler, Winter, Zach,Zin-
             zinger, Hämerlein, Kinzinger, Kobrich, Madlseder, Druschez-
             ky, Gresa (?), and several anonymous works.

399a   --- FELLERER, Karl Gustav. Thematische Verzeichnisse der fürst-
☐   bischöflichen Freisingischen Hofmusik von 1796, *Festschrift Otto
       Erich Deutsch* (Kassel: Bärenreiter, 1963) 296-302.

FREISING (Germany), Dom [Catalogue II]

400　Themata/ Von jenen Musicalien, Welche vom Jahre I789 bis/ I796
▿　inclusive theils neu angekauft, theils darzu/ hergeschenkt, auch
einige wenige Nro., son [schon] vor-/ handen gewesene diesem Catha-
logo einverleibt worden, / und ebenfalls im Musicalien Kasten auf
den Dom/ Chor, stundig sind　(D Kreisarchiv München: Handschriften-
sammlung HL III F. 41 nr. II) [8p.] (manuscript)

> A supplement to Nr. I (see above entry). Incipits arranged
> by genre for 51 Masses, 6 Requiems, 12 Offertories, 5 Ves-
> pers, 2 Litanies, 1 Salve Regina, 1 Regina Coeli, 1 Tantum
> ergo, 1 Te Deum, 1 Pange Lingua, 1 Miserere, and 11 sympho-
> nies. Composers represented are as follows: Alexi, Anger-
> maÿr, Brandl, Demler, Dischner, Ditters (Dittersdorf),
> Drexel, Dreÿer, Fichtl, Gallingstein, Gleisner, Groll, Groz,
> Grueber, Haffeneder, Hasse, Haÿdn, Michael Haÿdn, Holzman,
> Hubauer (Huebauer), Jaumann, Lachnitt, Laucher, Megelin,
> Michl, Mozart, Oberaltach, Pausch, Pleÿel, Reicha, Richini,
> Schlemer, Schmidbauer, Schmitt, Stadler, Stökl, Ullinger,
> Wera, Zimmermann.

FRESCOBALDI, GEROLAMO, 1583-1643

401　MOREL, Fritz. **Gerolamo Frescobaldi, Organista di San Pietro di
Roma I583-I643.** Ein Beitrag zur Struktur der Aufführungspraxis und
Bibliographie der Werke für Tasteninstrumente (Winterthur: Verlag
des "Organist", 1945) 56, 4p.
Thementafel, 4 unnumbered pages.

> Incipits for toccate, ricercari, and canzone.

401.1　ZIMMERMAN, Franklin B. **Thematic and first-line indexes to the complete works of Girolamo Frescobaldi.** Computer produced.

FRIEDRICH II. der GROSSE, 1712-1786

402　SPITTA, Philipp. **Friedrichs des Grossen Musikalische Werke.** Erste
kritisch durchgesehene Ausgabe (Leipzig: Breitkopf & Härtel, 1889)
3v., xxii, 115, 48; 116-211, 49-95; 93, 86p.
Thematisches Verzeichniss der Flötensonaten Friedrichs des Grossen,
v. 1, xix-xxii.
> Double staff incipits of 121 flute sonatas.

402a　--- Edition in 1 volume. SPITTA, Philipp. **Musikalische Werke Friedrichs des Grossen** (Leipzig: Breitkopf & Härtel, 1889) xxii, 307p.

FRIML, RUDOLF, 1879-?

403　**Educational commentary and catalogue. Piano compositions** (New York:
Schirmer, n.d. ca. 1919) 57p.
> Sales catalogue of about 100 works with first pages (in re-
> duced size) of 23 of them.

FROBERGER, JOHANN JAKOB, 1616-1667

404　FUCHS, Aloys. **Thematisches Verzeichnis über sämmtliche Compositio-
▿　nen von Johann Jakob Froberger, k.k. Hoforganist** (D Bds: HB VII,
Mus. ms. theor. Kat. 559) [vi, 16p.] Compiled 1838. Microfilm
copy in US NYcg. (manuscript)
> Double staff incipits for: *Libro 2do di Toccate, Fantasie,*

Canzone...(1649); *Libro IV. di Toccate, Ricercari, Capricci*...(1656); *Libro III. di Capricci, Ricercati*...; Toccaten-Ricercare-Capriccio's (misc.).

405   BEIER, Franz. Über Johann Jakob Froberger's Leben und Bedeutung für die Geschichte der "Klaviersuite." *Sammlung musikalischer Vorträge* V (1884), ed. by Paul WALDERSEE (Leipzig: Breitkopf & Härtel, 1879-1898) 386p.
Thematisches Verzeichnis der Suiten von Froberger, 357-86.
Incipits for all movements of 23 suites, arranged by published editions and MS collections.

406   SCHOTT, Howard M. (Wadham College, Oxford). The life and works of Johann Jakob Froberger (1616-1667)
Thematic catalogue.

FUCHS, Aloys   (compiler)

407   Thematisches Verzeichniss der sämmtlichen Compositionen von a) Hyero-
▽   nimus Frescobaldi, Organist b. St. Peter zu Rom, b) Georg Muffat und c) Gottlieb Muffat, k.k. Hof-Organisten zu Wien... (D Bds: HB VII, Mus.ms. theor. K. 556) [25p] Compiled 1838. Copy in US NYcg.
Double staff incipits for Frescobaldi: "Libro primo di toccate, canzone, partite...(1637)"[*], "Il secondo libro di toccate, canzone...(1637)"[**], "Fiori Musicali...(1635)", "Il primo libro di capricci, canzon francese e recercari (1626/1642)"; Georg Muffat: "Apparatus musico-organisticus...(1690)"; Gottlieb Muffat: "Componimenti Musicali per il cembalo...(1728)", "72 Versetten sammt 12 Tocatten (1726)", "Toccate...di Teofilo Muffatt".

[*] First edition: 1615; [**] First edition: 1627

408   Thematisches Verzeichnis über die Compositionen von: I. Antonio
▽   Vivaldi, II. Archangelo Corelli, III. Giuseppe Tartini (D Bds: Mus. ms. theor. K. 828) [49p] Compiled 1839. Copy in US NYcg. [see reproductions on following pages]
Double staff incipits for: Vivaldi [ii, 13p.], several sets of concerti, including Op.8, 10, 11; Corelli [ii, 13p.], two sets of sonatas, trios, Op. 1-4, concerti grossi, Op. 6; Tartini [ii, 11p.], four sets of sonatas, 6 concerti Op. 1, an Adagio and variations, a trio.

409   [Thematic catalogue] (D Berlin Staatsbibliothek: MS 98, according
▽   to Eitner) Compiled 1850 (manuscript)
This catalogue was not located in the Berlin Staatsbibliothek, and its whereabouts is unknown. Eitner states "In der B.B. [Berlin, Staatsbibliothek], Ms. 98, befindet sich ein thematisches Verzeichnis von 70 Orgelkompositionen (Praelud. u. Fug.), gezeichnet mit G. Bayer und Beyer und angefertigt von Aloys Fuchs 1850..."
Reference: Robert EITNER, Quellenlexikon I, 390.

FÜHRER, ROBERT JAN NEPOMUK, 1807-1861

410   KOLOWRAT, Bohuslav Hraběz. Robert Führer jeho život a dílo [Robert Führer, his life and works] (Praha: Knihtiskárna Cyrillo-Methodějská V. Kotrba, 1912)

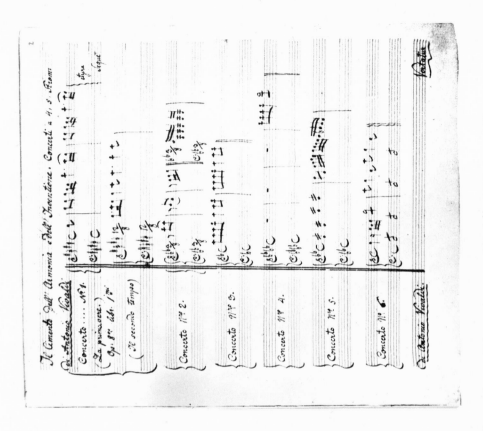

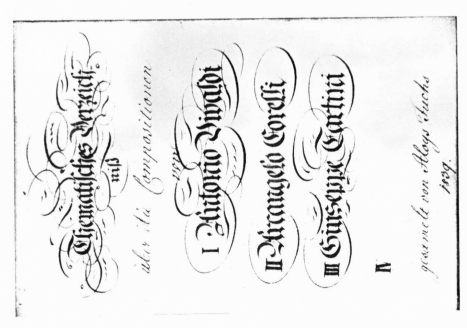

VIIIa. Fuchs, *Thematisches Verzeichnis... Compositionen von: ...Vivaldi*, 1839, no. 408

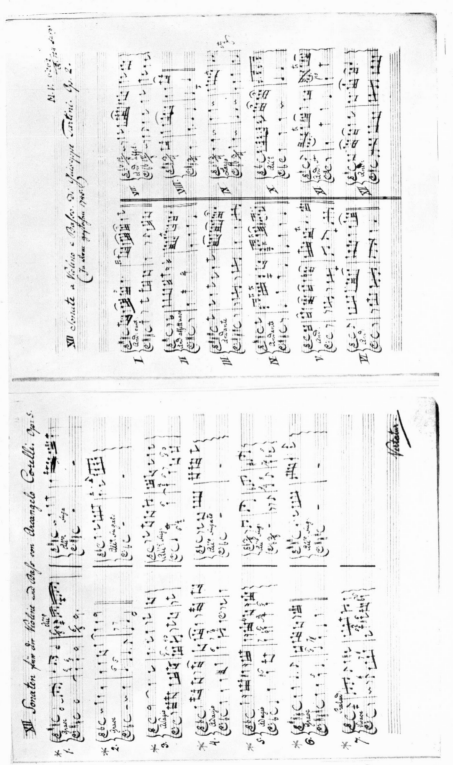

VIIIb. Fuchs, *Thematisches Verzeichnis... Compositionen von: ...Corelli, Tartini*, 1839, no. 408

Seznam jeho skladeb, 28-151.
>   Incipits for oratorios, Masses, Litanies, Graduals, and
>   several secular songs.

FUHRMANN, Roderich (compiler)

411   Mannheimer Klavier-Kammermusik   (PhD diss.: Marburg; Marburg: Mauers-
▽   berger, 1963) 2v. (typescript)
       [Thematic catalogue], v. 2, Anhang, 1-126.
>   Incipits for duo sonatas, trios, quartets, quintets, di-
>   vertimenti, sonatas for two keyboards, and symphonies by
>   the following composers: Eichner, Filtz, Forstmeyer, Holtz-
>   bauer, Le Brun, Liber, Richter, C. Stamitz, J. Stamitz,
>   Sterkel, Tantz, Toeschi, and Vogler. Information given on
>   dates, dedications, publishers, manuscripts, important edi-
>   tions, and occassionally, recordings. Ca. 500 incipits for
>   all movements.

FUKAČ, Jiří

412   Inventarien böhmischer oder mährischer Provenienz: J. Fukač: Křižov-
□▽   nický hudební inventář (Diplomarbeit, Brno, 1959) (typescript)

412a   Inventáře hudební, *Československý hudební slovník osob a institucí* I
□   (Praha, 1963) 550-51.

413   Tschechische Musikinventare, trans. by Adolf LANGER. *Tschechische*
□   *Musikwissenschaft.Geschichtliches. Musica Antiqua Europae Orientalis*
       (Praha: Tschechoslovakisches Musik-Informationszentrum, 1966) 1-64.
>   Discusses beginnings of Czech thematic inventories in the
>   18th century, as well as the historical and sociological im-
>   port.

FULLER, Julia D. (compiler)

414   An introduction to the study of the ballet de cour   (MA diss.:
▽   Columbia U., 1940) (typescript)
>   Incipits of 73 ballets from the collection, *Dansez sous le*
>   *règne de Henry 4me*, from volume 2 of the Philidor Collection.

FUX, JOHANN JOSEPH, 1660-1741

415   FUCHS, Aloys. Thematisches Verzeichniss der sämmtlichen Composi-
▽   tionen der k.k. Hofkapellmeister Johann Joseph Fux....(D Bds: HB VII,
       Mus. ms. theor. K. 566) [44p.] Compiled 1835. Copy in US NYcg.
>   Double staff incipits for 1. Vocal chamber music (religious),
>   Oratorios, operas; 2. Church music; 3. Instrumental music.
>   Each group further subdivides by genre; includes brief an-
>   notation.

416   KÖCHEL, Ludwig. Johann Joseph Fux Hofcompositor und Hofkapellmeister
       der Kaiser Leopold I., Josef I., und Karl VI. von I698 bis I740 (Wien:
       Hölder, 1872) 584, 187p.
       Thematisches Verzeichniss der Compositionen von J.J. Fux, 187p.
>   Single and multiple staff incipits for 405 works arranged
>   by genre: 57 Masses, 57 Vespers, 22 Litanies, 12 Graduals,

14 Offertories, 22 motets, 106 hymns, 10 oratorios, 18 operas,
79 partitas and overtures, and 8 clavier works. Information
given on location of sources. Index of first lines of vocal
works.

417   FUX, Johann Joseph. **Concentus musico-instrumentalis,** bearb. von
       Heinrich RIETSCH, *DTÖ* 23/2   (Wien: Artaria, 1916) 105p.
       Thematisches Nachschlageverzeichnis, p. 97.
              70 entries of orchestral works, arranged according to melodic
              interval of first line.

417   --- Reprint (Graz: Akademische Druck-u. Verlagsanstalt, 1960)

418   LIESS, Andreas. **Johann Joseph Fux; ein steirischer Meister des
       Barock**   (Wien: Doblinger, [1948])90p.
              **Verzeichnis der in den Jahren I942-I947 neu aufgefundenen Werke
              und Manuskripte von J.J. Fux,** [57]-89.
                     Partially thematic. Entries arranged by genre, according
                     to the cities in which the library sources are located.

419   FEDERHOFER, Hellmut. **Unbekannte Kirchenmusik von Johann Joseph
       Fux,** *Kirchenmusikalisches Jahrbuch,* Jahrg. 43 (1959) 113-154.
              [Thematic catalogue], 144-154.
                     Incipits of one vocal or instrumental part for each of 95
                     newly found church compositions and 20 doubtful works which
                     are supplemental to the works indexed by Köchel and Liess.
                     Appendix gives data on vocal parts and instrumentation,
                     plus location of copies, dates, and approximate dates of
                     performance.

419a   --- Supplement. Hellmut FEDERHOFER; Friedrich W. RIEDEL, **Quellen-
       kundliche Beiträge zur Johann Joseph Fux-Forschung,** *AfMW* XXI/2
       (Aug 1964) 111-140.
              Additional source material and incipits.

420   RUTHERFORD, Charles Leonard. **The instrumental music of Johann Joseph
  ▽   Fux (1660-1741)** (EdD diss., Music: Colorado State Col., 1967) 450 p.
       (typescript) (*RILM* 68 1891)
              Thematic catalogue.
                     Contains a list of libraries owning MS copies.

GABRIELI, GIOVANNI, 1557-1612

421   BENVENUTI, Giacomo. **Andrea e Giovanni Gabrieli e la musica strumen-
       tale in San Marco,** *IM* II/2 (Milano: Ricordi, 1932) 240p.(see no.102)
              Indice tematico [delle canzone e sonate contenute nelle "Sacrae
              symphoniae" del 1597], iii-viii.
                     Incipits for all voices of the 14 canzonas and 2 sonatas of
                     G. Gabrieli included in the volume.

Key: ✱ in preparation; ▽ manuscript; ☐ literature; ☆ Library of Congress

422   KENTON, Egon. **Life and works of Giovanni Gabrieli,** *Musicological Studies and Documents* XVI (Roma: American Institute of Musicology, 1967) 557p.
   Thematic index, 223-51.
     Chapter IV contains a complete thematic catalogue of Gabrieli's motets, magnificats, madrigals, and instrumental pieces comprising 82 printed works, listed chronologically, and 25 unpublished manuscripts. In old or new notation according to source, with tables and concordances between old and modern prints.

GADE, NIELS WILHELM, 1817-1890

423 **Registratur over N.W. Gade claveer Compositioner** (DK Kk: mu 6510.
▽ 2962) 46 slips (manuscript)
     Approximately 84 double staff incipits for Op.2-57.

GALLO, ALBERTO (da Venezia), first-half of the 18th c.

424 DEARLING, Robert J. (Dunstable, Bedfordshire). **[Thematic catalogue]**
▽ Index cards (manuscript) (see no. 282)
     Incipits for 47 symphonies, sonatas, and balletti from the Breitkopf Catalogue, Königsberg Staats- und Universitätsbibliothek (some of whose 15 anonymous symphonies are listed elsewhere as by Gallo), Haas' Estensischen catalogue, and Walsh's 12 "Sinfonie or Sonatas", Op. 2, in the British Museum.

GALUPPI, BALDASSARE, 1706-1785

425 TORREFRANCA, Fausto. **Per un catalogo tematico delle sonate per cembalo di B. Galuppi detto il Buranello,** *RMI* XVI (1909) 872-81.
     Incipits of all movements of 29 sonatas, with tempo indications, from MS sources in Venice (1782) and editions published by Walsh in London (1741).

426 BORREN, Charles van den. **Contribution au catalogue thématique des sonates de Galuppi,** *RMI* XXX (1923) 365-70.
     A continuation of Torrefranco's catalogue, giving incipits of all movements of sonatas 29-33, with tempi but no dates. Correlations given in the Brussels Conservatory Library MS where they appear. (see no. 425)

427 RAABE, Felix. **Galuppi als Instrumentalkomponist** (PhD diss.: Frankfurt a.d.O., Müller, 1929) 58p.
   Thematisches Verzeichnis bisher nicht katalogisierter Sonaten, [57-58].
     18 incipits of the upper voice for all movements. Additional information to the catalogues of Torrefranca and van den Borren on p. 54-56.

427.1 BOLLERT, Werner. **Die Buffoopern Baldassare Galuppis.** Ein Beitrag zur Geschichte der italienischen komischen Oper im 18. Jahrhundert (PhD diss.: Berlin; Bottrop: Postberg, 1935) 160p.
   Notenbeispiele, 139-60.
     234 incipits of arias from operas by Galuppi.

428   Baldassare Galuppi, detto il Buranello...Sonate per cembalo. Vol. I.
✡   Musiche vocali e strumentali sacre e profane sec. XVII-XVIII-XIX
      "Bonaventura Somma" a cura di Hedda Illy Vignanelli, No. 37 (DK Kk:
      [U24] U2; Roma: de Santis, 1969) xxviii, 111p.
          Indice tematico delle sonate,...dei concerti, iv-xvi.
              Incipits for all movements of 103 sonatas and 9 concertos.
              Provides list of sources and editions.

GARMS, J.H. Jr.

429   Het maken van een inhoudsopgave van melodieën,*Gedenkboek aange-*
☐   *boden aan Dr. D.F. Scheurleer* ('s-Gravenhage: Martinus Nijhoff,
      1925) 123-28.
              Discusses a system of classifying major, minor, and modal
              tonalities.

GASCONGNE, MATHIEU, c. 1470-c.1535

430   SWING, Peter Gram (Swarthmore College). **Mathieu Gascongne (c. I470-**
*   **c. I535). A thematic catalogue with concordances**
              Incipits for voice parts not in score. For masses, incipits
              for all movements, and duos and trios within movements.
              Incipits for both *prima* and *secunda pars* of motets. Works
              catalogued thus far include: 8 Masses, 21 motets, 2 (possibly
              3) Magnificats, and 19 chansons.

GASSMANN, FLORIAN LEOPOLD, 1729-1774

431   KOSCH, Franz. **Florian Leopold Gassmann als Kirchenkomponist** (PhD
▽   diss.: Wien, 1924) viii, 157*l*. (Typescript)
          Thematisches Verzeichnis, 28-91.
              68 double staff incipits for all movements of 5 Masses,
              1 Requiem, 10 Graduals, 1 Stabat Mater, 7 Offertories,
              hymns, Vespers, motets.

431a --- *Studien zur Musikwissenschaft.* Beihefte der *DTÖ* Bd. 14 (Wien,
☐   1927) 213-40.
              Text only.

432   LEUCHTER, Erwin. **Die Kammermusik Florian Leopold Gassmanns** (Phil.
▽   diss.: Wien, 1926) 207p. (typescript).
          [Thematic catalogue of instrumental works], 11-110
              Incipits for chamber and some orchestral works.

433   HILL, George R. (New York U.) **The concert symphonies of Florian**
*   **Leopold Gassmann**
          Thematic catalogue.
              Will include between 80 and 100 entries.

GATTI, LUIGI, 1740-1817

434   GEHMACHER, Monika. **Luigi Gatti. Sein Leben und seine Oratorien**
▽   (PhD diss.: Wien, 1959) iv, 314p. (typescript)
          Thematischer Katalog des Gesamtschaffens, v. II, 160-314.

Incipits for oratorios, Masses, and lesser church works, operas, cantatas, songs, and instrumental works (symphonies and chamber works). Incipits for all movements, with data on chronology and sources of MSS.

GAUKSTAD, Øystein (compiler)

435   Melodi-og tekstregister til Catharinus Ellings opptegnelser av folkemusikk [Melody and textregister to Catharinus Elling's collections of Norwegian folk music] (Oslo, 1953) vi, 114*l*. (stencil-mimeo)
        Melodiregister, 80-114*l*.
              Employs slashes for barlines, no duration, and numbers to indicate pitches.

435a --- Ludv. M. Lindman's collection of folk music (manuscript)
▽   Employs slashes for barlines, no duration, and numbers to indicate pitches.

GAUKSTAD, Øystein

436   Registrierung von Volksmusik. *Zweiter Weltkongress der Musikbiblio-*
☐   *theken Lüneburg* 1950. *Kongress-Bericht* (Kassel: Bärenreiter, 1951) 38-40.
              Discusses the classification of some 10,000 folk melodies, and proposes classification system based on intervallic melodic structures within the octave.

GEBAUER, JOHANN CHRISTIAN, 1808-1884

437   FOG, Dan   (København)   A thematic catalogue of his printed works
✱   "Bibliographical description of first edition, dates of composition and first edition, contemporary editions, arrangements and versions by the composer and others, important later editions.......chronological and systema-tical listing, index of titles and first-lines, and of names of persons and locations."

GEERING, Arnold (Bern)

438   [Thematic catalogue of Swiss folk songs in print]
✱

GELINEK (ABBÉ), JOSEPH, 1758-1825

439   Gelinek Werke (A Wst: MH 9177/c) 7p. (manuscript). Microfilm copy in
▽   US NYcg.
              Double staff incipits for keyboard works: 41 sets of varia-tions and 1 sonata.

440   Verzeichniss (thematisches) von Gelinek's erschienenen Variationen (Wien. S.A. Steiner, [181-]).
              Cited in *Handbuch der Musikalischen Litteratur* (Leipzig: A. Meysel, 1817) p. 590.

441   Thematisches Verzeichniss der Variationen des Abbé Gelinek für das
      pianoforte von No. I bis I00 (Offenbach: André, [18 20?]).
              Other versions of Gelinek catalogues exist without incipits
              and only indication of key (A Wgm: VII. 48251). No copy of
              the *Thematisches Verzeichniss* has been located.

442   PROIER, Gerlinde. Abbé Joseph Gelinek als Variationenkomponist
▽   (PhD diss.: Wien, 1962) 3v. (typescript)
          Thematischer Katalog der Variationenwerke von Abbé Joseph Gelinek,
          v. 3.
              Double staff incipits for 120 works arranged by opus number.

GELNAR, Jaromír

442.1 Nad katalogy písňových nápěvu, *Český lid* 49 (Brno, 1963) 241f.
☐   On classification.

GEMINIANI, FRANCESCO, bapt. 1687-1762

443   BACHMANN, Alberto. Les grands violinistes du passé (Paris: Fisch-
      bacher, 1913) 468p. (see no. 65)
          [Thematic catalogue], 90-91.
              Incipits for all movements of 3 sonatas and 1 *Amoroso*.

444   McARTOR, Marion E. Francesco Geminiani, composer and theorist
      (PhD diss.: U. of Michigan, 1951) Univ. Micro. 2363. (typescript)
          Thematic index, Appendix B, 311-22.
              Incipits of Geminiani's known solos and concertos which
              were published during his lifetime.

GENET, ELZÉAR, c. 1470-1548

445   RIGSBY, Oscar Lee. The sacred music of Elzéar Genet (PhD diss.:
      U. of Michigan, 1955) 2v. Univ. Micro. 11,346.(typescript)
          Thematic index, v. 1.
              Index of Genet's sacred music not included in the four-volume
              Avignon edition (1532-1537) of his works in the Austrian
              National Library of Vienna.

GERSON, GEORGE, 1790-1825

446   Verzeichniss/ über/ Zwei Hundert/ meiner/ Compositionen (DK Kk:
▽   George Gerson's Collection, mu 7105.0962) 22,88p. Compiled Nov. 1823.
          [Thematic catalogue], 88p.
              200 numbered works with exact dates and places of composition,
              dedications, authors of texts, etc. on left hand pages, facing
              musical incipits on right hand pages. Musical notation varies
              according to genre: piano notation, song notation (3 staves),
              score notation for chamber music, score or particel notation
              for orchestral works. Not included are 16 songs and 1 small
              cantata for men's voices and piano.

GESUALDO, DON CARLO, 1560-1613

447   HALPERN, Sylvia. Thematic catalogue of the complete works edition
▽   of Gesualdo (Queens College, N.Y.) v, 20p. (typescript). Xerox
      copy in US NYcg.
              Employs the *Simplified Plaine and Easie Code* (see no. 188).
              Incipits arranged by volume number of the complete works edi-
              tion. Provides index for the first lines of madrigals.

GILBERT, HENRY F., 1868-1928

448   LONGYEAR, Rey M. and Katherine E. (U. of Kentucky) **Thematic cata-**
*   **logue of the music of the American composer Henry F. Gilbert**
          Incipits will supplement the presently incomplete list in
          Katherine LONGYEAR,Henry F. Gilbert: His life and works
          (PhD diss.: Eastman, 1968). The catalogue will contain
          accounts of unpublished and unrecorded works, fragmentary
          MSS, sketches, mention of lost works, and corrections of
          misattributions.

GIORGI, GIOVANNI, d. 1725?

449   FEININGER, Father Laurence. **Catalogus thematicus et bibliographicus**
⚒   **Joannis de Georgiis operum sacrarum omnium.** *Repertorium liturgiae*
    polychoralis I (Tridenti: Societas Universalis Sanctae Ceciliae,
    1962) 156p.
          Incipits of all vocal, organ (figured bass), and any string
          parts of all Giorgi's sacred works. Arranged by genre, with
          alphabetical index by title.

          Reviews: Oscar MISCHIATI, *RItalianaMusicol* I/1 (1966) 145-47;
          Edwin HANLEY, *MQ* LIII/2 (1967) 270-76; Wendelin MÜLLER-BLATTAU,
          Mf XXI/1 (1968) 140-41.

--- Supplementum I (1965) of 24 additional works.

GIORNOVICHI, GIOVANNI MANE, 1740-1804

450   [4] **Concerti Viotti,** [5] **Concerti Giernovigh** (US BE: It. 1018c.)
▽   (manuscript) (see no. 107)
       [Thematic catalogue of concerti].
          Incipits for the first fast movement.

451   WHITE, Chappell. **Thematic catalogue of the violin concertos of**
*   **Giovanni Mane Giornovichi**
          Contains 17 concertos, plus 5 that have survived only in
          piano arrangement, and 2 spurious attributions.

GIULIANI, MAURO, 1781-1828

452   **Thematisches Verzeichnis der sämtlichen Original-Werke von Mauro**
       Giuliani welche in der Kunst- und Musikhandlung der k.k. pr. chemi-
       schen Druckerey und des S.A. Steiner & Comp: zu Wien am Graben No.
       612...zu haben sind (Wien: Steiner, [1815])
          Incipits for 68 works with opus numbers, and 12 works with-
          out opus numbers.

453   **Catalogue thématique des Oevres** [sic] **composées par Mauro Giuliani**
       (Wien: Artaria & Co., [1819]). Behind the title page of an edition
       of Giuliani's "Studio per la Chitarra, Opera Prima, a Vienna presso
       Artaria e Comp., Pl. Nr. 2246".
          Incipits, titles, and original publishers (with some plate
          numbers) of Giuliani's works through Op. 102. Does not in-
          clude works without opus number.

          Facsimile: HECK, T.M., **The birth of the classic guitar and its**
          cultivation in Vienna, reflected in the career and composi-
          tions of Mauro Giuliani (d. 1829) v. 2, p. x,202 (see no.455)

454 Oeuvres complets (Thematic catalogue advertised in the Artaria catalogue of 29 Nov. 1856).

> *Reference:* Alexander WEINMANN, Vollständiges Verlagsverzeich-
> nis Artaria & Comp. (Wien: L. Krenn, 1952) 154.

455 HECK, Thomas F. The birth of the classic guitar and its cultiva-
tion in Vienna, reflected in the career and compositions of Mauro
Giuliani (d. 1829) (PhD diss.: Yale U., 1968; New Haven, Conn.,
1970) ix, 286p.; xiv, 218p.

> Thematic catalogue of the complete works of Mauro Giuliani, v.2.
> Over 700 single and double staff incipits for all movements.
> Works arranged first by opus number (1-151), and then by
> works without opus number.

GLASS, Phyllis Watson (compiler)

456 Orchestral music for school and community orchestras by Viennese and
Bohemian composers, 1750-1800 (PhD diss.: U. of Southern Calif.,
1962) 370p. Univ. Micro. 62-6057. (typescript)

> Thematic index of works from 34 European libraries indicates
> instrumentation and library sources.

GLINKA, MIHAIL IVANOVIČ, 1804-1857

457 ALBRECHT, Konstantin-Karl. Thematic list of romances, songs and
operas of M.I. Glinka (Moscow: Jurgenson, 1891) 37p.

> Incipits, in chronological order with metronomic indica-
> tions, for 87 romances and songs and 53 pieces from operas.

458 FINDEIZEN, Nikolai. Catalogue of musical manuscripts, letters and
portraits of M.I. Glinka in the Manuscript Division, Imperial
Public Library, S. Petersbourg (St. Petersburg: 1898) 133p.

> Thematic index, 113-33.
> Incipits of 41 vocal and instrumental works.

GLUCK, CHRISTOPH WILLIBALD RITTER VON, 1714-1787

459 FUCHS, Aloys. Gluckiana (D Bds: Kat. ms. 575) 25*l*. (manuscript).
▽

> *Reference:* Richard SCHAAL, Quellen zur Musiksammlung Aloys
> Fuchs, *Mf* XVI (1963) 72. (see no. 1159)

460 FUCHS, Aloys. Thematisches Verzeichniss der sämmtlichen Musik-Stücke
▽   aus nachbenannten Opern von Gluck: I. Armida....II. Orfeo ed Euridice..
... III. Iphegenie en Aulide... IV. Iphigenie en Tauride...V. Alsceste
... VI. Il Trionfo di Clelia... (D Bds: HB VII, Kat. ms. 577) [46p]
Compiled 1843. (manuscript*)*. Microfilm copy in US NYcg.

460a --- Thematisches Verzeichniss der sämmtlichen Stücke aus nachbenannten
▽   Opern von Christoph Ritter von Gluck: I. Il Re Pastore...II. La
Semiramide...III. Echo et Narcisse... IV. Paride ed Elena...V. Ezio
[38p.]   (sources, date, etc. as above).(manuscript)

460 b --- Thematisches Verzeichniss der sämmtlichen Stücke von Gluck's
▽   nachbenannten Opern: I. Il Telemacco...II. Tetide...III. La Corronna
       ...IV. L'Innozenza giustificata...V. Le Cadi dupe...VI. Die Pilgrim
       von Mecca [52p.] (see above).(manuscript)

460 c --- Airs noveaux zu nachstehende Opern von Gluck: rechtmöglich
▽   componirt von Ebendemselben: I. L'arbre enchante...II. Cythere
       assiege...III. Le Cade dupe...IV. L'Yvrogne corrige...V. L'Isle
       de Merlin [27p.] (see above).(manuscript)

460 d --- Thematisches Verzeichniss über verschiedene einzelne, zerstreute
▽   Vocal= u Instrumental=Compositionen von Christoph Ritter von Gluck...
       [14p.] (see above).(manuscript)
                Incipits for several arias, Lieder, and Sinfonie.

461   FUCHS, Aloys. **Thematisches Verzeichniss sämmtlicher Compositionen
       des K.K. Hof-Componisten Christoph Ritters von Gluck,** zusammengestellt
       mit Angabe der erschienenen Partitur-Ausgaben und der Zeit der Erschaf-
       fung (der Opern) von Aloys Fuchs, Mitglied der K.K. Hof-Kapelle in
       Wien, mitgetheilt von Dr. F.S. Bamberg in Paris, *Neue Berliner Musik-
       zeitung* V (1851) 207-10.
                Double staff incipits for the overtures of 22 operas and bal-
                lets. Provides information on dates of composition, first
                performances, and sources.

462   WOTQUENNE, Alfred. **Catalogue thématique des oeuvres de Chr. W. v.
       Gluck** (Leipzig: Breitkopf & Härtel, 1904) 249p.
                The first part (p. 1-181) includes full incipits of all
                sections, acts and movements of compositions. Second part
                gives information on the works, publishers, first performances,
                and locations of sources. Arranged by genre.

462 a --- Deutsche Übersetzung by Josef LIEBESKIND. (1904)

462 b --- Ergänzungen und Nachträge by Josef LIEBESKIND. Translated into
       French by Ludwig FRANKENSTEIN (Leipzig: Reinecke, 1911) 20p.
                Incipits of additional works, 9 authentic and 1 doubtful.

462 c --- AREND, M.A. Ergänzungen und Berichtigungen, *Die Musik* XIII/49
       (Dec 1913) 288f.

463   HOPKINSON, Cecil. **A bibliography of the works of C.W. von Gluck,
       1714-1787** (London: Harding & Curtis, 1959, limited to 300 copies)
       xv, 79p.
                A bibliographical supplement to the Wotquenne thematic cata-
                logue (see no. 462), with a few thematic listings.

463a   --- Second edition, revised (New York: Broude, 1967)

GOFFERJE, Karl

464   **Über lexikalisch geordnete Melodieverzeichnisse zum mehrstimmigen
☐   deutschen Lied des 15. und 16. Jahrhunderts--Ein neuer Versuch,**
       Vetter Festschrift, ed. by Heinz WEGENER (Leipzig, 1969) 37-44.
                Describes the organization of 3 complementary files arranged
                according to melody, text incipit, and composer (or other
                relevant persons). Discusses advantages and disadvantages
                of this procedure.

GORDON, Edward

465   Themography   (US LC: ML 113/ .G7)
☐

GORZANIS, GIACOMO, 16th century

466 HALBIG, Hermann. **Anfänge der Sätze [des "Libro de Intabulatura di Liuto, I567"].** Eine handschriftliche Lautentabulatur des G. Gorzanis, *Theodor Kroyer Festschrift* (Regensburg: Bosse, 1933) 102-17.
Includes description and inventory of 24 lute tablatures

GOSSEC, FRANÇOIS-JOSEPH, 1734-1829

467 MACDONALD, Robert J. **François-Joseph Gossec and French instrumental music in the second half of the eighteenth century** (PhD diss.: U. of Michigan, 1968) 3v. Univ. Micro. 69-12,175.(typescript)
    Thematic catalogue, Appendix A, v. II, 1-93: " A study on catalogues of Gossec's instrumental music."
        "Includes 142 numbered entries indicating type of MS or published edition, issue, transcription, etc., at least a single staff incipit for the first movement, listing of movements (tempo, time signature, key), instrumentation, date with supporting documentation, full title, catalogue references, and sources. Divided into two parts: Part I, "Additions and corrections to the catalogue of instrumental compositions by François-Joseph Gossec cited by Barry S. Brook (see no. 185) in La symphonie française (II, 265-339); Part II, "Supplement of additional instrumental compositions".

468 MACDONALD, Robert J. (Grosse Ile, Michigan) **Thematic catalogue of**
*   **the vocal and instrumental music of Gossec**
        Incipits for all movements.

GOSTYŃ POZNAŃSKI, Poland. **Archivium des Oratoriums des heiligen Philipp**

469 IDASZAK, Danuta. **[Symphonies, 18th c.]** 10ℓ. (manuscript). In pos-
▽   session of Jan LaRue.
        Incipits for all movements of 21 symphonies (18th c. MS) located at this archive. Annotations repeat data on the title pages and provide MS measurements, call numbers. Composers: E. Eichner, [Antoni] Habel, J. Haydn (Hayden), Hoffmeister, J. Lachnitt, Pichl, I. Pleyel, Ferd. Riess, Ant. Rosetti, Carl Stamitz (C. Stamitz).

GOTTSCHALK, LOUIS MOREAU, 1829-1869

470 DOYLE, John Godfrey. **The piano music of Louis Moreau Gottschalk** (PhD diss.: New York U., 1960) 172p. Univ. micro. 61-107.(typescript)
    Thematic index, Chap. III, 46-88.
        An alphabetical thematic index of the composer's published piano compositions, including those under pseudonym, with brief commentaries on the incipits.

GÖTTWEIG, Austria. **Benediktinerstift**

471 WONDRATSCH, R.D. Henricum. **KATALOGUS/ OPERUM MUSICALIUM/ in/ Choro**
▽   **musicali/ MONASTERII/ O.S.P.B. GOTTWICENSIS/ R.R.D.D./ ALTMANNO/ AB-BATE per R.D./ HENRICUS WONDRATSCH/ p.t. chori regentem, conscriptus./ Anno MDCCCXXX Tom. 1.** (A GÖ) (manuscript)

Contains instrumental and sacred vocal works. Catalogue entries generally note the complete scoring specifications of
works, the name of the copyist (or purchasor), and the date
of acquisition. Composers: Aigner, Albrechtsberger, Arbesser, Aufschnaitter, Aumann, Ahm, Abel, Amon, Anfossi, Ber-
thali, Beethoven, Behr, Berghofer, Becker, Boog, Brentner,
Beyer, Blumenthal, Baradies, Bassani, Bergolgi, Bibern, Bla-
hack, Beer, Berkhamer, Bonno, Bechterley, Bicherle, Bürkho-
fer, J.S. Bach, C.E. Bach, Beati, Benda, Cadis, Caldara,
Candus, Carl, Crudeli, Cherubini, Caldarini, Conrad, Czerno-
hofke, Cherzelli, David, Ditters, Donnberger, Ebner, Eibler,
Eberlin, Erber, Ehrenhard, Ertl, Einwaldt, Ender, Feichter,
Fleischmann, Feger, Fogel, Fritz, Freytag, Fux, Furbe, Fai-
telli, Fauner, Frieberth, Fuchs, Fischer, Fils, Fegurini,
Fröhlich, Frumann, Fügerl, Fraeta, Gassmann, Geyer, Graff,
Grasl, Gsur, Gänsbacher, Gisolamo, Galuppi, Graun, Gyrowetz,
Giocatore, Gletle, Gossel, Gavinies, Gegenbauer, Habegger,
Hacker, Haltenberger, Haslinger, Hasse, J.Haydn, M. Haydn,
Hoffmann, Holzbauer, Huber, Hummel,Hahn, Hausser, Hörger,
Hofer, Hugl, Hochenreitter, Jacob, Joseph, Ivaschitz, Jansa,
Jomelli, Kampfl, Kimmerling, Klima, Kluger, Kohaut, Krammer,
Kranschnabl, Krommer, Krottendorfer, Kreutzer, Kayser,
Kircher, Kirnberger, Königsperger, Krumpholz, Kraus, Körzl,
Klaus, Kopp, Kinninger, Lenghamer, Leo, Linner, Lippamon,
Laugthaller, Liebl, Laube, Lolli, Mozart, Mazzoni, Müller,
Minner, Mancini, Manna, Molitor, Maschek, Mosel, Maldere,
Mitscha, Monn, Mislivecek, Novotny, Neckh, Nopaur, Naumann,
Öttl, Orlandini, Ordonez, Panny, Pfeiffer, Pratzner, Preindl,
Paumon, Petri, Pichler, Prixi, Pusserhofer, Predieri, Pre-
glauer, Pruneder, Prustmann, Pasterwitz, Pachschmidt, Pau-
mann, Pampani, Pergolese, Peyer, Planitzki, Porpora, Porfili,
Prantl, Prota, Pudler, Preinich, Presl, Pacher, Perkhammer,
Prentner, Pitoni, Pözl, Purchard, Palestrina, Paumgartner,
Pichl, Pleyel, Prachensky, Purksteiner, Raab, Rathgeber,
Reidinger, Reutter, Righini, Ratzky, Reichenauer, Reinhardt,
Richter, Rieder, Riepl, Rignaldi, Rinaldo, Reicharzer, Roset-
ti, Ratschy, Roy, Scheibl, Schenk, Scherbaum, Schmid, Schmidt-
bauer, Schneider, Schollenberger, Schopf, Schorn, Sengmüller,
Schubert, Sechter, Seuche, Sonnleithner, Strasser, Stadler,
Süssmayer, Stoll, Salieri, Santolapis, Sarry, Scarpi, Schum-
böck, Schnell, Schneck, Seyfried, Sölner, Steffan, Stieffat-
ter, Spies, Stocksmayer, Stand, Schöffer, Schramek, Scarlat-
ti, Schlöger, Schragner, Staimitz, Starzer, Stephan, Tuma,
Tschoblar, Tschortsch, Teller, Umlauf, Umstatt, Ulbrich, Vanhal, Vogel, Vinci, Vogler, Venatsrino, Wagenseil, Weinwurmb
Weber, Wenzely, Werner, Widder, Wiederhofer, Winter, Wöger,
Wittaszek, Wittmann, Wrastil,Weigl, Wenser, Widmann, Will-
komm, Weiss, Witt, Zechner, Ziegler, Zimmermann, Zacher,
Zeiller, Zoneka, Zoppis, Ziani, and Zach.

GOULD, Murray

472 A keypunchable notation for the Liber Usualis, *Elektronische Daten-*
☐   *verarbeitung in der Musikwissenschaft*, Harald HECKMANN, ed. (Regens-
     burg: Gustav Bosse Verlag, 1967) *RILM* [67] 2297.
          An expansion of the *Simplified Plaine and Easie Code*. (see
          no. 188)

GRAAF, CHRISTIAN ERNST, 1726-1802/04

473   HASSELT, Ludwig van (Amsterdam) Biography of Christian Ernst Graaf
*   [Thematic catalogue].

GRANDI, ALESSANDRO, ?-1630

474   INTALI, Domenic (Indiana U. of Pa.) The vocal music of Alessandro
*   Grandi

GRAUMANN, Dorothea

475   Catalogue de Musique/ pour/ Mad[emoise]lle D[orothe]a Graumann/ 1797
▽   (A Gu) 88, [2]p. (manuscript)
                Catalogue of printed music in Dorothea Graumann's possession
                (aged 16-17). Includes sonatas, trios, songs, quartets, quin-
                tets, concertos, listed by name of composer or editor (with-
                out first names). Many are keyboard arrangements of stage
                works. Beethoven, Mozart, and Haydn represent about one-third
                of the ca. 170 works. Incipits are double staff.

475   FEDERHOFER, Hellmut. Ein thematischer Katalog der Dorothea Graumann,
☐   *Festschrift Joseph Schmidt-Görg zum 60. Geburtstag* (Bonn, 1957) 100-
      110.

GRAUN, JOHANN GOTTLIEB, 1703 -1771

476   MENNICKE, Carl H. Hasse und die Brüder Graun als Symphoniker (Leip-
      zig: Breitkopf & Härtel, 1906) 568p.
            Thematisches Verzeichnis von II5 Orchesterwerken, 536-47.
                Incipits, arranged by key, for 17 overtures, 96 symphonies,
                a suite and a concerto grosso, with location of scores and
                parts and an index of printed works.

GRAUN, KARL HEINRICH, 1704-1759

477   MENNICKE, Carl H. Hasse und die Brüder Graun als Symphoniker (Leip-
      zig: Breitkopf & Härtel, 1906) 568p.
            Thematischer Katalog der Symphonien..., 525-536.
                32 works arranged by key, with information on sources, first
                performances, librettos and librettists, and an index of
                printed works.

477.1 GRUBBS, John Whitfield. An eighteenth-century passion pasticcio
      based on a passion cantata of Carl Heinrich Graun (MA Thesis, U. of
      Calif. at Los Angeles, 1964) 2 vols.
            Thematic catalogue

GRAUPNER, CHRISTOPH, 1683-1760

478   NAGEL, Wilibald. Christoph Graupner als Sinfoniker. Zusammenfassende
      Bemerkungen (nebst thematischem Kataloge der Sinfonien), *Musikalisches
      Magazin* Heft 49 (1912) (Langensalza: Beyer & Söhne, 1912) 31p.
            Thematischer Katalog der Sinfonien Christoph Graupners, [18]-31.
                Incipits of 113 works arranged by instrumental ensemble.

GYÖR, Hungary. Arch. Mus. Cathedralis

479   BARTHA, Dénes. [Instrumental music, 18th c.] 89 cards (type-
▽   script)
            Incipits for all movements of 89 works, mainly symphonies
            (18th c. MS) housed in the archives at Györ. Reproduces
            information on the title page, also providing call num-
            bers, and MS measurements. Composers include: Franz As-
            pelmayer, Bach, Bach [John Christian], Karl Ditters von
            Dittersdorf, Ernst Eichner, Anton Fils, Baldassare Galup-
            pi, Adalbert Gyrowetz, Joseph Haydn, Hellmich, Ignaz Holz-
            bauer, Ignaz Malzat, Martin [y Soler?], Georg Matthias
            Monn, Wenzel Raimund Pirck, Christoph Sonnleithner, Joseph
            Anton Steffan, Carlo Giuseppe Toeschi, Franz Tuma, Jan
            Vanhal, Georg Christoph Wagenseil, Weigerth, Anton Zimmer-
            mann.

GYROWETZ [JÍROVEC], ADALBERT, 1763-1850

480   SCHOENBAUM, Camillo (Denmark). **Adalbert Gyrowetz (Jírovec),**
▽   **Thematischer Katalog.** Compiled 1950-1968 (manuscript)
            253 single and double staff incipits for all movements of
            dances (46), concerti (3), notturni (13), overtures (11),
            quartetti (50), quintetti (8), serenate & divertimenti (7),
            sinfonie (39), sonate (54), sonatine (12), trii (6), di-
            verse (4).

HAARKLOU, JOHANNES, 1847-1925

481   BENESTAD, Finn. **Johannes Haarklou. Mannen og verket.** [Johannes
      Haarklou. The man and his work] (Oslo & Bergen, 1961) xiii, 338p.
            Pages 241-93 contain a chronological list of works with
            thematic incipits.

HAENSEL, PIERRE, 1770-1831

482   **Oeuvres complets** (Thematic catalogue advertised in the Artaria cata-
      logue of 29 Nov. 1856).

            Reference: Alexander WEINMANN, **Vollständiges Verlagsver-
            zeichnis Artaria & Comp.** (Wien: L.Krenn, 1952) 154.

Key: * in preparation; ▽ manuscript; □ literature; ☆ Library of Congress

HALTENBERGSTETTEN, Schloss Haltenbergstetten b. Niederstetten. Fürst zu
Hohenlohe-Jagstbergsche Bibliothek

483 Catalogus/ Musicorum/ pro Choro Bartenstein/ 1797// (D BAR) paginated
▽   folios 1-10, 25-30; 11-24 are missing. (manuscript) Copy in US NYcg.
          113 incipits of church-music in print or manuscript existing
          today in Bartenstein and Haltenbergstetten(38 works). Compos-
          ers: Beethoven, Boodeé, Bott, Bradelli, Brandl, Bühler, Dit-
          ters, Emmert, Fasoldi, Gensbacher, C.H. Graun, Hamel, M.Haydn,
          J. Haydn, Knischek, Kreuser, Madlseder, Martin, Michel, Mozart,
          Neubauer, Prag, Röder, Rolle, Rosetti, Sales, Schiedermaier,
          Schlecht, Schmittbauer, Schwindel, Seyfried, Stengel, Teradel-
          eas, Ulinger, Vanhal, Vogl, Vogler, Gottfried Weber, Winter,
          Witt. Folios 29v-30v list printed works without incipits.
          Entries continued to be added until at least 1824.

484 Catallogo/ Delle Opere, Sinfonie, Cantate,/ Ariette, Duetti, Terzetti,
▽   Quartetti,/ Quintetti, ed altre Musicaglie/ appartenenti all
     orghestra della/ Corte di Haltenbergstetten/Nell' Anno 1807 (D Hl;
     copy in US NYcg) 228 numbered p. (some blank or partially blank)
     Entries continued to be added until at least 1821.
          285 incipits, 215 of which represent works that exist today
          in print or manuscript in the library of Haltenbergstetten.
          Composers inventoried: André, Anfossi, Beecke, [Beethoven]
          Bethoven, Botteine, Brandl, Contin, Danzi, Endres, Eibler,
          Franzl, Fries, [Gyrowez] Girovez, Gleisner, Gluck, Hänsel,
          [Haydn] Hayden, [Hoffmeister] Hoffmeister, Krommer, Malte,
          Massoneau, Mozart, Neubauer, Paisiello, [Pleyel] Pleÿl,
          Rode, Romberg, Sacchini, Sales, Salieri, Schenk, Schneider,
          Stamitz, Süssmair, Vienne, Viotti, Weiss, Winter, Wranizkÿ.
          Names are variously spelled. Several others, not included,
          have no incipits.

HAMAL, JEAN-NOËL, 1709-1778

485 SMET, Monique de. **Jean-Noël Hamàl**, chanoine impérial et directeur
     de la musique de la Cathédrale Saint-Lambert de Liège; vie et oeuvre
     Académie Royale de Belgique. Classe des Beaux-Arts. Mémoires.
     (Bruxelles: Palais des Académies, 1959) Collection in-8°, 2. sér.,
     t. 11, fasc. 1. 336p.
          Catalogue thématique, 183-207.
          Inventories 253 compositions. Incipits for all movements
          of instrumental works; opening bars of violin and melodic
          vocal line for vocal works. Genres include: Masses 46, motets
          83, Psalms 23, Oratorios 4, Litanies-Lamentations-Responses
          39, oratorios 4, cantatas 17, operas 4, instrumental music
          41 (overtures 21, grave & fugue 1, symphonies 18, piéce pour
          cembalo 1). Tempo indications, instrumentation, text under-
          lay are given. "Inventaire descriptif", p. 115-75, provide
          full bibliographical apparatus.

HÄNDEL, GEORG FRIEDRICH, 1685-1759

486 FUCHS, Aloys. **Thematisches Verzeichniss über sämmtliche Compositionen**
▽   **von Georg Friedrich Händel**...(D Bds: HB VII, Mus. ms. theor. K. 595)
     [86p.] Compiled 1837. Microfilm copy in US NYcg (manuscript)

An incomplete catalogue, providing double-staff incipits for vocal and instrumental music. Gives performance and composition dates.

487 FUCHS, Aloys. **Thematisches Verzeichniss über sämmtliche Compositionen**
▽ **von Georg Friedrich Händel**...(D Bds: HB VII, Mus. ms. theor, K. 597) [ii, 72p.] Compiled 1837. Microfilm copy in US NYcg (manuscript)
Systematic arrangement of incipits for vocal and instrumental works, arranged by genre. Includes: operas, anthems, miscellaneous vocal works for church, oratorios, cantatas, chamber duets...Concerti grossi, works for full orchestra, concertos for oboe, for organ, trio sonatas, duets, suites and fugues for organ and clavier.

488 CHRYSANDER, Friedrich, ed. **Werke** (Leipzig: Breitkopf & Härtel, [1858-1902]) 94v.
[Thematic indexes of selected instrumental works], in the following volumes:
Instrumental-Concerte, v. XXI [1865], 2p. before p. 1; Sonate da Camera, v. XXVII [1879], 6p. before p. 1; 12 Orgel-Concerte, v. XXVIII [1868] 1p. before p. 1; 12 Grosse Concerte, v. XXX [1869] 1p. before p. 1; [Orchester-Werke], v. XLVII, 1p. before p. 1.

489 KAHLE, Felix. **Georg Friedrich Händels Cembalosuiten** (PhD diss.:
▽ Berlin, 1928) (D Mbs: Mus. th. 4755 wb) 217p., 34ℓ. Notenanhang.
Die Abschriften von Cembalocompositionen G. Fr. Händels auf der preussischen Staatsbibliothek zu Berlin, 53-65.
Ca. 25 incipits for "unknown" works.

490 COOPERSMITH, Jacob M. **An investigation of Georg Friedrich Händel's**
▽ **orchestral style** (PhD diss.: Harvard U., 1932) 12v. (typescript)
A thematic index of the printed works of Georg Friedrich Händel, v. II-XII, 4114p.
Works arranged by genre, with indications of the composer's borrowings from his own works, an extensive cross-reference system, and bibliography.

491 SEDLACZEK, Viktoria. **Orgelkonzerte von G.F. Händel** (PhD diss.: Wien,
▽ 1938) 206ℓ. (typescript)
Thematisches Verzeichnis der Orgelkonzerte, 34-41.
Double staff incipits of 11 organ concertos.

492 SMITH, William C. **The earliest editions of Handel's "Water Music"**,
☐ *MQ* XXV (Jan 1939) 60-75.
Thematic catalogue of the first editions for orchestra and harpsichord, p. 74-75.

493 MANN, Alfred; KNAPP, J. Merrill. **The present state of Handel re-**
☐ **search**, *ActaMusicol* XLI/1-2 (Jan-June 1969) 4-26.
Contains brief survey of the history and difficulties of preparing thematic catalogues of Händel's works.

494 BASELT, Berend (Halle). **Thematisch-systematisches Verzeichnis der**
∗ **Werke G.F. Händels**, *Händel-Handbuch,* Bd. I (To be published in 1973, Walter- und Margret-Eisen-Stiftung)
Will contain several indexes including a numbered thematic and systematic index, index of instrumental themes, and an index of first-lines.

495   COOMBS, G.H.   Thematic catalogue
*   Last reported in 1964, in typescript.

496   WALKER, Arthur D. (Manchester, England). [Thematic catalogue]
*   Incipits (ca. 300p. thus far) of Händel material in the Sir
             Newman Flower Collection which the Manchester Central Library
             has acquired.

497   ZIMMERMAN, Franklin B.   G.F. Handel: Index of themes, titles, and
*   first-lines (New York: Vienna House, announced for 1973) 3v.
             "22,000 themes from 640 works, numbered according to a new
             system devised by the compiler; with computerized concordances
             to the Arnold Edition (1787-97); to the Händel Gesellschaft
             Edition (1856-94) edited by Chrysander; to the new Halle Hän-
             del Edition (1955-); and to the autograph MSS. Each theme
             is indexed by pithches (vol. I), by intervals (vol. II), and
             by titles and first-lines (in vol. III)."

HARBURG, Germany. Fürstlich Oettingen-Wallerstein'sche Bibliothek

498   KOHLER, Caspar. [Thematic catalogue] (D HR) 14*l*. Compiled ca. 1830.
▽   (manuscript)
             Catalogue inventories part of the library of Schloss Harburg.
             About 150 incipits without order of works by the following
             composers: J.S. Bach, Karl Spazier, Ernst Weinrauch, Benedikt
             Aufschnaiter, Brixi, Jaumann, Allexi, Naumann, Bühler, Reinegg,
             J. Haydn, Vogler, Foerster, Romberg, Mozart, Mehul, Beecke,
             Gluck, M. Haydn, Luigi Gatti, Witt, Sartini, Ernst Wilhelm
             Wolf, Leopold Hoffmann, Dietter, Cajetan Vogl, Demler, Laube,
             Schacht, Schermer, Michl, Wineberger, Handl (Händel?), Feld-
             meyer, Zach, Righini, Paisiello, Carlo Monza, Salieri, Sacchini,
             Zanetti, Kozeluch, Benda, Martin, Guglielmi, Martini, Anfossi,
             Fischietti, P. Wranitzky, Rosetti, Lohelio, Jomelli, Brandl.

HARTMANN, JOHAN PETER EMILIUS, 1805-1900

499   Themat: Register (DK Kk: 6510. 2961) c. 100 slips (manuscript)
▽   115 incipits for piano works, songs, cantatas, etc.   71 in-
             cipits for piano works Op. 6-65 on two staves.

HASSE, JOHANN ADOLF, 1699-1783

500   Catalogo della Musica di Chiesa composta di Giov. Adolfo Hasse.
▽   Armaro VI (D Dl) 25p. Compiled c. 1800. Copy in US NYcg (manuscript)
             Incipits for Masses (p. 4-15) and motets (p. 16-24). There
             is a biographical note on Hasse in the hand of Franz Schubert
             (of Dresden) on page 1.

501   MENNICKE, Carl H. Hasse und die Brüder Graun als Symphoniker (Leip-
       zig: Breitkopf & Härtel, 1906) 568p. (see no. 476).
             Thematischer Katalog der Symphonien, 500-25.
                    Incipits for 86 works arranged by key with information on

sources, first performances, librettos and librettists, plus
chronological index (p. 493-497) and index of printed works
(p. 548-51).

502   MÜLLER, Walther. **Johann Adolf Hasse als Kirchenkomponist.** Ein
Beitrag zur Geschichte der Neapolitanischen Kirchenmusik (PhD diss.:
Leipzig; Breitkopf & Härtel, 1910) 179p. [*PIMG* 11/9 (1911)].
   Thematisches Verzeichnis der Kirchenmusik J.A. Hasse's, [147]-
   176.
        Double staff incipits for all sections of 10 Masses, 5 Mass
        parts, 3 Offertories, 3 Requiems, 5 Psalms, 4 Miserere, 20
        Hymns, 3 Litanies, 10 motets, etc.

503   KAMIEŃSKI, Lucjan. **Die Oratorien von J.A. Hasse** (Leipzig: Breitkopf &
Härtel, 1912) 366p
   Thematischer Katalog der Oratorien von J.A. Hasse, Notenbeilage I,
   1-43.
        Includes 11 oratorios arranged chronologically.

503.1 SONNECK, Oscar George. **Die drei Fassungen des Hasse'schen "Arta-
serse",** *SIMG* XIV (Leipzig: Breitkopf & Härtel, 1912) 226-42.
   [Thematic catalogue], 236-40.
        Incipits for overtures and arias of the three versions of
        Artaserse (Venezia 1730, Dresden 1740, Warszawa 1760).

504   HOFFMANN-ERBRECHT, Lothar. **Deutsche und italienische Klaviermusik
zur Bachzeit.** Studien zur Thematik und Themenverarbeitung in der Zeit
von 1720-1760. *Jenaer Beiträge zur Musikforschung,* Bd I, hrsg. von
Heinrich BESSELER (Leipzig: Breitkopf & Härtel, 1954)145p.
   Thematisches Verzeichnis der Klavierwerke J.A. Hasses, 137-42.
        Two staff incipits of 17 "Klaviersonaten" and 3 "sonstige
        Klavierstücke", with sources and a list of published works
        given.

505   HANSELL, Sven Hostrup. **Works for solo voice of Johann Adolph**[sic]
Hasse. *Detroit Studies in Music Bibliography* 12 (Detroit: Informa-
tion Coordinators, 1968) viii, 110p. (*RILM* 68/1940/bm[26])
   Thematic catalogue of the solo vocal works of Johann Adolf [sic]
   Hasse, 29-101.
        One and two staff incipits, usually of all sections, of most
        of the 132 listed cantatas, motets and antiphons.

HÄSSLER, JOHANN WILHELM, 1747-1822

506   WALKER, Helen Siemens. **Johann Wilhelm Hässler (I747-I822); I8th
▽   century solo keyboard literature for amateurs** (MA diss.: Smith college,
1968)   (typescript)
   Thematic catalogue,

HATTING, Carsten E. (compiler)

507   **Piano sonatas in manuscript from the I8th century in Czech collections** (Brno: Colloquium Musica bohemica et europaea, in press)
   Thematic list, 18p. Copy in US NYcg.
        Incipits for all movements of sonatas from the Doksy and
        Kroměříž collections. Includes sonatas not found in the
        catalogues by Wilhelm Fischer (Mann), Wörmann (Alberti),

and Newman (Marcello). Composers represented are Alberti,
Galuppi, Hofman, Marcello, Mann, Monn, and Urban. Tempo
markings, number of measures, and MS sources provided.
(see also Doksy no. 989 and Kroměříz no. 699).

HAYDN, JOSEPH, 1732-1809

508   Thematisches Verzeichniss der sämtlichen Quartetten für 2 Violinen,
      Viola und Violoncello von J. Haydn (Dresden: [n.d.]).

509   Indice tematico/ Delle Sinfonia a grande orchestra/ de Maestro/ Giu-
 ∇   seppe Haydn (I Mc : Noseda M 41-18) 4*l*. (manuscript)
               Incipits for symphonies numbered 1-53 and then lettered A-K.

510   HAYDN, Joseph; ELSSLER, Joseph. [Entwurf Katalog] (D Bds: mus. ms.
 ∇   607) Compiled ca. 1765-1805. 17*l*. (manuscript).
               Prepared mainly by Haydn, whose entries date from ca.
               1765-1805. The remainder is primarily in the hand of
               Joseph Elssler, court copyist of Prince Esterházy (en-
               tries from ca. 1765). Consists of 3 sections: the first,
               begun ca. 1765, is arranged according to genre: sympho-
               nies, divertimenti, baryton works, string trios, operas,
               secular cantatas, concertos, hymns, Te Deum, and piano
               works. The second section (begun in the 1770's), is in
               the hand of Schellinger as well as Haydn, and is a sup-
               plement to the first part, containing mostly symphonies
               as well as a piano trio and several songs. The third
               section (begun ca. 1790), consists only of symphonies.
               A great number of compositions are missing, especially
               works before ca. 1765.

510a --- Facsimile. Jens Peter LARSEN, Drei Haydn Kataloge (København:
      Munksgaard, 1941) 3-36. (see no. 550)

511   Six quartettos for two violins, a tenor and a violoncello, Op. 44
      (i.e. Op. 50) (London: Forster, [1785?]).
         A catalogue of the works of Giuseppe Haydn.
               A full page thematic catalogue, listing 34 "overtures" and
               12 quartets, Op. 33 and 44.

512   [Contract with William Forster, London publisher, signed by Haydn]
 ∇   "I acknowledge to have received seventy pounds... for 20 symphonies,
      sonatas, and other pieces of music composed by me..." 1786 (GB Lbm:
      Eg. 2380. f.12) Full text in H.C. Robbins LANDON, *The collected
      correspondence and London notebooks of Joseph Haydn* (London: Barrie
      & Rockliff, 1959) 53-56.
         "Haydn's subjects"
               Incipits of twenty works. This document, Landon indicates
               (p.55, n.2), was used as evidence against another London
               publisher, Longman and Broderip, who imported Artaria prints
               of the same works; the document shows that Haydn had granted
               Forster "exclusive" rights to the said works.

513   Catalogo/ Del Sinfonien/ Del Sig: Giuseppe Haydn [Katalog Kees]
 ∇   (D Rtt, Sign. J. Haydn 85) Compiled 1790-92. 10*l*. (manuscript).
               A catalogue of 94 symphonies prepared for the Viennese
               musical amateur Franz Bernhard Ritter von Kees by the same
               (unidentified) scribe who wrote entries in the last part of

the Entwurf Katalog. It has not been determined whether or
not Haydn actually supplied material for the catalogue.

513a --- Facsimile. Jens Peter LARSEN, Drei Haydn Kataloge (København:
Munksgaard, 1941) 39-49. (see no. 550)

514   [Agreement with Johann Peter Salomon, London impressario, signed by
▽   Haydn] "...Salomon shall have exclusive rights pertaining to the
following specific Overtures..." 1795 (GB Lbm: Add. 38071. f.5) Full
text in H.C. Robbins LANDON, *The collected correspondence and London
notebooks of Joseph Haydn* (London: Barrie & Rockliff, 1959) 146.
        Incipits for the first six London symphonies, Nos. 93-98.

515   Collection complette des quatuors d'Haydn [dédié au Premier Consul
Bonaparte] (Paris: Pleyel, 1802)
        Catalogue thématique de tous les quatuors d'Haydn, avoués par
        l'Auteur [et classés selon l'ordre dans lequel ils ont parus],
        1 leaf before page 1, 1st violin part.
            There were 2 editions and 2 issues of the first edition, all
            without dates. First edition, first issue, contains incipits
            for 80 quartets up to Op. 76, no. 6. Second issue (c. 1805)
            has 2 more quartets listed. Third issue probably 1810.

515a --- Nouvelle edition. (Paris: Pleyel & Fils ainé, [1820?])
            Incipits for 83 quartets, including the unfinished Op. 103.

515b --- A complete collection of Haydn's quartets, being a corrected
copy of the Paris edition (London: Collard & Collard, [1853?]).

            Reference: Otto Erich DEUTSCH, Theme and variations with
            bibliographical notes on Pleyel's Haydn editions, *MR* XII
            (1951) 63-71.

516   [Haydn, J. and] ELSSLER, Johann. Verzeichniss aller derjenigen
▽   Compositionen, welche ich mich beyläufig erinnere von meinem I8ten
bis in das 73te Jahr verfertiget zu haben (Budapest: Fürstl. Ester-
házysches Archiv) Compiled in 1805. 132*l.* (manuscript).
            An important catalogue of Haydn's works though not complete
            (a number of omissions of works before ca. 1765 and after
            the 1770's). Single and double staff incipits for 118 sym-
            phonies, 125 baryton trios, 38 baryton compositions, 20 di-
            vertimenti, 2 marches, 21 string trios, 3 flute sonatas,
            6 duets for violin and viola, 11 concertos (various instru-
            ments), 14 Masses, 12 vocal works, 4 choral works, 83 string
            quartets, 1 organ concerto, 3 clavier concertos, 18 cembalo
            divertimenti, 48 trios, sonatas etc. for pianoforte, 43 Lieder,
            40 canons, and incipits (some missing) for various vocal works,
            365 Scottish Lieder. Contains a few works of questionable
            authenticity.

516a --- Facsimile. Jens Peter LARSEN, Drei Haydn Kataloge (København:
Munksgaard, 1941) 53-119. (see no. 550).
            Contains all but the "Schottische Lieder", p. 68-132.

516b --- Manuscript copies of the "Schottische Lieder" portion of the
1805 catalogue include one formerly beloging to Köchel now in
A Wgm (Film A Wn: Photogrammearchiv nr. 705) and a second copy
formerly belonging to Otto Jahn now in D Mbs: Mus. ms. 2991.

517   Quatuors pour deux violons, alto et basse, mis en collection
(Paris: Sieber, [c. 1806]).
            Table thématique [des quatuors].

518   Collection complette des quatuors (Vienna: Artaria, [c.1810]).
      Catalogue thématique de la collection des quatuors de Jos.
      Haydn disposes par ordre chronologique, 1st violin part, 1 leaf
      before page 1.
            Incipits for 58 quartets.

519   Oeuvres choisies (Paris: Janet et Cotelle, [1815?])
      Catalogue thématique de tous les quatuors, 1st violin part, 1
      leaf before page 1.
            Incipits for 56 quartets.

520   Verzeichniss der Symphonien von Jos. Haydn welche bei Carl Zulehner
▽   in Mainz zu haben sind [1820] 13p. Copy in B Bc.(manuscript)
            136 incipits arranged by key, including duplications, cassa-
            tions, and divertimenti.

521   FUCHS, Aloys. Thematischer-Spezial-Catalog über Joseph Hayd's [sic]
▽   Opern und Cantaten. 1830 (D Bds: Mus. ms. theor. K. 614)(manuscript)
            Twelve 4° volumes bound together. The ordering of incipits
            follows that of the title, i.e. operas followed by the can-
            tatas.

522   FUCHS, Aloys. Thematisches Verzeichnis der sämtlichen Kompositionen
▽   von Joseph Haydn zusammengestellt von Alois Fuchs 1839 (D Bds: Mus.
      ms. theor. K. 180) Copy in D Mbs: Mus. Mss. 6367.(manuscript)

522 a --- Facsimile. Richard SCHAAL, Quellen-Kataloge zur Musikgeschichte
      (Wilhelmshaven: Heinrichshofen's Verlag, 1968) ix, 204p.

522 b --- Thematisches Verzeichnis......von Alois Fuchs. Wien, 1840. (D Bds:
▽   Mus. ms. theor. K. 606).(manuscript)
            A revision of the 1839 catalogue.

523   Collection complète des sonates d'Haydn, pour piano (Paris: Mme.
      Vve. Launer, [1840]) Cahiers 1-7.
      [Thematic catalogue of the sonatas].
            Each cahier includes "table thématique" of double staff
            incipits for sonatas in that cahier.

524   Partition des quatuors (Berlin: Trautwein, [1844]).
      Deux tables thématiques et chronologiques des quatuors.

525   FUCHS, Aloys. Thematische Verzeichniss der sämmtlichen Kirchen-
▽   Compositionen von J. Haydn für meinem freund Raymond zusammen gestelt
      am 14ten Juli 1850 von A. Fuchs (D Bds: Mus. ms. K. 612). Micro-
      film copy in US NYcg. (manuscript)

526   Les Quatuors (Thematic catalogue advertised in the Artaria catalogue
      of 29 Nov. 1856)

            Reference: Alexander WEINMANN, Vollständiges Verlagsver-
            zeichnis Artaria & Comp. (Wien: L. Krenn, 1952) 154.

527   WEBER, Carl Maria von. Mass in E^b (London: J.A. Novello, 1858)
      Thematic catalogue of Haydn's celebrated masses, nos. I-XVI,
      showing the commencement of the five principal movements in
      each, last page.

528   [Thematisches Verzeichniss der sämmtlichen Quartetten für 2 Violinen,
      Viola und Violoncelle von Joseph Haydn]. Neue Ausgabe in 25 Heften

revidirt von Hub: RIES Königl: Concertmeister (Berlin: Bote und Bock,
[1861]) 2l.
> Incipits (1st vln.) for the complete 83 string quartets
ordered by their appearance as published by Bote and Bock.

529 **Katalog Berlin (A. Fuchs?)** (D Bds) 19p. Compiled ca. 1865.
▽ This catalogue has no title page, and is not by Fuchs.
It lists autographs (nos. 1-4) and copies (nos. 1-52)
of Haydn's works. The MS is probably by Franz Espagne.

530 **Katalog Berlin (O. Jahn?)** (D Bds: Mus. ms. theor. K. 616) 38p.
▽ Also without title page, this catalogue is not by Jahn.
Incipits for 49 symphonies and chamber works of Haydn.

531 P[OHL], [Karl Ferdinand]. **Thematischer Catalog der Autografe Haydn's**
▽ **im fürstl. Musik-Archiv zu Eisenstadt.** Die ganze Sammlung neu
geordnet von [Karl Ferdinand] P[OHL] (1867) 11p. Copies of autograph MS in US LC, US NYPL.(manuscript)
Incipits of a few compositions in each of the following
genres: arias, lieder, choral music, masses, symphonies,
military music, and keyboard music.

532 POHL, Karl Ferdinand. **J. Haydn** (Berlin: Sasso, 1875-1927; Leipzig:
Breitkopf & Härtel, 1882) 3v.
Chronologisch-thematisches Verzeichniss der in den Jahren 1766-
1790 entstandenen Tonwerke J. Haydn's, v. II, 14p. at end.
Indexes compositions published under Haydn's name (including
spurious works). Incipits for 183 symphonies.

533 POHL, Karl Ferdinand. **[Thematic catalogue]** (A Wgm) ca. 1000 index
▽ cards (manuscript)
A complete thematic catalogue arranged by genre with bibliographical information.

534 POHL, Karl Ferdinand. **[Thematic catalogue of Haydn materials in**
▽ **the Breitkopf Archives]** (manuscript)
Manuscript catalogue destroyed during the Second World War.
According to the Beilage of Hoboken's **Joseph Haydn**, v.II
(1971) p. xv, there is a MS thematic catalogue from the ·
collection of Pohl entitled: "copirt Juli 872. Nach Haydn's
eigenhändiger Angabe, nicht chronologisch geordnet."

535 **Collection de quatuors pour 2 violons, viola et violoncelle.** Édition
nouvelle (Leipzig: C.F. Peters, [1868]) 4v.
A finding list with incipits for quartet volume.

536 GUARINONI, Eugenio de'. **Indice generale dell' Archivio musicale**
Noseda (Milano: Reggiani, 1897) 419p.
[Thematic list], 162-67.
Incipits for less than half of the early symphonies of Haydn.

537 MANDYCZEWSKI, Eusebius. **[Thematic catalogue]** (A Wgm) (manuscript).
▽ Compiled ca. 1900.

538 MANDYCZEWSKI, Eusebius. **Werke.** Erste kritische durchgesehene Gesamtausgabe, Ser. I, Bd. I (Leipzig: Breitkopf & Härtel, [1907])
[Thematisches Verzeichnis von Eusebius MANDYCZEWSKI], iv-vii.
Incipits for 104 symphonies, 16 overtures, 38 spurious and
36 doubtful works, arranged in chronological order, with

composition dates and numbering in the Haydn, Pohl, Fuchs,
Wotquenne, and Zulehner catalogues. "M" numbers still in
use for the symphonies, and correspond directly to the Hoboken
numbers for Part I.

538a --- Revised by Helmut SCHULTZ. **Werke**, Ser. I, Bd. 4 (1933) 4p.
following p. xii.

539   WOTQUENNE, Alfred. **Catalogue de la Bibliothèque du Conservatoire
Royal de Musique de Bruxelles** (Bruxelles: Coosemans, 1898-1912)
4v.
[Thematic list], v. 2 (1902), 7p. laid in between 464-65.
Incipits for 149 Haydn symphonies. For duplicate themes,
only the key and meter are given with a reference to the
number of the full incipits. Incipits for 15 doubtful
works appear at end.

540   **Thematisches Verzeichniss der Sinfonien von J. Haijdn** [sic] (A Wmi:
▽   c 3617) 27ℓ. Compiled early 20th century. (manuscript)
107 incipits of symphonies published by Trautwein, Simrock,
and André, plus a chronological ordering of the symphonies
that appear in the Breitkopf Catalogo 1766-1780.

541   MOSER, Andreas; DECHERT, Hugo. **30 Berühmte Quartette für 2 Violinen,
Viola und Violoncello** (Leipzig: C.F. Peters, [1918]) 8v. bound in 4.
[Thematic index of 30 string quartets].
Four-part incipits of each quartet in score at beginning of
each volume.

542   PÄSLER, Karl. **Werke**. Erste kritische durchgesehene Gesamtausgabe,
Ser. XIV, Bd. 3 (Leipzig: Breitkopf & Härtel, [1918])
[Thematisches Verzeichnis der Klaviersonaten von J. Haydn], p.
154.
Incipits of sonatas no. 1-52. Forward contains incipits for
8 lost sonatas.

543   Joseph Haydn, *Grove's dictionary of music and musicians,* 3rd ed.
(1927), v. II, p. 585-589.
[Thematic list of IO4 authentic symphonies].
Incipits arranged in chronological order, with indications
as to the catalogues in which they are located. Based on
1907 edition of E. MANDYCZEWSKI, and the (London) Philharmonic
Society catalogue of 1828, with MS additions in 1831.

544   SCOTT, Marion. **Haydn's "83": a study of the complete editions,** *MLetters* XI (1930) 216-19.
[Thematic index of the string quartets].
Incipits of quartets arranged by opus number. Comparison of
a large number of quartet editions.

545   LACHMANN, Robert. **Die Haydn-Autographen der Staatsbibliothek zu
Berlin,** *ZfMW* XIV (1932) 289-98.
Includes 66 entries of which only 9 have incipits.

546   **Jos. Haydn: Werkverzeichnis** (Leipzig: Breitkopf & Härtel, ca.1933)
Partially thematic; includes themes for 37 symphonies, 15
string quartets, 31 piano trios in the catalogue of the
Breitkopf Edition.

547   HINDERBERGER, Adolf. Die Motivik in Haydns Streichquartetten
        (PhD diss.: Bern , 1933; Turbenthal: Robert Furrers Erben, 1935)
        87p.
                A detailed study of theme formation in the Haydn quartets,
                with 169 themes through the text.

548   LARSEN, Jens Peter. Haydn und das kleine Quartbuch [and the famous
□   ensuing interchange with Adolph SANDBERGER], *ActaMusicol*, VII/3
        (1935) 111-23; VIII/1-2 (1936) 18-29; VIII/3-4 (1936) 139-54; IX/1-2
        (1937) 31-41.

549   LARSEN, Jens Peter. Die Haydn Überlieferung (København, 1939)
□   182-85.
                Discussion of importance of the *Breitkopf Thematic Catalogue*
                and the *Gerber Haydn Verzeichniss*, which had been based in
                part on the thematic catalogue sent him (in 1792?) by West-
                phal, the Hamburg music dealer, made up of incipits of all
                the Haydn printed works that had passed through his shop.
                (see GERBER, *Neues Lexicon* II, 560)

550   LARSEN, Jens P. Drei Haydn Kataloge in Faksimile; mit Einleitung
        und ergänzenden Themenverzeichnissen (København: Munksgaard, 1941)
        138p.
                Anhang, 122-28.
                To supplement the 3 facsimiles (see nos. 510, 513, and 516),
                Larsen has prepared a catalogue of works attributed to Haydn,
                but listed in neither the Elssler, Entwurf, or Kees cata-
                logues, nor in Pohl's biography of Haydn (vol. II), nor in
                the complete edition (Mandyczewski, et al.). Material cited
                is drawn form ca. 50 European archives. No attempt is made
                to substantiate authenticity, but works are ranked accord-
                ing to the number of confirming sources or catalogue refer-
                ences attributing them to Haydn. The catalogue is organized
                by genre, and within genre, by key. MS sources, printed
                works, and/or catalogue references for each listing are cited
                in an inventory of sources.(p. 136-38).

551   LARSEN, Jens Peter; LANDON, H.C. Robbins. Joseph Haydn: the complete
        works, ser. 1, v. 9 (Boston: Haydn Society Inc., 1950) xii, 343p.,
        Supplement 2*l*.
                [Thematic catalogue of] the symphonies, x-xii.
                Incipits of 104 symphonies in chronological order, with
                references to sources, MSS, and publishers.

552   LARSEN, Jens Peter; LANDON, H.C. Robbins. Joseph Haydn; the complete
        works, ser. 23, v. 1 (Boston: Haydn Society Inc., 1951)
                [Thematic catalogue of] the masses, x.
                Incipits of 12 Kyries and 2 lost Masses.

553   GEIRINGER, Karl. A thematic catalogue of Haydn's settings of folk-
        songs from the British Isles (Superior, Wisc.: Research Microfilm
        Publishers, 1953) xxxiiip., 438 cards. Copies deposited in US Wc:
        Microfilm/ML 19 and GB Lbm).
                Incipits for Haydn's 445 British folksongs.

                Reviews: Vincent DUCKLES, *Notes* XIII (Sept 1956) 650-52.

                Reference: Karl GEIRINGER, Haydn and the folksong of the Bri-
                tish Isles, *MQ* XXXV/2 (Apr 1949) 179-208.

554   LANDON, H.C. Robbins. **The symphonies of Joseph Haydn** (London: Uni-
      versal Edition, 1955) 862p.
            Thematic catalogue, 605-823.
                  Appendix I, p. 605-777, contains incipits of 107 authentic
                  symphonies, with commentary. Appendix II, p. 795-823, contains
                  incipits of 134 doubtful and spurious symphonies attributed
                  to Haydn, with names of correct or probable composers where
                  these are known.Discussion of early thematic catalogues,p.1-26.

                  Reviews: G.A., *Monthly Musical Record* LXXXVI (May-June 1956)
                  110-11; Ronald EYER, *MAmerica* LXXVI (Sept 1956) 16-17; H.H.,
                  MOpinion LXXIX 'Feb 1956)281; Rosemary HUGHES, *MLetters* XXXVII
                  (April 1956) 173-75, *MTimes* XCVII (June 1956) 296-97; Paul
                  Henry LANG, *MQ* XLIII (July 1957) 411-15; Jan LA RUE, *Notes*
                  XIV (Dec 1960) 103-04; Donald MITCHELL, *Tempo* (Spring 1956)
                  32-33; C.G. Stellan MÖRNER, *SvenskTMf* XLII (1960) 148-50;
                  Harold SCHONBERG, *MCourier* CLIV (Dec 1956) 39; Geoffrey
                  SHARP, *MReview* XVII (May 1956) 162-63; Howard TAUBMAN, *New
                  York Times* CV/Sect 2 (June 17 1956); Helmut WIRTH, *Mf* IX/4
                  (1956) 471-73.

554a --- Supplement. (London: Barrie & Rockliff; New York: Macmillan,
      1961) 64p.
                  Contains a few incipits from Czech and other sources on p.
                  28, 30, and 60.

                  Reviews: Strad LXXII (July:1961) 101; H.H., *MOpinion* LXXXIV
                  (1961) 679; Andrew PORTER, *MTimes* CII (June 1961) 362; J.A.
                  WESTRUP, *MLetters* XLII/3 (1961) 274-75.

555   HOBOKEN, Anthony van. **Joseph Haydn. Thematisch-bibliographisches
✡   Werkeverzeichnis. I. Instrumentalwerke** (Mainz: B. Schott's Söhne,
      1957) xxi, 848, 20p.(for Vol. II see no. 555d)
                  Incipits for all movements of Haydn's authentic and spurious
                  instrumental works, arranged according to genre and perform-
                  ing medium, with information on names, nicknames, instrumen-
                  tation, autographs, early MS copies, and prints issued in
                  Haydn's lifetime. Compositions are assigned cardinal numbers
                  which are occasionally preceded by the key of the composition.

                  Reviews: ActaMusicol XXIX (Apr-Sept 1957) 106-07; *Notes* XIV
                  (1957) 185; *Das Musikleben* IV (May 1957) 137-38; Otto Erich
                  DEUTSCH, *MR* XVIII (Nov 1957) 330-36; Karl GEIRINGER, *NeueZM*
                  CXVIII (Dec 1957) 693, *Notes* XIV (1957); Leopold NOWAK,*Öster-
                  reichischeMz* XII (Dec 1957) 489-90; Wouter PAAP, *MensMelodie*
                  XII (May 1957) 145-56; Otto RIEMER, *Musica* XI (Dec 1957) 768;
                  RassegnaMCurci XXVIII (Mar 1958) 634; M.B., *RBelgeMusicol* XII
                  (1958) 92-94; J.H. DAVIES, *MTimes* 99 (Feb 1958) 80-81; Rose-
                  mary HUGHES, *MLetters* XXXIX (Apr 1958) 186-90; Willi KAHL,
                  Mf XI/4 (1958) 525-29; *ÖsterreichischeMz* XIV (May-June 1959)
                  202-05.

555a --- **Der erste thematische Haydn-Katalog,** *Das Musikleben* V/4 (May 1951
☐   137-38.

555b --- **The first thematic catalog of Haydn's works,** *Notes* IX/2 (Mar 1952)
☐   226-27.
                  Articles written before the actual publication of the author's
                  catalogue describing the circumstances of its compilation
                  and its organization.

555c   --- Die Entstehung des "Thematischen Verzeichnisses der Werke von
☐   Joseph Haydn", *ActaMusicol* XXIX (1957) 106-08.

555d   --- Joseph Haydn. Thematisch-bibliographisches Werkverzeichnis. II.
       Vokalwerke   (Mainz: B. Schott's Söhne, 1971) 602p.
            Follows same organizational plan as Vol. I (no. 555).

555e   --- The first thematic catalogue of Haydn's works- volume II, *Notes*
☐   28/2 (Dec 1971) 209-11.

556   WHITE, Sarah Quillan. The solo songs of Joseph Haydn: A stylistic
▽   study (MA diss., Musicology: U. of North Carolina, 1958) 94, 11p.
            Supplement, 1-11.(typescript)
               Incipits include text for the songs.

557   VÉCSEY, Jenö. Haydn's Werke in der Musiksammlung der Nationalbiblio-
       thek Széchényi in Budapest (Budapest: Verlag der Ungarischen Akademie
       der Wissenschaften,1959) 168p.   English edition trans. by Sándor
       ORSZÁGH, 1960.
               Contains a few incipits along with other material on contem-
               porary MS copies.

558   IDASZAK, Danuta. Eine Haydn-Sinfonie in Gnesen?, *Mf* XX/3 (1967)
       287-88.
               Concludes with inventory of incipits of all movements. [The
               symphony, however, has been shown to be <u>not</u> by Haydn]

559   BECKER-GLAUCH, Irmgard. Neue Forschungen zu Haydns Kirchenmusik,
       HaydnStud II/3 (May 1970) 167-241.
               Incipits for sacred works of the Viennese period up to 1756;
               sacred contrafacta based on early works written for use at
               the Esterházy court in Eisenstadt.

560   DEARLING, Robert (Dunstable, Bedfordshire). [Thematic catalogue
▽   of keyboard sonatas] Index cards (manuscript).
               Cross-indexed thematic catalogue (Breitkopf & Härtel, Haydn
               Society, Hoboken, Peters 1, Peters 2, Augener, and Christa
               Landon editions).

HAYDN, MICHAEL, 1737-1806

561   LANG, Nikolaus, copyist. [Thematic catalogue]   (D Mbs: Mus. ms.
▽   2988) 38p. (manuscript)
               "Incipits for 363 works, plus an index of fifty-four titles
               for canons and part-songs. Themes are cited in order: sacred
               vocal compositions (Graduals for fixed feasts, Graduals for
               movable feasts, Offertories, Latin Masses and Requiems,
               Hymns, Litanies, Antiphons, Responses, and so forth); secular
               vocal compositions (operas, oratorios, arias, and Latin *ap-
               plauses*); and instrumental works (dance suites, symphonies,
               serenades, divertimenti, marches, etc.). There follow several
               themes for German 'Masses' and other pieces for the vernacular
               liturgy. A set of interleaves, added by Joseph Julius Maier
               cross-reference the entries in this manuscript to the Michael
               Haydn holdings of the Bavarian State Library." (Charles Sher-
               man)

561a   --- [Thematic catalogue] (D Mbs: Mus. ms. 2989) (manuscript)
▽   Although less complete, duplicates the arrangement of the
            previous entry.

561   --- Kathalock von den Michael Haÿdnischen Werken (D Mbs: Mus. ms.
▽   3765) (manuscript)
             Short catalogue citing themes for twenty Latin Masses.

561c   --- [Thematic catalogue] (D Mbs: Mus. ms. 3767) (manuscript)
▽   A short catalogue citing a number of Latin Masses, Requiems,
             and Offertories, but showing themes for three works only.

561d   --- [Thematic catalogue] (Benedictine Abbey of Michaelbeuern, Salz-
▽   burg province, Austria) 58p. (manuscript)
             Incipits for 458 works in the same order as D Mbs: Mus. ms.
             2988 (no. 561) except that Latin Masses and Requiems are
             cited first.

561e   --- [Thematic catalogue] (D Mbs: Mus. ms. 2990) (manuscript)
▽   Exact duplicate of D Mbs: Mus. ms. 3765 (no. 561b).

561f   --- [Thematic catalogue] (A Wn: MS 2103) (manuscript)
▽   A short thematic list of works drawn up to accompany a letter
             by Magdalena Haydn, dated November 25, 1808, offering certain
             of her husband's compositions for sale to Carl Zelter in Ber-
             lin.

562   Chataloc von dennen Michael Haydnischen Werke [sic]. (D Mbs: Mus.
▽   ms. 3766) 19p.(manuscript)
             Incipits for 20 Masses, 109 Graduals and Offertories,
             1 Pange Lingua, 3 Te Deums, 10 Litanies, 1 Vesper, 6
             Salve Reginas, 1 Ave Regina, 1 Alma Redemptoris, 1 Regina
             Coeli, 1 Sub Tuum, and 3 Responsories.

562.1 Catalogus/ omnium operum ecclesiasticor.   / authore/ Michaele
▽   Haydn   (A KN; III^D 435) 41p. (manuscript)
             Incipits for the following works dated between 1758 and 1806:
             Graduals (118), Offertories (70), Masses (35), Te Deums (5),
             Litanies (8) and smaller works.

563   FUCHS, Aloys. Thematisches Verzeichniss über sämmtliche-Compositionen
▽   von Michael Haydn (D Bds: Mus. ms. theor. K. 622) [ii, 88p.]
       Microfilm copy in US NYcg. (manuscript)
             Double staff incipits, organized by genre. Composition
             dates included.

564   Thematisches Verzeichniss derjenigen Compositionen von Michael Haydn,
▽   welche sich unter den Musik-Manuscripten der kgl. Hof & Staatsbiblio-
       thek in München befinden (D Bds: HB VII, Mus. ms. theor. K. 624)
       [28p.] Microfilm copy in US NYcg. (manuscript)
             Incipits for both secular and sacred vocal works and instru-
             mental works.

565   Johann Michael Haydn's Kirchen-Compositionen welche sich in H. schrift
▽   im Stifte St. Peter in Salzburg befinden (D Bds: HB VII, Mus. ms.
       theor. K. 626) [23p] Microfilm copy in US NYcg. (manuscript)
             Incipits for sacred vocal works arranged by genre with dates.

566   STRNISCHTIE, Gerlaci [Gerlak]. Themata/ Michael Haydn'scher Messen
▽   etc/ nebst Anzeige einiger unter...Kompositionen von eb... selben.
       (Nach einigen aus Salzburg mitgeschribten Blättern kopiert.) (CS:

Strahof Archivum Musicum)   Compiled 1784-1855.(manuscript)
Each page is divided in half and includes name of work, number and/or title, sometimes the date, and the incipit with a
tempo marking. Contains 26 Masses, 2 Te Deums, 1 Gradual,
and 3 Litanies. Cites additional titles without incipits.

567 Joh. Michael Haydn's Kirchencompositionen im Stifte St. Peter/ zu
▽   Salzburg (US LC: ML 134/ -H28A2/case) 16 unnumbered pages. Compiled
early 19th c. (manuscript).
Incipits for Introitus 1, Missa 107, Sequentia 67, Post-
communiones et Communio 4, Responsoria-Passiones-Miserere etc.
22, Vespere 11, Te Deum 18, Lytania 10, misc. 49. Altogether
289 works are inventoried.

568 RETTENSTEINER, Werigand. Catalog/ über/ die bekannten Compositionen
▽   des Herrn/ Michael Haÿdn/ des grossen, einzigen, und unnachahmlichen
Meisters/ im Kirchenstile./ zusammengesezt und niedergeschrieben/
von dessen erklärten Freunde Werigand Rettensteiner/ 1814 (Salzburg:
Benedictine Abbey of Michaelbeuern) (manuscript).

569 PERGER, L.H. Instrumentalwerke, *DTÖ* Jahrg. 14/2   (Wien: Artaria,
✰   1907)
Thematisches Verzeichnis der Instrumentalwerke von M. Haydn,
xv-xxxix.
Incipits for 136 instrumental works.

570 KLAFSKY, Anton. Kirchenwerke , *DTÖ* Jahrg. 32/1 (Wien: Universal,
1925)
Thematischer Katalog der Kirchenmusikwerke von M. Haydn, v-xiii.
Incipits of compositions arranged by Latin and German text
and genre, with dates, sources, and voice and instrument
indications.

570a --- Reprint (Graz: Akademische Druck-u. Verlagsanstalt, 1960).

570b --- PAULY, Reinhard G. Some recently discovered Michael Haydn manuscripts, *JAmerMusicolSoc* X/2 (Summer 1957) 97-103.
Addenda and corrigenda to Klafsky's thematic catalogue of Michael
Haydn's sacred vocal works (*DTÖ* 62), Appendix.
93 additions and corrections, chiefly indicating location of
autograph scores, with 6 incipits.

571 HESS, Reimund. Serenade, Cassation, Notturno und Divertimento bei
Michael Haydn (PhD diss.: Mainz, 1963) 214,99p. (Fotodruck)(typescript)
Ergänzungen zu Pergers thematischem Katalog, 200-07.
36 incipits for all movements of 8 divertimentos and 3 noc-
turnes not found in Perger's thematic catalogue (see no.569)

572 SHERMAN, Charles Henry. The masses of Johann Michael Haydn; a
critical survey of sources (PhD diss.: U. of Michigan, 1967) 246p.
Univ. Micro. 68-7724.(typescript)
[Thematic catalogue of the masses].
Corrects inaccuracies in Klafsky's 1925 catalogue. Cites
39 autograph copies of 29 masses and over 1000 MS copies.

HECK, JOHANN, b. 1740-?

573 KRABBE, Wilhelm. Das Liederbuch des Johann Heck, *AfMW* IV (1922)
420-38.
Partially thematic index, with text.

HECKMANN, Harald

574   Neue Methoden der Verarbeitung musikalischer Daten, *Mf* XVII/4 (1964)
☐   381-83.

575   Elektronische Datenverarbeitung in der Musikwissenschaft (Regens-
☐   burg: Gustav Bosse Verlag, [1967]).

HEINICHEN, JOHANN DAVID, 1683-1729

576   SEIBEL, Gustav A. Das Leben des königl. polnischen und kurfürstl.
      sächs. Hofkapellmeisters J.D. Heinichen. Nebst chronologischem
      Verzeichnis seiner Opern... und thematischem Katalog seiner Werke.
      (PhD diss.: Leipzig, 1912; Breitkopf & Härtel, 1913) vii,102p.
          Thematisches Verzeichnis der Werke, 39-96.
              Single and double staff incipits arranged by genre. Gives
              source, instrumentation, and text underlay.

577   HAUSSWALD, Günter. Johann David Heinichens Instrumentalwerke
      (PhD diss.: Dresden; Wolfenbüttel, Berlin: Kallmeyer, 1937)172p.
          Werkverzeichnis, 146-68.
              Incipits with library sources and movement titles for 24
              concertos, 2 suites, 21 sonatas, 5 symphonies, plus 4
              doubtful works, 2 fragments, and 1 printed work.

HEINITZ, Wilhelm

578   Eine lexikalische Ordnung für die vergleichende Betrachtung von Melo-
☐   dien, *AMw* III (1921) 247-54.
              An early suggestion that institutions share, through a peri-
              odical, their card files of melodies, using a universally
              recognizable key to notation of intervals for cataloguing
              and comparison. Objects to systems offered by Koller and
              Krohn *(q.v.)*.

HELL, Helmut (compiler)

579   Die Neapolitanische Opernsinfonie in der ersten Hälfte des I8.
      Jahrhunderts. Porpora- Vinci- Pergolesi- Leo- Jommelli, *Münchner
      Veröffentlichungen zur Musikgeschichte* Bd. 19 (Tutzing: Schneider,
      1971) 623p.
          Anhang. Incipitkatalog, [503]-606.
              Incipits for all sections of 220 opera overtures, symphonies
              and oratorios by N. Porpora, L. Vinci, G.B. Pergolesi, L.
              Leo, and N. Jommelli.

HERBECK, JOHANN FRANZ, 1831-1877

580   HERBECK, Ludwig. Johann Franz Herbeck: ein Lebensbild (Wien:
      Gutmann, 1885) 417p., Anhang 172p.
          Thematisches Verzeichnis der Compositionen, Anhang, 117-62.
              Incipits by his son for all movements of instrumental and
              vocal music with dates of composition and performance.

HERDRINGEN, Bibliotheca Fürstenbergiana: Sonsfeld

581   Des Herren General Major Frey Herrn von SonsFeldt Musicalisches
▽   **Cathallogium** (D Schloss Herdringen: Fü 3720a) Compiled ca. 1728, en-
      tries added through 1760. (manuscript)
                    Catalogue of the music collection of the Prussian general
                    Friedrich Otto von Wittenhorst-Sonsfeld (1678-1755). In
                    1755 the collection, part of which is extant, was bequeathed
                    to Freiherr von Fürstenberg-Herdringen. For a long period
                    it was located in the Erzbischöflichen Akademischen Biblio-
                    thek Paderborn. Since 1970 it has been housed in the collec-
                    tion of the Bibliotheca Fürstenbergiana at Schloss Herdringen.
                    The catalogue contains 365 works with incipits for over 130
                    concertos in addition to numerous sonatas, overtures, and some
                    symphonies. Composers include: Abel, Albinoni, Bach, Bau-
                    stetter,F. Benda, Biber, Bigaglia, Blum, S. Bodino, Bonporti,
                    J.J. Brand, Califano, Capelli, Croeber, Dümler, Emmerling,
                    J.F. Fasch, Feresch, Chr. Förster, Freytag, Galli, Galuppi,
                    Geraso, Graun, Händel, J.A. Hasse, Heinichen, Hencke, E.C.
                    Hesse, F. Hunt, E. Kegel, Krug, J.G. Linike, A. Lotti, Majo,
                    B. Marcello, Martini, Mattheson, Meyer, D. de Micco, Muffat,
                    Pepusch, J. Pfeiffer, Pichler, Plavert, Quantz, Rätzel, Reindl-
                    off, Richter, Rick, Riehmann, C.F. Rolle, Scher, Schiassi,
                    Schickhard, Solnitz, Stölzel, Streller, A.R. Stricker, Stulick,
                    Suhl, Syareck, S.P. Sydow, Telemann, Teloni, Tessarini, Trolle,
                    Vivaldi, J.S. Weiss, H. Weisse, Werner.

581a --- DOMP, Joachim,Studien zur Geschichte der Musik an westfälischen
☐   Adelshöfen im XVIII. Jahrhundert, *Freiburger Studien z. Musikwissen-*
      schaft I (Regensburg: Pustet, 1934) 122-31.

581b --- KÜNTZEL, Gottfried. Die Instrumentalkonzerte von Johann Fried-
☐   rich Fasch (Tutzing: Hans Schneider, 1965) (see no. 370)

HERZOGENBURG, Austria. Chorherrenstift Bibliothek und Musikarchive: [I]

582   Catalogus/ Selectiorum Musicalium/ Chori Ducumburgensis/ Quibus acce-
▽   dunt/ Instrumenta musica/ Diarium Cantus Figuratio/ Aliarumq functi-
      onum musicae/ totus anno/ e/ Index Generalis Catalogi/ Conscripti An-
      no 1751 (A H) 207*l*. (manuscript). Microfilm copies in A Wn:9026;
      US NYcg. [The 1751 date indicates when the catalogue was begun.]
                    Organ (bass clef) incipits for 1697 sacred vocal works, or-
                    ganized by genre, with instrumentation for each entry. Tran-
                    scripts of this catalogue were made in the later 18th and
                    early 19th centuries; they are also located at the abbey.
                    Composers include the following: Albrechtsberger, Altovad,
                    Bernardo d'Aprile, Arbesser, Aufschnaiter (Aufschnaitter,
                    Auffschnaitter, Affschnaiter), Aumann (Aumon, Aumonn, Franc.
                    Aumonn), Baumgartner (Paumbgartner, Alberto Baumgartner, Al-
                    berto Paumgartner), Baumonn (Baumon, Paumann, Paumon, Pau-
                    monn) [Paumann], Pietro Beretto, Bergolesi [Pergolesi], Ber-
                    nasconi, Bertali, Domino Bertali, Beyer, Ingatio Beyer, Joan.
                    Ignatio Beyer, Bichler [Pichler], Boog, Joa. Boog, Bonno (Bo-
                    no), Boscher, Brioschi, Brixi (Prixi), Bruneder, Caldara (An-
                    tonio, Anton., Ant., Caldara), Francesco Campeggi, Candus,
                    Carl, Carlman, Cherzelli (Cherzel, Cherzell), Compos, Conti

Francesco Conti, Corneli, Cunath, David, Ditters, Donberger (Georg, Giorgi, Giorg, Giorgio Donberger, Gerogio Donberg, Joseph Donberger), Domberger, Draghi, Ehrenhard (Ehrenhard, Ernhardt, Erenhardt, Erhardt), Ender, Era, Ertl (Franc. Ant. Ertl), Fago, Fardini, Fauner, Fernanda, Finckh [Finck] (Xaviero Finckh, Ferd. Finckh, Xaveri Finck), Fiorilli (Fiorilo), Carlo Fodi Roma, Freytag, Frischauff, Fritz, Ant. Fruemann, Fux (Jos. Fux), Galuppi, Gäsmann [Gassmann] (Geismann), Gottwald (Gottwaldt), Graff (Franc. Graff), Grasel (Adam Grasel, Adam Grasl, Adamo Grasse), Graun, Pietro Grua, Math. Grudeli, Gsur, Tobia Gsur, Hasse (Hässe), Haydn (Hayden, Heyden, Guisepp Hayden) Michael Hayden (Mich. Haydn), Hengsperger, Hoffmann (Hoffman, Leop. Hoffmann), Holzbauer (Holzbaur, Holapaur, Holtzbaur), Höndl [Händel?], Ildefonso, Ivanschitz, Jacomelli, Jomell, P.Jos.Ord.S. Aug. (Josep August Disc.), Kaiser, Rob. Kimmerling, Klimma, Kohaut (Kohauth), Körzl (Körzel), Krottendorfer (Giuseppo Krottendorffer, Kottendorffer), Lamberth, Lampugnani, Lapis, Laube, Legrenzi, Liebl (Carl Liebl, Carlo Liebl, Carlo Frid. Liebl, Libl), Magschitz, Mahaut, Maria, Mayr, Melzer, Molitor (Georg, Giorgio Molitor, Joan. Molitor, Joan. Georg Molitor), Monn, Firmino Mörger, Müller (Myller), Naumann, Neckh (Antoni Neckh), Novotni (Novottni), Orsler, Öttl (Oettl), Ottone, Pachschmidt, Palestino, Pampani, Pauli, Paumann (Paumon, Paumonn, Baumonn, Baumon), Perckhamer (Perghamber, Car. Perckhamer), Perghof, Giov. Batta Pergolesi (Bergolesi), Pernasconi [Bernasconi], Piccino, Pichler (Bichler, Püchler), Pfeiffer, Porsille, Poscher, Pratti, Prazner, Predieri (Praedieri), Preglauer, Prentner (Josepho,Jos. Prentner), Prixi (Brixi), Pruneder (Franc. Pruneder), Prustman (Prustmann, Prustmon, Ignati Prustman), Reidinger, Reinhard (Reinhardt, Reinharth, Giorg. Reinhard, Giorgio Reinhardt, Giorgio Reinharth), Reutter (Reütter,Reuttern, Reuttern, Reitter, Giorg de Reuttern, Giorg de Reutter, Giorgio Reitter), Ferd. Richter, Sarri Italo, Sassone, Schamböck (Schämpöck, Schämböck), Scheibl (Scheübl), Schenck (Schenckh, Leopoldo Schenck), Schlöger, Schmid (Schmidt, Ferdinando,Schmid, Ferd. Schmidt), Schneider, Schonauer, Schorn, Sengmüller (Sengmiller, Sengmülner), Seüche (Seuche), Singer, Somberger, Sonnleithner (Sonnleitner, Sonleitner), Stephan (Steffan), Strasser, Techeti, Tuma (Thuma, Francesco Tuma), Ulbrich, Umstatt (Umstadt), Vinci, Vogl, Wagenseil (Wagenseill, Christofforo Wagenseil, Christ. Wagenseill), Giorgi Wenesgÿ, Werner, Wider, Widerhoffer, Wisner, Wöger,Wrastill (Wrastrill), Zäher, Zechner, Georg (Giorg, Giorgio) Zechner, Ziani, Ziegler (Josepho Ziegler) Zwifloher (Zwifelhoffer), and anonymous works.

HERZOGENBURG, Austria. Chorherrenstift Bibliothek und Musikarchive: [II]

583 CATALOGUS/ Selectiorum Musicalium/ chori Ducumburgensis/ Instrumenta
▽   Musica in fine (A H) (manuscript)   Typewritten copy in A Wn: S.m.
     9027. Microfilm in US NYcg.
          A nearly identical copy of A Wn: S.m. 9026 (see above entry).

HERZOGENBURG, Austria. Chorherrenstift Bibliothek und Musikarchive: [III]

584 MUSICALIEN KATALOG/ .../ Für den Musik-Chor des lobl. Stiftes Her-
▽   zogenburg. (A H) 6 parts, 128p. Compiled 1844-46 (manuscript). Type-

written copy in A Wn: S.m. 9028. Microfilm in US NYcg.
The 6 parts contain double staff incipits (violin and organ)
for: 1) Masses (267), 2) Graduals (229), 3) Offertories (210),
4) Requiems, Te Deum (70), 5) antiphons, responsories, litanies etc., 6) symphonies, oratorios, overtures. Composers:
Achleitner, Aigner, Albrechtsberger, Allegri, Arbesser, Ass-
mayer, Aumann (Aumon); Beethoven, Berghofer, Bergolesi [Per-
golesi], Bernhart, Biebl, Blahak (Blahac), Bondera, Bonno,
Boog, Brixi, Bühler, Caldara, Cherubini, Danzi, Diabelli,
Derlet, Ditters (Dittersdorf), Dobldorf (Dobldof), Doblhof,
Dohnat, Donberger (Donnberger), Dont, Drechsler, Durante,
Ehrhardt, Eigner, Eybler, Fank, Fribert, Fritz, Robert Führer, Fux, Gaensbacher, Gassmann (Gasmann, Geismann), Geiger,
Goll, Graff, Grassel, Graun, Gyrowetz, Tobias Haslinger,
Hasse, Jos. Haydn (Haiden, Hayden), Mich. Haydn (Haiden, Hayden), Hoffmann, Hoffmeister, Holzbauer, Huber, Hummel, Jan-
sa, John, P. Joseph, Katzer, Kempter, Kimerling, Komenda,
Kracker, Krebs, Krinner, Krommer, Krottendorfer, Franz Lachner, Lamberth, Lang, Lasser, Lickl, Linner, Lobinger, Maschek, Mendelssohn-Bartholdy, Mozart, Müller, Naumann, Nehr-
zart, Neugebauer, Novotni (Nowotny), Otto, Paisello, Pasterwitz, [Pergolesi], Pernsteiner, Petzina, Plaimschauer, Pleyel, Polster, Preindl, Prixi [Brixi], Proch, Pueder, Raab,
Rath, Reinhardt, Resch, Reutter (Reuttern), Rieger, Righini,
Roeder, Rosen, Rosenecker, Sachini, Salieri, Scheibl, Schie-
dermayer(Schiedermayr), Schmidt, Schnabel, Schnaubelt, Schei-
der, Schubert, Sechter, Seyfried, Sonnleithner, Spangler,
Stadler (Abbé Stadler), Starke, Steffan, Steppanovsky, Stohl,
Strasse, Süssmayer(Süsmayer), Tomaschek (Tomascheck), Tumma,
Ulmayer, Umlauf, Vogel, Vogler, Wanhal, Wavra, C.M. Weber,
Weigl, Weiss, Wiederhofer, Winter, Wittaseck (Wittasseck),
Wozet, Wranizky, Ziegler, Zimmermann.

HERZOGENBURG, Austria. Chorherrenstift Bibliothek und Musikarchive: [IV]

585 MUSICALIEN-KATALOG/ in diesem Cataloge erscheinen die vom Jahre 1855
▽   angefangen/ neu angeschafften Kirchen-Musikalien eingetragen./ und
     zwar:/ Messen, Gradual- und Offertorien, / Te Deum, Regina-Coeli, Ave
     Maria etz./ Für den Musik-Chor des löblichen Stiftes Herzogenburg./
     errichtet im Jahre 1857 (A H) 12ℓ. (manuscript). Typewritten copy
     in A Wn: S.m. 9029. Microfilm in US NYcg.
          A partially thematic index of sacred vocal music containing
          double staff incipits for 21 works. Annotation cites instru-
          mentation and, where available, copyists and acquisition date.
          An inventory of contents is appended. Composers: Drobisch,
          Robert Führer, L. Geppert, Michael Haydn, F.S. Hoelzl, Albi-
          nus Maschek, W.A. Mozart, Preindl, Ignaz Reimann, Roeder,
          Schiedermaier, Carl Seyler.

HEUGEL, JOHANNES, c. 1500-1585

586 KNIERIM, Julius. **Die Heugelhandschriften der Kasseler Landesbiblio-**
▽   **thek.** Eine bibliographische Studie als Grundlage einer Monographie
     des hessischen Hofkapellmeisters Johannes Heugel (um 1500-1585)
     (PhD diss.: Berlin, 1943) (typescript)
          Thematischer Katalog aller Stimmen und Teile.
               Entry # 1216 in Schaal VIMD. Only one copy exists in the
               hand of the author.

HEUSSNER, Horst (Marburg/Lahn)

587   Die Klaviersonate in Deutschland bis ca. 1765
*   Will include bibliography and thematic catalogue for sonatas
              by German composers.

HINGESTON, JOHN, ca. 1610-1683

588   BOCK, Emil W.   The string fantasias of John Hingeston (ca. I6I0-
      I683) (PhD diss.: State U. of Iowa, 1956) 2v. Univ. Micro. 64-5496.
      Thematic index to Hingeston's fantasies, v. 2, 1-29.(typescript)
              Incipits for the fantasies and accompanying allemandes are
              arranged by number of parts and instrumentation.

HODSOLL, William (publisher)

589   Catalogue thematique of symphonies and overtures by Mozart, Haydn,
      Rossini, Pleyel, etc. Arranged by S.F. Rimbault (London: ca. 1824)
      1p. (GB Lbm: B.M.h. 276. (3.))

      --- (London: ca. 1824) 1p. (GB Lbm: B.M.h. 276. (8.))

      --- (London: ca. 1825) 1p. (GB Lbm: B.M.h. 276. (12.))

590   No. 1. Catalogue thematique, of symphonies and overtures by Mozart,
      Haydn, Beethoven, Himmel, Weber and Mehul. Arranged by S.F. Rimbault
      (London: ca. 1827) 1p. (GB Lbm: B.M.h. 276. (9.))

591   No. 2. Catalogue thematique, of symphonies and overtures by A. Rom-
      berg, Pleyel, Winter, Rossini, Kreitzer [i.e. Kreutzer], Handel,
      Paer, and Mozart. Arranged by S.F. Rimbault (London: ca. 1827) 1p.
      (GB Lbm: B.M. 276. (10.))

                  Reference: HUMPHRIES, Charles; SMITH, William C. Music pub-
                  lishing in the British Isles (Oxford: Blackwell, 1970) 182-
                  83.

HOFFMANN, ERNST THEODOR AMADEUS, 1776-1822

592   ALLROGGEN, Gerhard. E.T.A. Hoffmanns Kompositionen. Ein chrono-
▽   logisch-thematisches Verzeichnis seiner musikalischen Werke nebst
      einer Einführung in seinen musikalischen Stil (PhD diss.: Hamburg,
      1967) 2v., 319p. (typescript)

592a --- E.T.A. Hoffmanns Kompositionen. Ein chronologisch-thematisches
      Verzeichnis seiner musikalischen Werke mit einer Einführung, *Studien
      zur Musikgeschichte des 19. Jahrhunderts,* Bd. 16 (Regensburg: Gustav-
      Bosse-Verlag, 1970) (95), 143p.
      Chronologisch-thematisches Verzeichnis der Kompositionen E.T.A.
      Hoffmanns, 1-137.
                  Double staff incipits for all movements and sections of 85
                  works (operas, vocal music, instrumental works, etc.), arranged
                  in chronological order.

                  Reviews: Pippa DRUMMOND, *MTimes* 112/1545(1073.

HOFFMANN, HEINRICH ANTON, 1770-1842

593   MICHELS, Egmont. Heinrich Anton Hoffmann. Leben und Werk, *Beiträge*

zur mittelrheinischen Musikgeschichte Bd. 13 (Mainz, 1971)
Thematischer Katalog sämtlicher Werke.

HOFFMEISTER, FRANZ ANTON, 1754-1812

594   Catalogue/ Thematique/ de tous les Oeuvres/ pour la/ Flute tra-
      versiere/ Composés/ par Mͬ:/ F.A. HOFFMEISTER/ MAITRE de CHAPELLE./
      à Vienne./ 1800 (Vienna: chez l'auteur, 1800) 9p.
           315 incipits for all pieces for flute (soli, duetti, terzetti,
           quartette, quintette, concertos) arranged by genre and opus
           number.

594 a --- Facsimile. Alexander WEINMANN, Die Wiener Verlagswerke von Franz
      Anton Hoffmeister, (see next entry)

595   WEINMANN, Alexander. **Die Wiener Verlagswerke von Franz Anton Hoff-
      meister,** *Beiträge zur Geschichte des Alt-Wiener Musikverlages* II/8
      (Wien: Universal Edition, 1964) 252[+253-72]p.
           Pages 36-232 consist of the following, most of which is given
           in thematic form: Prints of the Musical Typographic Society,
           Listings 1785-1800, Hoffmeister's publishing house's dealings
           with Artaria & Co., Synoptic list: Artaria-Hoffmeister, Des-
           cription of Artaria's editions, Non-placeable works, Works
           in manuscript, Wrongly attributed works, Prints from I. Amon
           publishing house in Heilbronn, and Last publishing period of
           1801-1806.

HOFFSTETTER, JOHANN URBAN ALOIS, 1742-1818 ; ROMAN, 1742-1815

596   GOTTRON, Adam; TYSON, Alan; UNVERRICHT, Hubert. **Die beiden
      Hoffstetter. Zwei Komponisten-Porträts mit Werkverzeichnissen**
      (Mainz: Schott, 1968) 80p.
           [Thematic catalogue], 45-75.
                Contains a thematic catalogue of the works of Roman
                Hoffstetter (45-60), and Johann Urban Alois Hoffstetter
                (61-75).

HOFMANN, LEOPOLD, 1738-1793

597   PROHÁSZKA, Hermine. **Leopold Hofmann und seine Messen,** (PhD diss.:
      Wien, 1956), *StMW* XXVI (1964) [79]-139.
           Thematisches Verzeichnis der Messen, 106-39.
                Soprano line with occasional orchestral introduction is given
                for all sections of 36 masses. Text underlay, instrumentation,
                and location of manuscripts provided. 213 incipits.

598   KREINER, Viktor. **Leopold Hofmann als Sinfoniker (1738-1793)** (PhD
▽   diss.: Wien, 1958) 202, 40*l*. (typescript)
           Thematisches Verzeichnis, 40.
                Double staff incipits for all movements of 51 symphonies.

HOFMEISTER, Friedrich (publisher)

599   Thematisches Verzeichniss von CLXXII vorzüglichen Sinfonien und
      Overtüren für Orchester, welche von berühmten Tonsetzern unseres
      Zeitalters gedruckt erschienen sind (Leipzig: Fr. Hofmeister, 1831)
      25p.

Composers include the following: Beethoven, Louis Böhner, Cherubini, Max Eberwein, F.E. Fesca, C.A. Göpfert, J. Haydn, A. Hesse, J.W. Kalliwoda, Fr. Krommer, J. Kueffner, J.L. Kunerth, H.G. Lentz, H. Marschner, Mozart, Th. A. Müller, F. Nohr, C. Richter, F. Ries, A. Romberg, B. Romberg, Seyfried, F.W. Sörgel, Spohr, F.E. Thurner, C.M.v. Weber, F. Witt.

HOLBORNE, ANTONY, d. 1602

600   JEFFERY, Brian. **Antony Holborne,** *MDisciplina* XXII (1968) 129-205. **Thematic catalogue,** 175-205. (*RILM* 68 238)
> Incipits for the composer's 144 instrumental works and 2 songs.

--- Supplement. Review by JEFFERY of KANAZOWA's "The complete works" v. I, *JAmerMusicolSoc* XXII/1 (1969) 125-26.

HOLZBAUER, IGNAZ, 1711-1783

601   LEHMANN, Ursula, **Instrumentale Kammermusik.** *Das Erbe deutscher Musik*, Bd. 24 (Kassel: Nagels Verlag, 1953) Vorwort, 124p.
Thematisches Verzeichnis der in diesem Band nicht aufgenommenen bezw. der nicht erhaltenen Kammermusik I. Holzbauers., Anhang I, p. 107.
> Incipits for all movements of 8 chamber works.

HOPKINSON, Cecil; OLDMAN, C.B.   (compilers)

602   **Thomson's collections of national song, with special reference to the contributions of Haydn and Beethoven,** *Edinburgh Bibliographical Society Transactions* II, part I (1938-1939) 1-64.
> Incipits of 187 Haydn settings (p. 25-47) and 126 Beethoven settings (p. 48-64) of Scottish, Irish, and Welsh airs and melodies, with collations of the various editions. Text incipits are those that first appeared in Thomson's collections.
> *Reviews:* Rosemary HUGHES, *MLetters* XXXVI (July 1955) 272-74.

HOWELER, Casper   (compiler)

603   **Sommets de la musique. Version française de R. Harteel.** 5e ed. rev. et aug. (Paris: E. Flammarion, 1956)
> A biographical dictionary with a 25-page thematic catalogue of symphonic works by Beethoven, Berlioz, Franck, Mozart, Schubert and Wagner.

HUGHES, David G.; BRYDEN, John   (compilers)

604   **An index of Gregorian chant** (Cambridge, Mass.: Harvard U. Press, 1969) 2v.: xvi, 456; v, 353p. (see no. 202)
> Two indices both containing basically the same information, but in Volume I the entries are arranged in the alphabetical order of the textual incipit, while in Volume II they are arranged in the numerical order of the melodic incipit. Includes all information as to category of melody, use (anti-

phon, responsory, etc.),mode, and all sources for each chant.
Chants having verses are indexed for the verse as well as
the main chant. Incipit code employed is that prescribed by
Nanie BRIDGMAN.(see no. 174)

Reviews: RMusicol LVI/1 (1970) 90-95; *American Recorder
Guild* XXXVI (May 1970) 773; *Sacred Music* XCVII/2 (1970) 32.

HÜLLMANDEL, NICHOLAS JOSEPH, 1751-1823

605   BENTON, Rita. Nicholas Joseph Hüllmandel and French instrumental
music in the second half of the eighteenth century (PhD diss.: U. of
Iowa, 1961) 384p. Univ. Micro. 61-4019.(typescript)
Thematic catalogue of original works, Appendix A, 256-78.
Arranged in order of opus nos. 1-12. Keyboard incipits with
violin obligato or *ad libitum* for each movement.
Reviews: R. KAMIEN, *CurrentMusicol* (Spring 1965) 95-97.

HUME, Alexander

606   Index to The Scottish Psalm Tune Book   (Edinburgh, 184?)
☐   An early attempt at devising a code system for indexing
hymns. Briefly discussed by Maurice FROST in *Musical Times*
(July 1949) 247.

HUMISTON, Robert Groff (compiler)

607   A study of the oboe concerto of Alessandro Besozzi and Johann
▽   Christian Fischer with a thematic index of 201 eighteenth century
oboe concertos available in manuscript of eighteenth century editions
(PhD diss.: U. of Iowa, 1968) xviii, 338p. (typescript)
A thematic index of 201 eighteenth-century oboe concertos avail-
able in manuscript or eighteenth-century editions, 107-302.
Incipits for all movements and solo passages of concertos
by the following composers: Adam, André, C.P.E. Bach, J. Chr.
Bach, Baumgarten, Bem, C. Besozzi, A. Besozzi, Bigaglia, Braun,
Cherzelli, Chiesa, Ciampi, Deller, Dimler, Dittersdorf, Don-
ninger, Elmi, Fasch, Fehr, Feldmayr, Fiala, Fischer, Förster,
Frick, Fries, Gabellone, Gajarek, Garnier, Gilles, Giraneck,
Gosel, J.G. Graun, Gretsch, Händel, Haymann, Heinichen, Hoff-
mann, Holzbauer, Horneck, Körzl, Küffner, Laschansky, Loeillet,
Marcello, Milling, Molter, Pachschmidt, Pesch, Pla, Platti,
Pokorny, Postel, Reicha, Reichenauer, Richter, Ristori, Ritschel,
Röttig, Rosetti, Sammartini, Schacht, Schneider, Secchi, Sommer,
C. Stamitz, Stölzel, Stulick, Thiel, Thoniger, Tortti, Valen-
tini, Vanhal, J. Chr. Vogl, Vogler, Wiedner, Wineberger, Zach.

HUMMEL, J.J. and B. (publisher)

608   Catalogue thématique ou commencement de touttes les oeuvres de musique
qui sont du propre fond de J.J. & B. Hummel, publié à la commodité
des amateurs, par où ils pourront voir, si les pièces qu'on leur présente pour original, n'ont pas déjà été imprimées. Le supplement de
ce catalogue consistant en une feuille de nouveautez, paroîtra chaque
anné[e]. [Avec] suppl. 1-6. 1 vol. +6 fasc. Amsterdam, J.J. Hummel,

IX. Hummel, *Catalogue thématique...prem: supplemént*, ca. 1769, no. 608

124

[1768-74], 72p. (continuous paging: 36; +37-40, 41-48, 49-52, 53-60, 61-64, 65-72). Published without date of printing.[reproduction opposite]
> Contains incipits arranged by genre,of instrumental music published by J.J. & B. Hummel in 1754-74. A seventh supplement was advertised (see next entry), but no copy has been located. It is quite possible that it was never published.

608a --- Een magazijn-catalogus van J.J. Hummel te Amsterdam en B. Hummel
□ te 's Gravenhage, 1778, *Tijdschrift der Vereeniging voor Noord-Neder-lands Muziekgeschiedenis* VIII (1908) 262-86.
> Contains a non-thematic list of the works in the Hummel catalogues. Cites a title which refers to a *seventh* supplement: "Catalogue thématique, ou commencement des oeuvres suivantes, pour la Commodite des Amateurs, afin de voir tout d'un coup, si les Pieces qu'on leur presente en Manuscrit, n'ont pas déjà été imprimé, proprement gravé, du premier jusqu'au septième Supplement."

608b --- JOHANSSON, Cari. J.J. & B. Hummel
*
> The Hummel catalogue with the six known supplements will be published 1972/73 in facsimile as vol. 3 of a monograph on J.J. & B. Hummel.

HUMMEL, JOHANN NEPOMUK, 1778-1837

609 Catalog/ J. Nep. Hummel sämmtlicher gestochenen Werke. (A Wst: MH
▽ 9178/c) 16p. No date (manuscript). Microfilm in US NYcg.
> Double staff incipits for 91 works, primarily instrumental works for soloist, chamber group, or orchestra. Lists 127 opus numbers with publisher.

610 Werke von J.N. Hummel welche Artaria u. Compag/ in Wien als Eigenthum
▽ von dem Compositeur an sich Kauften (autograph, 18 May 1820) (A Wst: MH 9170/c) [4p.] Microfilm in US NYcg. (manuscript)
> Double staff incipits for 37 work, prepared by the composer, for either piano solo or chamber ensemble.

611 ZIMMERSCHIED, Dieter. Thematischer Katalog
*
> As a companion to his PhD dissertation (Mainz, 1967), which does not contain incipits, he is preparing a thematic catalogue to be published by Hans Schneider, Tutzing.

HUND, Joannes (compiler)

612 Catallogus symphoniarum et trisonantium, I753, I754. (GB Lbm:
▽ Add. 31994.) 10p.(manuscript)
[Thematic catalogue of symphonies and trios].
> Incipits in compressed score of the following composers: Abel, [Johann] Agrell, [Tommaso] Albinoni, [Andrea?] Berna-sconi, Bernas, Biechler, [Christian Siegmund] Binder, Corelli, Frey, Gebel, [Karl Heinrich and Johann Gottlieb] Graun, Händel, Hasse, Kamerlocher, [Franz Xaver?] Richter, [Giambattista or Giuseppe] San Martino, [Giuseppe] Scarlatti, [Christoph] Schaffrath, Teradellas (Dominico Terradeglias?), [Joseph] Umstatt, and Zücka (Carlo Zuccari?).

HUSTVEDT, Sigurd Bernhard (compiler)

613   A melodic index of Child's ballad tunes. Publications of the University
      of California at Los Angeles, Languages and Literatures, v. 1, no. 2.
      (Berkeley: U. of California Press, 1936) 51-78.
           Uses a notation that is a combination of numbers and letters.
           The first musical phrase is represented by letter names of
           the notes including accidentals and a rhythmic outline.
           No allowance is made for the inclusion of melodic ornaments.

IMBAULT (publisher)

615   Catalogue/ THÉMATIQUE/ des/ Ouvrages de Musique/ Mis au Jour/ Par
      Imbault/ M^d de Musique au Mont d'Or Rue S. Honoré pres l'Hotel d'Aligre
      No. 627/ À PARIS// ca. 1792. (Sole known print in D Bds; microfilm
      copies in F Pn and US NYcg) 141p.[reproduction on facing page]
           Arranged by genre, spaciously printed. The works in this
           thematic catalogue are virtually identical to the non-thematic
           Imbault publisher's catalogue reproduced as Facsimile Appendix
           I in Cari JOHANSSON, French music publishers' catalogues of
           the second half of the eighteenth century (Malmö, 1955).
           Genres include: simfonies en OEuvre, simfonies Périodique,
           simfonies concertantes, sonates pour clavecin, duos pour deux
           violoncelles, duos pour deux flutes, and concertos pour violon.

INGEGNERI, MARCO ANTONIO, c. 1545-1592

616   Liber sacrarum cantionum. Vidi speciosam. Monumenta Liturgiae Poly-
      choralis Sanctae Ecclesiae Romanae,ser. IV, n. 1 (Trento: Societas
      Universalis Sanctae Ceciliae, 1968)
           Index sacrarum cantionum, 7-11.
                Incipits of every voice in the 25 seven-to sixteen-part works
                of *Liber sacrarum cantionum,* 1589

ISAAC, HEINRICH, c. 1450-1517

617   JUST, Martin. Studien zu Heinrich Isaacs Motetten (PhD diss.:
▽   Tübingen, 1961) 2v., 219, 131l. (typescript)
           Werkverzeichnis, v. 2, 30-114.
                272 incipits for all sections and all voices of motets,
                arranged in alphabetical order according to text incipit.

618   STAEHELIN, Martin. Quellenstudien zu Heinrich Isaac und seinem
▽   Messenoeuvre (PhD diss.: Basel, 1967)(typescript)
      [Thematic catalogue].

Key: ✱ in preparation; ▽ manuscript; ☐ literature; ✰ Library of Congress

CONCERTOS DE CLAVECIN

KOZELUCH. prix 4ᵗ - 4ˢ

Ier. Allegro

Adagio poco

Rondo poco presto

VION . prix 6ᵗ

Ier. Allegro moderato

Adagio

c. ♯.

X. Imbault, *Catalogue thématique...*, ca. 1792, no. 615

127

Incipits for all voices of all sections for the Masses, including the doubtful ones.

618 a   --- Published version of the above is scheduled to appear in 1973 in
*   the *Publikationen der Schweizerischen Musikforschenden Gesellschaft*.

IVES, SIMON, 1600-1662

619   MEYER, Ernst Hermann. **Die mehrstimmige Spielmusik des 17. Jahr-**
✡   **hunderts in Nord- und Mitteleuropa**   (Kassel: Bärenreiter, 1934)
       258p. (see no. 821)
         [Thematic catalogue], 154.
             Incipits for 4 fantasias à 4, 1 fantasia à 5, 1 innomine
             à 5.

JAEGGI, STEPHAN, 1903-1957

621   STRÄSSLE, Josef. **Stephan Jaeggi** (Kirchberg: Benziger, 1967) 94p.
       (*RILM* 69/ 4433^{bm})
             A biography of the composer and music director, with a thema-
             tic catalogue.

JANÁČEK, LEOŠ, 1854-1928

622   VOGEL, Jaroslav. **Leoš Janáček, his life and works**, trans. by
       Geraldine Thomsin-Muchová (London: Paul Hamlyn, 1962) 426p.
             456 thematic entries which appear in historical sequence
             can be utilized by consulting title of work in index.

JÁRDÁNYI, P.

623   **Die Ordnung der ungarischen Volkslieder,** *StudMusicol* II/3-4 (1962)
☐   3-32.
             Discusses organization of Hungarian folk songs according to
             melodic shape and form. Also discusses research of Kodály
             and Bartók.

JASOV, Premonstratensian Monastery.

624   ORMISOVÁ-ZÁHUMENSKÁ, Božena (Martin, ČSSR). **Súpis hudobnín z**
       bývalého premonštrátskeho kláštora v Jasove. I. Zbierka z bývalého
       jezuitského kláštora sv. Trojice v Košiciach [Inventory of musical
       prints and MSS from the former Premonstratensian Monastery in Jasov]
       (Martin: Matica slovenská, 1967) 125p. (*RILM* ^{67} 1696)

Key: * in preparation; ▽ manuscript; ☐ literature; ✡ Library of Congress

"The first part of the inventory contains a thematic catalogue
of 102 items (24 editions and 78 MSS) mainly the work of
18th century Jesuit composers." (Juraj Potúček)

JENA, Universitäts-Bibliothek

625   ROEDIGER, Karl E. **Die geistlichen Musikhandschriften der Universitäts-Bibliothek Jena** (Jena: Biedermann, 1935) 2v.: 139p.; 207p.
⌊Thematic catalogue], v. 2, 207p.
>Incipits, original clefs, old notation, for sacred vocal
>works arranged by Chorbuch. Provides text underlay.
>Composers include: A. Agricola, J. Barbiriaro, N. Bonl-
>dewijm (Bauldenyn), A. Brumel, N. Champion [Campion], L.
>Compère, Josquin des Prez, A. Divitis (de Rijcke), A. de
>Févin, M. Forestier, J. Gascoing (Gasscoring), J. Ghiselin,
>H. Isaac, Petrus la Rue, J. Martini, J. Mouton, J. Obrecht,
>M. de Orto, M. Pipelare, J. Prioris, Rerniger (derselbe
>wie Rener?), Adam Reneri, G. Weerbecke.

JENKINS, JOHN, 1592-1678

626   MEYER, Ernst Hermann. **Die mehrstimmige Spielmusik des 17. Jahr-
✡ hunderts in Nord- und Mitteleuropa** (Kassel: Bärenreiter, 1934)
258p. (see no. 821)
[Thematic catalogue], 154-57.
>Incipits for 5 fantasias à 3, 27 fantasias à 3 (2 discan-
>tus and bass), 22 fantasias à 4, 19 fantasias à 5, 12 fan-
>tasias à 6, 2 Innomines à 6.

627   ASHBEE, Andrew. **The four-part instrumental compositions of John
▽ Jenkins** (PhD diss.: U. of London, 1966) 3v. (typescript)
Thematic checklists, v. III, 51-69.
>Incipits for all four parts of fantasias (17 works), airs
>(52 works), and spurious and doubtful works (13 pieces).
>Lists the sources for each work and "states which instru-
>mental part or parts is to be found in each source."

628   COXON, Carolyn (Edinburgh, Scotland). **A complete index of John
* Jenkins' music**

JENSEN, ADOLF, 1837-1879

629   MÜNSTER, Robert (München). **Thematisches Werkverzeichnis**
*

JEPPESEN, Knud (compiler)

630   **Die mehrstimmige italienische Laude um 1500** (Leipzig: Breitkopf &
Härtel; København: Levin & Munksgaard, 1935) 168p.
>Contains the following thematic indexes: Works by Dammonis
>from Petrucci's *Laude Libro Primo* (1507), p. lvi-lix. (In-
>cludes only those works not printed in full in the edition.);
>Udine MS 165, containing works by Hedus, p. lxii; Index of
>frottola melodies according to three rhythmical types, p.xxxi-
>xxxiii. Composers named are: Adam Antiquis Venetus, Brocus,
>Caprioli, Cesena, Cara, Eustachius de Monte, Filippo de Lurano,
>Jo. Lurano, Honophrius Patavinus, Nicolo Pifaro, Piero da Lodi,
>Rossinus, Stringarius, Tromboncino.

631   Die italienische Orgelmusik am Anfang des Cinquecento (København:
       Munksgaard, 1943) 130,82p.
       [Thematic index], 59-61.
            Incipits of *Frottole intabulate da sonare organi*, published
            by Andrea Antico da Montona (1517), including works by Cara,
            Ranier, Tromboncino, Michael Vicentino.

631a --- 2nd edition. (København: Wilhelm Hansen, 1960)
            Thematic index (p. 50-53) lists several changes in libraries,
            and possibly in authorship.

JERKOWITZ, Joseph (compiler)

632   Thematisches/ Verzeichniss/ der/ dem Unterzeichneten/ angehörenden/
▽   Musikalien./ Jos. Jerkowitz./ Schasslowitz/ den 1. Juli/ 1832./
       (D Mbs: Mus. Mss. 6330) 41*l*. (manuscript) [reproduction opposite]
            Ca. 500 incipits on one and two staves, arranged by genre.
            Composers: Jos. de Blumenthal, B. Campagnoli, F. Clement,
            Ferd. Kauer, Jos. Klauser, H. Köhler, Franz Krommer, Carl
            Stamitz, Karl Wlczek (!), F. Pössinger, G. Albrechtsberger,
            Jaques Conti, G. Druzeki, Fodor, Giornowichi (Gronovichi),
            F.A. Hoffmeister, Ant. Lacroix, J. Pleyel, Pierre Rode, Al-
            lex. Rolla, Louis Spohr, Smettana, J.B. Viotti, Franc. Weiss,
            Wutky, Mussini, J. Pirlinger, W. Pichel, Louis Boccherini,
            C. de Ditters, Frc. de L'amotte, Gaetano Pugniani, J. Weigl,
            F.A. Baumbach,Agnello Giuara, Adami, Ferliga, Flath, Pierre
            Fux, Carlo Khym, F. Worzischek, Ant. Wranitzky, J. Amon,
            Louis v. Beethoven, R. Kreutzer, F. Kuhlau, Montelli, J.B.
            Polledro, Felix Radicati, Giov. Wendt, Paul Wranitzky, Adam-
            mer, F. Fraenzl, A.E. Förster, F. Gleisner, Jos. Haydn, Hur-
            ka, J. Mayseder, W.A. Mozart, A. Romberg, B. Romberg, Christ.
            Sonnleithner, F.A. Lorenz, H.C. Schmiedigen, P.Giov.Battiste
            Martin, W. Müller, Nicolo Isouard, Mich. Haydn, G. Lickl, L.
            Jos. Borghi, Jos. Bürebl, Em. Faulhaber, Duc de l'Aine [Le-
            duc?], Ant. Lolli, Ch. Lundowig, Jos. Misliwetschek, Stamitz,
            Tauber, Giov. Wanhall, Westerhof, Woldemar, Jos. Wolfram,
            P.F. Fuchs, C. Nicola, J. Brandl, A. Gyrowetz, Baron de Kos-
            pot, Ant. Reicha, F. Witt, R. Collauff, K. Gruttmann, Ant.
            Kozelluch, Carlo Kreith, Vinc. Maschek, J. Nudra, L. Maurer,
            J. von Seyfried, F. Volkert, Louis Dussek, Jos. Sardi, L.
            Cherubini, F. Ries, J.N. Hummel, F. Kalkbrenner, Paul Resch,
            W. Tomaschek, Binder, J.Cibulka, J. Dankawsky, Ant. Diabelli,
            Jos. Drechsler, Melch. Dreyer, Freklaw, Evermod. Groll, Him-
            mel, Kohl, Ant. Laufka, J. Lasser, Ant. Lohr, P. Mattausch,
            G. Naumann, R.P.E.B., Pausewang, Eug. Pausch, W. Pokorny,
            D. Preisler, V. Righini, Rösler, Joh.B. Schiedermayr, Jos.
            Schuster, Schwertner, Fr. Stark, Taschke, Adrien Tonolieur,
            Caj. Vogel, Joh.N. Witasek, Joh.N. Wozet, J. Drobisch, R.
            Bertoni, V. Franchi, F. Paer, Paesiello, Pietro de Bologna,
            G. Rossini, Ryba, P. Winter, Jos. Gellert, Nanke, A.P.D.,
            Pfeiffer, Nerzad, Ant. Kargl, J.K. Klaus, Ant. Kraft, and
            many other works without incipits.

JOACHIM, JOSEPH, 1831-1907

633   BACHMANN, Alberto. Les grands violinistes du passé (Paris: Fisch-
       bacher, 1913) 468p. (see no. 65)
            [Table thématique], 111-16.
                 Incipits for Op. 11 and 12, and "oeuvres sans numéro d'opus".

XI. **Jerkowitz**, *Thematisches Verzeichniss...*, ca. 1792, no. 623

JOHNSON, David N.M.

634   A hymn tune index, *The Hymn* XI (Apr 1960) 45-50.
☐   Announces the scheduled publication of a hymn tune index.

JOHNSON, Jane Troy (compiler)

635   The English fantasia-suite, ca. I620-I660 (PhD diss.: U. of Calif.,
▽   Berkeley, 1971)(typescript)
          Thematic catalogue, Appendix C.
              Incipits of the first violin part are given for each of the
              three movements (fantasia, almaine or ayre, galliard or
              corant) of 136 suites. Works are organized by composer in
              approximate chronological order. Composers include the fol-
              lowing: [John Cooper] Giovanni Coperario, William Lawes, John
              Jenkins, John Hingston, John Birchenska, Christopher Gibbons,
              Christopher Simpson, [Jenkins] anonymous.

JOMMELLI, NICCOLO, 1714-1774

636   PATTENGALE, Robert (U. of Michigan). The cantatas of Niccolo
*   Jommelli
          Thematic catalogue.
              Includes "title, musical and textual incipit for each reci-
              tative and aria, instrumentation, date of composition, au-
              thor of text. Arias marked "da capo" or "del segno" are i-
              dentified. All known autographs and manuscript sources are
              listed. The catalogue is 26p. long in its present state."

JOZZI, GIUSEPPE, 18th c.

636.1 8 sonate pour clavecin (Amsterdam: A. Olofsen, 1761)
              Contains a thematic table of contents; the 8 works are contra-
              facta of Domenico Alberti's Op. 1.
              Reference: Otto Erich DEUTSCH, Thematische Kataloge (see page
              74 of no. 297).

KACAROVA-KUKUDOVA, Raina

637   Le classification des mélodies populaires en Bulgarie, *StudMusicol*
☐   VII (1965) 293-99.

KÁJONI, JÁNOS

638   PAPP, Géza. Kájoni János orgonakönyve [The organ books of János
      Kájoni] Klny.: Magyar Zenei Szemle (Budapest: Magyar Kórus, 1942)
      23p.
          [Thematic catalogue]

Key: * in preparation; ▽ manuscript; ☐ literature; ✪ Library of Congress

KÁLMÁN, EMMERICH, 1882-1953

639   MOSKOVIC, Carl (Queens College of C.U.N.Y.). Thematic catalogue
*   of Emmerich Kálmán's vocal music
            Incipits for all vocal themes of the operettas.

KARŁOWICZ, MIECZYSŁAW, 1876-1909

640   DZIEBOWSKA, Elżbieta; MICHAŁOWSKI, Kornel; ŻACZKIEWICZ, Barbara.
*   Mieczysław Karłowicz. Katalog tematyczny dzieł i bibliografia
      [Mieczysław Karłowicz. Thematic catalogue of works and biblio-
      graphy.] (Kraków: Polish Music Publications, ca. 1972) ca. 200p.
            Fully harmonized incipits for the complete works in chrono-
            logical order. Provides date and place of composition,
            dedication, autograph, edition, performance, transcriptions,
            recordings, and literature. Bibliography lists (500 items)
            musical and literary works on his life and work printed in
            Poland and abroad between 1892-1970.

KARLSRUHE, Badische Landesbibliothek: Catalogues A-C, and E

            [There are five MS catalogues of the Karlsruhe collection
            identified here by the letters A-E, as in the Jenkins-Chur-
            gin Sammartini thematic catalogue. All the catalogues are
            thematic except catalogue D, and many of the works have dis-
            appeared.]

641   [Catalogue A] (D KA) [10p.] (manuscript). Microfilm copy in US
▽   NYcg.
            Catalogue A is in the hand of J.M. Molter (ca. 1695-1765),
            Kapellmeister in Karlsruhe 1722-1733 and 1743-1765. His
            catalogue probably dates from the period ca. 1750-1765.
            Incipits, with instrumentation, are provided for chamber
            works, mostly for flute. Composers include: Agrel, Biavele,
            Bodinus, Castor, Fasch, Füscher, Gepusch [Pepusch], Gio-
            vanne, Giupe, Groneman (4), Hasse (17), Kelleri, Mahaut (32
            (32), Martini (2), Martino (2), Micco (Mico) 2, Molter (1),
            Näimann (5), Neinmetz (1), Nëumann (1), Pichter (2), Proschi
            (2), Quantz 17, Richter (1), Satzenhoven (2), A. Schek (2),
            Scherer (1), Schott (2), Spurni (1), Stöelzet (1), Stulk
            (1), Roman Suedese (3), Teleman (3), Thiela (Thÿela) (2),
            and Vogel (1).

642   [Catalogue B] (D KA) [16p.] (manuscript). Microfilm copy in US
▽   NYcg.
            Incipits for *sinfonies e quatri, sonate à 3, concerti*, and
            other chamber works by the following composers: Albertini
            (1), Bermegger (1), Besozzi (12), Bizzarini (2), Blavet (1),
            Santo Capis (1), Caputti (1), Chevalier (1), Coraucci (1),
            Enderle (6), Fischer (1), Hasse (47), Holzbauer (1), Köch-
            ler (1), Lampugnani (2), Mahaut (20), St. Martino (29),
            Messier (14), Neumann (6), Pernasone (1), Piarello (1),
            Quantz(12), Domenico Quintinori (1), Rösler (3), Schaffrath
            (Schafrath) (3), Schiatti (3), Schulz (5), Schütz (8), Sil-
            liti (1), Tarti (1), Tusco (1), Wendling (1), Wenseslaw Wo-
            ditzka (1).

643   [Catalogue C] (D KA) [6p.] (manuscript). Microfilm copy in US NYcg.
▽   Incipits for all movements of chamber music for winds, and
          incipits for first movements only of symphonies. Includes
          the following composers: Bach (9), Cannabich (6), Fils (26),
          Fräenzel (1), Jommelli (6), Kellerÿ (1), Malzath (1), Poc-
          korni (1), Schwindel (1), Toeschi (23).

644   [Catalogue E] (D KA) [25p.] (manuscript). Microfilm copy in US
▽   NYcg.
          Incipits for sacred vocal works and instrumental works by
          the following composers: Girolamo Abas (1), Balbi (1), Gio.
          Batta Bergolesi [Pergolesi] (1), Campani (4), Carcani (1),
          Chiesa (18), Christoforo Cluch [Gluck] (1), Cröner (1),
          Fedrici (10), Galimberti (2), Galuppi (12), Gasparin. (1),
          Gizielo (1), Hasse (13), Jommelli (2), Lampugnani (5, Leo-
          nardo Leo (4), Mahaut (7), Marchi (1), Martino (35), Mozart
          (1), Ometta (2), Paldino (5), Pencini (1), Perez (14), Pes-
          cetti (3), Pesozzi (5), Porpora (2), Prota (1), Rhoda (2),
          Reina (1), Richter (16), Reyter (1), Scarlatti (4), Schiliny
          (2), Carlo Sola (1), Statder (1), Angufano Stopol (1), Ter-
          radellas (3), Volpert (38), Zach (1), and Nepolitano (1).

KASSEL, Landesbibliothek

645   ÉCORCHEVILLE, Jules. Note sur un fonds de musique française de la
      Bibliothèque de Cassel, *SIMG* V (1903-1904) 155-71
          [Thematic catalogue], 158-66.
          This index and the one following deal with the same MS
          differing somewhat in order and in a few minor details.

645a --- Vingt suites d'orchestre du XVIIe siècle français (Paris: Fortin,
      1906) 2v.
          Table thématique, v. 2, 263-68.
          Incipits for 20 suites with usually 10-12 dances in each by
          Arne, Belleville, Bruler [Bruslard], Dresen [Drese], Du Ma-
          noir, Herwig, La Croix, La Haye, La Voye, La Zarin [Lazzari-
          ni], Mazuel, Nau, Pinel, Pohle, Werdier [Verdier], de Hesse
          [Wilhelm VI of Hessen]. Page 268 contains 33 incipits in
          3 groups for *Suites incomplètes*.

KASSLER, Michael

646   A representation of current common musical notation-manual for key
☐   punchers (Princeton: Princeton U., 1963) (mimeographed report)

647   MIR, a simple programming language for musical information retrieval
☐   (Princeton: Princeton U., 1964) (mimeographed report)

KAUER, FERDINAND, 1751-1831

648   MANSCHINGER, Kurt. Ferdinand Kauer. Ein Beitrag zur Geschichte des
▽   Wiener Singspiels um die Wende des 18. Jahrhunderts (PhD diss.:
      Wien, 1929) 252ℓ. (typescript)
          Thematisches Verzeichnis der auf öffentlichen Bibliotheken
          erhaltenen Singspiele, 179-252.
              Double staff incipits for all numbers (overtures, arias,
              duets, choruses, etc.) of 14 Singspiele.

649   WEINMANN, Alexander (Wien). **Ferdinand Kauer**
*   Inventory of works (partially thematic) with biographical
         information.

KAUN, HUGO, 1863-1932

650   Hugo Kaun's Kompositionen aus dem Musik-Verlage von Richard Kaun,
      17 Grüner Weg, Berlin O 27 [and] W^m· A. Kaun Music Co., 209 Grand
      Ave., Milwaukee, Wis, Vollständig bis 1. Oktober 1908. Musikali-
      scher Führer No. 2 (Leipzig: C.G. Röder 1908) 24p.
               Incipits (3 staves) for 30 Lieder (voice and piano) by
               Hugo Kaun. Also includes a list of works.

651   SCHAAL, Richard. **Hugo Kaun, Leben und Werk (I863-I932)** (Regensburg:
      Habbel, [1946])185p.
         Das Werk, 41-140.
               145 themes, mostly incipits, are cited in the course of dis-
               cussion of the composer's entire, varied, output.

KELLER, MAX, 1770-1855

652   **Katalog über die Kompositionen des Max Keller** (Schülers Michael
▽   Haydn's) (Von dem Komponisten selbst zusammengestellt u. ge-
      schrieben in den Jahren 1840-1850) 16, 196p. Copy in D Mbs.
         Nach der Art der Kompositionen geordnet, 196.
               Multiple staff incipits for sacred vocal works, Lieder, Sing-
               spiel, organ and clavier works,etc. Arramged by genre. Part 1,
               161.,is a chronologically ordered non-thematic index. Auto-
               graph (from which the D Mbs xerox copy was made) in the pos-
               session of the administration of the Hl.Kapelle in Altötting.

KELLNER, JOHANN PETER, 1705-1772

653   FECHNER, Manfred. **Die Klavier- und Orgelwerke J.P. Kellners,** ein
▽   Beitrag zur Stil- und Quellenforschung der Musik für Tasteninstru-
      mente im 18. Jahrhundert (Diplomarbeit: Leipzig, 1965)(typescript)
         Thematisches Verzeichnis der Klavier- und Orgelwerke.

KERÉNY, György

653.1 **The system of publishing the collection of Hungarian folksongs:** *Corpus*
□   *Musicae Popularis Hungaricae.* *Studia Memoriae Belae Bartók Sacra*
      (Budapest, 1956) 453-68.
               Discusses the history of folk music classifications leading
               to the current system developed by Kodály and (especially)
               Bartók.

KERLE, JACOBUS de, 1531 or 1532-1591

654   MACHOLD, Robert. **Ausgewählte Werke,** *DTB* Jahrg. 26 (Wiesbaden: Breit-
      kopf & Härtel,1972)[Only the reprint edition contains thematic cat.]
         Thematisches Werkverzeichnis, lxx-lxxvii.
               Incipits, all movements and all voices, for the complete
               works. Grouped according to individual, collected, and
               MS works, then chronologically arranged within groups.

KERLL, JOHANN KASPAR von, 1627-1693

655   Modulatio Organica super Magnificat octo Ecclesiaticis tonis respon-
      dens. Monachii, Apud Michaelem Wening, M.D.C. LXXXVI (D Mbs: 4°Mus.
      pr. 37847) 71, 10p.[reproduction on page opposite]
          Subnecto initia aliarum Compositionum mearum pro Organo et Clavi-
          cymbalo, in eum, quem dixi finem [I attach below the beginnings
          of some of my other compositions for organ and clavicembalo for
          the reason which I have stated], [Supplement, 10p.].
              Double staff incipits for 22 keyboard works not related to
              the *Modulatio Organica*. This beautifully engraved thematic
              catalogue was published in 1686 as a supplement to the *Modu-
              latio Organica*, a collection of Magnificat organ versets.
              It is the second known printed thematic catalogue and the
              first devoted to the works of a single composer. Its 32 inci-
              pits, unrelated to the *Modulatio*, are for 22 *other* keyboard
              works of Kerll's, which had been appearing under the names
              of other composers, and which he wished to proclaim as his
              own. Included are 8 toccatas, 6 canzonas, capriccio sopra
              il cucu, battaglia, ciaccona variata, passacaglia variata,
              and 4 suites.

              Reference: Barry S. BROOK, The first printed thematic cata-
              logues, *Festskrift Jens Peter Larsen* (København, 1972) 103-
              12. (see no. 193). Contains reproductions from the Kerll
              Catalogue.

656   FUCHS, Aloys. Orgel-Compositionen von Kasper v Kerl (D Bds: HB VII
▽   Mus. ms. theor. K.559, second part) [2p.] Compiled 1838. Microfilm
      copy in US NYcg. (manuscript)
              Double staff incipits for several toccatas, canzonas, and
              miscellaneous pieces.

KIDD, Ronald R. (Purdue U.)

657   Thematic indices of the obbligato keyboard and violin sonatas published
▽   in the second half of the 18th century. Index cards. (manuscript)
              Incipits for keyboard-violin sonatas by Abel, J.C. Bach,
              Clementi, Schroeter, Rush, Just, F.T. Schumann, Giardini,
              Giordani, Raupach, Piozzi, Vento, Steibelt, Rauzzini, Sacchini,
              Hook, Dussek, Barthelemon, etc., and all the keyboard chamber
              music of F.X. Sterckel. Files also include themes for all
              of the instrumental works in the Lady Hamilton Papers at the
              Beineke Library of Yale University.

KIEL, Schleswig-Holsteinische Landesbibliothek, Universitätsbibliothek,
Musikwissenschaftliches Institut der Universität

658   HORTSCHANSKY, Klaus. Katalog der Kieler Musiksammlungen; die Noten-
      drucke, Handschriften, Libretti und Bücher über Musik aus der Zeit
      bis 1830 (Kassel: Bärenreiter, 1963) 270p.
              Main catalogue of music holdings in the above-mentioned li-
              braries of Kiel. Incipits for MSS only.
              Reviews: Imogen FELLINGER, *Mf* XIX/1 (1966) 74-76.

KING, A. Hyatt

659   The past, present and future of the thematic catalogue, *Monthly*

XII. **Kerll,** *Subnecto initia...* of the *Modulatio Organica*, 1686,
title page and page 5, no. 655

☐   *Musical Record* LXXXIV/953, 954 (1954) 10-13, 39-46.
A survey of thematic catalogues from the earliest to the
present, discussing their function and offering suggestions
for their organization.

KIRSCH, Winfried (compiler)

660   Die Quellen der mehrstimmigen Magnificat-und Te Deum-Vertonungen bis
zur Mitte des I6. Jahrhunderts (Tutzing: Hans Schneider, 1966) 588p.
[Thematic catalogue], part IV, 421-86.
Incipits of the uppermost voice with text are arranged according to mode. Includes concordances in MSS and early prints,
modern editions, library locations, and chronological tables
of sources and composers. Over 1000 incipits.

Reviews: James ERB, *JAmerMusicolSoc* XXII/1 (Spring 1969)
122-25.

KJELLBERG, Erik

661   En tematisk katalog med Numericode. Ett projekt vid SMA, *SvenskTMf*
☐   (1968) 125-32. In Sv; summary in En.
Discusses the card types to be used at the Swedish Archives
of Music History in connection with Ingmar Bengtsson's "Numericode". The card types will be used to develop a thematic
catalogue of anonymous Swedish sources.

KJERULF, HALFDAN, 1815-1868

662   WENDELBORG, Hans. Halfdan Kjerulfs mannskorsanger med hovedvekten
▽   på et systematiseringsforsök av harmonikken   [Halfdan Kjerulf's
songs for male chorus, with special reference to the systematisation
of harmony] (MA diss.: Oslo, 1971) 190p. (typescript)
[Thematic catalogue].

KLEIN, Deanne Arkus (compiler)

663   Le quatuor à cordes français au I8e siècle (PhD diss.: U. of Paris,
▽   1970) 2v., 479p. (typescript)
Catalogue thématique de principaux quatuors à cordes français
de I768-I793, v. 1.
Incipits of 238 original works "available in Paris libraries
and listed in the catalogues of others, composed by French-
men and those foreigners who made their home in France during
the years listed above." Information concerning other movements, title pages, sources, and dates is included. Composers represented are: Baudron, Gossec, Saint-Georges, Davaux,
Vachon, Barrière, Breval, Chartrain, D'Alayrac, and Fodor.

KLIER, Karl M.

663.1 Entwurf zur Anlage eines Melodien-Registers (Wien, 1956) (typescript)
☐ ▽   On folk tune classification.

KLITZ, Brian Kent (compiler)

664   Solo sonatas, trio sonatas, and duos for bassoon before I750.
(PhD diss.: Chapel Hill, U. of North Carolina, 1961) iv, 151, 66p.
Univ. Micro. 61-6125. (typescript)
Not strictly a thematic catalogue. Themes present throughout.

KLÖCKER, Dieter (Köln)

665   Thematisches Verzeichnis der Klarinettenliteratur I750-I850
*

KLÖFFLER, JOHANN FRIEDRICH, 1725-1790

666   GÖTZE, Ursula. **Johann Friedrich Klöffler (I726-I790)** (PhD diss.:
▽   Münster, 1965) 253, 37p. (typescript)
         Thematisch-bibliographisches Werke-Verzeichnis, 23-202.
              Over 300 multiple staff incipits for all movements for the
              collected works. Arranged first by opus number (Op. 1-7),
              then by works without opus number.

KLOSTERNEUBURG, Austria. Augustiner-Chorherrenstift Bibliothek [I]

667   Musicalien Verzeichniss vom Stift Klosterneuburg (A Wgm: 788/18)
▽   2v.: v, 26ℓ.; iv, 55ℓ. (manuscript) Microfilm copy in US NYcg.
              The first volume contains incipits for 183 Masses and 48
              other religious works with text. Composers include: Al-
              brechtsberger, J. Haydn, M. Haydn, Mozart, Salieri, Nau-
              mann, Pasterwitz, Brixi, Gasmann, Hasse, Kainz, Schneider,
              Hofmann, Pfeiffer, Sonnleithner, Mosel, Grasl, Preindl,
              Leuttern, Wannhall, Ditters, Novotni, Tuma, Monn, Holz-
              bauer, Krottendorfer, Carl, Aumann, Fux, Ziani, Fleyda,
              Werner, Jomellÿ, Ehrenhardt, Ziegler, Novack, Pruneder,
              Caldara, Firmino, Donnberger, Brustmann, Schmidt, Steg-
              maÿer, Seuche, Gsur, Zimmerman, Arbesser, Grasel, Bono,
              Schenk, Pergolesi, Boog. The second volume contains
              incipits with text for 59 motets, 128 Offertories and
              Graduals, and over 200 other sacred works. Composers in-
              clude: J. Haydn, M. Haydn, Krottendorfer, Hofmann, Spangler,
              Gassmann, Leuttern, Ziegler, Hasse, Kainz, Monn, Sonnleit-
              ner, Vannhall, Campion, Händel, Zechner, Körzel, Lochelli,
              Aumon, Metz, Palzka, Oberfson, Kauer, Stegmayer, Kreutzer
              et Bondra, Salieri, Ehrenhardt, Mozart, Winter, Hofmann,
              Holzbauer, Peitzger, Hueber, Pasterwitz, Luigi, Carl,
              Tuma, Cramer, Bonno, Jacobi, Brustmann, Breindl, Jomelli,
              Zimmermann, Herculano C.P.C., Novotni, Baumon, Reinhardt,
              Vogl, Ziani, Domaseditz, Gozl, Caldara, Schlöger, Giovanni
              Zifser, Ulbrich, Paizger, Hengsberger, L. Schmid, R.D.
              Haveris C.P.C., Dittersdorf, Ferd. Schmidt, Ertl, Heyda,
              Franc: Maria, Pozizka, Hörger.

KLOSTERNEUBURG, Austria. Augustiner-Chorherrenstift Bibliothek [II]

668   Catalogus/ Deren auf Diesem Löbl. Stift Chor/ befindlichen Musicalien
▽   und Instrumenten./ Verfasst von Leopold Joseph Schmidt/ derzeit Or-
         ganist, und Chor Regent/ Stift Closterneuburg den 20ten 8bris 790.
         (A KN) 168p. (manuscript)
              Incipits for sacred vocal music (Masses, Litanies, Regina
              Coeli, Ave Regina, etc.) by the following composers: Albrechts-
              berger, Aumon, Arbesser, Bono, Brixi, Bogner, Battoni, Brust-
              man, Boog, Bruneder, Baumonn, Bach, Birek, Bondra, Caldara,
              Carl, Cramer, Cul, Cetto, Campion, Creutzer, Donnberger,
              Dittersdorf, Ehrenhardt, Ertl, Fux, Freytag, Grasl, Gassmann,
              Grottendorfer, Gosl, Gsur, Gözl, Hasse, Hoffmann, Haumon,

Jos. Haydn, Höger, Heyda, Mich. Haydn, Haydenreich, Händel,
Holzbauer, Hörtner, Hörger, Himmelpauer, Hengsberger, Habeg-
ger, Hanke, Huber, Hüber, Hendorfer, Jomelli, Kruchl, Kainz,
Kozeluch, Krottendorfer, Körzl, Kindermann, Reutter, Rein-
hardt, Roozizka, Rieppe, Seuche, Schneider, Sonnleithner,
Schorn, Schmidt, Schenk, Scheibl, Spangler, Salieri, Scheup-
flug, Schamböck, Stephan, Schlöger, Schumbock, Tuma, Umlauf,
Ulbrich, Luigi, Laube, Müller, Mosel, Metz, Monn, Martini,
Novotny, Novack, Naumann, Mislivetzek, W.A. Mozart, Ötte,
Ordonez, Obersson, Pfeiffer, Preindl, Prustmann, Pasterwitz,
Pergolese, Pruneder, Paumonn, Pichler, Paizger, Palzka, Phil-
lippo, Vanhal, Vogl, Wusner, Werner, Wrastrill, Wagenseil,
Wöger, Wanke, Weigart, Winter, Zechner, Ziegler, Ziani, Zim-
mermann.

KLUGE, Reiner

669 **Faktorenanalytische Typenbestimmung an einstimmigen Volksmelodien**
* □   (Berlin: Humboldt-Universität zu Berlin, project in progress)
     Computers and the Humanities II/2 (Nov 1967) 88.

670 **Versuch einer typologischen Systematik altmärkischer Volkslieder**
* □   **durch Faktorenanalyse mit Hilfe eines elektronischen Rechenauto-**
     maten ZRA 1 (PhD diss.: Musikwissenschaftliches Institut der
     Humboldt-Universität, Berlin, in progress)

KØBENHAVN, Det Kongelige Bibliotek: Giedde Collection

671 **Anonymes de la collection Giedde** (DK Kk) (manuscript). Copy US NYcg.
▽   Photocopy of handwritten list of incipits of 36 works
        in the Giedde collection. Other photocopies have been
        distributed on request.

KODÁLY, ZOLTÁN, 1882-1967

672 EÖSZE, László. **Zoltán Kodály, his life and work,** trans. by István
      FARKAS and Gyula GULYÁS (London: Collet's Holding Ltd., 1962) 166p.
      Thematic catalogue, 97-166.
          Indexed thematic catalogue, incomplete (73 incipits, numbered
          according to medium, following and illustrating the text).

KODÁLY, Zoltán

673 **Eine Vorbedingung der vergleichenden Liedforschung,** *Studia memoriae*
□   *Bela Bartok sacra* (Budapest, 1956) 7-8.
          States need for a system of organizing the musical part of
          folk music, aside from text. Gives a few examples of collec-
          tions that are attempts at systematic classification of the
          melodies.

673a --- English trans. **A pre-requisite condition of comparative song**
      research (1959 ed.) 11-12.

KOGOJ, MARIJ, 1895-1956

674 LOPARNIK, Borut. **Prvine melodične dikcije v Kogojevih otroškikh**
      pesmih [Elements of melodic diction in the children's songs of

Kogoj], *Musikološki Zbornik— Musicological Annual* V (Ljubljana, 1969) 54-82.   In Cs; English summary, p. 82.
> Melodični Primeri, 70-79.
>> Incipits of varying lengths for 80 children's songs. Incipits usually for opening themes , but sometimes include other sections.

KÖHLER, Karl-Heinz (compiler)

675 Die Triosonate bei den Dresdener Zeitgenossen Johann Sebastian Bachs
▽   (PhD diss.: Friedrich-Schiller-Universität, Jena, [1956]) 151*l*., 51 plates (typescript)
>> Incipits for trio sonatas by Johann Dismas Zelenka (6), Johann David Heinichen (15), Johann Joachim Quantz (47), Johann Adolf Hasse (19), Nicolo Antonio Porpora (8), Johann Baptist Neruda (8), Johann Gottlieb Goldberg (3). Lists MS sources (mainly Dresden) and printed works.

KOLLER, Oswald

676 Die beste Methode, Volks- und volksmässige Lieder nach ihrer melodi-
☐   schen Beschaffenheit lexikalisch zu ordnen, *SIMG* IV (1902) 1-15.
>> Discusses methods of thematically and textually indexing folksongs. On p. 9-15, the first 300 numbers from BÖHME's *Altdeutsches Liederbuch* are indexed using a system of Arabic and Roman numerals. (see Ilmari Krohn's response, no. 698 and Scheurleer's original *Preisfrage,* no. 1162).

KÖLN, Erzbischöfliche Diözesanbibliothek: Leiblsche Sammlung

677 GÖLLER, Gottfried. Die Leiblsche Sammlung. Katalog der Musikalien der Kölner Domcapelle, *Beiträge zur rheinischen Musikgeschichte* 57 (Köln: Arno Volk-Verlag, 1964) 133p.
>> Pages 1-123 contain 290 incipits, indexing the music in the Domcapelle of Cologne.
>> *Reviews:* Winfried KIRSCH, *Mf* XX/1 (1967) 95.

KÖNIGSBERG. Staats- und Universitäts-Bibliothek

678 MÜLLER, Jos. Die musikalischen Schaetze der Koeniglichen- und Universitaets-Bibliothek zu Koenigsberg in Preussen (Bonn: Marcus, 1870) 431p.
>> Contains a thematic list of fifteen anonymous symphonies.

KÖNIGSPERGER, MARIANUS, 1708-1769

679 ZWICKLER, Friedhelm. Frater Marianus Königsperger OSB (1708-1769).
▽   Ein Beitrag zur süddeutschen Kirchenmusik des 18. Jahrhunderts (PhD diss.: Mainz, 1964) 298p.(typescript)
> Thematisches Verzeichnis, 190-298.
>> Incipits of all movements of complete works.

KONOLD, Wulf   (Kiel)

680   Untersuchungen zur weltlichen Kantate im 20. Jahrhundert
*   Will include a thematic catalogue of German language works
                 (Germany, Austria, Switzerland). It is scheduled for pub-
                 lication in 1973.

KOŽELUCH, LEOPOLD, 1752-1818

681   LÖBL, Gertrud. Die Klaviersonate bei Leopold Kozeluch (PhD diss.:
▽   Wien, 1937) 144ℓ. (typescript)
             Thematisches Verzeichnis, 133-41.
                 49 double staff incipits of the clavier sonatas, arranged by
                 opus number.

682   POSTOLKA, Milan. Leopold Koželuh, Život a dílo [Leopold Koželuh, his
        life and works]   (Praha: Státní Hudební Vydavatelství, 1964) 387p.
             Thematický katalog, 161-365.
                 Incipits for all movements of ca.450 works "preserved in al-
                 most all important Czechoslovak and foreign archives, librar-
                 ies and museums", arranged by genre. "Every section of the
                 catalogue contains primarily authentic compositions by Leo-
                 pold Koželuh in chronological order (as far as chronology
                 was ascertainable; where it was impossible to estimate it at
                 least approximately, the composition is listed at the end of
                 the group of authentic compositions); moreover, doubtful and
                 spurious compositions arranged according to keys (C major,
                 C minor, C sharp major, C sharp minor, D major, D minor etc.)
                 and, finally, compositions documented only by bibliographical
                 literature or unidentifiable compositions." (English résumé,
                 153-58)

682a   FLAMM, Christa. Leopold Koželuch. Biographie und stilkritische
□▽   Untersuchung der Sonaten für Klavier, Violine und Violoncello
        nebst einem Beitrag zur Entwicklungsgeschichte des Klaviertrios
        (PhD diss.: Wien, 1968) 3v. (typescript)
             Richtigstellungen und Ergänzungen zum thematischen Verzeichnis
             der Werke Leopold Koželuchs, v. 2, 228-32.
                 An enlargement of Postalka's catalogue. Without incipits.

KRAJEWSKI, Klemens

683   Kolbergowska metoda notowania melodii ludowych [Oskar Kolberg's
□   method of folk-tune indexing], Lud XLII (1955) 425-30.

KRAKÓW, Biblioteka Polskiej Akademii Nayk: Jan Z Lublina [Johannes de Lub-
lin]

684   WILKOWSKA-CHOMIŃSKA, Krystyna. Tabualatura organowa Jana z Lublina
        Indeks tematyczny, indeks alfabetyczny, facsimile, pt. I (Kraków:
        Polish Music Publications, 1964) 578p.
             Index thématique, 17-46.
                 345 incipits.

684a   WHITE, John R. The tablature of Johannes of Lublin MS 1716 of the
□   Polish Academy of Sciences in Cracow, MDisciplina XVII (1965) 137-62.

684 b   WHITE, John R. Original compositions and arrangements in the Lublin
☐   keyboard tablature, *Essays in Musicology, a birthday offering for
       Willi Apel* (Bloomington, Ind.: Indiana U. Press, 1968) 83-93.

KRAUS, JOSEPH MARTIN, 1756-1792

685   ANREP-NORDIN, Birger. Studier över Joseph Martin Kraus. III. Instru-
       mentalmusik I Cyklisk Form, *SvenskTMf* VI/2 (1924) 49-93.
              Incipits (p. 92-93) of 29 instrumental works, including sona-
              tas and symphonies. Data on location of MSS and scoring.

685a   --- Studier över Joseph Martin Kraus by Birger ANREP-NORDIN (Stock-
       holm: Isaac Marcus' Moktryckeri-Aktiebolag, 1924) Musikbilaga, 126-27.
              Same as previous entry, but separately published.

KREBS, JOHANN LUDWIG, 1713-1780

686   HORSTMAN, Jean. The instrumental music of Johann Ludwig Krebs
       (PhD diss.: Boston U., 1959) 314p. Univ. Micro. 59-3465. (typescript)
              Thematic catalogue of J.L. Krebs' clavier and chamber music, 249-
              87.
                     Incipits for all movements. Gives MS location and modern
              editions.

KREISLER, FRITZ, 1875-1962

687   Fritz Kreisler, vollständiges Verzeichnis seiner Werke (Mainz: Schott,
       193-?)
              Partially thematic.

687a   --- Reprint. Louis P. LOCHNER, Fritz Kreisler (New York: Macmillan,
       1950) 445p.
       [Thematic catalogue], 407-16.
              Incipits for all movements or sections of most compositions,
              including "arrangements" later admitted to be original.

KREMSMÜNSTER, Austria. Benediktiner-Stift

688   FLOTZINGER, Rudolf. Die Lautentabulaturen des Stiftes Kremsmünster
▽   mit musikgeschichtlicher Auswertung der Handschriften L 64 und L 81
       sowie Thematischem Katalog des Gesamtbestandes (PhD diss.: Wien,
       1965) 2v. (typescript)
              The printed version below encompasses the contents of volume
              2 of this typewritten dissertation. Here, however, the in-
              cipit transcriptions are on 2 staves and numbering is not al-
              ways identical (ordered according to number of parts while
              in printed version according to MS).

689   --- Die Lautentabulaturen des Stiftes Kremsmünster. Thematischer
       Katalog, *Tabulae Musicae Austriacae* II (Wien: Böhlaus Nachf., 1965)
       274p.
              1329 incipits, transcribed from French and Italian lute
              tabluture, of nine 17th and 18th century MSS in the Bene-
              dictine abbey of Kremsmünster. Works include instrumental
              pieces (preludes, toccatas, arias, dances, and transcriptions

of chansons) and vocal airs de cour by the following composers: (Jacques?, Pierre, and Denis) Gautier, DuFault, DuPré,
C. Mouton, Gallot, Peri, Caccini, Fr. Lambardi, G. Bataille,
Vincent, P. Guédron, Farnaby, Scheidt, Sweelinck, Chevalier,
and Mace.

Reviews: Musikhandel XVIII/2 (1967) 88; Ian HARWOOD, *MTimes*
CVIII (Mar 1967) 233; André VERCHALY, *RMusicol* LIII/1 (1967)
69-70; Hans RADKE, *Mf* XXI (1968) 242-44.

KREUSSER, GEORG ANTON, 1746-1811

690　PETERS, Edith (Mainz).　**Georg Anton Kreusser. Leben und Werk**　(Will
*　be published in the series *Beiträge zur mittelrheinischen Musik-
geschichte*).
Thematischer Katalog sämtlicher Werke.

KREUTZER, RODOLPHE, 1766-1831

691　BACHMANN, Alberto.　**Les grands violinistes du passé**　(Paris: Fischbacher, 1913) 468p.　(see no. 65)
Table thématique des concertos, 121-31.
Incipits for all movements of 19 concertos arranged by opus
number.

692　MAYERHOFER, Herwig.　**Thematischer Katalog der Violinkonzerte**　(PhD
*　diss.: Mainz)

KRIEGER, ADAM, 1634-1666

693　OSTHOFF, Helmut. **A. Krieger, neue Beiträge zur Geschichte des
deutschen Liedes im I7. Jahrhundert** (Leipzig: Breitkopf & Härtel,
1929) 107p.
**Thematisches Verzeichnis der Ariensammlung Adam Kriegers von
I657,** 55-60.
Melodic incipits with figured bass.　Arranged by song number
within each of 5 groups.

KRIEGER, JOHANN, 1651-1735

694　SEIFFERT, Max.　**Gesammelte Werke für Klavier und Orgel,** *DTB* 18
(Leipzig: Breitkopf & Härtel, 1917)
**Verzeichnis der kirchlichen und weltlichen Vokalwerke Joh.
Kriegers,** xxxiv-xxxviii.
Thematic for Magnificats and Masses only.

KRIEGER, JOHANN PHILIPP, 1649-1725

695　SEIFFERT, Max.　**2I Ausgewählte Kirchenkompositionen,** *DDT* 53-54
(Leipzig: Breitkopf & Härtel, 1916) (see no. 1200)
**Verzeichnis der I684-I725 von J. Ph. Krieger in Weissenfels
aufgeführten eigenen Kirchenstücke,** sowie der in Bibliotheken
handschriftlich erhaltenen Werke, xxiv-lii.
Thematic for Magnificats and Masses only.

695a　--- Neuauflage (Wiesbaden: Breitkopf & Härtel, 1958), revidiert **von**
H.J. MOSER.

KRIENS, CHRISTIAN, 1881-1934

696   Catalogue of the works of C. Kriens   (New York: Carl Fischer, n.d.)
            Partially thematic. Does not include some of the larger
            works, such as operas, oratorio, symphonies, tone poems,
            overtures, suites, etc.

KROGMANN, CARRIE WILLIAMS, 1860-1943

697   A thematic catalogue of musical compositions by C.W. Krogmann (Boston:
      B.F. Wood, 1913) 43p.
            Double staff incipits of 175 piano compositions "grades 1a-
            3c", including 5 songs.

KROHN, Ilmari

698   Welches ist die beste Methode, um Volks- und volksmässige Lieder
□   nach ihrer melodischen (nicht textlichen)Beschaffenheit lexikalisch
      zu ordnen?, *SIMG* IV (1903) 643-60.
            Discusses Koller's article (no. 676); sets up a system for
            melodic incipits with generous examples. See Scheuleer's
            original *Preisfrage* (no. 1162).

KROMĚŘÍŽ, Czechoslovakia. Zámecký hudebni archiv

699   [Thematic catalogue]   (CS KRa) Compiled 1759. (manuscript)
▽   Not examined. According to letter from Dr. Jiří Sehnal, the
            catalogue has incipits for the "Leichtensteinsche Sammlung,
            Colloredsche Sammlung, Piaristensammlung, St.Mauritz-Sammlung,
            Sammlung der Marienkirche und Erzherzog-Rudolph-Sammlung (ein
            Torso)." The collections are still in Kromĕříž although the
            "alte Katalog" is in Brno.

KROMMER, FRANZ, 1759-1831

700   Kromer Werke (A Wst: MH 9179/c) [6p.] No date   (manuscript). Mi-
▽   crofilm in US NYcg.
            Incipits for 52 string quartets, 4 quintets, and a Hungarian
            dance.

      HORST, Walter. Franz Krommer (I759-I83I). Sein Leben und Werk mit
      besonderer Berücksichtigung der Streichquartette (PhD diss.: Wien,
      1932) 262*l*. (typescript)
         [Thematic catalogue of the complete instrumental works],93-262.
            Over 500 incipits for all movements of symphonies, concertos,
            and chamber works, Op. 1-110.

KUHLAU, FRIEDRICH [DANIEL FRIEDRICH RUDOLPH],1786-1832

702   FOG, Dan (København).   A thematic catalogue of his printed works
*   "Bibliographical description of first edition, dates of
            composition and first edition, contemporary editions,
            arrangements and versions by the composer and others,
            important later editions......chronological and systema-
            ical listing, index of titles and first-lines, and of names
            of persons and locations."

KUHNAU, JOHANN, 1660-1722

703 FUCHS, Aloys. Thematisches Verzeichnis über sämtliche Klavier- und
▽   Orgel-Kompositionen. 1830 (D Bds: Kat. ms. 656) 2*l*. (manuscript).

> *Reference:* Richard SCHAAL, Quellen zur Musiksammlung Aloys
> Fuchs, *Mf* XVI (1963) 72. (see no. 1159)

KUKLINSKA, A. Cechanowska

704 Polish mathematical methods in classification of slavic folk songs,
☐   *Tenth congress of the International Musicological Society, Ljubljana*
     (1967), Dragotin CVETKO, ed., 440-43.

KUNDIGRABER, HERMANN, 1879-1944

705 HAINZ, Anton. Hermann Kundigraber. Leben und Werk (PhD diss.:
▽   Graz, 1950) (typescript)
          Bibliographischer Anhang, 62-108.
               Incipits for works.

LABOR, JOSEF, 1842-1924

706 KUNDI, Paul. Josef Labor. Sein Leben und Wirken, sein Klavier- und
▽   Orgelwerk nebst thematischem Katalog sämtlicher Kompositionen (PhD
     diss.: Wien, 1962) 2v., 336, 114*l*. (typescript)
          Thematisches Verzeichnis der Kompositionen Josef Labors, v. 2.
               Multiple staff incipits for all movements. Works include:
               cantatas, oratorios, Masses, motets, choruses with piano-
               forte accomp., chamber works, organ chorale preludes, and
               pianoforte concertos.

LACHNER, FRANZ, 1803-1890

707 WAGNER, Günter. Franz Lachner als Liederkomponist nebst einem
     biographischen Teil und dem thematischen Verzeichnis sämtlicher
     Lieder, *Schriften zur Musik* Bd. 3 (Giebing üb. Prien a. Chiemsee:
     Katzbichler, 1970) 313p.
          Thematisches Verzeichnis, 141-304.

LAMBACH, Austria. Benediktiner-Stift Lambach

708 Catalogus/ Musicalium et Instrumentorum/ ad Chorum Lambacensem per-
▽   tinentium conscriptge (=conscriptum)/ MDCCLXIIX/ 1768 (A LA) [94p]
     (manuscript). Microfilm copy in US NYcg.

Key: ✱ in preparation; ▽ manuscript; ☐ literature; ☆ Library of Congress

Incipits for instrumental and sacred vocal works, with no-
tations of complete scoring specifications. Composers in-
clude: Aumann, Benda, Boccherini, Bode, Brioschi, Bugnani
[Pugnani], Caldara, Calvi, Camerlocher, Cherzelli, Chiesa,
Conrad, Contrapunti, Crisstelli, Desslbruner, Dilletante,
Ditters, Donberger, Eberlin, Fauner, Fiamenghino, Fischer,
Fonelli, Galimberti, Galuppi, Gassmann, Giacomelli, Grauner,
Hamp, Harrer, J. Heyden, Hoffmann, Holzbauer, Ivanschiz,
Jommelli, Kimmerling, Kohaut, Korzl, Kramel, Laub, Leo,
Mahaut, Martino, Matscheko, Mayr, Monn, Mozart, Negri, Neu-
mann, Obermayer, Olalbi, Ordenez, Orfler, Ortl, Pachi, Per-
boni, Pergolesi, Pernafion, Peÿer, Piacentino, Pichl, Piz-
zossi, Prioli, Pugnani, Reitter, Reluzzi, Richter, Riepl,
Rosmarin, Roy, Scheibl, Seidl, Siberer, Sleindt, Sonnleüth-
ner, Stamitz, Tartini, Vinstatt, Vogl, Wagenseil, Werner,
Wrastil, Zani, Zach, Zechner, Ziegler.

LANG, JOHANN GEORG, 1722-1798

709   DAVIS, Shelley G. **The keyboard concertos of Johann Georg Lang (I722-**
▽   **I798)** (PhD diss.: New York U., 1971)(typescript)
         Thematic catalogue
              36 incipits with outline description for each movement (in-
              cluding tempo, meter, structure and length, and for slow
              movements, the key), list of sources, discrepancies among
              the sources.

LANGNAC, Albert (compiler)

710   **Collection complète des leçons d'harmonie** (Paris: Lemoine, [19--])
      3v.
         Table thématique, v. 1, ii-v.
              Incipits for the 208 exercises in the 3 volumes.

LANSKY, Josef; SUPPAN, Wolfgang

711   **Der neue Melodien-Katalog des Deutschen Volksliedarchivs,** *FontesArtisM*
□   X/1-2 (1963) 30-34.
              The Deutsche Volksliedarchiv in Freiburg im Breisgau maintains
              a carefully-classified Inzipit-Katalog of 202,000 tunes [as of
              1963]. Article gives the background of the Archive and des-
              cribes the classification system. Includes useful bibliography.

LaRUE, Jan (compiler)

712   **Union thematic catalogue of 18th-century symphonies,** Index cards.
▽   Begun ca. 1954. (manuscript)
              Includes symphonies from numerous large and small libraries,
              18th-century manuscript and printed catalogues, and modern
              catalogues of collections. An estimated 12,000 to 13,000
              works are included. Approximately 800 of these are anonymous
              but many have been identified through use of the Union Cata-
              logue. Three large files of 3 x 5 cards make up the cata-
              logue: the composer, locator, and disputed paternity (DP)
              files. The composer cards are arranged alphabetically, and
              give the attribution, musical incipit for the first move-
              ment, brief information on the remaining movements, and the

library and catalogue sources for the composition. The locator cards are organized by key, mode, and time signature,
then according to the principle of least melodic motion from
the initial pitch. The DP cards currently number about 650,
and include all symphonies attributed to two or more composers. These multiple attributions have been discovered
through use of the main locator file. A one-tonality master file of the symphonies and a fully computerized
system are proposed for the future.

712a A union thematic catalogue of 18th century symphonies, *FontesArtisM*
☐   VI/1 (1959) 18-20.
> Discusses the need for a union catalogue and proposes a
> system for notating incipits.

712b Major and minor mysteries of identification in the 18th century
☐   symphony, *JAmerMusicolSoc* XIII/1-3 (1960) 181-96.
> States the need for LaRue's forthcoming union thematic cata-
> logue of 18th century symphonies, citing examples of errors
> in identification, attribution and other areas, and citing
> in particular the false attribution to G.M. Monn of a symphony
> by F.X. Pokorny.

713   Union thematic catalogue of concertos, Index cards. Begun ca. 1959
▽   (see no. 712) (manuscript)
> Contains some 8,000 entries for concertos composed between
> 1740 and 1810. Its three main divisions are the alphabeti-
> cal composer file, the key file, and the union file. The
> latter two are locator files; they differ from the locator
> files of the Symphony Catalogue in that they use numerical
> incipits instead of musical notation. The key file is ar-
> ranged along the principle of least melodic motion, but al-
> ways in reference to degrees 1-7 of the major scale, using
> sharps or flats as needed. The union file uses the same
> principle, but as if all incipits were in a single major to-
> nality. The DP catalogue has a limited amount of entries
> thus far.

713a Union thematic catalogues for 18th century chamber music and concertos,
☐   *FontesArtisM* VII/2 (1960) 64-66.
> Stresses need for union thematic indexes and discusses merits
> of numerical system vs. regular notation for incipits.

LaRUE, Jan

714   Significant and coincidental resemblance between classical themes,
☐   *JAmerMusicolSoc* XIV (1961) 224-34.
> Demonstrates the important role of his union thematic catalogues
> of 18th century symphonies and chamber music in a study of
> melodic relationships in classical themes.

715   Gluck oder Pseudo-Gluck?, *Mf* XVII/3 (1964) 272-75.
☐
> Discussion of varying attributions in various sources of an
> overture ascribed to Gluck by Wotquenne. Conclusion attri-
> butes the work to Bernasconi, and remarks on the typical
> difficulties in establishing accurate ascriptions.

716   *Review of:* KÖCHEL, Ludwig Ritter von. **Chronologisch-thematisches**
☐   **Verzeichnis sämtlicher Tonwerke Wolfgang Amadé Mozarts.** Sechste

Auflage bearbeitet von Franz Giegling, Alexander Weinmann, Gerd
Sievers (Wiesbaden: Breitkopf & Härtel, 1964), *JAmerMusicolSoc*
XX (1967) 495-501.
> Outlines principles for the production of future thematic
> catalogues.

717 The thematic index: a computer application to musicology, *Computers*
☐ *and the Humanities* II/5 (May 1968) 243.

LaRUE, Jan; RASMUSSEN, Mary

718 Numerical incipits for thematic catalogues, *FontesArtisM* IX/2 (1962)
☐ 72-75.
> Description of system using the normal typewriter symbols
> as a less expensive method of replacing the musical notation
> in thematic catalogues.

LaRUE, Jan; LOGEMANN, George W.

719 E[lectronic] D[ata] P[rocessing] for thematic catalogues, *Notes* XXII/4
☐ (June 1966) 1179-86.

LA RUE, PIERRE de, 1460?-1518

720 ROBYNS, Jozef. **Pierre de La Rue, een bio-bibliographische studie**
(Brussels: Palais des Académies, 1954) 251p.
Thematische catalogus, 177-231.
> Incipits in original clefs, arranged by genre. Index lists
> all sources, and notes on dates of each composition.

LASSUS, ROLAND de, 1532-1594

721 EITNER, Robert. **Chronologisches Verzeichniss der gedruckten Werke
von Hans Leo Hassler und Orlandus de Lassus,** nebst alphabetisch
geordnetem Inhaltsanzeiger (Beilage zu den Monatsheften für Musikgeschichte V. und VI. Jahrg.) (Berlin: Bahn, 1874) cxxxvip.
**Alphabetisch geordnetes Verzeichniss aller Gesänge des Orlandus
de Lassus,** lxxvii-cxxxiv.
> Partially thematic; chiefly for lections, Magnificats, and
> Masses. Cantus firmi only.

LATROBE, CHRISTIAN IGNATIUS, 1758-1836

722 STEVENS, Charles. **The musical works of Christian Ignatius Latrobe**
▽ (PhD diss.: U. of North Carolina, 1971) 388p. (typescript)
Thematic index, Appendix B, 261- 372.
> 295 entries. "Latrobe's extant works include about ten
> works of cantata proportion, many German and English
> anthems, several solos, three piano sonatas, and nine
> organ preludes." Incipits for most important voice (i.e.
> soprano or 1st violin). Full bibliographical apparatus.

LECHLER, BENEDIKT, 1594-1659

723 KELLNER, P. Altman. **Benedikt Lechler.** Seine Tätigkeit als Komponist
▽ und Leiter der Stiftsmusik von Kremsmünster (PhD diss.: Wien, 1931)

234*l*. (typescript)
   Verzeichnis der Kompositionen Lechlers (chronol.), [217]- 224.
      Incipits of 28 works (Masses, Hymns, canzonas,etc.)

LECLAIR l'aîné, JEAN-MARIE, 1697-1764

724   BACHMANN, Alberto. Les grands violonistes du passé (Paris: Fisch-
      bacher, 1913) 468p. (see no. 65)
         Table thématique, 157-60.
            Incipits for sonata à trois (1), duo, trio, sonatas (16),
            sonatas for 2 violins (12), concertos (12), & sonate en sol.

725   ZASLAW, Neal A. Jean-Marie Leclair l'aîné; biography and chrono-
▽   logical thematic catalogue (MA diss.: Columbia U., 1965) 177p.
            Lists 102 works with incipits for all except 12 that are lost.
            Information on MSS, editions, and misattributions.

LEFKOFF, Gerald (compiler)

725.1 Five sixteenth-century Venetian lute books (PhD diss.: Catholic U.;
      Washington, D.C.: The Catholic U. of America Press, 1960) xv, 208p.
            Contains a thematic index for each of the following printed
            collections: *Intabolatura de lauto de diversi autori. Di
            Francesco da Milano. Di Alberto da Mantoa. Di Marco da
            Laquila. Di io Iacomo Albutio da Milano. Di Pietro Pauolo
            Borono da Milano. Con alcune padovane et saltarelli novi.*
            Scotto (1563); *Intabolatura...di Bernardino Balletti. Divarie
            sorte di balli...*Gardane (1554); *La intabolatura...dell'
            eccellente P. Paulo Borrono...di saltarelli. Padovane, balli,
            fantasie, et canzon francese...*Scotto (1563); *Intabolatura
            ...di Iulio Abundante de ogni sorte di balli...*Gardano (1563);
            *Libro primo...de M. Antonio di Becchi...con alcuni balli,
            Napolitane, madricali, canzon francese, fantasie, ricercari
            ...*Scotto (1568).

LEFKOWITZ, Murray (compiler)

725.2 The English fantasia for viols (MM Thesis, U. of Southern California,
      1951) v, 421p. (typescript)
         Thematic catalogue (Byrd through William White).

LEHÁR, FRANZ, 1870-1948

726   Katalog der Bühnenwerke von Franz Lehár (Wien: Glocken,1955) 62p.
            Publisher's catalogue. Gives personnel and orchestration
            for operettas. Incipits with text underlay and notes on
            first performances for each aria or piece.

LEIPZIG, Universitätsbibliothek: Apel Codex

727   RIEMANN, Hugo. Der Mensural-Codex des Magister Nikolaus Apel von
      Königschofen, *KmJb* XII (1897) Abhandlungen und Aufsätze, 1-23.
            Description of the Codex (D LEu: MS 1494); index in letter
            notation of 188 compositions by: Adam von Fulda, Aulen, Broda,
            Finck, Florigal, Hohenems, Isaac, R.de Mol, Resinarius,
            Rupsch, Stolzer, and Verbene.

LE JEUNE, CLAUDE, 1528-1600

728   LEVY, Kenneth J. **The chansons of Claude Le Jeune** (PhD diss.: Prince-
      ton U., 1955) 356p. Univ. Micro. 13,705.(typescript)
          Thematic index of Le Jeune chansons, 316-41.
              Incipits of each voice given in semi-modern notation. Chansons
              are arranged alphabetically, and number of voices, date of
              publication, and any modern editions are noted.

LE SUEUR, JEAN-FRANÇOIS, 1760-1837

729   MONGRÉDIEN, Jean (Paris). **Jean-François Le Sueur (I760-I837).**
 *   ca. 250p.
              Will contain approximately 500 incipits for the complete
              works of this composer. Will provide information regarding
              autographs, editions etc., and other bibliographical apparatus.

LESURE, François

730   **Musique et musicologie dans les bibliothèques Parisiennes,** *Bulletin*
 □   *des bibliothèques de France* III (1958)   265.
              Mentions use of data processing techniques in the establish-
              ment of a thematic index as a possible direction in future
              research.

LEVY, Lester S. (compiler)

731   **Some pre-I80I imprints in the Lester S. Levy collection of American**
 ▽   **sheet music: A thematic catalogue and subject index** (Peabody Insti-
      tute, typescript)
              "The thematic catalogue contains 264 entries, a few of them
              subdivided, with references to their Sonneck-Upton locations
              and Wolfe numbers, or if an entry is found in neither bibli-
              ography, an indication that it is unrecorded." (Geraldine
              Ostrove)

LEWIS, Leo R.

732   **The possibilities of thematic indexing,** *Proceedings of the Music*
 □   *Teachers National Association* VII (1912) 180-88.
              Describes the advantage of a melodic index of tunes in library
              card files and publishers' catalogues. Offers a system of
              his own.

LINCOLN, Harry B., (State U. of N.Y. at Binghamton)

733   **Indices of the frottola repertory**
 *   A computer generated catalog of the printed sources of ap-
              proximately 1,000 frottola compositions from the period
              1504-1530, including computer-printed incipits of the music,
              indices of composers and titles, and a listing of incipits
              in music notation, in interval sequence order.

              Reference: **The frottole repertory, a pilot study in informa-**
              tion retrieval, paper read to *American Musicological Society,*
              New Orleans, La. (Dec 1967)

734   [Thematic catalogue]
*   35,000 incipits of 16th century works other than frottola,
               including madrigals, motets, complete works, and modern
               editions. (see above entry).

735   Some criteria and techniques for developing thematic indices, *Der*
☐   *Computer in Musikwissenschaft und Musikdokumentation,* Harald Heck-
      mann, ed. (Regensburg: Gustav Bosse, 1967)

736   Thematic index of I6th century Italian music, *Computers and the*
☐   *Humanities* II/2 (Nov 1967) 86.

737   Musicology and the computer: the thematic index, *Computers in human-*
☐   *istic research: Readings and perspectives,* BOWLES, Edmund A., ed.
      (Englewood Cliffs, N.J.: Prentice Hall, 1967) 184-93.

738   The thematic index: a computer application to musicology, *Computers*
☐   *and the Humanities* II/5 (May 1968) 215-20.

LINDPAINTNER, PETER JOSEPH von, 1791-1856

739   Thematisches Verzeichniss meiner sämtlichen Werke   (D S; copy in D
▽   Mbs) 4v. 91; 79; 96; 44*l.* (manuscript)
               Multiple staff incipits for all movements of 483 works, arranged
               in chronological order (1808-1855).

LIST, George

740   An approach to the indexing of ballad tunes, *The Folklore and Folk*
☐   *Music Archivist* VI/1 (1963) 7-16.

LISZT, FRANZ, 1811-1886

741   Thematisches Verzeichniss der Werke von F. Liszt,Bearbeitungen und
      Transcriptionen (Leipzig: Breitkopf & Härtel, 1855) 162p.

741a --- Neue vervollständigte Ausgabe. [1877].

741b --- Reprint. (London: for H. Baron, 1965).
               Thematic index by genre, with 6 indexes and cross-referencing.
               Incipits for all movements, with text underlay where pertin-
               ent. Provides occasional dates of composition, dedications,
               publishers and publication price, transcriptions, and editions.

742   SEARLE, Humphrey. Liszt article, *Grove's Dictionary of Music and*
      Musicians, 5th ed., v. 5, p. 256-316.
      Thematic quotations, 312-13.
               Gives some themes to differentiate between versions, or
               between compositions with several settings of the same text.

LITOLFF, HENRY CHARLES, 1818-1891

743   BLAIR, Ted M. Henry Charles Litolff: (I8I8-I89I): his life and
      piano music (PhD diss.: U. of Iowa, 1968) 287p. Univ. Micro. 68-10,
      647.(typescript)
      Thematic indexes, 78-165, 178-239.

Index of the "Concertos Symphoniques" is found on p. 78-165,
and "Thematic catalogue of Henry Litolff's solo piano music"
is found on p. 178-239. 110 multiple staff incipits with
publisher's numbers, sources of MSS, general description, and
suggested performance aids.

LITOLFF, Henry Charles (publisher)

744   Führer durch die Collection Litolff. Verzeichniss der in Henry
Litolff's Verlag in Braunschweig erschienenen Musikalien mit
stufenweis geordneter Folge der Clavier-, Orgel-, Harmonium- und
Violin-Werke nebst Anhang eines thematischen Verzeichnisses und
einer kleinen Harmonie-Lehre. 2. verm. Auflage. (Braunschweig:
Henry Litolff's Verlag, [1884]) x, 396p.
    [Thematic catalogue], 361-76.
        495 incipits, arranged by genre, of instrumental works by
        the following composers: Beethoven, Clementi, J.L. Dussek,
        J. Haydn, J.N. Hummel, Fr. Kuhlau, W.A. Mozart, Fr. Schubert.

LJUBLJANA [LAIBACH], Yugoslavia

745   Musicalien-Catalog der Philharmonischen Gesellschaft in Laibach....
1 Nov. 1794 bis letzten Juni 1804.
        Printed title-page and format sheets, filled in with MS
        incipits of orchestral, chamber, and vocal music.
        Reference: communication from Jan LaRue (1968).

LOBAUGH, H. Bruce (compiler)

746   Three German lute books: Denss's *Florilegium,* 1594; Reymann's *Noctes
musicae*, 1598; Rude's *Flores musicae*, 1600 (PhD diss.: Musicology,
U. of Rochester, 1968) 2v. Univ. Micro. 68-13,806.(typescript)
    Thematic catalogues,
        See listings under individual composers.

LOCATELLI PIETRO-ANTONIO, 1695-1764

747   BACHMANN, Alberto. Les grands violonistes du passé (Paris: Fischbacher, 1913) 468p. (see no. 65)
    Table thématique des caprices de Locatelli.
        Incipits for 24 works arranged by opus number.

748   KOOLE, Arend. Leven en Werken van Pietro Antonio Locatelli da Ber-
gamo (PhD diss.: Utrecht, 1949; Amsterdam: Jasonpers, 1949) 291p.
    Thematische catalogus, 240-275.
        Incipits of each movement arranged in order of opus number.

749   DUNNING, Albert; KOOLE, Arend. Pietro Antonio Locatelli: Nieuwe
bijdragen tot de kennis van zijn Leven en Werken, *TVerNederlandseMg*
XX/1-2 (1964-65) 52-96.
    Bibliographische, deels thematische catalogus van de werken van
    P.A. Locatelli, 76-96.
        Opera Authentica, p. 76-86; complete bibliography for Op. I-
        IX, with thematic incipits for variants in Op. II. *Opera Du-
        bia,* p. 87-96: 46 works, with incipits and sources, includ-
        ing concerti, symphonies, and chamber works.

750   CALMEYER, John H. The life, times, and works of Pietro Antonio
      Locatelli (PhD diss., Musicology: U. of North Carolina, 1969)ix,
      469p. Univ. Micro. 70-3210. (typescript)
            Thematic index, 411-31.
                Incipits for all movements of Locatelli's complete works.

LOCKE, MATTHEW, 1630-1677

751   HARDING, Rosamond E.M. A thematic catalogue of the works of Matthew
*   Locke (Oxford: Blackwell, 1972) 177p.
                Reviews: Times Literary Supplement no. 3,658 (Apr 1972) 387.

LOEILLET, JEAN-BAPTISTE, 1680-1730?, JOHN (dates?), JACQUES, 1685-1746?

752   PRIESTMAN, Brian. Catalogue thématique des oeuvres de Jean-Baptiste,
✡   John et Jacques Loeillet, *RBelgeMusicol* VI /4 (1952) p. 219-274.
                Flute and figured bass incipits for each movement of Jean-
                Baptiste's flute sonatas. Similar incipits for John's in-
                strumental works, plus 2-staff incipits for keyboard composi-
                tions and single staff for dances. Instrumental and figured
                bass incipits for each movement of Jacques' sonatas and con-
                certos. 18th century editions, plus current editions and
                some library locations are provided. The compositions of the
                three composers are numbered in one series of Roman numerals,
                i.e. Priestman I for John's op. I, Priestman XV for Jacques'
                op. 5, etc.

LÖHLEIN, GEORG SIMON, 1725-1781

753   GLASENAPP, Franz von. Georg Simon Löhlein; sein Leben und seine
      Werke (PhD diss: Halle-Wittenberg; Leipzig: Frommhold & Wendler,
      1937) 247p.
            [Thematisches] Verzeichnis der Werke G.S. Löhleins, 224-36.
                Incipits of all instruments that appear in first-movement
                opening bars of instrumental music; piano reduction with
                text of vocal works. Arranged chronologically, with lo-
                cation of sources.

LOLLI, ANTONIO, 1730-1802

754   MELL, Albert (Queens College of C.U.N.Y.). Thematic catalogue
*

LONDON, British Museum: Mulliner Book

755   STEVENS, Denis. [The Mulliner Book: thematic catalogue] (GB Lbm:
▽   Mus. Add. Ms. 30513 and Add. Ms. 4900) (manuscript)

LONDON, British Museum: Add. MS. 40011 B.

756   BUKOFZER, Manfred F. The Fountains fragment, *Studies in medieval
      and renaissance music* (New York: Norton, 1950) 86-112.
                Multiple staff incipits for the contents of British
                Museum Add. MS. 40011 B. All of the compositions
                are anonymous, but one has been identified as by
                Rowland, a second tentatively assigned to Pennard.

LONDON, British Museum: Egerton MS 3307

756.1 SCHOFIELD, Bertram; BUKOFZER, Manfred. **A newly discovered 15th-century manuscript of the English Chapel Royal,** *MQ* XXXII (1946) 509-36; XXXIII (1947) 38-51.
> Part I contains a thematic index of Egerton MS 3307 (Meaux Abbey MS), p. 526-36 (anonymous works). Incipits are for all voices and in original notation. Emendations to this index have been made by BUKOFZER in his **Studies in Medieval & Renaissance Music** (New York: Norton, 1950) 115-17.

LONDON, British Museum: Tregian's anthology

756.2 SCHOFIELD, Bertram; DART, Thurston. **Tregian's anthology,** *MLetters* XXXII/3 (July 1951) 205-16.
> **Incipits of the new instrumental pieces in Egerton MS 3665,** 216.
> 35 incipits from the over 1,000 villanelle, madrigals, and instrumental pieces mostly by English and Italian 16th and 17th century composers contained in this MS, which is probably copied by Francis Tregian. Composers include: Bassano, Deering, Ferrabosco I & II, Lupo, Morley, Mundy, and Philips.

LONDON, British Museum: Tudway Collection

757
▽ BURNEY, Charles. **Index in notation to the 6 vols 4** to **of Dr. Tudway's MS collection of English Church music [1715-1720] in the British Museum.** Bibl. Harl. 7337 to 7342 (GB Lbm: Br. Mus. Add. 11587 and 11589) Compiled after 1794. (manuscript)

LONDON, Philharmonic Society.

758 CALKIN, Joseph. **Catalogue of the library belonging to the Philharmonic Society, London,** instituted 1813. (London: Engraved by C. Maund, 1824) 42p.
> Incipits to symphonies and overtures which are owned by the Philharmonic Society, by the following composers: Andre, Beethoven, Blymä, Burghersh, Burrowes, Catel, Cherubini, Crotch, Eberl, Eibler, Eler, Fesca, Fiorillo, Fraenzl, Gallus, Gluck, Haydn, Himmel, Jomelli, Kreutzer, Krommer, Martini, Méhul, Mozart, Paer, Piccini, Pleyel, Reicha, Ries, Rigel, A. Romberg, B. Romberg, Rossini, Soliva, Spohr, Spontini, Teyber, Vogel, Weber, Winter, Woelfl, Wranizcky.

LONDON, Public Record Office

759 STEVENS, Denis. **A part-book in the public record office,** *Music Survey* II (1950) 161-70.
> Discussion of contents of bassus part-book found in 1948, dating from the time of Henry VIII. The MS is compared with the Mulliner Book of keyboard transcriptions. Thematic index of the bassus part of 25 songs (S.P.I., v. 246, ff. 16-29) appears on pages 169-70. (see no. 755).

LONDON. Westminster Abbey Library.

760 SQUIRE, William Barclay. **Musik-Katalog der Bibliothek der Westminster-Abtei in London,** Beilage zu den *MfMG* 35 (1903) (Leipzig: Breitkopf &

Härtel, [1903]) 29-40.
> Partially thematic for works in manuscript. Contains a listing of sacred and secular vocal music; collected works arranged in chronological order. Instrumental works arranged alphabetically by composer. Author and subject index is provided.

LOTZ, Andrew J.

761   **The death of the alphabet.** Musical notation for standard typewriters
☐   and how to dictate the notation (New York: Carleton Press, c. 1965)
> A number notation system upon which is based a derivative vocabulary for discussing theory and harmony. The author's eventual goal is "the development of a system of musical shorthand founded on mathematical principles."

LÖWENTHAL, Siegbert (compiler)

762   **Die musikübende Gesellschaft zu Berlin und die Mitglieder Joh. Philipp Sack, Fr. Wilh. Riedt, und Joh. Gabr. Seyffarth** (PhD diss.: Basel, 1927; Laupen, 1928) 98p.
> **Thematisches Verzeichnis** der Kompositionen Joh. Ph. Sacks, chronologisch geordnet, 40-43.
>> Incipits for 15 Lieder, and 8 dances for clavier.
>
> **Verzeichnis der Werke** Fr. Wilh. Riedts, chronologisch geordnet, 62-64.
>> 10 incipits of duets, trios and quartets for flute and other instruments.
>
> **Thematisches Verzeichnis** der Kompositionen Johann Gabriel Seyffarths, chronologisch geordnet, 91-94.
>> 21 incipits for 6 Lieder, 4 cantatas, 10 dances for clavier, and 1 symphony.

LÜBECK, Hendrich, 16th c. (compiler)

763   **[202 trumpet "sonatas" and fanfares for] C.K.C.D.** [Christian König zu
▽   Dänemark] 1598 [appears on binding which also shows the royal arms] (DK Kk: Gl. kgl. S. 1874. 4°) 115*l.* (manuscript). On folio 1 the compiler has written "Henrich Lübeckh gehört diss Buch zu mit Recht vnd ist mir lieb."
> **Register,** folios 3-4v contain incipits to the first group of 64 plus 38 sonatas (fanfares) in quadruple metre, divided into those which begin on the first beat and those with an upbeat. Folios 108-09 contain incipits to the 100 additional fanfares in triple metre, but only for those beginning on the downbeat.
>> With the exception of the melodic incipit listings in medieval tonaries (see no. 1310), this collection of trumpet pieces contains the earliest extant thematic index. (For the earliest example of a *printed* thematic catalogue, see Barton no. 73). This "register" was simply a practical method of indexing the incipits of the pieces included in the volume. Lübeck, and his compatriot and fellow trumpeter Magnus Thompsen, brought the well-developed art of German trumpet playing to the sumptuous court of Christian IV. They were among the 64 musicians (including 17 trumpeters from Germany) that participated in King Christian's coronation in 1596. Lübeck's volume, and the similar collection compiled by Magnus Thomp-

sen (DK Kk: Gl. kgl. S. 1875. 4 ; without thematic index),contain a rich and varied trumpet repertoire for court and field, with titles like: Sonate, Sonada, Siegnate (Signal), Aufzug, Post, Rotta, Pottesella (Boute selle), Montacawalla à cheval). *References:* Angul HAMMERICH, Musik am Hofe Christains IV (København, 1898). Georg SCHÜNEMANN, Sonaten und Feldstück der Hoftrompeter, *ZfMw* XVII/4 (1935) 147-70.

XIII. Lübeck, *Register [202 trumpet sonatas and fanfares]*, 1598, no. 763

LUDWIG, Friedrich (compiler)

764   Repertorium organorum recentioris et motetorum vetustissimi stili. (Band II. Musikalisches Anfangs-Verzeichnis des nach Tenores geordneten Repertorium.) Besorgt von Friedrich GENNRICH. Summa Musicae Medii Aevi, hrsg. von Friedrich GENNRICH, Band VIII (Langen bei Frankfurt, 1962).

> Thematic catalogue of 515 motets based on 50 tenors taken from the liturgy of the Mass of the Ars Antiqua period. Reprinted under Friedrich Gennrich's guidance from a portion of Ludwig's unpublished proof copy.

765   --- DITTMER, Luther. 2nd rev. & enl. ed. 1964, 4v.
          "The unpublished index of incipits prepared by Ludwig
          will follow..."

LULLY, JEAN-BAPTISTE, 1632-168 7

766   ELLIS, Helen Meredith, The dances of J.B.Lully (1632-1687)(PhD diss.:
          Stanford U., 1967) 269p. Univ. Micro. 67-17, 418. (typescript)
          [Thematic catalogue], n.p.
                Incipits of his 268 pieces with specific dance titles.
                Sources given for printed and MS copies.

LUND, Sweden. Universitetsbiblioteket

767   Card catalogue with thematic incipits of music collections Engelhardt
▽   (MSS and prints before 1780), Kraus (mainly MSS, late 17th-early 18th
          century) and Wenster (MSS and prints mainly 18th century). Copies
          in S Skma; S Sma; S Uu.(manuscript)
                The collections are rich in anonymous works, many of which
                are now being identified

LUND, Sweden. Universitetsbiblioteket: Kat. Wenster Litt. 1/1-17b

768   RASMUSSEN, Mary. The Manuscript Kat. Wenster Litt. 1/1-17b (Uni-
          versitetsbiblioteket, Lund), a contribution to the history of the
          Baroque horn concerto, *BrassQ* V (1961-62) 135-52.
                Incipits for all movements of the 18 horn concertos in the
                manuscript by the following composers: Forster, Gehra, Graun,
                Knechtel, Quantz, Reinhardt, Röllig, Scheibe, and 5 anony-
                mous works.

LÜNEBURG, Ratsbücherei

769   WELTER, Friedrich. Katalog der Musikalien der Ratsbücherei Lüne-
          burg (Lippstadt: Kistner & Siegel & Co., 1950) xi, 332p.
                1324 incipits of works in manuscript located at Lüneburg.

LUPO, THOMAS, d. 1628

770   MEYER, Ernst Hermann. Die mehrstimmige Spielmusik des I7. Jahr-
✡   hunderts in Nord- und Mitteleuropa   (Kassel: Bärenreiter, 1934)
          258p. (see no. 821)
              [Thematic catalogue], 157-59.
                    Incipits for 25 fantasias à 3, 13 fantasias à 4, 28 fan-
                    tasias à 5, 1 Miserere à 5, 13 fantasias à 6.

LUZZASCHI, LUZZASCO, c. 15 45-1607

771   SPIRO, Arthur G. (Youngstown State U.) Thematic catalogue of the
*   collected works of Luzzaschi
                    Concerned with all published madrigals- numbered volumes,
                    collections and posthumous publications. Will also include
                    additional information on sacred vocal music (published and
                    in MS).

MACDOUGALL, Hamilton C. (compiler)

772　Early New England psalmody (Brattleboro: Stephen Daye Press, 1940)
179p.
　　Tunes from Ainsworth, The Bay Psalm Book, Tufts, and completed
　　by Walter in modern hymnals, 151-60.
　　　　Of the 42 tunes indexed, three are by named composers as
　　　　follows: Croft or Händel, Este, and O. Gibbons.

--- Reprint. (New York: Da Capo Press, 1969).

MADRID, Biblioteca Medinaceli

773　TREND, J.B. Catalogue of the music in the Biblioteca Medinaceli,
　　Revue hispanique LXXI (1927) 485-554.
　　　　34 items fully described, with inventories of contents and
　　　　biographical sketches of the composers. Includes an appen-
　　　　dix of musical settings of famous poets. This library con-
　　　　tains the complete body of Spanish (Castilian) madrigals.
　　　　Includes 6 themes by Vasquez.

MAHLER, GUSTAV, 1860-1911

774　BEIBL, Thomas. A study of the contrapuntal style in the fifth sym-
▽　　phony of Mahler (MM diss.: Indiana U., 1971) 74p. (typescript)
　　Thematic catalogue.

775　MARTNER, Knud. Gustav Mahler's Werke. Chronologisches und systema-
*　　tisches Verzeichnis seiner gedruckten Werke, nebst einer Aufstellung
　　seiner frühen und fragwürdigen Werke und einer Diskographie (To be
　　published by Armido Verlag, Lucerne) ca. 260p.
　　　　"Following information will be given for every work: musical
　　　　incipit and tempo; composition place and date; playing time;
　　　　instrumentation; performances: (a) by Mahler, (b) by other
　　　　conductors during Mahler's lifetime; editions: (a) original,
　　　　(b) arrangements ....;literature regarding each work (i.e.
　　　　only separate analyses etc.); quotations regarding each work
　　　　from primary sources.....; annotations-name and title index.
　　　　Appendix A: Text to all Mahler's vocal works; B: Plate Nos.
　　　　list (or ed. nos.) of his publishers; C: literature in gen-
　　　　eral on Mahler."

MAIER, Julius Joseph (compiler)

776　Unbekannte Sammlungen deutscher Lieder des XVI. Jahrhunderts, *MfMG*

Key: * in preparation; ▽ manuscript; □ literature; ☆ Library of Congress

XII (1880) 6-13, 17-22.
> Contains a thematic catalogue of the anonymous works in the
> second *Liederbuch* of Peter Schöffer, p. 17-22.

MANCHICOURT, PIERRE DE, ca. 1510-1564

777   WICKS, John D. The motets of Pierre de Manchicourt (ca. 1510-1564)
▽   (Phd diss.: Harvard, 1959) 2v. (tyepscript)
> Thematic index of the complete works of Manchicourt, v. II,
> Appendix Z, 228-47.
>> "Each work is quoted polyphonically for the first two or
>> three measures. It is an alphabetical index according to
>> genre - motet, chanson, and Mass. Each work is numbered.
>> Both "prima" and "secunda partes" are given."

MANCINI, FRANCESCO, 1672-1737

778   WRIGHT, Josephine. The secular cantatas of Francesco Mancini
*   (PhD diss.: New York U.) in prep
>> Ca. 225 entries.

MANN [MONN], JOHANN CHRISTOPH, fl. 1766

779   FISCHER, Wilhelm, ed. Wiener Instrumentalmusik vor und um I750,
      DTÖ 19/2   (Wien: Artaria, 1912) xxxix,122p. (see nos. 844 & 507)
> Thematischer Katalog der Instrumentalwerke von....J.C. Mann,
> xxxiv-xxxix.
>> Incipits for all movements of instrumental divertimenti.
>> Double-staff incipits for all movements of sonatas and
>> minuets and trios. Arranged by key.

--- Reprint. (Graz: Akademische Druck-U. Verlagsanstalt, 1959) Bd. 39.

MARAZZOLI, MARCO, 1619?-1662

780   CALUORI, Eleanor. [Thematic catalogue of cantatas] (Wellesley:
▽   Wellesley College, 1964)(manuscript)
>> Proposed addition to the *Wellesley Edition Cantata Index*
>> *Series*.

781   WITZENMANN, Wolfgang. Autographe Marco Marazzolis in der Biblioteca
      Vaticana I, *Studien zur italienisch-deutschen Musikgeschichte* VI
      (1969) [36]-86, and VII (1970) [203]-294. (*AnalectaMusicol* 7 & 9)
> Katalog.
>> Ca. 450 incipits for all sections of sacred vocal music,
>> operas, and vocal chamber music.

MARCELLO, BENEDETTO, 1686-1739

782   FUCHS, Aloys. Thematisches Verzeichniss über sämmtliche Compositionen
▽   von Benedetto Marcello (D Bds: HB VII, Mus. ms. theor. 674) [5p]
      Compiled 1840. (manuscript) Microfilm copy in US NYcg. [reproduction
      on facing page]
>> Double-staff-incipits for 29 vocal works, 23 of them psalms.

XIV. Marcello, *Thematisches Verzeichniss...*(Fuchs), 1840, no. 782

783   Thematischer Catalog der 50 Psalmen von Marcello   (D Bds: HB VII,
▽   Mus. ms. theor. K. 675) [9p]. (manuscript) Microfilm copy in US NYcg.
               Incipits given in score.

784   NEWMAN, William S. **The keyboard sonatas of Benedetto Marcello,**
        ActaMusicol XXIX/1 (1957) 28-41. (see also no. 507)
               [Thematic index], 31-32.
                     Ex. 1 is "a thematic index of the 46 movements and *La Ciacona*
                     that make up the 13 sonatas in the Paris MS [Bibliothèque
                     Nationale Vm7 5289], plus 2 other movements...to be found
                     in Malipiero's assortment of keyboard sonata movements by
                     Marcello."

784a   --- Thematic Supplement. William S. NEWMAN, **Postscript to "The key-**
        board sonatas of Benedetto Marcello", *ActaMusicol* XXXI/3-4 (1959)
        192-96.
                     Additional incipits from MS 13,550, now in the Deutsche Staats-
                     bibliothek, and correlation with the Paris MS.

MARCHAND, LOUIS, 1669-1732

785   PIRRO, André. **Louis Marchand,,** *SIMG* VI (1904-1905) 154-59.
               Table des airs.....trouvés dans les bibliothèques de Paris.
                     Texted incipits with continuo found in 6 collections.

MARENZIO, LUCA, 1553-1599

786   JACKSON, Roland (Claremont, Calif.). **Thematic catalogue of the**
*   **sacred music of Luca Marenzio**

MARTIN, PHILIPP, fl. ca.1730-1733

787   NEEMAN, Hans. **P. Martin; ein vergessener Lautenist,** *ZfMW* IX/7 (1927)
        545-59.
               [Thematisches Verzeichnis der Lautentrios].
                     Full score incipits, arranged numerically.

MARTINI, PADRE GIOVANNI BATTISTA, 1706-1784

788   BROFSKY, Howard. **The instrumental music of Padre Martini**   (PhD diss.:
        New York U., 1963) 357p. Univ. Micro. 64-6452.(typescript)
               Thematic index, Appendix, 237-333.
                     Contains a complete "thematic source index" to over 600 works,
                     "the most important of which are the concertos, symphonies,
                     and sonatas." Incipits for all movements.

MARTINŮ, BOHUSLAV, 1890-

789   SAFRANEK, Miloš. **Bohuslav Martinu, his life and works,** English
        trans. by Robert Finlayson-Samaourova (London: Wingate, 1961)
               [Thematic catalogue], 334-58.
                     Incipits for 109 early works, and 276 major works, arranged
                     chronologically. Indicates publishers, MSS, and locations
                     of autographs.

790   HALBREICH, Harold. **Bohuslav Martinu** (Zürich: Atlantis, 1968) 384p.
      [Thematic catalogue]
              Two-thirds of this work is a thematic catalogue, including
              a recently discovered violin concerto (dated 1932 and listed
              as missing in Safranek's catalogue).

              Reviews: Gerald ABRAHAM, *MLetters* L/4 (1969); *NeueZM* XVIII/3
              (1969) 12.

791   PERRY, R. Kent (U. of Illinois). **The violin-piano sonatas of**
*   **Bohuslav Martinu**

MARX, ADOLPH BERNHARD, 1795-1866

792   HIRSCHBERG, Leopold. **Der Tondichter A.B. Marx,** *SIMG* X (1908-1909)
      1-72.
          [Descriptive catalogue of works with thematic quotations.]
              Themes and incipits quoted throughout text. Arranged by
              opus no.; vary from single staff to all vocal parts or
              piano reduction.

MASCHERA, FIORENZO, 16th century

793   BENVENUTI, Giacomo. **Andrea e Giovanni Gabrieli e la musica strumentale
      in San Marco,** *IM* II/2 (Milan: Ricordi, 1932) 240p. (see no. 421)
          Titoli e temi delle canzone del Maschera, lvi-lx.
              Melodic scheme and 4-voice incipits of the 21 instrumental
              canzone serve as a basis of comparison with the canzone of
              G. Gabrieli in his "Sacrae Symphoniae".

MASCITTI, MICHELE, ca. 1664-1760.

794   DEAN, Robert H. **The music of Michele Mascitti (ca. I664-I760): A**
▽   **Neapolitan violinist in Paris** (PhD diss.: U. of Iowa, 1970)(typescript)
          Thematic index, Appendix D, 279-331.
              510 incipits for all movements of 99 separate works.

MATTEIS, NICOLA, Sr., fl. 1672-1699

795   PROCTOR, George A. **The works of Nicola Matteis, Sr.** (PhD diss.:
▽   U. of Rochester, 1960) 2v.(typescript)
          Thematic catalogue of extant works, v. I, 145-81.
              "385 incipits which include all of the movements on single
              staff except for the twelve songs which include also the
              figured bass."

MATTEIS, NICOLA, jun., ca. 1675/77-1737

796   KEUSCHNIG, Peter. **Nicola Matteis Junior als Ballettkomponist** (PhD
▽   diss.: Wien, 1968) 2v., 247*l*.; v, 102*l*. (typescript)
          Thematischer Katalog der Werke Nicola Matteis jun., v. 2.
              Single and double staff incipits for all movements of 2 violin
              sonatas, 2 solo violin sonatas, and 49 ballets. The ballets
              are arranged in chronological order.

MATYSIAK, Waldemar (compiler)

797 Breslauer Domkapellmeister von 1831-1925   (PhD diss.: Breslau,
     1934; Düsseldorf: Nolte, 1934) 90p.
         Thematisches Verzeichnis der Messetext-Kompositionen Breslauer
         Domkapellmeister und Beispielsammlung, 35p. at end.
             Contains short biographies of the Domkapellmeister Brosig,
             Cichy, Filke, and Hahn, as well as an examination of the
             stylistic characteristics portrayed in their music. Complete
             bibliographies of their works and incipits of their masses
             are included. Other composers inventoried: Greulich, Max,
             Moritz, and Siegfried.

MAYSEDER, JOSEPH, 1789-1863

798 J. Mayseders Werke (autograph 15 March 1819) (A Wst: MH 9171/c)
▽   [3p.]   Microfilm in US NYcg.
             A catalogue prepared by the composer for the Viennese publish-
             er Artaria. Lists 15 chamber works for which publishing
             rights were given to the firm.

799 [Chamber works] (autograph, 17 April 1830) (A Wst: MH 9172) [5p.]
▽   Microfilm in US NYcg.
             Another catalogue prepared for Artaria. Incipits for 37
             chamber works.

800 Oeuvres complets (Thematic catalogue advertised in a catalogue by
     Artaria, 11/29/1856)

         Reference: Alexander WEINMANN, Vollständiges Verlagsver-
         zeichnis Artaria & Comp. (Wien: L. Krenn, 1952) 154.

801 HELLSBERG, Eugen. Joseph Mayseder (Wien 1789 bis 1863) (PhD diss.:
▽   Wien, 1955) 2v., 92, 84; 83, 85, 25ℓ. (typescript)
         Thematischer Katalog der Kompositionen von Joseph Mayseder, v. 2,
         [part 2], 1-85.
             Double staff incipits for all movements of string quartets
             and quintets, violin sonatas and concertos, etudes, variations
             etc. for violin. Works arranged by opus number (op. 1-67).

McCUTCHAN, Robert G. (compiler)

802 Hymn tune names (New York: Abingdon Press, 1957) 206p.
         Melodic index, 175-87.
             A letter-system index is provided for first lines of hymns
             discussed in the book.

MECK, JOSEPH, 1690-1758

803 BECKMANN, Klaus (Recklinghausen) Joseph Meck, Hofkapellmeister in
*   Eichstätt/Bayern. Thematisches Verzeichnis.

MÉHUL, ETIENNE-HENRI-NICOLAS, 1763-1817

804 FRAGGI, H. ed. Catalogue thématique des overtures et symphonies
     par ordre alphabétique. Collected and annotated from documents of
     Nicolo, Kreutzer, and Daussoigne Méhul. Compiled 19—.

the Bibliothèque du Conservatoire and the Bibliothèque de l'Opéra
de Paris. (F Pc) Xerox copy in possession of Barry S. Brook.
Incipits of overtures, plus incipits of each movement of
symphonies, arranged alphabetically by title. Includes
alternate versions from different sources, and cites dup-
lication in overtures to different compositions. Also includes works in collaboration with Cherubini, Boieldieu,
Nicolo, Kreutzer, and Daussoigne Méhul.

MEIER, Adolf (compiler)

805   **Konzertante Musik für Kontrabass in der Wiener Klassik.** Mit Beiträgen
zur Geschichte des Kontrabassbaues in Österreich, *Schriften zur Musik*
Bd. 4, hrsg. Walter Kolneder (Giebing über Prien: Katzbichler, 1969)
203p.
Thematisches Verzeichnis der behandelten Konzertanten Sinfonien,
Konzerte und Arien, Anhang II, [141]-158.
Incipits for all movements of 3 symphony concertantes, 27
concertos for contrabass, and 3 arias with obligato contra-
bass, by the following composers: Dittersdorf, F.A.Hoffmeister,
W. Pichl, Johannes Sperger, J.B. Vanhal, and A. Zimmermann.

MELANI, ALESSANDRO, b. ?-d. 1703

806   WEAVER, Robert (George Peabody College, Tenn.). **The cantatas of**
*   **Alessandro and Atto Melani** (To be published in the *Wellesley Edition Cantata Index Series*, [1972])
Incipits, with text, for approximately 116 cantatas and
single arias by Alessandro, and 285 arias, duets, and
other ensembles from the operas. Cantatas are divided
between reliable and unreliable attributions, and further
subdivided between or among compositions for one, two, or
three voices. Within these groups the arrangement is alphabetical. Complete bibliographical apparatus is provided.

MELANI, ATTO, 1626-1714

807   WEAVER, Robert (George Peabody College, Tenn.). **The cantatas of**
*   **Alessandro and Atto Melani** (To be published in the *Wellesley Edition Cantata Index Series*, [1972])
Incipits, with text, for 16 cantatas by Atto Melani (see
no. 806).

MELK, Austria. Benediktiner-Stift Melk

808   HELM, P. Rupert. **Katalog von Musikalien beim Regenschoriat zu Melk**
▽   **787.** [Part I: 1787]; **Catalogo delle Sinfonie, Concerti, Quintetti**
Quartetti, Trio, ed Soli [Part II: s.d.] (A M) (manuscript)
The earliest known catalogues for Melk, they are dated July
14, 1787, though some works included are known to have been
composed later. Part I is an inventory of music in use at
Melk in the 18th century. It includes listings for sacred
and secular vocal music, instrumental music, music books,
as well as a listing of musical instruments in the monastery's

possession. Part II is a thematic catalogue which, with a
few exceptions, corresponds to works listed in the inventory.
Composers: Haydn, Pleyel, Naumann, Paysiello, Paradeiser,
Stadler, Franc. Benda, Georgio Benda, Carlo Steinmetz, Carlo
Stamitz, Antonio Steinmitz, Giornovichi, Dieters, St. George,
Leop. Hofmann, Raimondi, Vanhal, Pichl, Kramer, Duc l'aine,
Scheller, Rolli, Syrmen, Michale Haydn, Hofmeister, Capuzzi,
Mozart, Cambini, Albrechtsberger, Ivanschitz, Ditters, Be-
sozzi, Bach, Huber, Lidarti, Ordonnez, Bocherini, Mislivocek,
Kerzel, Breunig, Lolli, Everard, Tretter [Traetta?], Ruge,
Marigi, Woborzil, Piantenido.

808a FREEMAN, Robert N. **Zwei Melker Musikkataloge aus der zweiten Hälfte**
☐   **des 18. Jahrhunderts,** *Mf* XXIII (1970) 176-184.
      Description of the above catalogues in Melk.

MELK, Austria. Benediktiner-Stift: Alte Kataloge (without call numbers)

809   [AK I] Catalogo delle Sinfonie, Concerti, Quintetti, Quartetti,
▽   Trio ed Soli (A M) 16*l*.,.15p. (manuscript).
      Contains entries for 18 symphonies, 49 violin concertos, 9
      quintets and sextets, 72 quartets, 92 trios, 44 duets. Com-
      piled by Rupert Helm around 1790-1792.

810   [AK II] Catalogo delle Sinfonie, Concerti, Quintetti, Quartetti,
▽   Trio ed Soli (A M) 8*l*., 22p. (manuscript)
      Contains themes for 18 symphonies, 50 violin concertos, 37
      string quartets, 310 quartets, 83 trios, 95 duets and 113
      solo sonatas (mostly for strings). This catalogue is an
      expanded version of AK I above, dating from 1820-25. Robert
      N. Freeman believes the probable author is Rupert Helm (see
      Weinmann no. 812)

811   [AK III] Gesang- und Schlagstücken (A M) 4*l*., p. 2 blank (manuscript)
▽   Contains over 200 entries for works for keyboard and voice.
      Dates from 1820-1825. Alexander Weinmann is preparing an
      edition of AK II and AK III. He believes the compiler of
      these catalogues to be Maximilian Stadler (1764-1833).
      (see Weinmann no. 812)

      Reference: Alexander WEINMANN, **Musikalische Schatzkammern in**
      Niederösterreich, *ÖsterreichischeMz* 25/2 (1970) 115-20.

812   WEINMANN, Alexander (Wien). **Alte Thematische Kataloge**
*   Photographic reprint of a modern draft with current call
      numbers and bibliographical commentary.

MENDELSSOHN-BARTHOLDY, FELIX, 1809-1847

813   Thematisches Verzeichniss der im Druck erschienenen Compositionen von
      Felix Mendelssohn Bartholdy (Leipzig: Breitkopf & Härtel, [1843])
      87p.
      Incipits arranged in piano score with text underlay where
      applicable, plus orchestration and publisher information.
      Arranged by opus number, followed by works without opus
      number and various indexes.

813a --- Neue vervollständigte Ausgabe [1873] 86p.

813b --- 3. vervollständigte Ausgabe (1882) 100p.

813c --- Reprint (London: H. Baron, 1966) 100p.

814 [Copy I] **[Thematic catalogue]** (GB Ob) 76p. (manuscript)
▽
         Prepared by a copyist for Mendelssohn's heirs. Contains
the following remark by Heinrich Conrad Schleinitz on the
inside of the cover: "Thematic catalogue of Felix Mendelssohn B's compositions and music. Studies, most of which
occur in the green books that he himself compiled; also,
MSS found after his death, prepared by him in the summer of
1848 in Leipzig. Schleinitz." Contents: volumes 1-44 of
the "green books", which were acquired by the Königliche
Bibliothek in Berlin in 1878; 4 additional works were added.
Incipits are given for all movements of each work, with
brief annotations (including instrumentation). Later additions in pencil concern composition dates and dedications.
These additions were probably made by Mendelssohn's older
daughter, Marie Benecke. The copy was first in possession
of Mendelssohn's brother Paul, then of Adolph Wach, Mendelssohn's brother-in-law. In 1965, it came into possession of
Margaret Deneke (Oxford), a descendant of Wach. Since 1971,
it has been at the Bodleian Library, Oxford.

814a [Copy 2] **[Thematic catalogue]** (D Berlin Staatsbibliothek Preussi-
▽   scher Kulturbesitz:Mendelssohn-Archiv) 76p. (manuscript)
         Prepared from Copy 1. Ownership mark on inside of cover:
"G. Grove 1871", next to it an entry by Grove: "This Catalogue was copied (by Peschkau 2nd bassoon of the Palace) by
permission from that in the possession of the Mendelssohns.
The volumes to which it refers are now in the Royal Bibliothek at Berlin. Nov. 14, 1886." Then an additional entry:
"Given to me by Lady Grove, Sept. 27, 1900. F.J. Edwards."
It is now at the Mendelssohn-Archiv, Berlin.

814b [Copy 3] **[Thematic catalogue]** (D Bds, Musikabteilung: Mus. Ms.
▽   theor. K. 681) 91p. (manuscript)
         Prepared according to Copy 1; copied 1877 for Königliche Bib-
liothek, Berlin, on the occasion of the purchase of the"green
books'. Contents are the same as Copy 1, with additions and
corrections in a librarian's hand (different format from copies 1 and 2). At the end, critical remarks by Espagne (29 Oct
1877), Kopfermann (Feb 1878, 1880, and 1888).

814c [Copy 4] **[Thematic catalogue]** (London, in possession of descen-
▽   dents of Paul Mendelssohn-Bartholdy) Copy of no. 1. (manuscript)

815 **Themat(isches) Verz(eichnis) d(er) Werke von Felix Mendelssohn**
▽   (D Bds: HB VII, Mus. ms. theor. K. 681) [92p.] Copy in US NYcg.
         In 44 brief sections, with dates from 1820-1845. Incipits
in single and multiple staves, normally for all movements,
along with references to 19th-century publications.
         [reproduction of section I, 1820, on following page]

816 WERNER, Rudolf. **Felix Mendelssohn Bartholdy als Kirchenmusiker**
         (PhD diss.: Frankfurt a.M., 1929; Frankfurt a.M.: Selbstverlag des
Verfassers, 1930) ix, 191p.
         Thematisches Verzeichnis der nicht veröffentlichten Kirchenmusik

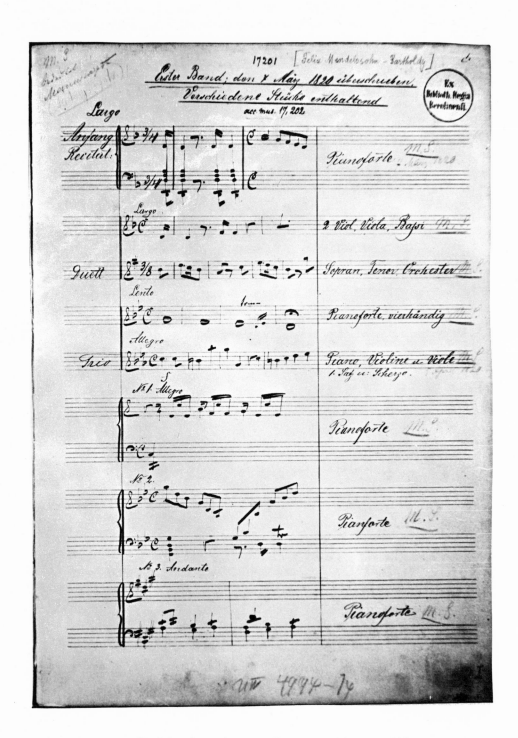

XV. Mendelssohn, *Themat...Verz...*, 1820, no. 815

Mendelssohns, 173-82.
 Vocal and organ works arranged chronologically. Incipits of
each vocal and instrumental section. P. 169-72 give numbers
of parts, date of composition, and concordance of Preussische
Staatsbibliothek MSS with Breitkopf & Härtel Gesamt-Ausgabe
numbers.

817
▽ LEAVITT, Michael. **Thematic index of Mendelssohns Werke** (Flushing,
N.Y.: Queens College of C.U.N.Y., 1966) 31p. (typescript).
 Designed for use with the Breitkopf & Härtel complete works
edition, edited by Julius Dietz (Leipzig, 1874-77). Incipits
are given in "The Simplified Plaine and Easie Code System for
Notating Music". (see no. 188).

818
▽ McDONALD, John A. **The chamber music of Felix Mendelssohn-Bartholdy**
(PhD diss.: Northwestern U., 1970) 2v.(typescript)
 Thematic catalogue.

MERSMANN, Hans

819
☐ **Grundlage einer musikalischen Volksliedforschung,** *AMw* IV (1922)
141-54, 289-321; V (1923), 81-135; VI (1924), 127-64.

MERULO, CLAUDIO, 1533-1604

820
 DEBES, Louis Helmut. **Die musikalischen Werke von Claudio Merulo
(1533-1604)** (PhD diss.: Würzburg, Julius Maximilians Universität,
1964; Tutzing: Hans Schneider, 1967) lviii, 483p.
 Quellennachweis und thematischer Katalog, 141-453.
  Over 700 2- to 4-staff incipits of all voices of vocal and
instrumental works. Arranged according to manner of publication (individually or in collections) of MS, and indexed
by title, subject, and author of text.

MEYER, Ernst Hermann (compiler)

821
 **Die mehrstimmige Spielmusik des I7. Jahrhunderts in Nord- und Mittel-
europa.** Mit einem Verzeichnis der deutschen Kammer- und Orchester-
musikwerke des 17. Jahrhunderts. *Heidelberger Studien zur Musik-
wissenschaft* II, hrsg. von Heinrich BESSELER (Kassel: Bärenreiter,
1934) 258p.
 **Verzeichnis der mehrstimmigen freien Spielmusikwerke des I6. und
I7. Jahrhunderts in England,** 130-64.
  Over 450 incipits for English fantasias and In nomines by
Brewster, Byrd, Coleman, Coperario, Deering, Ferrabosco,
Ford, Gibbons, Gill, Ives, Jenkins, Lupo, Mico, Morley,
Parsons, Peerson, Poynt, Ravenscroft, Strogers, Tallis,
Tomkins, Tye, Ward, R. White, W. White.

MEYER VON SCHAUENSEE, FRANZ JOSEPH LEONTI, 1720-1789

822
 KOLLER, Eugen. **Franz J.L. Meyer v. Schauensee, sein Leben und seine
Werke** (Frauenfeld & Leipzig: Huber, 1922) 138p.
 Thematisches Verzeichnis, 90-130.
  Generic arrangement by opus numbers, preceded by chronological

index. 2-staff incipits of each section of sacred works and
of songs, with distribution of vocal and instrumental parts.
Gives dates, MS and publication information, library location,
and tempo.

MEYLAN, Raymond (Zürich)

823   Thematic catalogue of concertos for flute and oboe
*   File cards are arranged by composer, first movement incipit,
                 and chronologically by publication of entry. Contains ça.
                 3000 cards for 1600 flute concertos and 400 oboe concertos.

                 Reference: "Documents douteux dans le domaine des concertos
                 pour instruments à vent au XVIIIe siècle", *RMusicol* XLIX
                 (1963) 47-60.

MEYLAN, Raymond

824   Utilisation des calculatrices électroniques pour la comparaison
☐   interne du répertoire des basses danses du quinzième siècle, *Fontes-
        ArtisM* XII/2-3 (May-Dec 1965) 128-35.

825   Symbolisierung einer Melodie auf Lochkarten, *Elektronische Daten-
☐   verarbeitung in der Musikwissenschaft,* Harald HECKMANN, ed. (Regens-
        burg: Gustav Bosse Verlag, 1967) 21-24. *RILM*[67] 2299.

MIASKOVSKIĬ, NIKOLAI IAKOVLEVICH, 1881-1950

826   ВИНОГРАДОВ, Виктор С. [VINOGRADOV, Viktor S.]. СПРАВОЧНИК-ПУТЕВОДИ-
        ТЕЛЬ ПО СИМФОНИЯМ Н.Я. МЯСКОВСКОГО [Reference guide to the symphonies
        of N.I. Miaskovskiĭ] (Moskva: State Music Publishing Co., 1954) xii,
        205p.
                 Piano reduction incipits for all movements, with instrumental
                 indications of the themes. Employs numbers, apparently
                 rehearsal numbers of Russian score, with brief indications
                 of what happens between numbers.

MICHI, ORAZIO, ca. 1595-1641

827   CAMETTI, Alberto. Orazio Michi "dell' Arpa", *RMI* XXI (1914) 203-77.
           Indice tematico delle arie di O. Michi, 272-77.
                 43 incipits, arranged alphabetically by first line of text,
                 with source location.

MICHL, JOSEPH WILLIBALD, 1745-1810

828   ZEHELEIN, Alfred. Joseph Michl (I745-I8I0). Ein vergessener
        südbayerischer Komponist. (Sein Leben und seine Werke). (München:
        Berntheisel, 1928) 62,28p.
           Musik-Anhang, 28p. at end.
                 Selected full-staff quotations, some incipits, of all
                 instruments and voices, with tempo and dynamic indica-
                 tions. Other single staff quotations scattered through
                 text.

MIES., Paul

829   Komponisten-Werkverzeichnisse. Ein Hilfsmittel für Musiker, Musik-
☐   liebhaber und Musikalienhändler, *Musikhandel* VI/4-5 (1955) 102-03,
      VI/6-7 (1955) 156-57.

830   Tematické seznamy hudebních skladeb [Thematic indexes of musical
☐   compositions], *HudR* XII/4 (1959) 146-48.
            List of important thematic catalogues, mainly of individual
            composers, complete or selected works.

MILANO, Collezione Alida Vardi: Medici Codex

831   LOWINSKY, Edward E. The Medici Codex, a document of music, art and
      politics in the Renaissance, *Annales Musicologiques* V (1957) 61-178.
            Incipits for the following composers: Mouton, Willaert, Jos-
            quin, Andreas de Silva, Festa, Moulu, Lafage, Lupus, Richa-
            fort, Boylean, Bruhier, Brumel, Brunet, Divitis, Elimot,
            Erasmus (Lapicida), M. Jan, Jacotin, Le Santier, Lhiretier,
            Therache, Pierre de la Rue, Ockeghem, Matthaeus Pipelare,
            Alexander Agricola, Prioris, Strus, Marbriano de Orto, Gas-
            par van Weerbecke, Compère, Hayne van Ghizeghem, Isaac, Nino
            Lepetit, Obrecht. Contains an alphabetical list of text in-
            cipits (p. 160). The codex is now in the possession of Ali-
            da Vardi of Milan.

            Reference: LOWINSKY, Edward E. The Medici Codex of 1518 (3
            vols.), *Monuments of Renaissance Music* vol. III-V (Chicago:
            U. of Chicago Press, 1968)

MILLER, James Earl (compiler)

832   The life and works of Jan Václav Stich (Giovanni Punto)- a check-list
      of eighteenth-century horn concertos and players- an edition for study
      and performance of the concerto no. VI in E-flat by Giovanni Punto
      (PhD diss.: State U. of Iowa,1962) 2v.   Univ. Micro. 62-4986.
            [Thematic index], v. 1, part II, Appendix C.
                  Incipits of 46 eighteenth-century horn concertos (not composed
                  by Punto), which are listed with annotations in Appendix A
                  and examined for this study.

MILLER, Janet (compiler)

832.1 The Anglo-Genevan Psalter of 1558; its place in Reformation psalmody
      (MA thesis, U. of Southern Calif., 1950) (typescript)
            Thematic catalogue

MITCHELL, JONI

833   BURGER, David (Queens College of the C.U.N.Y.). The songs of Joni
▽   Mitchell: A thematic catalogue. 28p. (manuscript)
            Contains all themes and sub-themes for songs arranged accord-
            ing to the order in which they appear in her discs.   Pro-
            vides alphabetical indexes of titles,first lines, and themes.

MITTERER, IGNAZ, 1850-1924

834   CORAZZA, Rupert. Ignaz Mitterer als Kirchenkomponist (PhD diss.:
▽   Wien, 1938) 177*l*. (typescript)

Mitterers Kirchenkompositionen. Thematischer Katalog der Messen
und Requiem, 13-24.
>Multiple staff incipits for 33 Masses and 10 Requiems arranged
by opus number. Contains list of works without incipits.

MODENA, Archivio Capitolare: MSS I, III, IV, IX, XI, and XII

836 CRAWFORD, David E. Vespers polyphony at Modena's Cathedral in the
▽   first half of the sixteenth century (PhD diss.: U. of Illinois,
     1967) 507p. (typescript)
     [Thematic catalogues], 66-134.
     >182 incipits in original notation for all *partes* and sections
     of motets and Mass Ordinairies with all voices given. In-
     cipits are from MSS I, III, IV, IX, XI, and XII of the Ar-
     chivio Capitolare at Modena, and include works by: Bruhier,
     Brumel, Compère, Eustachius de Monteregali, la Fage, Fevin,
     J. Fogliani, L. Fogliani, Genet (Carpentras), Isaac, Jachet
     of Mantua, Pope Leo X, Moulu, Mouton, Richafort, Fran Ros,
     de la Rue, de Sermisy, de Silva, Verdelot, Verzalia, and
     Willaert.

MOGIŁA, Poland. Cistercian Abbey

837 GOLOS, George. [Symphonies, 18th c.] 2 booklets, [23, 16p.] Com-
▽   piled 1962. (manuscript). In possession of Jan LaRue.
     >Incipits for all movements of 38 symphonies (18th c. MS)
     located at the Abbey. Annotations provide instrumentation,
     dates (where available), and call numbers. The following
     composers are inventoried: Abel, Anfossi Romano, [Bach],
     Benda, Brixi, Ditters (Carolo Ditters), J. Gotabek, Graun,
     Pietro Guglielmi, Hayden (Heyden), Iwanschitz (Iwanszchitz),
     Antonio Kamel, Giovanni Lampagnanii, Neumann (Neuman),
     Pach [Bach], Paisiello, Schir, Antoni Schmidt, Schwindl
     and several anonymous works.

MOLIQUE, BERNHARD, 1802-1869

838 SCHRÖDER, Fritz. Bernhard Molique und seine Instrumentalkompositionen
     (PhD diss.: München, 1922; Stuttgart: Schwerdtner, 1923) ix, 125p.
     Thematischer Katalog von Molique's Kammermusik, Orchesterwerken
     und Konzerten, 109-12.
     >Incipits arranged numerically within genre.

MOLLER, JOHN CHRISTOPHER, 1755-1803

839 STETZEL, Ronald D. John Christopher Moller and his role in early
     American music (PhD diss.: U. of Iowa, 1965) 2v.   U. Micro. 65-
     6712.(typescript)
     [Thematic index], v. II, Appendix B, 10-32.
     >The 115 multiple staff incipits for all movements are ar-
     ranged in three sections: (1) German works of unproven
     authorship; (2) works published in England; and (3) works
     published in the United States.

MOLTER, JOHANN MELCHIOR, ca. 1695-1765

840 LaRUE, Jan. [The symphonies of Molter] [43, 2p.] (microfilm,
▽ xerox).(manuscript)
        Reproduces the opening bars of 169 symphonies (18th c. MS),
        mostly in score, attributed to Molter in sources at the
        Badische Landesbibliothek, Karlsruhe (BRD). Provides li-
        brary call numbers.

841 DEARLING, Robert (Dunstable, Bedfordshire). [Thematic catalogue
▽ of symphonies] Index cards (manuscript).
        Incipits for ca. 150 symphonies in Badische Landesbibliothek
        Karlsruhe.

MOMIGNY, JÉRÔME-JOSEPH de, 1762-1842

842 PALM, Albert. Jérôme-Joseph de Momigny. Leben und Werk. Ein Beitrag
    zur Geschichte der Musiktheorie im 19. Jahrhundert. (Köln: Volk-Verlag,
    1969) 455p.
        Bibliographie, 329-419.
        Catalogue of complete works (theoretical, compositions, and
        editions). 130 incipits, two and three staves, for clavier
        sonatas, sonatas for clavier and violin, string quartets, and
        lieder.

MONIUSZKO, STANISŁAW, 1819-1872

843 NOWACZYK, Erwin, ed. Pieśni solowe S. Moniuszki. Materiały do Biblio-
    grafii Muzyki Polskiej, t. 2 (Krakow: Polskie Wydawnictwo Muzyczne,
    1954) 332p.
        Katalog tematyczny.
        Harmonized incipits of all songs, with data on dedications,
        voice ranges, dates of publication, autographs, and editions.

MONN, GEORG MATTHIAS, 1717-1750

844 FISCHER, Wilhelm, ed. Wiener Instrumentalmusik vor und um I750,
    DTÖ 19/2 (Wien: Artaria, 1912) xxxix,122p. (see no.779)
        Thematischer Katalog der Instrumentalwerke von G.M. Monn...,
        xxxiv-xxxix.
        Single and double staff incipits of each movement, arranged
        by genre.

MONTEVERDI, CLAUDIO, 1567-1643

844.1 BONINO, Mary Ann Teresa. Monteverdi's use of musical and dramatic
      expression in his first four books of madrigals (M.A.: U. of Southern
      California, 1963) iii, 103p.
          Thematic catalogue

845 ZIMMERMAN, Franklin B. Thematic and first-line indexes to the com-
 * plete works of Claudio Monteverdi. Computer produced.

MONTPELLIER, Bibliothèque de l'Université: Codex Montpellier

846 KUHLMANN, Georg. Die zweistimmigen französischen Motetten des Kodex
    Montpellier, Faculté de Médecine H. 196 (Würzburg: Triltsch, 1938)
    2v.

Volume 1 contains: "Die Motettentenores mit ihren Quellen
nach dem Liber Gradualis und dem Graduale Sarisburiense,"
p. 201-14.

MOORE, Earl V.; HEGER, T.E. (compilers)

847   The symphony and the symphonic poem; analytical and descriptive
      charts of the standard symphonic repertory (Ann Arbor, 1952) 238p.
           Gives a graphic representation of the overall design or
           pattern of a composition. Not for use as a thematic index,
           but rather a listener's guide supplementing the orchestral
           score. Contains 86 symphonic works from the standard
           repertoire.

      --- 4th rev. ed. (Ann Arbor, 1962).

MORTENSEN, Carl (compiler)

848   [Thematic catalogue of songs]   (DK Kk: Ny kgl. Samling 2159 fol)
▽   index cards. (manuscript)
           Carl Mortensen (1832-1893) compiled this thematic catalogue
           of songs, mostly Danish. Contains ca. 6800 index cards
           with text incipits and ca. 4800 index cards with musical
           incipits arranged after compiler's own system, which is
           described and enclosed with the index cards. Indicates
           composer, author, title of song, and sources.

MOSCHELES, IGNAZ, 1794-1870

849   THEMATISCHES VERZEICHNISS/ Sämmtlicher Werke von IGNAZ MOSCHELES/
      welche bey Artaria und Comp:... zuhaben sind (Wien: Artaria, n.d.)
      [2p.] (A Wst: Mc 26086) [reproduction on facing page]
           Single, double, and multiple staff incipits for 48 instru-
           mental works — piano and chamber pieces.

850   Catalogue thématique des ouvrages d'Ignace Moscheles, Arrangé et
      revu par l'auteur I825 (Leipzig: Probst [1825]) 11p.
           Two and four staff incipits arranged by opus no. (1-64)
           followed by 11 additional works without opus number. Mostly
           piano works, plus a few songs and chamber pieces.

851   I. Moscheles Werke (autograph, 17 May 1829) (A Wst: MH 9173/c) [4p.]
▽   Microfilm in US NYcg.(manuscript)
           A catalogue prepared by the composer for the Viennese publish-
           er Artaria. 20 double staff incipits for solo piano works
           and chamber music sold to the firm.

852   Oeuvres complets (Thematic catalogue advertised in the Artaria ca-
      talogue of 29 Nov. 1856)
           Reference: Alexander WEINMANN, Vollständiges Verlagsver-
           zeichnis Artaria & Comp. (Wien: L. Krenn, 1952) 154.

853   Thematisches Verzeichniss im Druck erschienener Compositionen von
      Ignaz Moscheles (Leipzig: Kistner, 1862) Nouvelle Edition revue
      et corrigée par l'Auteur (Leipzig: Friedrich Hofmeister[1885]) 66p.
           Arranged by opus numbers with double staff incipits. Pages

XVI. **Moscheles,** *Thematisches Verzeichniss...* (Wien: Artaria, n.d.) no. 849

1-42 contain works to opus 135. Works without opus numbers
on pages 53-60, Opus 136 and three other works without opus
numbers on page 61.

--- Reprinted for H. Baron (London: Stephen Austin & Sons, 1966)

MOZART, LEOPOLD, 1719-1787

854 SEIFFERT, Max, editor. Ausgewählte Werke, *DTB* 9/2 (Leipzig: Breitkopf
     & Härtel, 1908)
         Erhaltene Werke L. Mozarts...Verschollene Werke L. Mozarts, xli-
         lv.
             Incipits arranged by genre. Provides publication information,
             tempo and dynamics, library location.

MOZART, WOLFGANG AMADEUS, 1756-1791

856 Verzeichnüss aller meiner Werke vom Monath Febraio 1784 bis Monath...
▽   1..[15 November, 1791] (manuscript)
             This autograph catalogue has appeared numerous times in print
             and facsimile as seen below.

856a --- ANDRÉ, Johann Anton, ed. Thematisches Verzeichniss sämmtlicher
     Kompositionen von W.A. Mozart, so wie er solches vom 9ten Februar
     1784 an, bis zum 15ten November 1791 eigenhändig niedergeschrieben
     hat. Nach dem Original-Manuscripte. (Offenbach: André, [1805]) 63p.
             Published catalogue of Mozart's own 1st movement, double staff
             incipits, with dates of composition (and first performance,
             and singers for operas), and instrument indication.

856b --- Nebst einem erläuternden Vorbericht von A. ANDRÉ. Neue mit dem
     Original-manuscripte nochmals verglichene Ausgabe. [1828] 63p.

856c --- Neue Ausg. 185-.

856d --- Reprint [of information only, not incipits]. Alexander ULIBISCHEFF
     Mozart's Leben und Werke, 2nd ed. (Stuttgart: C. Conradi, [1859])
     v. 1, 310-25.

856e --- Reprint. Mozart's eigenhändiger Katalog, *Mitteilungen für die
     Mozart-Gemeinde in Berlin* XVI (1903) 189-219.

856f --- Mozart's Werkeverzeichnis, 1784-1791, ed. Otto E. DEUTSCH (Wien:
     Herbert Reichner, 1938) facsimile. 29p.
             Deutsch pamphlet includes Köchel numbers.

856g --- Verzeichniss aller meiner Werke. Reprinted in E.H.MÜLLER VON
     ASOW, Briefe und Aufzeichnungen W.A. Mozarts (Berlin: Metzner, 1942)
     v. 2, 515-65.
             Includes Köchel numbers, instrument indication, tempo,
             dynamics.

856h --- Separate publication of above   (Wien: Doblinger, 1943)

856i --- Mozart's Catalogue of his works, 1784-1791, ed. Otto E. DEUTSCH
     (New York: Herbert Reichner, [1956?])
             English version of the above.

856j --- Mozart; Briefe und Aufzeichnungen, Wilhelm A. BAUER and Otto Erich
     DEUTSCH (Kassel: Barenreiter, 1962) 4 vols. *passim.*

857 ANDRÉ, Johann Anton. [Thematic catalogue of Mozart's works composed
     before February, 1784] (GB Lbm: Add. 32412, ff 1-53) (Ist half of
     the 19th century). 36p.

Compiled prior to 1833. See Otto E. DEUTSCH, "Mozart's catalogue of his works, 1784-1791" (New York: Herbert Reichner,
[1956?] 3-4.

858 Mozart Werke (A Wst: MH 9181/c) 16p. No date (manuscript). Microfilm
▽   in US NYcg.
>   Single and double staff incipits for 106 orchestral, chamber,
>   and solo piano works.

859 Mozart Werke/ fürs Forte Piano/ nach Pleilische Auflage (A Wst: MH
▽   9182/c) [17p.] No date (manuscript). Microfilm in US NYcg.
>   Single and double staff incipits for 83 works, either piano
>   solo or chamber works with piano.

860 Les oeuvres complets/ de/ W.A. Mozart/ Catalogue thematique (A Wst:
▽   MH 9183) 364, [14p.] No date (manuscript). Microfilm in US NYcg.
>   A catalogue of works, with many omissions, arranged by genre.
>   Cites publisher and price. The appended section lists a se-
>   lection of works (arranged by opus [sic] number), making re-
>   ference to the publishers.

861 Catalogue thematique of Mozart's works (London: Monzani, ca. 1805)
     2p. (GB Lbm: B.M. 7896. h. 40. (12.))
>   *Reference:* HUMPHRIES, Charles; SMITH, William C. Music pub-
>   lishing in the British Isles (Oxford: Blackwell, 1970) 237.

862 FUCHS, Aloys. Thematisches Verzeichnis von einigen älteren Composi-
▽   tionen aus den Jahren 1760 bis 1784. 1837 (D Bds: Kat. ms. 694)
     19*l.* (manuscript).

863 --- Thematisches Verzeichnis der sämtlichen Compositionen. Nach
▽   Classen geordnet. 1837 (D Bds: Kat. ms. 700) 152*l.* (manuscript).

864 --- Thematisches Verzeichnis über sämtliche Opern und Serenaden.
▽   1837 (D Bds: Kat. ms. 704) 45*l.* (manuscript).

865 --- Thematisches Verzeichnis über sämtliche Klavier-Conzerte mit
▽   Orchester zur Sammlung des A. Fuchs gehörig. 1830 (D Bds: Kat. ms.
     710) 2*l.* (manuscript).
>   *Reference:* Richard SCHAAL, Quellen zur Musiksammlung Aloys
>   Fuchs, *Mf* XVI (1963) 72 (see no. 1159)

866 Thematisches Verzeichniss derjenigen Originalhandschriften von W.A.
     Mozart......welche Hofrath André in Offenbach a.M. besitzt (Offen-
     bach: André [1841]) 79p.
>   Double staff incipits of 280 compositions arranged by genre.
>   Provides instrument indications.

867 POTTER, [Philip] Cipriani. A thematic catalogue of Mozart's piano-
     forte works, with and without accompaniment (London: Coventry &
     Hollier, 1848)
>   Thematic contents of the 9 volumes of the pianoforte works,
>   previously issued in separate fascicules as *Chefs d'oeuvre
>   de Mozart* with partial thematic catalogue. (See also HOLMES,
>   Edward no. 868)

867a OLDMAN, Cecil B. Cipriani Potter's edition of Mozart's pianoforte
□   works, *Festschrift Otto Erich Deutsch (80th B.d.),* Gerstenberg et
     al., ed. (Kassel: Bärenreiter, 1963) 120-27.

868   HOLMES, Edward. Analytical and thematic index of Mozart's piano-
       forte works, *MTimes* (July 1851)
                 Incipits of 87 compositions, sonatas and chamber works with piano,
                 arranged according to the 9 volume edition that Novello purchased
                 from Coventry & Hollier. In 1851, Novello bought out the publish-
                 ing firm of Coventry & Hollier [1836-1846] who published editions
                 of Mozart's piano works edited by Cipriani Potter and containing
                 pages of thematic catalogues. Novello commissioned Edward Holmes
                 to annotate this thematic index. Holmes' version first appeared
                 in the July 1851 *Musical Times*. Novello reprinted it in 1852
                 separately or as part of his complete works.

868a   --- Published in J.A. Novello's Catalogue of music printed and pub-
       lished by J.A. Novello (London, 1852) 138-61.
                 See notation above.

869   Collection de quintuors pour 2 violons, 2 violas et violoncelle
       (Leipzig: C.F. Peters, 1854) 1p.
                 Catalogue thématique de la collection complete des quintuors.
                     Incipits for 8 string quintets, 1 quintet for clarinet and
                     strings, plus 1 quintet for horn and strings.

870   Thematisches Verzeichniss werthvoller meist noch ungedruckter Original-
       handschriften W.A. Mozart's; zu beziehen durch jede Buch-und-Musik-
       handlung (Berlin: F. Stage, [1856]). 15p.
                 Double staff incipits of 1st movements or overtures for most
                 of list of 38 compositions. Instrument indications, dates,
                 number of movements, and André catalogue numbers.

871   KÖCHEL, Ludwig Ritter von. Chronologisch-thematisches Verzeichniss
       sämmtlicher Tonwerke W.A. Mozart's (Leipzig: Breitkopf & Härtel,
       1862) xviii, 551p.

871a   --- Nachträge und Berichtigungen, *AMZ* neue Folge II (1864) columns
       493-99.

871b   --- Nachtrag (Leipzig: Breitkopf & Härtel, 1889) 32p.

871c   --- 2. Aufl. bearb. und ergänzt von Paul Graf von WALDERSEE (1905)
       xxxv, 789p.

871d   --- 3. Aufl. bearb. von Alfred EINSTEIN (1937) xlix, 984p.

871e   --- EINSTEIN, Alfred. Mozartiana und Köcheliana. Supplement zur
       dritten Auflage von L.v. Köchel's Chronologisch-thematischem Ver-
       zeichnis, *MR* 1/4 (1940) 313-42; *MR* II/1-4 (1941) 68-77, 151-88, 235-
       42, 324-31; *MR* IV/1 (1943) 53-61; *MR* VI (1945) 238-42.
                 Scattered incipits.

871f   --- 3. Aufl. with supplement "Berichtigungen und Zusätze" (Ann Ar-
       bor, Mich.: Edwards, 1947) xlix, 1052p.

871g   --- 4. Aufl. (Leipzig: Breitkopf & Härtel, 1958) xlix, 1019p.

871h   --- 5. Aufl. (Leipzig: Breitkopf & Härtel, 1961)

871i   --- 6. Aufl.bearb. von Franz GIEGLING, Alexander WEINMANN, und Gerd
☆   SIEVERS (Wiesbaden: Breitkopf & Härtel, 1964) cxliii, 1024p.
                 Reviews: H.D., *MOpinion* LXXXVII (Jul 1964) 603; Ludwig FIN-
                 SCHER, *FontesArtisM* XI (1964) 95-98; Bernard WILSON, *Notes*
                 XXI/4 (1964) 531-40; A. Hyatt KING, *Mf* SVIII/3 (1965) 307-

13; M.von HASE,*Börsenbl.*XVI(26 Feb. 1965)282.;G.A.TRUMPFF,*Neue
ZM* CXXVII(Apr 1966)164-65; Jan La RUE,*JAmerMusicolSoc* XX/3
(1967)495-501; Stellan MORNER,*Svensk-TMf* XLIX (1967)211-14.

872 --- Der kleine Köchel; chronologisches und systematisches Verzeichnis sämtlicher musikalischen Werke von Wolfgang Amadeus Mozart, ed.
by H. von HASE (Wiesbaden: Breitkopf & Härtel, 1951) 96p.

872a --- Le Petit Köchel...d'après la 3e edition...texte français de
Raoul Celly (Paris: Guide du Concert, 1956) 119p.

872b --- Le Petit Köchel...d'après la 6e edition...texte français de
Raoul Celly (Paris: Leduc, 1968) 142p.

873 LORENZ, Franz. W.A. Mozart als Clavier-komponist (Breslau: Leuckart,
1866) 63p.
  Thematisches Verzeichnis der im Texte angeführten Mozartschen
  Clavier-Werke, 8p.at end.
   Incipits of 60 compositions.

874 WYZEWA, Teodor de; St. FOIX, Georges de. W.A. Mozart: sa vie musicale et son oeuvre (Paris: Desclée de Brouwer & Cie., [1936-46]) 5v.
  Concordance du nouveau classement des oeuvres de Mozart avec
  leur classement dans le catalogue de Koechel, v. II, 437-41; v. V,
  341-43.
   All five volumes include incipits in numbered chronological
   order interspersed through text.

875 HUTCHINGS, Arthur. A companion to Mozart's piano concertos (London &
New York: Oxford U. Press, 1948)
  Thematic guide to Mozart's concertos for clavier, xi-xiv.
   Incipits arranged by Koechel numbers, with dates and publishers.
   Includes early arrangements from sonatas by other composers.

876 MÜLLER, K.F., ed. W.A. Mozart. (Gesamtkatalog seiner Werke; "Köchel-
Verzeichnis.") (Wien: Verlag P. Kaltschmid, 1951) 448p.
  Incipits of all authentic and complete works arranged according
  to category.
   Reviews: N.B., *MQ* XXXIX (April 1953) 304-06; Richard S. HILL,
   Notes X (Mar 1953) 278-80.

877 MÜLLER von ASOW, E.H., ed. Verzeichnis aller meiner Werke (von W.A.
Mozart.) Verzeichnis der Jugendwerke W.A. Mozarts, von Leopold Mozart.
(Wien & Wiesbaden: Ludwig Doblinger, 1956) 103p.
  104 incipits with Koechel numbers, tempo, dynamics, and opus
  numbers for the earliest sonatas (p. 4-13). Pages 4-30 contain Leopold's catalogue of Wolfgang's early works. Pages
  41-97 is a catalogue by Wolfgang of his own works, with
  several intervening works to be found on pages 32-38.
   Reviews: A. Hyatt KING, *MLetters* XXXVII (April 1956) 191-92;
   SvenskTMf XLIX (1967) 211-14.

878 Koechel ABC. Chronological and classified listing of W.A. Mozart's
works. English intro. by Robert SABIN (New York: A. Broude, 1966)
97p.
  Arranged by Köchel numbers; classified by genre and performers
  required. Includes thematic incipits of works with similar
  titles and in the same key.

879   FEDERHOFER, Hellmut. **Mozartiana im Musikaliennachlass von Ferdinand Bischoff,** *Mozart-Jahrbuch* 1965-66 (1967) 15-38.
        Pages 19-35 contain incipits of works arranged by Köchel numbers taken from the Bischoff collection. Provides tempo indications, dynamics, location of facsimiles, and autographs.

880   HILL, George R.; GOULD, Murray. **A thematic locator for Mozart's works as listed in Koechel's Chronologisch-Thematisches Verzeichnis Sixth Edition,** *Music Indexes and Bibliographies* No. 1 (Hackensack,N.J.: Joseph Boonin, Inc., 1970) 76p.
        Contains two complete thematic locators produced by computer printout. The first is arranged by lettered and numbered interval size (similar to Payne *Bach,* no. 60), the second alphabetically by pitch name (similar to Barlow/Morgenstern, no. 68). The volume uses the simplified "Plaine and Easie" code (see no. 188).

881   FLOTHIUS, Marius. **Köchel problemen,** *MensMelodie* 9/3 (1954) 76-78.
☐   Discusses discrepencies between Köchel and Saint-Foix.

MUFFAT, GEORG, 1653-1704

882   GORE, Richard Taylor. **The instrumental works of Georg Muffat**
▽   (PhD diss.: U. of Rochester, 1955) 260p. (typescript)
        Thematic catalogue of Florilegia, 231-46.

MUFFAT, GOTTLIEB, 1690-1770

883   RIEDEL, Friedrich (Mainz). **Thematischer Katalog** (MS in possession
▽   of compiler).(manuscript)
        Incipits for 500 keyboard works.

MÜNCHEN, Bayerische Staatsbibliothek : Maria Anna, Kurfürstin von Bayern

884   **Catalogo/ De Libri di Musica/ Di S.A.S.E./ Maria Anna/ Elettrice de**
▽   **Baviera/ La prima colonna denota il/ Numero del Libro/ La Seconda le Arie L'opre/ Oratori, Serenate etc:/ La Terza gl'Autori/** (D Mbs:Mus. Mss.1648) 58*l.* Compiled ca. 1750-90. (manuscript). Copy in US NYcg.
        Over 400 incipits of arias, duets, trios, and cantatas, in addition to a list of opera scores. Composers: Vinci, Terradellas, Hasse, Albertis, Giay, Scalabrini, Pampino, Jomelli, Cocchi, Galuppi, Ferrandini, Carlo Croener, Bernasconi, Perez, Pescetti, Casali, Francesco Maggiore, Almedia, Aliprandi, Negri, Manna, Porpora, Pulli, Carcani, Porta, Ciampi, Wagenseil, Conforti, Rinaldo di Capua, Rumling, Schürer, Gluck, Francesco Maria Pace, Adolfatti, Principe Sta. Croce, E.T.P.A. [Maria Antonia Walpurgis], Scarlati, Graun, Lampugnani, Jacomelli, Latilla, Scolari, Prusa, Zoncha, Bonna, Mazanti, Lapière, Carpani, Costantiny, Leo, Santarelli, Giamelli, Ruge, Trajetta, Naumann, Sales, Guglielmi, Sacchini, Tozzi, Gius. Michl, Holzbaur, Misliwecek, Bertoni, Anfossi, Cimarosa, Kyrmair, Gazaniga, Schuster, Boroni, Valentini, Sarti, Giomelli, Alessandri, Majo, Grua, Guardini, Turini, Schubaur, Kreusser, Schmitbaur, Prati, Paisiello, Reichardt, Tarchi, Bianchi, D'Ettore, Gasparini, Aurisicchio, Piazza, Piccini, Balbi, Pazzaglia, Rauzzini, Beme, Mango, Pugnani, Giordanielle, Zinga-

relli, Andreozzi, Monza, Calegari, Rust, Fabrizi, Giordani,
Caruso, Mortellari, Gatti, Nicolini, Cherubini, Insanguineo,
Ottani, Righini, Pach, Marineli, Robuschi, Tritto, Pleyel,
Rutini, and Salieri.

MÜNCHEN, Bayerische Staatsbibliothek: Königliche Hofcapelle

885 Catalog über saemtliche Kirchenmusik, welche sich in dem Magazine
▽   der Königl: Hofcapelle befindet. (D Mbs) 386*l* [some blank] Compiled
     ca. 1810-1850   (manuscript).
             Over 1500 incipits of first movements (sometimes all movements,
             or sections) of Masses, Offertories, Graduals, Vespers, Lita-
             nies, Requiems, etc. with information on settings and extant
             parts. Includes list (without incipits) of operas, oratorios,
             and choral works. A portion of the works are deposited
             in München, Bayerische Staatsbibliothek. The following compos-
             ers are represented: Aiblinger, Albrechtsberger, Allegri,
             Baaden, Beethoven, Benelli, Bernabei, Bernasconi, Caldara,
             Carlo VI, Cherubini, Piedro Chiarini, Danzi, Diabelli, Durante,
             Eberlin, Eybler, Juan a Fossa, Ferd. Fraenzl, Fux, Gaensbacher,
             Galuppi, Gasparini, Gassmann, Gazzaniga, Jos. Grätz, Carlo
             Grua, Paul Grua, Tobias Gsur, Händel, Haeser, Hammel, Hasse,
             Gius. Haydn, Mich. Haydn, Holzbauer, Holzmann, Hummel, Jaches
             de Mantua, Jomelli, Kienlen, Kirchero, Kirnberger, Lasso, Leo,
             Lindpaintner, Lotti, Part. Lustrini, Mantei, Marianna Martines,
             Martini, Martino, Stanislao Mattei, Maximilian Joseph von
             Bayern, Michl, W.A. Mozart, Neuner, Neyser, Pallaestrina, Pa-
             vona, Pergolesi, Perti, Poissl, Giov. Porta, Preindl, L. Rein-
             wald, Fr. Xav. Richter, Röder, Röth, Giov. Rovetta, Sabbatini,
             Ant. Sacchini, Pomp. Sales, Scarlatti, Schinn, Schneider, Greg.
             Schürer, Schuster, Spiess, Sterkel, Stözel, Hartmann Stuntz,
             Tozzi, Trajetta, Valotti, Vogler, Winter, Wenceslao Wodiczka,
             Disma Zelenka.

MÜNCHEN, Bibliothek des Metropolitankapitels (Erzbischöfliches Ordinariat mit den Beständen der Frauenkirche)

886 [Thematic catalogue]
*   Incipit catalogue in preparation under the auspices of the
             Deutschen Forschungsgemeinschaft (DFG), and under the gener-
             al direction of Robert MÜNSTER.

MÜNCHEN, Gräflich zu Toerring'sches Archiv

887 WALLNER, Bertha Antonia. [Catalogue] (On loan by the *DTB* to D Mbs)
▽   Compiled ca. 1910-1930. (manuscript)
             One of many partially thematic inventories prepared by the
             compiler under Adolf Sandberger's direction for the *Denkmäler
             der Tonkunst in Bayern*. The collection is supposedly lost.

MÜNSTER, Robert; MACHOLD, Robert (compilers)

888 Thematischer Katalog der Musikhandschriften der ehemaligen Kloster-
     kirchen Weyarn, Tegernsee und Benediktbeuern, *Kataloge Bayerischer
     Musiksammlungen* 1 (München: Henle, 1971) 196p.
             A carefully prepared inventory of about 1000 manuscript works

by 18th and early 19th c. composers, mostly church music.
The greatest part of the catalogue is from the important collection of Weyarn. Church and secular music of each collection is separated. Incipits are given on 2 or 3 staves, with
all pertinent information including watermarks. The volume
also contains a systematic index, plates for the watermarks,
short titles of the existing printed works in the three collections, plus short biographical notes about the hitherto
unknown composers. Present location of the collection: Weyarn (Dombibliothek Freising); Tegernsee (Katholisches Pfarramt Tegernsee); Benediktbeuern (Salesianer-Kloster Benediktbeuern).

MÜTHEL, JOHANN GOTTFRIED, 1728-1788

890   CAMPBELL, Robert Gordon. Johann Gottfried Müthel (PhD diss.: Indiana
      U., 1966) 2v. Univ. Micro. 66-14,807. (typescript)
      [Thematic catalogue of extant works], v. II.
            Incipits for keyboard works, 45 songs, a cantata, flute sonata,
            and bassoon concerto.

NÁDOR, Kálmán (compiler)

891   Jegyzéke a legújabb és legkevelteb zeneművek   zongorára [List of
      the newest and most popular works for piano], [Budapest, 1897], *Ver-
      band der deutschen Musikalienhändler Musik-Katalog. Gesammelte Ver-
      lags-Kataloge* II (Leipzig, 1895-97)
            A 20 page thematic catalogue of Hungarian popular composers.
            Part I of the index contains incipits with text of vocal
            works. Part II contains double staff incipits for Hungari-
            an piano works, with one English composer-Arthur Sullivan.

NAGEL, Willibald (compiler)

892   Zur Geschichte der Musik am Hofe von Darmstadt, *MfMG* XXXII (1900)
      1-16, 21-36, 41-57, 59-74, 79-89.
            This study, which discusses music of the Darmstadt court,
            16th-18th c., includes descriptions of several inventories
            and indexes of MSS. Partial thematic indexes are given for
            Beringer, J.S. Endler, W.G. Enderle, and C. Schetky.

NALDI, ROMULO, d. 1612

893   FEININGER, Laurentius. Ave regina celorum XVI vocum, *Monumenta Li-
      turgiae Polychoralis Sanctae Ecclesiae Romanae* IVa/2 (Tridentini:
      Sociatas Universalis Sanctae Ceciliae, 1969) ix, 26p.

Key: * in preparation; ▼ manuscript; □ literature; ☆ Library of Congress

Index thematicus [of motets], 1-5.
            32 incipits for 8, 12, and 16-voice motets.

NÁMEŠT Castle, Czechoslovakia

894   POHANKA, Jaroslav. Bohemika v zámecké hudební sbírce z Náměště n.
       Osl. [Bohemian material in the music collection of Náměšt castle],
       Acta Musei Moraviae XLVIII (1963) 235p.
                Includes thematic catalogue of 17th, and 18th century
                symphonies, concertos and quartets.

NANINO, GIOVANNI MARIA, 1545-1607

895   SCHULER, Richard J. The life and liturgical works of Giovanni
       Maria Nanino (PhD diss.: U. of Minnesota, 1963) 2v. U. Micro. 63-
       7953.(typescript)
          [Thematic index], v. 2.
                "A catalog giving incipits" and library location of MSS and
                early printed editions.

NARDINI, PIETRO, 1722-1793

896   PFÄFFLIN, Clara. Pietro Nardini, seine Werke und sein Leben (Plie-
       ningen-Stuttgart: F. Find, [1935]; Wolfenbüttel: G. Kallmeyer, 1936)
       96p.
          Thematischer Katalog von Nardinis Werken mit Nachweis der Neu-
          drucke, xxp. at end.
                Incipits for instrumental works only, arranged by genre.
                Gives time signatures for other movements, MS locations,
                and recent editions.

NAUDOT, JACQUES-CHRISTOPHE,   -1762

897   UNDERWOOD, T. Jervis. The life and music of Jacques-Christophe
▿   Naudot (PhD diss.: North Texas State U., 1970) xvi, 348p. (typescript)
          Thematic catalogue, complete works of Jacques-Christophe Naudot,
          168-348.
                Multiple staff incipits of all movements, with additional
                bibliographical material.

NAUMANN, JOHANN GOTTLIEB, 1741-1801

898   Verzeichniss der kirchen Musicalien vom Herrn Kapellmeister Naumann.
▿   Armaro VII (D Dl) 26p. Compiled c. 1801. Copy in US NYcg (manuscript)
                The catalogue was revised in 1812 by Franz Schubert (of Dres-
                den). He included a biographical note on p. 26. Incipits
                for 21 Masses and many motets, most of them dated.

NEBRA, JOSÉ de, 1702-1768

899   LEVASSEUR de REBOLLO, Yvonne (U. of Pittsburgh) Works by José Nebra
*   preserved at El Escorial
          Thematic index
                Incipits of the religious works.

900   SANTA-OLALLA de MUNOZ, Marta (Madrid). The works of José Nebra
  *   [Thematic catalogue]
              Will include incipits for keyboard, liturgical, extra-litur-
              gical, and secular works.

NEEFE, CHRISTIAN GOTTLOB, 1748-1798

901   LEUX, Irmgard Henschen. Christian Gottlob Neefe (Leipzig: Kistner
      & Siegel, 1925) 208p.

          Thematischer Katalog der Instrumental-Werke Christian Gottlob
          Neefes, 199-203.
              Multiple staff incipits arranged by genre, with original
              dates and publishers.

NEF, Walter R. (compiler)

902   Der St. Galler Organist Fridolin Sicher und seine Orgeltabulatur,
      SchJMW VII (1938) iii, 215p.
          Thematisches Verzeichnis der Sicherschen Orgeltabulatur, 159-209.
              Multiple. staff incipits, transcribed from tabulature, of
              176 compositions by mostly anonymous composers. Named
              composers include: Agricola, Bernhard, Brumel, Buchner, Bus-
              nois, Compere, Craen, Des Prez, Fuchswild, Grefinger, Hof-
              haimer, Isaac, Japart, Kotter, La Rue, Mouton, Obrecht,
              Pipelaire, Rischach, Schrem, Senfl, F. Sicher, H. Sicher,
              Silvanus, Stockem, and Weerbecke.

NERESHEIM, Benediktinerabtei [MS now in D Mbs]

903   SCHMID, Hans. Una nuova fonte di musica organistica del secolo
      XVII, *Organo* (1960) 108-13.

          Indice tematico del manoscritto di Neresheim.
              Incipits of fragments of keyboard (principally organ) music
              written between 1661 and 1682, contained in a MS from the
              Benedictine Abbey of Neresheim. Fragments arranged chiefly
              by ecclesiastical mode and notated in Italian organ tablature.

NERESHEIM, Benediktinerabtei [MSS now in D Rtt]

904   TSCHEUSCHNER, Eckart. Die Neresheimer Orgeltabulaturen der Fürstlich
      Thurn und Taxisschen Hofbibliothek zu Regensburg (PhD diss.: Erlangen-
      Nürnberg; Erlangen: Hogl, 1963) 217p., Notenanhang 63*l*.
          Die Initien der anonymen und unbekannten Kompositionen, Noten-
          anhang.
              Over 500 multiple staff incipits of anonymous works found in
              the Orgeltabulatur F.K. 21 and the Handschriften F.K. 22-24.

NEUBAUER, FRANZ CHRISTOPH, 1760-1795

905   SJOERDSMA, Richard Dale. The instrumental works of Franz Christoph
  ▽   Neubauer (1760-1795)(PhD diss.: Ohio State U.,1970) 2v. (typescript)
          Thematic index,v.2, 5-63.
              161 incipits for all of Neubauer's known instrumental works.

906   SJOERDSMA, Richard Dale (Carthage College) The vocal-choral works
*   of Franz Christoph Neubauer (1760-1795)
      Thematic index

NEUKOMM, SIGISMOND, 1778-1858

907   ARAUJO, Mozart. Sigismond Neukomm, Um músico austríaco no Brasil
      [Sigismond Neukomm, an Austrian musician in Brazil], *Revista Brasileira
      de Cultura* 1/1969, 61-74. In Pt.
      Le catalogue thématique de Sigismond Neukomm

NEURATH, Gustav Herbert (compiler)

908   Das Violinkonzert in der Wiener Klassischen Schule (PhD diss.: Wien,
▽   1926) 7, 209, 48*l*. (typescript)
      Thematischer Katalog der Werke Haydn's und seiner Zeitgenossen,
      48*l*.
            Incipits for all movements of 47 violin concertos by the
            following composers: Franz Aspelmayr (1), Giacomo Conti (1),
            Dittersdorf (2), Josef Fodor (4), Josef Haydn (6), Michael
            Haydn (1), Leopold Hoffmann (2), Franz Krommer (1), Josef
            Misliweczek (1), Simon Molitor (4), Wenzel Pichl (1), Ignaz
            Pleyel (1), Franz Pässinger (1), Josef Starzer (1), Anton
            Teyber (4), Josef Timer (1), Ferdinand Titz (1), Luigi Toma-
            sini (2), Christoph Wagenseil (1), Johann Wanhall (1), Anton
            Wranitzky (1), Josef Ziegler (1).

908 a --- Das Violinkonzert in der Wiener Klassischen Schule, *Studien zur*
□   *Musikwissenschaft* XIV (1927) 125-42.
            Summary of the text without incipits.

NEW YORK, New York Public Library at Lincoln Center

909   Catalogue of music available in black line print (New York: Public
▽   Library, 1935) 19p. Typescript in US NYpl: 312*; xerox in US NYcg.
            A typescript catalogue, partially thematic, of scores pre-
            pared on transparencies from 16th, 17th, and 18th century
            parts by W. P. A. (Works Progress Administration) copyists
            and others. Contains incipits for 17th century instrumental
            music (p. 3-8), 18th century orchestral music (p. 9-13),
            18th century chamber and solo instrumental music (p. 14-18).
            A total of 154 incipits of works by 88 composers as follows:
            Abel, Adson, Allison, Aloyson, Aniou, Artus, J.C. Bach, J.S.
            Bach, Baptiste, Bassani, Bianchi, Boccan, Boccherini, Boc-
            quet, Bull, Caresano, Caroso, Cavalieri, Constantin, Conver-
            so, Coperario, Derideau, Diomedes, Dittersdorf, Dowland,
            Du Manoir, Filtz, Finger, Fodor, Ford, Forqueray, Fuhrmann,
            Galilei, Giles, Graun, Grétry, G.F. Händel, Hassler, Hol-
            borne, Hooper, Hume, Jenkins, Johnson, Jomelli, Jones, Kinder-
            sley, Kozeluch, Kün, Laurencinas, Leclair, Leighton, Lupo,
            Maldere, Martin y Coll, Mercure, Mersenne, Mertle, Mestrino,
            Meyer, Milton (father of poet), Morley, Paisiello, Peerson,
            Pergamesco, Périchon, P. Philips, Pichl, Pilkington, Pleyel,
            Polonos, Porter, Pugnani, Reys, Richardson, Rosetter, G.
            Sammartini, Schew, Schultz, Schütz, Stamitz, Strobel, Tessa-
            rini, Valenciano, F. Valls, Vivaldi, Vogel, Wanhall, and
            Wesper.

910   Dictionary catalog of the music collection (Boston: G.K. Hall, 1964)
      33v. & Supplement, 1966)
              A significant number of the reproduced catalog cards include
              incipits. This was part of an uncompleted project to trans-
              cribe incipits on cards for works whose identification might
              not be clear. At one stage the project was enlarged to in-
              clude composers represented by Gesamtausgaben. Thus, for
              example, 300 incipits are included for works of Beethoven and
              a large number for the works of Mozart. John Blow has 24
              entries, C.P.E. Bach 2, etc.

NEW YORK, Queens College of the City University of New York

911   BROWN, Linda. Incipit catalogue of xeroxed scores in Queens College
▽   Music Library. Index cards. Compiled 1971. (manuscript)
              Incipits for all movements of works by Francesco Gasparini
              (1), Antonio Martinelli (1), Antonio Brioschi (1), Johann
              Gottlieb Graun (1), Wenceslas Pichl (3), Gaetano Pugnani
              (2), Leopold Antonin Tomas Kozeluh (1), Giovanni Battista
              Giovanni Battista Sammartini (17), Anton Filtz (1), Carl
              Friedrich Abel (24). Provides library call numbers.

NICHELMANN, CHRISTOPH, 1717-1762

912   LEE, Douglas A. The instrumental works of Christoph Nichelmann
      (PhD diss.: U. of Michigan, 1968) 2v. U. Micro. 68-13, 348. (typescript)
              Thematic index, Appendix I.
              Incipits for concertos for solo instrument and string
              orchestra, sonatas and miscellaneous pieces for solo
              keyboard, and works for instrumental ensemble. Based on
              microfilms of MS sources and first printed editions.
              Gives library location of sources, MS catalogue numbers,
              and verification of autograph copies.

912a --- The works of Christoph Nichelmann: a thematic index (Detroit:
      Information Coordinators, 1970).
              "The total index includes approximately seventeen keyboard
              concertos, twenty keyboard sonatas, roughly a dozen miscel-
              laneous keyboard pieces, a cantata, an opera, three sinfoni-
              as, a French ouverture, one keyboard fantasia, a set of vari-
              ations, and twenty-two eighteenth century German Lieder. An
              appendix presents all known publications of these works since
              1800."

              Reviews: G[erald] A[braham], *MLetters* 53/1 (Jan 1972), 84-85.

NIELSEN, CARL AUGUST, 1865-1931

913   HAMMER, Marilyn Joann (Eastman School of Music, Rochester, N.Y.)
*   Thematic index

NOBLE, Richard D.C.

914   Editorial [on thematic catalogues], *Consort* XXI (Summer 1964) 241-47.
□   Discusses the problems, aims and usage of thematic catalogues.

NOVELLO, Vincent (compiler)

915 [Rough thematic catalogues]. (GB Lbm: British Mus. Add. 33239,
▽   1832) 3v. (manuscript)
            Includes compositions by: (1) Orlando Gibbons, taken from
            Fitzwilliam MS x. 3.17 (in Dr. Blow's hand), from Boyce's
            Cathedral Music, and from Harl. 7337; (2) Pelham Humfrey,
            taken from Fitzwilliam MSS x. 1.26 and x. 3.17, from a MS
            belonging to the Rev. Dr. Goodenough of Westminster Abbey,
            from Add. 30931-30932, and from Harl. 7338; and (3) John
            Blow, from Fitzwilliam MS x. 3.17, Boyce's Cathedral Music,
            and from Harl. 7338-7340.

NUNAMAKER, Norman Kirt (compiler)

916 The virtuoso violin concerto before Paganini: the concertos of
▽   Lolli, Giornovichi, and Woldemar (PhD diss.: Indiana U., 1968)
     258p.(typescript)
            Incipits of the concertos of Lolli, Giornovichi, and Woldemar,
            Appendix C, 240-58.
                 Incipits for all movements of works by Lolli (13), Giorno-
                 vichi (18), and Woldemar (3).

NUNES GARCIA, JOSÉ MAURICIO, 1767-1830

917 PERSON de MATTOS, Cleofe. Catálogo temático das obras do Padre
     José Mauricio Nunes Garcia. Com informação biográphica (Rio de
     Janeiro: Gráfica Olímpica Editôra Ltda., 1970) 413p.
            Catálogo temático, Part III, 61-336.
                 Chronological arrangement of incipits classified in the
                 following groups: independent sacred vocal works; Masses;
                 Offices; and miscellaneous dramatic and instrumental com-
                 positions and arrangements. Alphabetical arrangement of
                 undated works, library locations of MSS, and biographical
                 and bibliographical information is provided. Double staff
                 incipits for all voices and all sections, with text under-
                 lay, of 237 works.

O'CONNELL, Charles (compiler)

918 The Victor book of symphonies (New York: Simon & Schuster, 1948)
     556p.
            Incipits or subjects of 138 symphonies recorded by the Vic-
            tor record company.

919 The Victor book of overtures, tone poems, and other orchestral works
     (New York: Simon & Schuster, 1950) 614p.
            Incipits or subjects of 318 orchestral works.

Key: ✱ in preparation; ▽ manuscript; ☐ literature; ✫ Library of Congress

OFFENBACH, JACQUES, 1819-1880

920   ALMEIDA, Antonio de (Paris). Catalogue thématique raisonné des
*   oeuvres complètes de Jacques Offenbach (To be published ca. 1973)
            Incipits, synopses, orchestrations, appendices on publishers,
            and librettists. In 1968, there appeared in certain periodi-
            cals a request for further information on lesser works and
            locations of MSS of Offenbach by a P. Gaudy who was acting
            for M. de Almeida.

d'OGNY, Le Comte   [Catalogue I]

921   Catalogue de la Musique de Monsieur Le Comte d'Ogny (GB Lbm: Hirsch
▽   IV. 1085) 52p., Supplement [66], 67p. (manuscript). Microfilm copy
      in US NYcg.
            D'Ogny, a French patron of Haydn, maintained a sizable musi-
            cal establishment of his own as may be seen from these two
            beautifully bound catalogues. The collection itself has
            been almost completely dispersed or lost. The catalogue is
            divided into three sections and contains single and double
            staff incipits for vocal music (52p., [66p]) and instrumen-
            tal chamber music and symphonies (67p.). (Operas are listed
            without incipits). Composers with incipits include: Anfossi
            82, Accorimbony 6, Aprile 1, Allessandri 2, Bach 4, Bust 1,
            Bertoni 2, Bianchi 1, Cambini 4, Cimarosa 3, Cazaniga 2, Col-
            la 2, D. 3, Franki 1, Guglielmi 8, Galuppi 6, Gossec 6, Gre-
            tri 8, Gluk [Gluck] 27, Jomelli 29, Langlé 35, Majo 13, Mon-
            za 5, Mazl 3, Martini 4, Mazzanti 1, Mortellari 6, Mislivesek
            2, Neumann 2, Piccini 49, Paeisiello 56, Philidor 4, Perez 2,
            Pergolesi 1, Pozzi 1, Ponzo 1, Ruttini 2, Sacchini 29, Sarti
            31, Salieri 1, Sassone [Hasse] 1, Traetta 25, Anfossi 25,
            Bianchi 3, Cambini 4, Carusio 1, Cherubini 1, Durante 1, Ga-
            luppi 2, Guglielmi 1, Gatti 1, Giordani 2, Gluck 2, Hasse 6,
            Haydn 9, Jommelli 37, Leo 4, Meraux 1, Majo 12, Monza 2, Maz-
            zoni 2, Martini 3, Monopoli 1, Mortellari 1, Marcello 1, Ot-
            tani 2, Paesiello 12, Piordaniello 1, Perez 1, Piccini 69,
            Ruttini 1, Rispoli 5, Rust 2, Sacchini 19, Sarti 3, Sterkel
            1, Schuster 1, Timarosa 8, Touchemoulin 1, Tarchi 1, Vogel 1,
            Anonymous 3; [Instrumental works], duets: Bar[rière] 6,
            Chartrain 6, Ernest Eichter 6, Guenin 6, Kammell 6, Navoi-
            gille 6, Rafaele 6, Stamitz 6; trios: Asslidl 6, Bach 6, Bre-
            val 6, Boccherini 6, Janson L'ainé 6, Kammel 6, Navoigille 12,
            Ricci 6; quartets: Abel 12, Breval 12, Boccherini 6, Bonesi
            6, Chartrain 18, Cambini 36, Davaux 18, De Giardini 66, D.L.C.
            12, D.B. 6, Eichner 6, Fiala 6, St. Georges 6, Gossec 12,
            Gluck 15, Graaf 12, Gugel 6, Haydn 12, Jadin 6, Kammell 6,
            Laurietti 6, Lorenzetti 12, Monsigny 8, Ordonnez 6, Piccini
            4, Philidor 4, Pugnani 3, Schuster 6, Sacchini 6, Signor-
            etti 6, Schmitte, Stamitz 24, Stamitz fils 6, Syrmen 6,
            Ritter 6, Rosetti 6, Traversa 6, Vachon 6, Del. Sig.r 12,
            Anonymous 6, Abel 6, Blasius 6, Boccherini 18, Cambini 30,
            Dalayrac 6, Giala 6, Gehot 6, Haydn 6, Mehnier, Zimmermann
            6; quintets: Boccherini 24, Kuchter (?) 6, Leistigb. (?) 3,
            Pugnani 3, Vanhall 6; symphonies: Cosare 1, Eichner 24, Gue-
            nin 3, Gossec 7, Haydn 34, Holzbauer 6, Navoigille 9, Sta-
            mitz 1, and Le Duc, Stamitz, Gossec; sinfonia concertante:
            Back 3, Breval 2, Cambini 5, Davaux 6, Gossec 1, Heina 1,
            Stamitz 7.

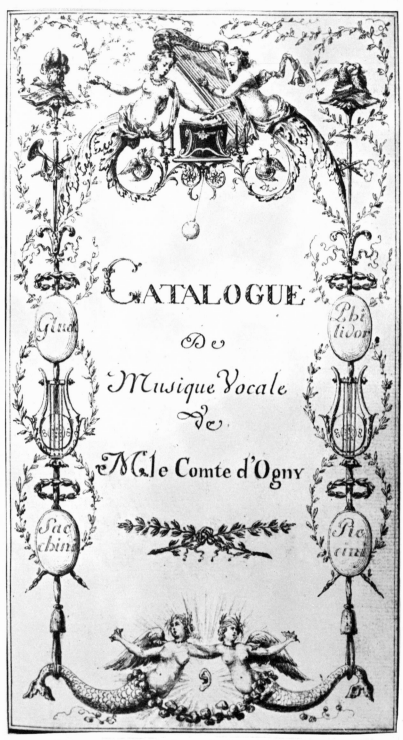

XVIIa. d'Ogny, *Catalogue de la musique vocale...*,
ca. 1785, title page, no. 922

Noms des auteurs	Parties Séparées	N°. des Morceaux	Motifs des Ariettes, Scènes, Duo, Trio, Quatuor, finales et Chœurs.
			andte Canzoncine ... 12 ...
Milico		I	ho Sparse tante Lacrime
Marcello		I	*andte* en mote. / che vvol far Ci vvol Pazienza.
Mereaux		I	*Largo Sosten:* Scene / o trop funeste Sort ... Ciel! ô / *allo Spirito.* / Ciel! ... qui nous donnas ce héros!
Méhul		I	*lent.* / Mi=nis=tres redoutés en plus bas
M.*.*.*			Motet françois.
		I	*allegro.* / Les Cieux instruisent La terre
Monret		I	Pirithoüs Tragédie

XVIIb. d'Ogny, *Catalogue de la musique vocale...*,
ca. 1785, page 120, no. 922

> *Reference:* Barry S. BROOK, La symphonie française dans la
> seconde moitié du XVIIIe siècle, v. I, 342-49. (see no.185)

d'OGNY, Le Comte [Catalogue II]

922   Catalogue de Musique Vocale de M. le Comte d'Ogny (US LC) 220p.
▽   (manuscript). Microfilm copy in US NYcg.
>   Single and double staff incipits, with text underlay, for
>   vocal works. Composers: Anfossi 139, Allessendri 4, Andre-
>   ozzi 3, Accorimboni 7, Aprile 5 (2 missing), Back 5, Baini
>   2, Bertoni 4, Benevolio 1, Bianki 9, Borghi 3, Bust 1, Ci-
>   marosa 70, Cambini 36, Caruso 6, Carlo 1, Casaniga 7, Cher-
>   ubini 3, Colla 2, Durante 2, David 2, Dr...2, Desaugier 3,
>   D...1, Edelmann 1, Franchi 1, Guglielmi 24, Giordani 5,
>   Giordanello 3, Giardini 1, Gatti 2, Gresnick 1, Gossec 3,
>   Gluck (Gluk) 23, Gretry 15, Graun 1,Galuppi 80, Haydn 63,
>   Hasse 9, Jommelli 83, Jadin 2, Kreüsser 2, Kraun (Graun) 1,
>   Langlé 7, Leo 4, Lepreux 2, Louet 5, Majo 40 (2 blank), Mis-
>   livesek 6, Mortellari 7, Masi 2, Monopoli 2, Mozart 25, Ma-
>   zanti 1, Martini 9, Monza 2, Mazoni 2, Milico 1, Marcello 1,
>   Mereaux 1, Méhul 1, M...1, Nauman 3, Nonini 1, Nicoli 1,
>   Ottani 4, Paesiello 218, Piccini 136, Prati 19, Pergolesi 3,
>   Perez 3, Pachierotti 2, Pozzi 1, Pugnani 1, Ponzo 1, Phili-
>   dor 6, Rispoli 13, Rusti 1, Ruttini 2, Rausini 2, Rust 3,
>   Reichard 4, Sacchini 111, Sarti 40, Schuster 10, Salieri 2,
>   Sterkel 1, Scolari 1, Traëtta 10, Tarchi 7, Tritta 3, Tomeoni
>   1, Touchemoulin 1, Vogel 1.[reproductions on preceding pages]

923   BROOK, Barry S. **Musical patronage in Paris: Le Comte d'Ogny**
*□   A study of the d'Ogny family as patrons of music, and of the
>   two d'Ogny thematic catalogues.

O' HARA, GEOFFREY, 1882-

924   **Catalogue of the works of Geoffrey O'Hara** (New York: M. Witmark,
>   1930?) 80p.
>   [Thematic catalogue], 40-80.
>   Complete list of published works contains many 3-stave in-
>   cipits (voice and piano). Also includes range and complete
>   text for each song.

OLD HALL, Catholic College of St. Edmunds: Old Hall MS

925   SQUIRE, William Barclay. **Notes on an undescribed collection of
>   early English 15th century music,** *SIMG* II (1900-1901) 356-73.
>   Contains a thematic list of the contents of the Old Hall
>   Manuscript, including works by the following: Aleyn, Burell,
>   Byttering, Chirbury, Cooke, Damett, Dunstable, Excetre,
>   Fonteyns, Forest, Gervays, Roy Henry, Lambe, Mayshuet, Oliver,
>   Pennard, Power, Pycard, Queldryk, Rowland, Sturgeon, Swynford,
>   Tyes, and Typp.

>   --- Revisions of the Barclay Squire catalogue are to be found in:
>   Manfred BUKOFZER **The music of the Old Hall Manuscript,** part I, *MQ*
>   XXXIV (1948) 514 and **Studies in medieval & renaissance music** (New
>   York: Norton, 1950) 36-37.

OLOMOUC [OLMÜTZ], Czechoslovakia

926 Cathallogus/ über/ die Hochfürstlichen Musicalia/ und Instrumenten.
▽   (CS: Olomouc Státní archiv. sign. C. kart. 504) 13p. Compiled 1759
     (manuscript). To be compared with the Kroměříč catalogue, no. 699.
                    The oldest inventory of the music collection belonging to
                    the Olmütz Bishop Leopold Egk. The music, now lost, was
                    obtained in the period 1758-1760. Description: consecutive
                    numbers, composer's name, instrumentation and voice setting
                    where appropriate, and thematic incipit. Contains 229 works,
                    arranged by genre, of which 130 are anonymous and 97 are by
                    the following composers: Beretti 6, Bucholtz 1, Caldara 1,
                    Campioni 1, Fux 1, Galuppi 1, Giulini (Conte Giulino) 2,
                    Haydn 1, Hoffmann (Hoffman) 4, Holtzbauer 8, Chiesa 1, Körzl
                    (Körtzl) 6, Maltzart 1, Martini 1, Motzard 2, Neumann 5,
                    Ordenez (Ordenitz) 1, Pescatore 1, Prioschi 1, Privio 1,
                    Relutzi 1, Engelberto Rendeux Czigese 1, Graf Rottal 1, Roy
                    7, Saliger 1, Savio 1, Sciroli 1, Schlöger 6, St: Martino
                    (S. Martino) 7, Stamitz 6, Steffan 2, Steinmetz 3, Wagenseil
                    9, Weigert (Weigerth) 2, Zach 1, Zechner 1, Zigler 1.

926a --- SEHNAL, Jiří. Kapela olomouckého biskupa Leopolda Egka (1758-60)
☐   a její repertoár [The capella of the Olmütz Bishop, Leopold Egk (1758-
      60) and its repertoire], *Časopis Moravského muzea-vědy společenské*
      50 (1966) 203-30.

ONSLOW, GEORGE, 1784-1853

927 Collection complète des quintetti et quatuors (Paris: Pleyel,
     [1830?])
                    Catalogue thématique des quatuors et quintetti composés pour
                    instrumens à cordes, 1st vln pt., 1 leaf before p. 1.

928 Quatrieme quintetto pour deux violons, alto, violoncelle & bass
     Oeuvre 17 (Paris: Dépot central de la librairie [ca. 1840]) 5 parts.
                    Catalogue thématique des quintetti pour deux violons, alto, et
                    deux violoncelles, ou violoncelle et contrebasse, vln 1 pt, title
                    page.
                    Incipits of 21 quintets Opp. 1-51. This is the Troupenas
                    edition with identification erased. It is the same as that
                    first published by Pleyel.

929 Collection complète des quatuors (Paris: Brendus et cie [1852]) 4v.
                    This is a "reissue of the earlier editions by Troupenas,
                    Schlesinger and Pleyel. It includes a thematic index of
                    the 36 quartets" at the front of the vln 1 part.

d'ORDOÑEZ, CARLOS, 1734-1786

930 BROWN, A. Peter (U. of Hawaii). Thematic catalogue for the music
 *   of Carlos d'Ordoñez
                    Includes "new material concerning the operas and chamber
                    music as well as some information governing the chronology
                    and dating of the symphonies.":Incipits for all movements
                    of 142 works catalogued thus far. Includes doubtful and
                    spurious works.

OREL, Dobroslav (compiler)

931　Der Mensuralkodex "Speciálnik".　Ein Beitrag zur Geschichte der
▽　　Mensuralmusik und Notenschrift in Böhmen bis 1540　(PhD diss.: Wien,
　　　1914) 460, 76*l*.　(typescript)
　　　　　　Thematischer Katalog, 76*l*.

OROLOGIO, ALESSANDRO, d. 1633

932　JUNKERMANN, Hilde H. (U. of Wisconsin-Milwaukee).　The madrigals of
*　　Alessandro Orologio
　　　　　　Incipits for　*Il secondo libro de madrigali à cinque voci*
　　　　　　(Venezia:Gardano, 1595).

OSEK, Czechoslavakia.

933　Syllabus/ seu/ Catalogus perutilis/ non Choralia,/ Verum figuralia/
▽　　pia festivi Chori proferens artificia,/ quae/ pro felici officij
　　　habiti fine/ in Bacchanalijs/ suavioris Instar Musicae/ filiali ex
　　　reverentia/ Reverendissimo, ac Amplissimo Domino Domino/ Cajetano/
　　　Sac: ac Exempti Ordinis Cisterciensis, Celeberrimi/ Monasterij B:
　　　V: Mariae de Osseco Abbati, Regni/ Bohemiae Praelato Dignissimo,
　　　Patri Suo Venerandissimo/ offert/ Filius obediens Fr/ nomine Nivar-
　　　dus Sommer cognomine dictus (CS Pnm) 122p. Compiled in 1754, 1802,
　　　and 1817. (manuscript)
　　　　　　A thematic catalogue of the music and musical instruments
　　　　　　of Osek Monastery in Bohemia. Description: consecutive
　　　　　　numbering, double staff incipits of first movements (Masses
　　　　　　have incipits for the various sections), title, instrumen-
　　　　　　tation, composer's name. Consists of 908 works: 559 ori-
　　　　　　ginal entries, 317 from 1802, and 32 from 1817. The cata-
　　　　　　logue is organized into 27 genres and contains 86 anonymous
　　　　　　works and 822 attributed works by the following composers:
　　　　　　R:P: Absolon 3, Andre 1, R:P: Angstenberger 13, Bach Milano
　　　　　　1, Bachschmid 2, Ballabene 2, Belli 2, Bencini 6, Boroni 7,
　　　　　　Brentner 2, Breünich 1, Brixi 114, Brunetter 1, Brunetti 1,
　　　　　　Caldara 11, Carpani 1, Cartellieri 1, Signore Celleberrino
　　　　　　1, Clemente 1, Constanzi (Costanzi) 4, Conti 6, Conti junior
　　　　　　2, Czecherini 1, Czerni 1, Debuini 2, Ditters d'Dittersdorff
　　　　　　12, Domberger 5, Duma 3, Durante 1, Eckert 1, Ehrenhardt 1,
　　　　　　Emmert 1, Eschler 1, Fago (Faggo) 3, Feo 16, Fiebig 1, Fils
　　　　　　4, Fischietti 1, Fux 4, Galerini 1, Galluppi 3, Giuseppe Ga-
　　　　　　zanigo (Gazzaniga) 2, Giacomelli 1, Gionelli 14, Graun 4,
　　　　　　Gsur 1, Guglielmi 1, Gyrovetz 4, Haan 2, Haas 1, Habbegger 1,
　　　　　　Habermann 6, Hahn 1, Händel 1, Hasse 11, Hatasch 1, J. Haydn
　　　　　　(Heijden) 24, Michele Haydn 10, Heinichen 1, Holtzbauer 1,
　　　　　　Jacob C:S:B: 5, R:P: Jancha 1, Jomelli 1, R:P: Wendelino
　　　　　　Karauscheck (Karaužeck) 6,　Kayser 3, Kern 22, Kluch 1, Klyma
　　　　　　10, Kohaut 1, Kohl 2, Kolz 1, Königsberger 2, Koprziva 4,
　　　　　　Leopodo Kozeluch 15, Kraus 1, Krommer 1, Landfelt 1, Lang 1,
　　　　　　Laube 1, Leo 5, Liberti 1, Linek (Lineck) 3, R:P: Lohelio
　　　　　　(Lohely, Lohelius, Loheli) 34, Loos 13, Lotti 11, Majer 2,
　　　　　　Majo 3, Mancini 13, Manchij 1, Manna ex Italia 1, Manschinger
　　　　　　2, Martino 2, Masi 1, Mederitsch 1, Mensy 2, Mentschel 1,
　　　　　　Mettiroti 1, Misliweczek (Misliwezeck) 19, Molieri 4, Mora-
　　　　　　weczek 1, Mozart 13, Müller 4, Naumann 1, Neruda 1, Nitsch

2, Nobis 1, Novak (Novack, Novac) 9, R:P: Oersler 1, Paesello
2, Peres 1, Pergolese (Pergolesi) 3, R:P: Petro 1, Petrucci
1, Piccini 2, Pignatelli 1, Pichl 5, Pichler 1, Pilaja 1,
Pinzger 4, R:P: Placido Fancka 1, Pleyel 10, Ponto 1, Porpora 3, Giovano Prachensky Maestro di Capella d'Lichtenstein
1, Prazak 2, Preindl 2, Püschel 1, Rautani 1, Reichnauer 16,
Reinhard 1, Reipert 1, Reütter 2, Aemil: Rikert Sac: Cister:
2, Ristori 3, Rofeld 1, Rolle 5, Romberg 1, Rosetti 1, Rosin
1, Rutini 1, Rautari 1, Sacchini 3, Salieri 1, Saputo 1,
Sarcuni 1, Sarri 8, Scarlatti 1, Seeliger 1, Sehling 23,
Seidelmann 1, Senati 1, Sheibl 1, R:P: Schenkirsch 4, Schie-
dermajer 3, Schmidt 6, Schretteri 1, Schubert 5, Schürer 7,
Schuster 3, Schwerdtner 3, R:P: Simone Piarum Scholar 4,
Söcka 3, Sordella 1, Soyka (Soijcka, Sojka) 8, Stamitz 1,
Strauhall 1, Swoboda 11, Syruczek 1, Tahettj 1, Taubner 1,
Techetti 1, Terraella 2, Traetta (Trajetta) 4, Umstadt 2,
Viennensis 1, Vignati 1, Vinci 2, Vogl 9, Walter 4, Wanhall
(Vannhall) 30, Wolff 1, Wozet 1, Paul Wranisky (Wranizki) 3,
Zach 8, Zarnetti 1, Zechner 3, Zelenka 5, Zimmermann 4, Zoppis
1.

OTT, Alfons

934 **Thematische Verzeichnisse,** *Die Musik in Geschichte und Gegenwart* XIII
☐   (1965) 311-21.
Historical survey beginning before Breitkopf catalogue and
including landmarks of publisher's cataloguing such as Artaria,
Pleyel, and Hofmeister; composer's catalogues of their own
works including C.P.E. Bach, Mozart, Haydn, Schumann, Brahms,
and Liszt; and mentioning giants of contemporary cataloguing
such as Deutsch, Robbins-Landon, Kinsky, Schmieder, and Hoboken. Discussion of symbolic-notation development. Major
thematic catalogues are listed in a comprehensive bibliography.

OXFORD, Bodleian Library: MS Canonici Misc. 213

935 STAINER, John F.R. and Cecie. **Dufay and his contemporaries;** Fifty
compositions (ranging from about A.D. 1400-1440) transcribed from
MS Canonici Misc. 213 in the Bodleian Library, Oxford (London: No-
vello; New York: Novello, Ewer and Co., 1898) xix, 207p.
Index to the whole contents of MS Canonici misc. 213, [199]-207.
The index, in letter notation, includes works by the following
composers: Acourt, Adam, Akany, Antonius de Civitate, Antoni-
us Romanus, Bartholomeus de Bononia, Baudet Corider, Benoit,
Billart, Binchois, Brassart, Briquet, Bruolo, Cardot, Carmen,
Cesaris, Charité, Chierisy, Coutreman, Dufay, Feragut, Domini-
cus de Feraria, P. Fontaine, Franchois, Francus de Insula,
Gallo, Gautier (Gualtier?), Grenon, Grossin, Hasprois, Hau-
court, La Beausse, A. de Lantins, H. de Lantins, Lebertoul,
Guillaume Le Grant, Joh. Le Grant, Gualterius Liberth, R. Lie-
bert, Loqueville, Joh. de Ludo, Malbecque, Passet, Paullet,
Prepositi.Brixiensis, Joh. de Quatris, Randulfus Romanus,
Rezon, P. Rosso, Ar. de Ructis, Hubertus de Salinis, Jo. de
Sarto, Tapissier, Tebrolis, R. de Vaux, Velut, Vide, Ant.
Zachara, Nic. Zacharias, and Zocholo de Portu.

--- Reprint (Amsterdam: Knuf, 1966).

OXFORD, Bodleian Library: Italian Chamber Music

936 ZIMMERMAN, Franklin B. A thematic catalogue of published seventeenth
▽   century Italian chamber music in the Music School collection, Bod-
     leian Library, Oxford (Typewritten research report: U. of Southern
     Calif., 1954) 2v. Xerox copy in US NYqc.
              Volume II contains the incipit catalogue with tempi; composers
              arranged alphabetically. Volume I is a notation index; repre-
              sentation of 12 semi-tones as nos. 1-9 and letters xyz, with
              modifications for rests and repeated figures. Indications
              are given for minor and major keys. Composers include: Alber-
              gati, degl'Antonii (G.B. and Pietro), Arresti, Baldassani,
              Bassani, Belisi, Boccaletti, Bononcini, Borri, Buoni, Caldara,
              Castello, Castro, Cazzati, Colombi, Fedeli, Fiore, Fontana,
              Gaudini, Gardano, Gaspardini, Gigli, Grossi, Guerrieri, Gus-
              sago, Iacchini, Laurenti. Legrenzi, Lolli, Mannelli, Marini,
              Matteis, Muzzolini, Merula, Pasino, Penna, Pesenti, Piazzi,
              Polaroli, Placuzzi, Ravenscroft, Rosenmiller, Rossi (S.),
              Sala, Sanmartini (P.), Silvani, Stiava, Tibaldi, Todeschini,
              Tonini, Torelli, Uccellini, Veracini, Viadana, Vinacese, Vi-
              tali, Viviani, and Ziani. The catalogue is in process of
              being indexed by computer.

937 STEVENS, Denis. [Thematic catalogue] (GB Ob: Ms Mus. Sch. D 228)
▽   (manuscript)
              Incipits of sonatas, 18th century, mostly anonymous.

OXFORD, Christ Church Library

938 ARKWRIGHT, G.E.P. Catalogue of music in the library of Christ
     Church, Oxford (London: Oxford U. Press, 1915-1923) 2v.
        Thematic catalogue, v. II,
              Incipits of anonymous vocal works, with speculation and
              commentary concerning their origins.

939 STEVENS, Denis. [Thematic catalogue] (GB Och: Mus. Ms. 371) (manu-
▽   script)
              Incipits of 16th century keyboard music.

940 --- [Thematic catalogue] (GB Och: Mus. Ms. 1034) (manuscript)
▽   Incipits of 16th century keyboard music.

PACKER, Dorothy (Dallas, Texas)

941 French vaudevilles of the late 17th and early 18th centuries.
*   Catalogue of songs arranged alphabetically by titles, first
              lines, and subject matter, accompanied by a numerical index
              file of the intervallic structure of each song. All texts,
              first lines of alternate texts, and sources given.

Key: * in preparation; ▽ manuscript; □ literature; ☆ Library of Congress

PAGANELLI, GIUSEPPE ANTONIO, 1710-c. 1765

942   SCHENK, Erich. G.A. Paganelli, sein Leben und seine Werke (Salz-
       burg: Waldheim-Eberle, 1928) 186p.
              Thematischer Katalog, 131-160.
                   Incipits for all movements of instrumental works. Dramatic
                   works, including aria and recitative incipits, have text
                   underlay. Data on MS locations and dedications. Incipits
                   for other composers included in the text: Christian Frie-
                   drich Döbbert (6 flute sonatas), Adam Falckenhagen (1 con-
                   certo, 6 lute sonatas), Johann Daniel Leuthard (6 partitas
                   for cembalo), and Johann Pfeiffer (1 trio sonata, 2 concer-
                   tos), p. 160-67.

PAGANINI, NICOLÒ, 1782-1840

942.1 BACHMANN, Alberto. Les grands violonistes du passé (Paris: Fisch-
       bacher, 1913) 468p. (see no. 65)
              Oeuvres de Paganini, 214-27.
                   List of works includes incipits for Op. 1, 6, 7-9, and 11.

PAISIELLO, GIOVANNI, 1740-1816

943   DELLA CORTE, Andrea. Settecento Italiano. Paisiello con una Tavola
       tematica. L'Estetica Musicale di P. Metastasio (Torino: Fratelli
       Bocca, 1922) x, 352.
              Tavola tematica Paisielliana, 4l. after p. 278.
                   67 single and multiple staff incipits for pieces from operas,
                   Masses, and instrumental works.

PAISLEY, William J.

943.1 Identifying the unknown communicator in painting, literature and music.
□   The significance of minor encoding habits, The Journal of Communication
       XIV/4 (Dec 1964) 219-37.
                   Describes a successful computerized theme-identification ex-
                   periment.

PALESTRINA, GIOVANNI PIERLUIGI DA, ca.1525-1594

944   HABERL, Franz X. [et al.] Werke (Leipzig: Breitkopf & Härtel, 1862-
       1907) 33v.
              Index musicus omnium operum Joannis Petraloysii Praenestini,
              v. 33, 97-129.
                   Short incipits in original notation, with text underlay.

945   JEPPESEN, Knud. The recently discovered Mantova masses of Pales-
       trina, ActaMusicol XXII (1950) 36-47.
              [Thematic list of ten Masses].
                   Four-voiced incipits for Masses from MS 164 and MS 166, Musica
                   già della capela di S. Barbara in Mantova.

PALISCA, Claude V.

946   American scholarship in western music, Musicology, Frank Ll. Harri-
□   son, Mantle Hood and Claude V. Palisca, compilers (Englewood Cliffs,
       N.J.: Prentice Hall, 1963) 163-66.
                   Survey of American developments in thematic cataloguing.

PANKIEWICZ, EUGENIUSZ, 1857-1898

947   PÓZNIAK, Włodzimierz. **Eugeniusz Pankiewicz.** *Studia i materiały
       do dziejów muzyki polskiej*, t. 5 (Wyd 1. Kraków: Polskie Wydawnictwo
       Muzyczne, [1958]) 167p.
          [Thematic catalog].
             Incipits for songs, choral works, and piano pieces.

947a   Dodatek nutowy. (Kraków: Polskie Wydawn. Muzyczne, [1958]) 38p.

PARADIS, MARIA THERESA, 1759-1824

948   ULLRICH, Hermann. **Thematisches Werkverzeichnis,** *Beiträge zur Musik-
       wissenschaft* II (1963) 117-54.
             Incipits for works arranged by genre: 3 stage works, 3 can-
             tatas, 30 vocal works, 19 piano pieces, 2 chamber composi-
             tions. Includes listings for works known to have existed
             but for which music is not extant. Provides full biblio-
             graphical apparatus.

PARIS, Bibliothèque nationale

949   ÉCORCHEVILLE, Jean. **Catalogue du fonds de musique ancienne de la
       Bibliothèque Nationale** (Paris: Terquem, 1910-14) 8v.
             Incipits for some early MSS. Arranged by composer and/or
             genre (for anonymi). Uneven coverage: volumes 1-4 include
             letters A-D; 5-8, E-Z.

PARIS, Bibliothèque Nationale: Catalogue thématique de la musique vocale
polyphonique des XVe et XVIe s., *see no.* 173 (Nanie Bridgman)

PARIS, Bibliothèque nationale: Fonds fr. 1597

950   **MS. (Fonds fr. 1597): A thematic inventory, an unpublished manu-
▽   script** (Cambridge, Mass., Harvard U.: Advanced Seminar in Musi-
       cology, under the direction of Gustave Reese, 1959) 59p. (xerox)
             Texted incipits of the 86 chansons in the 15th century MS,
             with concordances in 90 contemporary MSS and incunabulae,
             and a listing of modern editions. Included are transcrip-
             tions of 3 of the chansons, with critical commentary. Com-
             posers represented are: Agricola, Compère, Ghizeghem, Jos-
             quin des Prez, Ninot le Petit, Obrecht, Ockeghem, Pipelare,
             Prioris, Dufay, Binchois, and Fresneau.

PARIS, Bibliothèque nationale: Fonds fr. 12744

951   MOSKOWITZ, Gladys. **The monophonic chansonnier, Paris Bibliothèque
▽   Nationale, Fonds Française, 12744: An inventory** (MA thesis: Brooklyn
       College of C.U.N.Y., 1971) v, 96p. (typescript). Copy in US NYcg.
             Incipits, old notation and original clefs, for the 143 chan-
             sons in the manuscript. Provides folio number, form (text
             and music), concordances, and editions and remarks. Also in-
             cludes indices for text incipits, composers represented, and
             sources.

PARIS, Bibliothèque Nationale: Res. Vm7 676

952   BRIDGMAN, Nanie. **Un manuscrit italien du début du XVIe siècle à la
       Bibliothèque Nationale (Res. Vm7 676),** *Annales Musicologiques* I (1953)
       177-267.

Table des incipits, 191-259.
>Both music and text incipits for each voice, plus a list
>of concordances, and an annotation where appropriate.
>Inventories 114 sacred works. Composers: Agricola, Benedictus,
>Brumel, Colinet de Lannoy, Compère, Craen, Févin, Ghiselin,
>Hayne, Isaac, Janequin, Josquin, Lopicida, La Rue, Liégeois
>(Nicolas), Moulu, Ninot le petit, Obrecht, Ornitoparchus,
>Prioris, Souliaert (Carolus), Todinghem, Congiet, Jopart,
>Ockeghem, Martini.

PARIS, Bibliothèque nationale (Fonds du Conservatoire): Fonds Blancheton

953   LA LAURENCIE, Lionel de. **Inventaire critique du fonds Blancheton de la Bibliothèque du Conservatoire de Paris** (Paris: Droz, 1930-1931) 2v.
>Incipits and bio-bibliographical data for an important
>manuscript collection of mid-eighteenth century (largely
>Italian) symphonies and chamber music. A principal source
>for the symphonies of G.B. Sammartini.

PARIS, Bibliothèque nationale (Fonds du Conservatoire): Rés. 1185, 1186, 1186bis

954   MAAS, Martha. **Seventeenth-century English keyboard music, a study of Manuscripts Rés. 1185, 1186, and 1186bis of the Paris Conservatory Library** (PhD diss.: Yale U., 1968) 2v. Univ. Micro. 69-13,356.
A catalogue of MSS Rés. II85, II86, and II86bis of the Paris Conservatory Library, v. 1, 262-339.
>419 incipits for all the pieces in the MSS listed, in the
>order in which they occur in the MSS. Composers mentioned:
>Anonymous, Blow, Byrd, Bull, Churchyard, Clarke, Cosyns, Dow-
>land, Faranella, Formiloe, Gibbons, Johnson, LaBarre, Lawes,
>Lever (LaBarre?), Loosemore, Lugge, Morley, Price, "R.A.",
>"R.Cr.", Silver, Tallis, Tomkins, Tresure, Wilkinson, Yonge,
>and Yves.

PARMA, Biblioteca.

955   GASPARINI, Guido. **Catalogo generale delle opere musicali,** teoriche o pratiche, manoscritte o stampati, di autori vissuti sino ai primi decenni del XIX secolo, esistenti nelle bibliotheche e negli archivi d'Italia, *Associazione dei Musicologi Italiani* (Parma:Zerbini & Freshing, 1911--) 14v.
>Volume I contains a few scattered themes.

PARSONS, ROBERT, d. 1570

956   MEYER, Ernst Hermann. **Die mehrstimmige Spielmusik des I7. Jahr-**
✿   **hunderts in Nord- und Mitteleuropa** (Kassel: Bärenreiter, 1934) 258p. (see no. 821)
[Thematic catalogue], 160.
>Incipits for 3 Innomines à 4, 1 Innomine à 5, and 2 Inno-
>mines à 6.

PASQUINI, BERNARDO, 1637-1710

957   HAYNES, Maurice Brooks, ed. **Bernardo Pasquini. Collected works for**
✿

the keyboard (American Institute for Musicology, 1964-68) 2v.
   [Thematic catalogue]
         Double staff incipits for 11 imitative pieces (capricio,
         fuge, ricercare, fantasia, etc.), 17 suites, 3 Alemandes,
         1 corrente, 4 gigas, 4 bizzarrias, and 9 arias.

958   CRAIN, Gordon F.   **The operas of Bernardo Pasquini** (PhD diss.: Yale
      U., 1965) 2v. Univ. Micro. 65-15,026.(typescript)
         Thematic index, v. 2.
         600 musical incipits given in full scoring, plus 200 text
         incipits for lost items, "principally of arias and other
         ⁺set pieces', arranged in the order of their occurence in
         each opera (an alphabetical index of text incipits facili-
         tates location of any individual item). Also indexed are
         some 50-odd arias found in various MS collections, but for
         which no operatic source (if any) has been located."

959   CRAIN, Gordon F. (Rutgers U.). **Bernardo Pasquini cantata catalogue**
*   (To be published in the Wellesley Edition Cantata Index Series)
         "This index will include the solo and ensemble cantatas,
         the 'unattached' arias,....and newly located items." Approx-
         imately 100-150 items will be included, with full biblio-
         graphical apparatus.

PASSAU, Germany. Dom

960   LEHRNDORFER, Franz. **[Thematic catalogue]** (On loan by the *DTB* to D
▽   Mbs) (manuscript)
         One of many partially thematic inventories prepared by the
         compiler under Adolf Sandberger's direction for the *Denkmäler
         der Tonkunst in Bayern.*

PASTERWIZ, GEORG von, 1730-1803

961   KAAS, Walter. **Georg von Pasterwiz als Kirchenkomponist** (PhD diss.:
▽   Wien, 1925) 167l. (typescript)
         Leaves 18-21 contain double staff incipits for 10 Masses and
         1 Requiem. Leaves 60-61 contain double staff incipits for
         5 Introits. Leaves 65-155 contain double staff incipits for
         155 Graduals and Offertories. Leaves 114-17 contain double
         staff incipits for 12 Vespers.

PEER INTERNATIONAL CO. (publisher)

962   **Thematic catalogue of songs** (New York: Peer International Co.;
      Southern Music Publishing Co., 1952) 62p.
         Publisher's catalogue. Incipits (ca. 10 measures) in vocal-
         piano score for 59 songs, arranged alphabetically by composer.
         Composers include: R. Bales, J. Beeson, F.S. Bucky, H. Co-
         well, D. Diamond, L.Fernandez, W.Flanagan, L.Foss, I.Freed,
         D.R. Heitmann, C.E.Ives, G.Kubik, A.Lara, J.Lessard, P.Nor-
         man, J.Perry, M.Ponce, G.Read, W.Riegger, N.Rorem, M.Sando-
         val, S.Saxe, T.Serly, C.Shaw, E.Siegmeister, C.Sterne, C.
         Vauclain, H.Villa-Lobos, J.Wagner, R.Ward, and B.Wayne.

PELPLIN, (near Gdansk), Poland. Seminarium: Pelplin Tablature

963   SUTKOWSI, Adam; OSOSTOWICZ-SUTKOWSKA, Alina. **The Pelplin Tablature,**
       a thematic catalogue, *Antiquitates musicae in Polonia,* v. 1 (Warzawa:
       Graz, [1963]) xxii, 676p.
              Thematic catalogue of an important Polish organ tablature of
              the early seventeenth century containing over 900 compositions
              including some previously unknown works of important composers.

963a   ---_Supplement. SUTKOWSKI, Adam; MISCHIATI, Oscar. **Una prezosa**
       fonte manoscritta di musica strumentale: L'intavolatura di Pelplin,
       Organo II/1 (Jan-June 1961) 53-72.
              14 incipits of canzonas with unknown concordances, p. 71-72.

              Reviews: MQ L/4 (1964) 537-39.

PEPUSCH, JOHANN CHRISTOPH, 1667-1752

964   FRED, Herbert William. **The instrumental music of Johann Christoph**
       Pepusch (PhD diss., Musicology: U. of North Carolina, 1961) 102,
       155p. U. Micro. no. 62-3121.(typescript)
              Supplement, 1-154.
              Double staff incipits for works arranged by genre: solo works
              for violin, harpsichord, flute, oboe; trio sonatas; concerti
              grossi (incipits for all instruments).

PERGOLESI, GIOVANNI BATTISTA, 1710-1736

965   PAYMER, Marvin. **An index to the complete works of Pergolesi indi-**
▽   **cating misattributed and dubious works therein** (New York: Queens
       College, 1966) 16p. (typescript)
              Index to the *Opera omnia* (Roma,1941) in the *Plaine and Easie*
              Code (see no.188).To be published in the *MLA Index Series.*

PETERS, C.F. (publisher)

966   **Katalog der Edition Peters** (Leipzig: C.F. Peters, 1888) 267p.
       Thematisches Verzeichnis, 20p. at end.
              Incipits for 24 piano sonatas of Clementi; 83 quartets,
              24 symphonies and some piano sonatas of Haydn, the Peters
              edition of Mozart keyboard sonatas and sonatines. Also
              incipits for the soloist of the following violin concerti:
              Kreutzer (4), Rode (5), and Viotti (6). Reprints: 1900, 1917.

PETRUS JOANNELLUS, 16th c.

966·1 CRAWFORD, David E. **Petrus Joannellus and the motets in volume V of**
       his "Novus thesaurus musicus", 1568 (M.A. Thesis: U. of Kansas, 1964)
       125p. (typescript)
              Thematic catalogue

PEUERL, PAUL, c. 1575-1625?

967   GEIRINGER, Karl, ed. **Paul Peuerl: Neue Paduanen (1611),** *DTÖ* 36/2
       (Wien: Universal, 1929) 133p.
              Thematisches Verzeichnis der Anfänge aller Tänze in der Tenor-
              stimme [der "Ettlichen lustigen Padovanen", 1620], p.129.
                     Incipits for 44 dances for four instruments, classified by
                     title, with apparently original publication numbers.

PEYER, JOHANN BAPTIST, d. 1733

968 FUCHS, Aloys. **Thematisches Verzeichniss einer Sammlung Orgel Com-**
▽   **positionen von Beyer.** (D Bds: HB VII, Mus. ms. theor. K. 516) [4p.]
    (manuscript). Microfilm in US NYcg.
        Multiple staff incipits for preambles and fugues, as well
        as 2 capriccios. A list of anonymous works is appended.

PFITZNER, HANS, 1869-1949

969 RECTANUS, Hans (Heidelberg). **Thematisches Verzeichnis der Werke**
*   **Hans Pfitzners** (To be published. Tutzing: Hans Schneider, ca. 1972).

PICHL, WENZEL, 1741-1804

970 WOLF, Friedrich (Wien). **Thematischer Katalog der Kirchenwerke**
*

971 ZAKIN, Anita (New York U.) **The symphonies of Wenzel Pichl**
*   **Thematic index of Pichl's symphonies.** (PhD diss. in prep)
            Incipits of all movements of authentic works, and works of
            doubtful and spurious attribution, with a special locator
            index for quick identification.

PICTON, Howard (U. of Hull)

972 Eighteenth-century concertos in Prague libraries. Ca. 700 index
▽   cards (manuscript).
        "A private index-card file, compiled in 1969, cataloguing
        manuscript copies and printed editions of 18th-century con-
        certos (c. 1740-1830) in the Music Department of the National
        Museum, and incorporating the much smaller holdings of Prague
        University Library and the Music Archive of Czechoslovak Ra-
        dio. Contains approximately 700 cards for solo, double, con-
        certante concertos, concertinos, and works entitled concerto.
        Each card records the composer's name (conflicting attribu-
        tions; true author); catalogue number; a single-stave incipit
        of the first movement; tempo marking, key, time signature of
        other movements; whether printed (publisher, place, plate
        number), or manuscript (autograph or copy); whether score or
        parts; transcription of essential title-page material; scoring;
        details of ripieno, duplicate, or missing parts. Nearly 200
        additional cards record modern manuscript copies of parts,
        scored transcriptions, modern printed editions, and miscel-
        laneous items."

PIJPER, WILLEM, 1894-1947

973 KLOPPENBURG, W.C.M. **Thematisch-bibliografische catalogus van de**
    werken van Willem Pijper (Assen: Van Gorcum, 1960) xxxii, 199p.
        Multiple staff incipits for all movements arranged chrono-
        logically. Contains all data concerning all works, both
        original and arrangements, composition data, publishing
        information, dedications, and Pijper's own commentary or
        analysis.

        Reviews: Kees van BAAREN, *Sonorum Speculum* -/4 (1960) 147-49;
        Wouter PAAP, *MensMelodie* XV (Feb 1960) 51-53.

PLAYFORD, JOHN, 1623-1686

974   TRAFICANTE, Frank (U. of Kentucky). **Thematic index to the music**
▽   **for lyra viol contained in five publications by John Playford.** In-
       dex cards (manuscript).
              Incipits appear in the original tablature, arranged accord-
              ing to dates of publication, and transcribed into pitch
              (or staff) notation. Works are from the five following
              publication by John Playford: 1. *A musicall banquet,* 1651;
              2. *Musicks recreation: on the lyra viol,* 1652; 3-5. *Musicks
              recreation on the viol, lyra-way,* 1661, 1669, and 1682.

PLEYEL, IGNAZ, 1757-1831

975   **Quintetto per due violini, due viole, e violoncello....no. 8; Trois
       quatuors...**and other Artaria editions of Pleyel's works (Vienna:
       Artaria, 1789)
              **Catalogue thématique ou commencement de chaque quatuor, quintet,
              trios** [sic] **et duo compose par I. Pleyel, qui se vendent à Vienne
              chez Artaria Compagne.**

              116 incipits on one and a half pages preceding p. 1 of 2nd
              violin part. All of chamber music, arranged by genre, then
              opus number, with some works lacking opus numbers. The two
              plates for this thematic catalogue were used in many other
              Artaria editions of Pleyel's works (e.g. *Trois Quatuors,*Op.
              11) appearing around 1789 and later.

976   BENTON, Rita (U. of Iowa). **The life and works of Ignace Pleyel**
*   **Thematic catalogue.**

976a   --- **A la recherche de Pleyel perdu, or problems, perils, and pro-**
☐   **cedures of Pleyel research,** *FontesArtisM* XVII/1-2 (1970) 9-15.
              Discusses arrangement and scope of the catalogue.

POGLIETTI, ALESSANDRO, d. 1683

977   RIEDEL, Friedrich Wilhelm (Mainz). **Thematischer Katalog sämtlicher**
*   **Werke**

POKORNY, FRANZ XAVER, 1728-1794

978   BARBOUR, J. Murray. **Pokorny vindicated,** *MQuarterly* XLIX/1 (Jan 1963)
       38-58.
              **[Thematic index of] Disputed orchestral works by Pokorny in
              Regensburg,** 52-58.
                     Incipits of disputed works listed, as well as 35 other com-
                     posers to whom dubious works have been attributed.

979   BARBOUR, J. Murray. **Pokorny und der "Schacht-Katalog".** Ein Beitrag
       zur Geschichte der fürstlichen Hofmusik, *Thurn und Taxis-Studien* 3.
       Beiträge zur Kunst- und Kulturpflege im Hause Thurn und Taxis (Kall-
       münz, 1963) 269-98.
              Incipits der besprochenen Werke von Pokorny in der Fürstlichen
              Hofbibliothek zu Regensburg mit den dazugehörenden, jetzt gültigen
              Signaturen, 291-98.
                     Incipits of 109 symphonies located in the Hofbibliothek Regens-
                     burg.

POLLAROLO, CARLO FRANCESCO, ca. 1653-1722

980   TERMINI, Olga Ascher. **Carlo Francesco Pollarolo: His life, time, and**
▽   **music with emphasis on the operas** (PhD diss.: U. of Southern Calif.,
       1970) viii, 717p. (typescript)
           Thematic catalogue of extant operas and oratorios, Part III, Ap-
           pendix, 605-82.
                Incipits for all sections of 10 operas, 3 oratorios, 10 frag-
                ments of operas, and 45 arias and duets.

POMMER, Josef

980.1 **444 Jodler und Juchezer,** (Wien, 1903) iiif.
☐   On folk tune classification.

PORPORA, NICOLA ANTONIO, 1686-1768

981   MAYEDA, Akio. **Nicola Antonio Porpora als Instrumentalkomponist**
▽   (PhD diss.: Wien, 1967) 3v., 365*l*. (typescript)
           Thematischer Katalog der Instrumentalwerke, 118-30.
                Incipits for all movements of 6 symphonies, 12 violin sonatas,
                6 sonatas for 2 violins and 2 celli, 1 cello concerto, 1
                flute concerto, trios, etc.

981.1 SUTTON, Everett L. (U. of Minnesota). **The church music and chamber**
*   **cantatas of Nicola Porpora: an annotated thematic catalogue** (PhD
       diss. in progress)

POSCH, ISAAC, d. 1623?

982   GEIRINGER, Karl, ed. **Isaac Posch: Musikalische Tafelfreud,** *DTÖ*
       Jahrg. 36/2 (Wien: Universal, 1929) 133p.
           Thematisches Verzeichnis der Anfänge aller Tänze der "Musikali-
           schen Ehrnfreudt" nach der Altus-Stimme der "Musikalischen Ehrn-
           und Tafelfreudt" [1626], 130.
                Incipits of 16 dance suites in modern notation.

982a   ---Reprint   (Graz: Akademische Druck-u. Verlagsanstalt, 1960).

POZNAŃ, Poland. Archivum der Pfarrkirche.

983   IDASZAK, Danuta. **[Symphonies, 18th c.]** (PL Poznań: Archivum der
▽   Pfarrkirche) [13*l*.] (manuscript). Compiled ca. 1967. In possession
       of Jan LaRue.
                Incipits for all movements of 33 symphonies (18th c.MS) located
                in the Archive. Annotations repeat data on the title pages and
                provide MS measurements, call numbers, watermark information.
                The following composers are represented: Davaux, Ditters,
                Fischer, Greiner, Guillon (Guilon), Gyrowetz, Haydn (Joseph
                Haydn), Massonneau, Pasqua, Wenceslas Pichl, Pleyel (I.Pleyel,
                Ignac Pleyel, Ignace Pleyel), Rosetti, Schmidt, Schuster, L.
                Spohr, Stamitz; also contains an anonymous work.

PRAHA, Hudební oddělení národního Musea

984   **Katalog/ der/ Quintetten.//** [Statní Památková Správa Knižni Fond
▽   Radenin] (CS Pnm) 44p. (manuscript)

Incipits with tempo markings, and occasionally, dynamic markings or opus number, for works by Boccherini, Beethoven,
Kosboth, Krommer, Mozart, G. Onslow, and Vent.

985   Quarttetts. Posnan II. [Statní Památková Správa Kniźni Fond Rade-
▽   nin] (CS Pnm) (manuscript)
          Incipits with tempo markings, and occasionally dynamic mark-
          ings, instrumentation, and opus number for works by Onslow,
          Mozart, Spohr, Hofmeister, Girowetz, Beethoven, Haydn, Galup-
          pi, Neubauer, Wranitzky, Vanhal, Capuzzu, Pleyel, Boccherini,
          Cambini.

986   [Quartets]. Posnan III. [Statní Památková Správa Kniźni Fond Rade-
▽   nin] (CS Pnm) 128p. (manuscript)
          Incipits (as above) for works by Abel, Alday, Baisible, Boc-
          cherini, Cambini, Capuzzu, Dotzauer, Fodor, Gassmann, Gyro-
          wetz, Haydn, Haensel, Jansa, Klopp, Krommer, Onslow, Pleyel,
          Stamitz, Spohr, Tomasini, Wannhall, Wranitzsky.

PRAHA, Hudebni oddĕlení národního Musea: Clam é Gallas [I]

987   Catalogo/ Delle Carte di Musica/ appartenenti/ al Sige Conte Cristi-
▽   ano/ Clam e Gallas/ [Lower right] Da me per conservare/ Speer/
      Maestro di Musica// (CS Pnm) Compiled ca. 1810 (manuscript).
          Works are arranged by genre and numbered for each composer.
          (1) Sinfonie: Bach 23, Gossec 9, Davaux 4, Druschezky 11,
          Duscheck 19, Haydn 56, Maldere 10, Schmidbauer 21, Stamitz
          (C.) 18, Vanhal 45. (2) Cassationi: 28 listed in all, among
          them are Ditters, Koldinsky, etc. (3) Quartetti: Duschek
          12, Schmitt 17, Vanhal 18, and 90 entries miscellaneous.
          (4) Trios: Fyala 11, miscellaneous others-Vanhal, Wagenhofer,
          Schmitt,etc. (5) Concertini: Hoffmann 14. (6) Barthia (Par-
          thia):Aspelmayer 31, Bonno 30, Druschezsky 28, Vent 25.
          (7) Parthia Turcia. (8) Balli. (9) Airs. (10) Menuetti.
          (11) Arie. (12) Contredanse. (13) Ballo.

PRAHA, Hudebni oddĕlení národního Musea: Clam é Gallas [II]

988   Catalogo/ Delle Carte di Musica/ appartenenti alla Sige/ Contessa
▽   Carolina Clam=/ Gallas.// (CS Pnm) Compiled ca. 1810 (manuscript)
          Incipits for arias, organized by composer; each entry con-
          tains name of aria, accompanying instrumentation, dedica-
          tion, if any, incipit with tempo designation, and text.
          Composers include: Bonno 23, Sacchini 7, Salieri 10. The
          catalogue contains loose letters bearing the date March 1819.

PRAHA, Hudebni oddĕlení národního Musea: Waldstein-Doksy Music Collection

989   RUTOVÁ, Milada. [Waldstein-Doksy Music Collection; thematic catalogue]
▽   (PhD diss.: Praha, Charles U., 1971) 600, 170p. (see no. 507)(typescript)
          [Thematic catalogue], 170p.
          Items 1-1500 are incipits of chamber and orchestral works from
          the years 1750-1800 by the following composers: Agnesi, Agrell,
          Alayrac, Alberti, Albrechtsberger, Alessio, Aspelmayr, Johann
          Christian Bach, Balbi, Barba, Baroni, Bárta, Beethoven, Bern-
          asconi, Bertoni, Besozzi, Bicinino, Binder, Bioni, Bohrer,
          Brescianello, Brioschi, Brivio, Brixi, Camerloher, Cannabich,
          Cantu, Capponi, Caputi, Carcasio, Cardena, Castrucci, Cattaneo,

Caveani, Cervetto, Ciampi, Cimarosa, Cocchi, Conti, Corri,
Costa, Cupis, Czerny, Davesne, Dittersdorf, Duni, Dušek, Endel,
Faber, Fabri, Faghetti, Fantacci, Fasch, Fauner, Federici,
Fenoglio, Ferrandini, Fiaminghino, Fils, Florentino, Fraenzl,
Franchi, Friedrich der Grosse, Fuchs, Galdara, Galimberti, Ga-
luppi, Gasparini, Gassmann, Geweij, Ghibelli, Giulini, Gluck,
Gossec, Gottwald, Graaf, Grab, Graun, Grétry, Harre, Hartl,
Hasse, Hataš, Haydn, Hayer, Hoffmann, Holzbauer, Huberm Hup-
feld, Chiesa, Chintzer, Churfuerst, Ivanschitz, Jelínek, Jo-
melli, Klousek, Körzl, Kohout, Kraus, Krebs, Kreith, Kreusser,
Lampugnani, Lang, Laube, Leeder, Leemans, Lesson, Lidarti,
Logroscino, Lucchesi, Lully, Majo, Maldere, Malzart, Manna,
Marcello, Margiane, Maria, Micheli, Mozart, Muffat, Myslivecek,
Nardini, Naumann, Negro, Neruda, Neyni, Oberti, Ordoněz, Orsler,
Paganelli, Paisiello, Paladino, Pampani, Partsch, Pattoni, Paus,
Pazzolo, Pedrazzi, Perez, Pergolesi, Piccini, Pichl, Pleyel, Pre-
dieri, Pugnani, Pulli, Purcksteiner, Querfurth, Raynone, Ré, Re-
luzzi, Rendeux, Reutter, Ricci, Richterm, Rinaldo da Capua, Roy,
Saccini, Salernitano, Salieri, Salinger, Sammartini, Sarti, Satz-
enhoven, Scaccia, Scarlatti, Seger, Selva, Seyfried, Scheibel,
Schioppa, Schloeger, Schmidt, Schmittbauer, Schraub, Schwindel,
Simon, Somis, Sonnleithner, Stamic, Starzer, Stoelzer, Süssmayer,
Swieten, Stěpán, Thomas, Toeschi, Traetta, Troli, Tůma, Umstatt,
Valentini, Vanhal, Vranický, Wagenseil, Weigert, Werner, Winter,
Zach, Zcuvari, Zechner, Ziegler. Items 1500-2187 are incipits
of vocal and piano music, mainly 19th century,by the following
ccmposers: Abadie, Adam, Alkan, Alvensleben, Angel, Auber, Barth,
Baumann, Beauplan, Beecke, Beethoven, Bellini, Berat, Bériot,
Boehner, Bochsa, Bonn, Büchner, Bülow, Bukvička, Burgmüller,
Cavallo, Cibulka, Clementi, Coenen, Coló, Cramer, Crassus, Cünzer,
Czermak, Černý, Daniele, Daum, Diabelli, Döhler, Donizetti,
Drechsler, Dreyschock, Drštka, Durst, Dusík, Eberl, Engel, Ernesti,
Faust, Filtsch, Fischer, Foerster, Franz, Gänsbacher Gatayes,
Gerber, Giuliani, Glaser, Graziani, Guglielmi, Haas, Hackel,
Haibl, Haller, Hampel, Haslinger, Held, Heller, Herz, Hilmar,
Hlaváček, Hölzel, Holý, Hopp, Hoppe, Horzalka, Hünten, Hummel,
Cherubini, Chopin, Jaell, Jansa, Jany, Jullig, Kalivoda, Kalk-
brenner, Kammel, Kanne, Karas, Khünl, Kirmair, Kisch, Kittel,
Klingenbrunner, Köhler, Koželuh, Král, Kratzmann, Krebs, Kreutzer,
Krütner, Küvken, Labarre, Labitzký, Laffilé, Lachner, Lanner,
Lariviere, Lažanský, Lefébury-Wély, Leicht, Leopold, Leybach,
Lickl, Lindpaintner, Liszt, Lomický, Loschan, Marcucci, Masini,
Mašek, Mayer, Méhul, Mendelssohn-Bartholdy, Mercadante, Meyer,
Meyerbeer, Mittrowsky, Mladota, Mockwitz, Moscheles, Müller,
Nesvadba, Němec, Nicolini, Nürmberger, Offenbach, Ott, Pacini,
Paderewski, Paer, Panofka, Panseron, Parish-Alvars, Pecháček,
Pixis, Plachý, Pleyel, Polt, Pozděna, Preyer, Proch, Procházka,
Promberger, Puget, Reinthaller, Reissiger, Remy, Riem, Righini,
Roesler, Rosetti, Rossini, Rumler, Salieri, Sarti, Sechter, Sey-
ler, Schantl, Schoedl, Schulhoff, Sippel, Slansky, Spohr, Spon-
tini, Steibelt, Sterkel, Strauss, Strebinger, Svoboda, Škroup,
Šnor, Šťastný, Taubert, Tedesco, Teyber, Thalberg, Thiessen,
Titl, Tollemache, Tuvora, Uhlig, Ulver, Urach, Vaněk, Vanka,
Viardot-Garcia, Vitásek, Volánek, Weber, Wieschin, Willmers,
Zellner, Zillmann, Zingarelli, and Zumsteeg.

PRAHA, Hudební oddělení národního Musea: Kačina (Kuttenberg) [I]

990   Catalogo (CS Pnm) 151p. (many blank). Compiled ca. 1809 (manu-
▽   script)
        Catalogue and collection originally from Kačina castle east of
        Prague. All incipits given with bass (double staff) for: (1)
        Arias (88), p. 1-12, Gluck, Piccini, Gasmann, Traetta, Hiller;
        (II) Cembalo (28), p. 13-16, Deller, Gluck, Giuseppe Steffan,
        Starzer; (III) Chorus (30), p. 20-23, Handl, Zumsteg; (IV)
        Solos and duets (70), p. 25-33, Hofmann, Corolo, Thuma, Lidar-
        di, Bocherini, Gretsch, Campioni; (IV) Trios, p. 45-59 by
        Pugnani, Zannetti, Nardini, Boccherini, Ordonez, Filtz, Sta-
        micz; (V) Quartets (101), p. 79-91, by Richter, Haydn, Abel,
        Stamitz, Smith, Pugnani, Vanhal, Cambini; (VI) Operas, p. 98-
        102; (VI) Vocal works for 5 or more voices (32), p. 105-09,
        by Bach, Mislewitzeh, Cambini, Boccherini, Pichl, Romberg;
        (VII) Symphonies (41), p. 117-22, by Bach, Ordonez, Wagenseil,
        Sacchini, Kraus, Paesiello; Overtures (3), p. 123, by Romberg,
        Wranitzky; Church music (36), p. 136-40, by J. Haydn, Righini,
        Naumann, Eybler; (VIII) Balli (from operas), p. 141-43, by
        Gluck and Starzer; (IX) Grand operas and oratorios (21), p.
        146-48; non-thematic Verzeichnis on p. 149, dated 1813.

PRAHA, Hudební oddělení národního Musea: Kačina (Kuttenberg) [II]

991   Catalog der Kirchen Musicalien (CS Pnm) [19p.] (manuscript)
▽   Double staff incipits for: Graduals 22, by Winter, Haydn,
        Kraus; Offertories (34) by Haydn, Diabelli, Eybler, Cheru-
        bini; Masses (63) by Naumann, Haydn, Tomaschek, Beethoven,
        Cherubini, Diabelli, Carl Maria v. Weber; Arias; Te Deum;
        Stabat Mater; Salve Regina by Huberty and Danzi; Miserere;
        Dies Irae by Hasse; Requiems by Gossec, Mozart, Vogel; and
        Passion music by Pergolesi.

PRAHA, Hudební oddelení národního Musea: Kačina (Kuttenberg) [III]

992   Catalog der Opern Oratorien und einzelnen Singstücken (CS Pnm)
▽   [24p.] (some blank) (manuscript).
        Double staff incipits for: operas (25) by Philidor, Wranizky,
        Gasmann, Mozart; oratorios (12) by Bach, Händel, G. Winter,
        Kunzen; choral works (24) by Süssmayer, Cimarosa; arias (92)
        by Diabelli, Rossini, Gluck; duets, trios, quartets, quintets
        (Paesiello), sextets.

PRAHA, Hudební oddělení národního Musea: Kačina (Kuttenberg) [IV]

993   Catalog der Harmonie Stücke und Türkische Musik (CS Pnm) [10p.]
▽   (manuscript)
        Double staff incipits with tempo markings and occasional
        dynamic marks for: operas by Girowetz, Par, Winter, Mozart;
        ballets; arias; partitas by Druschezky, Winter, Krommer,
        Maschek, Pleyel. No works listed for "Türkische Musik".

PRAHA, Hudební oddělení národního Musea: Krakovský z Kolovrat

994   Verzeichniss/ Aller Musicalien Ihro Hochreichs Gräflichen Gnaden
▽   Herrn/ Herrn Philipp Krakowitz Grafen von/ Kollowrath// (CS Pnm)
    (manuscript) (Stamp on 2nd page reads:STATNI PAMÁTKOVÁ SPRÁVA KNIŽNÍ

FOND RADENIN.)

        Incipits for concertos, symphonie concertante, serenades, symphonies, sextets, quartets, trios, duets, sonatas, variations, minuets, German dances. Among the composers represented are: Lolli, Raimondi, St. George, Capuzzi, Pichl, Ditters, Ruprecht, Wanhal, Rosetti, Haydn, Bartta, de Pecker, Tomasini, Cambini, Hoffmeister, Paisible, Klopp, Davaux, Misliweczek, Abel, and Fodor.

PRAHA, Hudební oddělení národního Musea: Latin codices

995 PLOCEK, Václav. **Catalogus Codicum Notis Musicis Instructorum, qui in**
▽ **Bibliotheca Publica Pragensi SK ČSSR-UK Servantur** (Prague, 1965) 915p. (typewritten). Latin translation by Bohumil RYBA.

        Description of 243 Latin codices with notes (including some Latin-Czech codices contained in the same collection) in the possession of the State Library of the Czechoslovak Republic and University Library in Prague. The MSS once belonged to the most ancient College Libraries of the University of Prague, to the Jesuit University Library in Prague, and to libraries of monasteries abolished after 1782. Includes 2989 incipits, with text (mostly vocal music for one voice such as tropes, liturgical complexes, cantiones, liturgical plays, etc., with some many-voiced Masses and motets) of MSS dating from the 12th-18th centuries. For each codex there is a description of the general features of the MS (signature, material, age, number of folios, dimensions) and of its specifically musical features (voice parts, number of folios containing notes, writers and copyists, clef, color of the lines, type of notation, and the notae simplices).

PRAHA, Hudební oddělení národního Musea : Strahov

996 **Thematischer Catalog/ aller/ im königliche Prämonstratener Stifte**
▽ **Strahof in Pragvorhandenen/ Kirchenstücke.//** (CS Pnm) 3v. Compiled by Gerlak Strnischtie, choral director in Strahof. Dated 1.April 1833 (manuscript).

        Among the composers represented are the following: Volume I— Albrechtsberger-Ganster (?), fol. 1-161, Brixi 300, Caldara 15; Volume II— Gasmann-Kusfy (Kussy?), fol. 162-344, Gerlak 215, Händel 10, J. Haydn 19, Mich. Haydn 136, Kozeluch (T.A.) 75; Volume III— Lasfer-Zimmermann, fol. 345-497, Laube 15, P. Lohel 44, Los 11, Mozart 24, Palestrina 21, Pasterwitz 63, Posselt 19, Preindl 18, Schenkirž 14, Wanhall 12, Wanjura 13. Also contains a non-thematic Verzeichnis (Anhang A). The catalogue contains incipits of many other composers. Only those with 10 or more works have been listed above.

996a **Supplement/ zum thematischen Katalog/ von/ Kirchenstücken** (CS Pnm)
▽ Compiled 1847-1852 (manuscript).

        Double pages contain author, title, number, double staff incipits, voices, partitur, vocal parts, last performance, notes. The following composers are inventoried: Führer 66, Diabelli 1, Händel 1, Mendelssohn-Bartholdi 1, Florini 1, and Albin Maschek 1.

PRAHA, Hudební oddělení národního Musea: Strahov D.G. IV. 47

997 SNOW, Robert J. **The manuscript Strahov D.G. IV. 47** (PhD diss.: U.

▽   of Illinois, 1968) iv, 605p.   (typescript)
        Appendix II: Thematic index, 482-605.
                Incipits for all voices of 330 works. Genres include
                Mass movements, hymns, alleluias, sequences, Offertories,
                etc. Composers: Batty, Barbingant, Bartolomeo Brolo, Cecus,
                Johannes Cornago, Guillaume Dufay, Flemmik, Walter Frye,
                Francis Philipi, Johannes Pullois, Standly, Johannes Touront,
                Johannes Vincenet, and a large number of anonymous works.

PRAHA, Hudebnî oddělení národního Musea: Trolda Collection

998   BUCHNER, Alexander. **Hudebnî sbírka Emiliána Troldy.** Muzykal'noe
      sobranie Emiliana Trol'di. Music collection of Emilian Trolda
      (Praha: Sborník Národního Musea v Praze. A, sv. 8 Historický č. I,
      1954) 132p.
                An incipit catalogue of 520 vocal liturgical works by Czech
                and other composers active in Bohemia from 1550-1820, and
                by Czech composers of the same period outside Bohemia, com-
                prising the Emilian Trolda Collection. The collection is in
                the Musical Department of the National Museum in Prague.
                Arranged alphabetically by composer, with complete titles,
                full scoring, and text underlay given. Catalogue includes
                bibliography of Trolda's articles.

PRAHA, Hudebnî oddělení národního Musea: Žatec

999   Catalogues/ Musicaliorum/ Chori e Ecclesia...Beato/ virginis Maria
▽   in Coelum/ assumpto/ en Regia ao distriotuali Urbe/ Zatcoense/ Anno/
      quo/ laborem kune/ sub Glorioso Regimine/ Nobilium, Praenobilium ae
      Clarissimorum/ Dominarum Dominarum/ consule/ D. Joseph Hermanň/ Sena-
      toribus/ D. Josepha Hauner & D. Antonio Dvorak/ abtulet Minimus serv-
      orum kujus Regio/ & Districtualis Urbis Thomas Matczek/ Chori & Scho-
      la Rector die 1ma 8bris.// (CS Pnm) 56p. Compiled 1792 (manuscript)
                Incipits for sacred works arranged by genre. Some composers
                included are: Brixy [Brixi], Schenkirz, Lohelius [Lohelio].
                The catalogue and the collection are originally from the
                town of Žatec, approximately 100 Km northwest of Prague.

PRAHA, Loreta archiv

1000 PULKERT, Oldřich. **Domus Lauretana Pragensis.** Catalogus operum artis
 *   musicae [The Prague Loreta Musical archive. Thematic catalogue],
      To be published in the *Artis Musicae Antiquioris Catalogorum Series,*
      1972-73.
                Incipits for sacred compositions, primarily from the second
                half of the 18th century, that typify the repertoire of the
                Prague choirs in the St. Nichlas ad Loreta churches. A to-
                tal of 801 items. The most significant works are sacred
                compositions by Michael Haydn. Incipits are for first move-
                ments only; remaining movements and sections are included in
                the appendix and employ the *Simplified Plaine and Easie Code
                System* (see no. 188).

PRAHA. Státní Knihovna Československé Socialistické Republiky

1001 Souborný hudebnî katalog [Central catalogue of music]. (see no. 1072)
                Thematic cataloguing project initiated in 1965 at the incen-
                tive of *RISM,* and expanded to include all music material de-
                posited on the territory of the ČSR, and also Bohemicae, par-

ticularly the works of composers of Czech origin which are
deposited outside the ČSR. The catalogue will be composed
of manuscripts as well as printed music from medieval sources
to contemporary music documents. Medieval music will be
listed in an inventory system with a content specification
of convolutes. Manuscripts and printed music from the 17th
century onwards are listed in the catalogue in a detailed
analytical system: reference to the note or text incipits
of all parts or movements; all important bibliographical information. The project will be expanded to include the compilation of a picture documentation of works of art with
musical subjects and retrospective bibliography. To date
(Nov 1971), some 186,200 music compositions from 55 complete
archive funds have been catalogued, with 98,334 text incipits
and 162,388 music incipits.

1001a --- PULKERT, Oldřich. Souborný Hudebni Katalog. Pokyny ke katalogi-
□   zaci hudebnin [Collective music catalogue. Instructions to the ca-
       taloguing of music material] (Praha, 1966) 18, ix, [12p.]
            Describes the national cataloguing project and provides exam-
            ples (i.e. incipits) and a list of abbreviations for the ca-
            taloguing method.

PREDIERI, LUCA ANTONIO, 1688-1767

1002 FREUNSCHLAG, Heinz. Luc Antonio Predieri als Kirchenkomponist
▽   (PhD diss.: Wien, 1927) 119*l*. (typescript)
            List of works without incipits. Cites thematic catalogue
            in *Archiv des DTÖ*.

1003 ORTNER, Roman. Luca Antonio Predieri und sein Wiener Opernschaffen
▽   (PhD diss.: Wien, 1966) 4v., 147, v; 177; 114; 113*l*. (typescript)
         [Thematic catalogue], v. 1, 80-146; v. 2.
            Multiple staff incipits for 7 operas.

PREYER, GOTTFRIED von, 1807-1901

1004 BERNHAUER, Elfriede. Gottfried von Preyer. Sein Leben und Wirken,
▽   mit thematischem Katalog seiner Werke (PhD diss.: Wien, 1951) 4v.,
      772*l*.(typescript)
         Thematischer Katalog, v. 3 & 4.
            Multiple staff incipits for all movements of 23 Masses, plus
            Offertories, Lieder, instrumental music, etc.

PROCH, HEINRICH, 1809-1878

1005 Thematisches Verzeichnis sämmtlicher Werke von H. Proch
      (Wien: Diabelli, [1854]) 19, 3p.
            Incipits for opus 1-162, mainly songs and piano works, each
            with plate numbers and price in Kreutzer. Three MS pages,
            non-thematic for opus 163-222.

1006 VÖLKER, Inge-Christa. Heinrich Proch. Sein Leben und Wirken (PhD
▽   diss.: Wien, 1950) 2v., 411*l*. (typescript)
         Thematisches Verzeichnis, v. 2, 316-411.
            Double staff incipits for all movements of 266 compositions
            (Masses, Offertories, Lieder, operas, etc.).

PROCKSCH, GASPARD, d. 1789?

1007 CUCUEL, Georges. Études sur un orchestre au XVIIIme siècle (Paris:
      Fischbacher, 1913) 62, 54p.
          Les symphonies de Gaspard Procksch, 59-62.
              List of works includes incipits for chamber music.

PROTESTANT EPISCOPAL CHURCH IN THE U.S.A.

1008 The Hymnal 1940 Companion. Joint Commission on the Revision of the
      Hymnal (New York: Church Pension Fund, 1949) 741p.
          Melodic index, 715-718.
              Indexes groups of hymns in The Hymnal 1940 by verbal des-
              cription of approximate melodic progression of initial notes
              differing in pitch. Organized according to strong or weak
              beat‿opening, mode, and direction of first progression.

1008a --- 2nd ed. Revised (New York: Church Pension Fund, 1951).

1008b --- 3rd ed. Revised (New York: Church Pension Fund, 1955)
              No changes in thematic indexes.

PUGNANI, GAETANO, 1731-1798

1009 ZSCHINSKY-TROXLER, Elsa Margherita von. Gaetano Pugnani; ein Beitrag
 ☆   zur Stilerfassung italienischer Vorklassik (Berlin: Atlantis, 1939)
      254p.
          Thematisches Werkverzeichnis, [69]-[107].
              Incipits are arranged by genre, with tempi and time signa-
              tures given for other movements. Sources and locations of
              MSS, printed editions, and scoring are given.

1010 MÜRY, Albert. Die Instrumentalwerke Gaetano Pugnanis (Basel: Krebs,
      1941) vii, 109p.
          Thematisches Verzeichnis der bei Zschinsky nicht angegebenen
          Werke, 107-08.
              Incipits for 3 arias, 1 suite for orchestra, and 4 sonatas.

PULKERT, Oldřich

1011 Hudba, samočinné počítače a jiné novinky [Music, computers, and other
 ☐   novelties] Hudební věda 3 (1967) 479-84.
              A brief discussion of recent trends and publications in the
              U.S. concerning computer technology in the humanities, thema-
              tic catalogues, and woodwind music.

PURCELL, HENRY, 1659-1695

1012 NOVELLO, Vincent. Thematic catalogue of Purcell's church music
 ▽   (British Museum Add. 9074, c. 1831) ff. 1-16b.(manuscript)
              Includes references to the sources.

1013 ZIMMERMAN, Franklin B. Henry Purcell, 1659-1695, an analytical cata-
      logue of his music (New York: St. Martin's Press; London: Macmillan
      &Co., 1963) vii, 575p.
              Incipits for sacred and secular vocal works, dramatic works,

and instrumental music. Each section is arranged alphabetically by title. Contains an appendix with doubtful and spurious works, commentary, and dating information.

Reviews: Frank G. BARKER, *Music and Musicians* XII (Oct 1963)
47; Martin COOPER, *Daily Telegraph*(10 Aug 1963); Nigel FOR-
TUNE, *MTimes* CIV (Oct 1963) 710-11; *Music Journal Annual* (1964)
88p.; A. Hyatt KING, *Times Literary Supplement* (Sept 6, 1963);
George L. MAYER, *American Record Guide* XXX (July 1964) 1054-
55; Stanley SADIE, *Tempo* -/68 (Sprint 1964) 48-49; Halsey
STEVENS, *JResearchMEducation* XII/2 (1964) 180-81; Michael
TILMOUTH, *MLetters* XLV/1 (1964) 45-48; Rheinhold SIETZ, *Mf*
XVIII/3 (1965) 351-52; R.W., *MReview* XXVI/1 (1965) p. 74.

1014   ZIMMERMAN, Franklin B. **Henry Purcell (1659-1695): A thematic index**
*   **to his Complete Works.** (New York: Vienna House, announced for 1972)
3000 themes from 628 works numbered according to 1013 (above);
with concordance to the Purcell Society Edition. "Each theme
is indexed by pitches, shown in letter names, transposed to
C -Major-minor, and by intervals, represented numberically."
Prepared by computer.

QUANTZ, JOHANN JOACHIM, 1697-1773

1015   Thematisches Verzeichnis der Werke von Johann Joachim Quantz...
▽   (D Berlin, Deutsche Staatsbibliothek: Bibl. V Quantz)[6p] (manuscript)
A thematic catalogue for works by Quantz housed in the
Staatsbibliothek, West Berlin. Lists numerous concerti,
a sonata, a trio, 7 works for flute and cembalo, and two
vocal works.

1016   ZOELLER, Carli. Thematic catalogue of the compositions of Johann
▽   Joachim Quantz (British Museum Add. 32148, c. 1883). Taken from
the collections in the Neue Palast, near Potsdam, the Royal Libraries at Berlin and Dresden, and from Breitkopf's "Catalogo delle Sinfonie....1762-1784".(manuscript)
Compositions comprise the greater part of 300 flute concerti
(for 4,5,6,7, and 10 instruments), and about 150 out of 361
sonatas for flute and bass, written "Pour Charlottenburg,"
for the use of Quantz's pupil Frederick the Great, besides
miscellaneous duets for two flutes, trios, etc..

Key: * in preparation; ▽ manuscript; ☐ literature; ✵ Library of Congress

RACEK, Jan; POHANKA, Jaroslav (compilers)

1017 Antiqua Bohemica, Uvodní Studii napsal Jan Racek. Tematický Katalog
      sestavil Jaroslav Pohanka (Praha: Státní Hudební Vydavatelstvi, 1961)
      103p.
          Tematický Katalog sestavil Jaroslav Pohanka, [18]-90.
              Incipits for all movements of works by the following composers:
              Antonin Felix Bečvařovsky, František Benda, Jan Benda, Jiří
              Antonin Benda, František Xaver Brixi, Cibulka, Černahorský,
              Družecký, Jan Ladislav Dusik, František Xaver Dušek, Antonin
              Fils, Vojtěch Jirovec, Antonin Kammel, Kopřiva, Koutnik, Kože-
              luh, Kramář, Krommer, Kuchař, Linek, Losy, Mašek, Miča, Mich-
              alička, Milčinský, Mysliveček, Pichl, Pitsch, Rejcha, Rössler,
              Rosetti, Seger, Jan Václav Stamic, Skroup, Štěpan Tolar, Tomá-
              šek, Vanhal, Vejuanovský, Vitásek, Voříšek, Antonin Vranický,
              Pavel Vranický, Jan Zach.

RACEK, Jan

1018 Hudební inventáře a jejich význam pro hudebněhistorické bádání [Music
☐   inventories and their meanings for musicological research] *Acta Musei
      Moraviae* XLVII (1962) 135-62.
          Article discusses Czech inventories of music and instruments
          in castles, courts, convents, music chapels, some of which
          are thematic.

RAJHRAD Monastery, near Brno, Czechoslovakia

1019 Consignatio Musicalium/ id est/ Missarum: Offertoriorum Ariae/ Ves-
▽   perarum.....Antiphonarum/ Symphoniarum & reliquarum/ Parthiarum etc:/
      pro/ Monasterio Rayhradensi/ OSB/ in Moravia/ an. I77I (CS, Brno:
      Moravské Museum, sign. G 6.) 126p. (manuscript).
          Catalogue of the music collection from Rajhrad Monastery
          near Brno, 1771 (entries up to 1829). Description: consec-
          utive numbering, collection number, title key, instrumenta-
          tion, composer's name, copyist's name, double staff incipits
          with figured bass, text incipit, time signature, date (appar-
          ently date of acquisition). Consist of 1800 numbers (974
          original entries and 826 added ones). Contents arranged
          by genre, sacred and secular, into 39 groups. 97 anonymous
          works and 1703 attributed works. This collection contains
          two otherwise unknown Haydn keyboard sonatas discovered by
          Georg FEDER. Composers inventoried in the collection are
          as follows: Abos 1, Adani 1, Albertini 2, Ottavio Albutio 1,
          Andante 1, Anfossi 1, Antosch 1, Arcani 1, Aspelmayer 1,

Key: * in preparation; ▽ manuscript; ☐ literature; ✩ Library of Congress

212

Aumonn (Aumon, Auman, Aumann) 10, Bach (Baach, de Bach) 10,
Aloys Bach 1, Bachter 3, Bauer 1,Baumon 1, Beer (Bär) 11,
Franc. Berger 1, Bock 1, Bode 1, Bohacz 1, Bondra 1, Bonno 3,
Boog 1, Bragaczek 1, Brixi 40, Joan Brixides 24, Francs.
Bruneder 3, Buccini 5, Büchler 1, Buschmann 1, Caldara 23,
Call 1, Campi 5, Camrlocher 1, Cannabig 2, Capelli 3, di
Capua 1, Carassatti 2, Carcani 7, Carl 4, P. Carolus 2,
Cenaci 1, Cibulka 2, Constanti 5 (2 missing), Conti 2,
Crous 1, Czarda 2, P. Damasus (Damaso S.P. Piar.) 7, Dedler
4, A. Diabelli 14, Carol de Dittersdorf (Dietters) 53, Dom-
berger 6, Drahotusky 1, Josef Drayer 2, Giuseppe Drechsler 2,
Dreschler 1, Drexler 1, Druschetzky 2, Duport 1 (missing),
Edlinger 1, R.P. Edmund 1, Emert 1, Emmerling 1, Ender 1,
Engelsberg 1, Ignatio Erman 1, Essinger 1, Eybler (Eibler) 9,
Feo 1, Fils 5, Fischietto 1, Forti 1, Franchii 1, Carol De-
franchi 1, Frank (Francke) 3, Frauendorfer 1, Frenzl 1, Gae--
tano Freundthaler 1, Ignatio Fridrich 2, Frieberth (Fridbert,
Friebert) 6, Franz Fuchs 3, Joan Furbe (Fourbe) 58, Fux 17,
Gallina 1, Galuppi 14 (1 missing), Gasman 1, Geisler 1, Georgi
1, Gerl 1, Carlo Gevey 1, Giacomelli 1, Giavini 2, Giomelli 1,
Giraczek 1, Giranek 1, Girovetz (Gyrowetz) 6, Conte Giulini
1, Gluck 5, Quellus Gnono 1 (missing), Golletz 1, Graesel
(Gräsl) 2, R. Graff 1, Graun 24, Peregrino Gravani 7, Grigliry
1, Carol Grolich 1, Grüsman 1, Gsur 1, Habbeger 2, Habbiger 1,
Maurus Haberhauer O.S. Bened. 90, Habermann 1, Haensel 1,
Haibel 1, Hajek 1, Haslinger 1, Hasse 51, P. Hyron. Haura 3,
Hauser 5, Hayda 1, M. Haydn (Haiden) 25, J. Haydn (Haiden,
Heiden, Heyden) 114 (1 missing), C. Heimerich 2, Heimon 1,
Heinrich 2, Hendl 1, Hennicher 1, Leopold Hoffmann 27, Hof-
meister 6, Hollub 1, Holzbauer 16, Huber 5, Joan Nep. Hummel
1, Francesco Hur 1, Tobia Hur 2, Hybl (Hubl) 13, Chiarini 1,
Chiesa 2, Igomelly 1, Italo 4, Amando Ivantschitz 12,
P. Guntherus Jacob Benedik (Jacobi, Gacob) 11, Jommelli
4, R.P. Josepho Augustin (Josephus) 13, Kabelka 8, Kamml
1, Kauer 5, Kayser 5, Keller 19, P. Roberto Kemmerling OSB
(Kymerling, Kümmerling) 3, Klauseck 1, Klyma 1, Kohaut 15,
Königsberger 18, Körtzl 3, Kötzenthal 1, Kraft 3, Kracher
1, Krammer 3, Kratochvila 1, Kratovsky 1, R.P. Lambert Kraus
4, Kreith 1, Franz Krommer 11, Kubik 1, Kubitschek, Choralist
bei S. Jacob in Brünn (Kubitscheck) 3, Küffner 4, Joan Leo
Kuhnert 1, Kurzveil 1, Kutzera 1, Lamb 1, P. Lamberto OSB 1,
Batta Lampugnani 2, Lang 3, Lankisch 1, Lasser 3, Laub 10,
Laubel 2, Laufenmaier 1, Leo 5, Leopoldo M. Imperatore 1,
Carolo Libel 2, Likl 1, Linek 2, Loheli O. Premonst. (Lohelio)
8, Loos 4, Mark Mach 4, Malzart 2, Malzat 1, Batta d.S. Martini 1, Martino 1, Maschek 7, Maurus 1, Mayseder 2, Mazzoni
6, Meneghetti 1, Michl 6, Minuetti 1, Mislivecžek 3, Molieri
1, Monza 1, Moravetz 1, A.W. Mozart 24, Wences. Müller (Miller)
25 (2 missing), Nanke 10, Nanke Senior 1, Navratil 4, Nedo-
pitta 1, Neubauer 1, Neumann 5, Nith 1, Jos. Ant. Novotny 13,
Oetl (Öttl, Oettl, Oëtl) 11, Ordonez (Ordonez) 6, Örlinger
1, Pampani 1, Parzižech 1, Patella 1, Patti 1, Pausewang 1,
Eugen Pausch 3, Penda 1, Pernsteiner 1, Piazza 1, Piccini 3,
Piedrich 1, Pigilate 1, Pichel 1, Pichler 9, Piltmar 1,
Pinzger 2, Piscitti 1, Pleyel 12, Poccarini 2, Pögl 1, Predieri 1, Preindl 13, Prustmon 1, Giuseppe Puschman 2, Regini
2, Franz Reichart 1, Reichenauer 1, Reinhardt (Rainhard) 11,
Reinone 1, Reutter (Reiter, Reitter) 16, Rieder (Rider) 2,

Richlowsky 1, Richter 2, Rinaldo 1, Rosetti 1, Rossini 3,
Roy 2, Ruthini (Ruttini) 4, Matheo Rutka 11, Ryba 3, Sachini
1, Salieri 2, Sander 1, Sarri 2, Sarti 1, Sassone 3, Scar-
latti 2, Sedlak 2, Sedlaczek 3, Segneri 2, Seidl 1, Seiler 1,
Selliti 2, Seücher 1, Seyfried 1, Schapök 1, Schebetwosky 2,
Scheibl 6, Schenkirz 2, Scherer 1, Schey 1, Joan Schieder-
mayer 16 (1 missing), Leopold Schmidt (Schmied) 14, Schneider
3, Schönthal 1, Schoti 3, Schreier 2, Schubert 4, Schuster 1,
Schvertner 1, Sichra 1, Piar. Simon R.P. Scholar Piar. 5,
Sirmen 1, Sonnenleüthner 6, Soyka (Sogka) 2, Spermalogo 1,
Spihal 1, Spiller 3, Max Stadler 4, Stampi 1, Starke 6, Jos.
Steffan 7, Steinmetz 4, Stephan Optatus Ord.S.Francis. Minor.
9, Strasser 1, Stratzer 1, R.P. Strauhal 3, Stross (Stros)
12, Stumel 1, Stumreuter 2, Carol Suchanek 18 (1 missing),
Süssmayer 1, Ticini 4, Tini 2, Tonolier 1, Tomaso Traëtta 2,
Tuma 12, Tyly 1, Ulbrich 1, Umlauf 1, Umstadt 4 (1 missing),
Vinci 2, Cajet. Vogl 12, Vogler 1, Volkert 6, Volkmärchen 1,
Vulpizzio 1, Wagenseil 19, Wanhall 26, Weigerth 5, Weismann 1,
Werner 3, Franz Wessely 1, Winer 7, Joan Nep. Witassek 4,
Wöger 1, Wolff 4, Wranitzky 1, Wencel Wratny 1, Wrazlivci 1,
Zach 6, Francis Zappa 2, Zechner 48, Zelenka 1, Zelinger 1,
Zeman 1, Ziegler 4, Zieni 5, Zigani 1, Zimmermann 2, Zunk 1.

RANGSTRÖM, TURE, 1884-1947

1020 HELMER, Axel. **Ture Rangströms otryckta ungdomssånger, [Juvenile
songs of Ture Rangström in manuscript],** *SvenskTmf* XLII (1960) 76-91.
Thematic incipits of the 15 songs on p. 80.

RATHGEBER, JOHANN VALENTIN, 1682-1750

1022 HELLMUTH, Max. **Johann Valentin Rathgeber.** Ein mainfränkischer
▽   Barockkomponist 1682-1750. Leben und Werkverzeichnis (PhD diss.:
Erlangen, 1943) 135p. (typescript)
Gesamt-Katalog, 57-132.
Over 400 incipits for all movements of masses, psalms,
hymns, offertories, concertos, etc.

1023 DOTZAUER, Wilfried (Erlangen). **Die Kirchenmusik Valentin Rathgebers**
*   **Thematisches Verzeichnis**
Supplements HELLMUTH (see previous entry). Incipits for
previously lost works, MSS not identical to prints, and
Op. 16. (Antiphonale Marianum), Op. 19 (4 Masses), Op. 20
(Hortus noviter), and 1 Requiem.

RAU, Ulrich (Saarbrücken)

1024 **Die Kammermusik für Klarinette und Streichinstrumente im Zeitalter**
*   **der Wiener Klassik** (PhD diss. in progress).
Will include a thematic catalogue with incipits for all
movements.

RAUDNITZ, Czechoslovakia: Lobkowitz Collection

1024.1 NETTL, Paul. **Über ein handschriftliches Sammelwerk von Gesängen
italienischer Frühmonodie,** *ZfMW* II (1919) 83-93.
The index includes a few single and multiple staff incipits
by Peri and L. Rossi.

RAUZZINI, VENANZIO, 1746-1810

1025 REINDL, Johannes. Venanzio Rauzzini als Instrumentalkomponist
▽   (PhD diss.: Wien, 1961) 3v., 349*l*. (typescript)
         Thematischer Katalog der Instrumentalwerke, v. 2, 104.
                68 incipits for all movements. One symphony, 12 quartets,
                15 violin sonatas, etc.

RAVEL, MAURICE, 1875-1937

1026 ORENSTEIN, Arbie (Queens College of C.U.N.Y.). The life and works
*   of Maurice Ravel
         Thematic catalogue.
                Will include incipits for unpublished works and fragments.

REANEY, Gilbert (compiler)

1027 Manuscripts of polyphonic music: 11th-early 14th century, *RISM* B IV/1
      (München-Duisburg: G. Henle Verlag, 1966) 876p.
                Detailed description, bibliography and thematic incipits for
                contents of all known polyphonic manuscripts up to the begin-
                ning of the Ars Nova period. Original notation is used, con-
                cordances are given. Arranged alphabetically by country,
                and by libraries within countries. Indices of composers and
                text incipits are provided.

1028 Manuscripts of polyphonic music (c. 1320-1400), *RISM* B IV/2 (München-
      Duisburg: G. Henle Verlag, 1969) 427p.
                Continues from where the previous volume (above) left off.
                In these two *RISM* volumes the entire corpus of early poly-
                phonic music is inventoried.

REEVE, WILLIAM, 1757-1815

1029 DEARLING, Robert J. (Dunstable, Bedfordshire). [Thematic catalogue]
▽   Index cards (manuscript) (see no. 282)
                Incipits for 16 operatic overtures (from early editions in
                the British Museum), supplementing Cudworth by 14. (see no.
                273)

REGENER, Eric

1030 A linear music transcription for computer input (Princeton, N.J.:
☐   Princeton U. Department of Music, 1964)

REGENSBURG, Benediktinerkloster St. Emmeram [MS now in D Mbs]

1031 DÉZES, Karl. Der Mensuralcodex des Benediktinerklosters Sancti Emmera-
      mi zu Regensburg, *ZfMW* X (1927) [65]-105.
                Incipits, in mensural notation, of the Regensburg Codex
                (D Mbs: Mus. Ms. 3232) including works by Benet, Binchois,
                Biquardus, Blasius, Bosquet, Brassart, Dufay, Dunstable,
                Edlawer, Gemblaco, Grossin, Kungsperger, A. de Lantins, H.
                de Lantins, Liebert, N. de Merques, Portugal, Power, P.
                Roullet, Walonis, Waring, Wilhelmi, Zacharias.

REGENSBURG, Fürstlich Thurn und Taxissche Hofbibliothek

1032   CATALOGUS/ sämtlicher/ Hochfürstl. Thurn und Taxisch./ Sinphonien
▽   [Incipit-Katalog sämtlicher in der fürstl. Musikbibliothek vorhandenen
       Sinfonien, ca. 1782-1795] (D Rtt) unpaginated (manuscript).
              Virtually all of the symphonies inventoried in this thematic
              catalogue are extant in the Library. The composers are listed
              here with the number of incipits for each: Abel 12, Adlgasser
              6, Agrell 3, Ahlefeld 2, Albrechtsberger 18, Alessandri 6,
              Aspellmeyer 3, Bach 26, Bachschmidt 24, Ballavicini (Palla-
              vicini) 2, Barbella 2, Benda 6, Bernasconi 6, Bertoni 6,
              Besch 6, Beeke 12, Bode 3, Bono 3, Boroni 3, Brixi 3, Brusa
              3, Bullant 3, Brandl 3, Cambini 3, Cannabich 29, Cherzelli 3,
              Cocchi 3, Croes le Pere 6, Danzi 3, Davaux 6, Dechaye (Desnay)
              5, Deeke (Beecke?) 4, Ditters 34, Donninger 2, Le Duc 3,
              Eichner 3, Eisenmann 3, Fiala 3, Fils 14, Fischer 6, Fischietti
              3, Fridericus II, Galuppi 16, Gassmann 6, Giulini 3, Gluck 10,
              Gossec 14, Graun 13, Graaff 13, Gretry 3, Guenin 3, Guglielmi
              3, Gyrowetz 10, Händel 3, Hasse 22, J. Haydn 134, M. Haydn
              10, Hoffmann 12, Hoffmeister 16, Hoffstetter 6, Holzbauer 6,
              Huber 6, Jomelli 12, Kammel 1, Kalb 2, Klob 10, Klöffler 4,
              Kohaut 2, Kospoth 12, Kozeluch 7, Knecht 1, Krause 3, Kreuser
              12, Kürzinger 4, Lang 12, Latilla 3, Liber 1, Lippert 3,
              Luchesi 6, Martino 6, Maschek 3, Meunier 6, Michl 13, Misli-
              vetzek 7, Mitscha 8, Monn 4, Monsigni 2, Mozart 15, Naumann
              6, Navoigille 6, Neruda 3, Neubauer 3, Nopitsch 3, Ordonez 3,
              Orster 3, Paganelli 7, Paisiello 8, Perez 3, Peyerl 2, Phili-
              dor 1, Piccini 7, Pichl 16, Pleyel 32, Pokorni 25, Pugnani 7,
              Reluzzi 3, Richter 14, Riegel 2, Ripel 16, Righini 8, Ritschel
              1, Rodewald 1, Rosetti 23, Ruge 1, Rumling 1, Sacchini 3,
              Sales 1, Salieri 2, Sandel 8, Santalapis 1, Sartorius 1,
              Scarlatti 3, Schacht 24, Scheibel 1, Schierl 4, Schmid 3,
              Schmitbauer 6, Schubauer 6, Schuster 5, Schweizer 1, Schwindl
              13, Serini 9, Seemann 1, Sommer 1, Sonnleitner 1, Solnitz 12,
              Sperger 7, Spiller 2, Stamitz 21, Carl Stamitz 40, Sterkel 3,
              Tellemann 1, Teyber 6, Toeschi 20, Touchemoulin 14, Tour et
              Tassis 1, Umlauf 2, Vanhal 42, Vanswithen (Van Swieten) 7,
              Vent 1, Vogel 3, Vogler 1, Wagenseil 15, Waldstein 1, Wasmuth
              1, Winter 3, Witt 8, Wranizcky 10, Zach 15, Zannetti 1, Zimmer-
              mann 15.

REGENSBURG, Fürstlich Thurn und Taxissche Hofbibliothek: MS F.K. Musik. 76
II

1033   GOTTWALD, Clytus. Eine neuentdeckte Quelle zu Musik der Reformations-
       zeit, *AfMw* XIX-XX/2 (1962-1963) 114-23.
              [Thematic catalogue], 117-23.
                  Incipits, old notation, modern clefs, for "Regensburg,
                  Thurn- und Taxis'sche Hofbibliothek F.K. Musik. 76 II.
                  Abtlg Chorbuch (1530-38)". Composers include: Johann
                  Walter, L. Senfl, Conrad Rain, Jusquin [sic], Johannes
                  Galliculis, Jean Mouton, Cuncz Rein, and Adam Regneri.

REGENSBURG, Proske-Musikbibliothek: A.R. 940/41

1034   BRENNECKE, Wilfried. Die Handschrift A.R. 940/41 der Proske-Biblio-
       thek zu Regensburg, *Schriften des Landesinstituts für Musikforschung,*
       Kiel, 1. (Kassel & Basel: Bärenreiter, 1953)

Die Initien der unbekannten Kompositionen, Appendix, 11p.
Incipits of the 92 anonymous vocal compositions in the MS,
with their titles.

REGER, MAX, 1873-1916

1035 STEIN, Fritz. Thematisches Verzeichniss der im Druck erschienenen
Werke von Max Reger (Leipzig: Breitkopf & Härtel, 1934) 128p.

1035a --- Thematisches Verzeichnis der im Druck erschienenen Werke von Max
Reger einschliesslich seiner Bearbeitungen und Ausgaben. Mit systematischem Verzeichnis und Registern. Bibliographie des Reger-Schrifttums
von Josef Bachmair (Leipzig: Breitkopf & Härtel, 1953) viii, 617p.
Thematisches Verzeichnis, 3-495.
Single and multiple staff incipits of complete works. Works
are arranged by opus number, or by genre for works without
opus number. Information is provided for dates of composition
and publication, dedications, publishers, first and subsequent
editions, references by composer, duration of performances,
and place and artists of first performance. Some incipits in
open score; text underlay for vocal incipits. 10 appendices
containing various finding indices, bibliography, and publishers.

Reviews: Helmut WIRTH, *Mf* VIII/3 (1955) 363.

REGNART, JACOB, ca. 1540-1599

1036 PASS, Walter. Jacob Regnart (PhD diss.: Wien, 1965) 3v. (type-
▽   script).
Thematischer Katalog, v. III.
Incipits in score form for Masses as well as motets. Lists
of sources to extant part books included. This volume was
later published (see next entry).

1037 PASS, Walter. Thematischer Katalog sämtlicher Werke Jacob Reg-
narts (ca. 1540-1599), *Tabulae Musicae Austriacae* Band V (Wien:
Böhlau, 1969) 244p.
376 double and triple staff incipits for all voices of
motets and Masses.

Reviews: John A CALDWELL, *MLetters* LI/3 (1970) 315-16;
Musikerziehung XXIII/5 (1970) 240.

REICHARDT, JOHANN FRIEDRICH, 1752-1814

1038 DENNERLEIN, Hans. J. F. Reichardt und seine Klavierwerke (Münster:
Helios, 1930) 117p.
Thematisches Verzeichnis der Instrumentalwerke von J.F. Reichardt,
32p. at end.
Incipits for all movements, categorically arranged. Data
on place of publication, dates, and location of manuscripts
is given.

1039 PRÖPPER, Rolf. Die Bühnenwerke Johann Friedrich Reichardts; ein
Beitrag zur Geschichte der Oper in der Zeit des Stilwandels zwischen
Klassik und Romantik. In Verbindung mit dem Verzeichnis der litera-
rischen Werke und einem Katalog der Bühnenwerke Johann Friedrich

Reichardts (Bonn: H. Bouvier, 1965) Bd. 1: Textteil, 416p. ; Bd 2: Werkverzeichnis, 352p.
Katalog der Bühnenwerke J.F. Reichardts, v. 2, 69-339.
A detailed thematic catalogue, with incipits for recitatives and arias of the stage works of Reichardt.

REICHERSBERG, Austria. Bibliothek des Augustiner-Chorherrenstiftes

1040 Catalogus auctorum et eorundem Operum musicorum. Angelegt v...
▽   Herrn Pöll, Pfarrer u. Chorregenten des Stiftes Reichersberg. Fort-
     geführt v...Herrn Eduard Zöhrer, Cooper. u. Chorregenten d. Stifts-
     kirche. Stift Reichersberg 1830. (A Reichersberg) 189p. (some
     blank) (manuscript). Xerox copy in D Mbs.

Over 1000 incipits for Masses, Requiems, liturgical songs,
Graduals, Offertories, responsories, vespers, hymns, arias,
antiphons, litanies, psalms, oratorios, cantatas, secular
songs, sinfonies, chamber music, etc. Works arranged by
genre. Composers: Mich. Haydn, Jos. Haydn, Scarlatti,
Schack, W. Mozart, Fried. Schneider, Louis Spohr, Seifried,
Kochl, Preindl, Vogler, Haeser, Pichl, Pergolesi, Gaens-
bacher, Gottfr. Heinrich Stölzl, Lotti, Scandelli, Pet. Win-
ter, Fux, Praenestinus, Schubert, Morlachi, Carl L.B. de
Doblhof, Witassek, Tob. Haslinger, M. Stadler, Drobisch,
Carl Seyler, Fritz Zöhrer, Joan. August Dürrnberger, Anton
Schmidt, Franz Schneider, Göttersdorfer, Aloys Wolfgang Pass-
er, Pernsteiner (Bernsteiner), Aloys Bauer, Fr. X. Schmid,
Cherubini, Pfeiffer, Vogl, M. Henkel, Joh.Kasp. Aiblinger,
Donat Müller, Max Keller, Thad. Schiesl, Mich. Nugrzaun,
Fuss, A. Diabelli, Alex. Tusch, K.Kolb, M.Fischer, Gugler,
F. Bühler, Joh. Jaumann, Jos. Geist, Schiedermayr, Jos.
Kliebenschädl, Albrechtsberger, Kallaus, Schinn, Schicht,
Mayerbeer, Struk, Sörensen, Rochliz, S. Ambros, Jos. Schogg,
Heinr. Scheideman, Köchl, Mühling, S.G. Auberlen, Danzi,
Schuster, Himmel, Rolle, Em. Bach, Ranke, Graun, Häcker, W.
Speyer, Seegr, Eberwein, Herrkamer, Naumann, Grotz, H.Kunz,
M. Huber, Widemann, Byschofreiter, Kassner, Rechenmacher,
Eberlin, Schwarzmann, Benelli, Bernh. Klein, Hasse, Wanhall,
Zimmermann, Gatti, Jomelli, Brennich, Hochmayr, Händel, Ca-
simir Blumenthal, Hildenbrand, C.N. Fischer, Bonamico, Kürzin-
ger, Franz Lachner, Franz Broer, Jos. Lutz, Jos. Schnabel,
Caj. Vogl, Moser, Schubauer, Perez, Fasch, Zach, Bernasconi,
Thuma, C. Donizetti, Tomaschek, Perti, Georg Huber, Fuetsch,
Gossec, Rovetta, Reiter, Fel. Anerio, Robert Führer, Adlgass-
er, Allegri, Tom. Bay, Camerlocher, Nannini, Orlando Lasso,
Vittoria, Beethoven, Kunzen, Aug. Bergt, Herold, Neukomm, L.
B. Est, Bierey, A. Romberg, Zumsteeg, Rink, Fesca, Seb.Bach,
Kruft, C.M. Weber, Gottfr. Weber, Reicha, Moriz, Brixi, Ihler,
Witt, Schmitt, Reichardt, Salieri, Gluck, Wagner, Rossini,
Weigl, Stunz, Stegmann, Mehul, Spontini, Hauschke, Paradies,
Eisenhofer, G.Falk, Andre, Schelble, Knecht, Wölfl, Eybler,
Schulz, Präger, Schnyder, Plodter, Hofmeister, Rottmann,Pocci,
Schröfl, Ascher, Cramer, Lenz, Brauchle, Loehle, Ett, Mitter-
maier, K. Blum, Glaeser, Würfel, Joh.Mich. Bach, Joh.Chr.
Bach, Sarti, Lindpaintner, Miltiz, Harder, Luther, Heinr.
Isaak, Wilh. Schneider, G.W. Fink, Florschüz, Hummel, Gyro-
wez, Emmert, Call, Con. Kreutzer, Dussek, Martin, Pär,Ber-
ger, Paesiello, Blangini, Angrisani, Betscher, C.Cannabich,

A. Uber, Wesseli, Pleyel, Krommer, Rode, A. Pössinger, Mayseder, Angelo Benincorni, Boieldieu, Campagnoli, F.Blasius,
J.B. Viotti, Leop. Mozart, Beneduk.

REICHERT, Georg (compiler)

1041   Zur Geschichte der Wiener Messenkomposition in der ersten Hälfte
▽   des I8. Jahrhunderts (PhD diss.: Wien, 1935) 342*l*. (typescript)
       Thematisches Verzeichnis von Messen aus dem Kreise der Wiener
       Vorklassiker, 58-154.
              Over 400 double staff incipits of masses by: Ferd. Arbesser
              (1713-1794) (4), Ignaz Beyer (2), Franz Anton Candus (1),
              Anton Carl (13), Leop. Ferd. Christian (1717-1768) (1),
              Georg Donberger (1709-1768) (36), Franz Joh. Ehrehardt (26),
              Franz Anton Ertl (4), Feichter (1), Joh. Furbe (1), P. Alex-
              ander Giessel (5), Ignaz Jakob Holzbauer (23), P. Benedictus
              Klima (5), Carl Friedrich Liebl (3), Georg Matthias Monn (4),
              Matthias Oettl (1674-1725) (21), P. Carolomannus (Joseph)
              Pachschmidt (1700-1734) (7), Bernhard Paumon (5), Johann
              Pogg (1), Franz (Gerhard) Pruneder (c. 1692-1764) (8), Ignaz
              Prustmann (17), Joh. Georg Reinhardt (1677-1742) (36), Franz
              Rumpelneg (2), Ferdinand Schmidt (1694-1756) (21), Caspar
              Schollenberger (7), Joseph Timer (3), Franz Tuma (62), Joseph
              Umstadt (3), Georg Christoph Wagenseil (11), P. Joseph Wenser
              (2), Anton Werndle (1700-1754) (1), Gregor Joseph Werner (20),
              Wöger (1), Andreas Wid(d)er (4), Joh. Georg Zechner (53).

REIN (near Graz), Zisterzienserstift

1042   Thematischer Katalog (ca. 1820/30) (A R) (manuscript). Microfilm
▽   copy in D KNhi.
              This copy has not been examined.

REINDL, CONSTANTIN, 1738-1799

1043   JERGER, Wilhelm. Constantin Reindl, ein unbekannter Zeitgenosse
       W.A. Mozarts, *Mozart-Jahrbuch* 1954 (Salzburg 1955) 143-49.
              Incipits for all movements of 3 symphonies.

REUTTER JR., GEORG, bapt. 1708-1772

1044   HOFER, Norbert. Thematisches Verzeichnis der Werke von Georg
▽   Reutter Jr. (A Wn: S.m. 28,992) 247p. Compiled 1947. (typescript)
              Double staff incipits for all movements of 80 Masses,
              6 Requiems, 17 Graduals, 27 Offertories, 126 motets,
              151 Psalms and Canticles, 63 Hymns and sequences, 49
              Antiphons, 13 oratorios, 55 cantatas and opera, 14 suites
              and concertos for cembalo, 36 symphonies, partitas etc.
              with MSS sources. Includes an appendix of works (with
              incipits) incorrectly attributed to Reutter Jr., with
              information (where known) concerning the correct author-
              ship.

REYMANN, MATTHIAS, 1544-1597

1045 LOBAUGH, H. Bruce. **Three German lute books** (PhD diss., Musicology:
      U. of Rochester, 1968) 2v. Univ. Micro. 68-13,806 [see also 746]
      Noctes Musicae (1598), v. II, Appendix, 32-77.
           A thematic index or transcription in full of the entire con-
           tents. A total of 74 pieces appear, either in full (17) or
           in the thematic index (57). Incipits for "interior movements"
           are included in the thematic index (a total of 123 incipits).
           Works include 18 preludes, 12 fantasias, 10 passamezzo suites
           etc..

RHEDA, Fürst zu Bentheim-Tecklenburgische Bibliothek: Catalogue, 1750

1046 Catalogi musici/ Pars 1$^{\underline{ma}}$/ enthaltend/ 1) Waldhorn Concerte.../2)
 ▽   Violin Concerte.../3) Flaut Trav: et Flaut Abeo Concerte.../4)
      Hautbois Concerte.../5) Clavecin obligat Concerte.../6) Violin und
      Flauten Trio.../7) Violoncell Trio und Duetten.../8) Violin und
      Flaut=Trav: Solo.../ Limburg d. 22$^{\underline{ten}}$ Novembr./ 1750./ [Mit späteren
      Nachträgen] 101*l*.(On loan to D MÜu) (manuscript) Part I.
           Thematic catalogue of manuscripts in the Fürstlich zu Bent-
           heim-Tecklenburgischen Musikbibliothek Rheda. Since 1966,
           this manuscript has been located at Münster. Part I contains
           incipits for 577 instrumental works of the 18th century (364
           original entries, 213 added up to ca. 1785) by the following
           composers: 1) Aniely, Bigler, Bancratius, Bürger, Dömming,
           Fidler, Förster, Frey, Friderici, Fidele, Fiorillo, Graff,
           Graun, Gretsch, Gresser, Hasse, Hendel, Houbfelt, Lotti, Mo-
           zart,Stametz, Sterkel, Stierlein, Schweiniz, Schwaneberg,
           Teleman, Wagenseil, Zurlini; 2) Abell, Agrell, Albenoni,
           Appell, Baneratiy, Benda, Brescianello, Brioschi, Bürger,
           Cammerlocher, Dömming, Eberhard, Festing, Förster, Fiedler,
           Fabio, Ferdinand Fischer, Flotte, Förster, Giullini, Givani,
           Graff, Gresser, Graun, Guzinger, Giraneck, Hasse, Hece, Hoff-
           man, Hoffstätter, Janitsch, Kellery,Klöffler, Kunze, Labe,
           Locatelli, Lunichen, Mahaut, Meck, Martini, Martino, Meyer,
           Micheli, Neruda, Oglio, Pachmann, Pollozi, Pirckh, Pfeiffer,
           Rippel, Richter, Rezel, Roellig, Ritschel, Scaccia, Schwach-
           hofer, Scalabine a Venezia, Scala de Bona Gratia, Scheibe,
           Serta, Stamitz, Steinmetzer, Stierlein, Solnitz, Störlein,
           Tartini, Telemann, Tischer, Troll, Ursio [Bernasconi], Vi-
           valdi, Zach; 3) Adami, Albenoni, Baron, Bernasconi, Dömming,
           Fasch, Giay, Graun, Hasse, Heinry, Jomelli, Klöffler, Kunze,
           Labé, Locatelli, Lösel, Lucchesini, Luty, Magini, Mahaut, S.
           L. Martini, Meyer, Pachman, Quantz, Retzel, Scheibe, Scherer,
           Solnitz, Stelzel, Stulick, Telemann, Tischer, Zobell; 4) Bi-
           gler, Dömming, Förster, Graun, Heinichen, Messerschmid, Sal-
           vini, Scheibe, Schichard, Stölzel, Telemann; 5) Agrell, Döm-
           ming, Eberhard, Förster, Graun, Hertell, Janitsch, Leffloth,
           Pachman, Schaffroth; 6) Bernasconi, Bisqueto, Biarelli,
           Bichler, Bitzholt, Brandel, Dömming, Fasch, Förster, Grone-
           man, Graun, Hasse, Hamelbrüninck, Hendleni, Huppedepup, Kel-
           lery, Locatelli, Martini, Messerschmidt, Narale, Pagman,
           Pfeiffer, Polozzy, Quantz, Schlothauer, Schmalle, Scherer,
           Schultze, Solnitz, Sporny, Teleman, Thalman, Wilano, Zach;
           7) Albergetti, Antoinio, Dömming, Fidler, Ferdinando, Scala,
           Teleman; 8) Benda, Prince de Darnstadt, Dömming, Graff,

Hamel Brüninck, Kellery, Mahaut. Suiten et trio pro Mandora
ê gallichona et Harph: v. non et Flaut. Trav.: Gresser and
Hoffmann.

1046a --- Catalogi musici/Pars 2$^{\underline{da}}$/ enthaltend/1) Deutsche Cantates und..
▽   Arien.../2) Italiänische und Frantzösische Cantates...1750./ (D MÜu)
      27ℓ. (manuscript) Part II.
            Part II contains 220 incipits for sacred vocal music. This
            section is badly damaged, and only about one-third of it is
            usable. The German arias and cantatas are arranged alphabet-
            ically by text, and the Italian and French entries are arrang-
            ed by composer. The following composers are inventoried: 1)
            Teleman, Cesare, Dömming, Käffer, Keyser, Heinichen, Graun;
            2) Almeyda, Bononcini, Comte de Bückeburg, Cesare, Conti, Cos-
            tanzi, Dömming, Fabria, Fiore, Georgi, Graun, Hasse, Heinichen,
            Hendel, Köhler, Latila, Peretz, Porporini, Quantz, Romald,
            Rossetti, Tedeli, Teleman, Vacini, Venetiano, Vinci, Vivaldi.

RHEDA, Fürst zu Bentheim-Tecklenburgische Bibliothek: Index cards

1046b [Thematic catalogue of extant manuscripts] (Entire collection on
▽   loan to D MÜu since 1966) Index cards. Compiled 1968/69 by Erich
      Thurmann. (manuscript).
            Incipits for 985 extant manuscripts arranged alphabetically
            by composer. Composers represented are:C.F. Abel, Agrell,
            Albini, Albinoni, Almeida, J.A. André, P. Anfossi, Aniely,
            G.A. Appel, G. Arena, W. Attern, Auffeman, J.C. Bach, J.C.F.
            Bach, S. Bachman, Baron, J. Bauer, Beaty, Beck, F. Benda, F.
            L. Benda, G. Benda, Bernasconi, F. Bertoni, B.C.F. Bertram,
            Boccherini, J.J.C. Bode, Bononcini, Brescianello, Brioschi,
            Bürger, B. de Bury, Cambini, Camerloher, Cannabich, L. Caruso,
            G. Cavi, Cesare, Chelleri, M. Chiesa, Cimarosa, Clementi, G.
            Colla, F.B. Conti, G. Curcio, Davaux, Demachi, J.C. Dömming,
            J.M. Dömming, Duport, Dussek, Eberhard, E. Eichner, J.G. Eich-
            ner, A.A. Eisenmann, M. Esser, Fabricius, Fasch, Ferretti, M.
            C. Festing, M. Fiedler, A. Filtz, A.S. Fiorè, I. Fiorillo, F.
            Fischer, Flotte, J.A. Fodor, C. Förster, Forni, Friedrich d.
            Grosse, Fuchs, B. Galuppi, F.L. Gassmann, Georgii, Giaji, P.
            Gianotti, A. Giranek, G. Giulini, Givani, J. Graf, Graun, J.T.
            Greiner, Gresser, Grétry, J.K. Gretsch, A.H. Groene, J.A.
            Groenemann, S.D. Grosse, P. Guglielmi, J.P. Guzinger, A. Gyro-
            wetz, Gyrzichs, J. Hafeneder, J.A. Hasse, J. Haydn, J.D. Hein-
            ichen, Hendel, J. Herschel, Hertel, M. Hoffmann, F.A. Hoff-
            meister, I. Holzbauer, B. Hupfeld, J.G. Janitsch, G. Jarnovick,
            N. Jommelli, J.A. Just, A. Ivanschiz, F. Kauer, J.B. Kehl, R.
            Keiser, H.F.v. Kerpen, F.J. Kirmair, F. Kirsten, J.F. Klöffler,
            K.v. Kohaut, O.C.E.v. Kospoth, L.A. Kozeluch, Kuntze, Labé,
            J.G. Lang, Latilla, F. Lebrun, Lebutini, J.W. Leeder, Leffloth,
            H.N. Lepin, J.A. Liber, Liberati, P.I. Lichtenauer, J.G. Linike,
            P. Locatelli, Lotti, G. de Lucchesini, Luty, Magini, A. Mahaut,
            G.F. de Majo, Martini, M. Marx, Meck, Messerschmid, Meyer,
            Micheli, J.C. Moeller, F. Monani, C. Monza, L. Mozart, W.A.
            Mozart, Müller, Myslivecek, Narale, J.G. Naumann, C.G. Neefe,
            J.B.G. Neruda, F.C. Neubauer, J.G. Nicolai, V. Nicolai, Noel,
            A. Och, D. dall'Oglio, C.d'Ordonez, Pachmann, Paisiello, Palen-
            tini, F.W. Pannenberg, E. Pausch, Pecky, D. Perez, Pergolesi,
            Pescetti, K.A. Pesch, J. Pfeiffer, Pichler (Bigler), Pleyel,
            Pollozi, A. Polluzi, N. Porpora, J.G. Portmann, G. Pugnani,

J.J. Quantz, F.C. Rackmann, V. Rauzzini, Reichert, Retzel
Richter, J. Riepel, G.W. Ritschel, J.G. Roellig, V. Roeser,
J.A. Rosetter, F.A. Rosetti, F.W. Rust, G.M. Rutini, A. Sac-
chini, Salvini, Sammartini, G. Sarti, C.H.v. Sayn-Wittgenstein-
Berleburg, A.M. Scaccia, Scala de Bonagratia, P. Scalabrini,
C. Schaffrath, C.F. Schale, J.A. Scheibe, J. Scherer, Schichard,
Schlothauer, F. Schmitt, J.A. Schmittbauer, J. Schobert, J.S.
Schroeter, Schultz, J. Schuster, J.G. Schwanenberger, Schwei-
nitz,A. Schweitzer, F. Schwindel, M.L. Sirmen, A.W. Solnitz,
Spietal, A. Stamitz, C. Stamitz, J. Stamitz, Starck, J.F.X.
Sterkel, Stierlein, G.H. Stölzel, Stulick, G. Tartini, Tele-
mann, D. Terradellas, C. Tessarini, C. Textor, J.N. Tischer,
C.J. Toeschi, Troll, J.B. Vanhal, H.L. Vetter, Vinci, G.B.
Viotti, A. Vivaldi, G.C. Wagenseil, L. Weckbacher, J.B. Wend-
ling, E.W. Wolf, M. Yost, J. Zach, A. Zimmermann, W. Zimmer-
mann, C.L.D. Zinkeisen, Zobell, F. Zoppis.

1046c --- DOMP, Joachim. **Studien zur Geschichte der Musik an westfälischen**
☐   **Adelshöfen im XVIII. Jahrhundert,** *Freiburger Studien z. Musikwissen-*
     schaft I (Regensburg: Pustet, 1934) 7-35.

RHEINBERGER, GABRIEL JOSEF, 1839-1901

1047 IRMEN, Hans-Josef (Köln). **Thematisches Werkverzeichnis**
*

RHODES, Willard

1048 **The use of the computer in the classification of folk tunes,** *StudMusi-*
☐   *col* VII (1965) 339-43.

RICHTER, FRANZ XAVER, 1709-1789

1049 MATHIAS, Franz X. **Thematischer Katalog der im Strassburger Münster-**
     archiv aufbewahrten kirchenmusikalischen Werke Fr.X.Richters 1769-
     1789, *Riemann Festschrift* (Leipzig: Hesse, 1909) 394-422.
             Incipits for 104 sacred works, with scoring indicated.
             Kyrie incipits only for the 30 Masses. Indications of parts
             missing in collection in Strasbourg Cathedral.

1049a --- unveränderter Nachdruck der Ausgabe von 1909 (Tutzing: Hans
      Schneider, 1965) xl, 524p.

1050 GÄSSLER, Willi. **Die Sinfonien von Franz Xaver Richter und ihre**
▽   **Stellung in der vorklassischen Sinfonik** (PhD diss.: München, 1941)
     74p., 5ℓ. Notenanhäng (typescript).
     Nachtrag zum thematischen Katalog der Richter'schen Sinfonien
     in *DTB* 3/1, 1ℓ.
             Incipits for 7 symphonies not found in Riemann. One symphony
             is in *DTB* VII/1.

1051 SCHMITT, Eduard. **Thematischer Katalog der Kirchenmusik Richters,**
*   *Denkmälerreihe der Heidelberger Akademie der Wissenschaften*

RIEDEL, Friedrich Wilhelm (Mainz)

1052 **Thematischer Katalog der Wiener Klaviermusik von ca. I650-I750**
* ──

Approximately 1500 incipits of individual movements of keyboard works by : A. Caldara, F. Conti, W. Ebner, J.J. Froberger, J. J. Fux, J.K. Kerll, Gottl. Muffat, J.B. Peyer, A. Poglietti, F.A. Remer, J.G. Reutter, A.K. Richter, F.T. Richter, F.M. Techelmann, L. Tuner.

1053 Die Bibliothek des Aloys Fuchs, *Hans Albrecht in Memoriam*, Wilfried
☐ Brennecke, Hans Hasse, eds. (Kassel: Bärenreiter, 1962) 207-34 (see also 83a, 235, 1159)

1053 a Zur Bibliothek des Aloys Fuchs, *Mf* XVI (1963) 270-75
☐ Supplements information published in no. 1053

lit 1054 Zur Geschichte der Musikalischen Quellenüberlieferung und Quellen-
☐ kunde, *ActaMusicol* XXXVIII/1 (1966) 3-27.
Includes remarks on origins of thematic catalogues and older catalogues in MS.

RIEDER, AMBROS, 1771-1855

1055 BENEŠ, Gertrude. **Ambros Rieder. Sein Leben und sein Orgelwerk.**
▽ Nebst einem thematischen Verzeichnis seiner Werke (PhD diss.: Wien, 1967) 2v., 310, 194*l*. (typescript)
Thematisches Verzeichnis aller überlieferten Werke Ambros Rieders, v. 2.
Multiple staff incipits, arranged by opus number, for 17 Masses, 3 Requiems, 35 Offertories, 19 Graduals, 8 Tantum ergo, 1 opera, 16 choruses, 11 Lieder, string quartets, fugues, sonatas, etc.

RIEGER, Adam

1056 Zagadnienie leksykalnego indeksowania melodii ludowych [Problems of
☐ indexing of folk-tunes], *Lud* XLII (1957) 554-606.
Analyses principles of lexicographical indexing, reviews bibliographical literature on the subject, and proposes two of his own systems of indexing, one alphabetical and the other in numerical symbols.

RIEMANN, Hugo (compiler)

1057 Sinfonien der pfalzbayerischen Schule (Mannheimer Symphoniker),
DTB Jahrg. 3/1, 7/2   (Leipzig: Breitkopf & Härtel, 1902-1906)
2v.
Volume 1 contains a thematic catalogue, p. [xxxix]-liv; volume 2, pt. i, a supplement to the catalogue, p. [xxix]-xxxii. The above catalogues of works from the Mannheim School includes themes from works by the following composers: Johann Stamitz (58), Franz Xaver Richter (67), Anton Filtz (41), Ignaz Holzbauer (69), Joseph Toeschi (63), Christian Cannabich (101), Carl Cannabich (2), Carl Stamitz (72), Anton Stamitz (13), Ignaz Fränzl (4), Georg Zarth [Tzarth] (1), Franz Beck (19), Ernst Eichner (31), Thomas Alexander Erskine (14), Franz Danzi (8).

1058 Mannheimer Kammermusik des I8. Jahrhunderts, *DTB* Jahrg. 16
(Leipzig: Breitkopf & Härtel, 1915)
[Thematic catalogue], xxvi-lxiii.
Incipits for works by the following composers: Josef Bauer (9), Franz Beck (2), Christian Cannabich (49), Martin Fried.

Cannabich (9), Wilhelm Cramer (24), Johann Baptist Cramer
(52), Johann Friedrich Hugo Freiherr von Dalberg (6), Franz
Danzi (50), Margarethe Danzi (3), Anton Dimmler (8), Johann
Friedrich Edelmann (24), Ernst Eichner (33), Karl Michael
Esser (6), Anton Filtz (46), A.E. Forstmeyer (5), Ignaz
Fränzl (10), Ferdinand Fränzl (22), Ignaz Holzbauer (17),
Hugo Friedrich von Kerpen (6), Johann Küchler (6), Franzis-
ka Lebrun (12), Ludwig August Lebrun (6), Anton Joseph Liber
(7), Georg Metzger (1), Franz Metzger (1), Franz Xaver Rich-
ter (49), Anton Riegel(11), Peter Ritter (20), Valentin Rö-
ser (12), Joseph Schmitt (16), Anton Stamitz (66), Johann
Stamitz (40), Franz Xaver Sterkel (69), Ludwig Tantz (6),
Franz Tausch (3), Giuseppe Toeschi (60), Giovanni Battista
Toeschi (6), Georg Tzarth (8), Georg Joseph Vogler (86),
Johann Baptist Wendling (42), Peter Winter (3), Johann Zach
(7), Alexander Lord Erskine, Romanus Hoffstetter, Joseph
Götter, Georg Friedrich Fuchs, and Carl Stamitz.

1059   ALTMANN, Wilhelm.**Nachträge zu Hugo Riemanns Verzeichnis der Druck-
       ausgaben und thematischem Katalog der Mannheimer Kammermusik des
       I8. Jahrhunderts**, *ZfMW* I (1919) 620-28.
              Incipits arranged by key, following Riemann's format, for
              works by Wilhelm Cramer, Danzi, Edelmann, Kerpen, H.J. Riegel,
              P. Ritter, Sterckel, G. Toeschi, and P. Winter.

RIEMANN Musik Lexikon

1060   **Thematische Kataloge**, *Riemann Musik Lexikon* (1967) 952-53
☐   Provides brief listing and background, plus lists of major
              thematic catalogues.

RIEPEL, JOSEF, 1709-1782

1061   MERKL, Josef. **Josef Riepel als Komponist** (Kallmünz: Lassleben,
       1937) 88p.
              Thematisches Verzeichnis der Kompositionen J. Riepels, [67]-
       86.
              Incipits for all movements of instrumental works. Sacred and
              secular works listed separately, with no text underlay for vo-
              cal works.Scoring, tempi, and library locations are provided.

RIETSCH, Heinrich

1061.1 **Nachschlagverzeichniss für Tonweisen**, *Das dt. Volkslied* XVII, (Wien,
☐   1915) 2f.
              On folk tune classification.

RIES, FERDINAND, 1784-1838

1062   RIES, Franz. **Catalogue thématique of the works of Ferd^d Ries**
▽   (D Bds: HB VII, Kat. mus. 741) 105p. (manuscript)
              Double staff incipits arranged by opus number (169). Ries
              provides year and place of composition, as well as publisher.

1063   HILL, Cecil (U. of Calif., Santa Barbara). **Thematic catalogue**
*   Incipits for 186 opus numbers of Ries's, though about 15-20
              are missing. Catalogue will be much along the lines of
              Alan TYSON's **Thematic catalogue of the works of Muzio Cle-
              menti.**

RINALDO di CAPUA, ca. 1710- after 1770

1064   BOSTIAN, Richard Lee. **The works of Rinaldo di Capua** (PhD diss.,
       Musicology: U. of North Carolina, 1961) 257p. Univ. Micro. 61-6091.
            Incipits of overtures and symphonies, all movements, are
            incorporated into the text p. 173-92.

RINGMACHER, Christian Ulrich (compiler)

1065   **Catalogo de' soli, duetti,trii, quadri, quintetti, partito,** de'
       concerti e delle sinfonie per il cembalo, violino, flauto traverso
       ed altri stromenti che si trovano in manoscritto nella officina
       musica di Christiano Ulrico Ringmacher librario in Berelino, 1773.
            628 incipits, with instrumentation, are listed alphabetical-
            ly by composer within the various genres. Composers include:
            Abel, Adam, Agrell, Agricola, Anonymo, Aspelmeier, Aubert,
            C.P.E. Bach, Beck, G. Benda, F. Benda, Bertram, Binder, Boc-
            cherini, Boehm, Breidenstein, Brenneffel, Bümler, Campioni,
            Cannabich, Cirini, Cohn, Cramer, Diezel, Ditters, Doebbert,
            Dothel, Fasch, Feo, Fils, Fischer, Förster,Frederic, Frenzel,
            Galuppi, Gavinies, Gewey, Giardini, Gitaneck, Glösch, Graff,
            Gros, Graun, Guerini, Haindl, Hartmann, Hasse, Haydn, Heil,
            Hendl, Heinichen, Hertel, Hien, Hiller, Hoeckh, Hoffmann,
            Holzbogen, Houpfeld, Janitsch, Josefsky, Ivanschitz, Kirn-
            berger, Kleinknecht, Klöffler, Krafft, Krause, Krebs, Kyr-
            meyer, de la Lande, Lange, Lau, Leeder, Lizka, Locatelli,
            Mancini, Marpurg, Martini, Matthees, Menges, Mohrheim, Mon-
            signy, Müthel, Nauert, Neefe, Neruda, Neumann, Nichelmann,
            Ordonez, Palschau, Paulsen, Pergolesi, Petrini, Piazza, Plat-
            ti, Puci, Pugnani, Quantz, Rackemann, Rameau, Rathgeber,
            Raupach, Reichard, Reinards, Relluzi, Rezel, Richter, Riedt,
            Riepel, Rolle, Rosenbaum, Rossi, Roth, Schabolzky, Schaff-
            rath, Schale, Schedtel, Schetky, Scheuenstuhl, Schmid, Scho-
            bert, Schultz, Schwindl, Sebetosky, Sperontes, Stamiz, Stech-
            way, Steimetz, Traetta, Toeschi, Tübal, Tuscheck, Uber, Ude,
            Umstadt, Vallade, Veichtner, Vierling, Vivaldi, Wagenseil,
            Wanhall, Wenckel, Woerbach, Wolff, Zanetti, Zarth, Zicka,
            and Zinck.[reproduction on following page]

RINGMANN, Herbert (compiler)

1066   **Das Glogauer Liederbuch,** Erster Teil, *Das Erbe deutscher Musik,* Bd. 4
       (Kassel: Bärenreiter, 1936-37) xv, 134p.
            Musikalisches Anfangsverzeichnis des Glogauer Liederbuches, 102-19.
            Incipits for each part of 294 works in the book, cross-refer-
            enced to other editions. Among many anonymous works indexed
            are a few by known composers, including Bebrleyn, Broda, Bru-
            olo, Busnois, Caron, Dufay, Ghizeghem, Martini, Okeghem, Tinc-
            toris, and Vincenet.

1066a --- Manfred BUKOFZER, **An unknown chansonnier of the 15th century,** *MQ*
 □   XXVIII (1942) p. 17.
            Identifies anonymous works.

RIPA, ALBERTO da, ca. 1480-1551

1067   BUGGERT, Robert W. **Alberto da Ripa, lutenist and composer** (PhD

XVIII. Ringmacher, *Catalogo de' soli, duetti...*, (Berlin, 1773) title page and page 3, no. 1065

226

diss.: U. of Michigan, 1957) 440p. Univ. Micro. 21-154.(typescript)
[Thematic index], 184-202.
> Partial index of seven books of lute tablature, arranged
> by date of publication.

RISM   [Répertoire International des Sources Musicales]

> The entries below describe, country by country, the state of
> the work being done on *RISM* Series A/II, covering pre-1800
> manuscripts. The publication of Series A/I, the alphabetical
> catalogue of music printed between 1500 and 1800, was begun in
> 1971. When this series is completed, ca. 1975, *RISM* is expect-
> ed to begin publishing the A/II series for manuscripts. This
> will take many years. Several countries have not yet begun to
> work on A/II; some have indicated that they do not intend to do
> so. Meanwhile, in those countries where the work is proceeding,
> invaluable thematic cataloguing information is being gathered.
> Answers to specific questions may, under certain circumstances,
> be obtained by writing to the appropriate national chairman.
> In some countries, the thematic cataloguing has proceeded on an
> impressive scale, and has included materials from after 1800.
> In Sweden and Czechoslovakia (see special entries nos. 1001, and
> 1253),   virtually all manuscripts are being catalogued.

> For each entry below, we indicate the national chairman of the
> country, with his address, plus the names of collaborators work-
> ing specifically on thematic cataloguing for *RISM*. The *RISM*
> Zentralredaktion is presently concerned with printed editions
> only. It is under the direction of Karlheinz Schlager at 35
> Kassel, Ständeplatz 16, Germany (BRD).

> Catalogue cards prepared by *RISM* teams in each country or by
> outside collaborators are gathered in the national *RISM* centers.
> In most cases, a copy of the set of cards prepared for each li-
> brary is also deposited in that library. For certain libraries
> where we have had the opportunity to secure a complete list of
> composers, we have made complete entries which appear under the
> libraries name (e.g. Burgsteinfurt, Rheda, and Herdringen.)

> The present *RISM* regulations regarding manuscript cataloguing
> stipulate the inclusion of an incipit whenever the work cannot
> be otherwise specifically identified by existing printed thema-
> tic catalogues. In most countries, however, except in the most
> obvious cases (e.g. well-known works by Mozart) all incipits are
> recorded. The information below represents the state of affairs
> as reported toward the end of 1971. If a country is not listed
> this means that no work has been done there as yet, or that no
> answer to our questionnaire has been forthcoming. For the sake
> of completeness our questionnaire also included a request for
> information about the number of printed works catalogued for
> A/I and the number of those that were catalogued with incipits.

RISM: Austria (A)

1068   GRASBERGER, Franz, chairman (Augustinerstrasse 1, Wien I.); collaborator: Alexander Weinmann.
> 1.) No. of printed works catalogued: 66,790, none with inci-
> pits.

2.) No. of MSS catalogued: 9,780, all with incipits.
3.) Libraries or collections the MSS of which have been catalogued with incipits thus far: HE, M, SF, SEI, SCH, Wkh, Ww,
Wh, Wp, Wkann, Wweinmann.
4.) No. of years expected to complete project: 5-7.
5.) Major libraries or collections to be inventoried by 1975:
Wn, Wgm, Wst.

RISM: Belgium (B)

1069   LENAERTS, René Bernard, chairman (Seminarie voor Muziekwetenschap
K.W.L. Vlamingenstraat 83, Leuven); collaborators: Josef Robÿns,
Philippe Mercier, Ign. Bossingt, Jaak van Deun.
1.) No. of printed works catalogued: 5,850, none with incipits. A few hundred yet to be catalogued.
2.) No. of MSS catalogued: 1,600; no. with incipits: 400; no.
yet to be catalogued: over 2,000.
3.) Libraries or collections the MSS of which have been catalogued with incipits: no complete collections, but works of
De la Rue, W. de Fesch, Fiocco, De Croes, Van Maldere, Hamal,
Robson, Gresnick and others.
4.) No. of years expected to complete the project: 3-4.
5.) Major libraries or collections to be inventoried by 1975:
A, Bc, Br, Brc, Gc, Gu, Lc, Lu, M, K, MEa, MEs, Tc, Tr.

RISM: Brazil (BR)

1070   PERSON de MATTOS, Cleofe, chairman (Rue du Russel 32, Rio de Janeiro,
Brazil); collaborator: Mercedes Reis Pequeño.
1.) No. of printed works catalogued: not reported.
2.) No. of MSS catalogued: 237, all with incipits.
3.) Libraries or collections the MSS of which have been catalogued with incipits: no complete collections, but the works
of José Mauricio Nunes Garcia(see no. 917.1).

RISM: Canada (C)

1071   KALLMAN, Helmut, chairman (National Library of Canada, Music Division, Ottawa K2B 6L6).
1.) No. of printed works catalogued: 1,450, none with incipits.
2.) No. of MSS catalogued: 25, none with incipits.

RISM: Czechoslovakia (Bohemia and Moravia— CS)

1072   PULKERT, Oldřich, chairman (Státní knihovna ČSR-Universitní knihovna.
Hudební oddělení— Souborny hudební katalog. Praha 1, Klementinum,
čp. 190); collaborators: Jitřenka Pešková, Eva Dubová.(see no. 1001)
1.) No. of printed works catalogued: 94,556, all with incipits; Ca. 300,000 printed works yet to be catalogued.
2.) No. of MSS catalogued: 92,600, all with incipits. Ca.
200,000 MSS yet to be catalogued.
3.) No. of years expected to complete project: 5-8.
4.) To the grand total of incipits of printed and manuscript
music has been added incipits for a number of standard printed
thematic catalogues (e.g. Mozart [Köchel], Haydn [Hoboken]).
The grand total of incipits: 166,699 cards. In addition,
there is a catalogue of text incipits totaling 99,147.

RISM: Czechoslovakia (Slovakia—CS)

1073   MÚDRA, Darina, chairman (Slovenské národné muzeum, Musikabteilung,
        Bratislava, Hrad); collaborator: Emanuel Muntág. (see also no. 165)
        1.) No. of printed works catalogued: 800, all with incipits;
        800-900 printed works yet to be catalogued.
        2.) No. of MSS catalogued: 4,000, all with incipits; 5,000-
        6,000 MSS yet to be catalogued.
        3.) Libraries or collections the MSS of which have been ca-
        talogued with incipits: BRhs, Bre, Brnm, Brsa, Bru, J, KO,
        KRE, L, Mnm, Mms, N, NM, Pr, Rz, Sk, Snv, TR.
        4.) No. of years to complete project: 7-8.
        5.) Major libraries or collections to be completed by 1975:
        Bratislava Ursulinenkloster, Kremnica-Franziskanerkloster,
        Kremnica-sog. Cammer Kapelle, Bratislava-kathol. KMV, Bra-
        tislava evan. KMV, Dubnica-Pfarrkirche, Pruské-Pfarrkirche.
        6.) Thematic catalogues of major collections are scheduled
        to be published in individual volumes.

RISM: Denmark (DK)

1074   BIRKELUND, Palle, chairman (Det Kongelige Bibliothek, Chr. Brygge 8,
        1219 København K); collaborator: Nanna Schiødt.
        1.) No. of printed works catalogued: 4,500, none with inci-
        pits.
        2.) No. of MSS catalogued: 900, all with incipits; 3,000-
        4,000 MSS yet to be catalogued.
        3.) Libraries or collections the MSS of which have been cata-
        logued with incipits: Sa, Kmk, Km, Ou, Kv, Kc, As, Ku, DSch,
        Ch, Kk, Kt.
        4.) No. of years expected to complete the project: 2.
        5.) Libraries or collection to be completed by 1975: Kk, Kt,
        Ku, DSch, Ch.

RISM: Finland (Suomi—SF)

1075   HOLM, Marita, chairman (Sibeliusmuseum, Biskopsg. 17, 20500,Åbo 50)
        All questions should be directed to: Internationales Quellen-
        lexikon der Musik, D-3500 Kassel, Ständeplatz 16, Germany.

RISM: France (F)

1076   LESURE, François, chairman (Bibliothèque Nationale, Département de
        Musique, 2 Square Louvois, Paris II).
        Cataloguing of the prints is virtually completed with the
        collaboration of Paule Guiomar, among others. At the present
        time, France has no plans to catalogue manuscripts for *RISM*.

RISM: Germany, East (D-ddr)

1077   THEURICH, Jutta, chairman (Deutsche Staatsbibliothek, Musikabteilung,
        108 Berlin, Unter den Linden 8); collaborators: Ortrun Landmann,
        Wolfgang Reich, Renata Wuta-Blechschmidt, Eleonore Schmidt, Eva-Maria
        Koch, Ingeborg Stein, Jürgen Howitz.
        1.) No. of printed works catalogued: ca. 27,200, ca. 270 with
        incipits.
        2.) No. of MSS catalogued: ca. 25,300, ca. 1400 with incipits;
        ca. 15,000 yet to be catalogued.

        3.) Libraries or collections the MSS of which have been cata-
logued with incipits: some work has been done in virtually
all libraries given in *RISM* A/I.
        4.) No. of years expected to complete project: 8-10.
        5.) Libraries or collections to be completed by 1975: Dl, HER.

RISM: Germany, West (D-brd)

1078   STRIEDL, Hans, chairman (Deutsche Arbeitsgruppe des *RISM* München e.V.
      8 München 34, Bayer. Staatsbibliothek, Schliessfach); collaborators:
      Liesbeth Weinhold, Gertraut Haberkamp.
        1.) No. of printed works catalogued: 48,000, none with inci-
pits.
        2.) No. of MSS catalogued: 9,000, all with incipits; ca.
30,000 yet to be catalogued.
        3.) Libraries or collections the MSS of which have been cata-
logued with incipits: AB, BAR, HL, HR, LB, OB, RAd, RH, Zl.
        4.) No. of years expected to complete project: ca. 15.
        5.) Libraries or collections to be complete by 1975: B, MÜs,
Rtt, Tsch.

RISM: Great Britain (GB)

1079   KING, Alexander Hyatt, chairman (British Museum, Music Room, London).
        All Series A cataloguing has been completed without incipits.

RISM: Hungary (H)

1080   VAVRINECZ, Veronika, chairman (Hungarian National Library, Music De-
      partment, Budapest VIII. Muzeum Kr. 14).
        1.) No. of printed works catalogued: 3,000-4,000, a few hund-
red with incipits; a few thousand printed works yet to be
catalogued.
        2.) No. of MSS catalogued: ca. 400, 80-100 with incipits; ca.
8,000-10,000 yet to be catalogued.
        3.) Libraries or collections the MSS of which have been cata-
logued with incipits: KE, Helicon Library Györ, PH.
        4.) No. of years expected to complete project: ca. 10.
        5.) Libraries or collections to be completed by 1975: Bn, Bl,
Bb.

RISM: Italy (I)   [Reports received from three individual libraries only]

1081   **Roma: Biblioteca Musicale Governative del Conservatorio di Musica S.
Cecilia.**   ZANETTI, Emilia (Capo della Biblioteca); collaborator: Fla-
vio Benedetti Michelangeli.
        1.) No. of printed works catalogued: 2,400, none with inci-
pits; ca. 350 yet to be catalogued.
        2.) No. of MSS catalogued: none; ca. 4,900 yet to be cata-
logued.
        3.) No. of years expected to complete project: ca. 5 years.

1082   **Milano: Biblioteca del Conservatorio "G. Verdi".**   Collaborators: Gil-
da Grigolato, Agostina Zecca Laterza.
        1.) No. of printed works catalogued: ca. 3,000, none with in-
cipits; ca. 200,000 yet to be catalogued.
        2.) No. of MSS catalogued: none; ca. 15,000 to be catalogued
(without incipits).

1083   Torino: Archivio Musicale del Duomo. BOUQUET, Marie-Thérèse.
       Under the auspices of Ufficio Ricerca Fondi Musicali Milano,
       600-700 manuscripts from the 17th-19th centuries have been
       inventoried without incipits. No. of years to complete the
       work: 2.

RISM: Netherlands (NL)

1084   REESER, H.E., chairman (Instituut voor Muziekwetenschap, Drift 21,
       Utrecht 2501); collaborators: Clemens von Gleich, Marie H. Charbon,
       Frits Noske, Alfons Annegarn.
                1.) No. of printed works catalogued: 3,000, none with incipits.
                2.) No. of MSS catalogued: 400, none with incipits.
                3.) No. of years to complete the project: 2.
                4.) Libraries or collections to be completed by 1975: At, AN,
                DHgm, DHk, 'sH, La, Uim, Usg.
                5.) Specifically for the Gemeentemuseum in The Hague: 1,000-
                2,000 printed works catalogued, none with incipits, ca. 250
                yet to be catalogued.

RISM: Poland (PL)

1085   MENDYSOWA, Janina, chairman (Biblioteka Uniwersytecka, Warszawa Kra-
       kowskie Przedmieście 32); collaborators: Barbara Gołebiewska, Danuta
       Idaszak, Adam Mrygoń.
                1.) No. of printed works catalogued: ca. 6,000, none with in-
                cipits; 600 yet to be catalogued.
                2.) No. of MSS catalogued: 500, none with incipits; ca. 8,000
                yet to be catalogued.
                3.) Libraries or collections the MSS of which have been cata-
                logued with incipits: all MSS in Wu, but without incipits.
                4.) No. of years to complete project: 5.

RISM: Sweden (S)

1086   JOHANSSON, Cari, chairman (Kungliga Musikaliska Akademiens Biblio-
       tek, Postbox 16 265, S-103 25 Stockholm 16); collaborators: Anna-Le-
       na Holm, Vanja Klackenberg. (see also 1253)
                1.) No. of printed works catalogued: ca. 11,600, ca. 50 ano-
                nymous works with incipits.
                2.) No. of MSS catalogued: 12,500 all with incipits except
                those containing more than one work by one composer, and
                works identified by printed works or by reference literature.
                MSS catalogued before 1965 are without incipits. Will com-
                plete the cards on works not identified (by reference liter-
                ature) with incipits. No. of MSS to be catalogued: not more
                than 5,000.
                3.) Libraries or collections the MSS of which have been ca-
                talogued with incipits: B [Borås stadsarkiv], K, L, M, Skma,
                Ssr, St (cataloguing is proceeding), STr, V, Vx. MSS iden-
                tified with other references: N, VIl, ÖS.
                4.) No. of years expected to complete the project: 2.
                5.) Libraries or collections to be completed by 1975: all.

RISM: Switzerland (CH)

1087   BAUMANN, Max Peter, chairman (Musikwissenschaftliches Seminar, Uni-
       versität Bern, *RISM,* Länggass-Strasse 7, CH-3000 Bern).
                1.) No. of printed works catalogued: ca. 13,000, none with

incipits.
2.) No. of MSS catalogued: several hundred, all with incipits; no. of MSS yet to be catalogued: 10,000-15,000.
3.) Libraries or collections the MSS of which have been catalogued with incipits: Bu (work in progress).
4.) No. of years expected to complete the project: 10.
5.) Libraries or collections to be completed by 1975: Bu, E,
Zz, SGv, Sgs.

RISM: United States of America (US)

1088   SPIVACKE, Harold, chairman (Music Division, Library of Congress,
Washington D.C. 20540).
1.) No. of printed works catalogued: 53,000, none with incipits.
2.) No. of MSS cataloged: 4,000, none with incipits.

RISM: Yugoslavia (YU)

1089   CVETKO, Dragotin, chairman (61000 Ljubljana, Aškerčeva 12); collaborators: Josip Andreis, L. Zepič, Albe Vidaković.
1.) No. of printed works catalogued: 89, none with incipits.

RISTORI, GIOVANNI ALBERTO, 1692-1753

1090   MENGELBERG, Curt R.   **Giovanni Alberto Ristori; ein Beitrag zur
Geschichte italienischer Kunstherrschaft in Deutschland im I8.
Jahrhundert** (Leipzig: Breitkopf & Härtel, 1916) 151p.
Verzeichnis der Werke, [143]- 151.
Incipits for Masses and Requiems only. The date of com-
position, and the present location are given.

RITTER, PETER, 1763-1846

1091   GILREATH, Martha Jean. **The violoncello concertos of Peter Ritter**
▽   (MA diss., Musicology: U. of North Carolina, 1961) 76p.(typescript)
Thematic index, 62-65.
One line incipits for each movement of the concertos.

RODE, PIERRE, 1774-1830

1092   POUGIN, Arthur. **Notice sur Rode, violiniste français** (Paris:
Pottier de Lalaine, 1874) 64p.
Catalogue des oeuvres de Rode, 54-64.
13 incipits for violin concerti only.

1092.1 BACHMANN, Alberto. **Les grands violinistes du passé** (Paris: Fischbacher, 1913) 468p. (see no. 65)
[Thematic catalogue], 241-80.
Incipits for 24 caprices, 13 concertos, all sections of 3
variations, all movements of "deux quatuors ou sonates
brillantes" op. 24 & 28, 6 duos, 8 themes and variations.

ROESLER, JOHANN JOSEPH, 1771-1813

1093   WEINMANN, Alexander (Wien). **Johann Joseph Roesler**
*   A facsimile edition of Roesler's autograph thematic catalogue

and a complete modern inventory of his works is in preparation.

ROLLA, ALESSANDRO, 1757-1841

1094 SCIANNAMEO, Franco (Hartford, Conn.). **Catalogo tematico e descrit-**
* **tivo della opera di Alessandro Rolla** (To be published, Roma: Edizioni de Santis).
        Catalogo tematico, ca. 250p.
           Incipits for ca. 400 works arranged by genre.

ROMA, Biblioteca Apostolica Vaticana: Capella Sixtina: [I]

1095 HABERL, Franz Xaver. **Bibliographischer und thematischer Musikkatalog des Päpstlichen Kapellarchives zu Rom** (Leipzig: Breitkopf & Härtel, 1888) xi, 183p. (Beilage zu den *MfMG*, 19-20, 1887-88).
        Thematischer Katalog: die Themen der Choralbücher, auf die im ersten Teile hingewiesen ist, 76-79.
           22 incipits, old notation, modern clefs.
        Thematisches Verzeichnis in alphabetischer Anordnung der Autoren und Textanfänge, 80-174.
           Incipits, old notation, modern clefs, for works by composers of the Renaissance and later.

      --- Also issued separately as Volume II of HABERL's **Bausteine zur Musikgeschichte** (Leipzig: Breitkopf & Härtel, 1888).

ROMA, Biblioteca Apostolica Vaticana: Capella Sixtina [II]

1096 LLORENS, José Maria. **Capellae Sixtinae codices, musicis notis instructi sive manu scripti sive praelo excussi** (Città del Vaticano: Biblioteca Apostolica Vaticana, 1960) 555p.
        [Thematic catalogue], 474-98.
           A catalogue of all the musical holdings of the Sistine Chapel collection. An exhaustive description of 660 items. Incipits for anonymous polyphonic compositions: Masses, motets, Antiphons, psalms, and hymns. Catalogue supersedes Haberl's publication as one of the *Beilagen* to *Monatshefte für Musikgeschichte*.

ROMA, Biblioteca Apostolica Vaticana: Vat. Lat. 11953

1097 CASIMIRI, Raffaele. **Canzoni e mottetti dei sec. XV-XVI Codicetto Vat. Lat. 11953,** *Note d'Archivio per la Storia Musicale* XIV (1937) 145-60.
           Contains a thematic list of 48 works, mostly anonymous, but also including the names of Des Prez, Isaac, La Rue and Senfl. Van den Borren identifies a few of the anonymous works as by Brugier and La Rue, *Note d'Archivio* XVI (1939) [17]-18.

ROMA, Biblioteca Apostolica Vaticana: Cappella Giulia

1098 LLORENS, José Maria. **Le Opere musicali della Cappella Giulia. I: Manoscritti e Edizioni fino al'700,** *Studi e Testi* CCLXV (1971) xxiv, 412p., 7*l*.
           Contains 7*l*. with incipits for anonymous works. This cata-

logue was not available prior to publication. The Cappella
Giulia was a famous choir with à distinguished roster of
directors: Arcadelt, Ferrabosco, Animuccia, Palestrina,
Mozzocchi, Benevoli, Bernabei, A. Scarlatti, Guglielmi, and
Zingarelli; it continues to function today.

ROMA, Biblioteca Doria-Pamphilj

1099   HOLSCHNEIDER, Andreas. Die Musiksammlung der Fürsten Doria-Pamphilj
in Rom, *AMw* 18 (1961) [248]-264.
> 57 incipits for all movements of symphonies and chamber music
> by J. Chr. Bach and Johann Stamitz contained in this library.
> Also includes a list (without incipits) of madrigal collec-
> tions, sacred vocal works, and oratorios and operas of the
> 16th and 17th centuries.

1100 LIPPMANN, Friedrich. Die Sinfonien-Manuskripte der Bibliothek Doria-
Pamphilj in Rom, *AnalectaMusicol* 5, *Studien zur italienisch-deutschen
Musikgeschichte*, Bd. **V** (1968) 201-47.
> After a brief description of the collection, which contains
> 119 symphonies by 36 composers, there is a detailed thematic
> catalogue, p. 204-47, with incipits for all movements of this
> important MS source. Composers represented are: Aostino Ac-
> corimboni 1, Pasquale Anfossi 13, Antonio Aurisicchio 1, Maxim
> Sosonowitsch Beresowski 1, Marcello Bernardini 8, Ferdinando
> G. Bertoni 5, Giovanni B. Borghi 3, Giovanni Borgo 1, Antonio
> Boroni 2, Giovanni Cavi 1, Eligio Celestino 3, Francesco Sa-
> vero Cherzelli 3, Pietro Crispi 18, Gian Francesco De Majo 2,
> Bernardini Di Capua [Bernardini], Alessandro Felici 1, Carlo
> Franchi 1, Baldassare Galuppi 1, Giuseppe Gazzaniga 2, Andre
> Gretry 6, Pietro Guglielmi 8, Giacomo Insanguine 1, Niccolo
> Jomelli 2, Henri Moreau 1, Josef Myslivecek 1, Giovanni Paisi-
> ello 4, Nicolo Piccinni 8, Domenico Porta 1, Gaetano Pugnani,
> Giuseppe Radicchi 1, Antonio Sacchini 4, Pietro Sales 1,
> Giuseppe Sarti 2, Giovanni Schmid 2, Tommaso Traetta 2, Valen-
> tini 1, and Zannetti 1.

1101   LIPPMANN, Friedrich; FINSCHER, Ludwig. Die Streichquartett-Manus-
kripte der Bibliothek Doria-Pamphilj in Rom, *AnalectaMusicol* 7 ,
Studien zur italienisch-deutschen Musikgeschichte, Bd.VI(1969) 120-
144.
> Incipits for all movements of string quartets in this important
> MS source. Composers represented are: C.F. Abel 6, Michele
> Barbici 9, Boccherini 1 (lost), G. Demachi 6, Anton Kammel 9,
> Josef Myslivecek 6, G. Pugnani 5, Jan Vanhal 18.

1102   LIPPMANN, Friedrich; UNVERRICHT, Hubert. Die Streichtrio-Manuskripte
der Bibliothek Doria-Pamphilj in Rom, *AnalectaMusicol* 9, *Studien
zur italienisch-deutschen Musikgeschichte*, Bd.VII (1970) 299-335.
> Incipits for all movements of string trios in this important
> MS source. Composers represented are: Carlo Campioni 40,
> Josef Myslivecek 6, Giovanni Raimondi 4, Friedrich Schwindel
> 6, Mattia Stabinger 6, Francesco Zannetti 12.

ROMA, Biblioteca Vallicelliana: MS E. II. 55-60

1103   LOWINSKY, Edward E. A newly discovered sixteenth-century motet
manuscript at the Biblioteca Vallicelliana in Rome, *JAmerMusicol-
Soc* III (1950) 173-232.

Thematic catalogue of *unica* in Vall. S. Borr. E. II. 55-60, including works by Arcadelt, Corteccia, Festa, Jachet de Mantua, Lherithier, Lupus, Maistre Jan, Andreas de Silva, Verdelot, Willaert.

ROMAN, JOHAN HELMICH, 1694-1758

1104 VRETBLAD, Patrik. **Johan Helmich Roman, Svenska Musikens Fader [Johan Helmich Roman. The father of Swedish music.]** (Stockholm: Nordiska Bokhandeln, 1914) 2v.
Tematisk förteckning [Thematic catalogue], v. 2, 92p.
Incipits organized by genre.

1105 ☆ BENGTSSON, Ingmar. **J.H. Roman och hans instrumentalmusik, käll- och stilkritiska studier**, *Studia Musicologica Upsaliensa* IV (Uppsala: Almqvist & Wiksells, 1955) xxxi, 487, T1-T24p.
Tematisk Förteckning över J.H. Romans instrumentalverk [Thematic catalogue of J.H. Roman's instrumental works], T1-T24.
Works, including spurious compositions, arranged by genre.

1105a ▽ --- **[Thematic catalogue of vocal works]** (manuscript)
A complete catalogue of all vocal works ascribed to Roman is in the possession of Prof. Ingmar Bengtsson, Stockholm Sweden. Includes incipits.

ROSENMÜLLER, JOHANN, 1619-1684

1106 HAMEL, Fred. **Gestaltungs-und Stilprinzipien in der Vokalmusik Johann Rosenmüllers. Nebst einem vollständigen thematischen Verzeichnis seiner Werke** (unpublished paper, 1930)
In 1968, the late Dr. Hamel's thematic catalogue, originally appended to his unpublished paper, was in the possession of Martin Geck of the Bayerische Staatsbibliothek in Munich.

References: Fred HAMEL, **Die Psalmkompositionen Johann Rosenmüllers** (PhD diss: Giessen, 1930; Heitz, 1933) 126p.; Kerela J. SNYDER, **Johann Rosenmüller's music for solo voice** (PhD diss.: Yale, 1970).

ROSETTI, FRANCESCO ANTONIO [RÖSLER, FRANZ ANTON], ca.1746/50-1792

1107 KAUL, Oskar. **Ausgewählte Sinfonien**, *DTB* Jahrg. 21/1 (Leipzig: Breitkopf & Härtel, 1912)
Thematisches Verzeichnis der Instrumentalwerke von A. Rosetti, [lxi]-lxxxix.
Incipits for all movements of 60 symphonies, 27 ensemble works, 67 concerti, and 13 Klavierwerke.

1107a --- **Ausgewählte Werke, 2.Teil**, *DTB* Jahrg. 25 (Leipzig: Breitkopf & Härtel, 1925)
Nachtrag und Berichtigungen zum thematischen Verzeichnis der Instrumentalwerke A. Rosettis, [xvii]-xviii.
Supplements the above catalogue.

1107b ☆ --- Revised edition of 1107 and 1107a by Hans Schmidt (Wiesbaden,1968)

ROSSI, LUIGI, 1598-1653

1108 WOTQUENNE, Alfred. Étude bibliographique sur le compositeur napoli-
      tain L. Rossi (Brussels: Coosemans, 1909) xii,30,22p.
      [Catalogue thématique], 22p. at end.

1109 CAMETTI, Alberto. Alcuni documenti inedite su la vita de L. Rossi,
      SIMG XIV (1912-1913) 1-26.
          Composizioni di L. Rossi quali non sono elencate nell' Étude del
          Wotquenne, 18-20.
              Supplements Wotquenne catalogue. Partially thematic list.
              Works are arranged in order of number in the Chigiana Library
              where the manuscripts were found. (see no. 1108)

1110 GHISLANZONI, Alberto. Luigi Rossi (Aloysius de Rubeis). Biografia
      e Analise delle Composizioni (Milano; Roma: Bocca, 1954) 321p.
          Catalogo delle Canzoni, Arie e Cantate, 213-321.
              Multiple staff incipits for 388 works, arranged alphabetically
              by text.

1111 CALUORI, Eleanor.   Luigi Rossi [Thematic catalogue of cantatas]
      The Wellesley Edition Cantata Index Series, fasc. 3 (Wellesley:
      Wellesley College, 1965)
              Divided into 2 parts: 3a reliable attributions, 3b unreliable
              attributions. Contains 428 cantatas from more than 200
              manuscript collections arranged alphabetically by title.
              Original clefs and time signatures used. Concordances given
              for manuscripts and early prints. Appendix includes a list
              of sources and late and modern editions.

              Reviews: Claudio SARTORI, *Notes* XXIII/4 (1967) 734-37.

ROSSI, SALAMON, ca. 1570-1628

1112 NEWMAN, Joel; RIKKO, Fritz. A thematic index of Salamon Rossi's
  *   Works (Hackensack, N.J.: Joseph Boonin Inc., in press).
              Over 300 incipits in three categories: Jewish Service Music,
              Madrigals, and Instrumental Music (sinfonie, sonate, can-
              zone, dances).

ROSSINI, GIOACHINO, 1792-1868

1113 GOSSETT, Philip. (U. of Chicago) A Thematic catalogue of the works
  *   of Gioachino Rossini
              Will include operas, cantatas, instrumental music, songs,
              and péchés de viellesse, with a description of MS sources,
              modern editions of the music, and libretto editions.

ROVETTA, GIOVANNI, c. 1596-1668

1114 SELFRIDGE, Eleanor (Berkeley, Calif.). Thematic index of the
  *   works of Giovanni Rovetta
              Contains entries for all the published works and some of
              the MS works.

RÓZSAVÖLGYI (publisher)

1115 Rózsavölgyi és társa zene-és műkereskedésükben Pesten sajáti joggal megjelent zene-és műdarabok jegyzéke [The list of the music and artificial pieces which were published in the shop of Rozsavölgyi and his partner at Pest under their jurisdiction] (Pest: Druck Herz, 1859) 38p.
Verzeichnis

RUBANK, Inc. (publisher)

1116 Musica Rara guide (Miami, Fla., n.d.) 25p.
Incipits in full score for 134 instrumental solos, ensembles, and chamber music, ranging from the Renaissance to the present.

RUBIN, Emanuel L. (compiler)

1117 The English glee from William Hayes to William Horsley (PhD diss., Musicology: U. of Pittsburgh, 1968) 2v. Univ. Micro. 69-6423.
A check-list of published glees representing the period I760-I800, Appendix II, 62-868.
A computer-generated index "detailing individual compositions alphabetized according to their first line of text and numbered consecutively from one to approximately 2,600. Each is described and all of its known bibliographical locations is given. The music of the highest sounding voice of melodic interest is given with the text of the incipit underlayed for each of these pieces. This is accompanied by the name of the composer, arranger, poet, translator and by the title, sub-title, number and type of voices used, description of accompaniment and comments, all appearing as appropriate."

RUBSAMEN, Walter H. (compiler)

1118 Music research in Italian libraries. Third installment, *Notes* VIII/1 (Dec 1950) 70-99.
[Thematic index], 72-99.
Incipits of motets, masses, chansons, lamentations, and canons in an index of hitherto unknown or undescribed 15th and 16th century manuscripts and prints in the following libraries: Rome, Biblioteca Apostolica Vaticana (MSS Palatini Latini 1976-1979, 1980-1981, 1982); Modena, Biblioteca del Duomo (MSS IX, X); Padua, Biblioteca del Duomo (MS A 17, dated 1522); Florence, Biblioteca Marucelliana (print, Venice: Antiquis, 1520); Bologna, Biblioteca del Conservatorio Musicale "G.B. Martini" (R. 141-four prints). Composers included are: Acaen, Agricola, Balduin, Barbra, Brumel, Carpentras, Claudin, Compère, Deslonges, Dulot, Eustachius de Monte Regali, Festa, Fevin, Forestier, Gascongne, Gaspar, Hylaire, Isaac, Jachet, Josquin, LaFage, La Rue, Lebrune, Lhéritier, Lapus, T. Martini, Moulu, Mouton, Obrecht, Petit, Pipelaire, Prioris, Renaldo, Richafort, Silva, Verdelot, di Vitis, and Willaert.

RUDE, JOHANNES, 1555-1601

1119 LOBAUGH, H. Bruce. **Three German lute books** (PhD diss., Musicology:
U. of Rochester, 1968) 2v. Univ. Micro. 68-13,806 [see also 746   ]
Flores Musicae (1600), v. II, Appendix, 79-104.
"A thematic index or transcription in full of the fantasias,
entratas, and dance pieces (i.e. Nos. 77-136) found in Book
II only of Flores Musicae." A total of 60 pieces appear,
either in full (19) or in the thematic index (41). "The
variation to Galliardae Gregorij Huberti was not counted as
a separate piece." There is a total of 63 incipits (including 2 vocal tabulations, p.104-05). Works include 20 pavans,
paduanos, and padoanas, 15 galliards, etc..

RUDÉN, Jan Olof (Uppsala)

1120 **Lut- och gitarr-tabulaturer i svenska bibliotek och samlingar** [Lute
▽   and guitar tablatures in Swedish libraries and collections]
(Uppsala, 1967) (unpublished catalogue).
Includes incipits in Numericode of all movements in manuscript
sources from the 16th-18th centuries. A polyphonic transcription of the incipits is available.

RUGE, Filippo (compiler)

1121 **Catalogue de la collection symphonique établie par Filippo Ruge**
▽   **au Château de Seignelai.** Compiled ca. 1757 (manuscript). Currently
in the Frank DeBellis collection, San Francisco State College, 10p.
Incipits for works by Italian composers from the collection
brought to Paris by Ruge.   Genres includes symphonies,
overtures, instrumental works, and 1 cantata. Composers
represented are: anonymous 1, Abos 1, Auletto 2, Aurisichio
3, Ballabeno 1, Batirelli 1, Geo Gergo 1, Casali 1, Cluk
(Gluck) 1, Cocchi 2, Conforto 2, Crespi 6, Crisciaui 1,
Abb Deuossi 1, Enrichelli 3, Ferrandini 1, Frascia 3, Galuppi
10, Garzia 2, Guglelmi 1, Jomelli 5, Kohaut 1, Latillo 1,
Lustrini 6, Mattia Vento 1, Moro 1, N.N. 1, Pampani 3, Par-
zia 1, Perez 3, Pergolese 1, Piccini 2, Prata 1, Rendeux 2,
Rinaldo di Capua 8, Ruge 3, Ruge fils 1, Sala 1, Sarti 1,
Sciroli 8, Scolari 3, Traietta 3, Valentin 1.

1121a --- Barry S. BROOK, **La symphonie française dans la seconde moitié**
☐   **du XVIIIe siècle,** v. 1, 197-208. (see no. 185)
Discusses the compiler and the catalogue.

1122 --- LaRUE, Jan; COBIN, Marian W. **The Ruge-Seignelay catalogue, an**
☐   **exercise in automated entries,** *Elektronische Datenverarbeitung,*
Harald HECKMANN, ed. (Regensburg: Gustav Bosse, 1967) 41-46 (*RILM*
I/3 1376)
"Describes computer-aided preparation of thematic catalogues
for direct photo-offset reproduction. The *Ruge-Seignelay*
catalogue (a mid-18th century MS thematic list, mainly
orchestral works from the Italian repertory c.1750), once
owned by the Roman flutist, Filippo Ruge, serves as a model
and appears at the end of the article. Steps in preparing
the catalogue for photo-offset include: key-punching incipits
in the *Plaine and Easie* code (see no.188)on IBM data cards

and planning a display format for the data printout by an
IBM 407 Printer. Proofreading and correcting incipit cards
before the printout stage avoids further correction in galley
proof. The method thus described produces a catalogue containing all necessary scholarly information, in succinct
format, with minumum cost and maximum accuracy."

RUST, FRIEDRICH WILHELM, 1739-1796

1123 CZACH, Rudolf. **Friedrich Wilhelm Rust** (Essen: Kauerman, 1927) 156p.
        Thematisches Verzeichnis der Instrumentalkompositionen F.W.Rusts,
        p.3-18 at end.
                Incipits for all movements, with tempi, scoring, and dates. ,
                scoring, and dates given.

Rutini, Giovanni Marco, 1723-1797

        HIERONYMUS, Bess. **Rutini; the composer of pianoforte sonatas, to-
        gether with a thematic index of the sonatas** (MA thesis: Smith College,
        1948) 131p. (typescript)

RYBA, JAKUB JAN, 1765-1815

1124 NEMECEK, Jan. **Jakub Jan Ryba. Život a dílo.** [Jakub Jan Ryba, life
        and works] (Praha: Státní Hudební Vydavatelství, 1963) 356p.
        Tematický katalog Rybových skladeb [Thematic catalogue of Ryba's
        works], 261-356.
                559 incipits of sacred and secular vocal music and instru-
                mental works, arranged by genre. Gives bibliographical in-
                formation, voice and instrument entrances, text underlay.

SAINT-SAËNS, CAMILLE, 1835-1921

1125 **Catalogue général et thématique des oeuvres de C. Saint-Saëns**
        (Paris: Durand, 1897) 119p.
                Publisher's catalogue with prices. Multiple staff incipits
                arranged by genre, with text underlay for vocal works. Motifs
                are given for operatic items. Also provides dates of composi-
                tion and publication. Systematic index in appendix.

1125a --- Nouvelle édition (1908) 146p.

1125b --- [Supplément]
▽
                A MS supplement to the printed catalogue has been maintained
                by the firm of Durand in Paris.

1126 RATNER, Sabina (U. of Michigan). **The piano works of Camille Saint-**
 *   **Saëns.**
                Incipits for solo, duets, two-piano, and piano and orchestra
                works.

Key: * in preparation; ▽ manuscript; □ literature; ✫ Library of Congress

SALIERI, ANTONIO, 1750-1825

1127 NÜTZLADER, Rudolf. Salieri als Kirchenmusiker (PhD diss.: Wien, 1924)
▽   235*l*. (typescript)
        Thematisches Verzeichnis der Kirchenwerke, 111-35.
            80 single and double staff incipits for Masses, Offertories,
            settings of the Proper, Psalms, and Hymns.

1127a --- *Studien zur Musikwissenschaft*, Beihefte der *DTÖ* 14 (1927) 160-78,
☐   Anhang ix-x.
            Summary of the text without incipits.

1128 BOLLERT, Werner. **Antonio Salieri und die italienische Oper.** Eine
        Studie zur Geschichte der italienischen Oper im 18. Jahrhundert,
        Aufsätze zur Musikgeschichte (Bottrop: Postberg, [1938]) 43-93,
        115-28.
            Notenanhang, 115-28.
                Ca. 100 incipits of pieces (overture, arias, duetts, finales,
                etc.) from operas by Salieri.

SALZBURG, Austria. Dom-Musikarchiv

1129 Catalogus Mu=/ sicalis in ecclesia/ metropolitana./ (added ca. 1783:
▽   "Gatti") (manuscript)

1130 Catalogus/ Musicalis in Ecclesia/ Metropolitana:/ Archivium. Inside
▽   cover bears notation "anno./ 1791." (manuscript)

1131 Musicalis in Eccle=/ Sia Metropolitana/ conscriptus I3 Julÿ anno/
▽   MDCCCXXII/ ab Joachimo Fuetsch ppia Chori dirigente/ D.C.(manuscript).
            The 3 above manuscripts contain incipits for sacred vocal
            works only. Important listings for the following composers:
            Carl Biber, Andreas Hofer, Biechteler, Adlgasser, Eberlin,
            Gatti, Michael Haydn, Wolfgang and Leopold Mozart, Stadlmayer.

SALZBURG, Austria. St. Peter (Erzstift oder Benediktiner-Erzabtei), Musikarchiv

1132 Catalogus/ Rerum/ Musicalium/ pro choro figurato/ Ecclesiae/ S.
▽   Petrensis./ I822./ Tomus I^mus/ zusammen geschrieben von/ P. Martin
     Bischofreiter (added later: ', + 27/8. I845.8/ O.S.B.) (manuscript)
            Between 1819-1822, Martin Bischofreiter (1762-1845) compiled
            a thematic catalogue of the MS and printed sources (many of
            which are extant) of this cathedral. Incipits for sacred
            vocal works, with a few instrumental compositions. Includes
            works of many composers, mostly by the following Salzburg
            composers: Adlgasser, Eberlin, Gatti, Michael Haydn, Leopold
            and Wolfgang Mozart. Provides scoring specifications and
            dates of composition and/or acquistion.

            Reference: Manfred H. SCHMID, **Die Musikaliensammlung der
            Erzabtei St. Peter in Salzburg. Katalog.** Erster Teil. Leo-
            pold und Wolfgang Amadeus Mozart. Joseph und Michael Haydn.
            (Salzburg 1970) 15-16.

SAMMARTINI, GIOVANNI BATTISTA, 1700/01-1775

1133   SAINT-FOIX, Georges. **La chronologie de l'oeuvre instrumentale de Jean Baptiste Sammartini,** *Sammelbände der internationalen Musik-gesellschaft* XV (1913-1914) 308-324.

> Includes incipits of symphonies found in early English and French editions.

1134   TORREFRANCA, Fausto. **Le Origini della Sinfonia,** *RMI* XXII (1915) 431-46.
Elenco delle Sinfonie Sanmartiniane contenute nel Catalogo Breitkopf, 443-46.

> Incipits for 21 symphonies with MS sources and printed editions when available.

1135   CHURGIN, Bathia D. **The symphonies of G.B. Sammartini** (PhD diss.:
▽   Harvard U., 1963) 2v.(typescript)
A thematic catalogue of the symphonies of G.B. Sammartini, v. 2, 97p.

> The arrangement is according to key. The letter A before the number of a symphony is an indication to refer to Appendix A (which contains lost symphonies). Letter B before the number of a symphony refers to Appendix B (which contains doubtful and spurious works). Includes probable correct ascriptions.

1136   JENKINS, Newell; CHURGIN, Bathia. **Thematic catalogue of the works**
*   **of Giovanni Battista Sammartini (1700/01-1775).** Vol. I, Orchestral and vocal music (Cambridge: Harvard U.P., in press); Vol. II, Chamber music and solo sonatas, in progress. (Published under the auspices of the American Musicological Society).

> Incipits for all movements of 285 works. The extant authentic works are divided as follows: Orchestral works: symphonies (nos. 1-71), concertos (nos. 72-85), concertinos (nos. 86-92), marches and minuets (nos. 93-94). Secular vocal works: operas (nos. 95-97), other secular vocal works (nos. 98-106). Sacred vocal works: Masses (nos. 107-109), Mass sections (nos. 110-14), other sacred vocal works (nos. 115-30), oratorio (no. 131), cantatas (nos. 132-39). Appendix A lists 6 concerto arrangements; Appendix B, 11 contrafacta; Appendix C, 46 lost works; and Appendix D, 83 doubtful and spurious works. Appendix E presents a general chronology of the symphonies. Provides full scholarly apparatus; indexes.

SANDERS, Robert L. (Brooklyn College of C.U.N.Y.)

1137   **Dictionary of hymn-tunes**
*
> Works contained are derived from English-language hymnals published in the United States between the years 1901-1941 inclusive. The compiler is concerned only with what is clearly intended for congregational use, and of this only tunes set to metric hymns. The principal lexicon is not thematic, but is arranged by tune names in alphabetical order. There is, however, an adjunct finder-tool which is a type of thematic index based on the tonal profile of the melody. This skeleton profile includes 6 to 8 notes representing in turn the first, highest, lowest, and last notes

of each of the first two lines. A numerical code of 4 digits
is used to classify the tunes within the index's four auton-
omous sections: authentic major and minor, and plagal major
and minor. The ultimate objective of this compilation begun
in 1933 or 34 is to arrive at the musical parallel of John
JULIAN's Dictionary of Hymnology. Thus far, there are
approximately 6500 entries.

SANDERS, Robert L.

1138   Further thoughts on tune indexing, *The Hymn* II/2 (1951) 19-22.
□   Offers an alternate solution to Ellinwood's *(q.v.)* and supplies
             copious examples. Brief sketch of Sanders' proposed Dictionary
             to contain origins, variants, and resembances among tunes;
             to be indexed by tune names.

SANDVOLD, ARILD

1139   HERRESTHAL, Harald. Arild Sandvold og orglet [Arild Sandvold and
▽   the organ] (MA diss.: U. of Oslo, 1967) 75p. (typescript).
           [Thematic catalogue].
               "The author gives an analysis of each organ work and a complete
               list of Sandvold's works." (*RILM* 67/919^{dm})

SAN FRANCISCO, San Francisco State College: de Bellis Collection

1140   REESE, Gustave. An early seventeenth-century Italian lute manuscript
       at San Francisco, *Essays in musicology in honor of Dragon Plamenac
       on his 70th birthday,* ed. by Gustave REESE and Robert J. SNOW (Pitts-
       burgh: U. of Pittsburgh Press, 1969) 253-80.
           Thematic index, 258-72.
               Double staff incipits for 80 works in the MS presently located
               in the de Bellis Collection at San Francisco State College.

SARASATE, PABLO MARTÍN MELITÓN Y NAVASCUES, 1844-1908

1141   BACHMANN, Alberto. Les grands violonistes du passé (Paris: Fisch-
       bacher, 1913) 468p. (see no. 65)
           [Thematic catalogue], 283-88.
               List of works includes incipits for Op. 20-30, 32, 34-39,
               42-47.

SARTORI, Claudio (compiler)

1142   Il quarto codice di Gaffurio non è del tutto scomparso, *Collectanea
       Historiae Musicae* I (Firenze: L. Olschki, 1953) 25-44.
           [Thematic index], Liber Capelle Ecclesie Maioris Milani, 34-43.
               Incipits in original clefs and notation, tenor or bassus
               only, of 69 sacred works: Masses, motets, and magnificats.

SATIE, ERIK, 1866-1925

1143   GRABIE, Monica (Queens College of C.U.N.Y.) Thematic catalogue of
*   the works of Erik Satie

SAUZAY, Eugène   (compiler)

1144 Haydn, Mozart, Beethoven; étude sur le quatuor   (Paris: l'Auteur,
      1861) 173p.
         [Thematic catalogue]
              Incipits for chamber works for 4 instruments without piano.

1144a --- 2nd edition. (Paris: Librairie de Fermin-Didot, 1884)

1145 L'école de l'accompagnement   (Paris: Didot, 1869) 284p.
              Sequel to the above volume, containing a limited number of
              incipits for chamber works, concertos, and 4-hand music of
              Haydn, Mozart, and Beethoven (with piano).

SAVIONI, MARIO, c. 1608-1685

1146 EISLEY, Irving. The secular cantatas of Mario Savioni (1608-1685)
  ▽   (PhD diss.: U. of Calif. at L.A., 1964) 2v.(typescript)
         Thematic catalogue, v. I, 230-324.
              Incipits for the secular cantatas.

1146a --- Mario Savioni [Thematic catalogue of cantatas], *The Wellesley
      Edition Cantata Index Series*, fasc. 2 (Wellesley: Wellesley College,
      1964)
              Texted incipits, arranged alphabetically, with original
              clefs and time signatures. No index of sources.
              Reviews: Claudio SARTORI, *Notes* XXIII/4 (1967) 734-37.

SAYGUN, A. A.

1147 The classification of pre-modal melodies, *The Folklore and Folk Music
  ☐   Archivist* VII/1 (1964) 15-28.

SCALABRINI, PAOLO, 1713-1806

1148 MÜLLER, [von Asow], Erich H. Die Mingottischen Opernunternehmungen
      1736-1756 (PhD diss.: Leipzig; Dresden: Hille, 1915) xiv, 123,
      ccxiiip. (see next entry)
         Thematisches Verzeichnis der Werke von Paolo Scalabrini, ccv-ccxi.
              Single and double staff incipits for all movements of 7
              symphonies and 9 arias and duets.

1149 MÜLLER [von Asow], Erich H. Angelo und Pietro Mingotti; ein Beitrag
      zur Geschichte der Oper im XVIII.Jahrhundert (Dresden: Bertling,
      1917) xvii, 141, cccxp. (see also no. 381)
         Thematisches Verzeichnis der Werke von Paolo Scalabrini, Anhang
         VI, part 2, ccxxiii-ccxxxii.
              31 incipits for all movements of arias and symphonies.

SCARLATTI, ALESSANDRO, 1660-1725

1150 DENT, Edward J. A. Scarlatti: his life and works (London: Arnold,
      1905) x, 236p.
         [Thematic catalogue], 206-32.
              Incipits for the ten masses only (p. 227-29). Works arranged
              by genre, chronologically. Lists sources of the MSS.

--- New impression with preface and additional notes by Frank WALKER
(London: Arnold, 1960) xii, 252p.

1151 LORENZ, Alfred. **Alessandro Scarlatti's Jugendoper,** Ein Beitrag zur
Geschichte der italienischen Oper (Augsburg: Dr. Benno Filser-Verlag
G.M.B.H., 1927) 2v.: viii, 240; vi, 208p.
    [Thematic catalogue], v. 2.
            400 incipits arranged in chronological order. Each entry,
            whether solo, duet, trio, etc., has a segment of every voice
            part represented, as well as a bass line. Orchestral solos
            are included.

1152 HANLEY, Edwin H. **Alessandro Scarlatti's cantate da camera: a bib-**
▽   **liographical study** (PhD diss., History of Music; Yale U., 1963)
546p.(typescript)
            Analytical thematic catalogue of Scarlatti's cantatas.

SCARLATTI, DOMENICO, 1685-1757

1153 LONGO, Alessandro. **Tavola tematica/ Table thématique** (Milano,1906?)
            Thematic indices from Longo's editions. 545 incipits.

1154 GERSTENBERG, Walter. **Die Klavierkompositionen D. Scarlattis** (PhD
diss.: Regensburg, Schiele, 1931; Regensburg: Bosse [1933]) 158p.
    Thematischer Katalog, [151]-158.
            Includes works not in Longo. One is by Alessandro Scarlatti.
            Reference: Manfred BUKOFZER, **Music in the Baroque era** (New
            York: Norton, 1947) p. 239n, doubts completeness of Longo,
            calls Gerstenberg's No. 8b spurious.

1155 LONGO, Alessandro. **Indice tematico (in ordine di tonalità e di rit-**
mo) delle sonate per clavicembalo...(Milano: Ricordi, 1937) 7, 36p.
            Sonatas arranged by key. Reprint, 1952; German edition 1937.

1156 DICKINSON, George Sherman. **Thematic index of sonatas** (Vassar College,
1950?) card files.
            Incipits of over 500 sonatas (Longo edition), arranged by key,
            pitch, octave and duration. 2 copies at Vassar College.

1157 KIRKPATRICK, Ralph. **Domenico Scarlatti** (Princeton U. Press, 1953)
✡   473p.; (6th corrected printing, 1970) 482p.
    Catalogue of Scarlatti Sonatas, 442-59. Also published in v. 18
    of Ralph Kirkpatrick, ed., **Complete keyboard works in facsimile...**
    (New York: Johnson, 1972) [xi]p.
            Non-thematic, chronological listing of sonatas in pairings es-
            tablished by Kirkpatrick. Supercedes Longo in LC uniform titles.

1157.1 DEARLING, Robert J. (Dunstable, Bedfordshire). **[Thematic catalogue]**
▽   Index cards. (manuscript). Prepared in 1970.
            Cross-indexed catalogue of sonatas (Longo-Kirkpatrick).

1158 SHEVELOFF, Joel. **The keyboard music of Domenico Scarlatti: A re-eval-**
☐   **uation of the state of knowledge in the light of the sources** (PhD
diss.: Brandeis U., 1970) 3v. Univ. Micro. 70-24,658 (typescript).
            Non-thematic (except for the sonatas by ALBERO, see no. 9).
            Lists all 18th and 19th c. sources of authentic works, also
            of continuo-accompanied and doubtful compositions. Lists Kirk-
            patrick numbers in relation to categories established by Rita
            BENTON and by Kathleen DALE.

SCHAAL, Richard

1159 Quellen zur Musiksammlung Aloys Fuchs, *Mf* XVI (1963) 67-72.
☐   In an appendix entitled **Anhang: Manuskripte von Aloys Fuchs,**
    p. 71-72, Schaal provides a list of the manuscript thematic
    catalogues prepared by the indefatigable Aloys Fuchs. The
    indexes are of works by 21 composers which are in the col-
    lection of the Deutsche Staatsbibliothek in Berlin. Provides
    catalogue manuscript number, pagination, and date. Compos-
    ers include: J.G. Albrechtsberger, L.van Beethoven, A. Cal-
    dara, A. Corelli, G. Frescobaldi, J.J. Froberger, J.J. Fux,
    Chr. W. von Gluck, G.Fr. Händel, J. Haydn, M. Haydn, J.K.
    Kerll, J. Kuhnau, B. Marcello, W.A. Mozart, Gottlieb Muffat,
    Georg Muffat, J.B. Peyer (Beyer), L. Spohr, G. Tartini, and
    A. Vivaldi. Each of these catalogues is inventoried under
    the composer's name in this bibliography.

SCHEIN, JOHANN HERMANN, 1586-1630

1160 TARAKAN, Sheldon. **Alphabetical index with incipits [of the] complete**
▽   **works of Johann Hermann Schein,** ed., Arthur PRÜFER, 18p. Copies in
    US NYcg and US NYqc.(typescript)
       Works arranged by collection; dates and number of parts given.
       Musical incipits in the "Simplified Plaine and Easie Code",
       for instrumental works only. Vocal works arranged alphabet-
       ically by first line.

SCHENK, ÄGIDIUS

1161 BENCZIK, Edeltraud (Graz). **Ägidius Schenk. Leben und Werk** (PhD diss.
*   in progress) ca. 270*l*.

SCHEURLEER, Daniel

1162 **Preisfrage: Welches ist die beste Methode, um Volks- und volksmässige**
☐   **Lieder nach ihrer melodischen (nicht textlichen) Beschaffenheit lexi-**
   kalisch zu ordnen?, *ZIMG* I (1899) 219-20.
       A famous historic challenge to find the best method to classi-
       fy folk song materials (the prize was the complete works of
       Sweelinck). Earliest responses by Koller (see no.676) and
       Krohn (no.698) unleashed an as yet unresolved debate (see 354)

SCHIEGL, Hermann; SCHWARZMAIER, Ernst   (compilers)

1163 **Themensammlung musikalischer Meisterwerke.** Heft 1: Symphonische
    Musik der Klassik; Heft 2: Symphonische Musik der Romantik (Frank-
    furt am Main: M. Diesterweg, [1959]) Heft 2: 1964; 96, 12p.; 97p.
       Volume 1 covers some of the opera overtures and symphonies
       of Gluck, Haydn, Mozart, and Beethoven. A substantial amount
       of each movement with instrumental entries is given. Volume
       2 follows the same format and includes works of Schubert,
       Weber, Schumann, Brahms, Bruckner, Dvořák, Tschaikowsky, and
       Wagner. A numeric system shows all reprises.

       Reviews: Franz BLASL, *Musikerziehung* XIX/2 (1965) 95.
1163a--- 1967: 4. Auflage von Heft I: 2. Auflage von Heft 2.

SCHILDBACH, Martin (compiler)

1163.!Das einstimmige Agnus Dei und seine handschriftliche Überlieferung
    vom 10. bis zum 16. Jahrhundert (PhD diss.: Erlangen; Erlangen:
    Hogl, 1967) 208p. (*RILM* [68] 2928)
        [Thematic catalogue].
            "The thematic catalogue forms the main body of the work. It
            contains the incipits of 270 Agnus melodies, organized accord-
            ing to initial tones, with remarks on construction, final
            tones, ambitus, permanence of tradition, tropes, etc. The
            catalogue also includes a list of sources(486 MSS) organized
            according to country. The text comments on the liturgical
            conditions, the state of the sources, melodic forms, poly-
            phony, and Agnus tropes. Indices of sources, places of ori-
            gin of the MSS, and tropes are included."

SCHLAGER, Karl-Heinz (compiler)

1164 Thematischer Katalog der ältesten Alleluia-Melodien aus Handschriften
    des IO. und 11. Jahrhunderts, ausgenommen das ambrosianische, alt-
    römische und alt-spanische Repertoire, *Erlanger Arbeiten zur Musik-
    wissenschaft,* hrsg. v. Martin RUHNKE, Bd. 2 (München: Walter Ricke,
    1965) 270p.
            410 melodies. Entire melodies are arranged according to mode
            and, under mode, according to the starting note. The chants
            to which the alleluias belong are listed in alphabetical or-
            der and refer to the accompanying alleluia by number. Also
            note that the melodies are listed according to cities (entire
            alleluia chants are listed from these areas).

SCHLECHT, Raymund (compiler)

1165 Musik Geschichte der Stadt Eichstaett (Eichstätt, Erzbischöfliches
▽   Ordinariat; Copy in D Mbs) Bd. 1-4. Compiled 1883 (manuscript)
        Thematisches Verzeichniss der Compositionen Eichstaetter Musiker
        mit Angabe der Bibliotheken, wo sie sich befinden, Bd. 1, 21*l.*
            Over 300 incipits of sacred and secular works by the following
            composers: A. Bachschmid, J. Baumgärtner, A. Deichel, J.G.
            Fils, H. Knoeferle, H. Mango, R.I. Mayr, J. Meck, Ph. N. Meck,
            A. Rehm, J.N. Rehm, A. Schermer, L. Schermer, W. Schermer,
            J.P. Schiffelholz, G. Schinn, F. Schlecht, G. Steger, F. Sutor,
            M. Zeheter, J. Zink, M. Winkler. (see also nos. 348, 349)

SCHMIDT, FRANZ, 1874-1939

1166 SCHOLZ, Rudolf. Strukturelle und kompositionstechnische Untersuchungen
▽   an ausgewählten Orgelwerken von Franz Schmidt. Ein Beitrag zur
    Erkenntnis seines Personalstils (PhD diss.: Wien, 1962) 424*l.* (type-
    script)
        Thematischer Katalog sämtlicher Orgelwerke von Franz Schmidt,
        401-17.
            31 multiple staff incipits for all movements of fugues,
            toccatas, preludes, and choral music.

SCHMIEDER, Wolfgang

1167 Menschliches- Allzumerschliches oder einige unparteiische Gedanken
☐   über thematische Verzeichnisse, *Otto Erich Deutsch, Festschrift....*

zum 80.Geburstag, W. GERSTENBERG, ed. (Kassel, 1963) 309-18.
Discussion of great staples of thematic indexing (Kinsky, Jähns, etc.), brief history of thematic catalogues, and mention of their purpose.

SCHMITT, Eduard (compiler)

1168 Die Kurpfälzische Kirchenmusik im I8. Jahrhundert (PhD diss.: Heidel-
▽   berg, 1958) 414p. (typescript)
Incipits for church music and some instrumental works for the following composers: Carl Grua (p. 145-49), Johann Stamitz (166-73), Franz Xaver Richter (235-51), Ignaz Holzbauer (308-27), Anton Filtz (335-43), Johannes Ritschel (359-68), Joseph Rudolf Bodé (390-92), Joseph Wreeden (395-97), Johann Jakob Heckel (p. 401).

SCHMITT, JOSEPH, 1734-1791

1169 DUNNING, Albert. Joseph Schmitt, Leben und Kompositionen des Eber-
bacher Zisterziensers und Amsterdamer Musikverlegers (I734-I79I)
(Amsterdam: Heuwekemeyer, 1962) 135p.
Thematisches Werkverzeichnis; Anhang des Thematischen Werkver-
zeichnisses (Verzeichnis der zweifelhaften und unterschobenen Werke), 64-121; 122-25.
Catalogue and supplement arranged by genre.

SCHNEIDER, FRIEDRICH, 1786-1853

1170 KEMPE, Friedrich. Friedrich Schneider: ein Lebensbild (Berlin: Janke, 1864) 450p.
Chronologisches Compositionen-Verzeichniss (Schneider's eigen-
händiges thematisches Tagebuch in 5 Heften), [387]-450.
Partially thematic. Includes Schneider's own thematic diary.

SCHNERICH, Alfred (compiler)

1171 Messe und Requiem seit Haydn und Mozart (Wien, Leipzig: Stern,1909)

1172 Der Messen-Typus von Haydn bis Schubert (Wien: Im Selbstverlage des Verfassers, 1892) 23p. Offprint from St. Leopoldsblatt Nos. 1 & 2.
Thematic catalogues in these two volumes index the Masses and Requiems of Beethoven, Bruckner, J. Haydn, M. Haydn, Hummel, Liszt, Mozart, and Schubert. The Masses have the date of composition (if known), the voices, orchestration, and the incipits of the Kyrie.

SCHOBERT, JOHANN, ca. 1740-1767

1173 RIEMANN, Hugo. Ausgewählte Werke, *DDT* 39 (Leipzig: Breitkopf & Härtel, 1909) xxii, 177p.
Thematischer Katalog, [xxi]-xxii.
Incipits for 70 works arranged by opus number, 12 without opus number. Sources of manuscripts given.
1173a --- Neuauflage hrsg. und kritisch revidiert von Hans Joachim MOSER,
DDT 39/1 (Wiesbaden: Breitkopf & Härtel, 1958) xxvi, 177p.

1174 TURRENTINE, Herbert C. Johann Schobert and French clavier music from
      1700 to the revolution (PhD diss.: State U. of Iowa, 1962) 2v.
      Univ. Micro. 63-981.(typescript)
            Thematic catalogue, v. 1, Appendix A.
            Incipits of the clavier works.

SCHOECK, OTHMAR, 1886-1957

1175 VOGEL, Werner. Thematisches Verzeichnis der Werke von Othmar Schoeck
      (Zürich: Atlantis, 1956) 297p.
            Multiple staff incipits, fully annotated, arranged by opus
            number. 46 additional works without opus number are included.
            Works include vocal and instrumental, poetry by author, lieder
            and choral works. Discography given.

            Reviews: Hans EHINGER, *NeueZM* CXVIII (May 1957) 303.

SCHOENBAUM, Camillo (København)

1176 Collection C. Schoenbaum. Compiled 1946-1968 (manuscript)
 ▽   Ca. 200 double staff incipits for all movements of mostly
            Czech compositions from the 16th-19th c. in MSS (new copies
            and scores by compiler). Composers include: J. Angermayer (1),
            L.v. Beethoven ?(1), Fr. Benda (20), Fr.L. Benda (1), Joh.
            Benda (1), G. Benda (recte: Sarti, 1), G. Benda (2), J.J.
            Božan (1), J.G.FR. Braun (3), Fr.X. Brixi (5), Czarth (2),
            J.L.V. Dukát (2), Fr.X. Dušek (2), J.L. Dussek (1), F.A.
            Ernst (1), J. Fiala (3), A. Fils (6), G. Finger (16), J.J.
            Fux (3), Pietro Fux (1), Harant de Polschitz (2), J. Haydn
            (2 mss.), P. Gunther Jakob (2), V. Jírovec (1), V. Kopřiva-
            Urtica (1), J.A. Kozeluh (1), Leop. Kozeluh (5), K. Chr.
            Kriedel (1), Fr. Krommer (1), Krumlovský (1), J.B. Krumpholtz
            (1), A. Laube (1), J.J. Linek (10), Fr. A. Míča (3), Fr. V.
            Míča (5), J. Myslivecek (16), Fr. Navrátil (1), J.B. Neruda
            (1), V. Pichl (8), J.E. Planický (1), Pokorný (1), J.Rejcha
            (1), F.X. Richter (4), J.J. Ryba (4), Schaffard (1), Chr.
            Simpson (4), J.N. Skroup (1), Spourni (3), V.J. Stamic (10),
            J.B. Vanhal (12), C. Vaňura (1), P.J. Vejvanovský (4), V.
            Vodička (7), J.I.Fr. Vojta (1), J.D. Zelenka.

1177   Bohemica [Thematic catalogue of various works by Bohemian composers
 ▽   in Czech libraries] Compiled 1950-1960. (manuscript)
             300 single and double staff incipits, mostly all movements,
             for instrumental and vocal works by the following composers:
             G. Benda, F. Benda, Joh. Benda, G. Czart, J.L. Kussek, J. Fi-
             ala, A. Fils, Fl. L. Gassmann, D. Hatasch, A. Kammel, Fr.
             Krommer, V. Mašek, J. Myslivecek, J.B. Neruda, Niemeczek, W.
             Pichl, F.X. Richter, A. Rosetti, V. Stich, J.B. Vanhal, P.
             Wranitzky, J. Zach, J.D. Zelenka.

SCHUBERT, FRANZ PETER, 1797-1828

1178 Thematisches Verzeichnis der im Druck erschienenen Compositionen von
      Franz Schubert (Wien: Diabelli, [1852]). 49p.
            Arranged by publisher's opus number. Publisher's prices
            (as of 1852) listed.

1179 NOTTEBOHM, Gustav. Thematisches Verzeichnis der im Druck erschienenen
      Werke von F. Schubert (Wien: Schreiber, 1874) 280p.
            Partially thematic, arranged by publisher's opus numbers.
            Lists out-of-print dance collections (as of 1874), series
            and provides various bibliographies and indexes.

1180 --- FRIEDLAENDER, Max. Beiträge zur Biographie Franz Schubert's.
  □   (PhD diss.: Berlin, Haack [1889]) 56p.
            Ergänzungen und Berichtigungen zu dem Thematischen Verzeich-
            niss der im Druck erschienenen Werke von F. Schubert, hrsg.
            von G. Nottebohm. Wien 1874, 52-56.
            Contains no incipits.

SCHUBERT, FRANZ PETER, 1797-1828

1181 DEUTSCH, Otto Erich; WAKELING, Donald R. Schubert: Thematic catalogue
  ✡   of all his works in chronological order (London: Dent; New York:
      Norton, 1951) xxiv, 566p.
            965 dated compositions; undated works (Nos. 966-92); addenda
            (Nos. 993-98). Accompanied with a full compliment of appen-
            dices and indices. This will remain the standard catalogue
            until the publication of Neue Schubert-Ausgabe's fully re-
            vised edition.

            Reviews: Maurice J.E. BROWN, *MTimes* XCII (June 1951) 264;
            Richard CAPELL, *MLetters* XXXII (July 1951) 267-68; Alfred
            EINSTEIN, *Notes* VIII (Sept 1951) 692-93; Richard G. APPEL,
            MQ XXXVIII/1 (Jan 1952) 157-59; Hans REDLICH, *Mf* VI/1 (1953)
            73-75; Helen Joy SLEEPER, *JAMS* VI (Fall 1953) 247-49.

1181a --- Corrections and additions by Otto E. DEUTSCH, *MLetters* XXXIV
      91953) 25-32.

1181b --- Reprint. Kalmus edition (1970?).

1181c --- Interim edition, with Deutsch's additions (Tübingen: Walther Dürr)

1181d --- Completely new edition is projected under the auspices of Inter-
      national Schubert-Gesellschaft as part of the Neue Ausgabe sämtlicher
      Werke, approximately 1980.

SCHUBERT, JOSEPH, 1757-1837

1182 Missae Composta per Josephum Schubert (D D1) ca. 1840 (manuscript)
  ▽   Incipits for the Kyrie only, in double staff notation, for
            13 Masses. The notation is most likely in the hand of the
            composer or his brother Franz Schubert of Dresden.

SCHULHOFF, JULIUS, 1825-1898

1183 Thematisches Verzeichnis sämmtlicher Compositionen für das Piano-
      forte von J. Schulhoff (n.p., n.d.)
            Cited in the catalogue of St. Peterskirche, Vienna, 1908,
            p. 73.

SCHUMANN, ROBERT, 1810-1856

1184 Thematisches Verzeichniss sämmtlicher im Druck erschienenen Werke
Robert Schumann's (Leipzig: Schuberth, n.d.) 20, 110p.
> Incipits in piano score of works arranged by opus number
> (nos. 1-148), followed by works without opus number. Pre-
> ceded by 4 indices: systematic by genre, piano works by
> name, songs by title, songs by first line.

1184a --- 2.Aufl. 1860.

1184b --- 3.verb. u. verm. Aufl. 1863.

1184c --- 4.verb. u. verm. Aufl. 1868.

1184d --- Reprint by Stephen Austin and Sons (London: H. Baron, 1966)
112, 22p.

SCHÜRER, JOHANN GEORG, 1720-1786

1185 Catalogo della Musica di Chiesa composta da Giovanni Georgio Schürer.
▽   Armaro IV(D Dl) 78p. Compiled ca. 1765. Copy in US NYcg (manuscript)
> Incipits for Masses and motets. Most are dated and range
> from ca.1750 to ca.1765.

1186 Catalogus derer Schürerischen Kirchen Musicalien; [Alternate title]
▽   Catalogo della Musica di Chiesa (D Bds: HB VII, Kat. ms. 782) [ii],
163, 22p. (manuscript) Microfilm copy in US NYcg.
> Written in part by Schürer. Incipits for 40 Masses, 3 Requiem
> Masses, and 308 other sacred works, among them 140 psalms.
> Gives incipits for subdivisions of large-scale works, and in-
> cludes performance dates. Arranged by genre.

SCHÜRER, Johann Georg, et al. (compiler)

1187 Catalogo thematico della Musica di Chiesa catholica in Dresda com-
▽   posta Da diversi Autori secondo l'alfabetto, 1765 (D Bds: HB VII,
Kat. ms. 186) In three parts: 53, 55, 52p. (manuscript) Microfilm copy in US NYcg.
> Incipits for vocal and instrumental works by a wide selec-
> tion of composers ranging from Renaissance to the early Clas-
> sical period. Fairly large representation for Galuppi, Has-
> se, Ristori, and Zelenka. Incipits for a group of anonymous
> works are appended.

SCHUSTER, JOSEPH, 1748-1812

1188 Catalogus deren Kirchen Musicalien des Herrn Capell Meister Joseph
▽   Schuster. Armaro III (D Dl) 26p. Compiled ca.1812. Copy in US NYcg
(manuscript)
> Incipits for 19 Masses, motets psalms, etc. Page 3 gives
> the contents and includes 28 pages when in fact there are
> only 26. The catalogue has a handwritten notation on the
> cover indicating a review or revision by Franz Schubert (of
> Dresden) in 1823.

SCHÜTZ, HEINRICH, 1585-1672

1189 BITTINGER, Werner. Heinrich Schütz-Werke-Verzeichnis (SWV), kleine

Ausgabe. Im Auftrage der Neuen Schütz-Gesellschaft (Kassel: Bärenreiter, 1960) xxx**i**, 191p.
>Not a thematic catalogue, but a finding list to be used with
>the new Schütz collected edition. It is a preliminary version
>of a full-scale thematic Werke Verzeichnis which will appear
>after the completion of the Neuen Schütz-Gesellschaft Ausgabe.
>It summarizes the state of the Schütz sources research. (see
>next entry)

1190 **Heinrich-Schütz-Werke-Verzeichnis**
*   A thematic catalogue to be published after the completion of
         the new Schütz collected edition.

1191 PATRICK, Robert L. **A computer-based thematic index to the works of**
▽   **Heinrich Schütz** (PhD diss.: U. of Kentucky, 1971) vi,355p. (manu-
     script)
>Employs Zimmerman code (see nos. 936 & 1439) for 1933 incipits,
>1344 of which are vocal. Incipits are given for the open-
>ing outer parts and when such parts are not texted, the be-
>ginning of the vocal sections are included. "The index is
>printed in three appendices. Appendix I is a listing of the
>data from which the other two appendices are produced. Appen-
>dix II is an alphabetical index to the first line of text for
>each vocal incipit. Appendix III is a listing of the incipits
>arranged in order of increasing interval size."

SCHWERIN, Mecklenburgische Landesbibliothek

1192 KADE, Otto. **Die Musikalien-Sammlung des Grossherzoglich Mecklenburg-
     Schweriner Fürstenhauses aus den letzten zwei Jahrhunderten.** Alpha-
     betisch-thematisch verzeichnet und ausgearbeitet von Otto Kade
     (Schwerin: Sandmeyer, 1893) 2v., viii, 484; 424p.
>Incipits of the music collections of Duke Friedrich Franz III,
>and Mecklenburg-Schwerin houses. Works are listed in two sec-
>tions: (1) anonymous (religious.vocal, secular vocal, instru-
>mental);(2) alphabetical by composer (similarly subdivided).

1192a--- Supplement. **Der Musikalische Nachlass...der verwittweten Frau
     Erbgrossherzogin Auguste von Mecklenburg-Schwerin...** (Wismar: Hin-
     storff; Schwerin: Sandmeyer, 1899) vii, 142p.
>Bound in with volume 2 above, and similarly organized.

1193 MEYER, Clemens. **Nachtrag** (D SW) 295p. Compiled 1908. (manuscript)
▽   Xerox copy in US NYcg.
>Supplements the Kade catalogues, 1893 & 1899 (see above en-
>tries) with single and multiple staff incipits for 600 works
>added to the collection through 1908.

1194 --- **[Thematic catalogue]** (D SW) 482p. (many blanks). Compiled ca.
▽   1950. (manuscript) Xerox copy in US NYcg.
>This large MS catalogue is a supplement to both the Kade
>catalogues and the Meyer *Nachtrag* (see above entries).

SCHWINDL, FRIEDRICH, 1737-1786

1195 DOWNS, Anneliese (New York U.). **The symphonies of Friedrich Schwindl**
*   Thematic catalogue as supplement to dissertation in progress.

SCRIABIN, ALEXANDER, 1872-1915

1196 GLEICH, Clemens-Christoph von. Die sinfonischen Werke von Alexander
Skrjabin, *Utrechtse Bijdrage tot de Muziekwetenschap* III (Bilthoven:
A.B. Creyghton, 1963) 136p.
Partially thematic. Gives themes and sub-themes of symphonic
works, with chronological table.

Reviews: V. FÉDOROV, *RMusicol* LIII/1 (1967) 84-85.

SECHTER, SIMON, 1788-1867

1197 TITTEL, Ernst. Simon Sechter als Kirchenkomponist (PhD diss.: Wien,
▽   1935) 290p. (typescript)
Thematischer Katalog, 100-43.
Double staff incipits of 171 works arranged by genre, including 35 Masses, 3 Requiems, 49 Offertories and Graduals, 13
hymns, antiphons, etc..

SEIDELMANN, FRANZ, fl. ca. 1770

1198 Thematischer Catalogus: derer Kirchen Musicalien des Herrn Capell
▽   Meister Franz Seidelmann (D Bds: HB VII, Mus. ms. theor. K. 788)
[i, 21p] Microfilm copy in US NYcg. [reproduction on facing page]
185 sacred works arranged by genre, including 36 Masses,
37 Offertoria, and 40 psalms. Gives incipits for subdivi-
sions of large-scale works.

1199 Catalogus derer Kirchen Musicalien des Herrn Capellmeister Franz
▽   Seidelmann. Armaro IX (D Dl) 35p. Compiled c. 1800. Copy in US
NYcg (manuscript)
Presumably most or all of Seidelmann's sacred vocal music is
included. Incipits for 36 Masses and many other genres.

SEIFFERT, Max (compiler)

1200 J.P. Krieger, 21 ausgewählte Kirchenkompositionen, *DDT* 53/54 (Leipzig: Breitkopf & Härtel, 1916).
Verzeichnis der von J. Ph. Krieger in Wiessenfels aufgeführten
Werke fremder Komponisten.
The catalogue, partially thematic, includes themes for settings
of the Credo, Domine ad adjuvandum, Magnificat, and Mass by:
Albrici, Bernhard, Bertali, Brückner, Carissimi,Caventi, Caz-
zati, Cossoni, Danner, Erlebach, Fedeli, Ferdinand III, Filip-
pini, Foggia, Forchheim, Gianettini, Gratiani, Grünewald,
Kerll, Knüpfer, Kress, Legrenzi, Nanino, Palestrina, Palla-
vicini, Peranda, Piocchi, Pittoni, Pohle, Porta, Rigatti,
Rosenmüller, Rovetta, Schiefferdecker, Schwenkenbecher, Theile,
Thieme, Valentini, Victoria, and Ziani.

1201 Das Mylauer Tabulaturbuch von 1750, *AfMW* I (1919) 607-32.
Contains thematic index of works by the following: Garthoffen,
Kniller, J. Krieger, Kuhnau, Monteforte, Pachelbel, Pestel,
Vetter, Werckmeister, and Witte.

XIX. Seidelmann, *Catalogus derer Kirchen Musicalien...*,
page 14, ca. 1800, no. 1199

1202 Das Plauener Orgelbuch von 1708, *AfMW* II (1920) 371-93.
        325 works are listed, not all of which are thematic incipits,
        but are titles of the chorales and works. The works, listed
        by name, are not in alphabetical order, nor are the composers.
        The index gives the number of the work .next to the works
        listed in alphabetical order. Composers represented are:
        Armsdorff, J.B. Bach, Buttstett, Buxtehude, Erich, Pachelbel,
        Walther, J.S.Bach, Böhm, J. Michael Bach, and J.W. Zachow.

SEITENSTETTEN, Austria. Stift

1203 Index Missarum Ordine Alphabetico 807 [1807] [Folio 12" x 17"]
▽   2v. (A Seitenstetten) (manuscript)
        Incipits in MS on preprinted thematic catalogue page forms.
        Contains entire 18th century repertory of the Abbey. Works
        themselves are largely still extant. All sacred music (Mass-
        es, Motets, etc.) arranged in alphabetical order by composer.
        There are three separate groups (names in 2nd and 3rd groups
        not repeated): Volume I, A--Z; Volume I, Nachtrag A-Z; Volume
        II, A-Z. The following composers are represented: Volume I—
        Albrechtsberger, Brixi, Boog, Bruneder, Brustmann, Biber,
        Caldari, Carl, P. Paulis Conrad, Melchior Dreÿer, Carl Ditters,
        Donberger, Philipp Eder, Ehrenhard, Enter, Joseph Eybler, Eber-
        lin, Fischer, Fux, Fraundorfer, Gensbacher,·Gassmann, Martinus
        Gerbert, Grasl, Michaele Grätzer, Habegger, P. Gregor Hauer,
        Joseph Haydn, Michaele Haydn, Leopold Hoffmann, Georgio Hueber,
        Adolph Hasse, Joseph Hockenreiter, Hieronymus Hueber, Ivanschiz,
        P. Joseph, Kaiser, Giusseppe Kainz, Robert Kimerling, Andreas,
        Krikel, Gius. Kracher, Krottendorfer, Klima, Kohaut, Franz
        Kurz, Franz Kromer, Lasser, Franz Leitner, Loss, Luigi, Mann,
        W. Mozart, L. Mozart, Nauman, Neubaur, Neumann, Novotni,
        Obermeyer, Öttl, Pauman, Joseph Pfeiffer, Pichler, Pleyel,
        Preglaner, Preindl, Puchinger, Philipp Pusterhofer, Georg
        Pasternitz, [Brixi] Prixides, Predieri, Pascher, Stanislaus
        Reidinger, Reinhardt, Resch, Reitter, Reüter (Reütter), Ro-
        ser, Runc, Sartori, Adam Scheibl, Valentin, Scheibeflueg,
        Aegidius Schenck, Schmid, Schmidt, Schmidbauer, Franz Schnei-
        der, Schorn, Schramek, Seuche, Sonleitner, Maximilian Stadler,
        Strasser, Strobel, Süssmayer, Johann Schuber, Schiedermayr,
        Thuma, Ignaz Umlauf, J.B. Vannhall, Vogl, Florian Wastril,
        Franc Weigl, Weis, Werner, Widman, Wissner, Widerhofer, Wein-
        wurm, Zechner, Anton Zimerman; Volume I, Nachtrag- Aufschei-
        ter, Ehrenhardt, Guess, Himelbaur, Köberl, Loheli, Franc Raab,
        Bonno, Boslaus, Chochi, Leopold Diernberger; Volume II—Tha-
        deus Eckel, Einwald, Joseph Fierlinger, Matheus Frumann, Gluck,
        Paul Gottersdorfer, Dionisius Grätz, Hieronimus, Leopold Hoff-
        man, Holzbaur, Hörger, Nicola Jomellÿ, Kraus, Joseph Kriner,
        Anton Paiizger, Poog, Predieri, Michael Preunich, Perez, Ri-
        naldo di Capua, Franc Richter, Scarlatti, Joseph Senft, Span-
        ler, Vollcert, Wagenseil, Walder, Wrattni, Winter, Ziegler.
        A completely new thematic cataloguing of the extensive Seiten-
        stetten holdings is being prepared (and almost complete) by
        Alexander Weinmann for *RISM*.

SEITZ, Alipius (compiler)

1204 [Liederbüchlein, Geschenk für Marcus Seitz] (D Mbs: Mus. Mss. 7098)
▽   118p. (manuscript) Xerox copy of the thematic portion in US NYcg.

This manuscript, containing the text of many Lieder mostly
with melodies, was given as a gift to Seitz's nephew Marcus
Seitz. Date given on page 71, 13 Nov. 1804. Pages 91-110
contain the thematic catalogue of a music collection with
78 sacred vocal works, 33 symphonies, several Singspiel, etc.
Composers include: Anfossi, Beitinger, Binter, Brixi, Buch-
wieser, Bühler, Camerloher, Cannabich, Dimmler, Dittersdorf,
Drexel, Fischer, Gleisner, Grätz, Grueber, Guenin, Guglielmi,
Gyrowetz, Haltenberger, Haydn, Hoffmeister, Holler, Holzmann,
Kalcher, Keller, Knežek, Kozeluch, Kriebaum, Lidl, Malzat,
Michl, Neubauer, Pausch, Pergolesi, Pleyel, Pittrich, Rhei-
neck, Rosetti, Sales, Schmittbaur, Schmid, Schuster, Schwin-
del, Sterkel, Stollreiter, Ullinger, Vanhall, Vogler, Winter.

1205 --- MÜNSTER, Robert. **Die Musik im Augustinerchorherrenstift Beuer-**
berg von 1768 bis 1803 und der thematische Katalog des Chorherrn
Alipius Seitz, *Kirchenmusikalisches Jahrbuch* (München, 1970) 47-76.
In addition to providing a great deal of background information, the catalogue reproduces all incipits except those
that have been fully identified in standard thematic catalogues. Several additional incipits of works belonging
to the former Klosterkirche Beuerberg are added at the end.
Composers: Johann Drexel, Haydn (?), and 3 anonymous works.

SELFRIDGE, Eleanor (compiler)

1206 **Venetian instrumental ensemble music in the seventeenth century**
▽   (D. Phil. diss.: Oxford, 1969)(typescript)
       [Thematic catalogue], v. 1, Appendix II, 276-97.
Incipits for 110 works of canzonas and sonate da chiesa for
3 or more instruments (plus basso continuo) in the following
17 publications between 1612-1656 inclusive: 1-2, Dario Cas-
tello, *Sonate concertate,* Bk. I, 1621, Bk. II, 1699; 3. Fran-
cesco Cavalli, *Musiche sacre,* 1656; 4. Gio. Battista Grillo,
Sacri concentus, 1618: 5-7. Biagio Marini, *Affetti musicali,*
Op. 1, 1618 (sic), *Madrigali et symfonie,* Op. 2, 1618, *Di-*
versi generi di sonate, Op. 22, 1655; 8-9. Massimiliano Neri,
Sonate e canzone, Op. 1, 1644, *Sonate,* Op. 2, 1651; 10. Gio.
Picchi, *Canzoni da sonar,* 1625; 11-13. Gio. Battista Riccio,
Il primo libro delle divine lodi, 1612, *Il secondo libro*
delle divine lodi, 1614, *Il terzo libro delle divine lodi,*
1621 (sic); 14. Giovanni Rovette, *Salmi concertati,* Op. 1,
1627 (sic); 15. Giuseppe Scarani, *Sonate concertate,* Op. 1,
1630; 16-17. Franceso and Gabriel Spongie detto Usper, *Messa*
et salmi, 1614, *Compositioni armoniche,* 1619.

SELLE, THOMAS, 1599-1663

1207 GÜNTHER, Siegfried. **Thomas Selle; Thematisches Verzeichnis seiner**
▽   **geistlichen Konzerte, geordnet in Anlehnung an die Werkfolge in Sel-**
       les Opera Omnia (D Bds: Mus. Ms. theor. Kat. 790) [ii], 48p. Com-
       piled 1935 (manuscript). Microfilm copy in US NYcg.
Double staff thematic incipits and text incipits for the *Con-*
certuum latine sacrorum (4 books) and the *Deutsche geistliche*
Konzerte (3 parts). Often provides the source of the text,
sometimes gives the entire text.

SENFL, LUDWIG, ca. 1490-1545

1208   CHANCEY, Tina (Queens College of C.U.N.Y.). Thematic catalogue of
*   Senfl's Lieder in modern editions

1209   GERBOTH, Walter; BROWN, Dean (Brooklyn College of the C.U.N.Y.). The-
*   matic index to the complete works of Ludwig Senfl in the "Sämtliche
       Werke" edition. Punched cards.
              Incipits are given in the *Simplified Plaine and Easie Code
              System* (see no. 188).

SÉVERAC, DÉODAT DE, 1873-1921

1210   BRODY, Elaine. The piano works of Déodat de Séverac: a stylistic
▽   analysis (PhD diss.: New York U., 1964) 2v. 487p. (typescript)
              Thematic index, v. II, 446-57.
              Incipits for suites, collections, and four-hand pieces are
              arranged by genre. Title, dedication where applicable, per-
              formance instructions, pedalling etc. all appear in multiple
              staff arrangement.

SEVILLA, Biblioteca capitular Colombina: MS a.Z. 135.33

1211   ANGLÈS, Higini. El Chansonnier français de la Colombina de Sevilla,
       Estudis Universitaris Catalans XIV ([1929]) [227]-258.
              Incipits of the Colombina MS a. Z. 135.33, including works
              by Agricola, Binchois, Busnois, Caecus, Caron, Cornago,
              Dufay, Dunstable, Gaspar, Joh. Martini, Mureau, Ockeghem,
              Pyllois, Tinctoris, Touront, Vincenet, Zuny.

SHARP, William, James, and Granville (compilers)

1212   The Sharp catalogue. (US NYp: Drexel 1022) (manuscript).
▽   100 incipits for compositions dating from c. 1710-1760 are
              scattered through pages 45-123, and represent Eng-
              lish, Italian, German, French, Bohemian, Dutch, Scottish,
              Spanish, Irish, and Russian composers. 59 of the incipits
              are anonymous. The remaining 41 are by the following compos-
              ers: Rabbi Kimili (2), Pepusch (3), Purcell (1), Kirhoff (1),
              Jones (1), Weideman (11), Cecere (1), Defesch (1), Geminiani
              (1), Seibert (1), Hasse (2), Linicke (2), Lenike (3), Brew-
              nitz (1), Finger (1), Benegar (1), Davis (1), de Fesch (1),
              Eccles (1), Lamp (1), Abandane (2), Batta Somis (1), Lineke
              (Linike?) (1). Most of the incipits include information
              about instrumentation, and are arranged by the following
              divisions: (1) Full concerto, concerto, overture, sonatas
              from...opera airs, symphony, and quartetto; (2) Hautboy
              concertos, bassoon concertos, French horn and trumpet con-
              certos. The Collection, the Catalogue of which is dated on
              the title page 1759, once belonged jointly to 3 brothers,
              Messrs William, James, and Granville Sharp, in London.

1213   HOLLAND, Jeanette B.; La RUE, Jan. The Sharp manuscript, London
       1759-c1793: a uniquely annotated music catalogue, *NYPL Bulletin*
       LXXIII/3 (Mar 1969) 147-66.
              Catalogue entries that include incipits, 156-62.

The 100 incipits included in the catalogue are here reprinted
using the "Plaine and Easie Code" for which an explanatory
note is provided. In addition, the article includes a history
of the manuscript, illustrations of its various features,
a subject index and a list of the composers found in the catalogue.

SIBELIUS, JEAN, 1865-1957

1214 TANZBERGER, Ernst. **Jean Sibelius. Eine Monographie mit einem Werkverzeichnis** (Wiesbaden: Breitkopf & Härtel, 1962)
Werke, section C, 70-246.
> An examination of his works in 10 parts arranged by genre.
> In the body of the text are notations of themes. This is
> not strictly an index, but is systematically organized, and
> usable. The section on Klaviermusik, p. 244-46, contains no
> themes.

1215 VESTDIJK, Simon. **De symfonieën van Jean Sibelius** (Amsterdam: De
Bezige Bij; 'sGravenhage, Rotterdam: Nijgh & Van Ditmar, 1962) 262,
[15p.]
[Thematic catalogue], [15].
> Incipits for all important motifs in all movements of each
> symphony, with scoring indicated for each melody.

SIGMARINGEN, Germany. Fürstlich Hohenzollernsche Hofbibliothek: [Cata-
logue I]

1216 CATALOGUS/ Über die/ Sämtliche Musicalische Werck,/ und derselben
▽   Authorn, nach Al-/phabetischer Ordnung: Welche von/ Ihro Hochfürstl.
Durchlaucht/ dem/...Fürsten und Herrn/ Herrn Carl Friederich Erb-
prinzen/ zu Hohenzollern angeschafft worden seynd. 1766 (D SI: Hausarchiv Hohenz. Sigmaringen, 23,3. Mikroaufnahme Nr. 52-58) 189p.(including 92 blanks) (manuscript). Compiled in 1776 by Sigmaringen
music director Johann Michael Schindele.
> An inventory of 570 works from a collection, now lost, once
> located at the Hohenzollern Castle in Sigmaringen. A mostly
> alphabetical arrangement, by composer, of 18th century in-
> strumental works; provides instrumentation. Composers are:
> Abas, Abel, Aspelmaÿer, Auffmann, Aumonn, Bach, Barba, Ber-
> nasconi, Berner, Besch, Bierlinger, Bode, Bonno, Breünich,
> Brioschi, [Brixi], Bruchhausen, Cambioni, Cammerlocher (Ca-
> merlocher), Cannabich, Demachi, Demmel, Dischner, Ditters
> (Diters), Enderle, Ferandini, Fils, Forni, Freünd, Fux,
> Gallo, Galuppi, Gassman, Geweÿ, Giombatti, Gossec, Graff,
> Grimmer, Guilano, Hanser, Harsch, Hartenfels, Hasse, Haydn,
> Hofmann, Holzbauer, Holzbogen, Ivanschiz, Jomelli, Kamll
> [Kammel], Klöffler, Kohaut, Kraus, Kraÿser, Kÿrmaÿer, Lang,
> Laube, Leibgi, Mahaut, Maldere, Marass, Maria Theresia,
> Martino, Mayer, Meder, Miling, Miller, Mozzart, Nardini,
> Neruda, Ordonez, Pfeiffer, Pockorni, Pockorini , Polazzi,
> Prixi [Brixi], Puci, Pugnani, Reluzi, Richter, Ricli, Rip-
> pel, Rosencranz, Roy, Runck, Sander, Schindele, Schmid,
> Schmidbaur, Schubert, Schwindel, Seifert (Seÿfert, Seÿf-
> fert), Solniz, Sommer, Stain, Stamitz, Stainmez (Stein-
> mez), Stumpf, Surmonti, Tassino, Toeschi (Toesci), Uhl-
> man, Vogel, Wagenseil, Wanhal, Weiss, Wodizka, Wrosschki.
> Also includes several anonymous works.

SIGMARINGEN, Fürstlich Hohenzollernsche Hofbibliothek: [Catalogue II]

1217 WERNHAMER, Georg. [Thematic catalogue] (D SI: Hausarchiv Hohenz.
▽   Sigmaringen 23,4. Mikroaufnahme Nr. 50) 177p. including 136 blanks.
      Compiled 1768. (manuscript)
              Compiled by Georg Wernhamer who was Schindele's successor
              as music director. Incipits for church works by 40 compos-
              ers.

SIGMARINGEN, Fürstlich Hohenzollernsche Hofbibliothek: [Catalogues I & II]

1218 SCHÜLER, Annelise. Zwei thematische Musikkataloge aus Sigmaringen.
☐   Ein Beitrag zur Geschichte der Musik am Hofe zu Sigmaringen im 18.
      Jahrhundert (unpublished *Examensarbeit*:Freiburg i Br., 1957).

SKARA, Sweden. Stifts- Och Landsbiblioteket

1219 Card catalogue of the music collection of Skara Högre Allmänna
▽   Laroverk (16th.c.- ca. 1800) (prepared for *RISM*). Copies in S Uu;
      S Sma. (see no. 1086).
              Incipits of works in manuscript.

ŠKROUP, FRANTIŠEK, 1801-1862

1220 PLAVEC, Josef. František Škroup (Melantrich, 1941; Praha, 1946)
      659p.
              Notové ukázkey, iii-xxxii (inserted between p. 640-41).
              121 single and double staff incipits for songs, chamber music,
              and opera in pre-mid 19th c. style.

SLEEPER, Helen Joy, et al. (compilers)

1221 A check list of thematic catalogues,prepared by a committee of the
☐   *Music Library Association, NYPL Bulletin* LVII (Jan 1953) 23-37, (Feb
      1953) 88-94, (Mar 1953) 134-43.

1221a --- Also published as a separate pamphlet by *Music Library Associa-*
☐   *tion* (1954) 37p.
              Contains 350 items in 4 categories: **1.** Individual composers
              (238); 2. Collections (62); 3. Libraries (23); 4. Publishers
              (27)
              Reviews: Vincent DUCKLES, *Notes* XI (Sept 1954) 552-53; Scott
              GOLDTHWAITE, *JAmerMusicolSoc* VIII (Spring 1955) 58-59.

1221b --- BROOK, Barry S. Queens College supplement (1966) to the Music
☐   Library Associations's check list of thematic catalogues (1954)
      (Flushing, N.Y., 1966) 45p.
              Includes 229 additional items; a special category on litera-
              ture *about* thematic catalogues has been added. Both **Supple-**
              ment and original **Check List** are superceded by the present
              volume.

SOLER, ANTONIO, 1729-1783

1222 Soler harpsichord Sonatas (Musical Heritage record MHS 707).
              Incipits on record jacket for 7 sonatas. With a view to the
              establishment of a catalogue, Soler's sonatas have all been
              allotted numbers, preceded by the letter M (Marvin).

12 23 LEVASSEUR de REBOLLO, Yvonne (U.of Pittsburgh). **Works of A. Soler**
*   **Thematic index of all known sonatas**

SOUTHERN, Eileen (York College of the City University of New York)

    A computer-assisted thematic index of anonymous secular music of the years ca. 1450-1475
        Music and text incipits of 1421 compositions from 16 MSS and
        1 printed source: Berlin, Staatsbibl., MS 60413 (Lochamer
        Liederbuch); Berlin, Kupferstichkab. MS 78 C28; Brussels,Bibl.
        royale, MS 9085; El Escorial, MS IV.a.24 and V.II.24; Florence,
        Bibl.naz.cent., MS Magl. XIX 176; Florence, Riccardiana, MS
        2356; Monte Cassino, Arch. della Badia, Cod. 871N; Munich,
        Bayerisches Staatsbibl. Cim 351a (Schedelsches Liederbuch)
        and Cim 352b (Buxheimer Orgelbuch); Paris, Bibl.nat.fonds.fr.
        15123 (Chansonnier Pixérécourt), and Rothschild MS 2973 (Chan-
        sonnier Cordiforme); Rome, Bibl. Apostolica Vaticana, Capella
        Giulia, Cod.Urb.Lat. 1411; Pavia, Bibl.univ., Cod.Aldini 362;
        Seville, colombina, Cod. 5.1.43 and Part 1 of Paris, Bibl.nat.
        nouv.acq.fr. 4379; Trento, Castello del Buon Consiglio, MS 90;
        Toulouse,Library of the Royal College of Physicians,"L'art et
        instruction de bien danser."

SOWERBY, LEO, 1895-1968

1224 KIERMAN, Marilois Ditto. **The compositions of Leo Sowerby for organ solo** (MA diss.: American U., 1967) 141p. Univ. Micro. M-1098.
        Incipits for organ works appear in thematic index.

SPERGER, JOHANN MATTHIAS, 1750-1812

1225 **Tema von Contrabass Concerte** (D SW: W. Ab. 3065/8).(manuscript)
▽   Incipits represent a series of concerted and chamber
        works involving the contrabass. (see no.1227)

1226 **Catalog über verschückte Musicalien (1777-1802)** (D SW: W. Ab. 3065/3)
▽   22x29.5 cm employs only 14 of its pages. (see no. 1227)(manuscript)
        83 incipits of 35 symphonies. Presents details of date,
        dedicatee, location, and reason for the dedication.

1227 McCREDIE, Andrew D. **Mecklenburg sources for a historiography of the**
□*   **era of Ludwig van Beethoven,** *Gesellschaft für Musikforschung, Inter-*
     nationaler Musikwissenschaftlicher Kongress, Bonn, 1970 (Kongress-
     Bericht in press). (see nos. 1225 and 1226).
        Discusses the two Schwerin thematic catalogues of Sperger's
        works listed above.

1228 McCREDIE, Andrew D. **Sperger thematic catalogue**
*
SPOHR, LOUIS, 1784-1859

1229 FUCHS, Aloys. **Materiale zur Verfassung eines themat. Catalogs über**
▽   **sämmtliche Werke von Louis Spohr** (D Bds: HB VII, Kat. ms. 795) [60p]
     Compiled 1846. Microfilm copy in US NYcg.(manuscript)
        Single and multiple staff incipits arranged by genre. In-
        cludes vocal music: oratorios, cantatas, Masses, and operas;
        instrumental music: sinfonie, chamber music, and orchestral
        music.[reproduction on following page]

1229.1[Thematic Catalogue] (Leuckardt, 1859)
    Reference A. Hyatt King (no. 659) p. 40

1230 BACHMANN, Alberto. **Les grands violonistes du passé** (Paris: Fisch-
    bacher, 1913) 468p. (see no. 65)
        [Thematic catalogue], 301-09.
            List of works includes incipits for all movements of 11 con-
            certos.

SPOHR, LOUIS, 1784-1859

1231 GÖTHEL, Folker (Augsburg). **Thematisches Verzeichnis der Werke von**
*   **Louis Spohr** (Tutzing: Hans Schneider, ca. 1973)

STÄBLEIN, Bruno

1232 **Der thematische Katalog der mittelalterlichen einstimmigen Melodien,**
☐   *Zweiter Weltkongress der Musikbibliotheken Lüneburg* 1950, (Kassel,
    1951 ?) 52-54.
            A discussion of what a catalog of medieval single-line music
            should contain and how it should be organized.

STADLMAYR, JOHANN, ca. 1570-1648

1233 JUNKERMANN, Hilde H. **The Magnificats of Johann Stadlmayr** (PhD diss.:
    Ohio State U., 1967) 2v. Univ. micro. 67-6330.(typescript)
        Incipit index of Johann Stadlmayr's magnificat settings, v. 1,
        275-79.
            38 incipits with original clefs, mensuration, and note values,
            arranged chronologically according to the original six publi-
            cations containing Stadlmayr's settings.

1234 --- [Thematic catalogue]
*   Incipits for other works (probably all of those now known) by
            Stadlmayr. Incipits for all sections of Masses, in some cases
            including more than one vocal or instrumental part.

STAMITZ, ANTON, 1754-1809

1235 KAISER, Fritz [=Friedrich Carl]. **Thematischer Katalog**
▽   Although completed, publication is still in abeyance.

STAMITZ, CARL, 1745-1801

1236 KAISER, Friedrich Carl. **Carl Stamitz (1745-1801).** Biographische
▽   Beiträge. Das symphonische Werk. Thematischer Katalog der Orchester-
    werke (PhD diss.: Marburg, 1962) 95, 98, 101*l*. (typescript)
        [Thematischer Katalog], 101*l*.
            Over 400 single and double staff incipits for all movements
            of 52 symphonies, 38 sinfonia concertantes, 22 violin con-
            certos, 8 viola concertos, 6 violoncello concertos, 15 flute
            concertos, 11 clarinet concertos, 7 bassoon concertos, 3
            horn concertos, 2 clavier concertos, 4 arias for soprano and
            orchestra.

1237 KAISER, Fritz [=Friedrich Carl]. **Thematischer Katalog**
▽   Although completed, publication is still in abeyance.

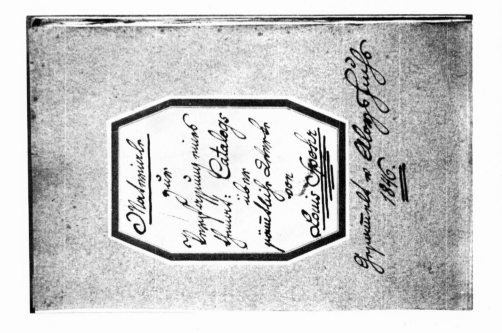

XX. Spohr, *Materiale zur Verfassung eines themat. Catalogs...(Fuchs)*, 1846, no. 1229

STAMITZ, JOHANN [STAMIC, JAN VACLAV], 1717-1757

1238 SCHOENBAUM, Camillo (Denmark). Stamic Sinfonier Tematisk Katalog
▽   19, 88ℓ. (manuscript) Copy in US NYcg.
            166 incipits (in some cases first movements only, in other,
            all movements) of both MS and printed symphonies with indi-
            cations of sources and editions.

1239 DÜRRENMATT, Hans-Rudolph. Die Durchführung bei Johann Stamitz (1717-
       1757), *Publikation der Schweizerischen Musikforschenden Gesellschaft*
       II/19 (PhD diss.: Bern, 1967; Bern: Paul Haupt, 1969) 156p.
            [Thematic catalogue], 56-82.
            Incipits for all movements of symphonies 1-30 (Riemann's num-
            bering).

1240 GRADENWITZ, Peter. Thematischer Katalog
▽   Mentioned in *MGG* as to be published within the series
            Veröffentlichungen der Arbeitsgemeinschaft für mittel-
            rheinische Musikgeschichte, this catalogue, first pre-
            pared before the Second World War, has not been updated,
            and the compiler has abandoned the project.

1241 LEBERMANN, Walter (Bad Homburg). Thematischer Katalog der Instru-
*   mentalkonzerte.
            Incipits for all movements of concertos.

1242 WOLF, Eugene K. (Syracuse U.) The symphonies of Johann Stamitz:
*   authenticity, chronology, and style.
            [Thematic index], Part III.
            Incipits for all movements of 57 symphonies and 10 orches-
            tral trios, 20 lost symphonies (i.e. known only from cata-
            logue references), and 38 symphonies with doubtful or spur-
            ious attributions. "The listing of authentic symphonies and
            orchestral trios generally follows the arrangement and num-
            bering established by Hugo RIEMANN in *DTB* III/1 (1902) and
            VII/2 (1906)."

STEFFAN, JOSEPH ANTON [ŠTĚPÁN, JOSEF ANTONÍN], 1726-1797

1243 PICTON, Howard (U. of Hull). The keyboard concertos of Joseph Steffan
*   (1726-1797) 5v.: v. 1-2, text; v. 3-5, music.
            [Thematic catalogue]
            "Catalogues over 80 manuscripts and printed sources for Stef-
            fan's 38 keyboard concertos. Information for each work in-
            cludes: a single-stave incipit (and total number of bars) for
            each movement; scoring; date of composition; catalogue refer-
            ences; list of sources (location; catalogue number; whether
            manuscript or print, score or parts; transcription of title
            page; description of paper and reference to masterlist of
            watermarks; reference to masterlist of copyists; details of
            autograph editions, corrections; cadenzas; missing parts;
            different versions; arrangements); literature; modern editions,
            etc."

1244 --- Complete works of Joseph Anton Steffan (1726-1797) index cards
*   "An in-progress private manuscript catalogue of about 240
            items arranged by genre: solo keyboard works; keyboard con-
            certos; chamber music; orchestral works; church music; Sing-

spiel; Lieder. Includes detailed descriptions of manuscript
and printed sources, and references to modern editions and
literature. The beginning of each movement is given in short
score."

1245 ŠETKOVÁ, Dana (Praha). **J.A. Štěpáns Klavierwerk**
*   The catalogue will include incipits for 138 works (41 sonatas,
           40 concertos, chamber music etc.) mostly in manuscripts.
           More than half of the works are deposited in Kroměříž (Krem-
           sier in Moravia), then Marburg, Wien, Brussels, etc.

STEFFANI, AGOSTINO, 1654-1728

1246 EINSTEIN, Alfred; SANDBERGER, Adolf. **Agostino Steffani. Ausgewählte**
      Werke *DTB* 6/2 (Leipzig: Breitkopf & Härtel, 1905)
           Thematisches Verzeichnis der Kammerduette und Scherzi, [xx]-xxvi.
           Original clefs used. Contains revision of the manuscripts,
           and part of the texts of the cited vocal works.

1247 TIMMS, Colin R. (Queen's U., Belfast). **The chamber duets of Agos-**
*   **tino Steffani; a thematic catalogue** (To be published in the *Welles-*
      ley Edition Cantata Index Series)
           Incipits for all movements of duets arranged according to
           reliable attributions, unreliable attributions, and duets
           from Steffani's operas found in sources of the chamber duets.
           Entries are arranged alphabetically by the first line of the
           text, with concordances to the numbering system used by Ein-
           stein in his catalogue (*DTB* 6/2).

STEIBELT, DANIEL, 1765-1823

1248 **Oeuvres/ de Steibelt** (A Wst: MH 9180) [37p.] No date (manuscript).
▽   Microfilm in **US** NYcg.
           Double staff incipits for 155 works for keyboard solo, cham-
           ber group and piano, and orchestra and piano.

STENZEL, Jürg (Villars sur Glâne, Switzerland)

1249 **[Catalogue of concerti for 1-2 oboes to 1800]**
*   Partially thematic.

STERKEL, JOHANN FRANZ XAVER, 1750-1817

1250 WAGNER, Heinz (Mainz). **Thematisches Verzeichnis der Werke von Johann**
*   **Franz Xaver Sterkel**

STESZEWSKI, Jan

1251 **Ébauché de l'histoire des classifications ethnomusicologiques en**
□   **Pologne,** *StudMusicol* VII (1965) 345-48.

STOCKER, STEFAN, 1845-1910

1252 SINKOWITZ, Elvira. **Der Klavierkomponist Stefan Stocker (1845-1910).**
▽   Mit Biographie und thematischem Katalog seines Gesamtwerkes. (PhD
      diss.: Wien, 1955) 2v., 259, 13*l*.; 131*l*. (typescript)

Thematischer Katalog sämtlicher Werke nach Gattungen geordnet, v. 2.

Over 200 multiple staff incipits for all movements. Works include 1 symphony, 1 violin concerto, 2 quartets, and over 215 Lieder, etc.

STOCKHOLM, Kungliga Musikaliska Akademiens Bibliothek

1253 [Card catalogue now consisting of 36,000 incipits in Ingmar
▽   Bengtsson's Numericode] (S Skma) (manuscript)

Incipits of MSS catalogued in Sweden for *RISM* since 1968 and also from: 39 published thematic catalogues (22 of them as parts of biographies and of *DDT*), Hallardt's sångsamling (thematic catalogue in MS), all compositions in "Le delizie dell'opere" v. 1-4 (London: I. Walsh), all compositions in "A select collection of the most admired songs, duetts, &c. from operas" (London: Corri), a few "Complete works" such as Georg Friedrich Händel's Werke (Chrysander), and music examples in some works on music in the 18th century. The selection of incipits is made with regard to the holdings of music in MSS before 1800 in Swedish libraries. Consequently, up till now almost all music inventoried is 18th century. With a few exceptions, only incipits for first movements. The catalogue is increasing in size as new incipits of the MSS that are being catalogued for the *RISM* are being added. Thus far the following works have been coded in the card catalogue of incipits:

A. Incipits of thematic catalogues in print and MS.
   1. Collections: The Breitkopf thematic catalogue (New York, 1966); BROOK, B.S., La symphonie française, t. 2 (Paris, 1962); *DTB* 3/1, 7/2, 16; V. DUCKLES and M.ELMER, Thematic catalogue of a manuscript collection of eighteenth century music (Berkeley, 1963); Hallardts sångsamling.Thematisk förteckning 1-2 Ms.; J.J.&B. Hummel, Catalogue thématique.
   2. Composers: Albinoni (Giazotto, 1945), C.Ph.E. Bach (Wotquenne, 1905), J.C. Bach (Terry, 1967), Boccherini (Gérard, 1969), Camerloher (Ziegler, 1919), Corelli (Rinaldi, 1953), Dittersdorf (Krebs, 1900), Fasch (Küntzel, 1965), Galuppi (Torrefranca, 1909), Geminiani (McArtor,1951), Gluck (Wotquenne, 1904), Graun & Hasse (Mennicke, 1906), Hasse (Hansell, 1968), Haydn (Hoboken, 1957), Heinichen (Seibel, 1913), Locatelli (Koole, 1949), Mozart (Köchel,only the instrumental works), Paganelli (Schenk, 1928), Pugnani (Müry, 1941), Pugnani (Zschinsky-Troxler, 1939), Reichardt (Pröpper, 1965), Roman (Bengtsson, 1955), Roman (Vretblad, 1914), Rosetti (Kaul, 1968), Schmitt (Dunning, 1962), Tartini (Capri, 1945), Telemann (Kross, 1969), Torelli (Giegling, 1949), Viotti (Giazotto, 1956), Vivaldi (Rinaldi, 1945), Vivaldi (Fanna, 1968), Wagenseil (Michelitsch, 1966).

B. Incipits of published music.
   1. Collections: Le delizie dell'opere Vol.1-4. London: I. Walsh; Musikaliskt tidsfördrif. Stockholm 1789-1834;

A select collection of the most admired songs, duetts, &c
from operas... By D. Corri. London.
  2. Composers: D. Buxtehudes Werke. Rd 1-8; F. F.
Dall'Abaco. In *DDT*, Folge 2: Bd 1 & 16/17 and in *DTB*, Neue
Folge, Bd 1; Friedrich II [the Great]; G. F. Händel's Werke.
Hrsg. von F. Chrysander. Leipzig 1858-1902. All movements;
B. Marcello, Estro poetico armonico. Vol.1-8. Venezia 173..

C. Incipits of music in MSS since Dec. 1968 catalogued in
Sweden for the RISM.

D. Incipits published as music examples in different works
on composers and music from the 18th cent.

STOCKHOLM, Kungliga Musikaliska Akademiens Bibliothek: Hallardt's Collection.

1254 Hallardt's sångsamling. Tematisk förteckning (S Skma: MS 37: 1-2)
▽   2v.: 1, (16), 84; 141*l*.(manuscript)
        Thematic incipits of the vocal works in J.F. Hallardt's
        collection (mainly MSS, 18th century) that was acquired
        by the above-mentioned library in 1795.

1255 --- DAVIDSSON, Åke. Cultural background to collections of old music
☐   in Swedish libraries, *FontesArtisM* (1964) 21-28.

STOCKHOLM, Kungliga Musikaliska Akademiens Bibliothek: Mazer Collection

1256 Catalogue thématique de musique (S Skma: Mazer Collection) 7v.
▽   (manuscript).
        Thematic catalogue by genre of the Mazer collection in the
        Library of the Royal Swedish Academy of Music, Stockholm.
        Contains about 4550 instrumental and vocal works in score
        and parts from the 18th and first half of the 19th centuries,
        including symphonies, concertos, chamber music, choral works,
        and arias. Mostly from printed sources, but some manuscripts
        are included.

1256a--- JOHANSSON, Cari. Något om Mazers Musiksamling i Kungl. Musik-
☐   aliska Akademiens Bibliothek, *SvenskTMf* (1951) 143-46.

STOLTIE, James M. (compiler)

1257 A "symphonie concertante" type: the concerto for mixed woodwind
      ensemble in the classical period (PhD diss.: U. of Iowa, 1962)
      2v. Univ. Micro. 63-974.(typescript)
        Volume I, p. 63-254, contains a formal outline and analysis
        of extant concertos arranged alphabetically by composer.
        Not a thematic catalogue *per se*, but includes incipits and
        in some cases other important themes from all movements in
        works by 27 composers.

STOLTZER, THOMAS,ca. 1475-1526

1258 HOFFMANN-ERBRECHT, Lothar. Thomas Stoltzer: Leben und Schaffen, *Die
      Musik Im Alten und Neuen Europa* V (Kassel: Johann Philipp Hinnenthal-
      Verlag, 1964) 213p.

Initien der bisher nicht neugedruckten Werke, 192-99.
> Incipits, in original notation, for all voices of 51 works
> with author's numbering. The index, complete as of 1962, is
> of works not included in new editions.
>
> *Reviews:* Fred BLUM, *Notes* XXIII/3 (Mar 1967) 541; *MReview*
> XXVIII/1 (Feb 1967) 75-76.

STONE, David Leon (compiler)

1259 The Italian sonata for harpsichord and pianoforte in the eighteenth
▽   century (I730-I790) (PhD diss.: Harvard U., 1952) 3v.(typescript)
        Thematic index, v.II, 103p.
> Incipits for works in the collection of the Library of Con-
> gress, and in the Einstein Collection of Smith College.

STRADELLA, ALESSANDRO, 1642-1682

1260 JANDER, Owen. **Alessandro Stradella** [Thematic catalogue of cantatas]
      The Wellesley Edition Cantata Index Series, fasc. 4 (Wellesley:
      Wellesley College, 1966) 2v.
> Catalogue divided into two parts: 4a-reliable attributions
> (195 works); 4b-unreliable attributions (205 works). Intro-
> duction, 69p., lists all sources, grouped according to de-
> pendability.

1261 McCRICKARD, Eleanor Fowler. **Alessandro Stradella's instrumental**
▽   **music: A critical edition with historical and analytical commen-**
      tary (PhD diss.: U. of North Carolina, 1971) 2v: x, 97p; 420p.
      (typescript)
        Thematic catalogue.

STRASBOURG, Bibliothèque nationale et universitaire : MS M. 222 C. 22

1262 BORREN, Charles van den. **Le Manuscrit musical M. 222 C. 22 de**
      la Bibliothèque de Strasbourg, *Annales de l'Académie Royale*
      d'archéologie de Belgique (1923-1927) v. LXXI-LXXIV 7ᵉ sér., t. 1,
      343-74; t. 2, 272-303; t. 3, 128-96; t. 4, 71-152.
        [Thematic index], t. 2-4.
> Uses solfège syllables for works by Alanus, Antonius Cleri-
> cus Apostolicus, Binchois, Borlet, Bosquet, Camaraco, Car-
> lay, Cesaris, J. de Climen, Cornelius, Dufay, Egidius de
> Pusiex, Egidius de Thenis, P. Fontaine, Grenon, Grimache,
> Henricus de Libero Castro, Henricus Hessmann, Lampens,
> Landino, A. de Lantins, Henri Lauffenbourg, C. Liebert,
> Machaut, N. de Merques, P. de Molins, Nucella, Passet (?),
> Jugis Philomena, Prunet, Richart, Royllart, Hubertus de
> Salinus, Senleches, Vaillant, Vide, Vitry, N. Zacharius,
> and Zeltenpferd.

STRATICO, MICHELE, ca. 1721- ca. 1782

1263 [87] Concerti Del Sig:ʳ Tartini [52] Sonate con il Basso Del Sig:ʳ
▽   Tartini [16] Sonate à Violino solo [4] Sinfonia à 4. del Sig:ʳ Tar-
      tini [26] Concerti del Sig:ʳ Stratico [2] Concerti à Due Violini
      Obbligati [59] Sonate dello Stesso. Segue N:°6 Sonate Stampate in

Londra [e 6] **Duetti**   (I AN: ms. n. inv. 16154). (manuscript)
This thematic catalogue is in the hand of hand A, the copyist
who has also written the thematic catalogue now in Berkeley
(U. of Calif. Music Library: ms. It. 1018a, see no. 1264   ).
The copyist is certainly from Padua. Incipits are given for
the first fast movement of each work.

1264 [55] **Concerti del Sig.**^{re} **Giuseppe Tartini,** [50] **sonate a Violino e**
▽   **Basso del Sig.**^{re} **Giuseppe Tartini,** [16] **Concerti del Sig.**^{re} **Michiele**
Straticò, [26] **Sonate a Violino e Basso del Sig.**^{re} **Michiele Straticò**
(Berkeley, Calif., U. of Calif. Music Library, It. 1018b.)(manuscript)
Incipits for the first fast movement of a composition (1st
movement of the concerto, 2nd movement of the sonata). The
listings in this catalogue correspond to a large extent to
the collection of Tartini and Stratico MSS in the Music
Library of the University of California at Berkeley. It is
in hand B, the copyist who assembled part of the Berkeley
collection; this copyist is peculiar to the Berkeley holdings
and cannot be found in any other collection of Tartini MSS.
Reference: Vincent DUCKLES et al., (see no. 107) p. 385.

STRAUBING, Germany. Pfarramt St. Jakob

1265 WALLNER, Bertha Antonia. **[Catalogue]** (On loan by the *DTB* to D Mbs)
▽   Compiled ca. 1910-1930. (manuscript)
One of many partially thematic inventories prepared by the
compiler under Adolf Sandberger's direction for the *Denk-
mäler der Tonkunst in Bayern.*

STRAUSS, JOHANN, 1804-1849

1266 SCHÖNHERR, Max; REINÖHL, Karl. **Johann Strauss Vater; ein Werkver-
zeichnis,** *Das Jahrhundert des Walzers,* 1. Band (London, Vienna,
Zürich: Universal, 1954) 368p.
Incipits of 252 works with annotations. Includes dates,
instrumentations, editions, commentary and illustrations.
Reviews: Wilhelm ZENTNER, *Zeitschrift für Musik* CXV (Nov
1954) 681-82; Helen Joy SLEEPER, *Notes* XII (Mar 1955) 228-29;
Hans F. REDLICH, *MReview* XVII (May 1956) 171-72; Reinhold
SIETZ, *Mf* IX/1 (1956) 104-05; *RassegnaMCurci* XXVII/2 (1957)
184-85.

STRAUSS, RICHARD, 1864-1949

1267 STEINITZER, Max. **Richard Strauss** (Berlin: Schuster & Loeffler, 1911)
202p.
Ungedruckte Jugendwerke, [176]-202.
Partially thematic. Works arranged by opus number.

1267a--- 9.-12. durchges. und erg. Aufl. (Berlin: Schuster & Loeffler,
[1920?]) 260p.
Verzeichnis der Werke, 222-56.

1268 SPECHT, Richard. **R. Strauss und sein Werk** (Leipzig: Tal, 1921) 2v.
Thementafeln [der Opern], 50p. laid in at end of v. 2.
Incipits of lieder, choralworks, and operas. The operas are
arranged chronologically, with a complete listing of motives
as they appear in the opera. Orchestration is often included.

1269 MUELLER VON ASOW, Erich H. **Richard Strauss. Thematisches Verzeichnis**
(Wien, Wiesbaden, München: L. Doblinger, 1955-1968) I.-XXV. Lieferung,
1452p.

> Comprehensive thematic catalogue of works listed first by
> opus numbers in piano-vocal form, then works without opus
> numbers. Provides full bibliographical apparatus.

> *Reviews:* Eric BLOM, *MLetters* XXXVI (July 1955); Erich VALEN-
> TIN, *Zeitschrift für Musik* CXVI (June 1955) 273-74; Andreas
> LIESS, *Neue ZM* CXXI (1960) 398; Erik WERBA, *ÖsterreichMz* XIX
> (Aug 1964) 387-88; *StudMusicol* IX/1-2 (1967) 241-46; *Musik-
> handel* XIX/5 (1968) 244.

STREICHER, THEODOR, 1874-1940

1270 WURSTEN, Richard (U. of Wisconsin). **Theodor Streicher, life and**
*   **works**
Thematic catalogue.
> Incipits for a piano piece, string trio, piano trio, string
> sextet, and vocal works (over 100 Lieder, choral pieces *a
> capella* and for various combinations of voices and instru-
> ments, and 2 unpublished operas).

STUTTGART, Landesbibliothek

1271 GOTTWALD, Clytus. **Codices Musici (Cod. Mus. Fol. I I-7I)** Die
Handschriften der Württembergischen Landesbibliothek Stuttgart,
1. Reihe, 1. Bd., Codices Musici I (Wiesbaden: Harrassowitz, 1964)
xvi, 184p.
Incipitverzeichnis, [167]-184.
> Incipits without text for all voices of 117 anonymous
> compositions in Codices 1-48.

SUCHOFF, Benjamin

1272 **Computerized folk song research and the problems of variants,** *Com-*
☐   *puters and the Humanities* II/4 (Mar 1968) 155-58.

SULLIVAN, ARTHUR, 1842-1900

1273 HODGSON, Julian. **Thematic catalogue of the works of Arthur Sullivan**
*   Main section lists works in order of composition giving title,
designation, opus number, incipit, dedicatee, words (if any),
dates of composition and publication, date and place of first
performance, performers at first performance, orchestration
(if not included in title). In addition, there will be listings of periodical articles for each work and a discography.
Autographs (where extant) will be noted and locations given,
plus a bibliographical description of the first edition.
Appendices will include a classified list of works, a bibliography of books and periodicals, and a bibliographical index.

SUSATO, TYLMAN, d. 1561-1564? (publisher)

1274 KLIEWER, Jonah C. **Tylman Susato and his "Ecclesiasticarum Cantionum"**
(MA diss.: U. of Kansas, 1957). U. of Rochester Press Microcard
UR-58, 433-37.(typescript)

Thematic catalogue.
> Incipits for all sections of 266 motets published by Susato
> in his 15 books. Incipits are listed by number, and the title,
> name of composer, book and folio number are provided. Compos-
> ers represented: Anonymous, Adrian Willaert, Clemens non
> Papa, Lupus Hellinck, among others.

SÜSSMAYR, FRANZ XAVER, 1766-1803

1275 KECSKEMÉTI, István. **Süssmayr-Handschriften in der Nationalbibliothek Széchényi, Budapest** (Budapest: Studia Musicologica, part I, 1962;
part II, 1966).
> Originally published in *Studia Musicologica Academiae Scien-
> tiarum Hungaricae* II/1962, p. 283-320 (part I), and VIII/1966
> p. 297-378 (part II). Works listed by genre, including
> theatre works, cantatas and church music, lieder, instrumental
> music, and Süssmayr autographs of works by other composers.
> Works are listed in chronological order within genre, with
> text underlays, instrumentation, and other pertinent biblio-
> graphical material.

SWIETEN, GOTTFRIED van, 1745-1784

1276 SCHMID, Ernst Fritz. **Gottfried van Swieten als Komponist,** *Mozart-
Jahrbuch* 1953 (Salzburg, 1954) 15-31.
> [Thematic index], 24-26.
> Incipits for all movements of 7 extant and 1 lost symphonies.

SZYMANOWSKI, KAROL, 1882-1937

1277 MICHAŁOWSKI, Kornel. **Katalog Tematyczny Dzieł i Bibliografia**
[Thematic catalogue of works and bibliography] (Kraków: Polskie
Wydawnictwo Muzyczne, 1967) 248p.
> [Thematic catalogue], 21-281.
> Incipits in piano score of 240 finished compositions, arranged
> by opus number. Information on total number of bars of each
> composition, dates and circumstances of composition, dedica-
> tion, MSS, editions, transcriptions, recordings, and perfor-
> mances is given.
>
> *Reviews:* Maria PROKOPOWICZ, *Muzyka* XIII/3 (1968) 78-82.

TARTINI, GIUSEPPE, 1692-1770

1278 ROBERTI DEGLI ALMERI, Andrea. **Tutti motivi de concerti del caro Signor**
▽ **Maestro Tartini fatone copia per esso da Andrea Roberti degli Almeri**
Anno MDCC.LXI a di....giugno stando in Padova (I MO1: ms. G.A. 595
bis). (manuscript)
> The index gives incipits of 120 concerti of Tartini arranged
> chromatically by key starting from A major. The last 13 con-
> certi are not arranged by key. Incipits for 8 works do not
> correspond to any concerto listed by DOUNIAS, but agree with
> other Tartini sources.
>
> *Reference:* P. PETROBELLI, **Problemi di cronologia tartiniana,**
> in progress.

1279 [MENEGHINI, Giulio]. **Temi, ho sia motivi di tutte le Sonate, Concerti,**
▽ **ed Opere del Sig:ʳ Giuseppe Tartini** (F Pc: Ms. 9796 [former signature
4386]) *l.* 407-10.(manuscript)
> This thematic catalogue, in the hand of the pupil and successor
> of Tartini to the position of First Violin at the Chapel of the
> Basilica del Santo in Padua, is actually the description of the
> collection of Tartini MSS now located in the Bibliothèque du
> Conservatoire. It is subdivided in the following parts: *l.*
> 407: "Sonate Vechie, ho sia Composte ne primi suoi anni" (in-
> cipits for second movements of 10 sonatas) and "Meno Vechie"
> (incipits of 27 sonatas); *l.*408: "Segue ultime recenti composte
> negl'ultimi anni della sua vitta cioè dell'anno 1765, e 1766"
> (incipits of 6 sonatas), and "Altre Sonate a Violino e Basso,
> cioè: Opera Prima Sonate N:•12 Stampate in Abstardan [Amster-
> dam]. Opera Seconda Sonate N;•12 Stampate in Roma Opera Terza
> Manoscrita in libro con Sonate N⁰ 28, e con molto agiunte in
> fine, adatabili alle Sonate stesse. Viariazioni [sic] sopra
> la Gavotta del Corelli."; *l.* 408-10: "Tema de Concerti" (in-
> cipits of 84 concerti, one incipit is repeated twice.)
>
> *Reference:* P. BRAINARD, **Die Violinsonaten Giuseppe Tartinis,**
> 204-06 [see no.1288]; P. PETROBELLI, **Giuseppe Tartini- Le**
> **fonti biografiche,** s.l., Universal Edition (1968), p. 76, note
> 1.

1280 Mottivi de [105] **concerti** [e 82 sonate] di Tartini (US. BE: It.
▽ 1018a) (manuscript).
> The content of this thematic catalogue corresponds to a part
> of the collection of Tartini MSS kept in the University of
> California's Music Library. It is in hand A, the main copy-
> ist of the Berkeley collection, active in Padua in the Tar-
> tini circle in the second half of the eighteenth century.
>
> *Reference:* Vincent DUCKLES et al., (see no. 107) p. 385.

Key: ✱ in preparation; ▽ manuscript; ☐ literature; ✫ Library of Congress

1281 ⌐55⌐ Concerti del Sig.^{re} Giuseppe Tartini, ⌐50⌐ sonate a Violino e
▽   Basso del Sig.^{re} Giuseppe Tartini, ⌐16⌐ Concerti del Sig.^{re} Michiele
      Stratico, ⌐26⌐ Sonate a Violino e Basso del Sig.^{re} Michiele Stratico
      (Berkeley,Calif., Univ. of Calif. Music Library, It. 1018b.)(manuscript)
           The listings in this catalogue correspond to a large extent to
           the collection of Tartini and Stratico MSS in the Music Library
           of the University of Caligornia at Berkeley. It is in hand B,
           the copyist who assembled part of the Berkeley collection; this
           copyist is peculiar to the Berkeley holdings, and cannot be
           found in any other collection of Tartini MSS.
           Reference: Vincent DUCKLES et al.,(see no.107) p.385.

1282 ⌐87⌐ Concerti Del Sig.^{r} Tartini ⌐52⌐ Sonate con il Basso Del Sig:^{r}
▽   Tartini ⌐16⌐ Sonate à Violino solo ⌐4⌐ Sinfonia à 4. del Sig:^{r} Tar-
      tini ⌐26⌐ Concerti del Sig:^{r} Stratico ⌐2⌐ Concerti à Due Violini Ob-
      bligati ⌐59⌐ Sonate dello Stesso. Segue N:$^{°}$6 Sonate Stampate in Lon-
      dra ⌐e 6⌐ Duetti (I AN: ms. n. inv. 16154). (manuscript)
           This thematic catalogue is in the hand of hand A, the copyist
           who has also written the thematic catalogue now in Berkely
           (U. of Calif. Music Library: ms. It.1018a, see no. 1280).
           The copyist is certainly from Padua. Incipits are given for
           the first fast movement.

1283 FUCHS, Aloys (?). [Seven Tartini catalogues] Apparently append-
▽   ed to Spohr catalogue (D Bds: Kat. ms. 795) 13 loose sheets. (manu-
     script). Microfilm in US NYcg.
1283a   (1) Index tematico dei Concerti del Sgr Tartini
▽   Incipits for 97 concerti.

1283b   (2) Motivi degli Concerti Del Signor Giuseppe Tartini
▽   A copy of No. 1.

1283c   (3) Concertos pour Violon avec acc. de quatuors par Tartini
▽   Incipits for 26 works.

1283d   (4) Concerti
▽   Partial copy of Nos. 1 & 2 (62 incipits).

1283e   (5) Inventaire general des [???touts mon Bien???] herités
▽   dal Sgr. Giuseppe Tartini (In upper left-hand corner: Le
         12 sonate stampata con la Pastorale).
             Lists 48 works.

1283f   (6) Motivi d'egli Concerti del Sr. Giuseppe Tartini
▽   Incipits for 9 concerti, all movements.

1283g   (7) [Violin sonatas op. 1-9]
▽

1284 TEBALDINI, Giovanni. L'Archivio musicale della Cappella Antoniana
▽   in Padova (Padova: Libreria Antoniana, 1895).
         [Thematic catalogue of autographs of Tartini sonatas and concer-
         tos], 140-44.
             8 incipits, of which 6 are violin sonatas. Also lists
             sinfonias, trios for 2 violins and continuo, and miscellaneous
             incomplete works. Very incomplete.

1285 BACHMANN, Alberto. Les grands violinistes du passé (Paris: Fisch-
     bacher, 1913) 468p. (see no. 65)

Catalogue thématique des oeuvres de Tartini se trouvant à la Bibliothèque du Conservertoire de Paris, 320-65.
>Incipits for all movements of 14 concertos, violin sonatas Op. 1, 2, 3, 5, 6, and 7, and 3 unnumbered sonatas.

1286 DOUNIAS, Minos. **Die Violinkonzerte G. Tartinis** (PhD diss.: Berlin; München: Druck der Salesianischen Offizin; Wolfenbüttel: Georg Kallmeyer, 1935) viii,307p.
>**Thematisches Verzeichnis der Violinkonzerte Tartinis**, 243-97.
>>Incipits for all movements of 125 violin concerti arranged chromatically by key. Provides sources and a special index for doubtful works. The best thematic catalogue of Tartini's violin concerti, however the list of works and the sources are not complete. At least one "doubtful" concerto (Anhang VII) is authentic, the autograph having been found in Padova.

1286a --- Reprint of Kallmeyer (Wolfenbüttel: Möseler Verlag, 1966).

1287 CAPRI, Antonio. **Giuseppe Tartini; con 22 illustrazioni e un catalogo tematico** (Milano: Garzanti, 1945) iv, 582p.
>**Catalogo tematico delle musiche tartiniane esistenti nell'archivio della Cappella Antoniana di Padova**, 525-55.
>>Incipits for 108 works. Several MSS however are not listed, and some incipits appear more than once.
>>*Reference:* P. BRAINARD, **Die Violinsonaten**, p. 9, note 1; p. 213 note 1. (see no. 1288)

1288 BRAINARD, Paul. **Die Violinsonaten Giuseppe Tartinis** (Diss.:Göttingen, 1959) 3v.: 351*l.* (typescript)
▽
>**Thematic catalogue**, v. 3, 238-337.
>>Incipits of each movement of every work plus the number of bars in each section; repeats and length are thus indicated. The autographs and other manuscript sources (with library sigla) early printings and modern editions are described in detail. Works are dated on stylistic grounds and the principal variant features of each version are noted. Arranged by key with individual numbering within each key.

1289 BRAINARD, Paul. **Le Sonate a tre di Giuseppe Tartini- Un sunto Bibliografico**, *RItalianaMusicol* IV (1969) 102-26.
>**Catalogo tematico**, 114-26.
>>Incipits for all movements of every work plus the number of bars in each section (repeats and length are thus indicated). Arranged by key with individual numbering within each key. Autographs and other MS sources (with library sigla), and early printings are described in detail.

1290 DEARLING, Robert (Dunstable, Bedfordshire). [Thematic catalogue of
▽ concerti] Index cards (manuscript).
>Cross-indexed catalogue (Dounias-Capri).

TAUSIG, CARL, 1841-1871

1291 TAPPERT, Wilhelm. **Carl Tausig, sämmtliche, gedruckte Werke. Thema-**
▽ **tischer Catalog** (D Bds: HB VII, Mus. ms. theor. Kat. 815) [12p]
Compiled 1873. Microfilm copy in US NYcg.[reproduction on facing page]
>>Double staff incipits for Tausig's published keyboard music, both original works and arrangements of works by other composers, including Wagner, Bach, and Beethoven.

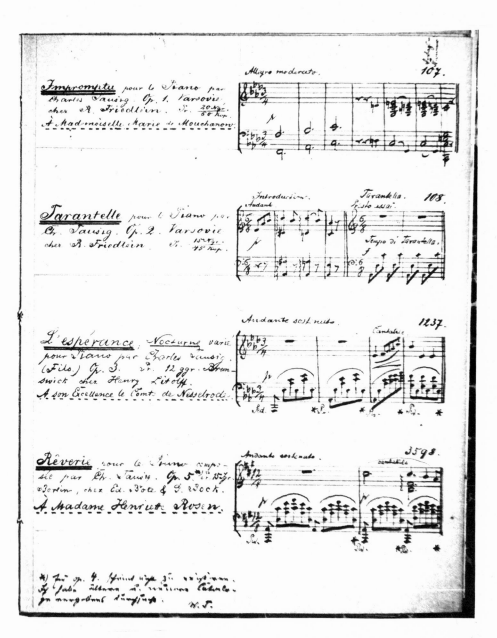

XXI. **Tausig**, ...*sämmtliche gedruckte Werke.*

Thematischer Catalog, 1873 (Tappert), no. 1292

TCHAIKOVSKY, *see* ČAJKOVSKIJ

TECHELMANN, FRANZ MATHIAS, 1649-1714

1292 KNAUS, Herwig. **Franz Mathias Techelmann. Sein Leben und seine**
▽   **Werke** (PhD diss.: Wien, 1959) 204*l*. (typescript)
          Thematischer Katalog, 164-89.
                124 double staff incipits for keyboard works found in manu--
                scripts Cod. 19167, 18593, and 192442/135 and 135a located
                in the Österreichische Nationalbibliothek and the Göttweig
                MS "Kerl 2" (ricercare, suites, canzonas).

TELEMANN, GEORG PHILIPP, 1681-1767

1293 SCHAEFER-SCHMUCK, Käthe. **Georg Philipp Telemann als Klavierkomponist**
      (PhD diss.: Kiel, 1932; Borna-Leipzig: Noske, 1934) 70, 38p.
          Thematisches Verzeichnis der Klavierwerke G.P. Telemanns, 38p.
          in pocket.
                Two staff incipits for all movements of keyboard works,
                arranged by genre.

1294 HÖRNER, Hans. **G. P. Telemanns Passionsmusiken** (PhD diss.: Kiel;
      Borna-Leipzig: Noske, 1933) 157, 136p.
          Thematischer Katalog der erhaltenen Passionsmusiken G.P. Tele-
          mann's, 136p. at end.
                Multiple staff incipits for all sections with text under-
                lay. Works are divided into two categories: liturgical
                and oratorio, with works in the former arranged chrono-
                logically.

1295 RUHNKE, Martin. **Telemann-Forschung 1967.** Bemerkungen zum "Telemann-
☐   Werke-Verzeichnis", *Musica* XX/1 (1967) 6-10.
                Discusses the comprehensive catalogue now in preparation (see
                no. 1298).

1296 HOFFMANN, Adolf. **Die Orchestersuiten Georg Philipp Telemanns,**
      Telemann-Werke-Verzeichnis Gruppe Orchestersuiten (TWV 55)
      (Wolfenbüttel-Zürich: Möseler Verlag, 1969) 187p.
          [Thematisches Verzeichnis], 79-183.
                Incipits for all movements of 135 orchestral suites.

1297 KROSS, Siegfried. **Das Instrumentalkonzert bei Georg Philipp Telemann**
      (Tutzing: Hans Schneider, 1969) 172p.
          Thematisch-bibliographisches Verzeichnis der Konzerte Telemanns,
          121-72.
                Incipits arranged by genre.

1298 **Telemann-Werke-Verzeichnis (TWV)**
*   A complete catalogue prepared in conjunction with the Tele-
                mann, *Musikalische Werke*, (Kassel: Bärenreiter, 1950–).

1299 THALER, Alan (New York). **Thematic catalogue**
*

TENAGLIA, FRANCESCO, 17th c.

1300 CALUORI, Eleanor (Manhattan School of Music) **Thematic catalogue**
*   **of the works of Francesco Tenaglia**

TERRADELLAS, DOMINGO, 1713-1751

1301 GROEPPE, Kenneth (Boston, Mass.). **Domingo Terradellas. Thematic**
 *   **catalogue of works, and bibliography**
                Incipits of melodic line only for all sections or movements
                of operas (125 arias), and sacred music (approx. 35 pieces).
                Three incipits are provided for da capo arias (opening ritor-
                nello, beginning of 1st phrase, beginning of "B" section).

THANNABAUER, Peter Josef (compiler)

1302 **Das einstimmige Sanctus der römischen Messe in der handschriftlichen**
      Überlieferung des 11. bis 16. Jahrhunderts (Erlanger Arbeiten zur
      Musikwissenschaft, hrsg. v. Martin RUHNKE, Bd. 1) (München: Walter
      Ricke, 1963) 263p.
            Initienkatalog, 109-211.
                Incipits of 230 Sanctus melodies referred to in the text,
                giving variants of melodies and sources.

THIEL, Eberhard

1302.1 **Thematisches Verzeichnis**, *Sachwörterbuch der Musik. Kröners Taschen-*
 □   *ausgabe* Bd. 10 (Stuttgart: Kröner, 1962) viii, 602p.

THIEME, CLEMENS, 1631-1668

1303 BUCH, Hans Joachim. **Bestandsaufnahme der Kompositionen Clemens**
      Thiemes, *Mf* XVI/4 (1963) 367-78.
                Partially thematic. Single and multiple staff incipits,
                arranged by genre and library, for first movements. Tempi
                and instrumentation given for other movements. Includes
                information on MSS and lost works.

THOMAS, Christian Gottfried, 1748-1806 (compiler)

1304 **"Der grosse thematische Catalogus".** Available for sale in manuscript
 ▽   at Thomas' Notenverlag in Leipzig in 1778. 16 parts, 115½ leaves
      (manuscript copies, none located thus far) (First part, symphonies,
      20*l*.; 2nd part, "partien", 4*l*.; 3rd, piano pieces, 18*l*.; 4th, violin,
      29*l*.; 5th, viola, 2*l*.; 6th, cello, 6*l*.; 7th, "flauto traverso", 15*l*.;
      8th, oboe, 2½*l*.; 9th, bassoon, 2*l*.; 10th, French horn, 2*l*.; 11th,
      trumpet, 1*l*.; 12th, trombone, 2*l*.; 13th, clarinette, 2*l*.; 14th, harp,
      2*l*.; 15th, operas "and other wordly pieces", 4*l*.; 16th, church music,
      passion-oratoria, motets, 4*l*.).
                Thomas, an eccentric idealist, was trying to establish a
                large copying business and catalogue to rival those of Breit-
                kopf (see no. 167), his Leipzig contemporary. Although Thomas
                announced that this catalogue would be printed in 1778, it
                never was. Furthermore, no manuscript copy has been located
                thus far. A complete description, from which the above de-
                tails were obtained, is given in his 64p. pamphlet *Praktische*
                Beyträge zur Geschichte der Musik, musikalischen Litteratur
                und gemeinen Besten bestehend vorzüglich in der Einrichtung
                eines öffentlichen allgemeinen und ächten Verlags musikali-
                scher Manuscripte [Practical contributions to the history of
                music, to musical literature and to the general welfare, con-
                sisting primarily of the establishment of a public, general
                and authentic storehouse of music manuscripts to the advan-
                tage of composers and buyers; as in other literary transac-
                tions that relate to music].

1304a --- BROOK, Barry S. The dissemination of music in the Eighteenth
□   Century, *Charles Warren Fox Festschrift,* Eastman School of Music,
     50th Aniversary Celebration (Rochester, N.Y.: Eastman School of Music,
     in press)
> Discusses Thomas' career, copying storehouse, thematic cata-
> logue, and includes translations of extensive sections from
> the *Praktische Beyträge.* A version of the latter portion of
> this paper was presented at the 31st annual meeting of the
> American Musicological Society: "On the dissemination of
> music during the classic period: Christian Gottfried Thomas
> (1748-1806)", *Abstracts of papers...*Lawrence F. Bernstein,
> ed. (St. Louis, 1969).

1304b --- [Supplement] Des musikalischen summarischen Verzeichnisses erster
     Nachtrag von Sinfonien, Partien, Concerten, Divertimenten, Quintetten,
     Quartetten, Trios, Duetten, und Solos auf allen Arten Instrumenten,
     etc., die zu bekommen sind bey Christ. Gottfr. Thomas (Leipzig, 1779)
     32p.
> This printed, *non-thematic*, supplement is organized in the
> same sixteen parts as the main catalogue, and, according to
> the preface, contains only *neue Sachen.*

TITUS, Robert Austin (compiler)

1305 The solo music for the clarinet in the eighteenth century (PhD diss.:
     State U. of Iowa, 1962) xiv,604p. Univ. Micro. 62-2412. (typescript)
> "Appendix A presents a thematic index of all solo works ex-
> amined in the study," including "all available concertos,
> double concertos, and sonatas for clarinet thought to have
> been composed by about 1800."

TOCH, ERNST, 1887-1964

1306 JOHNSON, Charles A. (U. of Calif. at LA) The unpublished works of
*   Ernst Toch
        Thematic catalogue, Appendix.
> Incipits for all movements of all known works, arranged by
> genre. 171 works with all pertinent bibliographic informa-
> tion are listed.

TOESCHI, CARLO GIUSEPPE, ca.1722-1788

1307 MÜNSTER, Robert. Die Sinfonien Toeschis. Ein Beitrag zur Geschichte
▽   der Mannheimer Sinfonie (PhD diss.: München, 1956) 414p. (typescript)
> Biographies of Carl Joseph, Johann Baptist, and Karl Theodor
> Toeschi. Thematic lists appear on p.361-87; A-Chronologisches
> Verzeichnis der gedruckten Sinfonien, a catalogue of prints
> arranged chronologically with incipits not included in *DTB*
> 3/1 and 7/2; B- Verzeichnis der handschriftlich erhaltenen
> Sinfonien, a catalogue of symphonies in manuscript with inci-
> pits not in *DTB* 3/1 and 7/2; C- Thematisches Verzeichnis der
> Konzerte von Toeschi, all instrumental concertos with inci-
> pits.

TOMASINI, LUIGI, 1741-1808

1308 ▽ KORCAK, Friedrich. **Luigi Tomasini (1741-1808).** Konzertmeister der fürstlich Esterhazyschen Kapelle in Eisenstadt unter Josef Haydn (PhD diss.: Wien, 1952) iii, 245, 31*l*. (typescript)

Thematisches Verzeichnis der Werke Luigi Tomasinis, pt. II, 15*l*.

Over 100 incipits for all movements of 2 violin concertos, 10 string quartets, 24 trios, etc.

TOMKINS, THOMAS, 1572-1656

1309 ▽ BAKER, J. Anne. **The consort music of Thomas Tomkins** (MA diss.: U. of Toronto, 1968) iii, 183p. (typescript)

List of works and sources, 78-84.

Incipits for each work, with MS locations, early prints, and modern editions.

1309.1 * WALKER, Arthur D. (Manchester, England). **Thomas Tomkins [Thematic catalogue]**

TONARIES (tonaria, tonalia)

1310 These important medieval treatises were written to explain the theory of chant psalmody in terms of tonal modes. They served to guide the reader in the choice of the proper Tone (i.e. formula) to be used to connect the end of the psalm verse with the antiphon or other free melody. To accomplish this, they usually provided a listing of chant melodies arranged according to mode. When these listings are accompanied, as they often are, by musical incipits, given in neumes or other notation, they must be considered the first true thematic catalogues.

The oldest known tonary (with one minor exception) was Aurelian of Reôme's *Musica Disciplina*, ca. 850, which includes only *verbal* descriptions of the melodies. However, in the 10th century, for practical and mnemonic purposes, musical notation for the incipits (or of entire melodies) was usually added. Some of the most important early *tonaria* are those by Regino of Prüm,ca. 900, Odo of Clugny, d. 942 ,and Guido d'Arezzo, ca. 995-1050.

References: The tonaries mentioned above have been published in COUSSEMAKER, **Scriptorum**, and GERBERT, **Scriptores**.See also: Fr. X. MATHIAS, **Die Tonarien** (Diss.: Graz, 1903); Carlton T. RUSSELL, **The Southern French Tonary in the Tenth and Eleventh Centuries** (Diss.: Princeton U., 1966) and review by Clive W. BROCKETT, Jr., *CurrentMusicol*.13 (1972) 107-13; Michel HUGLO, **Les Tonaires: Inventaire, Analyse, comparaison** (Paris:Heugel, 1972)

TORELLI, GIUSEPPE, 1658-1709

1311 ✡ GIEGLING, Franz. **Giuseppe Torelli; ein Beitrag zur Entwicklungsgeschichte des italienischen Konzerts** (Kassel: Bärenreiter, 1949) 88p.

Thematisches Verzeichnis, supplement.

22 incipits are given in the 36 page index. Works listed are secular and primarily instrumental.

TORRES y MARTINEZ BRAVO, JOSEPH, 1665-1738

1312   LEVASSEUR de REBOLLO, Yvonne (U. of Pittsburgh) The Latin liturgi-
*   cal works of Joseph Torres y Martinez Bravo
          Thematic index
                Gives list, description, and incipits of Torres' extant works
                with transcriptions of those available.

TRENT CODICES

1313   Sechs [i.e. seven] Trienter Codices. Geistliche und weltliche Com-
       positionen des XV. Jahrhunderts, *DTÖ* Jahrg. 7, 11/1, 19/1, 27/1, 31,
       40 (Wien: Artaria, 1900-1933) 6v.
                Volume 1, (294p.) ed. by Guido ADLER and Oswald KOLLER, con-
                tains a thematic catalogue. Supplements in v. 2 (130p.) ed.
                by ADLER and KOLLER, and v. 5 (135p.) ed. by Rudolf von
                FICKER. The composers include the following: de Anglia,
                Anglicanus, Ariminio, Bassere, Battre, Bedingham, Benet,
                Benigni, Binchois, Bloym, Bodoil, Bourgois, Brassart, Bruolo,
                Brugis, Busnois, Caecus, Caron, Christopherus, Ciconia, Collis,
                Compère, Constans, Cornago, Cousin, Domarto, Driffelde, Du-
                fay, Dunstable, Dupont, Faugues, Forest, Frye, Gaius, Ghi-
                zeghem, Grenon, Grossin, Hermannus de Atrio, Hert, Isaac,
                Joye, Krafft, H. de Lantins, G. Le Grant, J. Le Grant, Lie-
                bert, Loqueville, Ludo, Johannes de Limburgia, Maior, Mark-
                ham, Martini, C. de Merques, N. de Merques, Ockeghem, Opili-
                onis, Piamor, Piret, Polmier, Power, Pugnare, Pyllois, Rouge,
                J. Roullet, Salice, Sandley, Sarto, Simon de Insula, Sorbi,
                Spierink, Tallalfangi, Teramo, Touront, Tressorier, Tyling,
                Velut, Verbene, Vide, Villete, Vincenet, Vitry.

TSCHAIKOWSKY, *see* **ČAJKOVSKIJ**

TSCHIEPE, Rudolph

1314   Auxiliary catalogues in the music library, *FontesArtisM* VI/1 (1959)
☐   7-9.
                Explains a numerical system for thematic cataloguing and
                states a few important cataloguing necessities for libraries.

TUMA, FRANZ, 1704-1774

1315   VOGG, Herbert. Franz Tuma (1704-1774) als Instrumentalkomponist.
▽   Nebst Beiträgen zur Wiener Musikgeschichte des 18. Jahrhunderts
       (Die Hofkapelle der Kaiserin- Witwe Elisabeth Christine) (PhD
       diss.: Wien, 1951)3v.:vi, 448p. (typescript)
          Thematischer Katalog der Instrumentalwerke, v. 3, 384-448.
                Incipits for liturgical as well as instrumental works.
                Provides lists of sources of MSS.

1316   PESCHEK, Alfred. Die Messen von Franz Tuma (PhD diss.: Wien, 1956)
▽   306p. (typescript)
          [Thematic catalogue], 141-306.
                Incipits provided for all movements in a given work, plus a
                short descriptive analysis. Includes information on sources,
                chronology, and total number of measures.

TÜRK, DANIEL GOTTLOB, 1750-1813

1317   HEDLER, Gretchen Emilie. **Daniel Gottlob Türk (1750-1813)**   (PhD diss.:
▽   Borna-Leipzig, Noske, 1936) 111p.(typescript)
         Werkeverzeichnis, 95-111.
               Index of theoretical and practical works. 77 incipits for
               clavier sonatas, lieder, cantatas. This dissertation has on
               occasion been listed under the name of THIEME, Dr. Hedler's
               married name.

TURNER, WILLIAM, 1652-1740

1318   FRANKLIN, Donald O. **The anthems of William Turner (1652-1740); an
         historical and stylistic study** (PhD diss.: Stanford U., 1967) 467p.
         Univ. Micro. 67-17,418.(typescript)
         A thematic and source catalogue of the anthems of William Turner,
         220-307.
               "Lists 35 full and verse anthems, arranged alphabetically,
               and gives a series of musical incipits in short score (243
               incipits), with two staves and text written out below all
               appropriate voices. The source listing, which immediately
               follows the incipits, contains all printed and MSS sources
               which I had discovered by 1967."

1318a --- Supplement. Additional anthems and source listings that have
 *   been uncovered since 1967. Private file.

UNVERRICHT, Hubert (compiler)

1319   [Thematic catalogue of trios]   (manuscript).
 ▽   Ca. 3000 cards deposited in München Bayerische Staatsbiblio-
               thek. Thematic catalogue of string trios, also with wind
               instruments, of the period 1740-1830, and some later, avail-
               able in print, manuscript, or only known from catalogues.
               Incipits, sometimes for all movements, arranged alphabetically
               by composer.

UPPSALA, Universitetsbiblioteket: Codex carminum gallicorum

1320   HAMBRAEUS, Bengt. **Codex carminum gallicorum.** Une étude sur le volume
         "Musique vocale du manuscrit 87" de la Bibliothèque de l'Université
         d'Upsala. (Uppsala: Studia musicologica Upsaliensia, 1961) 158p.
         Incipits des pièces anonymes, 146-58
               The MS is a 16th-century anthology, in lute tablature, of
               mainly French and Italian pieces, sacred and secular. Pages

Key: * in preparation; ▽ manuscript; □ literature; ☆ Library of Congress

79-145 include "Transcriptions complètes" (of selected pieces).
The "Incipits des pièces anonymes" are given in the order of
the manuscript. Text incipits are given on pages 21-25

UPPSALA, Universitetsbiblioteket: Düben Collection

1321 KJELLBERG, Erik. **Instrumentalmusiken i Dübensamlingen. En över-**
▽   **sikt** [Instrumental music in the Düben collection. A survey] (MA
     diss.: Uppsala, 1968) 51, 69p. (typescript, mimeographed).
          Katalogdel [Catalogue section], 69p.
             On pages 43-65, there are 109 incipits, given in Numericode,
             and taken from the catalogue of the Uppsala University Li-
             brary. Anonymi are listed by composer's initials, which
             are sometimes available, or when completely anonymous, by
             title. Incipits for several hundred other works inventoried
             in the Katalogdel have been prepared by the compiler but
             are not included.

UPPSALA, Universitetsbiblioteket: Düben Collection Supplement

1322 DÜBEN, Gustaf. **Ett nyfunnet komplement till Dübensamlingen** [A newly-
     discovered supplement to the Düben collection], *SvenskTMf* XLVII (1965)
     51-58.
          [Thematic catalogue], 52-53.
             A manuscript tablature book in the hand of Gustaf Düben, con-
             taining mainly dance movements from the 17th century. Inci-
             pits in the order of the MS.

UPPSALA, Universitetsbiblioteket: Gimo Collection

1323 **Catalego di Musica/ Mandata à casa** (S Uu: Gimo 360) 64p. (some
▽   blank) Compiled mid-18th c. Microfilm copy in US NYcg. (manu-
     script)
             This 18th century MS thematic catalogue inventories the
             Gimo Collection of Italian manuscript music, and is now
             preserved in that collection at Uppsala. Incipits for
             instrumental works (40 duets, 140 trios, 65 symphonies,
             15 concerti, 6 quintets) and 95 arias with text underlay.
             Some works in the collection are missing from the cata-
             logue. Composers include: Antinoni 1, Giovanni Bachi 10,
             Bannino 1, Barbella 8, Alessandro Besozzi 5, Antonio Bis-
             cogli 1, Brescianello 2, Gio. Gualberto Brunetti 1, Bura-
             nello 36, Pasquale Cafaro 1, Camerlocker [Camerloher].1,
             Campion 23, Gio. Battia Casali 1, Domenico Caudioso 1,
             Carlo Cecere 2, Chiabrano 11, Chrichielli 1, Vicenzo Ciam-
             pi 1, Gio. Ciurache 1, Gioacchino Cocchi 2, Comolo 1,
             Nicolo Conforti 1, Costanzi 1, Pietro Crispi 4, Diletti 1,
             Egidio Duni 1, Frascini 1, Gasparo Gabbellone 1, Galeotti
             2, García 1, Gasman [Gassmann] 2, Gasparini 9, Gio. Batta
             Gervasio 8, Ghelardi 1, Giovanni 1, Giubilei 1, Giuseppe
             Giulino 1, Grosci 1, Pietro Guglielmi 4, Hager 1, Gio.
             Adolfo Hasse Sassone 12, Nicolo Jommelli 8, Latilla 1,
             Ciccio Lecce 1, Leonardo Leo 1, Lidarti 10, Logroscino
             1, Lustrini 1, Magherini 1, Francesco di Majo 1, Carlo
             Marini 2, Martinelli 2, Bortolemo Menesini 5, Menesistris
             1, Meucci 1, Millich [Millico] 7, Minuti 1, Fran. Moroni
             1, Antonio Moselle [mosel] 1, Nardini 2, Vito Pgilo 1,
             Pergolese 2, Perillo 5, Niccolo Piccini 12, Pietro Piom-

banti 1, Tommaso Prota 3, Pugnani 6, Pietro Pulli 1, Ri-
naldo di Capua 1, Paolo Risi 2, Sabatini 19, Sacchini 1,
Sala 1, Salulini 6, Gius. Sarti 2, Schleger 2, Giuseppe
Sellitti, Simoncini 1, Giuseppe Tartini 4, Tommaso Trajetta
1, Vito Ugolino 1, Uttini 1, Mattia Vento 11, Vetrai 9,
Zannetti 26, Zuckitz 1, and 9 anonymous works.

Reference: DAVIDSSON, Åke. Catalogue of the Gimo Collection of
Italian manuscript music in the University Library of Uppsala,
Acta Bibliothecae R. Universitatis Upsaliensis XIV (Uppsala:
Almqvist & Wiksell, 1963) 101p.
This modern catalogue also inventories the Gimo collection,
but unlike the above 18th century catalogue, it is without
incipits. Davidsson describes the earlier thematic catalogue
on p. 15-16 and reproduces a page from it as frontispiece.

URBANA, Illinois. University of Illinois

1324 TROWBRIDGE, Lynn Mason. [Thematic catalogue of 15th c. chanson-
▽   niers]

Part of an on-going project for the University of Illinois
Musicological Archive for Renaissance Manuscript Studies
whose present goal is to construct a census of MS sources
from ca. 1400 to 1550. The catalogue is in 5 sections:
inventory listing, composer index, text index, pitch-inter-
val sequence order, and pitch-rhythm segment order. Indexes
2116 incipits, the lengths of which are based on their mensural organization, of the following 8 chansonniers: Berlin
78C28, Copenhagen, Dijon, Mellon, Pixérécourt, Nivelle de la
Chausée, Laborde, and Wolfenbüttel. A second index of early
16th c. motets has also been produced. Additional MSS will
be included as they are coded.

Reference: Directory of Scholars Active, *Computers in the
Humanities* IV/5 (May 1970) 343-44; V/5 (May 1971) .

VAET, JAKOB, 1529-1567

1325 STEINHARDT, Milton. Jacobus Vaet and his motets (East Lansing:
Michigan State College Press, 1951) vii, 189p.
Thematic index of the motets of Jacobus Vaet, Appendix B, [141]-
185.
76 incipits for all voices in closed (two octave) format.
No orderly system of numbering of the motets.

Key: ✱ in preparation; ▽ manuscript; □ literature; ✫ Library of Congress

VALEN, FARTEIN, 1887-1952

1326 KORTSEN, Bjarne. Thematical list of compositions by Fartein Valen
     (Oslo: Bjarne Kortsen, 1962) 141*l*.
               Incipits are fully annotated, multiple staff, including all
               parts, and arranged by opus number. Publisher and dating
               information with critical commentary provided. Gives themes
               and motives, not only incipits.

               Reference: Bjarne KORTSEN, Fartein Valen: life and music
               (Oslo: Johan Grundt Tanum, 1965) 3v.

VANHAL, JOHANN [VAŇHAL, JAN KŘTÍTEL], 1739-1813

1327 BRYAN, Paul Robey. The symphonies of Johann Vanhal (PhD diss.,
 ⚡   Musicology: U. of Michigan, 1956) 2v., 524l. Univ. Micro. 21-134.
      [Thematic catalogue], v. 1, 270-280.
               Incipits of 90 symphonies arranged by key.

1328 DEARLING, Robert J. (Dunstable, Bedfordshire). [Thematic catalogue]
 ▽   Index cards (manuscript) (see no.282).
               Incipits for symphonies, quartets, string sonatas, etc.
               Some 200 works in all.

1329 WEINMANN, Alexander (Wien). Thematischer Katalog
 *

VEA, Ketil (compiler)

1330 Tema-boka, *Oslo Norsk Musikforlag* (1969) 102p.
               Intended for pedagogical use. Incipits of composers in
               standard repertoire plus Norwegian composers e.g. Klaus
               Egge and Fartein Valen.

VERDELOT, PHILIPPE, d. 1552

1331 BÖKER-HEIL, Norbert. Die Motetten von Philippe Verdelot (PhD diss.:
     Frankfurt-am-Main, 1967) 414, 26p.
          Verzeichnis der Motetten mit ihren Incipits,Anhang III, 266-326.
               Incipits, in original notation, for each voice of 75 works.
               Incipits include all mensuration changes throughout a work.
               Sources and references in text.

VERONA, Società Accademia Filarmonica

1332 TURRINI, Giuseppe. Catalogo descrittivo dei manoscritti musicali
     antichi della Società Accademia Filarmonica di Verona, *Atti e memorie*
     della Accademia di Agricoltura Scienze e Lettere di Verona 5, v.XV
     (Verona: La Tipografica Veronese, 1937) 167-220.
          Manoscritti musicali antichi, 171-216.
               Most often works include incipits, though a substantial num-
               ber are listed by title and source only. Includes anonymous
               works of the 16th and 17th centuries, as well as works by
               Verdelot, Orazio Vecchi, and Corregio.

VERONA, Società Accademia filarmonica: MS 218

1332.1 BÜKER-HEIL, Norbert. **Zu einem frühvenezianischen Mottenrepertoire,**
Osthoff Festschrift. Frankfurter musikhistorische Studien. Helmuth
Osthoff zu seinem siebzigsten Geburtstag überreicht von Kollegen,
Mitarbeitern und Schülern, ed. by Wilhelm STAUDER, Ursula AARBURG,
and Peter CAHN (Tutzing: Schneider, 1969) 59-88. (*RILM* 69595)
[Thematic catalogue].
Incipits for works in this manuscript. "Presumably written
at Padua about 1536, the collection includes a Mass 'a 7' by
Andrea de Silva and 24 motets (7 to 10 voices), mostly by
French composers of the post-Josquin generation. Twelve of
the motets seem to unica. Along with some reworkings of
older compositions the MS preserves 2 hitherto unknown poli-
tical pieces which obviously deal with Pope Clemens VII."

VERONA, Società Accademia filarmonica: MS 220

1333 KENTON, Egon. **A faded laurel wreath.** *Aspects of Medieval & Renais-
sance Music, a birthday offering to Gustave Reese,* ed. by Jan LaRUE
(New York: Norton, 1966) 506-10.
A report on MS 220, a collection of 22 five-and six-part 16th
century Italian madrigals, in the library of the Accademia
Filarmonica in Verona. Texted incipits in modern notation,
some with C clefs. Composers include: Asola, Bell'Haver,
Carteri, P. da Monte, A. Gabrieli, G. Gabrieli, Guami, Ingeg-
neri, Lasso, Massaino, Marenzio, Merulo, Pordenone, Ruffo,
Sfogli, Striggio, Valenzola, and Vecchi.

VETTERL, Karel

1334 The method of classification and grouping of folk melodies, *Stud-*
☐   *Musicol* VII (1965) 349-55.

VIADRINA CODEX

1335 STAEHELIN, Martin. **Der Grüne Codex der Viadrina.** Eine wenig
beachtete Quelle zur Musik des späten I5. und frühen I6. Jahrhunderts in Deutschland, *Akademie der Wissenschaften und der
Literatur zu Mainz, Abhandlungen der Geistes- und Sozialwissen-
schaftlichen Klasse,* Jahrgang 1970, Nr. 10 (Mainz/Wiesbaden, 1971)
140 incipits for all voices of all sections of the works
in the manuscript.

VIANO, Richard J. (Graduate School of the C.U.N.Y.)

1335.1 The origin and early development of the violoncello sonata: a thema-
✶   tic catalogue. Index cards.
Incipits for all movements of ca. 100 works thus far. Will
include manuscript and printed works, with full bibliographical apparatus.

VIERNE, LOUIS, 1870-1937

1336 [BOUVARD, J.]. In memoriam Louis Vierne, 1870-1937. (Ses souvenirs,
suivis d'un hommage par ses confrères, élèves et amis.). (Paris:
Desclée de Brouwer, 1939) viii, 228p.
50 Thèmes d'improvisation de Louis Vierne, [195]-201

1337 LONG, Page Carroll. Transformations of harmony and consistencies
      of form in the six organ symphonies of Louis Vierne (PhD diss.:
      U. of Arizona, 1963) 259p. Univ. Micro. 63-6725.(typescript)
          Thematic index, Appendix A.
              Incipits, numbered 36 through 95, for the organ symphonies.

VIETORIS CODEX

1338 ABELMANN, Charlotte. Der Codex Vietoris. Beitrag zur Musikgeschichte
▽   des ungarisch-tschechoslowakischen Grenzgebietes (PhD diss.: Wien,
      1946) 3v., 97*l*.; 127p.; 49*l*. (typescript)
          Indices des Codex Vietoris, v. 3, 49*l*.
              364 incipits of all vocal and instrumental works contained
              in the codex.

VIEUXTEMPS, HENRI, 1820-1881

1339 BACHMANN, Alberto. Les grands violinistes du passé (Paris:
      Fischbacher, 1913) 468p. (see no. 65)
          [Thematic catalogue], 382-91.
              Themes for concertos and etudes from Op. 10, 16, 19, 28,
              35, and 37.

VIOLA DA GAMBA SOCIETY

1340 [Provisional thematic index of music for viols]
              The index is published annually in the *Viola da Gamba
              Society Journal* (England).

VIOTTI, GIOVANNI BATTISTA, 1755-1824

1341 [4] Concerti Viotti, [5] Concerti Giernovigh (US BE: It. 1018c) (see
▽   no. 107) (manuscript)
          [Thematic catalogue of concerti].
              Incipits for the first fast movement.

1342 POUGIN, Arthur. Viotti et l'école moderne de violon (Paris: Schott,
      1888) 190p.
          Catalogue des oeuvres de Viotti, [163]-188.
              157 incipits. Works include 29 violin concerti, 12 violin
              sonatas, 3 songs, plus 2 staff incipits for selected piano
              concerti and 9 piano sonatas.

1343 BACHMANN, Alberto. Les grands violinistes du passé (Paris:
      Fischbacher, 1913) 468p. (see no. 65)
          [Thematic catalogue], 403-36.
              Incipits for 61 works.

1344 GIAZOTTO, Remo. Giovanni Battista Viotti (Milano: Curci, 1956)
☆   390p.
          Catalogo tematico e cronologico delle opere, [289]-368.
              Incipits with dating and publishing information given for
              157 works . Primarily chamber works for violin and other
              strings.

VIOTTI, GIOVANNI BATTISTA, 1753-1824

1345   WHITE, E. Chappell. **Giovanni Battista Viotti and his violin concertos** (PhD diss.: Princeton U., 1957) 2v. Univ. Micro. 23,887.
   [Thematic catalogue], v. II.
        Incipits for each movement of the 29 violin concertos.

VIVALDI, ANTONIO, 1678-1741

1346   BACHMANN, Alberto. **Les grands violinistes du passé** (Paris: Fischbacher, 1913) 468p.(see no. 65)
   [Table thématique], 441-56.
        Incipits for 110 concertos, 9 symphonies, and 16 sonatas,
        arranged by number.

1347   ALTMANN, Wilhelm. **Thematischer Katalog der gedruckten Werke A.**
   Vivaldi's, *AfMW* IV (April 1922) [262]-279.
        Arranged by opus number. Manuscript sources given.

1347a --- Reprint. **La scuola veneziana, note e documenti,** *Siena, Accademia Musicale Chigiana* (Siena: Ticci, 1941) 65-73.

1347b --- Reprint. Mario RINALDI..**Antonio Vivaldi** (Milano: Istituto
   d'Alta Cultura [1943]) [409]-441.

1348   RUDGE, Olga. **A. Vivaldi, note e documenti sulla vita e sulle opere,**
   Siena, Accademia Musicale Chigiana (Siena: Settimana Musicale XVII,
   1939) 75p.
        Catalogo tematico delle opere strumentale di Antonio Vivaldi
        esistenti nella Biblioteca Nazionale di Torino, 47-59.
            An incipit listing of works in the Mauro Foà and Renzo
            Giordano collections of the Biblioteca Nazionale. Works
            are grouped according to genre and collection. Incipits
            are presented in fair, often illegible manuscript. No
            systematic grouping of works within collections and no
            indication of medium of performance is given.

1348a --- Reprinted in Mario RINALDI, **Antonio Vivaldi** (Milano: Istituto
   d'Alta Cultura ([1943]) [443]-490.

1349   RUDGE, Olga. **La Scuola Veneziana (Secoli XVI-XVIII).** Note e Documenti raccolti in occasione della Settimana Celebrativa (5-10 Settembre
   1941-XIX), *Accademia Musicale Chigiana* (Siena: Ticci, 1941)
   Opere vocali attribuite a Antonio Vivaldi nella R. Biblioteca
   Nazionale Torino-Catalogo di Alcuni "Microfilm" di MSS e stampe
   dell'Accademia Chigiana, proveniente da Biblioteche Estere, 74-80.
            Incipits for all sections of cantatas, arias, oratorios and
            concertos. The following title appears only in the Table
            of Contents: [Catalogo tematico delle opere vocali inedite
            e dei microfilms della B. Chigi Saracini].

1349a --- Reprinted in Mario RINALDI, **Antonio Vivaldi** (Milano: Istituto
   d'Alta Cultura, [1943]) [491]-523.

1350   RINALDI, Mario. **Catalogo numerico tematico delle composizione di**
   Antonio Vivaldi (Roma: Editrice Cultura Moderna, 1945) 311p.
            Employs a now obsolete system of numeration (use of opus
            numbers applied to works in Foà and Giordano collections
            at Turin). Incipits for each movement of instrumental

works listed. Includes table of sacred and secular vocal
works (some with incipits), tables of instruments and com-
binations, tonalities and a cumulative listing of works
by genre.

1351 PINCHERLE, Marc. **Antonio Vivaldi et la musique instrumentale** (Paris:
Floury, 1948) 2v.
    Inventaire-thématique, v. 2; vi, 75p.
        Includes instrumental compositions known to Pincherle up to
the time of publication. Works are listed according to genre,
various collections, and concertos both published and in MS
according to tonality. Incipits for all movements. Provides
Pincherle catalogue designations, a concordance of MS sources,
modern transcriptions, and"spuriosities."

1352 SALTER, L. S. **An index to Ricordi's edition of Vivaldi,** *Notes*
XI (June 1954) 366-74.
        A correlation between the Rudge, Pincherle, and Rinaldi
catalogues, and concordances between these and the Mali-
piero Ricordi Edition of the Works.

1353 KOLNEDER, Walter. **Zur Frage der Vivaldi-Kataloge,** *AfMW* XI/4 (1954)
☐ 323-31.
        A discussion of problems in preparing an accurate catalogue
of the works of Vivaldi. Efforts by Rinaldi, Fanna, and
Pincherle are examined in detail. Gives a listing of
Vivaldi manuscripts located in the Sächsische Landesbibliothek (Dresden), with a concordance of Dresden Library,
Pincherle, and Siena Microfilm-Archives catalogue designations, as well as contemporary printed editions and dupli-
cations found in the Biblioteca Nazionale (Turin). Brief
mention is made of a recent find of copies of the Dresden
manuscripts in Rome.

1354 **Indice tematico di 200 opere strumentali,** (Istituto Italiano
Antonio Vivaldi, serie 1 (Milano:Ricordi, 1955) 35p.
        Issued as an index of instrumental works published by the
Institute in its Collected Works edition up to 1955. Includes incipits for each movement, editor for each work,
duration of performance, and Fanna and Ricordi Edition
catalogue designations. Works grouped by genre, medium
of performance, and tonality, in subdivided order.

    Reviews: Notes XIV (Dec 1956) 44.

1355 JUNG, Hans Rudolf. **Die Dresdener Vivaldi-Manuskripte,** *AfMw* XII/4
☐ (1955) [314]-318.
        Includes Vergleichstabelle der Dresdener Vivaldi-Manuskripte,
additions to Kolneder and corrections to Pincherle lists.
No incipits.

1356 BRAUNSTEIN, Joseph. **Thematic index** on record jacket of "The complete Vivaldi" (New York: Library of Recorded Masterpieces [now
Musical Heritage Society], 1959?).
        Vol. 1, Index Record #1, contains incipits of each move-
ment of 52 works recorded, plus an index by keys and by
Ricordi, Pincherle, and Fanna classifications.

1357 CORAL, Lenore. A concordance of the thematic indexes to the instru-
☐   mental works of Antonio Vivaldi (Music Library Association, 1965)
      32p.
            Non-thematic. Three concordance sections built from the
            Rinaldi, Pincherle, and Fanna numbering schemes respective-
            ly. Works arranged by genre.

1358 FANNA, Antonio. Antonio Vivaldi: Catalogo numerico-tematico delle
✡   opere strumentali (Milano:Ricordi, 1968) 192p.
            The index of the instrumental works published in the Ri-
            cordi Edition of the works of Vivaldi, isssued concomitantly
            with the last volumes of the Edition. It is the most
            complete index available. Includes incipits for each move-
            ment, editor for each work, duration of performance, Fanna
            and Ricordi Edition catalogue designations, and location
            and call number of manuscripts an/or earlier editions.
            Spurious and unfinished works are omitted. Appendices
            include concordances for Fanna, Pincherle, and Ricordi
            Edition designations, table of comparison of various
            works, listing of works published during Vivaldi's life-
            time (bearing opus numbers), and an index of newly dis-
            covered works.

            Reviews: Stanley SADIE, Vivaldi catalogued, *MTimes* CX/
            1515 (May 1969) 492. Criticises failure to cross-reference
            other systems (Pincherle, Rinaldi) by which Vivaldi's
            works are often numbered; *RItalianaMusicol* III/2 (1968)
            328-29; *Musikhandel* XX/7 (1969) 350; *ÖsterreichischeMz* XXIV
            (Nov 1969) 662; *MensMelodie* XXIV (Dec 1969) 382; *MGes* XIX
            (Mar 1969) 214.

1359 DUNHAM, Sister Meneve. The secular cantatas of Antonio Vivaldi in
▽   the Foà Raccolta (PhD diss.: U. of Michigan, 1969) vi, 207p.(typescript)
      [Thematic index], Appendix B, [185]-197.
            Incipits of 36 cantatas. The works indexed are located in
            the Biblioteca Nazionale (Torino), the Biblioteca del Conserva-
            torio (Firenze), and the Sächsische Landesbibliothek (Dresden).

1360 MARTIN, Arlan Stone. Vivaldi violin concertos: a handbook (Metuchen,
      N.J.: Scarecrow Press, 1972) xii, 278p.
            Incipit guide, 23-262.
            Incipits for all movements of concertos arranged by key. Pro-
            vides all other cataloguing numbers, along with publications
            and recordings. Includes a cross-index.

1361 DEARLING, Robert J. (Dunstable, Bedfordshire). [Thematic catalogue]
▽   Index cards (manuscript) (see no. 282)
            "The catalogue is in Pincherle order. Appended to this is
            a cross-reference system incorporating Fanna and Ricordi
            numbers, together with Rinaldi's and the genuine opus num-
            bers, so that any work may be found immediately providing
            one of the numbers is known. Added are incipits for the
            concerti and sonatas published recently and undiscovered
            when Pincherle's catalogue appeared."

1362 RYOM, Peter (København). Verzeichnis der Werke Antonio Vivaldis
*   [short version] (scheduled for publication in 1972 by VEB Deutscher
      Verlag für Musik, Leipzig and Engstrøm & Sødring, København).
            A preliminary version of the Ryom-Verzeichnis (RV). Incipits

of first movements, together with only the essential descriptive information, references, and concordances.

1362a --- Verzeichnis der Werke Antonio Vivaldis [complete version] (To
 *　　be published a few years after the above by the same publishers.)
　　　　　　　Incipits for all movements including lost, incomplete, and
　　　　　　　spurious works with detailed source references, concordances,
　　　　　　　and complete bibliographic apparatus.

1362b --- Le premier catalogue thématique des oevres d'Antonio Vivaldi,
 ☐　　*Festskrift Jens Peter Larsen 1902 ⅞ 1972.* Studier udgivet af Musik-
　　　　videnskabeligt Institut ved Københavns Universitet. (København: Wil-
　　　　helm Hansen Musik-Forlag, 1972) 127-40.
　　　　　　　The article describes the Fuchs' Vivaldi catalogue. (see no.
　　　　　　　408)

VIVANCO, SEBASTIAN de, ca. 1550-1622

1363　ARIAS, Enrique Alberto. **The Masses of Sebastian de Vivanco (ca.**
 ▽　　**1550-1622): A study of polyphonic settings of the Ordinary in late**
　　　　Renaissance Spain (PhD diss.: Northwestern U., 1971) 2v.: x, 193;
　　　　329p. (typescript)
　　　　　　Thematic catalogue.

VOLKMANN, ROBERT, 1815-1883

1364　VOLKMANN, Hans. **Thematisches Verzeichnis der Werke von Robert Volk-**
　　　　mann (I8I5-I883), nebst Registern, Anmerkungen, Literaturnachweisen
　　　　und zwei Bildern (Dresden: W. Ramisch, 1937) 79p.
　　　　　　　Over 100 double staff incipits for all movements, arranged
　　　　　　　by opus number.

VOLLEN, Gene Earl (compiler)

1365　**The French cantata: A survey and thematic catalog** (PhD diss.: North
 ▽　　Texas State University, 1970) iv, 893p. (typescript)
　　　　　　Thematic catalog, 228-854.
　　　　　　　Single and double staff incipits for all sections of 409 can-
　　　　　　　tatas by 71 composers, including anonymi. Composers are ar-
　　　　　　　ranged in alphabetical order, and the cantatas appear below
　　　　　　　their composer in published order. Provides "Index of Com-
　　　　　　　posers"(p. 855-57) and "Index of Titles" (p. 858-74).
　　　　　　　Composers: Abeille, Anonymous, Jacques Aubert, Nicolas
　　　　　　　Bernier, Pierre Monton Berton, François Biferi, François
　　　　　　　Colin de Blamont, Boismortier, Thomas Louis Bourgeois, Jean-
　　　　　　　Baptiste Drouart de Bousset, René Drouart de Bousset, Fran-
　　　　　　　çois Bouvard, René de Bearn Brassac, Nicolas Antoine Bergi-
　　　　　　　ron de Briou, Sébastien de Brossard, Brulart, Brunet de Mo-
　　　　　　　land, Bernard Burette, Bernard de Bury, Buttier le fils, An-
　　　　　　　dré Campra, Jean-Baptiste Cappus, Marc-Antoine Charpentier,
　　　　　　　François Chauvon, Chavray, Chupin de la Guitonniere, Louis-
　　　　　　　Nicolas Clérambault, César-François Nicolas (le fils) Cléram-
　　　　　　　bault, Philippe Courbois, François David, Jean Desfontaines,
　　　　　　　André Cardinal Destouches, Louis Antoine Dornel, Dubois, Du-
　　　　　　　pré, Dupuits, Jean-Baptiste Dutartre, Pierre Février, Mr.
　　　　　　　Gxxx, Charles-Hubert Gervais, Laurent Gervais, Gomey, Nico-·

las Racot de Grandval, Honoré-Claude Guedon de Presles,Henri-Charles Guillon, Hubineau, Pierre de LaGarde, Elisabeth Claude Jacquet de La Guerre, Lejay, Louis Lemaire, C...François Lescot, Marchand Du Maine, Henriette de Mars, de Mongaultier, Michel Pignolet de Montéclair; Morel, Jean-Baptiste Morin, Jean-Joseph Mouret, Monsieur N., Louis Néron, Piffet le fils, Pipereau, Charles Piroye, Jean-Philippe Rameau, François Rebel, Nicolas Renier, André Richer, Jean-Baptiste Stuck, Louis Antoine Travenol, Jean-Claude Trial, Alexandre Villeneuve.

VOSS, Otto (compiler)

1366 Die sächsische Orgelmusik in der zweiten Hälfte des I7. Jahrhunderts (Jena: Neuenhahn, 1936) 99p.

>   Übersicht der erhaltenen Orgelkompositionen geordnet nach den vier oben aufgeführten Kreisen, 60-86.

>>   The partially thematic index (p. 60-86) includes themes, usually one staff, soprano or bass, from the works of Böhme, Edelmann, Fabricius, Garthoffen, Hammerschmidt, Heinichen, Kauffmann, Krieger, Kuhnau, Michael, Pestel, Petzold, Strungk, Vetter, Witte.

VRANICKÝ, ANTONÍN, 1761-1820

1367 BLAŽEK, Vlastimil. Bohemica v lobkovském zámeckém archivu v Roudnici n.L. (Praha: Knihovna Hudební Výchovy, 1936) 156p. [Thematic catalogue], 78-155.

>   Approximately 240 incipits for dances, trios, quartets, serenades, concerti, symphonies, vocal works with orchestra, Mass, motets, etc.

VRANICKÝ, PAVEL, 1756-1808

1368 BLAŽEK, Vlastimil. Bohemica v lobkovském zámeckém archivu v Roudnici n.L. (Praha: Knihovna Hudební Výchovy, 1936) 156p. [Thematic catalogue], 12-50.

>   Incipits for all movements of 11 symphonies, 3 quintets, 3 violin concerti, overture, 2 quodlibets, 4 quartets, and ca. 200 vocal works (mostly canons).

1369 POSTOLKA, Milan. Thematisches Verzeichnis der Sinfonien Pavel Vranickýs, *Miscellanea musicologica* XX (1968) 101-28.

>   Incipits for 51 symphonies, arranged by key with an index of opus numbers, and a chronological table.

WAGENSEIL, GEORG CHRISTOPH, 1715-1777

1370 MICHELITSCH, Helga. **Das Klavierwerk von Georg Christoph Wagenseil,** *Tabulae Musicae Austricae* III (Wien : Böhlaus, 1966) 163 p. **Thematischer Katalog.**
Over 600 double staff incipits for all movements of the clavier works.

Reviews: Musikhandel XVIII/4 (1967) 204; Bernhard HANSEN, *Mf* XXI/4 (1968) 530; A.Hyatt KING,*Erasmus* XIX (1967) 553-54.

1371 KUCABA, John. **The symphonies of Georg Christoph Wagenseil** (PhD diss.: Boston U., 1967) 543p. Univ. Micro. 67-13,319.(typescript) **[Thematic catalogue],** v. 2, 2-136.
Contains numerous examples and thematic incipits.

1372 DEARLING, Robert J. (Dunstable, Bedfordshire). **[Thematic catalogue]**
▽ Index cards. (manuscript) (see no. 282)
Incipits for 78 symphonies and string sonatas.

WAGNER, RICHARD, 1813-1883

1373 KASTNER, Emerich. **Wagner-Catalog. Chronologisches Verzeichniss der von und über Richard Wagner erschienenen Schriften, Musikwerke, etc., etc., nebst biographischen Notizen** (Offenbach: André, 1878) 140, 8, [30]p.
Catalogue musical et thématique de toutes les compositions gravées de R. Wagner, ainsi que des transcriptions, fantasies et arrangements dont elles ont été l'objet, [30p.]
Double and triple (voice and piano) incipits, with tempo indications, text underlay, available editions, dedications, and arrangements.

1374 PARKINSON, Frank. **Bibliography of Wagner's Leit-motives and preludes. With commentaries on Lohengrin and Parsifal** (London: Waterlow Bros. & Layton, 1893) 48p.

1375 DUBITZKY, Franz. **Von der Herkunft Wagnerscher Themen,***Musikalisches Magazin* L (1912) (Langensalza: Beyer, 1912)
A tracing of the origins of Wagnerian themes through works of other composers. Examples showing how two or more composers used the same thematic material.

1376 WINDSPERGER, Lothar. **Das Buch der Motive und Themen aus sämtlichen Opern und Musikdramen Richard Wagner's. In zwei Bänden. Für Klavier zu 2 Händen mit übergelegtem Text** (Mainz-Leipzig: B. Schott's Söhne, [1921]) 2v.: 58, 56p.
491 themes and motives of operas: Rienzi, Fliegende Holländer,

---

Key: ∗ in preparation; ▽ manuscript; ☐ literature; ☆ Library of Congress

Tannhäuser, Lohengrin, Tristan und Isolde, Meistersinger,
Rheingold, Walküre, Siegfried, Götterdämmerung, Parsifal.
Works arranged in chronological order. Manuscript sources
given, as well as various editions of piano arrangements of
the operas.

1377 TERRY, E.M. A Richard Wagner dictionary (New York: Wilson, 1939)
     Leading motives of the operas, [32p] at end.
          Entries vary from piano reduction to single lines and are
          usually 2 to 4 measures in length.

1378 GECK, Martin. [Thematic catalogue]
*   This catalogue will be one of the first volumes of Wagner's
          Complete Works to be published by Bayerische Akademie der
          Schönen Künste (München) and B.Schott's Söhne (Mainz) under
          the general editorship of Carl DAHLHAUS.

WAKELING, Donald R. (compiler)

1379 National anthems, *Grove's Dictionary of Music and Musicians* 5th ed.
     1954 VI, 14-29.
          Authors and composers and their dates given. Discussion of
          previous anthems; latest recognized anthem specified. 95
          incipits given.

WALDBURG-ZEIL, Fürstlich Waldburg-Zeil'sches Gesamtarchiv

1380 Musikalienkataloge (1767-ca.1786)   (D Zl) 77*l*. (manuscript)
          Single and double staff incipits for nearly 600 instrumental
          works (symphonies, concertos, trios, quintets, quartets, etc.)
          of the 18th century. Composers: Albrechtsberger, Bauer,
          Beecke, Bieling, Boccherini, Breval, Cambini (Campini), Can-
          nabich, Caspar, Cirri, Davaux, Ditters, Dolphin, Eisenmann,
          Esser, Fehr, Fieronj, Filz, Fischietti, Foghiti, Foder, Fran-
          cisconi, Fuchs, George, Giardini, Giordani, Giuliani, Grei-
          ner,Hanser, Hasse, Haydn (Heydn), Heyde, Hemberger, Himel-
          paur, Hoffman, Holzbauer (Holtzbauer), Holzbogen, Ivanschiz,
          Jacobi, Jommelli, Justen, Kaa, Kammel, Kraus, Kuchler, Kÿff-
          ner, Lacher, Lachnith, Lang, Liber, Maÿer, Mederitsch, Mozart,
          Müller, Navoigille, Neeffe, Neubaur, Neuman, Ordonez, Pam-
          pani, Pasqualini, Passero, Pattori, Pergolesi, Pfeiffer,
          Pleyel, Pokorni, Pugnani, Rigel, Rosetti, Sales, Salieri,
          Schiatti, Schmid, Schmitt, Schmittbaur, Schnizer, Schobert,
          Schwindel, Singer, Sperger, Stainmez, Stamitz, Stamitz (Ant.),
          Sterkel, Steffan (Stephen), Titz, Toeschi, Vanhal, Vetter,
          Wranizky, Zach.

WALIN, Stig (compiler)

1381 Beiträge zur Geschichte der schwedischen Sinfonik; Studien aus dem
     Musikleben des 18. und des beginnenden 19. Jahrhunderts (Stockholm:
     P.A. Norsted & Söper, 1941)
          Notenanhang, 24p.
          Incipits of 103 symphonies with MS locations.

WALTER, Georg (compiler)

1382   Verzeichnis von Werken der Mannheimer Symphoniker im Besitze der
       Universitätsbibliothek in Basel und der Allgemeinen Musikgesell-
       schaft in Zürich, *Festschrift zum Zweiten Kongress der Internationalen
       Musikgesellschaft* (Basel: F. Reinhardt, 1906) 87-103.
              Catalogue of works which are contained in both libraries.
              Only 32 works are with incipits. Composers: Johann Stamitz,
              Franz Xaver Richter, Anton Filtz, Ignaz Holzbauer, Joseph
              Toeschi, Christian Cannabich, Carl Stamitz, Fränzl [Ignaz
              Fränzl].

WANGERMÉE, Robert (compiler)

1383   Les maîtres de chant des XVIIe et XVIIIe siècles à la collégiale des
       SS. Michel et Gudule à Bruxelles, *Académie royale de Belgique. Classe
       des Beaux-Arts. Mémoires*, t. 7, fasc. 1 (Bruxelles: Palais des
       Académies, 1950) 310p.
              Catalogue thématique, 253-74.
                     Contains thematic catalogues for the following composers:
                     Pierre-Hercule Bréhy— 54 Masses, 6 lamentations, 13 sonatas,
                     2 misc.; Charles-Joseph van Helmont— 82 Masses & motets, 5
                     lamentations, 5 litanies, 1 oratorio, 13 instrumental works;
                     Adrien-Joseph van Helmont— 1 Mass, 2 motets, and 1 opéra
                     comique.

WARD, JOHN, 1571-1638

1384   MEYER, Ernst Hermann. Die mehrstimmige Spielmusik des 17. Jahr-
 ⋈   hunderts in Nord- und Mitteleuropa (Kassel: Bärenreiter, 1934)
       258p. (see no. 821)
              [Thematic catalogue], 162-63.
                     Incipits for 1 Innomine à 5, 8 fantasias à 6, 2 Innomines
                     à 6.

WARD, Tom R. (compiler)

1385   The polyphonic office hymn from the late fourteenth century to the
       early sixteenth century (PhD diss., Musicology: U. of Pittsburgh,
       1969) 509p. U. Micro. 70-4271 (typescript)
              Thematic catalogue, Appendix I, 203-509.
                     Incipits for 587 hymns include all voices on multiple staves.
                     "The entries are arranged alphabetically by the incipit of
                     the first stanza of the hymn regardless which stanza is un-
                     derlaid in a particular setting. All text underlaid is in-
                     dicated as well as the voices in which it is complete. The
                     traditional chant melody incorporated into each setting is
                     listed, and settings using the same melody form sub-groups
                     under each text. Within each sub-group the arrangement is
                     chronological. Only continental manuscripts have been in-
                     cluded."

WARREN, Charles Stevens (compiler)

1386   A study of selected eighteenth-century clarinet concerti (PhD diss.:
 ▽   Brigham Young U., 1963) 2v.(typescript)

Appendix A contains a thematic index of all movements of the
twenty concerti studied; Appendix B contains seventeen
clarinet solo parts.

WARSZAWA, Biblioteka: Krasinski Library

1386. JACHIMECKI, Zdzis. **Muzyka na dworze krola Władysława Jagiełły 1424-
1430** [Music in the court of King Vladislav Jagiello, 1424-1430],
Rozprawy Wydziału Filologicznego Akademii Umiejętnosci, t. 54 (Kraków: Reports of the Academy of Science, Philogical Department, v. 54,
1915) 38p.
> Includes a thematic index of MS no. 52 of the Krasinski Li-
> brary of Warsaw. 36 incipits for works by Mikołay z Radomia
> (Nicolaus de Radom), Ciconia, Zacharias, and others.

WASHINGTON, Catholic University of America. Music Library

1387 DOWER, Catherine A. **Eighteenth-Century Sistine Chapel Codices in
the Clementine Library of the Catholic University of America** (PhD
diss.: Catholic U., 1968) xiv, 176p. Univ. Micro. 69-9167. *DA* XXIX
12, p. 4516-a.(typescript)
Thematic catalogue, 103-73.
> Incipits for all voices of 32 motets, 6 antiphons, 5 psalms,
> 2 hymns, Masses, and a Mass setting by Palestrina.

WASHINGTON, Library of Congress, Music Division

1388 **Eddy hymn book index.** (US LC, Music Division.) Index cards.(manuscript)
▽
> About 6000 entries from 40 hymnals, mostly 19th-century
> American. First lines and incipits provided.

WASSERBURG/INN, Chorarchiv St. Jakob, Pfarramt

1389 **[Thematic catalogue]**
*
> Incipit catalogue in preparation under the auspices of the
> *Deutsche Forschungsgemeinschaft (DFG),* under the general
> direction of Robert MÜNSTER.

WAWEL, Poland. "Conservator's books"

1390 GLUSZCZ-ZWOLIŃSKA, Elżbieta, ed.. **Zbiory muzyczne proweniencji
wawelskiej, Tom I, zeszyt I** [Collections of music copied for use
at Wawel, V. 1, Fasc. 1] (Krakow: PWM, 1969) 40p., 61 leaves, 4p..
Katalog tematyczny rekopiśmiennych zabytków dawnej muzyki w Polsce,
[Thematic catalogue of early musical manuscripts in Poland],
SZWEYKOWSKI, Zygmunt M., general ed..
> First in a series of thematic catalogues of individual early
> MSS or groups of MSS extant in Poland, this volume will
> consist of 6 fascicles copied for use at Wawel. 128 multiple-
> staff incipits of 61 a capella sacred vocal works from the
> oldest extant set of part-books from the second half of the
> sixteenth century, known as the "conservator's books".
> Each entry gives title, text incipit, composer, number of
> voices, nature of text, concordances and editions. Most
> works are anonymous, but 6 composers are given: Borek,
> Krzysztof; Certon, Pierre; Felsztyna, Sebastian z; Gawara,
> Walentyn; Paligon, Marcin; Szadek, Tomasz.

WEBER, KARL MARIA FRIEDRICH ERNST, FREIHERR VON, 1786-1826

1391 [Thematic catalogue of works, incomplete] (D Bds: HB VII, Mus. ms.
▽   theor. K. 843) 84p. Compiled 19th c. (manuscript)
> Single, double, and multiple staff incipits arranged by opus
> number through Op. 75. Appends incipits for additional
> works, both with and without opus numbers. Gives publishers
> for some.

1392 JÄHNS, Friedrich Wilhelm. **Carl Maria von Weber in seinen Werken.**
Chronologisch-thematisches Verzeichnis seiner sämmtlichen Compositionen (Berlin: Schlesinger, 1871) 480p.
> A chronological arrangement of the works (by year only), with
> single and double staff incipits for all movements. Annota-
> tions include information on editions, autographs, instru-
> mentation etc. Main catalogue preceded by a list of first-
> movement incipits arranged by genre and provided with the
> number of the main entry. Includes incomplete, lost, and
> spurious compositions.

1392a --- Reprint. (Berlin:Lichterfelde, Lienau, 1967)

> *Reviews: MTimes* CIX (Oct 1968) 924; *Mf* XXII/2 (1969) 236-37.

WEBER, JACOB GOTTFRIED, 1779-1839

1393 LEMKE, Arno. **Jacob Gottfried Weber. Leben und Werk. Ein Beitrag
zur Musikgeschichte des mittelrheinischen Raumes,** *Beiträge zur mittelrheinischen Musikgeschichte* Nr. 9 (Mainz: Schott's Söhne, 1968) 320p.
Thematischer Gesamtkatalog, 55-167.
> Over 100 incipits, single and multiple staff, primarily of
> Lieder, cantatas, and variations.

WEIGL, Johann Nep. (compiler)

1394 [Quartbuch or Kleine Quartbuch (little folio book)] 2 Thematischer
▽   Cathalog [sic] verschiedener Compositionen von verschiedenen Mei-
stern,2 Bände   (original destroyed in 1944; copy in A Wn: suppl.
mus. 9040; Marion Scott's photocopy of the original in GB Cu; Microfilm copy of A Wn: suppl. mus. 9040 in US NYcg) 2v., 50ℓ. each. Compiled ca. 1775. (manuscript)
> According to H.C. Robbins Landon, the Quartbuch was destroyed
> in 1944 when the Esterházy Archives in Budapest were bombed.
> This entry is based on the copy in the Österreichische Na-
> tionalbibliothek. A fragmentary catalogue of a collection
> from an Austrian archive, possibly Melk. Incipits for sym-
> phonies and chamber works arranged by key. Contains a large
> number of Haydn's works including most of the early sympho-
> nies. Haydn looked through the catalogue and made a number
> of corrections, indicating on the first page of volume I:
> "94 Stück sind hierin angemerckt von Jos. Haydn" and on the
> first page of volume II: "Hierin sind 61 Sinfonien und 2
> Divertimenti von Jos. Haydn". Though Haydn made several
> corrections of spurious compositions, a number of doubtful
> works remain. Composers include: Abel, Albrechtsberger,
> Bach, Bartta, Ditters, Fils, Gassman, Gossec, Hoffmann, Hof-
> mann, Holzbauer, Hucker, Krottendorfer, Kymerling, Kyttner,
> Maldere, Ordonez, Piccini, Pichl, Schlöger, Schmid, Stamitz,

Vanhal, Wagenseil, Ziegler, Zimmermann, and some anonymous.

Reference: H.C. Robbins LANDON, The symphonies of Joseph Haydn, p. 12. (see no. 554).

WEIGL, JOSEPH, 1766-1846

1395 BOLLERT, Werner. Joseph Weigl und das deutsche Singspiel, *Aufsätze zur Musikgeschichte* (Bottrop: Postberg,[1938]) 95-114, 129-36.
Notenanhang, 129-36.
Ca. 50 incipits of Singspiel "numbers".

1396 GRASBERGER, Franz. Joseph Weigl (1766-1846). Leben und Werk mit
▽ besonderer Berücksichtigung der Kirchenmusik (PhD diss.: Wien, 1938)
179*l.* (typescript)
Thematischer Katalog, 104-13.
24 double staff incipits for 11 Masses, 6 Graduals, and 7 Offertories. Leaves 81-102 contain a list of works without incipits.

WEINER, Paul (compiler)

1397 Cyclopedia of music (New York, [19--]) 15v. (manuscript)
▽ Thirty looseleaf notebooks in typescript containing manuscript incipits with text of solo vocal materials: songs (arranged by nationality), opera excerpts, sacred music and some duets.
In the New York Public Library at Lincoln Center.

WEINWURM, RUDOLF, 1835-1911

1398 FRIEBEN, Johann. Rudolf Weinwurm (PhD diss.: Wien, 1962) 3v., 287*l.*;
▽ 211, 126*l.*; 333*l.* Notenbeilagen (typescript)
Chronologisches Werkverzeichnis, v. 3, 30-266.
Multiple staff incipits for all movements of over 600 works including choruses, Lieder, Masses, operas, clavier works, and other genres.

WEIRICH, AUGUST, 1858-1921

1399 CUDERMAN, Mirko. Der Cäcilianismus in Wien und sein erster Repräsen-
▽ tant am Dom zu St. Stephan August Weirich 1858-1921 mit thematischem Katalog seines Gesamtschaffens und Darstellung seiner Messen (PhD diss.: Wien, 1960) 2v., 218, 133*l.* (typescript)
Thematischer Katalog der Werke August Weirichs, v. 2.
Double staff incipits for all movements of 4 Masses, 1 Requiem, Mass Propers, Graduals, Offertories, hymns, motets, Lieder, organ works, and 1 symphony.

WELLESLEY EDITION CANTATA INDEX SERIES

1400 JANDER, Owen, general editor.
The following volumes have appeared, or will appear, in the series. Specific entries can be found under the composers' names: Pier Simone Agostini, Bononcini (see no. 101), Carlo Caproli, Giacomo Carissimi, Antonio Cesti, Alessandro Melani, Atto Melani, Bernardo Pasquini, Luigi Rossi, Mario Savioni, Agostino Steffani, Alessandro Stradella.

WERT, GIACHES DE, 1535-1596

1401 BERNSTEIN, Melvin. The sacred vocal music of Giaches de Wert
▽   (PhD diss., Music: U. of North Carolina, 1964) 2v. (typescript)
          Thematic catalogue, v. 2, iii, 191.
              Contains "only melodic incipits of opening sections (in-
              teresting in that they are not always the original first
              strophes). The subdivision of the catalogue of Wert hymns
              is by book (I and II) and period of the liturgical year
              of specific feastday. A further listing of texts only
              under the same headings indicates text incipits of follow-
              ing sections."

1402 --- The hymns of Giaches de Wert, *Studies in musicology. Essays
      in the history, style, and bibliography of music.* In memory of
      Glen Haydon, ed. by James PRUETT (Chapel Hill, N.C.: North Caro-
      lina P., 1969) 190-210.
              "Incipits arranged in order of hymns in two volumes, first
              strophe only. Correlations concerning melodic usage pro-
              vided."

WESLEY, SAMUEL, 1766-1837

1403 AMBROSE, Holmes. The Anglican anthems and Roman Catholic motets of
▽   Samuel Wesley (1766-1837) (PhD diss.: Boston U., 1969) 2v.: 756p.
      (typescript) (*RILM* 69/ 1007dd)
              Incipits for 23 English anthems and 31 Latin motets.

WEYSE, CHRISTOPH ERNST FRIEDRICH, 1774-1842

1404 FOG, Dan (Copenhagen). A thematic catalogue of his printed works
*   "Bibliographical description of first edition, dates of
              composition and first edition, contemporary editions,
              arrangements and version by the composer and others,
              important later editions.......chronological and systema-
              tical listing, index of titles and first-lines, and of
              names of persons and locations."

WIEN, Zentralarchiv des Deutschen Ordens

1405 Freudenthal. Catalogue Des Diverses Musiques (A Wdo) Late 18th c.
▽   (manuscript)
              Incipits of symphonies. Recent efforts to examine this cata-
              logue in person or through microfilm copy have been unsuccess-
              ful.

WIEN, Kunsthistorisches Museum: Estensische Sammlung

1406 HAAS, Robert. Die Estensischen Musikalien; thematisches Verzeichnis
      mit Einleitung (Regensburg: Bosse, 1927) 232p.
              A thematic catalogue of the musical works owned by the
              Este.-Habsburg family. Incipits of the first movements of
              works, with tempo and meter indications for subsequent move-
              ments. Entries are arranged alphabetically by composer
              within the following headings: Druckwerke; Handschriften:

Solosonaten, Sonaten a Due, Sonaten in stärkerer Besetzung, and Sinfonien und Konzerte (Benannte Werke, Unbenannte Werke). Partial list of composers: Dall'Abaco 10, Albinoni 12, Filippo Banner 2, Bella 3, Belisi, Boni 12, Bononcini 1, Brivio 1, Giuseppe Maria Brimi Bolognese 10, Buonporti 10, Caldara 9, Corelli 1, Garzaroli 6, Ferronati 10, Legrenzi 12, Locatelli 1, Marini 12, Mazzaferrata 12, Ruggieri 20, Vivaldi 12, and Zotti 12.

WIEN. Musikarchiv der Kirche St. Karl Borromäus

1407 ANTONÍCEK, Theophil. **Musikarchiv der Kirche St. Karl Borromäus**
▽   (manuscript)
This music archive contains approximately 3000 individual works. The compiler has all incipits for both printed works and MSS in a card file. The catalogue of the printed works has already been published *without* incipits [*Tabulae Musicae Austriacae* IV (Wien: Böhlau, 1968)]. A catalogue of the MSS *with* incipits will be published in the same series.

WIEN, Minoritenkonvent: Mus. MS 64, 67 and 139

1408 CALVIN, Edouard Ward. **Die Handschriften Mus. MS 64, 67 und 139 des**
▽   **Minoritenkonvents zu Wien.** Beitraege zur Geschichte der Wiener Kla-
vier- und Orgelmusik im ausgehenden 17. Jahrhundert (PhD diss.:Wien, 1955) 122*l.* (typescript)
[**Thematic catalogue**], 93-121.
135 incipits, single and double staff, for clavier and organ works contained in the 3 MSS. Genres include cadenzas, pre- ludes, toccatas, fugues, dances, passacaglias, suites and partitas. Composers represented are: Wolfgang Ebner, Johann Kaspar Kerll, Georg Muffat, Johann Pachelbel, Poglietti, Georg Reutter, Ferdinand Tobias Richter, and Franz Matthias Techelmann.

WIEN, Österreichische Nationalbibliothek: MS S.m. 2454 [catalogue]

1409 **Catalogo delle Opere, Serenade, Cantate, ed Oratori le quali Sua**
▽   **Imperiale Reale Maesta l'Imperadore Giuseppe II Si compia que di**
trasmetter nell' Archi-vio Musicale, dell' Imp.: Reale Capella,
L'Ano MDCCLXXVIII (A Wn: MS S.m. 2454) [Catalogue from the Hof-
musikkapelle of Joseph II. Includes no incipits, but has same sig- nature and is bound with:] [reproducion on following page]

CATALOGO/ delle/ Musiche Ecclesiastiche/ in Concerto e Pieno/ lequali si ritrovano nell'/ Archivio Musicale/ dell' Imp: e Reale Capella./ degl' Autori, e Maestri di Capella/ Reutter, Gasmann, e Bonno./ Um-
lauf. (A Wn: S.m. 2454) 117, [65]p. (manuscript). Microfilm copy in US NYcg.
Double staff incipits for sacred vocal works by Reutter (258), Gassmann (26), and Bonno (55). Arranged by genre for each composer; includes instrumentation. An appended section (in a different hand) provides incipits for 261 works by the fol- lowing composers: Albrechtsberger, Caldara, Doblhoff, Eÿbler,

Adolfo Hasse, Gius. Haydn (Haÿdn),(Mich.) Michaele Haydn
(Haÿdn), (L., Leop.) Leopol. Hoffmann, Hummel, Koželuch,
Krottendorffer, Wolf. Mozart, Pasterwitz, Preindel, Salieri,
Gior. Spangler, Süssmaÿer, Massimiliano (Massi., M.) Ulbrich,
Umlauf, Pietro (P.) Winter.

WIEN, Österreichische Nationalbibliothek: MS S.m. 2456 [catalogue]

1410   CATALOGO/ delle/ Musiche Ecclesiastiche/in/ Concerto e Pieno/ lequali
▽   si ritrovano nell'/ Archivio Musicale/ dell'Imp: e Reale Capella./
       degl' Autori, e Maestri di Cappella/ Reütter, Gasmann, e Bonno.
       (A Wn: S.m. 2456) 118p. (manuscript). Microfilm copy in US NYcg.
           A partial copy of A Wn: S.m. 2454, containing incipits for
           only Reutter (258), Gassmann (26), and Bonno (50).

WIEN, Österreichische Nationalbibliothek: MS S.m. 2457 [catalogue]

1411   Musiche/ Per la Chiesa/ In Concerto./ Aut: Reütter.   (A Wn: S.m.
▽   2457) [xxx], 72p. (manuscript). Microfilm copy in US NYcg.
           Double staff incipits, with instrumentation, for sacred vo-
           cal works by Reutter (167), Gassmann (26), and Bonno (48).
           Opens with a non-thematic inventory of vocal music by Reut-
           ter.

WIEN, Österreichische Nationalbibliothek : MS S.m. 2464 [catalogue]

1412   CATALOG/ der/ neueren gangbaren/ Kirchen-Musik/ für das/ k.k. Hof-
▽   Musik-Grafen-Amts-Archiv./ 1825   (A Wn: S.m. 2464) [vi], 185p.
       (manuscript). Microfilm copy in US NYcg.[reproduction on preceding page]
           A catalogue of sacred vocal works of the 18th and 19th cen-
           turies, organized by genre and alphabetically by composer
           within genre. Double staff incipits for 621 works, with in-
           dication of instrumentation. Includes a table of contents
           and a non-thematic inventory of additional sacred vocal works.
           Composers include: Anton Adelgasser, Georg Albrechtsberger,
           Ignaz Assmayer, Beethoven, Heinrich Graf Bombelles, Luigi
           Cherubini, Joseph Eybler, Joh. Bapt. Gansbacher, Florian
           Gassmann, Carl Heinrich Graun, Georg Friedrich Händel, Jo-
           hann Adolph Hasse, Joseph Haydn, Michael Haydn, Leopold Hof-
           mann, Joh. Nepom. Hummel, Pater Joseph Kaintz, Joh. Anton
           Kozeluch, Joseph Krottendorfer, Peter Lindpaintner, Wolfg.
           Amad. Mozart, Joh. Amad. Naumann, Joseph Panny, Georg Pas-
           terwitz, Joseph Preindl, Joseph Prentner, Benedict Rand-
           hartinger, Georg Reutter, Vincenzo Righini, Antonio Sacchini,
           Antonio Salieri, Schneider, Albert Schulz, Simon Sechter,
           Ignaz Seyfried, Georg Spangler, Abbé Maximilian Stadler,
           Stuntz, Franz Xaver Süssmayer, Anton Teyber, Maximilian Ul-
           brich, Ignaz Umlauff, Michael Umlauff, F.G. Vogler, Jos.
           Weigl, Peter v. Winter, Johann Wittasseck, Hugo Worzischeck.

WIEN, Österreichische Nationalbibliothek: MS S.m. 2465 [catalogue]

1413   Katalog/ der/ gangbaren/ KIRCHEN-MUSIK/ für das/ k.k. Hof-Musik-Gra-
▽   fen/ Amts-Archiv./ 1825. (p. 261: "Erneuert im July 1844– Frühwald,
       Archivar") (A Wn: S.m. 2465) [viii], 261p. (manuscript). Micro-

film copy in US NYcg.

        Double staff incipits for sacred vocal works from the 16th
to 19th c., with a listing of instruments for each entry.
Arranged alphabetically by composer, then by genre under
each composer's name. Contains a table of contents (arranged alphabetically) and a non-thematic inventory of Introits.
An updated version of SM 2464 (see above entry). Composers
inventoried: Adelgasser, Adler, Aiblinger, Albrechtsberger,
Anerio felice, Ignaz Assmayr, Mich. Bauer, Beethoven, Jul.
v. Belizay, Julius Benoni, Beraneck, Rudolf Bibl, Heinrich
Graf v. Bombelles, Moritz Brosig, Ant. Bruckner, Luigi Cheru-
bini, Anton Diabelli, Gaetano Donizetti, Josef Drechsler,
Eybler, Robert Führer, Joa. Jos. Fux, Joh. Bapt. Gänsbacher,
Gassmann, Constanze Geiger, Charles Gounod, Graun, Franz
Grutsch, Händel, Hasler, Hasse, Joseph Haydn, Michael Haydn,
Joh. Herbeck, Hoffmann, Horak, Hoven, Joh. Nep. Hummel, Leop.
Jansa, Kaintz, Kässmayer, Friedrich Kiel, Franz Kostinger,
Joh. Krall, Krottendorfer, Kozeluch, Josef Labor, Franz Lach-
ner, Orlando Lasso, Peter Lindpaintner, Franz Liszt, Anto-
nio Lotti, Friedrich Lux, Franz Mair, Joseph Mayseder, Wil-
helm Mittag, Mozart, Naumann, Neugebauer, Sigmund Neukomm,
Neuland, Nicolai, Pierluigi da Palestrina, Panny, Pasterwitz,
Car. Franc. Pitsch, Preindl, Prentner, Gottfried Preyer,
Heinrich Proch, Benedict Randhartinger, Reisinger, Reutter,
Righini, Ludwig Rotter, Sacchini, Salieri, P.Corn. Scherzin-
ger, H. Schnaubelt, Hans Schlager, Øchneider, Franz Schubert,
Josef Schubert, Schulz, R. Schumann, Sechter, Fr. Greg. Seeg-
ner, Seyfried, Carl Seyler, Spangler, Abbé Maximilian Stad-
ler, Stehle, Stuntz, Süssmayer, Teyber, Ignaz Umlauff, Mich.
Umlauff, Orazio Vecchi, Georg Vogler, Carl M.v. Weber, Joseph
Weigl, Winter, Wittassek, Hugo Worzischek, Franz Jos. Zierer.

WIEN, Österreichische Nationalbibliothek: MS S.m. 2466 [catalogue]

1414   **CATALOG/ der/ neueren gangbaren/ Kirchen Musik/ für das/ k.k. Hof-**
▽   **Musikgrafenamts=/ Archiv./ 1825/ Erneuert 1850.** (A Wn: S.m. 2466)[vi],
    225p.   (manuscript). Microfilm in US NYcg.

        A less inclusive version of A Wn: S.m. 2465. Contains 806
double staff incipits. Composers: Anton Cajetan Adelgasser,
Georg Adler, Aiblinger, Albrechtsberger, Ignaz Assmayr, Lud-
wig van Beethoven, Benoni, Beranek, Heinrich Graf Bombelles,
Ludwig Cherubini, Anton Diabelli, Cajetan Donizetti, Jos.
Edler v. Eybler, Joa. Fux, Joh. Bapt. Gänsbacher, Florian
Gassmann, Constanze Geiger, Carl Heinrich Graun, Grutsch,
Georg Friedrich Händel, Hasler, Joh. Adolph Hasse, Joseph
Haydn, Michael Haydn, Leopold Hoffmann, W.E. Horak, Johann
Hoven, Johann Nep. Hummel, Pater Joseph Kaintz, Kässmayr,
Johann Anton Kozeluch, Joh. Krall, Joseph Krottendorfer,
Lackner, Orlando di Lasso, Peter Lindpaintner, Antonio Lotti,
Joseph Mayseder, Wilhelm Mittag, Wolfgang Amadeus Mozart,
Johann Gottlieb Naumann, Neugebauer, Sigmund Ritter von
Neukomm, W. Neuland, Otto Nicolai, Giov. Pierluigi da Pales-
trina (Pranestiono), Pasterwitz, Carol. Franc. Pitsch, Jos.
Preindl, Prentner, Gottfried Preyer, Heinrich Proch, Bene-
dict Randhartinger, Carl Gottlieb Reissiger, Georg v. Reutter,
Vincenzo Righini, Ludwig Rotter, Antonio Sacchini, Antonio
Salieri, Schläger, Joseph Schubert, Schultz, Simon Sechter,

Ignaz Ritter v. Seyfried, Seyler, Georg Spangler, Maximilian
Stadler, Joseph Stuntz, Franz Xav. Süssmayer, Anton Teyber,
Ignaz Umlauff, Michael Umlauff, Orazio Vecchi, Georg Jos. Abbé Vogler, Joseph Weigl, Peter von Winter, Johann Nep. Witta-
sek, Joh. Hugo Worzischek, Fr. Jos. Zierer.

WIEN, Österreichische Nationalbibliothek: Ms. 16798

1415 SCHOTT, Howard M. (Wadham College, Oxford). [Thematic catalogue of
*   Vienna Ms. 16798]
          This manuscript was   " catalogued in part, somewhat in-
          accurately in Mantuani's listing of Vienna's musical mss. in
          the general mss. catalogue. In addition to a number of Fro-
          berger suites, Ms. 16798 includes a variety of other 17th-
          century keyboard works in German keyboard tablature, inter
          alia compositions otherwise unknown by Christian Grimm."

WIEN, Österreichische Nationalbibliothek: Chorbuch von 1544

1416 KIRSCH, Winfried. Ein unbeachtetes Chorbuch von 1544 in der Öster-
      reichischen Nationalbibliothek Wien, *Mf* XIV (1961) 290-303.
         . [Thematic catalogue], 295-303.
          Incipits with text of mainly anonymous works and of one com-
          position each by Heinrich Finck and Thomas Stolzer. Provides
          a table of concordances and an inventory of contents.

WIEN, Österreichische Volksliedarchive, *see nos.* 298, 298a (W. Deutsch)

WIEN, Schottenstift

1417 Verzeichnis/ der im Stift Schotten'schen Musicalien-Archiv/ vorhan-
▽   denen Compositionen/ Zusammengestellt nach den früheren Katalogen und/
      den neuen Anschaffungen unter Sr. Gnaden/ den Hochwürdigsten Herrn
      Prälaten/ Sigmund Schulter./ Abgeschlossen am 28. Jänner/ 1857/ I.
      Band (A Ws) 163p. (manuscript). Typewritten copy in A Wn: S.m. 9031.
      Microfilm in US NYcg.
          Double staff incipits for 1139 sacred vocal works from the
          16th to 19th c. Annotations include: instrumentation, number
          of voices, description of the condition of the source and,
          where available, copyists, copy dates, and date of composition
          (some of the entries bear dates beyond 1857). Contains an
          index of text incipits and an index of composers (with bio-
          graphical data). Composers: Wenzel Adam, Ant. Cajet. Adlgas-
          ser, J. Caspar Aiblinger (Ayblinger), Engelbert Aigner, J.G.
          Albrechtsberger, Gregor Allegri, Ignaz Assmayr, Emmanuel C.
          Th. Bach, Johann Sebastian Bach, Bauer, Ludwig van Beethoven,
          Andreas Bibl, Blahak (Blahack), Moric Brosig, Anton Cartelli-
          eri, Luigi Cherubini, Fr. Danzi, Anton Diabelli, Carl Ditters
          von Dittersdorf, Carl Freyherr von Doblhof-Dier, Joseph Dont,
          Jos. Drechsler, Drobisch, Francesco Durante, Daniel Eberlin,
          Josef Edler von Eybler, Johann Fuchs, Robert Führer, Johann
          Baptist Gänsbacher, Florian Leop. Gassmann, Luigi Abbate Gat-
          ti, Christoph Ritter von Gluck, Grasel, Karl Heinrich Graun,
          Tobias Gsur, Adalbert Gyrowetz, Bernard Hahn, Georg Fried.
          Händel, Johann Adolph Hasse, Joseph Haydn, Michael Haydn,
          Joh. Bapt. Henneberg, Franz Hiess, Leopold Hoffmann, W.L.
          Horak, J. Hoven, Hueber, Johann Nep. Hummel, L. Jansa, Nico-

lo Jomelli, Joseph Kaintz, Karl Kammerlander, Ferdinand Kauer, Karl Kempter, P. Maximilian Kerschbaum, Komenda (Kromenda), Conradin Kreutzer, Krottendorfer, Franz Krückl, Orlando Lasso, C.G. Lickl, Peter Lindpaintner, Hedwig Malfatti, Mariane Martinez, Albin Maschek, Etienne Henri Mehul, Molique, W.A. Mozart, Gottlieb Amadeus Naumann, Sigismund Ritter von Neukomm, Franz Novottni, Ortlieb, Fernando Paer, Pierluigi Aloisio Palestrina, Pater Georg Pasterwitz, H.L. Pearsall, Giov. Battista Pergolesi (Pergolese), C.F. Pitsch, Joseph Preindl, Gottfried Preyer, Prentner, Bened. Randhartinger, Rath, Reissinger (Reissiger), Georg Reutter (Reuter), Vincenz Righini, Ludwig Rotter, Antonio M.G. Sacchini (Sachini), Antonio Salieri, E. G. Salzmann, Santner, I.B. Schiedermayer, Joseph J. Schnabel, Franz Schneider, Ferdinan Schubert, Franz Schubert, Carl Schülle, Joh. Abr. Pet. Schulz (Schulze), Simon Sechter, Franz Georg Seegner, Franz X. Seidel (Seidl), Ignaz Ritter von Seyfried, Carolo Seyler, Johann Skraup, Ignaz Spangler, Luis Spohr, Max Abbé Stadler, Conrad P. Stöcklin, Allesandro Stradella, F.X. Süssmayer, Siegmund Ritter von Tomaschek (Tomascheck), Maxim Ulbrig, Franz Volkert, F. Walter, C.M.v. Weber, Joseph Weigl, Joseph Widerhofer, Peter von Winter, J.N. Witasek (Witaseck), Ciril Wolf, Joh. Hugo Worzischeck (Wozischek), I.N. Wotzet (Wozet), Benedetto Ziack (Ziak), I.B. Ziegler, Jos. Leop. Zvonar, and anonymous works.

WIENANDT, Elwyn A.; YOUNG, Robert H. (compilers)

col 1418   The anthem in England and America (New York: Free P., 1970) 495p. Thematic catalogue.

WIENIAWSKI, HENRI, 1835-1880

col 1419   BACHMANN, Alberto. Les grands violinistes du passé (Paris: Fischbacher, 1913) 468p. (see no. 65)
Table thématique, 459-64.
List of works includes 13 incipits.

WIESENTHEID, Musiksammlung des Grafen von Schönborn-Wiesentheid

coll 1420   ZOBELEY, Fritz. Die Musikalien der Grafen von Schönborn-Wiesentheid ...I. Teil: Das Repertoire des Grafen Rudolf Franz Erwein von Schönborn (1677-1754). Band 1: Drucke aus den Jahren 1676 bis 1738 (Tutzing: Schneider, 1967) xxiv, 143p.
Ca. 1300 incipits for all movements of chamber music (trios, duets, concerti grossi), church music (psalms, motets, litanies, Masses), cantatas, and orchestral works.
Reviews: W. Gordon MARIGOLD, *Notes* XXIV/4 (1968) 715-16.

prep 1420a --- Band 2. Handschriften (Tutzing: Hans Schneider, ca. 1971/72).

WILLAERT, ADRIAN, ca.1490-1562

1421   HABERL, Franz Xaver. Messen A. Willaert's gedruckt von Franc. Marcolini da Forli [1536. Mit einem thematischen Verzeichnisse], *MfMG* III (1871) [81]-89.
Two and three staff incipits of the masses. Information given on each work preceding each listing.

1422 BECK, H. Adrian Willaerts Messen, *AfMw* XVII/4 (1960) 215-42.
A thematic catalogue, interpolated throughout the text, of
cantus incipits from nine masses of Willaert, plus compositions of other composers which they resemble.

WILSON, JOHN, 1595-1674

1423 HENDERSON, Hubert Platt. The vocal music of John Wilson [with supple-
ment] (PhD diss.: U. of North Carolina, 1962) 388p. Univ. Micro.
63-3495.(typescript)
     Source index.
          This catalog contains over 300 incipits of vocal/choral music
          with accompaniment (primarily secular), with complete refer-
          ences to the manuscripts and printed sources.

WINSTON-SALEM, N.C., Peters Memorial Library, Moravian Music Foundation:
Johannes Herbst Collection

1424 GOMBOSI, Marilyn. Catalogue of the Johannes Herbst collection (Chapel Hill: U. of North Carolina Press, 1970) xix, 255p.
          This is the first volume in a series undertaken by the Mor-
          avian Music Foundation to catalogue its ca. 10,000 musical
          documents dating from the 18th to 19th centuries. The Jo-
          hannes Herbst Collection, preserved in Winston-Salem, con-
          tains 464 MSS of ca. 1000 anthems and arias used in Moravian
          worship services, plus 45 extended vocal works and a few
          volumes of miscellaneous pieces. The collection was part of
          the personal library of Johannes Herbst (1735-1812), Moravian
          minister and musician. Single and double staff incipits
          are given with instrumentation, dates, and text provided.

WINTER, PETER, 1754-1825

1425 LOEFFLER, Edmund. Peter Winter als Kirchenmusiker. Ein Beitrag zur
Geschichte der Messe (PhD diss.: Frankfurt a. M., 1929; Printed without indication of place or publisher]) 94p.
     Thematisches Verzeichnis, 38-60.
          Over 100 double staff incipits for all movements of 8 Masses,
          1 Requiem, 24 Mass movements, Psalms, 2 Te Deums, 1 Stabat
          Mater, hymns, etc. Works arranged by genre.

WOLFENBÜTTEL, Herzog August Bibliothek

1426 The Wolfenbüttel Chansonnier. Manuscript 287 Extravagantum (New York:
▽   New York U., Advanced Seminar in Musicology, under the direction of
Gustave Reese, 1966) (manuscript)
          Texted incipits of the 77 chansons in the 15th c. MS, with
          full concordances in 61 contemporary MSS and incunabulae,
          and listings of modern editions. Composers represented are:
          Barbireau, Basiron, Bedingham, Binchois, Busnois, Caron,
          Convert, Phillipot Despres, Dufay, Dunstable, Frye, Ghizeghem,
          Michelet, Morton, Ockeghem, Prioris, and Rubinus.

WOTQUENNE, Alfred (compiler)

1427 Thèmes des petits recueils Ballard 1695-1743 (US LC: ML 120/ .F7W7/
▽   case) 138*l*. (manuscript)
> A thematic catalogue of the music collections published by
> Christophe Ballard and Jean-Baptiste Christophe Ballard.
> Works included are: (1) *Parodies Bachiques, sur les airs et
> symphonies des opéra, recueillies et mises en ordre par M.
> Ribon*...1695; (2) *Nouvelles parodies Bachiques...recueillies
> et mises en ordre par Christophe Ballard*...1700-1702; (3)
> *Brunettes ou Petits air tendres...recueillies...par Chris-
> tophe Ballard*...1703-1704; (4) *Tendresses Bachiques...re-
> cueilles...par Christophe Ballard*...1712; (5) *La clef des
> chansonniers ou Recueil des vaudevilles depuis cent ans et
> plus...recueillies par J.-B. Ballard*...1717; (6) *200 chan-
> sons à danser extraites du recueil les rondes et chansons à
> danser*...1724....*100 contre-danses extraites du 2e volume du
> Recueil: Les rondes et chansons a danse*...1724; (7) *Les me-
> nuets chantants sur tous les tons, notes pour les instru-
> ments*...1725; (8) *Les parodies nouvelles et les vaudevilles
> inconnus*...1730; (9) *Nouveau recueil de chansons choisies,
> 1731-1743*...1700-1712; (10) *Recueil divers de danses par
> Feuillet. Pécour, Desais* **1700-1712.**

1428 Le chansonnier français, ou Recueil de chansons, ariettes, vaude-
▽   villes et autre couplets choisis, avec la musique (Paris) 1760-62
> Rare periodical publication: one volume appeared every 2 months,16v.
> (US LC: M 1730/.C323W7/case) 3v. Compiled 1917-18. (manuscript)
>> Incipits for 15 volumes of this periodical (v. 16 without in-
>> cipits), averaging 135 incipits per volume.

1429 Théâtre de la Foire. Thèmes des mélodies contenues dans 1. Le Thé-
▽   âtre de la Foire. 2. Les parodies du Nouveau théâtre italien. 3. Le
> nouveau théâtre italien (US LC: M 1507/.W8/case) 386*l*. Compiled
> 1918-1929. (manuscript)
>> Incipits are arranged alphabetically by text.

WROCŁAW (BRESLAU), Biblioteka Uniwersytecka

1430 Der Codex Mf. 2016 des Musikalischen Instituts bei der Universität
> Breslau; eine palaeographische und stilistische Beschreibung von
> Fritz FELDMAN (Breslau: Priebatsch, 1932) 2v.
>> Thematisches Verzeichnis, v. 2, i-xvii.
>>> Incipits in old notation, original clefs, for 96 sacred
>>> vocal works contained in the codex. Provides text incipits,
>>> folio numbers, number of voices, concordances, etc. Composers
>>> include: Agricola, Compère, Isaac, Josquin. The codex contains
>>> Masses and motets from ca. 1500.

ZACH, JOHANN, 1699-1773

1431 KOMMA, Karl Michael. Johann Zach und die tschechischen Musiker im
      deutschen Umbruch des I8. Jahrhunderts, *Studien zur Heidelberger
      Musikwissenschaft* VII, hrsg. Heinrich Besseler (Kassel: Bärenreiter,
      1938) 124p.
         Thematisches Verzeichnis der Werke Johann Zachs, [113]-124.
            Incipits of 61 works arranged by genre. All movements given
            for instrumental music, only Kyries for Masses.

1432 GOTTRON, Adam; SENN, Walter. Johann Zach. Kurmainzer Hofkapellmeister.
      Nachträge und Ergänzungen zum thematischen Verzeichnis seiner Komposi-
      tionen., *Mainzer Zeitschrift 1955* (Mainz: Verlag des Altertumsvereins)
      81-94.
            Incipits for all movements (instrumental music) of 69 works,
            arranged by genre.

ZECHNER, JOHANN GEORG, 1716-1778

1433 RIEDEL, Friedrich Wilhelm (Mainz). Thematischer Katalog sämtlicher
*   Werke

ZEIDLER, JOZEF, ca.1744-1806

1434 ZIENTARSKI, Władysław. Jozef Zeidler, *Muzyka* IV/12 (1967) 29-36.
         Katalog Tematyczny Kompozycji Józefa Zeidlera, 34-36.
            Incipits for 32 vocal and instrumental works.

ZELLBELL, FERDINAND the younger, 1719-1780

1435 BENGTSSON, Ingmar. A complete thematic catalogue of Ferdinand Zell-
▽   bell the Younger's works (manuscript)

ZEIDLER, JÓZEF,

1436 MALISZEWSKA, Maria. Kompozycje mszalne Józefa Zeidlera zachowane w
▽   archiwach Wielkopolski (MA diss.: Warszawa, 1969) 136p.(typescript)
         [Thematic catalogue].

ZELLNER, JULIUS, 1832-1900

1437 HERRMANN, Hellmuth Heinz. Julius Zellner, Leben und Werk (PhD diss.:

Key: ✱ in preparation; ▽ manuscript; ☐ literature; ✪ Library of Congress

▽   Wien, 1950) 3v., 225*l*.; *l*.226-400; *l*. 401-85. (typescript)
     Thematischer Katalog der Werke Julius Zellners, v. 3, 404-85.
          Multiple staff incipits for all movements of 67 works arranged
          by opus number (symphonies, concertos, quartets, sonatas, etc.).

ZELTER, CARL FRIEDRICH, 1758-1832

1438   BARR, Raymond A.   **Carl Friedrich Zelter: A study of the Lied in**
▽   **Berlin during the eighteenth and early nineteenth centuries** (PhD
       diss., Music: U. of Wisconsin, 1968) ii, 270p.(typescript)
          [Thematic catalogue], 165-270.
              Incipits are inserted into the text as the Lieder are dis-
              cussed chronologically.

ZIMMERMAN, Franklin B.

1439   **Melodic indexing for general and specialized use,** *Notes* XXII/4
□   (June 1966) 1187-92.
              Examines and suggests criteria and uses for a thematic in-
              dexing system.

1440   **Musical biography and thematic cataloguing: two opposing aspects of**
□   **musicology in the 21st century,** *Musicology and the computer,* Barry S.
       BROOK, ed. (New York: The City University of New York Press,1970)
       216-21.

ZODER, R.

1441   **Anordnung von Ländlern,** *Zeitschrift Vereinigung für Volkskunde* XVIII
□   (1908) 307ff.

ZULEHNER

1442   **Zulehner Ouverturen-Verzeichnis.** Manuscript. (Now in the possession
▽   of Ewald Lassen, Frankfurt.)

ZÜRICH, Zentralbibliothek

1443   WALTER, Georg. **Katalog der gedruckten und handschriftlichen Musi-**
       kalien des 17. bis 19. Jahrhunderts im Besitz der Allgemeinen Musik-
       gesellschaft Zürich (Zürich: Verlag der Allgemeinen Musikgesellschaft,
       1960) vii, 145p.
              187 incipits of the MSS and lost works.

ZWICKAU. Ratsschulbibliothek.

1444   VOLLHARDT, Reinhard. **Bibliographie der Musik-Werke in der Rats-**
       schulbibliothek zu Zwickau (Leipzig: Breitkopf & Härtel, 1893-1896)
       (Beilage zu den *MfMG,* 25-27.)
              Partially thematic index of MS and printed liturgical music
              by anonymous composers primarily from the Renaissance.

Using the Index

MAIN ENTRIES

Composer

Smith	first name absent
Dupont, Jacques	this first name always present
Bianchi, (Marco)	this first name sometimes present
Schmidt, Heinrich Georg	(H., H.G., Hendrick, Schmit, Schmitt) variants for what is *probably* a single composer's name

Compiler, Author

subject, genre, title

The index contains the following special subject entries:
classification and indexing: general; folk music
codes, computer input languages
computer applications
manuscripts, codices, & chansonniers (by title)
manuscripts, codices, & chansonniers (by library call number)
thematic catalogues: bibliography; contract; bill of sale; history
*   and function; titles; union cataloguing projects*
thematic catalogues of collections
thematic catalogues of library holdings
thematic catalogues used in Library of Congress uniform titles

NUMBERS

303	catalogue devoted entirely to that composer's works
404	entry *about* the composer (not a catalogue)
-323,676	collective catalogues dated *before* 1830
+454,909	collective catalogues dated *after* 1830
r505	review of the catalogue bearing that number

N.B. Numbers with added decimals are separate entries. Numbers followed by letters are related entries (e.g. second edition, supplement, descriptive literature). Unless a specific added letter appears, index numbers refer to all entries with added letters that share the same number in the Bibliography.

Index

A

A.P.D., 632
dall'Abaco, 1406
Abadie, 989
Abandane, 1212
Abas (Abbas), - 194, 1216
Abbos (Abos), - 313.3, 1019, 1121
Abeille, 1365
Abel, Carl Friedrich (Abell),1-4; - 279, 325, 471, 581, 612, 921, 986, 990, 994, 1046; + 75, 112, 657, 837, 909, 911, 1032, 1046b, 1216, 1394
Abelmann, Charlotte, 1338

Abof, Girolamo, 644
Abraham, Gerald, r790
Absolon, 933
Abundante, Iulio, 725.1
Acaen, 1118
Accorimbony (Agostino), - 921, 922; + 1100
Achleitner, 584
Acourt, 935
Adam, - 1065; + 607, 935, 989
Adam von Fulda, + 111.1, 727
Adam, Wenzel, 1417
Adami, - 1046; + 632
Adammer, 632
Adams, Robert Lee, 5
Adani, 1019
Addinsell, 208
Adler, George, 1413-14
Adler, Guido, 1313
Adler, I., 231
Adlgasser, Anton Cajetan (Adelgasser), 6; - 107.1, 183, 1032, 1040, 1131-32, 1412-14, 1416; + 32, 1417
Adolfati (Adolfatti), - 194,399, 884
Adson, 909
Aemil, Rikert Sac,(see also Rikert Sac), 933
Agnesi, 989
Agnus Dei, 1163.1
Agostini, Pier Simone, 7; 1400

Agrell (G., J., Agrel), - 194, 279, 641, 1032, 1046, 1065; + 205, 989, 1046b
Agricola (18th c.), 1065
Agricola, Alexander, - 111; + 111.1, 201, 387.1, 625, 831, 902, 950, 952, 1118, 1211, 1430
Ahlefeld, 1032
Ahm, 471
Aiblinger, Joh. Kasp. (Ayblinger), - 885, 1040, 1413-14; + 1417
Aigner, - 471; + 584
Aigner, Engelbert, 1417
air de cour, 689
airs (see also *arias*) 987,1427
Akany, 935
Alai, Mauro, 194
Alayrac, *see* Dalayrac
Alanus, 1262
Albéniz, Isaac, 8
Albergati (Albergetti), - 1046; + 936
Albero, Sebastian, 9; 1158
Albert, 166
Alberti, 272, 989
Alberti, Domenico, 10-11, *507*; 636.1
Alberti, G.M., 112
Albertini, 642, 1019
Albertis, 313.3, 884
Alberto da Mantoa, 725.1
Albini, 1046b
Albinoni, Tomaso (Albenoni),12-14; - 581, 612, 1046; + 1046b, 1253, 1406
Albrecht, Konstantin-Karl, 15, 457
Albrecht, Otto, r93
Albrechtsberger, Johann Georg, 16-21; - 183, 350, 471,582, 667-68, 808, 885, 1032, 1040, 1203, 1380, 1394, 1409, 1412-14; + 584, 989, 996, 1159, 1417
Albrichi, 1200

Albutio, Iacomo, 725.1
Albutio, Ottavio, 1019
Alday, 986
Alday l'aine, - 76; + 185
Alday le jeune, 185
Aleotti, 279
Alessandri, - 279, 884,1032
Alessandri, L., 205
d'Alessandro, Raffaele, 21.1
Alessio (Francesco), 310, 989
Alexandre, 185
Alexi (Allexi), 400, 498
Aleyn, 925
Alfonso el Sabio, 24
Alfvén, Hugo, 22
Aliprandi, 884
Alkan, 989
Allegri (Gregor), - 279, 885, 1040; + 584, 1417
alleluia, 997, 1164
Allessandra, 313.1
Allessandri (Allessendri),921-22
Allgemeine Musikgesellschaft, 1443
Allison, 909
Allorto, Riccardo, 251
Allroggen, Gerhard, 592
Almedia, 884
Almeida (Almeyda), -1046a; + 1046b
Almeida, Antonio de, 140, 920
Altmann, Wilhelm, 23, 24, 1059, 1347
Altovad, 582
Alvensleben, 989
d'Ambreville, 185
Ambros, S., 1040
Ambrose, Holmes, 1403
Amon (J.), - 471, + 32, 632
Andante, 1019
Anderson, Owen, r167c
André, - 484, 758, 933, 1040; + 607
André, J.A. (Joh.), 32, 1046b
André, Johann Anton, 856a, 857
André (publisher), 441

307

E

F

G

$$\mathscr{H}$$

J

ℳ

Manzvoli, 345

Marass, 1216

Marazzoli, Marco, 780-81

Marcello, (B., Benedetto),782-
84, *507;* - 279,309,313.1-2,
581,921-22; +607,989,1159

Marchand, Louis (du Maine),
785; 1365

Marchi, 279, 644

Marco da Laquila, 725.1

Marcucci, 989

Marenzio, (Luca), 786; 1333

Maretta, Luise, 21.1

Margiane, 989

Marguerite of Austria, 201

Maria, - 582; + 989

*Marina Anna of Bavaria collec-
tion,* 884

Maria Theresa, 1216

Marigi, 808

Marigold, W.Gordon, r1420

Marinelli, 884

Marini, 936, 1406

Marini, Biagio, 1206

Marini, Carlo, 1323

Markham, 1313

Markl, Jaroslav, 354

Maroti, 313.2

Marpurg, 1065

Mars, Henriette de, 1365

Marschner, H., 599

Marsh, John, 273

Martin, - 313.2, 483, 498,
1040; + 32, 185

Martin, Arlan Stone, 1360

Martin y Coll, 909

Martin y Soler, 479

Martin, P.Giov. Battiste, 632

Martin, Gerard, 32

Martin, Gius., 32

Martin, Philipp, 787

Martinelli, (Antonio), - 1323;
+ 911

Martines, Marianna, -885; +1417

Martinetti, 112

Martini, (*see also* Sammartini),
- 194,399,498,581,641,668,
758,885,921-22,926,1046,
1065; +75,952,1046b,1066,
1313

Martini, Batta d.S. (*see also*
Sammartini), 1019

Martini, Joh., 625, 1211

Martini, Padre Giovanni Battista, 788

Martini, S.L., 1046

Martini, T., 1118

Martino, - 76,399,641,644,708,
885,933,1019,1032,1046,
1216; + 112

Martino, St., 642

Martinů, Bohuslav, 789-91

Martner, Knud, 775

Marx, Adolph Bernhard, 792

Marx, Hans Joachim, 261

Marx, M., 1046b

Mascagni, 166

Masch, P.H., 205

Maschek, - 309, 471, 993, 1019,
1032; + 584

Maschek, Paul, 204

Maschek, Vinz., 310, 632

Maschera, Fiorenzo, 793

Mascitti, Michele, 794

Mašek, (V.), +989,1017,1177

Masi, - 399, 922, 933

Masini, 989

Mason, D.G., 207

Mass, 107.1,142,145,180-81,
183,194,400,584-85,667-68,
797,836,885,933,991,995,
997,1040-41,1118,1142,1171-
72,1200,1203,1332.1,1430,
1480

Massaino, 1333

Massoneau, - 484; + 185, 983

Mathias, Franz X., 1049, 1310

Mathurin, 185

Matscheko, 708

Mattausch, (P.), 166, 632

Mattei, Stanislao, 885

Matteis, 936

Matteis, Nicola, 795

Matteis, Nicola, jun., 796

Matthees, 1065

Mattheson, (J.von) - 581;+ 112

Mattia, Vento, 1121

Matysiak, Waldemar, 797

Maurer, L., 632

Maurus, 1019

Max, 797

Mayeda, Akio, 981

Mayer, (Mäyer), -1216,1380;+989

Mayer, George L., r1013

Mayer, Matthias, 219, 219a

Mayer, Ruperti, 183

Mayerbeer, 1040

Mayerhofer, Herwig,692

Mayr, - 313.2, 582, 708

Mayr, J.S., 32, 205

Mayr, R.I., 1165

Mayseder, Joseph (J.), 798-801;
- 1019, 1040, 1413-14; + 632

Mayshuet, 925

337

theme
 definition, 193,296-97,659,
  934
 identification by computer,
  943.1
 "theme catalogues" (dealing
  with true themes or melodies
  rather than incipits)
   concertos, 208
   film music, 358
   Haydn quartets, 547
   instrumental music, 68,
    943.1
   opera themes, 372
   Sibelius, 1214-15
   symphonic music, 207,1163
   symphonie concertante,
    1257
   trumpet, 338
   vocal music, 69
   Wagner, 1373-77

𝒱

W

𝒳𝒴𝒵